CONNECTIONIST MODELS IN COGNITIVE PSYCHOLOGY

Studies in Cognition Series
Published Titles

Series Editor
Glyn Humphreys, University of Birmingham, UK

Cognitive Models of Memory
Martin A. Conway (Ed.)

Language Processing
Simon Garrod & Martin Pickering (Eds.)

Knowledge, Concepts, and Categories
Koen Lamberts & David Shanks (Eds.)

Attention
Harold Pashler (Ed.)

Cognitive Neuroscience
Michael D. Rugg

Aspects of Language Production
Linda Wheeldon (Ed.)

The Cognitive Neuroscience of Memory
Amanda Parker, Edward L. Wilding & Timothy J. Bussey (Eds.)

Connectionist Models in Cognitive Psychology

Edited by

George Houghton
University of Wales

Ψ **Psychology Press**
Taylor & Francis Group

HOVE AND NEW YORK

First published 2005
by Psychology Press
27 Church Road, Hove, East Sussex BN3 2FA

Simultaneously published in the USA and Canada
by Psychology Press
270 Madison Avenue, New York NY 10016

Psychology Press is part of the Taylor & Francis Group

Typeset in Times by RefineCatch Limited, Bungay, Suffolk
Printed and bound in Great Britain by TJ International Ltd, Padstow, Cornwall
Cover design by Hybert Design

This publication has been produced with paper manufactured to
strict environmental standards and with pulp derived from
sustainable forests.

British Library Cataloguing in Publication Data
A catalogue record for this book is available from the British Library

Library of Congress Cataloging-in-Publication Data
Connectionist models in cognitive psychology / [edited by] George Houghton.
    p. cm. – (Studies in cognition)
  Includes bibliographical references and index.
  ISBN 1-84169-223-9
  1. Connectionism.   2. Cognitive psychology.   I. Houghton, George, 1957–
  II. Studies in cognition (Hove, England)

BF311.C62152 2004
153.1′2–dc22   2004012053

ISBN 1-84169-223-9

Contents

v

SECTION 3
Attention and cognitive control

SECTION 4
Language processes

List of contributors

John A. Bullinaria, School of Computer Science, University of Birmingham, Birmingham B15 2TT, UK

Morten H. Christiansen, 240 Uris Hall, Cornell University, Ithaca, NY 14853–7601, USA

Richard P. Cooper, Room 522, School of Psychology, Birkbeck, University of London and University College London, Malet Street, London WC1E 7HX, UK

Suzanne Curtin, Assistant Professor of Linguistics, Department of Linguistics and Psychology, 2806 Cathedral of Learning, University of Pittsburgh, Pittsburgh, PA 5260, USA

Gary S. Dell, Department of Psychology, 635 Psychology Building, University of Illinois, 603 E. Daniel, Champaign, IL 61820, USA

David W. Glasspool, Advanced Computation Laboratory, Cancer Research UK, 61 Lincoln's Inn Fields, London WC2A 3PX, UK

Dietmar Heinke, Behavioural and Brain Sciences Centre, School of Psychology, University of Birmingham, Birmingham B15 2TT, UK

George Houghton, School of Psychology, University of Wales, Bangor Adeilad Brigantia, Penrallt Road, Gwynedd LL57 2AS, UK

Glyn W. Humphreys, Behavioural and Brain Sciences Centre, School of Psychology, University of Birmingham, Birmingham B15 2TT, UK

John K. Kruschke, Department of Psychology, Indiana University, 1101 East 10th Street, Bloomington, IN 47405–7007, USA

E. Charles Leek, School of Psychology, University of Wales, Bangor, Adeilad Brigantia, Penrallt Road, Gwynedd LL57 2AS, UK

Randall C. O'Reilly, Department of Psychology, University of Colorado at Boulder, 345 UCB Boulder, CO 80309, USA

Mike Page, Department of Psychology, School of Psychology, University of Hertfordshire, College Lane, Hatfield, Hertfordshire AL10 9AB, UK

David R. Shanks, Department of Psychology, University College London, Gower Street, London WC1E 6BT, UK

Marco Zorzi, Department of General Psychology, University of Padova, Via Venezia 8, 35131 Padova, Italy

Series preface

Over the past 20 years enormous advances have been made in our understanding of basic cognitive processes concerning issues such as: What are the
basic modules of the cognitive system? How can these modules be modelled?
How are the modules implemented in the brain? The book series "Studies in
Cognition" seeks to provide state-of-the-art summaries of this research,
bringing together work on experimental psychology with that on computational modelling and cognitive neuroscience. Each book contains chapters
written by leading figures in the field, which aim to provide comprehensive
summaries of current research. The books should be both accessible and
scholarly and be relevant to undergraduates, post-graduates, and research
workers alike.

Glyn Humphreys

CHAPTER ONE

Introduction to connectionist models in cognitive psychology: Basic structures, processes, and algorithms

George Houghton
University of Wales, Bangor, UK

INTRODUCTION

This book aims to present an overview of the current state of connectionist modelling in cognitive psychology, covering a broad range of areas. All of the authors are specialists in their chosen topic, and most have been actively engaged in connectionist cognitive modelling for many years. In these chapters the reader will find numerous examples of the way in which theories implemented in the form of connectionist models have interacted, and continue to interact, with experimental data in an intellectually productive and stimulating way. I believe these contributions speak for themselves and that there is no need in this introduction to advance or defend any particular conception of the modelling enterprise. Instead, my purpose here is to provide an accessible introduction to some of the basic, and most frequently encountered, features of connectionist cognitive modelling, ones that recur throughout the chapters of the book. Readers new to connectionist modelling, or who encounter difficulty with technicalities in any of the chapters, will hopefully find the discussion presented here of some use.

The development of connectionist (or "neural network") models has a long history, involving contributions from scholars in many disciplines, including mathematics, logic, computer science, electronic engineering, as well as neuroscience and psychology. For instance, the ideas of Donald Hebb on modifiable connections go back at least to the 1940s; the "delta rule" learning algorithm discussed below dates to the early 1960s (Widrow & Hoff,

1

1960). However, despite influential work by such authors as Grossberg (1980), Kohonen (1984) and others, the impact of such ideas on cognitive psychology really began with the publication in 1986 of the two volumes by Rumelhart, McClelland and colleagues (Rumelhart & McClelland, 1986; McClelland & Rumelhart, 1986). These books, as well as describing numerous connectionist models and algorithms, including the well-known back-propagation learning rule, also contained programmatic chapters written with an "ideological" purpose. The authors clearly believed they were on to something new and exciting, something that would change the way theoretical cognitive psychology was done, and they wanted the rest of us to know about it.

Previously, during the 1970s and early 1980s, modelling in cognitive psychology was dominated by the idea, initially inspired by developments in linguistics and artificial intelligence, that all cognitive processes involved the rule-based manipulation of cognitive symbols (Charniak & McDermott, 1985). On this account, the dominant metaphor for the relationship between the brain and cognition was that of the hardware/software division of computing. The brain is the hardware (the physical machine) and the cognitive processes are the software (programs) being run on the machine. The crucial thing about this metaphor is that understanding how a piece of software works (i.e. understanding the rules of the program by which one can predict its behaviour) does not require knowledge of the machine it is running on. Indeed, the same program can run on very different physical machines, so long as each machine has a compiler for the program. Hence, an understanding of the program (predicting its behaviour) will be independent of the machine. It is a simple step from this view to the idea that the "rules" of cognition (our mental software) should be stated at an abstract, functional level, without reference to physical machine properties (Pylyshyn, 1984).

Neural network modelling involves a shift in this view, proposing rather that there is no such clear division in real brains: the way the brain physically operates will need to be taken into account to explain cognitive phenomena. To take one example, many phenomena in learning and memory can be accounted for by network models of associative learning, in which links are formed between "neurons" representing different aspects of the environment (see Shanks, Chapter 2; Kruschke, Chapter 4; O'Reilly, Chapter 5, this volume). In connectionist networks, this is not an accident; that is, it is not just one form of memory out of many that could be equally easily implemented. Associative memory is therefore "natural" to neural network models. At the same time, most current work on the neural basis of memory is dedicated to understanding how synaptic connections between neurons can be modified. It is hard to overestimate the importance of this coming together of the cognitive and neuroscientific levels of investigation; although scientists in each field will have their own specific issues, which may not easily translate into the terms of the other, there is nevertheless a central, common perspective (in this case, memory is in the connections) which is meaningful to both fields, and which allows the productive interchange of discoveries and questions. The theoretical "lingua franca" in which this interdisciplinary discourse takes place is that of connectionist networks.

Hence, the success of the connectionist program in cognitive psychology has not just been due to the empirical success of individual models. The push for a more "neurally-inspired" form of modelling came at the right time. By the mid-1980s the work of the cognitive neuropsychologists, investigating the patterns of breakdown in cognitive capacities as a result of brain injury, had become a major force in cognitive psychology (Shallice, 1988). This work not only led to revisions of traditional "box-and-arrow" models of cognitive architectures, but also produced a demand for computationally explicit models that could be artificially "damaged", while continuing to function at a suboptimal level (Bullinaria, Chapter 3, this volume). The disturbed behaviour of the model following various patterns of damage could then be compared to the behaviour of individual patients (Shallice, Glasspool, & Houghton, 1995). The symbolic approach to cognition was singularly unhelpful in this enterprise, as models based on it tend to either work perfectly (i.e. as programmed) or to crash, generating only error messages. Generating a damaged version of such a model, if it is feasible at all, typically involves extensive reprogramming to implement the hypothetical effects of the brain damage. For example, if the model involves the interaction of separate modules, then any disruption in the output of one module (the damaged one) will generally require reprogramming of any other modules receiving that output. If this output is not of the form expected, then it will cause the program to crash. Connectionist models, on the other hand, lend themselves easily to forms of damage: for instance, by the addition of random noise to weights or activations, loss or reduction of connections, and so forth. The models will always continue to function under such circumstances, but the patterns of breakdown will not be random.

THE NEURAL BASIS OF CONNECTIONIST MODELS

Connectionist models of cognitive functions are said to be "neurally inspired". However, it is fairly rare to come across models containing features specifically based on data regarding the brain mechanisms involved in the particular capacity being modelled. In most cases this is simply because nothing very specific is known about these mechanisms. Of course, in many cases a given psychological function can be reliably located within a circumscribed brain region, generally some part of the cerebral cortex in the case of higher perceptual and cognitive functions. However, this kind of simple localization (achieved by studies of the performance of brain-injured patients, and functional neuroimaging) does not provide much in the way of constraints on the mechanisms built in to the models. The simple fact is that we do not yet understand how specific cortical neural circuits work, or how to constrain functional principles on the basis of the kind of variation in cortical architecture that underlies brain maps of such as the classic Brodmann map.

Connectionist models are therefore neurally inspired in a more general sense. They are based on a set of widely held beliefs about what are the central functional characteristics of the way in which neurons represent, store, and retrieve information to construct our behaviour. These basic characteristics should not be thought of as being complete, or even undeniably correct. However, it is necessary to start somewhere, and current work has shown that very interesting and empirically successful models can be constructed using a handful of basic ideas.

Below I discuss the most common of these features, ones that appear repeatedly in the articles in this book. I hasten to add that the following is not intended to constitute an introduction to the basic principles of neuroscience, but simply to highlight the neural origins of the features most commonly found in connectionist models in cognitive psychology.

The neuron

The fundamental principle of neuroscience is the so-called "neuron doctrine", the first complete expression of which is typically attributed to the Spanish histologist Santiago Ramon y Cajal, in work published 1888–1991 (Shepherd, 1992). At the time, it was widely supposed that the nervous system was a single continuous network, the "reticular theory". Ramon y Cajal used microscopes to view nervous tissue stained by a method invented about 14 years earlier by the Italian physician Camillo Golgi, and recorded what he saw in hundreds of detailed drawing. These observations showed (to Ramon y Cajal, at least) networks made up of distinct cellular elements, typically containing a bulbous body; short, branching filaments (the dendrites); and a single elongated projection (the axon). The neuron doctrine thus states that the nervous system is composed of physically separate entities (neurons), and hence that understanding how the nervous system works requires an understanding of the neuron.

The neuron is an electrochemically excitable cell capable of sending spatially localized, invariant impulses (action potentials, discussed further below) throughout the brain and body. The prototypical (projection) neuron (Fig. 1.1) is comprised of: a cell body (*soma*) containing the cell nucleus; a set of branching elements emanating from the soma, known as *dendrites*, which act as input sites for connections from other neurons; and a single pronounced projection, the *axon*, which makes distant connections to other cells. The dendrites and cell body are the main "input sites" of the neuron, where

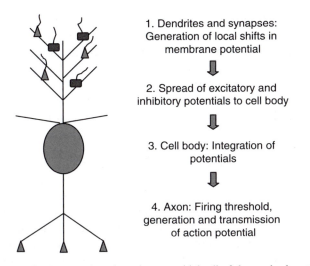

1. Dendrites and synapses:
Generation of local shifts in
membrane potential

⇩

2. Spread of excitatory and
inhibitory potentials to cell body

⇩

3. Cell body: Integration of
potentials

⇩

4. Axon: Firing threshold,
generation and transmission
of action potential

Figure 1.1.   An idealized neuron based on the pyramidal cell of the cerebral cortex. The function of the neuron is shown as transforming mixtures of excitatory and inhibitory dendritic
potentials into the production of action potentials with a given firing rate. In real pyramidal cells,
the cell body of the neuron also receives (mostly inhibitory) synapses.

connections from other neurons are made. The axon carries signals from the
neuron to other cells, hence acting as an output channel. Although neurons
have at most one axon, the axon can branch many times, allowing a single
neuron to make contact with many others.

How are these contacts between cells made? At the time of the formulation of the neuron doctrine this was not known, and it was not until as late as
the 1950s that the theory of the chemical *synapse*, the most common type of
connection throughout the nervous system, became firmly established.
Synapses are mainly formed between the axon terminals of one neuron (the
pre-synaptic neuron) and the surface of the dendrites and cell bodies of
others (*post-synaptic* neuron). Between the pre- and post-synaptic elements
there is a small gap, the synaptic cleft. How communication between neurons
takes place at synapses is discussed below.

This description of the neuron is fairly generic and best characterizes long-
axon, projection neurons, which send signals between brain regions, and
between the brain and the peripheral nervous system and spinal cord. However, the nervous system contains many variations on this theme, reflecting
specialization of function. For instance, the Purkinje neuron of the cerebellum has an enormous system of dendrites, which appears to be needed to
accommodate as many as 200,000 synapses (Llinas & Walton, 1990). All
brain regions contain *intrinsic* or *local-circuit* neurons, which do not send
signals out of their containing region, and hence have only relatively short

axons. The distinction between this latter type of cell and projection neurons (which send long axons between nervous system structures) is an important one. The projection neurons of any brain structure are often referred to as its *principal* neurons. Since these are the only neurons that leave a given area, they are the route by which the results of any "computations" carried out within the region are conveyed to other brain structures, or to the muscles. Since the only thing projection neurons appear to do is to produce action potentials (see below), it follows that the results of any significant kind of neural computation must eventually be coded in the firing pattern of these neurons. Of particular interest to cognitive psychology, the principal cell of the cerebral cortex is the *pyramidal cell*, which constitutes about 70% of all cortical cells. Moreover, the major input to any cortical region comes from other cortical regions, i.e. from cortical pyramidal cells (Douglas & Martin, 1990), and connections between cortical regions are usually reciprocal. This is true even of primary sensory regions (such as primary visual cortex, V1), and presumably indicates the importance of "top-down", or feedback, projections on even supposedly "low-level" sensory processing. A fair generalization, then, is that the "language" of the cerebral cortex, by which cortical areas talk to each other, and to other parts of the brain, is expressed in the firing patterns of pyramidal cells.

The action potential

The first nervous systems evolved in the sea, in water full of salts such as potassium and sodium chloride. Dissolved in water, the constituents of these salts separate into positively and negatively charged ions, and the cells of ancient sea creatures evolved to exploit these ions to create the local electrical potentials which underlie all neural activity. Although we have long since left the sea, in effect we continue to carry it around with us in the fluid which surrounds and permeates the neurons in the brain. The membrane of the neuron contains mechanisms which ensure that the positive and negative ions are unevenly distributed inside and outside of the cell, so that in its resting state a neuron has a net internal negative charge (of about −70 millivolts, the resting potential). This *polarization* leads to pressure on positive sodium ions in the extracellular fluid to enter the cell, which they can do so via specialized channels in the cell membrane. However, in a beautiful piece of natural engineering, whether the relevant channels are open or closed depends on the potential across the cell membrane, and at the resting potential the sodium channels are closed. However, at a slightly less negative potential, called the "firing threshold", the channels open, allowing positive charge, in the form of sodium ions, to enter the cell. Whenever this happens, there is a local "depolarization" of the neuron, as the potential turns from negative to positive. If the firing threshold is crossed at the initial part of the axon, then a kind of chain reaction is initiated whereby the depolarization of one part of the axon opens sodium channels in the adjacent part, leading to that part being depolarized, and so on. In this way a wave of depolarization travels down the axon from the cell body to the axon terminals, where contacts are made with other neurons (or muscles). It is this process that is referred to as the action potential (AP).

To summarize, the AP is "all-or-nothing" (thresholded), and does not decrease in strength as it travels down the axon. For this reason neurons have sometimes been modelled as binary threshold devices, i.e. they have two states, ON or OFF (1 or 0), and the transition from OFF to ON depends on some continuous variable crossing the threshold (Hopfield, 1982). However, it is not generally believed that the firing of a single action potential is a significant event in the nervous system, nor that it is only the presence or absence of APs in a neuron that matters. Rather it is the firing rate of a neuron, the number of APs produced per unit time, that matters.

Neurons can sum the effects of the signals they receive from other neurons over short time periods (temporal summation). Hence, the higher its firing rate, the greater the effect a neuron will have on any others to which it is connected, as the sum of its input over a given time window will be greater. In addition, if a local group of neurons shares the same function, they will tend to be active at the same time. The higher the average firing rate of the neurons in the group, the more of them that will produce an AP at the same time. Cells receiving inputs from all the neurons in the group can integrate their individual signals (spatial summation). This permits the strength of an aggregate neural signal to be assessed almost instantaneously.

Either method leads to the important idea that, rather than being all-or-nothing, behaviourally significant neural signals are continuously variable, and convey quantitative information in an analogue fashion. As discussed below, this idea has its connectionist equivalent in the idea of the *activation level*.

Neuronal communication and synaptic integration

In the chemical synapse, the arrival of an action potential at the axon terminals results in the release of chemical *neurotransmitters*, which cross the synaptic cleft and bind to receptor sites embedded in the membrane of the post-synaptic neuron. These transmitter receptors control the state of "ligand-gated" ion channels. For instance, the receptor may control a channel through which positive ions can flow. If activated by a neurotransmitter, the receptor opens the channel, allowing positive ions to enter, and consequently the membrane potential around the open channels become less negative (depolarized). Since this shifts the membrane potential nearer to the firing threshold, increasing the likelihood of producing an action potential, these responses are termed *excitatory post-synaptic potentials* (EPSPs). Similarly, other receptors gate channels that either allow positive ions to leave the cell or negative ions to flow in. Either event will *hyperpolarize* the cell (make the membrane potential more negative), pushing it away from the firing threshold. This is the basic mechanism of neural inhibition, and such events are called *inhibitory post-synaptic potentials* (IPSPs).

Unlike the AP, synaptic potentials are not all-or-nothing, but are graded (although they appear to occur in integer multiples of a "mini"-potential). Synaptic potentials are local, say occurring on a particular site on a dendrite, but spread passively (rather than actively like the AP) to neighbouring sites. All dendrites lead eventually to the neuron cell body, hence all local dendritic depolarizations will spread towards the cell body, where they combine. To a first approximation, it is usual to think of the cell body as adding the dendritic signals together, with the result that inhibitory and excitatory signals cancel each other out. If the sum of the dendritic inputs at any time is positive (net excitation), then the membrane potential will be shifted away from the resting potential towards the firing threshold. If this threshold is crossed at the initial segment of the axon, then an AP is initiated (by the opening of voltage-gated sodium channels in the axon membrane). Hence, the firing of a neuron is caused by there being sufficient net excitation (EPSPs) to shift it beyond the firing threshold. The greater and more sustained this excitation, the higher will be the neuron's firing rate.

There is now compelling evidence that the strength of synapses (measured as the size of the potential shift caused in the post-synaptic neuron when the pre-synaptic neuron fires) is variable.

COGNITIVE AND NEURAL INTERPRETATIONS OF CONNECTIONIST NETWORKS

Our knowledge of brain function is still at an early stage, and we should anticipate that there are many significant functional principles still to be discovered. It could still turn out that some currently cherished beliefs regarding the psychological significance of what we know about the brain (e.g. the role of synaptic change in memory formation) are mistaken. If such ideas proved wrong, what would be the consequences for the connectionist program? Some might argue that in fact it would not matter, as connectionist cognitive models are first and foremost cognitive; i.e. they are to be judged only on how well they explain and predict behavioural data from cognitive psychology experiments. From this point of view, the basic elements of connectionist models are to be interpreted only in abstract functional terms. A node in a network stands for some kind of isolable unit of cognitive representation; it does not matter whether, in the brain, the same cognitive content involves a few, clustered neurons or thousands of widely distributed neurons (or glial cells for that matter!). The activation level of a connectionist node represents the availability or current psychological strength of the cognitive unit represented by that node; it does not matter whether this corresponds in the brain to, say, the firing rate of a neuron, the number of simultaneously active neurons, or the number of neurons oscillating in phase. Connections and weights in a network represent patterns of functional interactivity between cognitive units, such that units that are cognitively related can activate each other, while units that are cognitively incompatible inhibit each other; it does not matter that the brain contains (modifiable) excitatory and inhibitory synapses—maybe the cognitively important task (generation of internally consistent states) is realized in some other way.

Such an abstract view has its attractions, and, in practice, many cognitive modellers will (at least some of the time) act in accordance with it. Indeed, in the absence of any specific neural constraints on the form that a cognitive model (e.g. of spelling) should take, it is the level of discussion of a network that is frequently most useful, since it talks directly in the kinds of terms that are relevant to the description of the only data we typically have, i.e. patterns of human behaviour.

Nevertheless, I believe that most connectionist cognitive modellers, however rarely a new neuroscientific finding actually impinges on their work, would reject the logical consequence of this view, in which the coarse analogy between artificial and real neural networks is entirely accidental, and of no practical or theoretical importance. Rather, the general belief is that a neurally-grounded cognitive psychology is both desirable and achievable. It is desirable for at least two reasons. First, if the brain is the generator of all cognition and behaviour, then we want neurally and cognitively based theories to be not only compatible but translatable, one into the other. For better or worse, the language and concepts of neural networks are the only theoretical "lingua franca" that the cognition and brain sciences have. Second, connectionism is, at least in practice, a genuinely constraining framework, and the constraints lead to fundamental theoretical questions that also make sense to neuroscientists; e.g. how can cognition arise from interactions between basic processors capable of only simple analogue computations? How are memories formed in a system limited to changing patterns of connectivity between these simple elements? How does binding of distributed information take place to produce unitary percepts? How does a parallel, distributed system (without a serial, central processor) control its own behaviour, in space (attention) and time (serial order)?

We now turn to the nuts and bolts of connectionist modelling, the way in which networks are implemented as computational structures and processes. The following account is far from exhaustive, but covers the most common mechanisms, in particular those found repeatedly in the chapters in this book.

Readers unclear about basic mechanisms referred to in these chapters will hopefully find what follows of some use.

BASIC STRUCTURES AND PROCESSES OF CONNECTIONIST MODELS

It is easy to describe the components of connectionist models; they are made of nodes (or units) and connections between them. The nodes are the basic processing elements, and each is associated with an *activation level*, represented by a number. The connections between nodes allow them to influence each other, so that their activations interact. Each connection is associated with a *weight*, also represented by a number. These two sets of numbers, activation levels and weights, are found in all connectionist networks, and in many cases they are the only numbers we need to be concerned with. This fundamental simplicity and uniformity of network models is of some importance to modellers, and is intended to correspond, to a first approximation, to the basic principles of neural architecture and processing outlined above.

Below we describe these components in more detail, and introduce typical equations which describe the way components of networks interact with each other. Connectionist models are mathematical models of a rather traditional sort, found in other areas of the natural sciences, i.e. they involve variables associated with continuous-valued numbers (activations, weights), and for a model to do anything, it is necessary to provide rules which describe how the values of the variables change as a function of other variables. Fortunately, the basic mathematics of most networks is fairly simple, often involving no more than arithmetical operations, such as addition and multiplication, and in what follows I have endeavoured not to go much beyond that.

However, using only the simplest mathematics, one is constrained to a "node level" account of how a network operates, i.e. an account in terms of how each node or connection functions and changes. Connectionist models contain different levels of representation, just as in informal, diagrammatic models. A level of representation in a connectionist net consists of a set of nodes, referred to as a *layer* in the network. The units in the layer should at least be able to distinguish, by virtue of differences in their overall activation *patterns*, between all the functionally distinct states required by the level of representation. Hence, it is frequently much more useful to discuss the processing carried out by a network at a higher level, involving, for instance, the pattern of activation over a whole set of units, and the way this pattern is affected by passing through a set of weighted connections. In this case, "higher-level" constructs involving vectors (sets of numbers) and matrices (two-dimensional arrays of numbers) are invaluable, and these are introduced below in separate sections.

To facilitate the description at the network level, we can introduce at this point a simple network architecture, the two-layer feedforward network (Fig. 1.2a). To briefly describe the wood before the trees, this consists of two layers of processing units, the input layer and the output layer. The units in each of these layers are used to represent the elements in some cognitive domain. For instance, in a model of reading aloud, the input units might represent letters, and the output units phonemes. The two layers are linked, in one direction only, by a set of weighted connections, such that every input unit is connected to every output unit. When the network performs, the input layer receives some signal from the network's "environment", which activates a subset of the input units (the network perceives a printed word). This activation is then fed forward to the output units via the weighted connections (which also

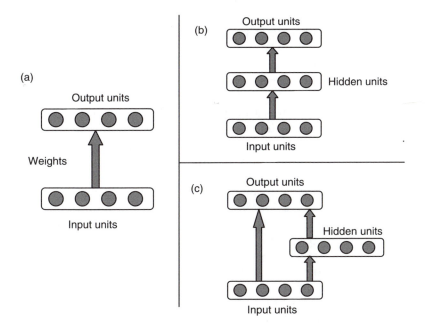

Figure 1.2.   Some common feedforward network architectures. Connections go in one direction only (indicated by the arrows) and each arrow represents "complete connectivity", i.e. every unit in the receiving layer has a connection from every unit in the sending layer. (a) The basic two-layer network. This is the simplest connectionist structure capable of performing a mapping (transformation) between two domains of representation, represented by the input and output units. (b, c) Two extensions of the two-layer network, which increase its computational power by adding an extra set of units (hidden units) between input and output. (b) The typical single-route multi-layer network employed in many cognitive models. As in (a), there is still only one pathway from input to output, but the direct linkage between the input and output layers seen in (a) has been removed. (c) The dual-route multi-layer network, in which the direct input–output connections of the two-layer network have not been removed. In contrast to both (a) and (b), the output units in (c) receive signals from two distinct pathways.

transform the input activation), leading to a pattern of activation on the output units (the network's pronunciation of the word).

Units and activation levels

The activation level of a unit corresponds to the idea of the degree of activation of some cognitive element represented by the unit (discussed further below). The activation of a single unit is represented by a single number, most commonly having a value from 0 to 1. An activation value of 0 means that the unit is not active at all; an activation value of 1 means that it is as active as it can possibly be. We will symbolize the activation levels of units with the letter a, with subscripts to denote the activations of particular units. For instance, the activation of two arbitrary units, u_i and u_j, have associated activation levels a_i and a_j. The activations of whole set of units, say the output units of a network, can be represented as a set of numbers, e.g. $\{a_1, a_2, \ldots, a_n\}$ for an arbitrary number (n) of units. In this case it is generally more convenient to use *vector* notation, described below.

In some models, units are limited to these two extreme states (0 or 1, OFF or ON). This is a *binary* representation, where the unit simply signals the presence (1) or absence (0) of whatever it stands for. Frequently, though, all activation values between the extremes are allowed; in this case activations are said to be *continuously variable*. This is a very important feature of many connectionist models, as it permits different units to be simultaneously active to different degrees. If the units represent incompatible cognitive elements, then it permits the model to represent states of uncertainty or ambiguity. With respect to the discussion of the neuron above, a continuously variable activation level corresponds to the idea that neurons can convey graded information, either by differences in firing rate or by the number of cooperating neurons that are simultaneously active.

Normally, an activation of 0 represents the *resting level* of a unit, i.e. the activation level it will have (or will return to) given 0 input from anywhere else. However, there are certain exceptions. Some models use units which, given 0 input, will actually have an activation level of 0.5 (halfway between maximum and minimum). In such models, these units have to learn when to be inactive as well as when to be active. Other models use resting levels below 0, i.e. negative activations. This is most commonly a way of implementing a frequency effect. The less frequently whatever the unit represents occurs, the lower (more negative) is its resting level. Negative activation can also be used to represent the *suppression* of a unit, as a result of inhibition (see e.g. Glasspool, Chapter 8, this volume; Houghton & Tipper, 1996). Since a unit with negative activation has been inhibited below the point at which it begins to be able to affect other units, negative activation does not propagate along connections (see below). Neurally, it corresponds roughly to a state of hyperpolarization or inhibition, where the membrane potential is being kept away from the firing threshold.

As noted, the units in a network model represent the cognitive elements relevant to the model's domain. To give a concrete example, a model of word reading will need to have some way of representing the letter pattern of a word presented to it, and individual units can be assigned (by the modeller) to represent, for instance, particular letters (see Bullinaria, Chapter 3; Zorzi, Chapter 13, this volume). Once a representation is established, the activation level of a unit corresponds to the mental activation of whatever the unit represents. For instance, in a reading model, suppose there is a unit that represents the presence of a letter *g* at the beginning of a word. If the model is presented with the word *grant*, then this unit should become activated, representing the fact that the initial *g* has been perceived. However if the input word is *rant*, the initial *g* will not be activated. In the context of behaviour (as opposed to perception), units participate in the representation of responses, or actions. So, in a spelling model, individual units may represent letter identities for the purpose of writing or typing them (Houghton, Glasspool, & Shallice, 1994; Rumelhart & Norman, 1982). In this case, the activation of such units represents, not a perception, but an intended action or response. If the response units have continuously variable activations, then their relative activation levels can be used to code the relative strengths of a set of simultaneously active responses (Rumelhart & Norman, 1982). This has proved to be an important factor in modelling, for instance, serial order errors in many domains (see e.g. Dell, Chapter 12; Glasspool, Chapter 8; and Page, Chapter 7, this volume).

Vector representation of activation patterns

We frequently want to talk about the *pattern* of activation over a whole set of units, e.g. the input unit activation pattern, or the output unit pattern. We mentioned above that such a pattern can be represented as a set of activations, e.g. $\{a_1, a_2, \ldots, a_n\}$, for n units. Formally, it is convenient to treat such sets of numbers as single objects, called vectors. A vector can be thought of geometrically as specifying a point in a space (better, a line from the origin to that point, Fig. 1.3). For instance, if we have an output layer with only two units, with activations a_1, a_2, both with minimum and maximum activations of 0 and 1, then the overall "state" (pattern of activation) of the output units will always lie somewhere in a square two-dimensional (2-D) state space. This state can be represented by the activation vector $\mathbf{a} = \{a_1, a_2\}$ (vectors are denoted with lower case bold letters). Fig. 1.3 shows an example where $\mathbf{a} = \{0.75, 0.5\}$. Any other possible pairs of activations can be represented as a vector in the same space. Note that if the units are constrained to be binary, having activations of only 0 or 1, then there are only four possible activation

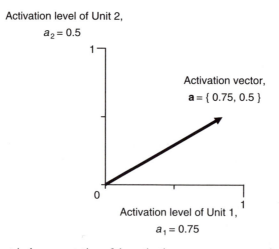

Figure 1.3.   Geometrical representation of the activation pattern over two units as a vector. The axes of the space are defined by the range of possible activation levels of the two units. Any given activation pattern over the units therefore corresponds to a point in the space whose coordinates are the activation levels of the two units. The activation *vector* is equivalent to the line from the origin to that point.

patterns ({0,0}, {0,1}, {1,0}, {1,1}), and they lie at the four corners ("vertices") of the state space.

The beauty of this geometrical interpretation of activation patterns is that it permits one to visualize important properties of such patterns which might otherwise be difficult to comprehend. For instance, considering Fig. 1.3, one could ask about the length of the activation vector (its magnitude), which we might use as a measure of the total "energy" in the activation pattern, longer vectors having more energy. If another activation vector were added to the space, one could ask how "similar" it was to the vector shown. Similarity can be interpreted, for instance, as the distance between the two vectors (the length of the straight line connecting the two endpoints), or alternatively, as the angle between the two vectors. At first sight, the idea of talking about the "angle" between representations might strike the reader as rather strange, but it is quite natural once the geometric interpretation of vectors is understood. The more components (active units) two representations (vectors) share, the smaller the angle between them will be. If they share no components, then we can say that the representations are independent of each other, or *orthogonal*. In this case, the vectors are at 90° to each other. It is straightforward to calculate these various properties from the vectors themselves.

Of course, we rarely deal with networks with only two units in a layer; however, the principles remain the same, however many units are involved. The state space of a set of units has as many dimensions as there are units in the set, and any pattern of activation over the set of units is equivalent to the "activation vector" in the high-dimensional space (although, of course, above three dimensions we can no longer visualize it). For instance, for an activation vector consisting of n binary units, the number of possible patterns is 2^n, and, just as for the 2-D case, they lie at the vertices of the n-dimensional state space. The lengths of, and distances and angles between, vectors (similarity) can also be calculated in the same way as in the 2-D case. As we shall see, the vector representation of activations is especially useful when combined with the matrix representation of weights described below.

Representation of cognitive elements by units

As mentioned several times above, the units in a network are used to represent the cognitive elements that are required in the domain being modelled. The simplest way to do this is to assign one unit to each identifiable element. For instance, in a model incorporating a mental lexicon (store of words), each known word would be represented by one unit. In a model of face processing, each unit would represent a known face. This is known as a *local* representation, as to find out to what extent a given mental entity is currently active we need only look "locally" at a single unit. From a more formal point of view, each element is represented *orthogonally* to all the others. Suppose we want to represent four individuals, John, Paul, George, and Ringo (Page, 2000), then we need four units, one for each individual. The activation pattern (vector) {1 0 0 0} would represent John, {0 1 0 0} would represent Paul, and so on. These activation patterns are all orthogonal to each other, meaning that they have *no* active elements in common. Mathematically, if we take the vector dot product of any pair of patterns (the sum of the products of corresponding elements, see below), the result is always 0. This lack of correlation between representations means that anything that happens to the activation of one unit (whether it goes up or down) will directly effect only one cognitive element.

Local representation requires as many units as there are things to be represented, and has been criticized for (amongst other things) being inefficient. An alternative is to use a *distributed* representation. In this case, cognitive elements are represented not by the activation of individual units, but by the pattern of activation over a set of units. In the above example, John might be {1 0 1 1}, Paul {1 1 0 0}, and so on. Thus, each entity is represented by many units, and each unit takes part in representing many entities. In the limit, as long as each pattern in a set differs from each of the rest by (at least) one unit, then it is distinct. Such a representation allows many more elements to be represented by a given set of units, as the number of possible patterns grows exponentially with the number of units (specifically, there are 2^n possible patterns of 0s and 1s for a set of n units). Of course, completely "packing" this space, so that every possible pattern represents a different entity, makes a system highly vulnerable to noise or damage, as a change in the state of just one unit (from 0 to 1, or vice versa) will change what is being represented.

The relative advantages of local and distributed representations have been the cause of debate, with some influential authors considering the use of distributed representations to be defining feature of the connectionist approach (see Page, 2000, and associated commentaries). In practice, many models use both forms of representation, and in many cases the use of distributed representations is restricted to the "hidden units", in networks trained using back-propagation or a related method (discussed below in the section on learning). In this case, the distributed representation employed by the hidden units is "discovered" by the network during learning, and considerable ingenuity may be required to analyse the representation (McClosky, 1991; Plaut et al., 1996).

From a psychology perspective, it is best to treat representations as embodying substantive claims about cognitive representation. Distributed representations can capture the similarity structure of a domain; items that are similar in some important respect will end up with similar (correlated) representations. This is important for generalization, as things learned (associatively) about one item will tend to generalize to items with similar representations. The central feature of local representation is not really "locality" *per se* (i.e. all the activations in one unit), but the more abstract property of orthogonality, or independence, mentioned earlier. That is, considered as activation vectors, any two local representations (over the same vector space) are orthogonal to (uncorrelated with) each other, so that anything that happens to one representation does not affect any other. Of course, at another level, involving different units, the two orthogonal items may be highly correlated. For instance, at the letter level the words *cat* and *sat* are very similar and the patterns (vectors) of letter unit activations representing the two words would be similar (they both contain activations of the units representing *at*; the vectors are not orthogonal to each other). Nevertheless, at the *word* level, *cat* and *sat* are distinct and unrelated, and local (i.e. orthogonal) lexical representations capture this perfectly. In general, it appears to be a fact about the world that distinct entities (e.g. identical twins, cars of the same make and model rolling off the same production line) can be virtually identical with respect to their constituent properties but be utterly separate as entities (and as equally separate as a pair of entities sharing no properties). If the brain were to use *only* distributed representations based on similarity structure, then in essence it would have failed to capture a pervasive and behaviourally significant feature of the world.

Connections and weights

There would be no "connectionism" without connections, and it is the "central dogma" of connectionism that all psychologically significant interaction and transformation of representations depends on the connections between the units that realise the representations. If the defining feature of cognitive processes is that they are knowledge-based, then the knowledge in a cognitive neural network is primarily contained in the pattern of connectivity between the units.

The connections in a network are pathways along which the activation of units may "flow", to influence the activation of other units. As noted, activation levels are represented by numbers. Connections introduce the second type of number found in networks, the *weights*. Each connection between two units in a network is associated with a weight, a number which may be positive, negative or 0. If the weight is positive, then the connection is *excitatory*; if the weight is negative, then the connection is *inhibitory*; if the weight is 0, then the connection is not functional (but still exists, and the weight might be changed as a result of *learning*). When the activation of a unit "spreads" along a connection from one unit to another, it interacts with the weight on the connection. By far the most common form of interaction is simply that the activation level is multiplied by the weight. The result of this multiplication of the two numbers is passed on to the receiving unit.

A very simple example consisting of two nodes and one connection is shown in Fig. 1.4. We label the "sending unit" *Unit 1*, and the "receiving unit", *Unit 2*. Letting w stand for a weight, the weight on the connection *from* Unit 1 *to* Unit 2 is written as $w_{1,2}$. If there was a connection going back from Unit 2 to Unit 1, that would be $w_{2,1}$ (the subscripts on the weights are often written the other way round, to be consistent with the matrix representation of weights, discussed below). Hence, the signal (or the *input*) Unit 2 receives from Unit 1 is given by the very simple rule (as above, we use the letter a to stand for activation, with a subscript, e.g. a_1, a_2, etc.) to denote the unit):

$$\text{Input to unit } 2 = a_1 \times w_{1,2} \qquad (1)$$

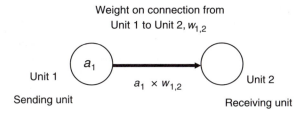

Figure 1.4. In most connectionist networks, the signal sent from one unit to another is computed as the activation level of the sending unit multiplied by the weight on the connection between them.

It is easy now to list all possible outcomes of this rule:

1. If either the activation, a_1, or the weight, $w_{1,2}$, is 0, then the input is 0. A zero weight always means a 0 signal is sent, whatever the activation level.
2. If the activation is not 0, then it is positive ($a_1 > 0$). Hence, the input to Unit 2 has the same *sign* (positive or negative), as the weight. Specifically:
   - If the weight is positive ($w_{1,2} > 0$), then the input is positive.
   - If the weight in negative ($w_{1,2} < 0$), then the input is negative.

The weight therefore determines the type of effect one unit has on another. By analogy with the neural case discussed above, a positive weight implements an excitatory connection (activation of one unit tends to increase the activation of another), while a negative weight implements an inhibitory connection (activation of one unit tends to reduce the activation of another).

The matrix representation of sets of weights

In discussions of connectionist models, it is common to find references to the "weight matrix" (or "matrices", plural). This is because the mathematical construct of a matrix (i.e. a 2-D array of numbers) provides a very convenient way of representing, and talking about, all the weights connecting sets of units. Take the two-layer network shown in Fig. 1.5. Connections go in one direction only, and every input unit is connected to every output unit (the figure explicitly shows only the connections to the first and last output units). As there are four input units in this network, then each of the six output units will receive four connections, 24 (6 × 4) weights in total. In general, any fully connected two-layer network will have a total of $n \times m$ weights, where n is the number of *output* units and m is the number of *input* units. Whatever the values of n and m, we can always represent the entire set of weights as a matrix, with n rows (one row per output unit) and m columns (one column per input unit). In this scheme, each row (horizontal array) of the matrix represents all the weights *to* a given output unit, and each column (vertical array) represents all the weights *from* a given input unit, (Fig. 1.5). The weight to output unit j from input unit i is thus located in row j, column i, e.g. the weight to output unit 6 from input unit 1 is in row 6, column 1 (Fig 1.5). Note that, in principle, the scheme could be reversed, the rows of the matrix representing the weights from input units, and the columns the weight to output units (the $n \times m$ matrix would become $m \times n$, known as the *transpose* of the original matrix). However, for mathematical reasons, this is not done.

Matrices are conventionally denoted in bold upper-case letters, hence we can denote a given weight matrix as **W**. As noted, each row of the matrix

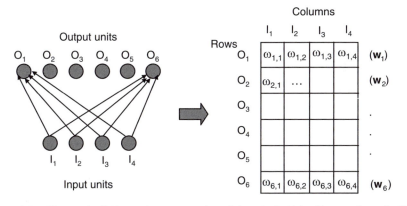

Figure 1.5.   The matrix (2-D array) representation of the set of weights in a two-layer feedforward network. The network is shown on the left and the matrix on the right. The input units are labelled I_1–I_4, and the output units O_1–O_6. The input and output units are completely connected, so that every output unit receives a connection from each of the four input units (only the connections to the first and last output units are shown). Each row of the matrix consists of the four weights to one output unit, the first row being the weights to the first output unit, the second row the weights to the second output unit, and so on. Hence, the matrix has as many rows as there are output units and as many columns as there are input units. Each row constitutes a vector, the weight vector for a given output unit, indicated by $\mathbf{w}_1$–$\mathbf{w}_6$ on the right of the matrix.

contains all the weights to a given output unit, thus consisting of a set of *m* numbers, where *m* is the number of input units. Just as with activations, above, we can think of this set of numbers (one row of the matrix) as a vector, in which case we can say that each row constitutes the input weight vector $\mathbf{w}_i$ to the output unit u_i.

Spread of activation and the net (summed) input

In the above example, Unit 2 only gets one input. In a typical model, a unit will have many connections to it, and any number of the units at the sending end of the connections may be active at the same time (Fig. 1.6). Hence, a unit can receive signals from many others in parallel. What does it do with them? By far the most common rule is that it simply adds them all up (cf. spatial summation in the neuron). As each individual input is the product of an activation and a weight [equation (1)], the *net input* is therefore a sum of products. The net input from a set of *n* units (1,2, . . ., n) to a unit *j*, net_j, is:

$$net_j = a_1\, w_{1,j} + a_2\, w_{2,j} + \ldots + a_n\, w_{n,j}$$

Using the sigma notation for summation (Σ), this can be written more succinctly as:

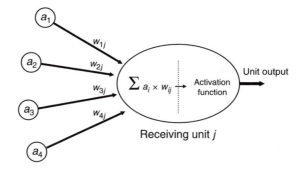

Figure 1.6. From input to output in a typical connectionist unit. The activation of every unit connected to the receiving unit (a1–a4 in the figure) is multiplied by the weight on the connection, and these individual signals are summed to produce the net input. This input passes through an activation function which determines the receiving unit's level of activation.

$$net_j = \sum_{i=1}^{n} a_i \times w_{i,j} \tag{2}$$

The summation is over all n sending units, i, from $i = 1$ to n.

   In the special case in which all the activations a_i are set to either 1 or 0 (this is often the case with at least the input units of a network), the rule becomes even simpler. Any unit with an activation of 0 produces an input of 0, while if the activation level is 1, then the activation times the weight equals the weight. So equation (2) reduces to simply adding up the weights on the connections from activated units.

Spread of activation using vector and matrix notations

Earlier we noted that a pattern of activation can be represented as a vector. In addition, the set of weights to a given output unit (one row of the weight matrix) constitutes a vector. In a fully connected net, the activation vector representing the input pattern and the weight vector to any output unit will have the same number of elements (obviously, as each input unit has one connection weight to the output unit). From this point of view, the spread of activation from the input units through the weights to a single output unit, u_j, can be considered an interaction between two vectors, the input activation vector $\mathbf{v}_{in}$, and the weight vector to u_j, $\mathbf{w}_j$. It turns out that there is a standard operation on pairs of vector, known as the vector *dot (or inner) product*, defined as the sum of the products of the corresponding vector components; i.e. for two vectors, $\mathbf{u}$ and $\mathbf{v}$, with the same number of elements, the dot product, $\mathbf{u}.\mathbf{v}$, is formed by multiplying the first element of $\mathbf{u}$ with the first of $\mathbf{v}$, the second with the second and so on, and then adding up all the products. If the vectors are the activation and weight vectors, $\mathbf{v}_{in}$ and $\mathbf{w}_j$, then this is just the net input rule stated in equation (2). Hence that equation can be written:

$$net_j = \mathbf{v}_{in}.\mathbf{w}_j \tag{3}$$

Equation (3) gives the net input to just one output unit. The same process has to be carried out for all output units (using the appropriate weight vector, or row, from the matrix). The result of this is a set of net inputs, $\{net_1, net_2, \ldots, net_m\}$, for m output units. Note that, once again, we have a vector, one which represents the signals all the output units receive once the activation vector passes through the weight matrix $\mathbf{W}$ [the activation vector is "multiplied" (dot product) by every row of the matrix]. Hence, we start with an activation vector over the input units $\mathbf{v}_{in}$. This interacts with a weight matrix $\mathbf{W}$, being multiplied by each row vector, generating as a result, another vector, let us say $\mathbf{v}_{out}$, which contains the signal each output unit receives. It would be handy to be able write one simple expression involving these three objects which captures the entire process. Happily, what has just been described corresponds to the multiplication of a vector (input pattern) by a matrix (weights). Hence, using vector–matrix notation, the whole process can be written:

$$\mathbf{v}_{out} = \mathbf{W}\mathbf{v}_{in} \tag{4}$$

This expression not only permits a very succinct representation of the processing carried out by a network, it is in fact the general form of a "linear" transformation of one set of variables, represented by components of the input vector, into another, represented by the output vector. Hence a single set of weights (matrix) can perform any linear transformation between two domains of representation. The question of the limits of such linear mappings is briefly addressed later.

Activation functions

Assuming that at least the weights in the network have continuous values, the net input to a unit is continuous, and may be positive (net excitatory), negative (net inhibitory), or zero. What does a unit receiving this input do in response to it? It has to decide on it own activation value, which will either be taken as part of the response (or output) of the network, or passed onto other units via further connections (possibly including "recurrent" connections). The rule for converting the input to a unit into an activation level is generally known as the *activation function*.

There are a number of activation functions in common use but, for units that sum their inputs, the general idea behind them can be stated very simply:

- The more excitatory the net input, the higher the activation level (nearer to its maximum value).
- The more inhibitory the net input, the lower the activation level (nearer to its minimum value, including negative, or suppressed, values).

Here we list a few common examples also found in articles in this book. Each example is shown graphically in Fig. 1.7. In each case the graphs plot the net input to a unit (*x* axis) against its activation level (*y* axis).

1. *Activation level is (linearly) proportional to the net input.* The simplest rule is just that the activation level of a unit is identical to (or proportional to) its net input, i.e. the activation function is given by equation (2). However, if there are no constraints on the size of the weights (and hence on the net input), this permits activation levels to be negative and/or arbitrarily large. If this is not desired, activations can be "clipped" at maximum (e.g. 1) and/or minimum values (e.g. 0). A linear activation function with clipping at 0,1 is shown in Fig. 1.7. The activation value can be made proportional to the net input (as opposed to identical to it) by simply changing the slope of the line. This can be done by multiplying the net input in equation (2) by a scaling parameter. The higher the value of this parameter, the steeper

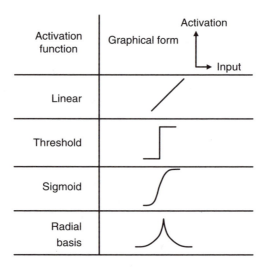

Figure 1.7.   Graphical forms of some commonly used activation functions. The horizontal axis represents the input signal to a unit, the vertical axis its response or activation level. In general, units increase their activation level as the strength of input increases. Radial basis functions, however, have a "preferred" input which produces the peak response. A change in the input in any direction reduces the response.

the slope of the curve and the more rapid the transition from activations of 0 to 1. Thus, the parameter might be thought of as controlling the "sensitivity" of the unit to changes in its net input.

2. *Binary threshold units.* If units are to have binary activations (0 or 1 only), then the continuous valued net input needs to be thresholded, so that if it is above the threshold, the unit is turned ON ($a_i = 1$), and if it is below the threshold the unit is turned OFF ($a_i = 0$). Fig. 1.7 shows a threshold function. The threshold is at the point θ on the x axis (net input). A threshold rule can be expressed by a conditional rule, such as the following:

$$a_i = \begin{cases} 1, \text{ if } net_i > \theta \\ 0, \text{ otherwise} \end{cases} \tag{5}$$

3. *Sigmoidal (S-shaped) activation functions.* A very common rule is to convert the continuous range of input values into a continuous range of activation values, but with "soft" limits on the activation, e.g. at 0,1 (or, say, $-1,1$ to represent "suppressed" states of activation using negative activation levels). Within these limits, the activations vary smoothly, with an overall S-shape (Fig. 1.7). The most commonly encountered mathematical form of this rule is (in its bare form):

$$a_i = \frac{1}{1 + exp(-net_i)} \tag{6}$$

The symbol *exp(.)* stands for the exponential function, i.e. the mathematical constant e ($= 2.714$) raised to the power of its argument, which in this case is the negative of the net input.

Some readers may find the mathematical form of the sigmoidal function a little puzzling, so we will briefly describe how it works. Suppose the net input is 0. Then $exp(0) = 1$ (any number raised to the power of 0 equals 1), and the value of the function is therefore ½ (0.5). That is, a unit with no input will have an activation level of 0.5 (see below). If the net input increases (becomes excitatory), the value of $exp(-net_i)$ falls (note the minus sign), and in the limit (minus infinity) is equal to 0. Thus, the maximum activation level is $1/(1 + 0) = 1$. Thus, excitatory input will increase the activation to a limit of 1. If the net input is inhibitory (negative, $net_i < 0$), then $-net_i$ becomes positive, $exp(-net_i)$ gets bigger than 1 and the denominator in the equation grows. As the denominator grows, the whole equation becomes a smaller and smaller fraction, with a value of 0 in the limit.

As noted, this rule produces an activation level of 0.5 for a net input of 0.0. In many feedforward multi-layer networks, the rule is used in this form. However, numerous variations on it are possible. For instance, it is a simple matter formally to shift the whole curve to the right (so to speak), so that a net input of 0 will produce an activation of about 0. Similarly, the minimum activation value can be easily changed to permit suppressed states of activation (activation levels below zero). Finally, the slope of the rising portion of the curve can be made more or less steep. If the slope is very steep, then the rule can be made to approximate a binary threshold rule.

A final mathematical note: the sigmoid function is continuous, i.e. it has no gaps or sudden jumps in value. Therefore, at every point in the curve we can say what the slope of the curve is (how fast the curve is rising at that point). Mathematically, this means that the sigmoid function is *differentiable*, that it has a *derivative*, a related function whose value at any point represents the slope of the sigmoid at that point. This is an important property, because gradient-descent learning rules for networks with hidden units (such as back-propagation) need the derivative of the activation function to calculate the "error" attributable to hidden units (Bullinaria, Chapter 3; Kruschke, Chapter 4, this volume).

Radial basis functions (RBFs)

The activation functions discussed above share the property that, as the net input to a unit becomes more positive (excitatory), the higher the expected activation value of the unit (the thresholded unit of course changes instantly once the threshold is reached, but as the net input increases, the more likely it is that the threshold will have been crossed). The last class of rule we discuss, radial basis function, does not have this property. Instead, we can think of a unit as having an optimal *pattern* of input, and as the actual input moves away from the optimal pattern, the activation level of the unit decreases (Fig. 1.7). In this case the activation of the input units is not multiplied by the weights. Rather, some form of comparison is made between the input activation pattern (vector) and the weights (weight vector) attached to given unit, such that the *distance* between the activation and the weights can be calculated. When the distance is zero, the input is the same as the weights; as the distance increases, the input is less similar to the weights. The activation level of the RBF unit should be maximal (e.g. = 1) when the similarity of the input pattern and the weights is maximal (distance = 0). The activation will decrease as the similarity becomes less in any way. Thus, the RBF can be thought of as implementing the idea of a "receptive field" in some space (the space can be an abstract feature space—Kruschke, Chapter 4, this volume). A unit with an RBF has a receptive field centred on some abstract "point" in the feature space, and responds more strongly as stimuli approach that point (from any direction).

Thus, an RBF rule consists of two parts: first, the "metric" rule, which compares the input pattern to the weights to derive the distance of the input from the optimal value; second, a typically symmetric "radial" function, which converts the distance value into an activation peaking when the distance is 0. An obvious measure of distance in the psychological space is the so-called Euclidean distance—the distance of a "straight line" from the point represented by the input to that stored in the weights. Suppose this distance is given by D, then the activation of an RBF unit with an "exponential" similarity gradient" is given by $exp(-D)$ (a parameter is usually added to change the slope of the gradient, i.e. the rate at which the activation falls off as the input moves away from the optimal one).

Activation decay and temporal integration

The rules discussed above convert the current net input to a unit to an activation value instantaneously. In none of the equations above is there any mention of time; in particular, no mention is made of the effect of the activation level of a unit at an immediately previous instant of time on its current activation. Units following such rules are "instantly reactive". To take a very simple example, if at some point in time t such a unit is given a "shot" of excitatory input, its activation will shift from 0 to a positive value, depending on the rule. If at the very next instant, that input is terminated, the activation will go immediately back to its resting level (typically 0). However, in many models, units do not behave like this (in particular models, with feedback or recurrent connections; See Fig. 1.11). Instead, if they are given an instantaneous jolt of activation, the activation then decays away gradually. If the unit receives no further activation within a given period of time, then its activation will return to the resting level. However, if it receives a further input before the activation returns to 0, then the new activation will be added to the current one. Hence, the units integrate their inputs both spatially and temporally.

LEARNING RULES

Learning, defined as the acquisition of knowledge and/or change in behaviour as a result of experience, is of great importance to connectionist models (see Christiansen and Curtin, Chapter 11; Kruschke, Chapter 4; Shanks, Chapter 2, all this volume). Learning takes place in the connections, by modification of the values of the weights. A wide variety of rules have been developed which, following exposure of the network to stimulus patterns, produce weight changes that are "useful", in the sense that if the same stimulus patterns are presented again, the response of the network will be better. How does one define what is a "better" response? In general, "better" means that the interaction with the environment is improved; that successful predictions can be made about it, on the basis of partial information. In the case of *category (or classification) learning*, experience leads to clustering of stimuli based on similarity—in brief, similar things go together, and should be treated in a similar manner. For instance, if one has learned from prior experience that some parts of plants taste good (e.g. fruits), and some bad (e.g. leaves) then the ability to classify a new stimulus as a fruit or a leaf, just by looking at it, will determine how one responds to it. To the extent that this prevents one from trying to eat an indigestible leaf or ignoring a succulent fruit, then the learning is useful (see Kruschke, Chapter 4, this volume, for discussion of category learning).

In the case of *associative learning*, the goal of learning is to associate disparate aspects of experience that occur together, hence enabling us to predict the structure of our environment on the basis of partial cues. For instance, faces and voices are processed in different brain areas, yet through experience we associate particular voices with faces of people that we know. On hearing a known voice, we look for the presence of a particular face. If we see a friend, we immediately notice any change in his/her voice (maybe he/she has a cold), or accent (who has he/she been talking to?). Hence, one form of perceptual input gives rise to learned expectations about another, and allows us to predict aspects of our environment ahead of time (and to detect changes in them).

In neural networks, a broad distinction is made between *supervised* and *unsupervised* learning. In supervised learning, the network is provided with some form of environmental feedback which indicates how well it is performing, and learning will only take place when the network performs badly, i.e. makes an error. In practice, the network is supplied during training with explicit target responses (outputs) to which its actual responses are compared. Useful weight changes are those that reduce the difference (error) between the actual output of the network and its target. In the case of unsupervised learning, there is no explicit comparison between actual and desired outputs. Rather, the network typically has implicit goals, such as forming a useful categorization (grouping) of sets of input stimuli, or extracting the co-occurrence relationships amongst features of the environment, which permit the prediction of features not actually present (e.g. Hebbian learning).

Below we discuss in more detail some of the more commonly used learning rules that occur in the articles in the current book. As stated, all learning rules change the weights between units, so we will write all the rules in the form $\Delta W_{ij} = \ldots$, by which we mean "on a given learning trial, the *change* (Δ) in the weight, W, between units u_i and u_j is equal to . . .". To derive the actual weight (following learning) the change in the weight is simply added to its existing value. If ΔW_{ij} is negative, then the weight will decrease; if it is excitatory, or become more negative, if it is inhibitory.

Unsupervised learning—the Hebb rule

The simplest learning rule is named after the psychologist Donald Hebb, who formulated an intuitive, physiologically based version of it in a work published in 1949. Hebb proposed that knowledge was stored in "cell assemblies", connected groups of neurons that would activate each other. Faced with the problem of how such assemblies could form on the basis of experience, Hebb proposed that if two cells that were connected repeatedly fired at the same time, then the strength of the connection between them (and hence the ability of one cell to activate the other) would increase. Thus, things that go together in one's experience (e.g. the face and voice of a friend) become associated, such that experiencing one thing can activate, or bring to mind, the other. In connectionist terms, the basic rule has the form:

$$\Delta w_{ij} = a_i \times a_j \qquad (7)$$

where a_i and a_j are the activations of two units connected by the weight w_{ij}. Hence, the weight increases (i.e. has a positive change) whenever the two units are active at the same time (if either unit has zero activation, then clearly $\Delta w_{ij} = 0$, and the weight does not change). In neural terms, the rule can be thought of as stating that the strength of (excitatory) synapses should increase whenever two neurons connected by such synapses fire (become depolarized) at the same time (or at least very closely in time). The phenomenon of *long-term potentiation* (LTP) of synapses has this characteristic (see e.g. Carlson, 2001, Chapter 14). The rule can be used to perform associative learning between mental entities that are active at the same time. For instance, Fig. 1.8 shows nodes from two layers of a simple reading model (e.g. McClelland & Rumelhart, 1981). In one layer each node stands for a letter (in a given position); in the upper layer each node stands for a word. If the letter nodes for "C", "A" and "T" are activated at the same time as the word node "Cat", then the weights on the connections (shown as solid, bold lines) between these units will be strengthened. Thus, the next time the same pattern of letter nodes is activated (without independent activation of "Cat"), the spread of activation from the letters to the word will be more likely to be able to activate the word (i.e. the letter pattern will be recognized as forming a known word).

The rule can be added to in various ways which complicate its mathematical expression (and for this reason have been omitted). For instance, a *learning rate* parameter is usually added, which scales the size of the weight change; lower values of the parameter produce more gradual learning, while higher values can produce rapid, even single-trial, learning. Single-trial learning is required, for instance, in modelling memory for single episodes, or short-term memory for stimuli presented just once (e.g. a list of words to be recalled in the correct order; see Page, Chapter 7, this volume). The activation values, a_i, a_j, can also be thresholded, so that learning only occurs if they are

Word units

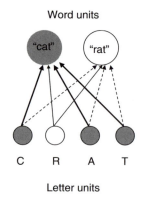

C   R   A   T

Letter units

Figure 1.8. A snapshot of Hebbian learning in part of a two-layer network mapping from letter units (spelling) to word units. Shaded units are active. When a set of letter units constituting a word is activated the appropriate word node should also become active, indicating what the word is. The letters "C" "A" and "T" are active at the same time as the unit representing the word "cat". Hebbian learning strengthens the weights on the connections between them (bold arrows). A contrasting "anti-Hebb" rule would also decrease the weights from the activated letter units to unactivated word unit "rat" (dashed arrows).

sufficiently high (this can avoid the learning of spurious coincidences, say due to random variation in activation levels).

In its basic form, the Hebb rule allows weights to increase indefinitely, whenever the two units are co-active. Given that the effect of the rule is to produce excitatory connections between the units, this could quickly become unavoidable, as the activation of one unit will be sufficient to activate the other, and hence the weight will increase even faster. Thus, there is a positive feedback relationship between the weight change and the likelihood that the two units will be co-active. Such a situation threatens to lead a network to be dominated by a few frequent patterns, which will be continuously activated whenever one part of a pattern is experienced. In the example shown in Fig. 1.8, if the connections from letter nodes "A", and "T" to "Cat" become strong enough then they will always activate the "Cat" node, even if they occur in another word, such as "Rat", "Mat", etc. This unwelcome outcome can be avoided in a variety of ways, e.g. weights can simply be given an upper value which they cannot exceed (clearly, biological synapses have some limit on their strength), or the summed weights of all inputs to a node can be fixed (weight normalization). More interestingly, the individual weights can be made to decrease actively by a so-called "anti-Hebb" rule, whereby the weight is decreased by some amount if the input unit (a_i) is active but the receiving unit (a_j) is inactive or only weakly active. In the example shown in Fig. 1.8, anti-Hebb learning would lead to a reduction in the weights (shown as dashed lines in the figure) from "C", "A", "T" to the word "Rat", as "Rat" was not activated. Interestingly, this proposal has physiological support in the phenomenon of *long-term depression* (LTD), in which firing of a pre-synaptic neuron combined with weak post-synaptic depolarization, or hyperpolarization, leads to a reduction in synaptic strength.

The Hebb rule, and its variants, typically alters excitatory connections between activated units to the extent that they "go together". The anti-Hebb rule, by decreasing weights, could in principle produce inhibitory connections between things that do not go together, by reducing the weight below zero (although there is no physiological support for such a change in the "sign" of a synapse). The development of inhibitory links is very important in many cognitive models, but they are generally produced using the delta rule or one of its generalizations, discussed next.

Supervised learning—the delta rule

The Hebb (and anti-Hebb) rules are considered examples of unsupervised learning, as no explicit feedback is given from the environment as to whether the network makes a correct response. More technically, there is no explicit *error signal*. Supervised learning, in contrast, only takes place when an error is detected in the output response of the network. For the error to be generated, the actual response of the network has to be compared with an externally provided "target" activation pattern (Shanks, Chapter 2, Zorzi, Chapter 13, this volume). Errors can be of two types, which we will refer to as "*omission*" and "*commission*" errors. In an omission error, the network fails to activate a node that should have come on. In a commission error, the network activates a unit that should have remained inactive. The two types of error frequently co-occur. For instance, suppose the network shown in Fig. 1.8 is being trained to read simple words. It is presented with the letter string "C" "A" "T" (i.e. the corresponding letter nodes are activated) but responds by activating the output node "Rat". In supervised learning, the "teacher" will specify that the node that should have been activated was "Cat". Hence, there is both a commission error ("Rat" was activated when it should not have been), and an omission error ("Cat" was not activated when it should have been). Both forms of error lead to weight changes, but in opposite directions:

- *Commission errors* lead to a reduction in excitatory weights (and/or increase in inhibitory weights) to the inappropriately active unit from all the input units that where activated by the input stimulus. Hence, if the same input pattern is repeated, the summed input [equation (2)] to the offending output unit will be less, so its activation level will fall (which is what is required).
- *Omission errors* lead to an increase in excitatory weights (and/or reduction in inhibitory weights) to the output unit that was not active enough, from all the input units that where activated by the input

stimulus. Hence, if the same input pattern is repeated, the summed input [equation (2)] to the under-active output unit will have increased, so its activation level will increase (which is what is required).

Let's now see how this actually works in practice. Here we give the standard formula for the Widrow–Hoff (or "delta") rule, for the weight change between an input unit, i, and an output unit, j (as with the Hebb rule, for simplicity we omit the learning rate parameter, which scales the size of any weight change):

$$\Delta w_{ij} = (target_j - actual_j) \times a_i \qquad (8)$$

The expression in brackets, $target_j - actual_j$, is called the *error term*, and is computed very simply by subtracting the actual activation of the output unit from the target activation provided by the teacher. The error term is then multiplied by the activation of the input unit from which the connection derives. Consequently, if the input unit is not active ($a_i = 0$), then no weight change takes place. Here we notice a similarity with the Hebb rule, discussed above—weight changes only take place when the "pre-synaptic neuron" is active. Indeed, if we denote the error term dj, the delta rule is $d_j \times a_i$, while the Hebb rule is $a_j \times a_i$.

Supposing the input "neuron" is active, Fig. 1.9 summarizes the possible

Actual activation of output unit

		Low (≈0)	High (≈1)
Desired (target) activation of output unit	Low (≈0)	Error ≈ 0 Wt change ≈ 0	(*Commission*) Error < 0 (negative) +ve wts decrease −ve wts increase
	High (≈1)	(*Omission*) Error > 0 (positive) +ve wts increase −ve wts decrease	Error ≈ 0 Wt change ≈ 0

Figure 1.9. A summary of weight changes produced by the delta rule. When actual and target activations are close (upper left, lower right quadrants), the error is small and little or no change takes place. In commission errors (upper right quadrant), a unit is more active than it should be, and the weights from active inputs are decreased (or made more inhibitory). In omission errors (lower left quadrant) a unit is less active than it should be, and the weights from active input units are increased (or made less inhibitory). Key: +ve = positive, −ve = negative, wt(s). = weight(s).

outcomes. The weights will change only if the target and actual activations of the output unit are different (if they are equal, then $dj = 0$, and hence $\Delta w_{ij} = 0$). A commission error (unit is active when it should not be) results in a negative error term, and hence a negative value for the weight change. Thus, positive (+ve) weights decrease, negative (−ve) weights increase (in absolute value). For an omission error (the output unit is not sufficiently active), the reverse happens. The value of the weight change is positive, positive weights become larger, and negative weights smaller. Hence, this very simple equation fulfils the requirements specified above.

The delta rule and the Hebb rule: A comparison

As noted above, the delta and Hebb rules look rather similar, especially if we use the notation dj for the error term. However, the delta rule has been presented (as is conventional) as an example of supervised learning, a process which apparently requires considerable machinery; a teacher is needed to supply the desired output, a comparison process must take place between the actual and desired outputs to generate an explicit error term, and finally the error term must be exported to the appropriate weight to determine the direction of the change. The Hebb rule, on the other hand, only requires that the input and output patterns be co-activated, and it will alter the associative weights between them, an example of unsupervised learning. However, this difference is really just a matter of how the rules are usually implemented. In fact, it is possible to implement the delta rule without explicitly computing the error. We can see this by applying some simple algebra. We can rewrite the delta rule [equation (8)] by multiplying out the error term in the bracket by a_i, which gives:

$$\Delta w_{ij} = (\text{target}_j \times a_i) - (\text{actual}_j \times a_i)$$

The rule now appears as two "Hebb-like" terms (actually, Hebb and anti-Hebb), with no direct comparison between a target and desired activation. The first term makes weights more positive (or less negative), while the second does the opposite (note the minus sign). The weight change due to the first term is precisely the Hebb rule, if we imagine the target activations instantiated on the output units, while the input units are active. This will make the connections to the output units that should be ON more positive. The second term can be computed by activating the input units and then *decrementing* the weights to any output units that are activated as a result. This is quite literally an anti-Hebb rule. Although it may appear odd to decrement all weights to active output units, this will especially affect those units that should not be activated (commission errors), as they will not have had the weights incremented by the Hebb term. Finally, note that when the target and actual activations are the same, then the Hebb and anti-Hebb components are equal and no learning will take place.

FURTHER EXTENSIONS OF THE DELTA RULE—MULTI-LAYER NETWORKS AND NONLINEAR MAPPINGS

The delta rule is defined for two-layer networks in which the input units are directly attached to the output units (Fig. 1.2a). Indeed, for any problem presented to such a network in the form of sets of input–target pairs (e.g. the pronunciation and spelling of the set of English monosyllabic words), the delta rule will find the "best" set of weights for making the associations between the two sets, in the specific sense that, over the whole set of input–target pairs, the total error will be as small as it possibly can be for a two-layer network. In the case of a problem that the network is in principle capable of solving, then the net error will be 0, i.e. for every stimulus pattern, the network will produce the correct response. However, the set of problems (defined as input–output mappings) that a two-layer network can solve *in principle* is limited. In technical terms, for a complete solution to be achievable by a two-layer net, the relationship defined by the mapping has to be *linear*. Explaining in detail what is meant by a linear mapping would require entering into too much mathematical discussion. Let us just note a couple of important properties of linear relationships (mappings). First of all, similarity (neighbourhood relationships) is preserved in the mapping. This means that input patterns that are similar will map to output patterns that are similar, e.g. the spellings of the words *cat, hat, flat, sat*, are similar (all end in "at"), and their pronunciations are also similar in an analogous fashion (all end in /& t/). Second, this sensitivity to similarity is combinatorial, in the sense that given two distinct input patterns, P_1 and P_2, that produce two output patterns, O_1 and O_2, respectively, then the combination of P_1 and P_2 (i.e. presented together) will produce an output similar to the combination of O_1 and O_2. For instance, to use the reading example again, if the network response to the separate inputs "sl" (P_1) and "at" (P_2) are /s l/ (O_1) and /& t/ (O_2), then the response to the combined input "slat" ($P_1 + P_2$) will be /s l & t/ ($O_1 + O_2$). Note that in a regular alphabetic reading system, such linearity is highly desirable, and will permit the network to correctly read most words, and correctly generalize to new words. However, it will lead to "regularization errors" when there are irregularly spelled words, as in English. For instance, the word *pint* will be pronounced to rhyme with *mint, hint, lint*, etc. (Zorzi, Chapter 13, this volume).

Exceptional items (such as *pint*) break the constraint of the preservation of similarity; it is not pronounced the way similarly spelled words are. Also, if we divide it up into $p + int$, then it breaks the combinatorial constraint, as (the nonword) *int* on its own would be pronounced with the short vowel of words like *hit*. More complex networks, with at least one additional layer of units (*hidden units*), are required to handle both the linear regularities and exceptional items (Seidenberg & McClelland, 1989). More generally, mappings that are not dominated by the linear properties sketched above (let us say, *nonlinear* mappings) require hidden units. To give a concrete example, the relationship between the spelling of a word and its meaning clearly violates linearity. For instance, *that, thin, spat* and *spin* are made up of combinations of onsets *sp, th* and rhymes *at, in*. However, there is clearly no corresponding relatedness in their meanings, or with the meanings of the words *at* and *in*, which they contain. This lack of "linear predictability" can extend to combinations of words, e.g. we cannot predict the meaning of the phrasal verb "to carry on" (i.e. continue) from the meanings of "to carry" and "on". Hence, models mapping between word forms and meanings must perforce include hidden units (e.g. Dell, Chapter 12; Leek, Chapter 6, this volume; Hinton & Shallice, 1991). Note that there are two possible ways in which these hidden units may be introduced (Fig. 1.2b,c). They may receive *all* the connections from the input units, so that the input and output units are no longer directly connected (Fig. 1.2a). In this case, as in the two-layer net, there is only one route between input and output. Or they may be added as an additional pathway between the input and output units, with the direct connections left in place (Fig. 1.2c). In the latter case, there are two routes from input to output, a linear and a nonlinear one. The single-route multi-layer network (Fig. 1.2b) is the form most frequently encountered in connectionist cognitive modelling, although the dual-route architecture is also found (Shanks, Chapter 2; Zorzi, Chapter 13, this volume). Although in purely computational terms the two architectures have the same "power", they are distinct cognitive architectures, and behave differently in simulation studies.

The addition of hidden units to networks permits them to handle arbitrary, nonlinear relationships (the hidden units must use a nonlinear activation function, such as the sigmoid, Fig. 1.7). Essentially the hidden units can re-map the input representations to a new representation, more appropriate for activating the appropriate output pattern. But how can this intermediate, hidden-unit representation be formed, if it is not specified *a priori* by the modeller? Ideally we would like to have a learning rule, like the delta rule, but applied to networks with hidden units. The immediate problem with applying the delta rule is that, although it could be adopted to change the weights from the hidden to output units (the activation of the input units in equation (8) could be replaced with the activation of the hidden units), it provides no way of adapting the weights from the input to hidden units. In particular, if we want to use a supervised learning rule, we need a way to define the *error* for the hidden units, so that the input-to-hidden weights can be changed to reduce the error. But how can this be done, given that the target activations are only defined for the output units? The *back-propagation* learning rule provides a solution for this (Rumelhart, Hinton, & Williams, 1986).

I do not intend here to provide a mathematical account of back-propagation, as it requires the use of concepts, notation and procedures from differential calculus. Instead I will try and provide an intuitive insight into how it works (this inevitably involves some simplification with respect to the details of the standard account of the algorithm; in particular, I have omitted any reference to the derivative of the activation function. Readers requiring a fuller account should consult O'Reilly & Munakata, 2000).

For a three-layer network such as that shown in Figure 1.2b, the problem is to change two sets of weights, from hidden-to-output, and from input-to-hidden, in such a way that, for a given input–target pair, the error at the output units will decrease once the changes have been made. The network is set up at the outset with random, nonzero weights. The hidden and output units use a sigmoidal activation function. If an input pattern is presented, activation will flow through the network, according to equations (2) and (6) above, leading to a pattern of activation first on the hidden and then on the output units. These patterns will initially be "wrong", being the result of the initial set of random weights. The output is compared to the target pattern (from which it will initially differ) and, on this basis, an error for each output unit can be calculated in essentially the same way as for the basic delta rule. This error is used to change the hidden-to-output weights, again as described above for the two-layer net (but with the input unit activation replaced by the hidden unit activation).

Now comes the tricky part, the assignment of "error" to the hidden units. Essentially, every output unit that made an error (i.e. did not produce the right activation) apportions "blame" to the hidden units (which is appropriate, as the output pattern is a direct result of the signal sent from the hidden units). If the output unit was more active than it should have been, then it received too excitatory a signal from the hidden units, and its error will be negative (target – actual < 0). If the unit was not as active as it should have been, it received an insufficiently excitatory signal, and will have a positive error (target – actual > 0). In the crucial step, these output error terms are now "propagated" back to the hidden units, modulated by a calculation of the way in which each hidden unit contributed to making the error. For instance, if an output unit was *less* active than it should have been, then a hidden unit having positive connections to it could reduce the error by being *more* active (sending more activation), and a hidden unit having negative connections by being *less* active (sending less inhibition). In the former case, the hidden unit will get a positive error signal, in the latter a negative signal. This is achieved by simply multiplying the output unit error (positive, in this case) by the weight from the hidden unit (Fig. 1.10). If the output unit was *more* active than it should have been, then the output unit error is negative, and the above situation is reversed (but the logic is the same).

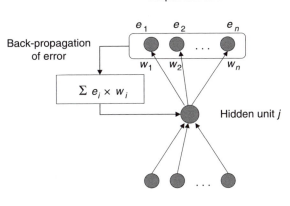

Figure 1.10. Back-propagation of error in multi-layer networks. The problem is to extend the delta rule to networks with hidden units (for clarity, the figure shows just one hidden unit, but the same process applies to all hidden units). For this, hidden unit error must be defined; however, unlike the output units, they have no externally defined target activation. Instead, each hidden unit is assigned a degree of "blame" based on an assessment of its overall contribution to the output unit error. All the output units "back-propagate" their errors (e_1, e_2, . . ., e_n) to each hidden unit via the hidden-to-output weights. Each hidden units sums these signals to derive its individual error term. The hidden unit error is then used to change the input-to-hidden weights in the same way that the output unit error changes the hidden-to-output weights.

Hence, a hidden unit receives an error signal from every output unit, which it sums up (Fig. 1.10). This summed signal (modulated by the hidden unit activation level) is the hidden unit error, which tells the hidden unit how, overall, it could best contribute to reducing the output error, by being more or less active than it actually was (or, in the case of a zero error signal, by staying the same). The hidden units then use this error just like the output units, by adding it to the weights from the input units that were active. For instance, if a hidden unit could have reduced the overall output error by being more active than it was, its error will be a positive number. Adding this to the weights from the active input units will make the excitatory weights stronger and the inhibitory weights weaker. Consequently, if the same input pattern is now presented again, the hidden unit will get a more excitatory input, its activation will increase, and this will lead in turn to a smaller error at the output units.

As with the delta rule, BP also has a learning rate parameter, scaling the size of the weight changes. For a given problem, a whole set of input–target pairs are presented to the network one after another. The algorithm performs a "gradient descent" with respect to the error, always changing the weights (as described above) in such a way that performance on the most recently presented input–target pair will improve (if it is not already perfect). In general the learning rate should be fairly low, leading to very gradual, incremental learning. If faster learning rates are used, each learning episode pulls the weights strongly towards the optimal setting for the most recently experienced input. For complex, nonlinear mappings, this is likely to interfere with the optimal weights for some other input–output pair (or pairs) in the learning set. When these other items are presented to the network, the error will consequently be high, and the large weight change will tend to pull the weights back in a different "direction". Hence, the network will tend to oscillate between different "local" solutions, rather than converging slowly on a global one.

This point leads us to a major difference between the delta rule and back-propagation (more strictly, between two-layer and multi-layer networks). We noted above that for a given learning task, the delta rule is guaranteed to find an optimal set of weights, in the sense that the overall error on the task will be a low as is possible for the network. If the mapping task contains significant nonlinearities, then the solution will not be perfect, but it will be the best the network can do (given the input–output representation chosen by the modeller). For multi-layer networks, there is no equivalent guarantee (more technically, there is no "convergence theorem"), i.e. a multi-layer network may have sufficient representational capacity (sufficient hidden units and associated weights) to solve a problem in principle, but the back-propagation algorithm may fail to find the solution. This is mainly due to what are known as "local minima" in the error space. If the network ends up in a local minimum, then the weight changes produced by improving performance on *any* individual input–output pair lead to an overall increase in error on the other patterns. This will lead to the change being cancelled out, as the other patterns pull the weights back to where they were. In this case, one talks of the network being "stuck" in the minimum. The network is still making errors, but whichever way it turns (so to speak) its overall performance worsens, so it stays where it is. In practice, this problem can often be overcome by simply starting again with a new set of random weights (and maybe changing the number of hidden units) and hoping for the best! Given sufficient redundancy in the network, there is every chance that next time round the local minimum will be avoided. However, many more principled developments and refinements of the basic algorithm have been produced which aim to make the learning altogether faster and more reliable. Although some of these methods have been used in the construction of cognitive models, they are not central to any of the chapters of this book, and will not be discussed here.

Finally note that the algorithm is not restricted to one set of hidden units. Once error measures have been derived for one set of hidden units, these can then be used to send error signals back to further sets of hidden units, which compute their own error using the same logic. However, further layers do not increase the computational power of the networks, and models in cognitive psychology rarely use more than one set of hidden units in mapping between two levels of representation.

FEEDBACK AND RECURRENT ARCHITECTURES

So far we have been concerned only with networks in which activation spreads in one direction only, i.e. *feedforward* networks. In such networks, processing of an input occurs in a single pass through the network, as the input vector is transformed into the output vector. In networks with more interesting dynamic properties, activation patterns change over time, usually have some form of feedback, so that pairs of units are connected in both directions, and the activation of either unit can affect the other. We finish this introductory chapter with a description of these architectures. We will divide feedback (or recurrent) architectures into two categories, within-layer feedback and between-layer feedback. It should not be supposed that there is any contrast intended between these categories, and single networks may employ both forms of recurrent connectivity (e.g. Grossberg's (1980) adaptive resonance model; McClelland and Rumelhart's (1981) related interactive activation model).

Within-layer feedback and winner-takes-all dynamics

As the name suggests, in within-layer feedback, units within a layer are connected to each other. Perhaps the most common form is *lateral inhibition*, which can be used to produce *winner-takes-all* (WTA) dynamics over a set of units (see Cooper, Chapter 10, Glasspool, Chapter 8, this volume). WTA is important in localist networks using continuous activation functions, e.g. the sigmoid function, equation (6). In such a network, more than one unit in a group of units may be active at one time. If the units represent mutually incompatible entities (e.g. object nodes in an object recognition network; Heinke & Humphreys, Chapter 9, this volume; responses in an action planning network; Cooper, Chapter 10, this volume), then the activation of multiple units represents uncertainty as to what is being perceived, or what to do. A decision has to be made, and this requires that only one unit remain active (or active above a threshold).

In WTA systems, the unit with initially highest activation eventually becomes the only active unit. This is achieved by the lateral interaction between the units in the layer. Each unit has an excitatory connection to itself (positive feedback) and lateral inhibitory connections to all the other units (Fig. 1.11a). Typically, the weights on these connections have fixed values for the network; all the positive feedback weights are the same, and all the

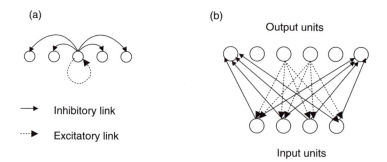

Figure 1.11.   Two forms of recurrent or feedback connectivity. (a) Within-layer feedback; every unit within the layer is connected to itself on to every other unit in the layer. The figure shows a "winner-takes-all" network in which each unit sends positive feedback to itself and lateral inhibition all other units. (b) Between-layer feedback; the output units send activation back to the input units via a separate set of connections (bold, dotted arrows). For clarity the figure only shows some connections, but all units in one layer are connected to all units in the other layer, in both directions.

inhibitory weights are the same. The "internal" input a unit j (Int_j) receives from within the layer is thus given by:

$$Int_j = a_j\, w^+ + w^- \sum_{i \neq j} a_i \qquad (9)$$

where a_j is the activation of unit j, a_i is the activation of other units in the layer, w^+ is the positive feedback weight, and w^- is the lateral inhibitory weight (Figure 1.11a). The first term on the right-hand side of equation (9) is the positive (self-) feedback, while the second represents the inhibition received from all other units in the layer (the constant lateral inhibitory weight is multiplied by the sum of the activation of all other units in the layer). This implements a form of competition for activation, and the initially most active unit has the advantage; it will send more activation to itself than any other unit (the size of the self-feedback term in equation (9) depends on the unit's activation); and will receive the least inhibition (the lateral inhibition depends on the summation over the activation of other units in the layer; this will be smallest for the most active unit, as it will contribute the most to the inhibition of other units, but does not inhibit itself). Thus, after an initial activation pattern is established by an external input, WTA leads to the gradual suppression of all but the most active unit, as the less active units get inhibited by the lateral inhibitory signals, and thereby become progressively less able to support their own activation via excitatory feedback. Note that the fact that this competitive process takes time allows a network to produce variations in response time, which is used for modelling human reaction times.

Between-layer feedback and attractor dynamics

In the case of between-layer feedback, connections run in both directions between two layers of units. In the case of a basic two-layer network, as well as connections from the input to the output units, there are connections from the output to the input units (Grossberg, 1980). The network thus has two weight matrices, the feedforward and feedback matrices. If the feedforward matrix has n rows and m columns, then the feedback matrix will have m rows and n columns. As with the within-layer feedback, this feedback will give the network a more complex dynamics, with the activation pattern changing over time (Dell, Chapter 12, this volume). After the output units are first activated by the initial forward pass of activation, this activation is fed back to the input units via the feedback weight matrix (which will transform the pattern of activation). The input units are now receiving a new pattern of input and their own activations will change. This will in turn change the signal the output units receive, which will then send a new signal to the input units, and so on. In short, the network's response to an initial signal to the input units is no longer computed in a single pass but evolves over time.

Where does it evolve to? Let us suppose that even though the activation in the network continues to pass back and forth between the layers of units, there comes a point when the activation pattern over all the units ceases to change (proving when this is bound to happen is mathematically challenging, and we will simply assume that it is the case). In the jargon of the field, we say that the network has "settled" to its final response, in which the pattern of activation over the whole network is stable (no longer changing). These stable states of recurrent networks, towards which they will spontaneously move, or be attracted, when "perturbed" by an external input, are known as "attractors" in the terminology of dynamic systems theory. Any network with recurrent connectivity will possess attractors, which, if the network is functioning properly, should correspond to the functionally meaningful states of the network (depending on the network, these may constitute the network's "memories", or its cognitive consistent states). For instance, for the WTA network discussed above, the attractors are (ideally) the states in which only one unit is active. Attractors that do not correspond to meaningful states are termed "spurious" attractors. As with WTA dynamics, the time taken for a recurrent network to settle can be used to generate reaction time predictions (Dell, Chapter 12, this volume; Grossberg, 1980; McClelland & Rumelhart, 1981).

The reader might note that if, following the presentation of a single input, a network passes through a series of "meaningful" states, then the network will have produced interpretable sequential behaviour. For instance, if the network has response units which (by whatever means) represent letters, then if it runs through the sequence of activations representing the letters "c", "a", and "t" then it will have spelled the word "cat". Recurrent network architectures specifically aimed at generating meaningful sequential behaviour have been produced, and are discussed by Glasspool, Chapter 8, and Christiansen & Curtin, Chapter 11, this volume.

REFERENCES

Carlson, N. R. (2001). *Physiology of behavior* (2nd ed.). Boston, MA: Allyn & Bacon.

Charniak, E., & McDermott, D. (1985). *Introduction to artificial intelligence*. Reading, MA: Addison-Wesley.

Douglas, R. J., & Martin, K. A. C. (1990). Neocortex. In G. M. Shepherd (Ed.), *The synaptic organisation of the brain* (pp. 389–438). Oxford: Oxford University Press.

Grossberg, S. (1980). How does a brain build a cognitive code? *Psychological Review, 87*, 1–51.

Hinton, G., & Shallice, T. (1991). Lesioning an attractor network: Investigations of acquired dyslexia. *Psychological Review, 98*, 74–96.

Hopfield, J. J. (1982). Neural networks and physical systems with emergent collective computational properties. *Proceedings of the National Academy of Sciences*, USA, 81, 3088–3092.

Houghton, G., Glasspool, D., & Shallice, T. (1994). Spelling and serial recall: Insights from a competitive queuing model. In G. D. A. Brown, & N. C. Ellis (Eds.), *Handbook of spelling: Theory, process and intervention* (pp. 365–404). John Wiley & Sons: Chichester.

Houghton, G., & Tipper, S. P. (1996). Inhibitory mechanisms of neural and cognitive control: Applications to selective attention and sequential action. *Brain & Cognition, 30*, 20–43.

Houghton, G. & Zorzi, M. (2003). Normal and impaired spelling in a connectionist dual route architecture. *Cognitive Neuropsychology, 20*(2), 115–162.

Kohonen, T. (1984). *Self-organisation and associative memory*. New York: Springer-Verlag.

Llinás, R. R., & Walton, K. D. (1990). Cerebellum. In G. M. Shepherd (Ed.), *The synaptic organisation of the brain* (pp. 214–245). Oxford: Oxford University Press.

McClelland, J., & Rumelhart, D. E. (1981). An interactive activation model of context effects in letter perception: Part 1. An account of basic findings. *Psychological Review, 88*, 375–407.

McClelland, J., & Rumelhart, D. (1986). *Parallel distributed processing: Explorations in the microstructure of cognition: Vol. 2. Psychological and biological models*. Cambridge, MA: MIT Press.

McClosky, M. (1991). Networks and theories: The place of connectionism in cognitive science. *Psychological Science, 2*, 387–395.

O'Reilly, R., & Munakata, (2000). *Computational explorations in cognitive neuroscience*. Cambridge, MA: MIT Press

Page, M. P. A. (2000). Connectionist modelling in psychology: a localist manifesto. *Behavioral and Brain Sciences, 23*, 443–512.

Plaut, D., McClelland, J. L., Seidenberg, M. S., & Patterson, K. (1996). Understanding normal and impaired word-reading: Computational principles in a quasi-regular domain. *Psychological Review, 103*, 56–115.

Pylyshyn, Z. (1984). *Computation and cognition: Toward a foundation for cognitive science*. Cambridge, MA: MIT Press.

Rumelhart, D. E., Hinton, G., & Williams, R. (1986). In D. E. Rumelhart, & J. L. McClelland (Eds.), *Parallel distributed processing: Explorations in the microstructure of cognition: Volume 1. Foundations* (pp. 318–362). Cambridge, MA: MIT Press.

Rumelhart, D. E., & McClelland, J. L. (Eds.). (1986). *Parallel distributed processing: Explorations in the microstructure of cognition: Vol. 1. Foundations*. Cambridge, MA: MIT Press.

Rumelhart D. E., & Norman, D. (1982). Simulating a skilled typist: A study of skilled cognitive-motor performance. *Cognitive Science, 6*, 1–36.

Seidenberg, M. S., & McClelland, J. L. (1989). A distributed developmental model of word recognition. *Psychological Review, 96,* 523–568.

Shallice, T. (1988). *From neuropsychology to mental structure.* Cambridge: Cambridge University Press.

Shallice, T., Glasspool, D. W., & Houghton, G. (1995). Can neuropsychological evidence inform connectionist modeling? Analyses of spelling. *Language and Cognitive Processes, 10,* 195–225.

Shepherd, G. M. (1992). *Neurobiology* (2nd Ed.). New York: Oxford University Press.

Widrow, G., & Hoff, M. E. (1960). *Adaptive switching circuits. Institute of Radio Engineers, Western Electronic show and convention record, Part 4* (pp. 96–104).

SECTION ONE

Learning

CHAPTER TWO

Connectionist models of basic human learning processes

David R. Shanks
Department of Psychology, University College London, UK

It is natural to believe that the current high level of interest in connectionist models of cognitive processes is attributable to the impressive accounts such models can provide of human competencies (e.g. reading, classification, skill acquisition) and that the (arguable) improvement such models provide in explanatory power over nonconnectionist models is the main impetus to their growing acceptance amongst cognitive psychologists. From a historical perspective, however, a more compelling reason for trying to understand high-level human abilities within a connectionist framework is that many decades of research, especially on elementary conditioning in animals, has led to an almost-universal consensus (although see Gallistel, 1990, for an alternative viewpoint) that learning involves moment-by-moment increments and decrements in mental associations. This connectionist view of elementary learning has achieved outstanding success (Dickinson, 1980; Fletcher et al., 2001; Hall, 1991; O'Reilly & Rudy, 2001; Schultz & Dickinson, 2000; Waelti, Dickinson, & Schultz, 2001) and thus, so long as one is willing to envisage some continuity between phylogenetically primitive processes such as conditioning and more "high-level" capacities such as reading acquisition, then pursuing a connectionist research program in cognitive psychology becomes all but mandatory.

In this chapter I discuss elementary learning processes in various human analogues of animal conditioning procedures and use the findings to draw conclusions about the basic properties required in realistic connectionist models. One might wonder what is to be gained by studying human learning in these tasks rather than the "real thing", namely animal Pavlovian conditioning itself, especially since the latter has been an immensely active field within psychology for three-quarters of a century, generating a vast stock of knowledge (in this chapter I do occasionally describe relevant animal Pavlovian conditioning findings). In response to this very fair point, I would argue, first, that researchers studying human associative learning tend to pay careful heed to the animal work and usually hesitate before making theoretical claims that are at variance with the latter. In fact, there is a remarkable degree of similarity between the principles governing Pavlovian conditioning and human associative learning (Shanks, 1995) and there seems little risk at present that theories of human and animal learning will diverge seriously. A second reason is more to do with persuasiveness: No matter how compelling the evidence is in Pavlovian conditioning for the involvement of connectionistic processes, there will always be a leap of faith involved in seeing a relationship between such processes and more high-level human abilities. Indeed, there have been those who have argued that there is no such thing in humans as Pavlovian conditioning, since conditioning always seems to be permeated by "cognitions" (Brewer, 1974). Studies of human associative processes provide an indispensable bridge spanning these two extreme fields, especially if high-level cognitive processes (e.g. causal induction) can be shown to obey the same rules as conditioning (Dickinson, 2001; Lober & Shanks, 2000).

Very many of the so-called "supervised" networks and architectures that have been most extensively studied in the last few years take as their input a pattern of activation across a set of input units, generate an output pattern across a set of output units, and then receive some sort of signal from the outside world, indicating what the output pattern generated by the system should have been. A learning rule adjusts the weights in the network, such that the actual and desired output patterns converge over time. This sort of simple situation provides a straightforward model for associative learning and memory tasks, which conform to this input–output mapping description. Some examples include generating the past tense of a verb from its stem, generating the pronunciation of a word from its written form, and deciding the category to which an object belongs. These competences are complex, however, in a number of ways. For instance, in the domain of past-tense learning (see Plunkett & Marchman, 1993), the input stimuli (verb stems) and outputs (past tense forms) require very sophisticated coding schemes; lengthy training is involved both for children acquiring this competence and for networks simulating it, and the critical phenomena to be accounted for in evaluating the model are subtle. Thus, even if a connectionist model is reasonably successful in such a domain, that success is bound to be a complex interaction of many of these factors and it is likely to be difficult to prove that the specific coding scheme, say, or learning algorithm, is psychologically appropriate.

In consequence, it is necessary to turn to much simpler situations in which the learning task is stripped down to its bare essentials in such a way that the coding scheme, learning algorithm, and so on can be more directly and independently studied. This is achieved, in the experiments described in this chapter, by using tasks such as the following. Participants are instructed to imagine that they are food allergists attempting to work out which foods various fictitious patients are allergic to. On each trial a meal is presented to the patient, comprising one or a small number of foods, and the participant has to predict whether an allergy ensues. Then feedback is given about the actual outcome and the participant goes on to the next trial. Over a series of trials (usually in the order of 50–200), various trial types are presented repeatedly in an intermixed order until the participant is correctly predicting the outcome on each trial. Finally, a transfer test is given to assess some aspect of the learning process. The parallel to Pavlovian conditioning should be clear, with the foods playing the role of conditioned stimuli (CSs) and the allergy the role of the unconditioned stimulus (US).

As we will see, despite the simplicity of the ability we are attempting to simulate, there are profound difficulties in creating an adequate connectionist theory, but a good deal of progress has nevertheless been made. Also, it should be mentioned that the experimental designs on which this chapter focuses can generally be solved without the need for selective attention, and the models I review do not incorporate attentional processes. Yet, as Kruschke makes clear in Chapter 4 of this volume, such processes are of considerable importance in associative learning more broadly. I assume that the models described below would need, in a more complete treatment, to be supplemented with attentional processes of the sort Kruschke describes.

LINEAR AND NONLINEAR CLASSIFICATIONS

A useful starting point is an analysis of the abilities (and more importantly, limitations) of the simplest connectionist device for performing supervised learning. Suppose we have a large set of potential cues (or "elements" or "micro-features") that define the to-be-learned item and a number of possible outcomes. We assume that each of the cues is represented by a unit in a homogeneous input layer of a large, highly interconnected network, such as that shown in Fig. 2.1. Each outcome is also represented by a unit in a separate output layer, and each input unit is connected to each output unit with a modifiable connection (for the moment, we ignore possible hidden units). Networks of this form are called *feedforward* networks or *pattern associators*.

On every trial, some item consisting of a set of cues is presented. We calculate the activation a_o of each output unit:

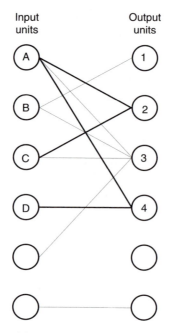

Figure 2.1. Pattern associator. A homogeneous layer of input units is connected in parallel to a layer of output units. The connections between the units have modifiable weights. When a pattern of activation (representing the input stimulus) is applied to the input units, activation spreads to the output units via the weighted links between the units. A learning algorithm adjusts the weights on a trial-by-trial basis until the correct pattern of activation is obtained on the output units. Solid lines represent links that have acquired positive or negative weights and dotted lines represent some of the potential links that may be strengthened on future training trials.

$$a_o = \sum_i a_i \, w_{io} \qquad (1)$$

where a_i is the activation of input unit i and w_{io} is the current weight from that unit to output unit o. For a binary-valued cue, a_i will be 1 if that cue is present and 0 if it is not, whereas for a continuous-dimension cue, a_i will take on a value corresponding to the value of the cue on that dimension. Next, we calculate the "error", d_o, on the output unit between the obtained output, a_o, and the desired output, t_o:

$$d_o = t_o - a_o \qquad (2)$$

Values of t_o are determined in a similar way to values of a_i and represent the feedback provided to the learner. Usually t_o takes the value 1.0 if the target outcome is present and 0.0 if it is absent.

Finally, we use the well-known "delta" rule (Stone, 1986) to change each of the weights in proportion to the error:

$$\Delta w_{io} = \alpha \, a_i \, d_o \qquad (3)$$

where Δw_{io} is the weight change and α is a learning rate parameter for the cue.

As described above, the procedure for training a connectionist network is to provide a set of input patterns (items) together with their associated target output patterns. As a result of incremental weight changes dictated by the delta rule, the network will come to produce the correct output pattern for each input pattern. It is important to note that the delta rule is guaranteed (given enough trials) to produce a set of weights that is optimal for the training stimuli (see Kohonen, 1977). That is to say, the rule will find a set of weights that minimizes the squared error between actual and desired output patterns. Often, this squared error will be zero, meaning that the network produces exactly the desired output for each input pattern. We will discuss below some cases where this is impossible unless extra units are included between the input and output units, but even without such units, the delta rule will minimize the squared prediction error. The ability to prove that a learning rule will *converge* in this way towards an acceptable solution is an important feature.

In pattern associators, associative knowledge is represented in weighted connections between elements of the stimulus and elements of the outcome. The model given in equations (1)–(3) is in fact formally equivalent to the well-known Rescorla–Wagner theory (Rescorla & Wagner, 1972) of animal Pavlovian conditioning, a theory that has dominated conditioning research for nearly 30 years (Hall, 1991; Miller, Barnet, & Grahame, 1995) and which has many proven empirical successes. While this learning algorithm has been successfully applied to many tasks, however, there is evidence to suggest that its "elemental" representational assumption is inadequate. In learning to associate one pattern with another, for instance, it appears that in addition to learning direct associations between the outcome and the separate elements that make up the stimulus, higher-order representations of the stimulus can also be involved in associations with the outcome.

The inadequacy of the notion that the elements of the cue are directly and independently associated with the outcome comes from a number of sources. Perhaps the most direct is evidence concerning summation in animal Pavlovian conditioning. According to the elemental coding assumption, a compound cue such as ABC, comprising three elements, should elicit a response that is proportional to the sum of the weights of the elements A, B, and C. If these elements have previously been separately paired with a US and have each acquired asymptotic weights of 1.0, then the compound ABC should evoke summation, that is to say, a level of responding that is far higher than that elicited by the elements themselves. Although the precise conditions remain to be clarified (Myers, Vogel, Shin, & Wagner, 2001; Rescorla, 1997), there is now convincing evidence against this prediction from studies that reveal no evidence of summation in experiments of this sort (Aydin & Pearce, 1997; Pearce, Aydin, & Redhead, 1997).

Another and more well-established source of evidence comes from the fact that humans can learn *nonlinearly separable* classifications. In single-layer networks, in which just one layer of modifiable connections exists between the input and output units, it is easy to see that the predicted outcome a_o must be a linear sum of the inputs. Consider a network consisting of two input units (denoted x and y) connected to one output unit, where the inputs and correct output, t_o, can take on values between 0.0 and 1.0, and where the network is trained to classify input patterns into one of two categories. Regardless of the weights, equation (1) tells us that the output a_o must always be a simple linear sum of the activations (a_x and a_y) of input units x and y:

$$a_o = a_x\, w_{xo} + a_y\, w_{yo}$$

It follows that the only types of classification such a system can learn are *linearly separable* ones in which the members of the two categories can be distinguished by a simple linear boundary. Specifically, for the delta rule model to learn a discrimination, it must be possible to construct a straight line in the x,y input space that exactly divides the stimuli into the correct categories. If such a line can be drawn, then there exist weights that will allow the model to produce greater outputs for members of one category than for members of the other category. The discrimination is solved by making one response whenever the output is greater than a threshold and the other response whenever it is less.

However, people have no difficulty learning nonlinearly separable dis-criminations that the delta rule model would be unable to master. Consider the following simple experiment. In this task, 16 participants (UCL students) had to learn relationships between foods people ate and allergic reactions caused by those foods. On each trial, a list of foods was described that the person had eaten, and the participant had to choose one out of a selection of possible allergies that the person suffered. The foods were such things as bananas, avocados, etc., and the allergies were called Type 1, Type 2, etc. Some of the people suffered no allergic reaction. After making their predic-tions, participants received feedback telling them the correct outcome for that trial. Embedded in the design were critical trials of the following sorts which conform to a *feature-neutral* discrimination (Rudy & Sutherland, 1995): A → O, BC → O, C → no O, and AB → no O, where A–C are different foods, O is an allergy, and no O is no allergy. Participants received 10 trials of each of these types in a fully randomized and intermixed fashion. In fact, the full design included three distinct sets of trials conforming to this design; we have collapsed the data across these three sets.

Examination of the trial types reveals that the discrimination is not linearly separable. Each of the elements (A, B, C) is equally often paired with the outcome and with no outcome, so the discrimination cannot be solved on the basis of summation of the weights of individual stimulus elements. A moment's thought reveals that a pattern associator like that in Fig. 2.1 cannot solve the discrimination, so the key question is, can people? The answer is "yes", as Fig. 2.2 shows.

The data plotted in the figure are percentages of allergy predictions, scored in the following way. On trials where an allergy was the correct outcome, a score of 1 was given to a correct response and zero to an incorrect response. On trials where no allergy was the correct outcome, a score of zero was given to a correct response and 1 to an incorrect response. The graph then plots the means of these scores transformed into percentages. With this scoring scheme, the chance level is 25% for trials associated with an allergy and 75% for trials associated with no allergy. At the outset, responding on the different trial types was approximately at chance, but by the end of training more allergy predictions were being made to A and BC, the trial types associated with the target allergy, than to AB or C, the trial types associated with no allergy. In fact, A and BC, which start out with much lower percentages of allergy predictions than AB and C, end up with much higher percentages.

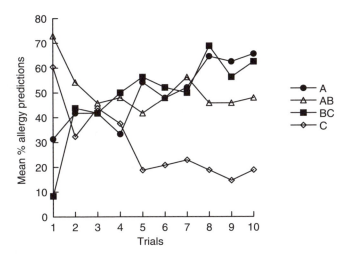

Figure 2.2. Discrimination results from an experiment in which participants received intermixed A → O, BC → O, C → no O, and AB → no O trials, where A–C = different foods, O = an allergy, and no O = no allergy. The figure shows that participants were able to solve this feature-neutral discrimination problem, since the percentage of allergy predictions increased across trials for A and BC and decreased for C and AB. The abscissa shows trials per trial type. The ability to learn a nonlinear discrimination of this sort is inconsistent with an elemental single-layer network model. See text for explanation of the scoring method.

Although our participants had clearly not learned the feature-neutral discrimination perfectly after 10 trials of each type, they were nonetheless making a high proportion of correct responses. This rules out the possibility that the human associative learning faculty is a simple single-layer pattern associator of the sort we have been considering thus far.

Plainly, our participants were able to learn that knowledge of *configurations* of foods was essential in determining the outcomes associated with the different trial types. The key question is, what form does this configural knowledge take? This question will be addressed shortly, but before leaving the simple model of Fig. 2.1 it is important to realize that people's ability to solve nonlinear discriminations is certainly not the only problem for single-layer pattern associators; some predictions concerning the learning of linear discriminations can be shown to be incorrect too (see Redhead & Pearce, 1995). Consider a discrimination of the form A → O, AB → O, ABC → no O. This is linear because it can be solved by giving a positive weight to A, a weight of zero to B, and a negative weight to C. The pair of trial types A and ABC are more dissimilar than the pair AB and ABC, so intuitively the discrimination between the former should be acquired more easily than the discrimination between the latter. To put it another way, the association between A and the outcome should be learned faster than the association between AB and the outcome. Yet a pattern associator governed by the equations given above makes the opposite prediction. The reason is that, according to the delta rule, B must always have a weight that is greater than or equal to zero, and hence the combined weight of AB will always be as great as that of A alone.

Fig. 2.3 shows that the intuitive prediction is correct, and the model incorrect. As in the earlier experiment, participants (38 further UCL students) saw 10 trials of each trial type in an intermixed fashion (the design included various filler trial types as well) and had no difficulty learning to predict the allergy on A and AB trials but not on ABC trials. As soon as the discrimination began to be solved, however, participants made consistently (and significantly) more correct predictions on A than on AB trials. This is a result that single-layer pattern associators governed by the delta rule is unable to explain.

UNIQUE CUES

It would be a mistake to give the impression that the learnability of the feature-neutral discrimination is especially surprising. Although human performance on this particular problem has not previously been studied, it has been known for many years that humans can solve nonlinear classifications (e.g. Medin & Schwanenflugel, 1981), and the problem this poses for single-layer networks has equally been long recognized (Minsky & Papert, 1969).

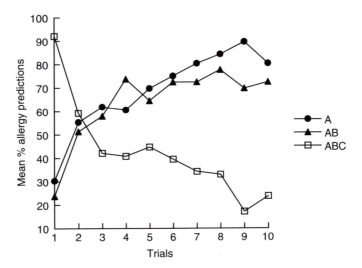

Figure 2.3. Discrimination results from an experiment in which participants received inter-mixed A → O, AB → O, and ABC → no O trials, where A–C = different foods, O = an allergy, and no O = no allergy. The figure shows that participants were able to solve this classification problem, since the percentage of allergy predictions increased across trials for A and AB and decreased for ABC. However, the important finding is that the rate of acquisition for A was greater than for AB, inconsistent with the predictions of a single-layer network model. A similar scoring method to that used in Figure 2.2 was employed here.

What is perhaps novel about the experiment is that the elements of the to-be-classified stimuli were so obviously decomposable (or "separable" in the jargon of categorization studies). Our participants surely knew that foods are independent entities, yet even so they had no difficulty in learning that the correct outcome was predicted by configural information.

Just as it has been recognized for many years that humans can solve such learning problems, so a simple account of how this is achieved has long been available. Wagner and Rescorla (1972) suggested that whenever two elements occur together, their combination gives rise to further "unique" elements which function much like the elements themselves. Wagner and Rescorla, studying animal conditioning, reasoned that when several conditioned stimuli are combined in an experiment, the perceptual experiences they create may be more than just the sum of their components. For example, tones and clickers are often used as CSs, but it is likely that, when combined together, the resulting stimulus contains a unique part which derives from the interaction of the stimuli.

In network terms, unique cue[1] theories are easy to implement. As elaborated by Gluck (1991), the idea would be to supplement the layer of input units with additional units that correspond to the unique cues. Thus, in addition to input units for elements A and B, there would be an AB unit which would only be activated when *both* A and B are present. What about higher-order configurations? Suppose that a stimulus presented for classification consists of elements ABC. One extreme possibility is that the network should contain seven input units (three for the elements, one each for configurations AB, AC, and BC, and one for configuration ABC) corresponding to the complete power set of elements. The problem with this sort of scheme is that the number of input units required accelerates at a tremendous rate as the number of elements increases. An alternative, therefore, is to constrain the unique cue units to consist of just the element-pairs AB, AC, and BC. Since none of the experiments we will be discussing hereafter used triplets of elements, we will not spend time trying to decide which of these alternatives is superior but will rather limit ourselves to evaluating the simpler version. Note that our conclusions about this sort of unique cue network apply equally to the first version, however.

It should be plain that the results of the experiment shown in Fig. 2.2 are readily accounted for by a unique cue analysis. In the A → O, BC → O, C → no O, AB → no O feature-neutral problem, none of the elements can become a reliable predictor of the category, but the unique cues can. When unique cues are included, the trial types become A → O, BCX → O, C → no O, and ABY → no O, where X is the unique cue created by the combination of elements B and C and Y is the unique cue created by the combination of A and B. It is simple to see that the discrimination is solved if cue A and the unique cue X acquire positive weights for the category, B and C have weights of zero, and Y has a negative weight.

Unique-cue networks have now been applied to a number of human category learning tasks. Thus, Gluck (1991) showed that such a network could correctly reproduce the rates of learning in some linearly-separable and non-linearly-separable problems, and Shanks and Gluck (1994) created a large unique-cue network for dealing with continuous-dimension stimuli.

CHALLENGING UNIQUE CUE MODELS

Despite the obvious predictive successes of unique cue models, it is fairly easy to show that the patterns of generalization predicted by such networks are inappropriate, and we can illustrate this with an experiment by Shanks, Charles, Darby, and Azmi (1998a, Experiment 3) which uses a design originally adopted in animal conditioning studies by Pearce and Wilson (1991; Wilson & Pearce, 1992). The basic idea is that participants learn an A → O, AB → no O discrimination in the first stage, which should establish A as a predictor of the outcome and B as an inhibitor of that outcome which counteracts A's influence. Then, participants learn that B by itself also predicts the outcome (B → O), and finally retention of the original discrimination between A and AB is tested. Unique cue theories, as we shall see, predict a dramatic influence of the B → O trials.

To provide adequate controls, the full design needed to be slightly more complex (see Table 2.1). The critical trial types in the first stage of the experimental condition were intermixed A → O_1, AB → no O, and AC → O_1 trials. In the second stage, participants saw B → O_1 trials, and then in the test phase they were presented with A, AB, and AC test stimuli. Once again, the to-be-learned items were foods or combinations of foods, and the outcomes were various allergies (or no allergy). What are the predictions about performance in the test phase? Let us begin by ignoring possible unique cues. In the first stage, element A should acquire a positive weight for outcome O_1, element B should acquire an equal but negative weight for the same outcome, and C should have a weight of zero. In the second phase, cue B's negative weight will be dramatically altered, since B now predicts the outcome whereas in the first stage it was negatively associated with it. In the test, we now have one compound (AB) each of whose elements is strongly connected to O_1, and another compound (AC) consisting of an element (A) which is connected to the outcome and another element (C) which should have a weight of zero. In sum, then, participants should be more likely to predict outcome O_1 on an AB test trial than on an AC one.

What are the predictions if unique cue inputs are added? Here, things are a little more complicated, but the conclusion is that participants are predicted to be at least as likely to select O_1 on an AB test trial as on an AC one. The difficulty with deriving predictions arises from the indeterminacy of the relative learning rate parameters [α in equation (3)] for the elements and the unique cues, but we can explore certain boundary conditions. If the salience and hence learning rate for the unique cues is zero, then the unique cue version reduces to the simple elemental model we have already considered. If

TABLE 2.1
Critical trial types in the two training stages and the test phase of
Shanks, Charles, Darby, & Azmi's (1998a) Experiment 3

Condition	Stage 1	Stage 2	Test
Experimental	A → O_1		A?
	AB → no O	B → O_1	AB?
	AC → O_1		AC?
Control	D → O_2		D?
	DE → no O		DE?
	DF → O_2		DF?

Note: The full design included various fillers not shown here. A–F = foods; O_1, O_2 = allergies; no O = no allergy.

the learning rate is the same for the elements and unique cues, then participants should again be more likely to predict O_1 on an AB test trial than on an AC one, just as in the pure elemental model. Stage 1 contains $A \rightarrow O_1$ and $ABX \rightarrow$ no O trials, where X is the unique cue created by the combination of A and B. In this situation, element B and unique cue X will have negative weights for O_1 which are equal in magnitude and, when added together, exactly oppose element A's positive weight. Thus, assuming that the weight at asymptote for element A is 1.0, B and X will each have a weight of –0.5. In stage 2, B's weight will go from –0.5 to +1.0 (assuming that training continues to asymptote). In stage 3 the trial types are ABX and ACY, where Y is the unique cue created by the combination of A and C. The combined weight of the ABX stimulus for outcome O_1 is 1.5 and that for ACY is 1.0 (both C and Y have weights of 0.0) and so participants should be more likely to predict outcome O_1 on the AB test trial than on the AC one.

Finally, if the learning rate or salience of a unique cue is much greater than that of an element, then X will acquire a strong negative weight (close to –1.0) in stage 1 and B will maintain a weight close to zero. B's weight will then increase to 1.0 in stage 2, and the ABX stimulus will have a combined weight of +1.0 in the test phase. For ACY, the weight will also be 1.0, since A's weight is 1.0 and C and Y have weights of zero. Thus, participants are predicted to respond identically to AB and AC at test.

To summarize, on any version of an elemental or unique cue theory, participants should be at least as likely to predict outcome O_1 on the AB test trial as on the AC one. Having derived this prediction, we can now turn to the data. Put simply, the outcome directly contradicts the prediction. Fig. 2.4 shows participants' performance in each of the three phases of the experiment. By the end of the first stage (Fig. 2.4a), participants had correctly learned to predict O_1 on A and AC but not AB trials. In stage 2 (Fig. 2.4b), they initially predicted no allergy on B trials, consistent with the inference from stage 1 that B is an inhibitor or preventor of the outcome, but they corrected this prediction across the trials of this stage until by the end they were reliably predicting O_1. The key stage 3 data are shown in Fig. 2.4c and reveal that participants predicted O on AC trials more than on AB trials. The prediction of the model is entirely falsified.

Examination of the trial types in Table 2.1 reveals that in one sense participants were behaving perfectly reasonably, however. Although from an elemental point of view the revaluation of element B during stage 2 should have had an effect on responding in the test phase to AB, the fact is that participants had direct experience of the outcome on AB trials: they know that no allergy occurs. The problem with unique cue (and elemental) theories, it seems, is the assumption that responding to an item is determined simply by the sum of the weights of its components. The fact that some of those components can be unique cues does not alter the summation assumption. What

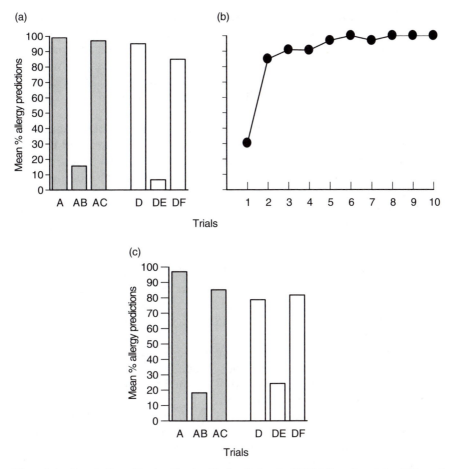

Figure 2.4.   Results from Shanks, Charles, Darby, & Azmi's (1998a) Experiment 3, which used the design shown in Table 2.1. The figure shows that by the end of stage 1 (a), participants had correctly learned to predict the allergy on A and AC but not on AB trials, and during stage 2 (b) cue B overcame its initial inhibitory association with the outcome and became strongly associated with the outcome. In the test stage (c), participants made many more allergy predictions on the AC than on the AB trials. This is exactly opposite to the predictions of a single-layer network model, even assuming that additional "unique" cues are formed by each stimulus compound. In fact, responding in the test is indistinguishable between the experimental (A, AB, AC) and control (D, DE, DF) cues.

our experiment indicates is that a component of a stimulus can be radically revalued without affecting to any great degree the associative connection between that stimulus and the original category.

   In fact, in this experiment and in other similar ones (Shanks, Darby, & Charles, 1998b) the revaluation trials actually had no detectable effect on the initial discrimination. As Table 2.1 shows, the full design of the experiment included a control condition in which the trial types (D $\rightarrow$ O$_2$, DE $\rightarrow$ no O, and DF $\rightarrow$ O$_2$) were functionally identical to the A, AB, and AC trials from stage 1 of the experimental condition, but for which cue E was not revalued in stage 2. Figure 2.4 shows that there was no difference at test in the levels of responding to the control stimuli D, DE, and DF compared to A, AB, and AC.

The results of this experiment can be viewed from a different angle. Consistent with a large amount of research on eyewitness memory and the misinformation effect (see Payne, Toglia, & Anastasi, 1994, for a review), as well as research on animal memory (see Bouton, 1993), the results show that genuine unlearning seems to play a rather minor role in normal forgetting. Participants were presented in stage 2 with information that should have had a strongly interfering effect on what they had learned in stage 1, since the negative connection between element B and outcome O$_1$ (deducible from the A $\rightarrow$ O$_1$ and AB $\rightarrow$ no O trials in stage 1) was contradicted by the B $\rightarrow$ O$_1$ trials seen in stage 2. Yet, participants did *not* alter their test trial expectations on AB trials. The fact that the networks we have been considering predicted a dramatic reversal on the test trials represents a phenomenon known as "catastrophic interference" (Lewandowsky, 1991; McCloskey & Cohen, 1989; Ratcliff, 1990; Sloman & Rumelhart, 1992), whereby target information is almost entirely overwritten or unlearned by later interfering information. But this interference is quite uncharacteristic of human performance. We found instead that the revaluation trials with B had minimal impact on responding to AB, compared to a control condition.

In fact, even when sizeable retroactive interference (RI) is found, it now appears that this need not be due to unlearning of the original information. As support for this claim, consider the results of some experiments conducted by Chandler (1993), which used a classic A–B, A–C design, with the elements of the associations being forenames and surnames. In Chandler's first experiment, participants initially read a series of A–B target names (e.g. Robert Harris) and were given an immediate cued recall test (Robert H—?) to ensure that they had learned them. Some of the targets were experimental items and some were control items: this refers to the fact that on a second list of names, which also had to be learned, there appeared A–C names (e.g. Robert Knight) that were similar to the earlier experimental names, but there were none on the second list that were similar to the earlier control names: instead, there were a number of unrelated X–Y names. Then, on a final memory test, participants were given a mixed-up list of the first names and surnames that had appeared in the original list (the A and B elements), and were asked to match them up. Note that on this test, the potentially-interfering surnames (e.g. Knight) from the second list did not appear. Chandler found that participants were able to correctly match 59% of the control names but only 46% of experimental names, representing a sizeable retroactive interference effect.

We obviously have evidence of interference-induced unlearning or forgetting in this experiment, in that participants were poorer at remembering names when they were followed by other similar names, but what is the basis of this RI effect? On an unlearning account, the effect is attributed to the fact that the similar names (Robert Knight) led to the earlier names being unlearned or overwritten in memory, with the A–B association being permanently lost. In contrast, Chandler proposed an alternative "retrieval failure" account, according to which the names from the second list simply blocked retrieval of the target names.

How can we discriminate these hypotheses? In a further experiment using the same general procedure, Chandler obtained a result that cannot be accounted for if the target words were really lost from memory. In this study, Chandler merely varied the delay interval between the two lists of names and the final memory test for different groups of participants. In one case, the delay between the first list and the test was 5 min (during which the second list was learned); in a second condition the delay was 15 min; and in a final condition it was 30 min. Once again, experimental names on the first list were followed on the second list by similar names, while the control names were not. For the groups tested after 15 or 30 min, the second list was presented immediately after the first list and was then followed by some filler tasks before the test took place.

The results showed that the amount of RI actually declined as the retention interval was increased. At intervals of 5 and 15 min, the results of the first experiment were replicated, with RI of about 8% being obtained. However, by 30 min, there was no evidence whatsoever of RI. Such a result is impossible to explain on an unlearning account, because the account has to attribute the RI obtained at the shorter retention intervals to genuine unlearning of the original experimental items, at least relative to the control items; but if the experimental items have to some extent been unlearned, they should still be harder to recall than the control items at the 30 min delay.

In sum, Chandler's results, which have also been obtained with pictorial stimuli (Chandler, 1991), suggest that forgetting is not, in the main, due to real unlearning of associative connections but is instead due to the fact that later information blocks the retrieval of earlier information. Although it is somewhat tangential to our current concerns, Chandler's results suggest that this blocking process only occurs when the potentially-interfering information is active in memory. As the delay before the test is increased, the interfering information becomes less active in memory and is less likely to block retrieval of the target trace. In a last experiment, this interpretation was confirmed. Chandler (1993) presented the final memory test 30 min after the original A–B list, but for different groups gave the second list either just after the original study list or just before the test. The outcome was that no RI occurred in the former case—replicating the result from the second experiment—but that RI did occur when the interfering list was learned just prior to the test. Such a result confirms the idea that blocking of the target items by subsequent items only occurs when the latter are active in memory. When the intervening items are learned long before the test, sufficient time has elapsed for them to become inactive in memory and hence unable to block retrieval of target names.

BACK-PROPAGATION MODELS

Up to this point, we have been considering network models that contain a single layer of modifiable weights connecting an outcome to the elements (and combinations of elements) making up the stimulus, and clearly, the assumption that responding to a stimulus is a function of the summed weights of its components is incorrect. It is for this reason that many feed-forward connectionist models incorporate a layer of "hidden" units that intervene between the input and output units. Such a network can operate exactly like a single-layer pattern associator if we continue to use the delta rule as the learning algorithm. One particular type of hidden-unit network has been extremely widely investigated and has been shown to have some very powerful properties. In such a "back-propagation-of-error" network, the delta rule applies exactly as before, except that it is refined in order to determine how much the input-hidden weights and the hidden-output weights should be changed on a given trial. The equations can be found in McClelland and Rumelhart (1988).

The development of multi-layer networks using the generalized version of the delta rule has provided a major contribution to recent connectionist modelling, since phenomena such as the learning of nonlinear classifications, which are impossible for basic single-layer networks, can be easily dealt with by multi-layer networks. Even more impressive than their ability to learn nonlinear classifications is the fact, proved by Hornik, Stinchcombe, and White (1989), that back-propagation networks can learn essentially any mapping between a set of input and output patterns that one cares to construct. Thus, for any set of mappings from arbitrary input patterns to arbitrary output patterns ($I_1 \rightarrow O_1, I_2 \rightarrow O_2, I_3 \rightarrow O_3, \ldots$), a back-propagation network with sufficient hidden units will construct a set of weights to learn the mapping to any desired degree of approximation. Hence, there is no question about the power of this sort of connectionist network for learning associative relationships. But the question remains, does it learn in the same way as humans?

There is undoubtedly evidence of persuasive correspondences between human behaviour and the predictions of back-propagation networks. Some of the best evidence concerns child language acquisition, where it is possible to provide a network with approximately the same sort of input that children receive and to see whether characteristics of the network's learning match those seen in children. One much-debated example concerns the learning of the past tense in English. While most verbs are regular in adding -*ed* to produce the past tense (e.g. *walk–walked*), a number of very common verbs are irregular (e.g. *go–went, send–sent, have–had*, etc.). Children, of course, are able eventually to learn the correct past tenses, but they also produce some interesting errors in that they occasionally "over-regularize" irregular verbs: they say "goed", "sended", and so on. It turns out that back-propagation networks are also able to produce such errors (Plunkett & Marchman, 1993). Because many more regular than irregular verbs are encountered, early on in training the network may inappropriately generalize the contingency between verb stems and the -*ed* past tense and apply it to irregular verbs.

From the more general perspective of human associative learning, however, the basic back-propagation system is inadequate, and the reason is simple: As McCloskey and Cohen (1989) showed, such networks predict catastrophic interference just like unique cue and elemental models. To illustrate, we ran a simple back-propagation simulation of the experimental condition in Table 2.1. There were three input units, corresponding to stimuli A, B, and C, and one output unit corresponding to the target outcome O_1. In the first stage, $A \rightarrow O_1$, $AB \rightarrow$ no O, and $AC \rightarrow O_1$ trials were presented repeatedly until correct responding was observed. In the second stage, $B \rightarrow O_1$ trials were presented and again, training continued until the correct output was obtained. Finally, stimuli AB and AC were presented in the test phase. In contradiction to the results illustrated in Fig. 2.4, AB evoked a stronger O_1 response than AC. We have tried many permutations of the network architecture and training regime but have been unable to find any circumstances in which this outcome is reversed.

The problem for back-propagation models is particularly starkly illustrated in an experiment and accompanying simulation conducted by López, Shanks, Almaraz, and Fernández (1998). This study again used a simple prediction task, but in this case the cues were symptoms and the outcomes diseases. The design is shown in Table 2.2. Participants received information about the symptoms that a particular patient presented and they had to diagnose the disease this patient was suffering from. Table 2.2 shows that across stages 1 and 2 the cues of interest, A and D, were followed by their respective outcomes, O_1 and O_2, exactly the same number of times and in compound with cues that had undergone exactly the same treatment. The only difference between A and D was that A was a better predictor of O_1 than its pairmate B in stage 1 and a worse predictor than its pairmate C in stage 2, whereas for D, this was reversed. That is, D was a worse predictor of O_2 than E in stage 1 and a better predictor than F in stage 2. The various trial types in each stage were

TABLE 2.2

Trial types in the two training stages and the test phase of López, Shanks, Almaraz, & Fernández's (1998) Experiment 3, mean percentages of predictions of the target disease (**bold** figures), and results from a simulation using Pearce's (1994) model (*italic* figures)

Stage 1	*Stage 2*	*Test*			
		Stage 1 Trials		*Stage 2 Trials*	
AB → O₁	AC → no O	AB	**48.8**	AC	**23.8**
			0.719		*0.037*
B → no O	C → O₁	B	**2.5**	C	**70.0**
			0.031		*0.946*
DE → no O	DF → O₂	DE	**21.3**	DF	**48.8**
			0.413		*0.970*
E → O₂	F → no O	E	**78.8**	F	**6.3**
			0.977		*0.026*

A–F = symptoms; O_1, O_2 = diseases; no O = no disease.

randomly intermixed. The critical component of the design is that, just as in the Shanks et al. (1998a) experiment shown in Table 2.1, the stage 2 contingencies indirectly contradict the ones presented in stage 1, inasmuch as stage 1 tends to suggest that A is a powerful predictor of the disease and that D prevents the disease, while stage 2 tends to suggest the exact opposite.

Participants learned to predict the correct outcomes during both stages 1 and 2. In the subsequent test stage, trials of each type from the two stages were re-presented without any feedback. The key issue is whether participants could remember the correct responses for the stage 1 trial types. If they have forgotten or unlearned the stage 1 trial types, they will obviously make many errors on test trials from stage 1. In fact the data, reported in Table 2.2 (bold figures), reveal good recall of the stage 1 contingencies. Participants tended to predict the target disease on AB and E trials and predicted no disease on B and DE trials, consistent with the phase 1 associations.

We then conducted a series of simulations using back-propagation networks, as described in McClelland and Rumelhart (1988). The training patterns coincided with the training trials participants received during the learning stage of the experiment and were also distributed in two blocks. Different parameters and network architectures (different numbers of hidden units) were tested in these simulations, but all of them showed the basic catastrophic forgetting effect, thus only the details of one of them will be described. The outcome of this simulation is presented in Fig. 2.5. A three-layered network was used, consisting of six input units, corresponding to the six cues (symptoms), 10 hidden units to allow an internal representation of the input information to be formed, and two output units corresponding to

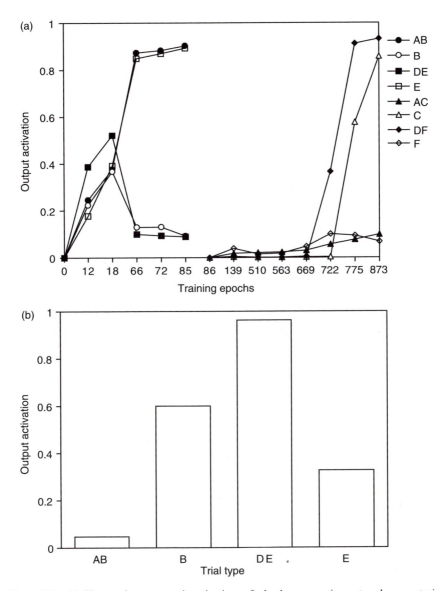

Figure 2.5. (a) Changes in output unit activations of a back-propagation network across training epochs for the different trial types of Table 2.2. An epoch consists of one presentation of each trial type. The activation of output unit O$_1$ is shown on AB, B, AC, and C trial types. The activation of output unit O$_2$ is shown on DE, E, DF, and F trial types. The learning rate was set to 0.2 and the momentum parameter to 0.9. The remaining free parameters were set to default values. Input biases were adjusted to all hidden and output units. The training of the network continued until a learning criterion had been met (sum squared error = 0.04). (b) Output unit activations after the training phase had been completed for the different trial types from stage 1. The network's performance during the test showed that it had catastrophically forgotten the relationships learned during the first learning stage. From López, F. J., Shanks, D. R., Almaraz, J., and Fernández, P. (1998). Effects of trial order on contingency judgments: A comparison of associative and probabilistic contrast accounts. *Journal of Experimental Psychology: Learning, Memory, and Cognition, 24,* 684. © 1998 by the American Psychological Association. Reproduced with permission.

the two outcomes (diseases) used in the training stage. "No disease" was coded as an output of zero on both output units. As can be seen, in stage 1 the activation values of the O_1 and O_2 output units increased across trials up to asymptote on AB and E trials, respectively. In contrast, on B and DE trials, the activation values of both output units remained low across this first block of trials. During stage 2, the activation values on the O_1 and O_2 output units on C and DF trials, respectively, increased across trials towards asymptotic values, but only if a very large number of trials was presented. The activation values of the output units were low on AC and F trials within the second block of trials.

The main results are the activation values of the output units on the different stage 1 trial types in the test stage (see Fig. 2.5b). The activation of the output unit corresponding to outcome O_1 was 0.05 on AB trials, while on B trials it was 0.60 on a scale of 0–1. Therefore, the network predicts outcome O_1 more often on B than on AB trials, despite the AB $\rightarrow O_1$, B $\rightarrow$ no O training presented in Phase 1. Similarly, the activation of the output unit corresponding to outcome O_2 was 0.96 on DE trials, whereas it was 0.33 on E trials. Therefore, the network predicts outcome O_2 more often on DE than on E trials. This pattern of results shows that, unlike the participants in the experiment, the network performed during the test stage according to the contingencies it had learned during Block 2 of the learning stage and had catastrophically forgotten the relationships programmed during Block 1.

Yet another problem with back-propagation networks as models of human associative learning is that they do not always appear to generalize in an appropriate manner. As an illustration, suppose that one classification problem consists of A $\rightarrow$ O and AB $\rightarrow$ no O trials, while a second consists of AC $\rightarrow$ O and ABC $\rightarrow$ no O trials. These problems are identical except that both trial types in the second problem have an added element, C. Just as in the experiment described earlier (Fig. 2.3), intuition suggests that adding such an element makes the trial types more similar and therefore must make the classification harder to learn, a prediction that has been confirmed empirically in an animal discrimination learning study by Pearce and Redhead (1993). However, Pearce (1994) showed that back-propagation networks are unable to reproduce this effect. It does not seem as though human associative learning and generalization are well accounted for by this sort of network model.

CONFIGURAL MODELS

The results we have reported carry a straightforward message: Representations of complex stimuli need to be bound quite tightly together in such a way that learning something new about one of the elements of a stimulus does not strongly transfer back to the stimulus itself. In other words, stimuli need to be coded in a configural rather than an elemental manner.

The basic idea behind configural networks is illustrated in Fig. 2.6. When a stimulus is presented, it is coded via the direct activation of a unique hidden unit dedicated to that stimulus. Thus, returning to the design shown in Table 2.1, stimulus AB activates a different hidden unit from stimulus B. Then, it is the hidden and not the input units that become connected to the outcome. The obvious benefit here is that knowledge of some association involving AB is protected against novel and competing knowledge concerning element B. Of course, as it stands, this model would be inadequate, since it does not allow any degree of generalization, so it needs to be supplemented with the idea that a hidden unit dedicated to a given stimulus can be activated by another stimulus to the extent that the two are similar.

Models based on these design characteristics have been explored by Pearce (1987, 1994, 2002) and Kruschke (1992, 1993). Although they differ in their details, each provides approximately the correct trade-off between

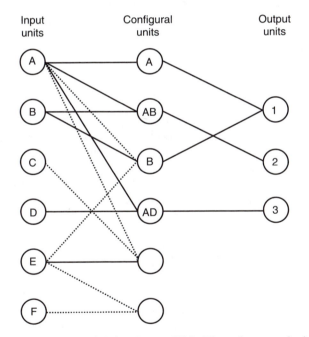

Figure 2.6.   A configural network (after Pearce, 1994). The to-be-categorized item activates input units corresponding to the elements of which it is constituted. Rather than being directly associated with the category output units (as in the model shown in Figure 2.1), the inputs are connected to internal configural units, each of which is selectively activated by a given conjunction of input elements. These configural units are then connected to the output units via modifiable weights. The figure shows configural units activated by items A, AB, B, and AD. Dotted lines represent some of the potential links that may be formed on future training trials.

generalization and protection from interference. Let us consider how Pearce's (1994) configural model can predict the absence of catastrophic forgetting. The model has been implemented as a connectionist network that includes four layers of units: an input layer, two layers of hidden units (an output layer and a layer of configural units) and a single-unit layer that represents the outcome. The activation level of this outcome unit determines the system response. The units in the input layer can be at an activation level of either 0 or 1, depending on whether the element of the stimulus pattern the unit is representing is absent or present, respectively. Each input unit is connected to a single output unit. The intervention of these output units ensures that each stimulus pattern activates maximally (an activation level of 1) a single configural unit. Henceforth, the configural unit can be regarded as representing a particular stimulus pattern. In addition, each stimulus pattern can activate more than one configural unit through a process of generalization. If we assume that configural unit x becomes maximally activated when input pattern X is presented, what will be its activation value when input pattern Y is presented? According to the model, the activation value a_x of configural unit x will be proportional to the degree of similarity between the stimulus patterns. Pearce (1987, 1994) assumes that the similarity of input patterns X and Y is a linear function of the number of elements they share:

$$a_x = n_C \left(\frac{1}{\sqrt{n_X}} \times \frac{1}{\sqrt{n_Y}} \right) \tag{4}$$

where n_C is the number of input units both patterns share and n_X and n_Y are the number of input units that are specific to each stimulus pattern.

Thus, the activation level of the outcome unit when pattern X is presented (V_x) has a double origin. Part of the activation is conveyed by the connection between the configural unit maximally activated and the outcome unit (w_x), and some of its activation comes through the connections between other configural units activated through generalization and the outcome unit:

$$V_x = w_x + \sum_{i=1}^{n} (S_{x,t} \times w_i) \tag{5}$$

where $S_{x,i}$ is the squared activation of these other configural units [see equation (4)] and w_i represents their connections to the outcome unit.

Associative learning involves modifications only in the weight of the connection between the configural unit maximally activated (one for each stimulus pattern) and the outcome unit. These modifications are governed by equation (6):

$$\Delta w_x = \alpha(t - V_x) \tag{6}$$

Note the similarity between equations (3) and (6). As in the

Rescorla–Wagner model, the modification of weights is proportional to an error term, α represents the learning rate, and t is set to 1 when the outcome is present and to 0 otherwise.

Pearce's model is able to account for a good deal of the data reviewed in this chapter thus far. Because stimuli are represented configurally, the model's predictions are unaffected by whether or not a particular classification is linear, and hence it can predict the learnability of the feature-neutral discrimination shown in Fig. 2.2. Also, the theory predicts the faster learning for A than for AB shown in Fig. 2.3, since there is less generalization between A and ABC than between AB and ABC (see Redhead & Pearce, 1995, for a detailed analysis of the results of a related design). Finally, it accounts, at least partially (see Shanks et al., 1998a) for the data in Fig. 2.4, as Wilson and Pearce (1992) have shown formally. The reason is that by relying purely on configural representations, the model predicts that learning the B $\rightarrow$ O association in stage 2 of the experiment only interferes minimally with the A $\rightarrow$ O and AB $\rightarrow$ no O associations learned in stage 1. Each stimulus configuration is represented by a unique configural unit with its own intrinsic associative strength. Only a modest interfering effect of the stage 2 trials is anticipated because of generalized associative strength. Since there is a degree of similarity between stimuli AB and B, the associative strength the latter acquires in stage 2 for the target category will generalize back to stimulus AB, leading to an increase in target outcome choices in the test stage. This effect is expected, however, to be fairly small. The one weakness of the account is that the experiment (see Fig. 2.5) failed to obtain any effect of the B $\rightarrow$ O trials.

What about the experimental situation given in Table 2.2? According to the model, the combination of cues A and B in a single compound will maximally activate a configural unit, which increases its associative strength on AB $\rightarrow$ O_1 trials. Moreover, a different configural unit will be activated maximally on AC $\rightarrow$ no O trials but no associative strength is gained by this unit, as it is never paired with the outcome. To illustrate specifically the model's predictions, López et al. (1998) simulated the main results of the experiment. The simulation results were averaged across 10 replications using an equal number of randomly selected sequences of trials. Different sets of simulations were run using different free parameters but, as the results did not substantially vary, we only present simulation data in which α was given a value of 0.5.

Table 2.2 (figures in italics) presents the mean activation values of outcome units O_1 and O_2 for the different trial types presented in the test stage. The results showed similar proportions of correct diagnoses for those trial types originally presented in stages 1 and 2 of the training session. The activations of the outcome units were high for those trial types that were paired with the target outcome and low for those trial types that were paired with the absence of any target disease, regardless of the stage in which they were originally presented. The fit of simulation to data is impressive. Other successful simulations of human associative learning results using Pearce's model are described by Perales & Shanks (2003), Vallée-Tourangeau, Murphy, & Baker (1998), and Vallée-Tourangeau, Murphy, Drew, & Baker (1998).

To conclude, Pearce's configural model allows us to give a degree of coherence to the pattern of results described so far. The absence of catastrophic forgetting can be understood in terms of the model. It provides a solution to the catastrophic forgetting problem, which involves a trade-off between two empirical constraints, namely, the fact that new information does not cause complete unlearning of prior knowledge and the ability to adapt to the new incoming information through a process of generalization. This particular solution (not the only one—see Lewandowsky, 1991, for further discussion) is based on the creation of semi-distributed representations of the incoming information by means of the assignment of exclusive configural representations to each new input pattern and the operation of a generalization mechanism based on pattern similarity. By abandoning the notion that stimuli are coded elementally, findings that are problematic for single-layer networks can be encompassed.

REPRESENTATIONAL FLEXIBILITY

At this point it would be nice to end the chapter with the conclusion that connectionist models incorporating some form of configural coding scheme provide powerful models of basic human learning processes. However, such models turns out to be lacking an absolutely key capacity, namely representational flexibility.

Some recent data reported by Williams, Sagness, & McPhee (1994) (see also Williams, 1996; Williams & Braker, 1999) raises the possibility that participants may only behave "configurally" under certain conditions: Sometimes, they may behave more in the "elemental" manner envisaged by single-layer networks. In their study, Williams et al. used an adaptation of the classic two-stage "blocking" design of Kamin (1968). In a blocking experiment (see Table 2.3), participants see AB → O and CD → O trials in which two cue combinations are separately paired with an outcome O, and are then tested on trials

TABLE 2.3
Trial types in a blocking experiment

Stage 1	Stage 2	Test
B → O	AB → O	A?
D → no O	CD → O	C?

A–D = cues; O = an outcome; no O = no outcome.

with cues A and C alone. In a preceding stage elements B and D have been respectively paired and not paired with the outcome (B → O, D → no O) prior to the compound trials. The result is that participants form a weaker association between element A and the outcome when B has previously been established as an independent predictor of the outcome than between C and the outcome when D has previously been established as a nonpredictor of the outcome, and this effect is readily explained by any theory in which association strengths are updated in accordance with an error-correcting rule, such as equation (3). The reason is that when B predicts the outcome in stage 1, it acquires a positive connection weight for the outcome. In the second stage, the error term on AB trials is now close to zero and hence no increments to the A → O connection are possible. In contrast, when D does not independently predict the outcome, the error term in stage 2 on CD trials is large and so a substantial positive C → O connection is formed.

Williams et al. (1994, Experiment 4) conducted a blocking experiment such as this, but pretrained various groups of participants in different ways. In one condition the pretraining was designed to foster an "elemental" strategy, whereby participants would to some degree analyse each cue separately. Specifically, the pretraining phase involved exposure to intermixed X → O and XY → O trials, where O is an outcome, and although the XY configuration is paired with the outcome, there is explicit information suggesting that it is the X element of the configuration that is the important one. In a second condition, pretraining was designed to foster a "configural" strategy. Here, participants received XY → O, X → no O, and Y → no O trials; clearly, in this case it is the XY configuration rather than either of its elements that predicts the outcome. The task involved predicting a change in the value of the stock market (the outcome, O) on the basis of whether or not certain stocks were traded on a given day (the cues).

After this pretraining phase, participants then went on to the main phase of the experiment in which they received a standard within-subjects blocking problem like that shown in Table 2.3, using a new set of cues. In the first stage B → O and D → no O trials were presented, followed in the second stage by AB → O and CD → O trials. What would we expect to happen in this situation when participants finally rate cues A and C? On the basis of the results of previous human blocking experiments (e.g. Chapman & Robbins, 1990; Dickinson, Shanks, & Evenden, 1984; Shanks, 1985), we might expect to see that cue A is blocked and receives lower ratings than cue C, and this is exactly what happened for participants who received the elemental pretraining. However, for those participants given the configural pretraining, no blocking was observed, and instead A and C received equal ratings.

To explain this intriguing result, Williams, Sagness, & McPhee (1994) argued that when participants saw the AB and CD trials, they could treat these compounds either as being composed of separable elements or as constituting configurations. In the former case, analysis will reveal that cue B is more likely than cue A to be the element most predictive of the outcome, and that cue C is more likely than cue D to be predictive, and hence blocking will be observed. In contrast, if the participants are inclined to treat the AB and CD configurations as being relatively unrelated to the B and D elements seen in the earlier stage, then they should treat them equally, since each is paired to the same extent with the outcome. In this case, no blocking would be expected. The success of Williams et al.'s pretraining manipulations to bias the way participants rated the cues in the blocking part of the experiment suggests that this strategic theory correctly describes what participants were doing. Alvarado and Rudy (1992) have documented the same basic phenomenon in animal discrimination learning experiments.

Williams et al. (Experiment 5) went on to provide a simpler but even more striking example of representational flexibility. In this study participants again received trials according to a blocking design similar to that described above, but half the participants received neutral experimental instructions, whereas the other half received modified instructions that suggested that some of the stocks (the cues) were "causal", in that they automatically triggered a market change, whereas others were "non-causal". These additional instructions were designed to encourage participants to process the individual stocks as separate entities with independent causal powers. Despite the minor nature of this change in instructions, it was sufficient to dramatically alter the outcome of the blocking procedure: In the "default" condition no blocking was observed, whereas in the condition with additional instructions blocking was observed. Apparently, the instructions were sufficient to overcome the default configural coding and instead evoke an elemental one, which in turn yielded blocking.

We (Shanks et al., 1998a, Experiment 5a) looked to see if we could reverse the "configural" behaviour seen in the experiment described in Table 2.1, using a rather different method suggested by another of Williams' (1995) studies. Participants were presented with the training trials depicted in Table 2.4. The similarity to the design in Table 2.1 should be apparent: In both cases, participants learned an A → O/AB → no O discrimination, followed by training trials (B → O) in which cue B was revalued, and the test comprised an assessment of the preservation of the initial discrimination. However, in this experiment there were two modifications which we, following Williams (1995), thought might encourage a greater degree of elemental processing. First, in an initial training stage (stage 1), only the elements were presented, so participants' initiation should have suggested to them that the task had an elemental nature. Second, during the stage in which the A → O/AB → no O discrimination was learned, participants also saw B → no O trials.

The results are shown in Fig. 2.7. In this experiment, in contrast to the earlier one, the B → O revaluation trials (Fig. 2.7b) had a very substantial

TABLE 2.4
Critical trial types in the three training stages and the test phase of Shanks,
Charles, Darby, & Azmi's (1998a) Experiment 5a

Condition	Stage 1	Stage 2	Stage 3	Test
Experimental	A → O	A → O	B → O	A?
	B → no O	B → no O		B?
		AB → no O		AB?
Control	C → O	C → O		C?
	D → no O	D → no O		D?
		CD → no O		CD?

Note: The full design included various fillers not shown here. A–D = foods; O = an allergy; no O = no allergy.

effect on retention of the initial discrimination. This is shown, first, by the fact that responding to AB in the test stage (Fig. 2.7c) was at a far higher level than it had been at the end of stage 2 (Fig. 2.7a; cf. the corresponding level of responding to AB in Figure 2.4) and second by comparison to the control stimuli. The experiment included control trial types (C, CD, and D) which were functionally identical to the A, AB, and B trials from stages 1 and 2, but for which B was not revalued in stage 3. Responding to these control stimuli was at approximately the same level in the test as it had been at the end of stage 2 and, crucially, responding to AB was far higher at test than to CD. Hence the effect of the B → O trials was selective to responding to AB.

The pair of results given in Fig. 2.4 and 2.7 confirms Williams et al.'s conjecture that the representation of a compound stimulus AB can be flexibly altered. In our task, configural processing appears to be the default in that responding to AB after AB → O/B → no O acquisition trials is unaffected by subsequent B → O revaluation trials. However, this default can be overcome in a functionally identical design in which the elemental properties of the stimuli are emphasized. Pinning down exactly what the factors are that tend to push people between configural and elemental coding remains a major target for future research, and until we have some answers to this question it will be difficult to take forward the theoretical modelling of associative learning. In the meantime, however, what we can say is that current connectionist models are missing an important feature in their inability to accommodate representational flexibility.

ROLE OF THE HIPPOCAMPUS IN STIMULUS CODING

Efforts to develop connectionist models of associative learning have commonly been informed by neuropsychological considerations, so in this section I briefly review the evidence concerning the neural substrates of learning. The

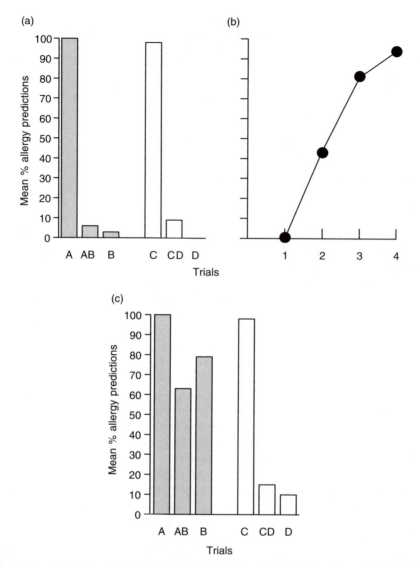

Figure 2.7. Results from Shanks, Darby, Charles, & Azmi's (1998a) Experiment 5a. The design is given in Table 2.4. The figure shows the percentage of allergy predictions on the final trial of stage 2 (a), on the stage 3 B → O trials (b), and on the test trials (c). During stage 2, participants learned to predict the allergy on the B trials. In contrast to the data shown in Figure 2.4, participants behaved "elementally" in the test stage, in that they made many more allergy predictions on the AB trials than they had at the end of stage 2 or than they did on the control CD trials.

starting point for this review is the universally accepted idea that of all brain regions it is the hippocampus, located in the medial temporal lobe, that most obviously plays a role in learning and memory. It has been known for decades that brain damage in this region has a profound effect on these abilities (see Parkin, 1997, Chapter 6) and recent histological studies have confirmed that damage limited to the hippocampus results in detectable memory impairment (Rempel-Clower, Zola, Squire, & Amaral, 1996). Indeed, paired-associate learning, which requires participants to learn arbitrary associations between word pairs, and which therefore resembles the sorts of tasks used in the experiments described here, is normally included in test batteries for detecting amnesia.

Despite this consensus, many researchers believe that the hippocampus does not contribute to all associative learning tasks and that instead its involvement is restricted to *declarative* memory tasks, in which successful performance requires conscious retrieval of facts or episodes. Squire (1994) is perhaps the best-known proponent of this view, and the key claim is that, despite their poor general memory, patients suffering from the classic amnesic syndrome have a variety of preserved learning abilities, namely those that do not require conscious retrieval. For instance, Squire and his colleagues have argued that repetition priming, in which processing of a stimulus (e.g. reading a word) is facilitated by an earlier occasion on which the same or similar processing was carried out, is entirely normal in amnesia (Hamann, Squire, & Schacter, 1995). The claim that amnesia is restricted to declarative memory deficits is controversial, however, for two reasons. First, there are no agreed behavioural measures for determining whether or not a particular test involves conscious retrieval (see Shanks & St. John, 1994), which leads to the danger of a circular definition of the term "declarative": a test is declarative because amnesics perform poorly on it, and the reason they perform poorly is that it is a declarative test. Second, it is far from proven that there are any learning tasks on which amnesics perform normally. For example, the claim for normal repetition priming is controversial (Ostergaard & Jernigan, 1996) and, more pertinently, it has now been very well established that simple Pavlovian conditioning, a prototypical nondeclarative task, is affected by hippocampal damage (McGlinchey-Berroth, Brawn, & Disterhoft, 1999) and that hippocampal activity can be detected in brain-imaging studies of normal participants during conditioning (Blaxton et al., 1996). Thus, it is possible that the hippocampus is involved in, and indeed is necessary for normal performance in, essentially all forms of associative learning task.

Putting that issue to one side, a more subtle and germane claim is that the hippocampus is particularly involved in tasks that require the formation of configural representations. This idea has a long history (Wickelgren, 1979) but was made most explicit by Sutherland and Rudy (1989) and is supported by a range of evidence, mostly from animal conditioning studies, to the effect that hippocampal lesions impair the acquisition of certain configural or non-linear discriminations but do not impair acquisition of elemental or linear ones. For instance, McDonald et al. (1997) found that lesions to the hippo-campus, but not fornix-fimbria (a major input–output pathway for the hippocampus), in rats impaired acquisition of a *negative patterning* discrimination (A → O, B → O, AB → no O), which cannot be solved elemen-tally. Rickard and Grafman (1998) provided confirmatory evidence from human amnesic patients, showing that they failed to learn a *transverse patterning* task, which again can only be solved if configural stimulus representations are formed.

The hippocampal-configural theory of Sutherland and Rudy is particu-larly attractive, not only because it grounds the elemental/configural distinc-tion on an underlying neural substrate but also because it hints that the representational flexibility described in the previous section may be attribut-able to differential loading of tasks on hippocampal function. Although the experimental manipulations that bring about a transition from configural to elemental processing may be quite subtle (e.g. the different instructions used by Williams et al., 1994, Experiment 5), it is possible that these manipulations have their effect by increasing or decreasing the demands placed on the hippocampus. Unfortunately, though, other evidence has failed to support the theory. Perhaps most clear-cut is evidence (Gallagher & Holland, 1992) that hippocampal lesions do not impair acquisition of the feature-neutral discrimination (see Fig. 2.2) and also evidence that human amnesic patients are no more impaired on the transverse patterning task than on a linear discrimination of equivalent difficulty (Reed & Squire, 1999).[2] It has been confirmed, on the other hand, that negative patterning is impaired (McDonald et al., 1997). Overall, therefore, it does not appear that the hippocampal-configural theory, as stated in its original form, is adequate.

However, there are two possible modifications of the theory that should be considered prior to its complete rejection. First, it may be the case that not all configural problems are solved in precisely the same configural way and that minor procedural variations affect the strategy adopted. For instance, per-haps unlesioned rats in Gallagher and Holland's experiment solved the fea-ture-neutral problem via the use of unique cues, whereas those in McDonald et al.'s experiment solved the negative patterning discrimination via true configural representations of the sort postulated in Pearce's theory. If hippo-campal lesions only affect performance on tasks that elicit full-blown con-figural representations, then perhaps this would explain why hippocampal lesions were found to affect the negative patterning discrimination but not the feature-neutral one. In support of this contention, there is now some good evidence that rats, like humans, can solve what looks like the same discrimin-ation in different ways, depending on minor design properties (Alvarado & Rudy, 1995).

A limitation of this suggestion is that it retains the essential idea behind the Sutherland and Rudy theory, namely that the hippocampus is essential for forming configural associations. Regardless of whether different "configural" problems are solved in different ways, it remains beyond dispute that hippocampal lesions do not make it impossible for animals to solve such problems, and so this idea needs to be weakened. Thus, the second possibility is to refine the proposed role of the hippocampus and to suggest that, instead of being involved in the solution of all configural discriminations, it acts instead to turn up the "gain" on the activity of configural units outside the hippocampus (Rudy & Sutherland, 1995). In Rudy and Sutherland's revised theory, circuits in the cortex are capable of forming configural representations (and unique cues), but the hippocampus can aid the solution of discriminations by amplifying the activation or salience of configural units. On this account, a hippocampal animal is like a unique cue network, whereas a normal animal may function like a configural network, in the extreme case solving a discrimination in a purely configural manner. In between these extremes, normal animals may solve some problems by reliance on a mixture of configural and elemental representations, depending on the demands placed on the hippocampus by the particular discrimination. Rudy & Sutherland (1995) have argued persuasively that this approach can account for much of the apparently conflicting evidence on the effects of hippocampal lesions, and O'Reilly & Rudy (2001) have extended it further by suggesting that the hippocampal gain process is particularly critical in situations that require the rapid formation of conjunctive representations. The details of how this proposal may be turned into an explicit computational model are beyond the scope of this chapter, but recent efforts (Gluck & Myers, 1997; O'Reilly & Rudy, 2001; Schmajuk & DiCarla, 1992) hold out considerable promise of integrating a wide range of data.

CONCLUSIONS

In this chapter we have considered a number of possible connectionist models of the mechanism by which humans learn simple associative relationships. While it is fairly easy to obtain evidence at variance with the predictions of elemental theories—including ones that incorporate unique cues—configural theories are much better supported by the data. Even so, these theories currently lack any capacity for representational flexibility, i.e. the ability to construct different representations of the same stimulus under different circumstances. In this final section we return to some more fundamental issues concerning the learning process.

One of the principal attractions of connectionist models is their use of distributed representations, which provides a natural explanation for the context sensitivity and gradedness of generalization (van Gelder, 1991). The astute reader will have noticed, however, that associative knowledge is far less distributed in a configural model than in, say, a standard back-propagation network. Whereas a given hidden unit in a back-propagation network is likely to be activated by many input stimuli and to "represent" only a complex configuration of elements in the input stimulus, in Pearce's (1994) model the internal units represent individual input stimuli in a very direct manner. Each configural unit corresponds exactly to one training item. Hence one could almost call configural networks "localist" rather than "distributed". Of course, the complex effects of generalization between stimuli means that knowledge is still to some extent spread across the nodes and connections in the network. But consider the two properties which, according to van Gelder (1991), are definitive of distribution, namely *superposition* and *equipotentiality*. According to the notion of superposition, in a distributed system the representations of different items are superposed on each other using a common medium. It is straightforward to see that a configural network fails to meet this criterion, since a new representational resource (i.e. a new configural unit) is required for each new item the system learns about. Equipotentiality refers to the fact that, in a distributed system, each part of the representational medium is equivalent to every other part in terms of the objects it represents. Again, a configural network will fail to meet this criterion, since different configural units represent different things: If such a network were split in half, this would not affect all input–output mappings equally.

Thus, it seems that the price to pay for a model in which knowledge is appropriately protected from interference is that the benefits of pure distribution of category knowledge are to some extent diluted. Whether a model such a Pearce's can display appropriate context sensitivity and gradedness is an open question.

Another general issue concerning models of associative learning is the possible distinction between *similarity-based* and *rule-based* behaviour, or (in other terminology) between "implicit" and "explicit" behaviour. The network models we have considered in this chapter all rely on the assumption that responding to a stimulus is a function of its similarity to previously encountered stimuli, with similarity being measured in terms of common elements. Where the models differ is in terms of exactly how similarity is computed. But there is another way in which decisions may be reached, namely via the application of a rule, where a rule is defined as a principle that specifies definitively whether or not an object or event is of a particular sort. To see how rule- and similarity-based behaviour may differ, consider a situation in which the stimuli are rectangles varying in width and height, and suppose there are two categories defined by a rule that unequivocally assigns a stimulus to category 1 if its width is greater than its height and to category 2 if its height is greater than its width. If participants are able to abstract this rule from exposure to some training examples, and if they respond according to the rule, then when they make a classification decision they should merely be interested in whether or not the stimulus is wider than it is high; its similarity to specific training items should be immaterial. And if responding is based on a decision as to whether or not the stimulus is wider than it is high, that decision (ignoring what happens when width and height are perceptually difficult to discriminate) should be performed equally rapidly and accurately for all stimuli, regardless of how similar they are to stimuli seen in the training phase. Generalization will be perfect up to the "decision boundary", at which point responses will switch from one category to the other.

There have now been a number of studies demonstrating that rule- and similarity-based responding are indeed dissociable (Johnstone & Shanks, 2001; Palmeri & Nosofsky, 1995; Regehr & Brooks, 1993; Shanks & St. John, 1994; Thomas, 1998) and powerful models of rule-based category learning have been proposed (e.g. Erickson & Kruschke, 1998; Nosofsky, Palmeri, & McKinley, 1994), in which hypotheses are formed and then rejected if they are disconfirmed. These models, which rely on symbolic descriptions of rules, are quite different in character from connectionist models. It will be an important part of future research to see whether network models can be constructed to deal with apparent rule-based responding, or whether their domain of application is limited to similarity-mediated behaviour.

ACKNOWLEDGEMENTS

The research described here was supported in part by a project grant from the UK Biotechnology and Biological Sciences Research Council (BBSRC). The support of the Economic and Social Research Council is also gratefully acknowledged. The work is part of the program of the ESRC Centre for Economic Learning and Social Evolution, University College London. I thank Richard Darby and Francisco López for their contributions to the experimental work described here and John Pearce for his helpful comments on an earlier version of the chapter. Correspondence concerning this chapter should be addressed to David R. Shanks, Department of Psychology, University College London, Gower St., London WC1E 6BT, UK. Electronic mail may be sent to: d.shanks@ucl.ac.uk.

Notes

1. What we term "unique cue" models are often referred to in the literature as "configural-cue" networks (e.g. Gluck, 1991). We use the former term here to avoid confusion with the "true" configural models that we describe later.
2. The basis for the discrepant findings of Rickard & Grafman (1998), who found that human amnesics were more impaired on transverse patterning than on an equally difficult elemental control problem, and Reed & Squire (1999), who did not, is unclear. Reed & Squire (p. 7) suggest that the control problem Rickard & Grafman used was not as difficult as the transverse patterning problem. Rats with

hippocampal lesions are undoubtedly impaired at solving the transverse pattern-ing discrimination (Rudy & Sutherland, 1995).

REFERENCES

Alvarado, M. C., & Rudy, J. W. (1992). Some properties of configural learning: An investigation of the transverse-patterning problem. *Journal of Experimental Psychology: Animal Behavior Processes, 18,* 145–153.

Alvarado, M. C., & Rudy, J. W. (1995). A comparison of "configural" discrimination problems: Implications for understanding the role of the hippocampal formation in learning and memory. *Psychobiology, 23,* 178–184.

Aydin, A., & Pearce, J. M. (1997). Some determinants of response summation. *Animal Learning and Behavior, 25,* 108–121.

Blaxton, T. A., Zeffiro, T. A., Gabrieli, J. D. E., Bookheimer, S. Y., Carrillo, M. C., Theodore, W. H., et al. (1996). Functional mapping of human learning: A positron emission tomography activation study of eyeblink conditioning. *Journal of Neuroscience, 16,* 4032–4040.

Bouton, M. E. (1993). Context, time, and memory retrieval in the interference paradigms of Pavlovian learning. *Psychological Bulletin, 114,* 80–99.

Brewer, W. F. (1974). There is no convincing evidence for operant or classical conditioning in adult humans. In W. B. Weimer & D. S. Palermo (Eds.), *Cognition and the symbolic processes* (pp. 1–42). Hillsdale, NJ: Lawrence Erlbaum Associates, Inc.

Chandler, C. C. (1991). How memory for an event is influenced by related events: Interference in modified recognition tests. *Journal of Experimental Psychology: Learning, Memory, and Cognition, 17,* 115–125.

Chandler, C. C. (1993). Accessing related events increases retroactive interference in a matching recognition test. *Journal of Experimental Psychology: Learning, Memory, and Cognition, 19,* 967–974.

Chapman, G. B., & Robbins, S. J. (1990). Cue interaction in human contingency judgment. *Memory & Cognition, 18,* 537–545.

Dickinson, A. (1980). *Contemporary animal learning theory.* Cambridge: Cambridge University Press.

Dickinson, A. (2001). Causal learning: An associative analysis (The 28th Bartlett Memorial Lecture). *Quarterly Journal of Experimental Psychology, 54B,* 3–25.

Dickinson, A., Shanks, D. R., & Evenden, J. L. (1984). Judgement of act–outcome contingency: The role of selective attribution. *Quarterly Journal of Experimental Psychology, 36A,* 29–50.

Erickson, M. A., & Kruschke, J. K. (1998). Rules and exemplars in category learning. *Journal of Experimental Psychology: General, 127,* 107–140.

Fletcher, P. C., Anderson, J. M., Shanks, D. R., Honey, R., Carpenter, T. A., Donovan, T., et al. (2001). Responses of human frontal cortex to surprising events are predicted by formal associative learning theory. *Nature Neuroscience, 4,* 1043–1048.

Gallagher, M., & Holland, P. C. (1992). Preserved configural learning and spatial learning impairment in rats with hippocampal damage. *Hippocampus, 2,* 81–88.

Gallistel, C. R. (1990). *The organization of learning.* Cambridge, MA: MIT Press.

Gluck, M. A. (1991). Stimulus generalization and representation in adaptive network models of category learning. *Psychological Science, 2,* 50–55.

Gluck, M. A., & Myers, C. E. (1997). Psychobiological models of hippocampal function in learning and memory. *Annual Review of Psychology, 48,* 481–514.

Hall, G. (1991). *Perceptual and associative learning.* Oxford: Clarendon Press.

Hamann, S. B., Squire, L. R., & Schacter, D. L. (1995). Perceptual thresholds and priming in amnesia. *Neuropsychology, 9,* 3–15.

Hornik, K., Stinchcombe, M., & White, H. (1989). Multilayer feedforward networks are universal approximators. *Neural Networks, 2,* 359–368.

Johnstone, T., & Shanks, D. R. (2001). Abstractionist and processing accounts of implicit learning. *Cognitive Psychology, 42,* 61–112.

Kamin, L. J. (1968). "Attention-like" processes in classical conditioning. In M. R. Jones (Ed.), *Miami symposium on the prediction of behavior, 1967: Aversive stimulation* (pp. 9–31). Coral Gables, FL: University of Miami Press.

Kohonen, T. (1977). *Associative memory: A system theoretical approach.* New York: Springer.

Kruschke, J. K. (1992). ALCOVE: An exemplar-based connectionist model of category learning. *Psychological Review, 99,* 22–44.

Kruschke, J. K. (1993). Human category learning: Implications for backpropagation models. *Connection Science, 5,* 3–36.

Lewandowsky, S. (1991). Gradual unlearning and catastrophic interference: A comparison of distrubuted architectures. In W. E. Hockley & S. Lewandowsky (Eds.), *Relating theory and data: Essays on human memory in honor of Bennet B. Murdock* (pp. 445–476). Hillsdale, NJ: Lawrence Erlbaum Associates, Inc.

Lober, K., & Shanks, D. R. (2000). Is causal induction based on causal power? Critique of Cheng (1997). *Psychological Review, 107,* 195–212.

López, F. J., Shanks, D. R., Almaraz, J., & Fernández, P. (1998). Effects of trial order on contingency judgments: A comparison of associative and probabilistic contrast accounts. *Journal of Experimental Psychology: Learning, Memory, and Cognition, 24,* 672–694.

McClelland, J. L., & Rumelhart, D. E. (1988). *Explorations in parallel distributed processing.* Cambridge, MA: MIT Press.

McCloskey, M., & Cohen, N. J. (1989). Catastrophic interference in connectionist networks: The sequential learning problem. In G. H. Bower (Ed.), *The psychology of learning and motivation* (Vol. 24, pp. 109–165). San Diego, CA: Academic Press.

McDonald, R. J., Murphy, R. A., Guarraci, F. A., Gortler, J. R., White, N. M., & Baker, A. G. (1997). Systematic comparison of the effects of hippocampal and fornix-fimbria lesions on acquisition of three configural discriminations. *Hippocampus, 7,* 371–388.

McGlinchey-Berroth, R., Brawn, C., & Disterhoft, J. F. (1999). Temporal discrimination learning in severe amnesic patients reveals an alteration in the timing of eyeblink conditioned responses. *Behavioral Neuroscience, 113,* 10–18.

Medin, D. L., & Schwanenflugel, P. J. (1981). Linear separability in classification learning. *Journal of Experimental Psychology: Human Learning and Memory, 7,* 355–368.

Miller, R. R., Barnet, R. C., & Grahame, N. J. (1995). Assessment of the Rescorla–Wagner model. *Psychological Bulletin, 117,* 363–386.

Minsky, M. L., & Papert, S. A. (1969). *Perceptrons: An introduction to computational geometry.* Cambridge, MA: MIT Press.

Myers, K. M., Vogel, E. H., Shin, J., & Wagner, A. R. (2001). A comparison of the Rescorla–Wagner and Pearce models in a negative patterning and a summation problem. *Animal Learning & Behavior, 29,* 36–45.

Nosofsky, R. M., Palmeri, T. J., & McKinley, S. C. (1994). Rule-plus-exception model of classification learning. *Psychological Review, 101,* 53–79.

O'Reilly, R. C., & Rudy, J. W. (2001). Conjunctive representations in learning and memory: Principles of cortical and hippocampal function. *Psychological Review, 108,* 311–345.

Ostergaard, A. L., & Jernigan, T. L. (1996). Priming and baseline perceptual identification performance in amnesia: A comment on Hamann, Squire, and Schacter. *Neuropsychology, 10,* 125–130.

Palmeri, T. J., & Nosofsky, R. M. (1995). Recognition memory for exceptions to the category rule. *Journal of Experimental Psychology: Learning, Memory, and Cognition, 21,* 548–568.

Parkin, A. J. (1997). *Memory and amnesia: An introduction* (2nd ed.). Oxford, UK: Blackwell.

Payne, D. G., Toglia, M. P., & Anastasi, J. S. (1994). Recognition performance level and the magnitude of the misinformation effect in eyewitness memory. *Psychonomic Bulletin & Review, 1,* 376–382.

Pearce, J. M. (1987). A model for stimulus generalization in Pavlovian conditioning. *Psychological Review, 94,* 61–73.

Pearce, J. M. (1994). Similarity and discrimination: A selective review and a connectionist model. *Psychological Review, 101,* 587–607.

Pearce, J. M. (2002). Evaluation and development of a connectionist theory of configural learning. *Animal Learning & Behavior, 30,* 73–95.

Pearce, J. M., Aydin, A., & Redhead, E. S. (1997). Configural analysis of summation in autoshaping. *Journal of Experimental Psychology: Animal Behavior Processes, 23,* 84–94.

Pearce, J. M., & Redhead, E. S. (1993). The influence of an irrelevant stimulus on two discriminations. *Journal of Experimental Psychology: Animal Behavior Processes, 19,* 180–190.

Pearce, J. M., & Wilson, P. N. (1991). Failure of excitatory conditioning to extinguish the influence of a conditioned inhibitor. *Journal of Experimental Psychology: Animal Behavior Processes, 17,* 519–529.

Perales, J. C., & Shanks, D. R. (2003). Normative and descriptive accounts of the influence of power and contingency on causal judgment. *Quarterly Journal of Experimental Psychology, 56A,* 977–1007.

Plunkett, K., & Marchman, V. (1993). From rote learning to system building: Acquiring verb morphology in children and connectionist nets. *Cognition, 48,* 21–69.

Ratcliff, R. (1990). Connectionist models of recognition memory: Constraints imposed by learning and forgetting functions. *Psychological Review, 97,* 285–308.

Redhead, E. S., & Pearce, J. M. (1995). Similarity and discrimination learning. *Quarterly Journal of Experimental Psychology, 48B,* 46–66.

Reed, J. M., & Squire, L. R. (1999). Impaired transverse patterning in human amnesia is a special case of impaired memory for two-choice discrimination tasks. *Behavioral Neuroscience, 113,* 3–9.

Regehr, G., & Brooks, L. R. (1993). Perceptual manifestations of an analytic structure: The priority of holistic individuation. *Journal of Experimental Psychology: General, 122,* 92–114.

Rempel-Clower, N. L., Zola, S. M., Squire, L. R., & Amaral, D. G. (1996). Three cases of enduring memory impairment after bilateral damage limited to the hippocampal formation. *Journal of Neuroscience, 16,* 5233–5255.

Rescorla, R. A. (1997). Summation: Assessment of a configural theory. *Animal Learning and Behavior, 25,* 200–209.

Rescorla, R. A., & Wagner, A. R. (1972). A theory of Pavlovian conditioning: Variations in the effectiveness of reinforcement and nonreinforcement. In A. H. Black & W. F. Prokasy (Eds.), *Classical conditioning II: Current theory and research* (pp. 64–99). New York: Appleton-Century-Crofts.

Rickard, T. C., & Grafman, J. (1998). Losing their configural mind: Amnesic patients fail on transverse patterning. *Journal of Cognitive Neuroscience, 10,* 509–524.

Rudy, J. W., & Sutherland, R. J. (1995). Configural association theory and the hippocampal formation: An appraisal and reconfiguration. *Hippocampus, 5,* 375–389.

Schmajuk, N. A., & DiCarla, J. J. (1992). Stimulus configuration, classical conditioning, and hippocampal function. *Psychological Review, 99,* 268–305.

Schultz, W., & Dickinson, A. (2000). Neuronal coding of prediction errors. *Annual Review of Neuroscience, 23,* 473–500.

Shanks, D. R. (1985). Forward and backward blocking in human contingency judgement. *Quarterly Journal of Experimental Psychology, 37B,* 1–21.

Shanks, D. R. (1995). *The psychology of associative learning.* Cambridge: Cambridge University Press.

Shanks, D. R., Charles, D., Darby, R. J., & Azmi, A. (1998a). Configural processes in human associative learning. *Journal of Experimental Psychology: Learning, Memory, and Cognition, 24,* 1353–1378.

Shanks, D. R., Darby, R. J., & Charles, D. (1998b). Resistance to interference in human associative learning: Evidence of configural processing. *Journal of Experimental Psychology: Animal Behavior Processes, 24,* 136–150.

Shanks, D. R., & Gluck, M. A. (1994). Tests of an adaptive network model for the identification and categorization of continuous-dimension stimuli. *Connection Science, 6,* 59–89.

Shanks, D. R., & St. John, M. F. (1994). Characteristics of dissociable human learning systems. *Behavioral and Brain Sciences, 17,* 367–447.

Sloman, S. A., & Rumelhart, D. E. (1992). Reducing interference in distributed memories through episodic gating. In A. F. Healy, S. M. Kosslyn & R. M. Shiffrin (Eds.), *From learning processes to cognitive processes: Essays in honor of William K. Estes* (Vol. 1, pp. 227–248). Hillsdale, NJ: Lawrence Erlbaum Associates, Inc.

Squire, L. R. (1994). Declarative and nondeclarative memory: Multiple brain systems supporting learning and memory. In D. L. Schacter & E. Tulving (Eds.), *Memory systems 1994* (pp. 203–231). Cambridge, MA: MIT Press.

Stone, G. O. (1986). An analysis of the delta rule and the learning of statistical associations. In D. E. Rumelhart, J. L. McClelland & the PDP Research Group (Eds.), *Parallel distributed processing: Explorations in the microstructure of cognition. Vol. 1: Foundations* (pp. 444–459). Cambridge, MA: MIT Press.

Sutherland, R. J., & Rudy, J. W. (1989). Configural association theory: The role of the hippocampal formation in learning, memory, and amnesia. *Psychobiology, 17,* 129–144.

Thomas, R. D. (1998). Learning correlations in categorization tasks using large, ill-defined categories. *Journal of Experimental Psychology: Learning, Memory, and Cognition, 24,* 119–143.

Vallée-Tourangeau, F., Murphy, R. A., & Baker, A. G. (1998). Causal induction in the presence of a perfect negative cue: Contrasting predictions from associative and statistical models. *Quarterly Journal of Experimental Psychology, 51B,* 173–191.

Vallée-Tourangeau, F., Murphy, R. A., Drew, S., & Baker, A. G. (1998). Judging the importance of constant and variable candidate causes: A test of the Power PC theory. *Quarterly Journal of Experimental Psychology, 51A,* 65–84.

van Gelder, T. (1991). What is the "D" in "PDP"? A survey of the concept of distribution. In W. Ramsey, S. P. Stich & D. E. Rumelhart (Eds.), *Philosophy and connectionist theory* (pp. 33–59). Hillsdale, NJ: Lawrence Erlbaum Associates, Inc.

Waelti, P., Dickinson, A., & Schultz, W. (2001). Dopamine responses comply with basic assumptions of formal learning theory. *Nature, 412,* 43–48.

Wagner, A. R., & Rescorla, R. A. (1972). Inhibition in Pavlovian conditioning: Application of a theory. In R. A. Boakes & M. S. Halliday (Eds.), *Inhibition and learning* (pp. 301–336). London: Academic Press.

Wickelgren, W. A. (1979). Chunking and consolidation: A theoretical synthesis of semantic networks, configuring in conditioning, S–R versus cognitive learning, normal forgetting, the amnesic syndrome, and the hippocampal arousal system. *Psychological Review, 86,* 44–60.

Williams, D. A. (1995). Forms of inhibition in animal and human learning. *Journal of Experimental Psychology: Animal Behavior Processes, 21,* 129–142.

Williams, D. A. (1996). A comparative analysis of negative contingency learning in humans and nonhumans. In D. R. Shanks, K. J. Holyoak & D. L. Medin (Eds.), *The psychology of learning and motivation: Causal learning* (Vol. 34, pp. 89–131). San Diego, CA: Academic Press.

Williams, D. A., & Braker, D. S. (1999). Influence of past experience on the coding of compound stimuli. *Journal of Experimental Psychology: Animal Behavior Processes, 25,* 461–474.

Williams, D. A., Sagness, K. E., & McPhee, J. E. (1994). Configural and elemental strategies in predictive learning. *Journal of Experimental Psychology: Learning, Memory, and Cognition, 20,* 694–709.

Wilson, P. N., & Pearce, J. M. (1992). A configural analysis of feature-negative discrimination learning. *Journal of Experimental Psychology: Animal Behavior Processes, 18,* 265–272.

CHAPTER THREE

Connectionist neuropsychology

John A. Bullinaria
University of Birmingham, UK

INTRODUCTION

The field of cognitive neuropsychology employs the patterns of performance observed in brain-damaged patients to constrain our models of normal cognitive function. This methodology was historically based upon simple "box and arrow" models, with particular cognitive deficits being taken as indicative of the selective breakdown of corresponding "boxes" or "arrows". In principle, within this framework, one should be able to piece together a complete model of mental structure by studying patients with complementary patterns of deficit (e.g. Caramazza, 1986; Shallice, 1988). The concept of *double dissociation* has been of particular importance for this enterprise, with its presence being taken to imply modularity across a whole range of systems. I shall review the technical details and provide specific examples later, but the basic inference is that if one patient can perform task 1 but not task 2, and a second patient can perform task 2 but not task 1, then a natural way to explain this is in terms of separate modules for the two tasks.

Cognitive modelling has now moved on, and the use of connectionist techniques to provide detailed models of the inner workings of these modules or "boxes" is becoming increasingly common. Typically, networks of simplified neurons loosely based on real brain structures are set up, with general architectures based on known physiology, and trained to perform appropriately simplified versions of the human tasks. The models are iteratively refined by requiring their learning process to match children's development,

their generalization performance to match human generalization performance, their reaction times to match human reaction times, and so on. These
individual network models can then be wired together in the manner of the
old box and arrow models, and all the old explanations of patient data can
carry through. The obvious advantage this provides is that one can now take
a more detailed look at the performance and degradation of the various
components, and the removal of neurons or connections in these models
constitute a more natural analogue of real brain damage (Farah, 1994). However, in addition to providing an elaboration of the previous models, one can
also question in detail the validity of the old assumptions of neuropsychological inference. In particular, Bullinaria & Chater (1995) have
considered the possibility that double dissociation does not really imply
modularity, but may also be possible as a result of damage to fully distributed
connectionist systems. They concluded that, assuming one successfully avoids
small-scale artefacts, only single dissociations are possible without modularity. Moreover, these single dissociations were seen to be rooted in natural
regularity effects, with regular mappings more robust than irregular mappings. These general arguments have since been extended from simple
abstract mappings through to more realistic single route models of reading,
which show how surface dyslexia-like effects can arise but phonological
dyslexia effects cannot (Bullinaria, 1994, 1997a,b).

Whilst finding a counter-example to the inference from double dissociation to modularity would clearly settle the matter, failing to find a counter-
example will always be less conclusive. There have also been some reports in
the literature containing conflicting conclusions concerning models from the
class investigated by Bullinaria & Chater (1995). Marchman (1993), for
example, has studied models of past tense production and seemingly found
dissociations with the irregular items more robust than the regulars. Moreover, Plaut (1995) has apparently found a connectionist double dissociation
without modularity. Naturally, these apparent contradictions have caused a
certain amount of confusion, particularly amongst researchers unfamiliar
with the detailed workings of connectionist models. In this chapter I shall
review and extend the work of Bullinaria & Chater (1995) with a view to
minimizing future confusion in this area.

The concrete illustrative models, on which the following discussion shall
be based, all have the same simplified structure of a fully-connected feedforward network, with one hidden layer trained using some form of gradient
descent error minimization algorithm on some combination of regular and
irregular mappings. A set of regular items (defined as such because they
follow consistent mappings in the training set) will naturally be easier to learn
than irregular items, and consequently they are learnt more quickly and
accurately. We shall see that this then results in more damage to be required
for them to be lost again. This sounds simple enough, but we have to be

careful about the details of our definition of regularity. In terms of network learning, a very high-frequency "irregular" item might be deemed more "regular" than a consistent set of regular items whose total frequency is still much less than the irregular item. Also, if an irregular item is very "close" in the input/output space to a regular set, then we might deem that item particularly irregular and the regular items less regular than usual (although talking about "consistency", rather than "regularity", is usually more useful in such cases). In the following sections I shall present explicit neural network simulation results and argue that, as long as one controls for such confounding effects, the basic conclusion of Bullinaria & Chater (1995) holds. We shall see how the opposite "regularity" effect found by Marchman (1993) arises, and argue that it would be more correctly labelled a "frequency" effect. We shall also see how Plaut's (1995) double dissociation is consistent with our findings, it being more a different use of terminology than a different conclusion. Our discussion will also reveal how it is possible to obtain a valid strong double dissociation between high frequency irregulars and low frequency regulars due to global damage of a fully distributed connectionist system without modularity. Since regularity and frequency do tend to anti-correlate in natural language, such potential confounds are seen to require particular care in many language processing experiments and models.

In the remainder of this chapter, I shall begin by reviewing the important relevant ideas from cognitive neuropsychology: the traditional inference from double dissociation to modularity, the types of system that may exhibit double dissociation, and the problem of *resource artefacts*. This will include a varied selection of examples from the neuropsychology literature to provide an idea of what is required of connectionist models in this area. Next I will outline the basic properties of the connectionist models most commonly employed in cognitive psychology. The general properties of these models then lead naturally to a range of explicit neural network learning and lesion simulations that explore those issues of particular relevance to connectionist neuropsychology. First, I explain the general consequences of network damage as originally discussed by Bullinaria & Chater (1995), then I bring the apparently contradictory results of Plaut (1995) and Marchman (1993) into the same framework, and finally I present some more recent simulations that explore the frequency–regularity confound which is at the root of many of the recent confusions. I will end with a more general discussion of connectionist dissociations and some conclusions. Throughout I shall concentrate on the general principles that may be applied to any of the models described elsewhere in this book, rather than on presenting a series of specific case studies.

COGNITIVE NEUROPSYCHOLOGY

Whilst data from individual normal subjects, or individual brain-damaged patients, can undoubtedly constrain cognitive models, certain patterns of deficit across populations of patients can provide much stronger constraints. If a patient A performs very much better on task 1 than on task 2, then we say that we have a strong *single dissociation*. If two patients, A and B, have opposite single dissociations, then together they form a *double dissociation*. This pattern of performance can be conveniently plotted as in Figure 3.1. The various types of dissociation and their implications have been discussed in

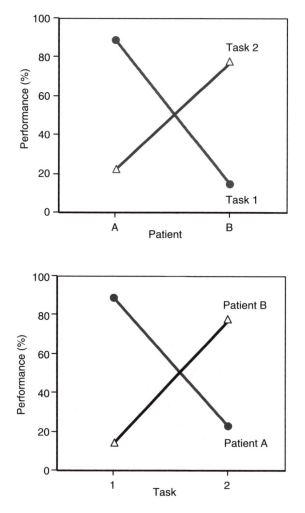

Figure 3.1.   A strong crossover double dissociation for Tasks 1 and 2, Patients A and B.

some detail by Shallice (1988) and Dunn & Kirsner (1988). Of particular relevance to us is the inference from double dissociation to modularity of function, which forms an important part of the foundations of cognitive neuropsychology (Teuber, 1955).

Any observed double dissociation (DD) of performance has a natural explanation in terms of the existence of separate modules associated with the two tasks, with the two patients suffering damage to a different one of them. A classic and well-known example occurs in the field of acquired reading problems. Extreme cases of surface dyslexia include patient KT, who could read 100% of nonwords and regular words but could only manage 47% of irregular words (McCarthy & Warrington, 1986). Conversely, the phonological dyslexic patient WB could read 90% of real words but was unable to read even the simplest of nonwords (Funnell, 1983). This loss of exception words by surface dyslexics, together with the loss of nonwords by phonological dyslexics, constitutes a DD which can be taken to imply separate lexical and rule-based modules in a dual route model of reading (e.g. by Coltheart, Curtis, Atkins, & Haller, 1993).

However, the modules do not necessarily have to operate in parallel like this—the same data could be taken to imply modules that operate in series (e.g. by Patterson & Marcel, 1992; Bullinaria, 1997b). In fact there could be any number of different modular accounts for a particular DD, and the account that appears most natural from the point of view of boxes and arrows might not look so natural from the point of view of connectionist systems. This is another reason why it is important to explore the more detailed models offered by connectionism. For our reading example, a rule-based box that can not deal with exception words seems less natural when it becomes clear that a neural network trained on all words will automatically learn to process the exception words as well as the regular words (Seidenberg & McClelland, 1989), and on damage result in surface dyslexia-type deficits, right down to the details of the regularization errors (Bullinaria, 1994, 1997a; Plaut, McClelland, Seidenberg, & Patterson, 1996). Furthermore, proficient reading using only a lexical/semantic route begins to look increasingly unnatural when we find that a neural network, trained to map between orthography, phonology, and semantics, prefers to access semantics from orthography via phonology, rather than by direct activation (Bullinaria, 1997b). Even if the details of these particular neural network models turn out to be inaccurate, they do highlight the fact that the assignment of modules is not as clear-cut as many would suggest, and show how connectionist models can be used to test the computational plausibility of the possible box and arrow frameworks.

We shall not delve into the details here, but other areas in which DD has been observed and taken to infer mental structure include: regular vs. irregular past tense production (e.g. Lavric, Pizzagalli, Forstmeir, & Rippon,

2001; Pinker, 1991, 1997); lexical vs. syntactic components of number processing (Caramazza & McCloskey, 1989); aspects of visual processing (De Renzi, 1986; Farah, 1990; Warrington, 1985); long-term vs. short-term memory (Shallice, 1979); episodic vs. semantic memory (Shoben, Wescourt, & Smith, 1978); and natural kinds vs. artefacts in picture naming (Warrington & Shallice, 1984), to name but a few. Often it seems that DD is taken quite generally to imply modularity, and this is despite Dunn & Kirsner (1988) having shown that this inference cannot generally be justified, and Shallice (1988, p. 249) providing a whole list of nonmodular systems that can produce dissociations (even double dissociations) when damaged (e.g. topographic maps, overlapping processing regions, coupled systems). Some early neural network models (Sartori, 1988; Wood, 1978) also seemed to indicate that DD was even possible in distributed systems, but these were very small-scale models and the effects have since been seen to be largely the consequence of individual neurons acting as "modules" in their own right. This led Shallice (1988, p. 257) to believe that "as yet there is no suggestion that a strong double dissociation can take place from two lesions within a properly distributed network".

Before moving on to test whether this claim has stood the test of time, we need to consider one further complication, known as the problem of *resource artefacts*. As illustrated in Figures 3.2 and 3.3, a DD with a crossover in terms of patient performance, but not in task performance, can be explained as a resource artefact in a single system. All that is required is for the two tasks to depend on a single resource in different manners, such that which task is performed better depends on the amount of resource that has been spared by the damage. Clearly, such a pattern of dissociation should NOT be taken to imply modularity (Shallice, 1998, p. 234). As we shall see later, DDs of this type are actually rather easily obtainable in connectionist models. Devlin, Gonnerman, Anderson, & Seidenberg (1998) have presented a particularly interesting example involving a connectionist account of category-specific semantic deficits. The importance of connectionist modelling here is not that we can get a form of DD which is not possible in other types of model, but rather that it provides a finer grain of detail that allows us to demonstrate explicitly that, given appropriate assumptions about the information and representations being processed, the observed DD really can arise in this manner.

NEURAL NETWORK MODELS

This section provides a review of the relevant features common to most neural network models used in cognitive psychology. This will prepare us for the later sections in which we discuss some explicit simulations that have been formulated to elucidate the properties that form the basis of *connectionist neuropsychology*.

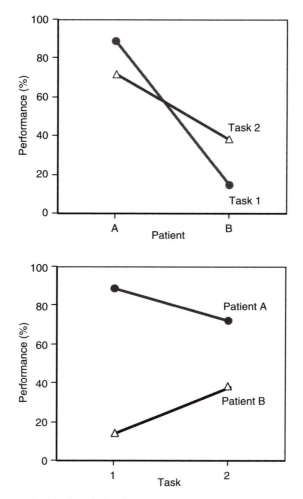

Figure 3.2. A weak double dissociation for Tasks 1 and 2, Patients A and B.

Most neural network models of human performance on psychological tasks tend to be based on simple feedforward networks that map between chosen simplified input and output representations via a single hidden layer, or have such a system as an identifiable subcomponent. For this reason I shall concentrate my discussion on such systems. Extensions to more complicated systems will be readily apparent. Whilst it is obviously important that the chosen representations are appropriate for the task in hand, allow that task to be accomplished in a sufficiently human-like manner, and have a reasonable degree of biological and psychological plausibility, the details will not affect the general discussion that follows.

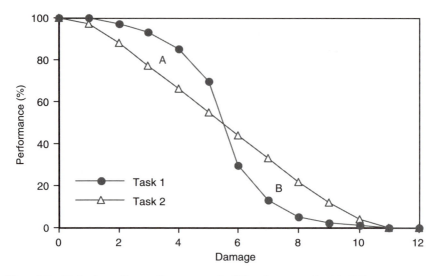

Figure 3.3. Tasks depending on the resources in different ways can lead to DDs.

Clearly, an important feature of connectionist models is that the networks *learn* to perform their given task by iteratively adjusting their connection weights (e.g. by some form of gradient descent algorithm) to minimize the output errors for an appropriate training set of input–output pairs. Generally, we simply assume that the quick and convenient learning algorithms we choose to use will generate similar results to those produced by more biologically plausible learning procedures. Comparisons between back-propagation and contrastive Hebbian learning by Plaut & Shallice (1993) provide some justification for this assumption. We can then compare the development of the networks' performance during training and their final performance (e.g. their output errors, generalization ability, reaction times, priming effects, speed–accuracy trade-offs, robustness to damage, etc.) with human subjects to narrow down the correct architecture, representations, and so on, to generate increasingly accurate models. Here, of course, we are particularly interested in simulating neuropsychological effects by lesioning our trained networks.

To ease the subsequent discussion it is worth defining some notation. Our networks will be set up so that the output of each processing unit i for each training pattern p is the sigmoid (or "squashing function") of the sum of the bias/threshold of that unit plus the weighted activations flowing into it from the units j of the previous layer. We write:

$$Out_i(P) = sigmoid(Sum_i(P)) \qquad Sum_i(P) = \sum_j w_{ij} \, Prev_j(P)$$

in which, for mathematical convenience, we define $Prev_0(P) = 1$, so that the bias w_{i0} can be treated in exactly the same way as the real connection weights. Then, to train the network, we specify a suitable error function E to minimize and iteratively update the weights w_{ij} (now including the biases) to reduce this error using gradient descent:

$$\Delta w_{ij} = -\eta \frac{\partial E}{\partial w_{ij}}$$

In other words, we take repeated steps Δw_{ij} in weight space in the direction that best reduces the error E. Typically for this we use either the sum-squared output error measure:

$$E = \frac{1}{2} \sum_P \sum_i |Target_i(P) - Out_i(P)|^2$$

or, for classification problems with binary outputs, the cross-entropy error measure:

$$E = -\sum_P \sum_i [Target_i(P)\cdot\log(Out_i(P)) + (1 - Target_i(P))\cdot\log(1 - Out_i(P))]$$

(Bishop, 1995; Hinton, 1989). Often it is also appropriate to add some form of regularization term to the gradient descent cost function to smooth the outputs or improve the generalization. For example, adding a term to E that is quadratic in the weights will result in a linear weight decay during training and restrict over-fitting of the training data (Bishop, 1995). Whilst such extra factors will not usually affect the kinds of results we are concerned with here, one should always check to make sure, because there are situations in which they can have a significant effect on how well the different training patterns are learnt (e.g. Bullinaria, Riddell, & Rushton, 1999).

A crucial feature of this learning approach, which underlies much of what follows, is that a network's performance on one pattern will be affected by its training on other patterns. It is helpful to begin by illustrating this with a concrete example originally presented by Seidenberg & McClelland (1989) for their reading model, but using data from my own reading model (Bullinaria, 1997a). In both cases we have a neural network model mapping from a simplified representation of orthography to a simplified representation of phonology via one hidden layer. Figure 3.4 shows how the output performance on the regular word "tint" varies as the result of further training of a partially trained network. First, training on the regular nonword "wint", that already has a very low error (0.000001), has no effect on the word "tint" because it generates very small weight changes. We have a ceiling effect. Compare this with three different word types with matched and relatively

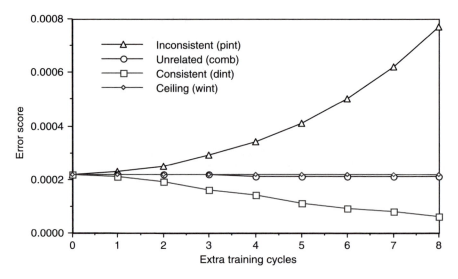

Figure 3.4.   The effect on the word "tint" of repeated training on other words.

high error scores. Training on the regular word "dint" (0.00252) improves performance, i.e. reduces the error, because the weight changes generated for the "int" ending are also appropriate for "tint". In fact, because of its relatively low error (0.00022), even training on "tint" itself has less effect than training on "dint". Training on the irregular word "pint" (error 0.00296) worsens performance because the weight changes generated for the "int" ending here (with a long "i" sound rather than the regular short "i" sound) are inappropriate for "tint". Finally, training on the control word "comb" (0.00296) has little effect because the weight changes have little relevance for "tint".

By considering the implications of these performance changes for a full set of training data, it is easy to understand why the network tends to learn to read consistent sets of regular words before exceptional words, and why it generally ends up performing better (i.e. with lower output activation error scores) on regular words than on exception words. Similarly, we can understand why having inconsistent neighbours will be detrimental to learning and final reading performance. It also reveals why high-frequency exception words should be learnt faster than low-frequency exception words, and why we should expect ceiling effects whereby the performance on the higher frequency exception words eventually catches up that of the regular words. All this is consistent with empirical data from humans.

Given this simple example, we can easily see what will happen in the general case. Amongst other things, it follows straightforwardly from adding up the network weight change contributions due to individual training patterns that:

1. High-frequency items are learnt more quickly than low-frequency items, because the appropriate weight changes are applied more often.
2. Regular items will be learnt more quickly than irregular items, because consistent weight changes combine and inconsistent weight changes cancel.
3. Ceiling effects will arise as the training items are mastered, because the sigmoids saturate and the weight changes tend to zero.

These fundamental properties of neural network learning lead automatically to many of the interesting successes of connectionist models, such as human-like age of acquisition effects, patterns of reaction times, speed–accuracy trade-off effects, and so on (Bullinaria, 1997a, 1999).

Once we have trained our networks and confirmed that they are performing in a sufficiently human-like manner, we can then set about inflicting simulated brain damage on them. Small (1991) has considered the various ways in which connectionist networks might be lesioned, and discussed their neurobiological and clinical neurological relevance. He identifies two broad classes of lesion: *diffuse*, such as globally scaling or adding noise to all the weights, and *focal*, such as removing adjacent subsets of connections and/or hidden units. Which of these we choose will naturally depend on the type of patient we are modelling. Focal lesions would be appropriate for stroke patients, whereas diffuse lesions would be required for diseases such as Alzheimer's. Clearly, for our abstract models it will be appropriate to examine all these possibilities. Finally, we should be aware that relearning after damage may affect the observed pattern of deficits, and so we must check this also (Harley, 1996; Plaut, 1996).

LEARNING AND LESIONING SIMULATIONS

In this section we shall explore in some detail the relation between the basic learning and lesioning effects that arise automatically in the class of neural networks outlined above. Fortunately, it proves feasible to do this by simulating some fairly small networks that are required to perform some rather simple sets of regular and irregular mappings of varying frequency.

Consider first a simple fully-connected feedforward network with 10 input units, 100 hidden units and 10 output units, with binary inputs and output targets trained on two sets of 100 regular items (permuted identity mappings) and two sets of 10 irregular items (random mappings). One of the input bits is used to signal which of the two regular mappings should be applied. The two sets of regular items used here are equivalent, since the ordering of the network's input and output units is arbitrary, but we shall have one set appearing during training with a frequency of 20 times the other. Similarly for the two irregular sets. Such frequency differences can be implemented naturally over many epochs by manipulating the probability that a given pattern is used for training in a given epoch, but we can also implement them within each single epoch by scaling the weight change contributions in proportion to the frequencies. As long as the weight changes per epoch are kept small, it seems to make little difference which method we choose. Clearly, though, if the training set contains some very low-frequency items and we use the many-epochs approach, we need to be careful that the network is trained over enough epochs for all items to be used a reasonable number of times. The network was actually trained using the many-epochs approach by gradient descent on a sum squared error measure with no regularization. The predicted regularity and frequency effects were found, as can be seen clearly in Figure 3.5 which shows how the mean output $Sum_i(P)$'s develop during training for each of the four item types (high-frequency regular, low-frequency regular, high-frequency irregular, low-frequency irregular) and two target activations (0, 1). If we set a particular correct response threshold for the $Sum_i(P)$'s, e.g. ± 2.2 corresponding to output activations less than 0.1 for targets of 0 and greater than 0.9 for targets of 1, we see that the more regular and higher-frequency items are the first to be learned during training and end

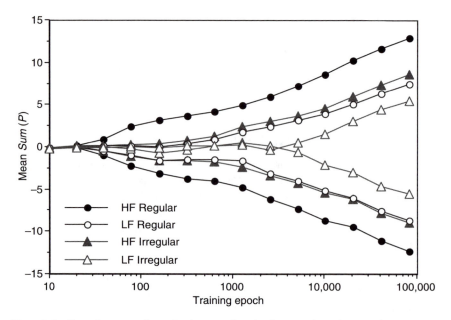

Figure 3.5.   Learning curves for a simple network trained on quasi-regular mappings.

up furthest from the thresholds when the training is stopped. If we add a regularization term to the gradient descent error function that leads to weight decay during training, the $Sum_i(P)$'s eventually level off rather than increasing indefinitely, as in Figure 3.5, but we still get the same clear item-type dependence. Bullinaria & Chater (1995) also found similar regularity effects for networks trained using the conjugate gradient learning algorithm on a training set of 224 regular items and 32 less regular items, and again for a set of 224 regular items and 16 random items that employed an error correcting coding. It seems that the pattern of results is quite robust with respect to the implementational details.

We can now turn to the consequences of lesioning these networks. Bullinaria & Chater (1995) found that damaging trained networks by removing random hidden units, removing random connections, globally scaling the weights, or adding random noise to the weights, all led to very similar patterns of results. Moreover, by plotting the $Sum_i(P)$'s against increasing degrees of damage, we could understand why. Figure 3.6 shows the effect of removing increasingly large numbers of connections from our network—we see that we get the reverse of the pattern of learning seen in Figure 3.5. If we set a particular correct response threshold for the $Sum_i(P)$'s as above, we see that the items that are first to be learnt during training and end up furthest from the thresholds when the training is stopped, tend to be the last to be lost

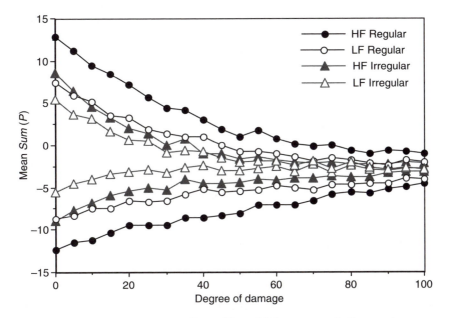

Figure 3.6. Damage curves corresponding to Figure 3.5 due to removal of connections.

during damage, and hence we get clear dissociations, with the regulars more robust than the irregulars, and high-frequency items more robust than low-frequency items. Removing random sets of hidden units, or globally reducing all the weights by repeated application of constant scale factors, result in a similar pattern. Adding random noise to all the weights produces more of a general random walk rather than a drift to zero $Sum_i(P)$, but still it is the patterns that start nearest the thresholds that tend to cross it first, again resulting in the regulars being more robust than the irregulars. These basic effects extend easily to more realistic models, e.g. surface dyslexia in the reading model of Bullinaria (1994, 1997a). Here we not only successfully simulate the relative error proportions for the various word categories, but also the types of errors that are produced. The closest threshold to an irregularly pronounced letter will be that of the regular pronunciation, and hence the errors will be predominantly regularizations, exactly as is observed in human surface dyslexics. The same basic considerations also allow us to understand various developmental and reaction time effects (Bullinaria, 1999).

After brain damage, patients often (but not always) show a rapid improvement in performance (Geshwind, 1985). This is important to connectionist modellers for two reasons. First, if relearning occurs automatically and quickly in patients, then we need to be sure that the same effects are observed in our models and that we are comparing patient and model data at equivalent stages of the relearning process. Second, our models may be of assistance in formulating appropriate remedial strategies for brain-damaged patients (Plaut, 1996; Wilson & Patterson, 1990). It has been known for some time that the information remaining after damage does allow rapid relearning in neural networks ranging from standard back-propagation models (Sejnowski & Rosenberg, 1987) through to Boltzmann machines (Hinton & Sejnowski, 1986). It is also clear from the discussion above that, since both learning and damage result in the same regularity and frequency effects, it is unlikely that relearning using the original training data will reverse this pattern; indeed, it is likely to enhance it (Bullinaria & Chater, 1995). Obviously, if some rehabilitation regime is employed that involves a very different set of training examples to that of the original learning process, then it is possible for different results to arise (Plaut, 1996). In this case our models may be used to predict or refine appropriate relearning strategies and the patients' responses should be used to validate our models. In the section on Regularity and Frequency Confounds (below) we shall see that more complicated outcomes of relearning are possible if two or more factors, such as regularity and frequency, are confounded.

The general point to be made here is that some items are naturally learnt more quickly and more accurately than others, and the effects of subsequent network damage follow automatically from these patterns of learning. There are actually many other factors, in addition to regularity and frequency, that can cause the differing learning and damage rates, and we can explore them all in a similar manner and use them in models of neuropsychological data in the same way. Consistency and neighbourhood density are the most closely related to regularity, and are commonly found in language models, such as the reading and spelling models of Plaut et al. (1996) and Bullinaria (1997a). Representation sparseness or pattern strength are often used to distinguish between concrete and abstract semantics, such as in the models of Plaut & Shallice (1993) and Plaut (1995). Correlation, redundancy and dimensionality are commonly used in models to distinguish the semantics of natural things vs. artefacts, such as in the model of Devlin et al. (1998). At some level of description, all these may be regarded as forms of regularity, and their effects can easily be confused. Which we use will depend on exactly what we are attempting to model, but clearly, if we want to make claims about neuropsychological deficits involving one of them, we need to be careful to control for all the others.

AVOIDING SMALL-SCALE ARTEFACTS

Modelling massively parallel brain processes by simulating neural networks on serial computers is only rendered feasible by abstracting out the essential details and scaling down the size of the networks. It is clearly important for all connectionist models to check that the abstraction and scaling process has not been taken so far that we miss some of the important fundamental properties of the system we are modelling, or introduce features that are nothing but small-scale artefacts. Bullinaria & Chater (1995) showed that such artefacts can arise particularly easily in the field of connectionist neuropsychology. This complication is of such importance that it is worth discussing in more detail here.

The damage curves of Figure 3.6 are relatively smooth because we have averaged over many output units and many training items, and because our network has many more hidden units and connections than are actually required to perform the given mappings. For smaller networks, however, the effect of individual damage contributions can be large enough to produce wildly fluctuating performance on individual items, which in turn can result in dissociations in arbitrary directions. Often these small-scale artefacts are sufficient to produce convincing-looking double dissociations. The early models of Wood (1978) and Sartori (1988) are classic examples of this. As soon as we scale up to larger networks, in which the individual contributions each have a small effect on the outputs, the "regulars lost" dissociations disappear (Bullinaria & Chater, 1995). We always find that the apparent double dissociations dissolve into single dissociations as the network is made more distributed. We are then left with a simple "regularity effect", as discussed above.

It would clearly make our modelling endeavours much easier if we had some independent procedure for determining when our networks are sufficiently distributed to obtain reliable results. In effect, we need to make sure that our individual processing units are not acting as "modules" in their own right, and the obvious way to do this is by checking to see that all the individual contributions $c_{ij} = w_{ij} \, Prev_j(P)$ feeding into to an output unit i are small compared to the total $Sum_i(P) = \Sigma_j \, c_{ij}$. Clearly, if the network damage corresponds to the removal of unit j or the connection ij, then the contribution c_{ij} to the output i will be lost. If the lost contribution is small compared to the corresponding total, i.e. the ratio $C = c_{ij}/\Sigma_k \, c_{ik}$ is much less than one, then the output activation will not be changed much and it will take many such lost contributions to result in an output change large enough to be deemed an error. This is the brain-like resilience to damage often known as *graceful degradation*. Fortunately, this distribution of information processing tends to occur automatically, simply by supplying the network with a sufficiently large number of hidden units.

Figure 3.7 shows the distribution of 10,000 typical individual contribution ratios C for the high-frequency regular outputs in networks with 30 and 100 hidden units trained on the quasi-regular mapping discussed above. For 100 hidden units, there are very few contributions with ratios C larger than one, but with only 30 hidden units, many contributions are much greater than their corresponding total and their removal will result in wild fluctuations in the outputs. The reduction in the number of large contribution ratios as we increase the number of hidden units is shown in Figure 3.8. Unfortunately, in

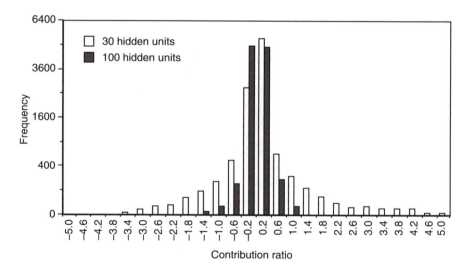

Figure 3.7.   The distribution of output contribution ratios C for two typical networks.

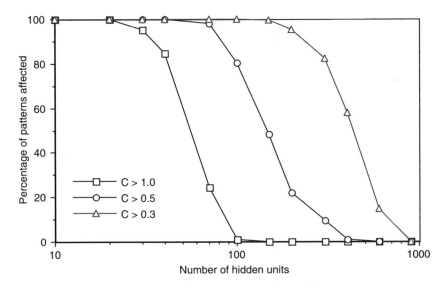

Figure 3.8. The fall-off of large contributions C with number of hidden units.

general, it seems that we really do need to use a surprisingly large number of hidden units to avoid the small-scale artefacts—tens, or even hundreds, of times the minimal number required to learn the given task.

It is natural to ask what can be done if limited computational resources render the use of sufficiently large numbers of hidden units impossible. Well, consider the effect of network damage on the histograms in Figure 3.7. Obviously, after removing a random subset of the hidden units or connections, the number of contributions will be reduced by some factor α. However, in large fully distributed networks, the mean contribution will not change much, and so the total contribution after damage is simply reduced to $\alpha\ Sum_i(P) = \alpha\ \Sigma w_{ij}Prev_j(P)$. Note that we can achieve exactly the same result by simply globally scaling all the weights w_{ij} by the same factor α. In smaller networks, of course, this equivalence breaks down because the means tend to suffer relatively large random fluctuations during damage. However, since global weight scaling does not suffer from such random fluctuations, it can be used to simulate a smoothed form of lesioning and give a reasonable approximation in small networks to what will happen in more realistic networks. Alternatively, if one wants to claim that each hidden unit in our model actually corresponds to a number of real neurons, then the weight scaling can be regarded as removing a fraction α of these corresponding real neurons. Either way, this procedure involves approximating a form of focal damage by a form of diffuse damage, and there are clear limits to the validity of the approximation. If this approach is pursued, we need to be careful not to lose sight of what type of brain damage we are modelling, and what the weight scaling really represents.

PLAUT'S DOUBLE DISSOCIATION WITHOUT MODULARITY

Given that we have just concluded that valid DD does not arise in fully distributed connectionist systems, it is not surprising that Plaut's well-known paper entitled "Double dissociation without modularity: Evidence from connectionist neuropsychology" (Plaut, 1995) is often taken as evidence that there must be something wrong with the above discussion. His work was based on the models of deep dyslexia of Plaut & Shallice (1993), which in turn were extensions of the earlier models of Hinton & Shallice (1991). Deep dyslexia is a well-known acquired reading disorder characterized by semantic errors, such as reading "forest" as "tree". Of particular relevance to us are two patients who provide a DD between abstract and concrete word reading. Patient CAV was able to read correctly 55% of abstract words but only 36% of concrete words (Warrington, 1981), whereas patient PW could read 67% of concrete words but only 13% of abstract words (Patterson & Marcel, 1977).

The Plaut & Shallice (1993) models consist of attractor networks that map from orthography to semantics via a layer of hidden units, and then from semantics to phonology via another set of hidden units, with additional layers of "clean-up" units at the semantics and phonology levels. The particular model used to investigate concreteness had 32 orthography units corresponding to letters at particular word positions, 61 phonology units corresponding to phonemes in a similar manner, and 98 semantic units corresponding to a hand-crafted set of semantic micro-features. Each hidden layer and clean-up layer contained 10 units. The network was trained on 40 words, using back-propagation through time, until it settled into the correct semantics and phonology when presented with each orthography.

Lesions at two different locations in the trained network were then found to produce a DD between concrete and abstract word reading if the concreteness was coded as the proportion of activated semantic micro-features. Specifically, removal of orthographic to hidden layer connections resulted in preferential loss of abstract word reading, whereas removal of connections to the semantic clean-up units primarily impaired performance on the concrete words. Although the two damage locations do not constitute modules in the conventional sense, it is not difficult to understand how they contribute to different degrees to the processing of the two word types and will give opposite dissociations when damaged. It is simply a consequence of the sparser representations of the abstract words making less use of the semantic clean-up mechanism, and depending more on the direct connections, than the richer representations of the concrete words (Plaut & Shallice, 1993). The performance of each location is fully consistent with the general discussion above, and the only disagreement concerns the appropriateness of using the word "module" to describe the two damage locations.

As Plaut (1995) himself points out, one of the problems when discussing "modularity" is that different authors use different definitions of the term. A Fodor (1983) module, for example, is hard-wired, innate and informationally encapsulated, whereas a Coltheart (1985) module is defined to have none of those properties. Moreover, the definitions provided are often imprecise, and sometimes they are even left totally implicit. A cynic, such as myself, might therefore suggest that the situation would be less confusing if we all confined ourselves to describing our models and their ability to account for the neuro-psychological data, and made a conscious effort to avoid using words like "module" altogether.

REGULARITY AND FREQUENCY CONFOUNDS

Another connectionist model that appears to be in even more direct conflict with the above discussion is the past tense model of Marchman (1993). She used back-propagation to train a feedforward network to map from 45 input units representing the stem phonology, to 60 output units representing the corresponding past tense phonology, via 45 hidden units. In contradiction to all our previous arguments, she concluded that "the acquisition of regular verbs became increasingly susceptible to injury, while the irregulars were learned quickly and were relatively impervious to damage". So what is at the root of this opposite conclusion?

The crucial feature of her simulations was that the irregular items were presented to the network with frequencies of up to 15 times those of the regular items. On the face of it, this might seem eminently reasonable, given that the irregular items *are* more frequent than the regular items in English. However, it presents us with two fundamental problems:

1. It is far from obvious how the real word frequencies should map to training pattern frequencies in our over-simplified network models.
2. It is clearly going to confound the regularity and frequency effects that are observed in the models.

Fortunately, it is not difficult to investigate the regularity–frequency con-found in our model, and hence understand what is happening in her model.

We have already noted that high frequency and high regularity both increase the rate of network learning and the subsequent robustness to dam-age. We can also see in Figures 3.5 and 3.6 that, in terms of the $Sum_i(P)$'s, it is possible to compensate for low regularity by higher frequency. By setting appropriate correct response thresholds on the output activations, it is straightforward to translate those $Sum_i(P)$ results into correct performance curves. Figure 3.9 shows how the performance of our simple model varies for the four item types during the course of learning. We see that our frequency ratio of 20 is sufficient for the frequency effect to swamp the regularity effect and allow the high-frequency irregulars to be learnt more quickly than the low-frequency regulars. This reversal of the natural regularity effect is exactly what Marchman found—although she confuses the issue by repeatedly referring to it as a "regularity effect" rather than a "frequency effect".

Taking global weight scaling as a smooth approximation to the removal of random network connections results in the pattern of performance loss shown in Figure 3.10. We see that the patterns of damage follow from the patterns of learning as discussed above, with the low-frequency regulars more susceptible than the high-frequency irregulars. Again we have replicated Marchman's result—a "frequency effect" that is often inappropriately called a "regularity effect". Interestingly, by our careful matching of the frequency ratio to the degree of regularity, we have generated a crossover of the frequency and regularity effects. We see that there is potential for a weak double dissociation here, caused by the frequency and regularity effects coming into play at different rates (remember the resource artefact graph of Figure 3.3). But it remains to be seen whether we can get stronger double dissociations in a similar manner.

It is actually quite straightforward to explore further the effect of different frequency ratios by explicit simulation. Again, we take our simple feed-

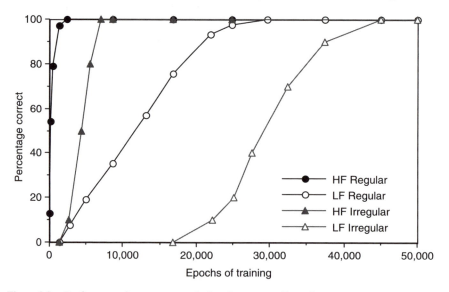

Figure 3.9. Performance improvements during the course of learning.

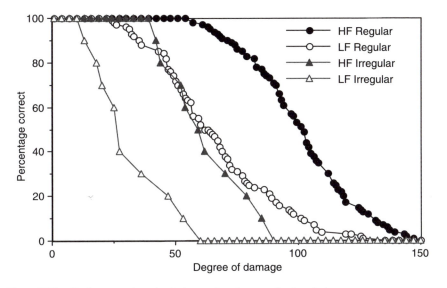

Figure 3.10.   Performance loss due to increasing degrees of network damage.

forward network with 10 input units, 100 hidden units and 10 output units, but now we train it by gradient descent on just one set of 200 regular items and one set of 20 irregular items with a variable (irregular:regular) frequency ratio (this guarantees that we avoid any potential confounds caused by having two sets of each regularity type). For each frequency ratio, we find that the learning curves take the familiar form of Figure 3.9, and lesioning the network continues to produce damage curves like Figure 3.10. The only unexpected result from this more systematic study is that the relative rates of fall-off in performance turn out to be rather dependent on the type of damage inflicted.

If each trained network corresponds to a typical normal subject, then the network after different degrees of damage can be regarded as corresponding to a typical series of patients with different degrees of brain damage. Naturally, it is the data from the patients with the clearest dissociations that are the most well known, as they place the clearest and strongest constraints on our models, and these cases will inevitably correspond to the largest dissociations. It therefore makes sense for us to look for the largest dissociations in damage curves such as those of Figure 3.10. For a given trained network we can define the maximum dissociation in each direction as the maximum absolute percentage difference in performance between the two item types as the performance on them is reduced by damage from 100% to 0%. We can then determine how this varies with the frequency ratio and the type of damage. Figure 3.11 shows the maximum dissociations obtained for hidden unit

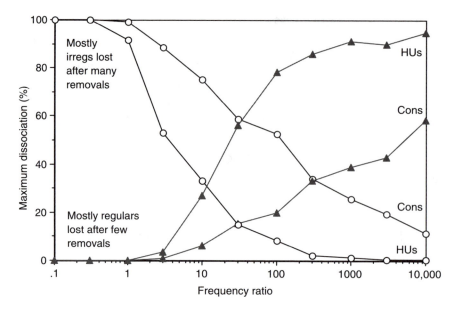

Figure 3.11. The dissociations depend on the frequency ratio and the damage type.

removal vs. connection removal as the frequency ratio varies over five orders of magnitude in our model.

We see that, by picking an appropriate frequency ratio, it is possible to get any dissociation we want. However, it is important not to take the frequency scale too literally. First, the precise frequency ratio at the crossover point will, of course, depend on the details of the regularity, which will rarely be as regular as the identity map that has been used in the simulations. In practice, in more realistic training sets, there will be a whole distribution of different regularities and frequencies to complicate matters. Second, matching real frequencies to appropriate training data distributions for networks that employ representations and learning algorithms of dubious biological plausibility is notoriously difficult. Seidenberg & McClelland (1989), for example, argued that a logarithmic compression of the real word frequencies was appropriate for use in the training data of their reading model, and this did produce good results. Later, more successful, reading models (e.g. Bullinaria, 1997a; Plaut et al., 1996) provide a better account for the empirical data if actual word frequencies are used. As Plaut et al. (1996) discuss in some detail, obtaining realistic interactions between frequency and regularity in a given model relies on coordinating the choice of input and output representations appropriate for the regularity, with the choice of training data frequencies. Getting this wrong can easily reverse the dissociation found in a given model. Conversely, a model that only gets the right dissociation by invoking doubtful choices of representations and frequencies should be viewed with some suspicion. Fortunately, there is plenty of non-neuropsychological data, such as reaction times and ages of acquisition, that will assist in constraining our models in this respect.

There are two further factors that will also affect the crossover frequency ratios in Figure 3.11, and whether we get the resource artefact style DD seen in Figure 3.10. First, as noted above, relearning after damage will tend to enhance a dissociation between types or frequencies. In cases involving opposing frequency and regularity effects, the consequence of relearning will depend on the details. For example, in the case of Figures 3.9 and 3.10, the high-frequency irregulars are learnt more quickly than the low-frequency regulars, so the regulars' lost dissociation will be enhanced and the irregulars' lost dissociation reduced by relearning. In extreme cases, then, relearning may convert a double dissociation into a single dissociation, or vice versa, and in a single patient a dissociation could be reversed. The second factor is the number of hidden units employed in the model, especially if it is near the minimal number required to perform the task in hand. It is well known from the field of modelling developmental disorders that dissociations can occur with poor performance on the last-learned items if resources are limited, such as by restricting the number of hidden units (e.g. Bullinaria, 1997a; Plaut et al., 1996). This will again be model-dependent, but is likely to have differential effects on frequency and regularity. It is perhaps worth noting that both these two factors apply to the past tense model of Marchman (1983) discussed above.

CONNECTIONIST DOUBLE DISSOCIATION

Given that "box and arrow" models have provided good accounts of all manner of DD; and since one can always implement modular "box and arrow" models in terms of neural networks, it is clearly possible to obtain DD as a result of damage to connectionist systems. Exactly how the modules emerge in biological neural networks is still a matter of some debate, but this is another area where connectionist modelling may be of assistance (e.g. Bullinaria, 2001; Jacobs, 1999). However, all this still leaves the question of whether connectionist models can allow DD without modularity. In fact, since we know that there exist nonconnectionist systems that can exhibit DD without modularity (e.g. Dunn & Kirsner, 1988; Shallice, 1988), and that these nonmodular systems too can be implemented in terms of neural networks, it is clearly also possible to obtain connectionist DD without modularity (for appropriate definitions of the word "modularity").

One kind of nonmodular system that sits particularly naturally within the framework of connectionist modelling, and yet can result in double dissociation when damaged, involves a continuum of processing space or topographic maps (Shallice, 1988, p. 249). These are not fully distributed systems in the sense used above, and so are perfectly consistent with our preceding conclusions. A particularly transparent example described by Shallice is that of the visual cortex. Damage resulting in deficits in different parts of the visual field can constitute a DD, yet there is no natural separation into modules. Such DD without modularity may also result from any other representations in the brain that take on a similar topographic form, and it is not difficult to see how these representations may arise naturally from restrictions on the neural connectivity with other subsystems. For example, if semantic representations are of this form, then it is easy to see how localized damage could result in all manner of category-specific and concrete–abstract deficits (Warrington & Shallice, 1984). An interesting connectionist model of optic aphasia involving topographic biases within semantics has recently been presented by Plaut (2002). More specific details of this type of system are highly problem-dependent, and would take us too far from our discussion of general principles, so I will not present any explicit models here. The challenge is not just to get the models to produce dissociations, as we have seen that this is fairly straightforward, but to justify the chosen representations and relative degrees of connectivity necessary to give dissociations that match the patients. This is another area where explicit connectionist models can take us to a new level of refinement beyond the old "box and arrow" models.

We are finally left with the question of whether we can get DD in fully distributed models that have no nonconnectionist analogue. We have seen above how it is possible to generate made-to-measure single dissociations in fully distributed networks, but it is not clear whether it is also possible to get double dissociations in this manner. Bullinaria & Chater (1995) suggest not, but they did not allow regularity–frequency confounds of the type discussed above. Consider the crossover point in Figure 3.11, where there are strong dissociations in both directions (i.e. around a frequency ratio of 30). The actual network performance levels here are plotted in Figure 3.12. For both lesion types, the pattern of dissociation reverses as we increase the amount of damage. We begin with a mostly regulars-lost dissociation but, after many removals, end with a mostly irregulars-lost dissociation. We see that, for particular degrees of damage, it is possible to obtain a crossover double dissociation between high-frequency irregulars and low-frequency regulars. However, to get it we need an interaction between two carefully balanced factors (e.g. regularity and frequency) that "act" in the same way but at different rates, and two different types of damage (e.g. hidden unit and connection removal) that "act" in the same way but at different rates.

So, by carefully balancing factors such as regularity and frequency, one *can* get crossover DD in a fully distributed system, and it is inevitable that other factors known to give dissociation (such as representation sparseness) will also be able to result in DD in a similar manner. Given the discussion of

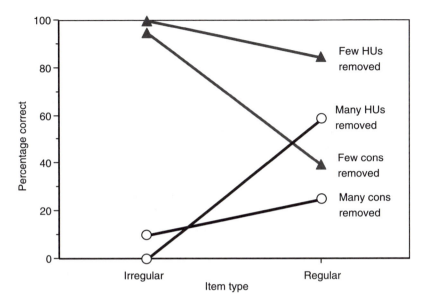

Figure 3.12.   Carefully chosen parameters can result in a connectionist crossover DD.

Dunn & Kirsner (1988), this should not be too much of a shock, but it does complicate our modelling endeavours. We are left with a number of questions. Is this not rather unnatural? Can it really happen like this in real life? And if so, what does it mean? In language, for example, the relation between word regularities and word frequencies is not just random. Hare & Elman (1995) have shown how language evolution naturally results in a correlation between irregularity and frequency, because irregular words tend to get lost from the language or regularized unless they are high-frequency. In this way, a balancing of the effects of frequency and regularity can really happen, and thus it seems that real language does have a built-in confound. Similar natural confounds are likely to arise as a result of evolution in other areas as well. Whether this is the right way to account for particular real DDs is something that will need to be investigated on a case-by-case basis. As always, the modeller simply needs to take each set of empirical data at face value and examine how it might be modelled, irrespective of any confounds the experimenter has failed to remove.

CONCLUSIONS

This work grew out of repeated questions and confusion concerning the consistency of the conclusions of Bullinaria & Chater (1995) with the properties of explicit network simulations by other researchers that apparently gave conflicting results. The work of Marchman (1993) and Plaut (1995) seemed to provide particularly strong counter-examples. Hopefully the above discussion has convinced the reader that all the network simulation results are actually in agreement—and that the apparent inconsistencies are merely in the terminology.

We have seen that a general feature of neural network models is that regularity and frequency and various related factors (such as representation consistency, strength and correlation) all result in increased rates and accuracy of learning, and these in turn result in increased resilience to network damage. This simple fact is at the root of most of the results that have come out of connectionist lesion studies. A major problem in comparing our connectionist models with empirical patient data is that the causes of these differential effects are easily confused. Clearly, if one wants to make reliable claims about one factor, such as regularity, one has to be very careful about controlling for frequency and the other factors. The model of Marchman (1993), for example, has a regularity effect that has been reversed by a larger frequency effect. Moreover, it is also probably worth noting here that the problematic confounds we have been discussing will automatically follow through to secondary measures, such as reaction times and priming. Unfortunately, this is not just a problem for connectionist modellers, it is at least equally problematic for experimenters on human subjects. As noted by Shallice (1988, p. 239), even basic questions, such as what frequency distributions did a given subject learn from, are generally unanswerable. And even if we did know, the nature of many natural tasks, like language, is such that it would be virtually impossible to control for all the potential confounds anyway.

In conclusion, it seems clear that connectionism has much to offer in the fleshing out of the details of earlier "box and arrow" models, or even in replacing them completely, to provide more complete accounts of cognitive processing. The resulting enhanced models and the new field of connectionist neuropsychology are not only producing good accounts of existing empirical data, but are also beginning to suggest more appropriate experimental investigations for further fine tuning of these models, and an ethical approach for exploring potential remedial actions for neuropsychological patients.

ACKNOWLEDGEMENTS

This chapter presents extensions of work originally carried out in collaboration with Nick Chater while we were both at the University of Edinburgh and supported by the MRC. I continued the work while at Birkbeck College, London, supported by the ESRC, and at the University of Reading, supported by the EPSRC.

REFERENCES

Bishop, C. M. (1995). *Neural networks for pattern recognition*. Oxford, UK: Oxford University Press.

Bullinaria, J. A. (1994). Internal representations of a connectionist model of reading aloud. *Proceedings of the Sixteenth Annual Conference of the Cognitive Science Society* (pp. 84–89). Hillsdale, NJ: Lawrence Erlbaum Associates, Inc.

Bullinaria, J. A. (1997a). Modelling reading, spelling and past tense learning with artificial neural networks. *Brain and Language, 59*, 236–266.

Bullinaria, J. A. (1997b). Modelling the acquisition of reading skills. In A. Sorace, C. Heycock, & R. Shillcock (Eds.), *Proceedings of the GALA '97 Conference on Language Acquisition* (pp. 316–321). Edinburgh: HCRC.

Bullinaria, J. A. (1999). Free gifts from connectionist modelling. In R. Baddeley, P. Hancock, & P. Földiák (Eds.), *Information theory and the brain* (pp. 221–240). Cambridge: Cambridge University Press.

Bullinaria, J. A. (2001). Simulating the evolution of modular neural systems. In *Proceedings of the Twenty-third Annual Conference of the Cognitive Science Society* (pp. 146–151). Mahwah, NJ: Lawrence Erlbaum Associates, Inc.

Bullinaria, J. A., & Chater, N. (1995). Connectionist modelling: Implications for cognitive neuropsychology. *Language and Cognitive Processes, 10*, 227–264.

Bullinaria, J. A., Riddell, P. M., & Rushton, S. K. (1999). Regularization in oculomotor adaptation. In *Proceedings of the European Symposium on Artificial Neural Networks* (pp. 159–164). Brussels: D-Facto.

Caramazza, A. (1986). On drawing inferences about the structure of normal cognitive systems from analysis of patterns of impaired performance: The case of single-patient studies. *Brain and Cognition, 5*, 41–66.

Caramazza, A., & McCloskey, M. (1989). Number system processing: Evidence from dyscalculia. In N. Cohen, M. Schwartz, & M. Moscovitch (Eds.), *Advances in cognitive neuropsychology*. New York, NY: Guilford Press.

Coltheart, M. (1985). Cognitive neuropsychology and the study of reading. In M. I. Posner, & O. S. M. Marin (Eds.), *Attention and performance XI*. Hillsdale, NJ: Lawrence Erlbaum Associates, Inc.

Coltheart, M., Curtis, B., Atkins, P., & Haller, M. (1993). Models of reading aloud: Dual-route and parallel-distributed-processing approaches. *Psychological Review, 100*, 589–608.

De Renzi, E. (1986). Current issues in prosopagnosia. In H. D. Ellis, M. A. Jeeves, F. Newcome, & A. Young (Eds.), *Aspects of face processing*. Dordrecht: Martinus Nijhoff.

Devlin, J. T., Gonnerman, L. M., Andersen, E. S., & Seidenberg, M. S. (1998). Category-specific semantic deficits in focal and widespread brain damage: A computational account. *Journal of Cognitive Neuroscience, 10*, 77–94.

Dunn, J. C., & Kirsner, K. (1988). Discovering functionally independent mental processes: The principle of reversed association. *Psychological Review, 95*, 91–101.

Farah, M. J. (1990). *Visual agnosia: Disorders of object recognition and what they tell us about normal vision*. Cambridge, MA: MIT Press.

Farah, M. J. (1994). Neuropsychological inference with an interactive brain: A critique of the locality assumption. *Behavioral and Brain Sciences, 17*, 43–104.

Fodor, J. A. (1983). *The modularity of the mind*. Cambridge, MA: MIT Press.

Funnell, E. (1983). Phonological processing in reading: New evidence from acquired dyslexia. *British Journal of Psychology, 74*, 159–180.

Geshwind, N. (1985). Mechanisms of change after brain lesions. *Annals of the New York Academy of Sciences, 457*, 1–11.

Hare, M., & Elman, J. L. (1995). Learning and morphological change. *Cognition, 56*, 61–98.

Harley, T. A. (1996). Connectionist modeling of the recovery of language functions following brain damage. *Brain and Language, 52,* 7–24.

Hinton, G. E. (1989). Connectionist learning procedures. *Artificial Intelligence, 40,* 185–234.

Hinton, G. E., & Sejnowski, T. J. (1986). Learning and relearning in Boltzmann machines. In D. E. Rumelhart, & J. L. McClelland (Eds.) *Parallel distributed processing: Explorations in the microstructures of cognition* (Vol. 1, pp. 282–317). Cambridge, MA: MIT Press.

Hinton, G. E., & Shallice, T. (1991). Lesioning an attractor network: Investigations of acquired dyslexia. *Psychological Review, 98,* 74–95.

Jacobs, R. A. (1999). Computational studies of the development of functionally specialized neural modules. *Trends in Cognitive Science, 3,* 31–38.

Lavric, A., Pizzagalli, D., Forstmeir, S., & Rippon, G. (2001). Mapping dissociations in verb morphology. *Trends in Cognitive Science, 5,* 301–308.

Marchman, V. A. (1993). Constraints on plasticity in a connectionist model of the English past tense. *Journal of Cognitive Neuroscience, 5,* 215–234.

McCarthy, R. A., & Warrington, E. K. (1986). Phonological reading: Phenomena and paradoxes. *Cortex, 22,* 359–380.

Patterson, K., & Marcel, A. (1977). Aphasia, dyslexia and the phonological coding of written words. *Quarterly Journal of Experimental Psychology, 29,* 307–318.

Patterson, K., & Marcel, A. (1992). Phonological ALEXIA or PHONOLOGICAL alexia? In J. Alegria, D. Holender, J. Junça de Morais, & M. Radeau (Eds.), *Analytic approaches to human cognition* (pp. 259–274). Amsterdam: Elsevier.

Pinker, S. (1991). Rules of language. *Science, 253,* 530–535.

Pinker, S. (1997). Words and rules in the human brain. *Nature, 387,* 547–548.

Plaut, D. C. (1995). Double dissociation without modularity: Evidence from connectionist neuropsychology. *Journal of Clinical and Experimental Neuropsychology, 17,* 291–321.

Plaut, D. C. (1996). Relearning after damage in connectionist networks: Towards a theory of rehabilitation. *Brain and Language, 52,* 25–82.

Plaut, D. C. (2002). Graded modality-specific specialisation in semantics: A computational account of optic aphasia. *Cognitive Neuropsychology, 19,* 603–639.

Plaut, D. C., McClelland, J. L., Seidenberg, M. S., & Patterson, K. E. (1996). Understanding normal and impaired word reading: Computational principles in quasi-regular domains. *Psychological Review, 103,* 56–115.

Plaut, D. C., & Shallice, T. (1993). Deep dyslexia: A case study of connectionist neuropsychology. *Cognitive Neuropsychology, 10,* 377–500.

Sartori, G. (1988). From neuropsychological data to theory and vice versa. In G. Denes, P. Bisiacchi, C. Semenza, & E. Andrewsky (Eds.), *Perspectives in cognitive neuropsychology.* Hove, UK: Lawrence Erlbaum Associates Ltd.

Seidenberg, M. S., & McClelland, J. L. (1989). A distributed, developmental model of word recognition and naming. *Psychological Review, 96,* 523–568.

Sejnowski, T. J., & Rosenberg, C. R. (1987). Parallel networks that learn to pronounce English text. *Complex Systems, 1,* 145–168.

Shallice, T. (1979). Neuropsychological research and the fractionation of memory systems. In L. G. Nilsson (Ed.), *Perspectives on memory research.* Hillsdale, NJ: Lawrence Erlbaum Associates, Inc.

Shallice, T. (1988). *From neuropsychology to mental structure.* Cambridge: Cambridge University Press.

Shoben, E. J., Wecourt, K. T., & Smith, E. E. (1978). Sentence verification, sentence recognition, and the semantic–episodic distinction. *Journal of Experimental Psychology: Human Learning and Cognition, 4,* 304–317.

Small, S. L. (1991). Focal and diffuse lesions in cognitive models. *Proceedings of the Thirteenth*

Annual Conference of the Cognitive Science Society (pp. 85–90). Hillsdale, NJ: Lawrence Erlbaum Associates, Inc.

Teuber, H. L. (1955). Physiological psychology. *Annual Review of Psychology, 9,* 267–296.

Warrington, E. K. (1981). Concrete word dyslexia. *British Journal of Psychology, 72,* 175–196.

Warrington, E. K. (1985). Agnosia: The impairment of object recognition. In P. J. Vinken, G. W. Bruyn, & H. L. Klawans (Eds.), *Handbook of clinical neurology.* Amsterdam: Elsevier.

Warrington, E. K., & Shallice, T. (1984). Category specific semantic impairments. *Brain, 107,* 829–853.

Wilson, B., & Patterson, K. E. (1990). Rehabilitation for cognitive impairment: Does cognitive psychology apply? *Applied Cognitive Psychology, 4,* 247–260.

Wood, C. C. (1978). Variations on a theme of Lashley: Lesion experiments on the neural model of Anderson, Silverstein, Ritz & Jones. *Psychological Review, 85,* 582–591.

CHAPTER FOUR

Learning involves attention

John K. Kruschke
Indiana University, Bloomington, IN, USA

INTRODUCTION

One of the primary factors in the resurgence of connectionist modeling is these models' ability to learn input–output mappings. Simply by presenting the models with examples of inputs and the corresponding outputs, the models can learn to reproduce the examples and to generalize in interesting ways. After the limitations of perceptron learning (Minsky & Papert, 1969; Rosenblatt, 1958) were overcome, most notably by the back-propagation algorithm (Rumelhart, Hinton, & Williams, 1986) but also by other ingenious learning methods (e.g. Ackley, Hinton, & Sejnowski, 1985; Hopfield, 1982), connectionist learning models exploded into popularity. Connectionist models provide a rich language in which to express theories of associative learning. Architectures and learning rules abound, all waiting to be explored and tested for their ability to account for learning by humans or other animals.

A thesis of this chapter is that connectionist learning models must incorporate rapidly shifting selective attention and the ability to learn attentional redistributions. This kind of attentional shifting is not only necessary to mimic learning by humans and other animals, it is also a highly effective and rational solution to the demands of learning many new associations as quickly as possible. This chapter describes three experiments (one previously published and two new) that demonstrate the action of attentional learning. All the results are fitted by connectionist models that shift and learn

113

attention, but the results cannot be fitted when the attention mechanisms are shut off.

Shifts of attention facilitate learning

A basic fact of learning is that people quickly learn new associations without rapidly forgetting old associations. Presumably this ability is highly adaptive for any creature that confronts a rich and complex environment. Consider a hypothetical situation in which an animal learns that mushrooms with a round top and smooth texture are tasty and nutritious. After successfully using this knowledge for some time, the animal encounters a new mushroom with a smooth texture but a flat top. This mushroom turns out to induce nausea. How is the animal to quickly learn about this new kind of mushroom, without destroying still-useful knowledge about the old kind of mushroom? If the animal learns to associate both features of the new mushroom with nausea, then it will inappropriately destroy part of its previous knowledge about healthy mushrooms, i.e. the previous association from smooth texture to edibility will be destroyed. On the other hand, if the old association is retained, it generates a conflicting response, i.e. eating the mushroom.

To facilitate learning about the new case, it would be advantageous to selectively attend to the distinctive feature, viz. flat top, and learn to associate this feature with nausea. By selectively attending to the distinctive feature, previous knowledge is preserved, and new learning is facilitated. Not only should attention be shifted in this way to facilitate learning, but the shifted attentional distribution should itself be learned: Whenever the animal encounters a mushroom with smooth texture and flat top, it should shift attention to the flat top, away from the smooth texture. This will allow the animal to properly anticipate nausea, and to avoid the mushroom.[1] The third example in this chapter describes a situation in which people use exactly this kind of attentional shifting during learning. The challenge to the theorist is expressing these intuitions about attention in a fully specified model.

Shifts of attention can be assessed by subsequent learning

The term "attention", as used here, refers to both the influence of a feature on an immediate response and the influence of a feature on learning. If a feature is being strongly attended to, then that feature should have a strong influence on the immediate response and on the imminent learning. This latter influence of attention on learning is sometimes referred to as the feature's *associability*. In this chapter, these two influences of attention are treated synonymously. This treatment is a natural consequence of the connectionist models described below, but the treatment might ultimately turn out to be inappropriate in the face of future data.

Because redistribution of attention is a learned response to stimuli, the degree of attentional learning can be assayed by examining *subsequent* learning ability. If a person has learned that a particular feature is highly indicative of an appropriate response, then, presumably, the person has also learned to attend to that feature. If subsequent training makes a different feature relevant to new responses, then learning about this new correspondence should be relatively slow, because the person will have to unlearn the attention given to the now-irrelevant feature. In general, learned attention to features or dimensions can be inferred from the ease with which subsequent associations are learned. This technique is used in all three examples presented below.

INTRA- AND EXTRADIMENSIONAL SHIFTS

A traditional learning paradigm in psychology investigates perseveration of learned attention across phases of training. In the first phase, participants learn that one stimulus dimension is relevant to the outcome while other dimensions are irrelevant. In the second phase, the mapping of stimuli to outcomes changes so that either a different dimension is relevant or the same dimension remains relevant. The former change of relevance is called *extra*dimensional shift, and the latter change is called *intra*dimensional shift. Many studies in many species have shown that intradimensional shift is easier than extradimensional shift, a fact that can be explained by the hypothesis that subjects learn to attend to the relevant dimension, and this attentional shift perseverates into the second phase (e.g. Mackintosh, 1965; Wolff, 1967). In this section of the chapter, a recent experiment demonstrating this difference is summarized, and a connectionist model that incorporates attentional learning is shown to fit the data, whereas the model cannot fit the data if its attentional learning mechanism is "turned off".

Experiment design and results

Consider the simple line drawings of freight train box cars shown in Figure 4.1. They vary on three binary dimensions: height, door position, and wheel color. In an experiment conducted in my lab (Kruschke, 1996b), people learned to classify these cars into one of two routes. On each trial in a series, a car would appear on a computer screen, the learner would make his/her choice of the route of the car by pressing a corresponding key, and then the correct route would be displayed. During the first few trials, the learner could only guess, but after many trials, she/he could learn the correct answers.

Figure 4.2 indicates the mapping of cars to routes. The cubes in Figure 4.2 correspond with the cube shown in Figure 4.1. Each corner is marked with a

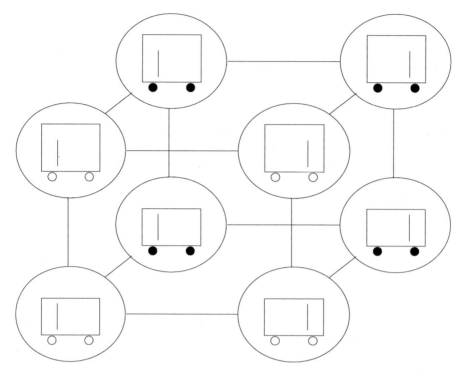

Figure 4.1.   Stimuli used for relevance shift experiment of Kruschke (1996b). The ovals merely demarcate the different stimuli and are not part of the stimuli *per se*. The lines connecting the ovals indicate the dimensions of variation between stimuli.

disk whose color indicates the route taken by the corresponding train; in other words, the color of the disk indicates the category of the stimulus.

The left side of Figure 4.2 shows the categorization learned in the first phase of training, and the right side shows the categorization learned subsequently. In the first phase, it can be seen that the vertical dimension is irrelevant. This means that variation on the vertical dimension produces no variation in categorization: The vertical dimension can be ignored with no loss in categorization accuracy. The other two dimensions, however, are relevant in the first phase. Some readers might recognize this as the exclusive-or (XOR) structure on the two relevant dimensions.

In the subsequent phase, some learners experienced a change to the top-right structure of Figure 4.2, and other learners experienced a change to the bottom-right structure. In both of these second-phase structures only one dimension is relevant, but in the top shift this relevant dimension was one of the initially relevant dimensions, so the shift of relevance is called intradimensional, whereas in the bottom shift the newly relevant dimension was initially irrelevant, so the shift of relevance is called extradimensional. Notice

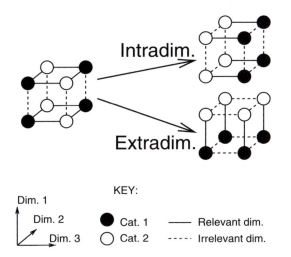

Intradim.

Extradim.

KEY:

Dim. 1

Dim. 2   ● Cat. 1   ——— Relevant dim.

Dim. 3   ○ Cat. 2   - - - - - Irrelevant dim.

Figure 4.2.   The structure of two types of relevance shifts. The cube at left indicates the initially learned categorization; the cubes at right indicate the alternative subsequently learned categorizations. Adapted from Kruschke, 1996b.

that the two second-phase category structures are isomorphic, so any differences in ease of learning the second phase cannot be attributed to differences in structural complexity.

This design is an advance over all previous studies of shift learning because no novel stimulus values are used in either shift. Thus, intradimensional and extradimensional shifts can be directly compared without confounded changes in novelty. In traditional studies of intradimensional shift, the shift is accompanied by introduction of novel values on the relevant dimension. For example, the initial phase might have color relevant, with green indicating category X and red indicating category Y. The only way to implement an intradimensional shift, without merely reversing the assignment of categories to colors, is to add novel colors; e.g. yellow indicates X and blue indicates Y. Unfortunately, if novel features are added to the initially relevant dimension, it might be the case that differences in learnability of the dimensions were caused by differences in novelty. If novel features are added to both dimensions, it might be the case that differences in learnability are attributable to differences in degree of novelty, or differences in similarity of the novel values to the previous values, and so forth (Slamecka, 1968). This new design solves these problems by making the initial problem involve *two* relevant dimensions, and no novel values at all in the shift phase.[2]

Human learning performance in this experiment is shown in Figure 4.3. It can be seen that people learned the intradimensional shift much faster than the extradimensional shift [$t(118) = 3.65$, $SE_{diff} = .026$, $p < .0001$ two-tailed].

Notice that the advantage of the intradimensional shift over the

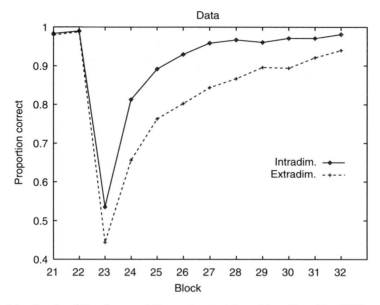

Figure 4.3.   Results of the relevance shift experiment. Adapted from Kruschke, 1996b.

extradimensional shift cannot be explained by the number of exemplars that changed their route, because in both shift types there were four exemplars that changed their route. Another possible explanation for the difference is that only one dimension changed its relevance in the intradimensional shift, but all three dimensions changed their relevance in the extradimensional shift. This explanation is contradicted by results from another condition in the experiment (not summarized here), in which only two dimensions changed their relevance but the learning was even more difficult than the extradimensional shift.

This advantage of intradimensional over extradimensional shift has been found in many previous studies in many other species, but the results here are particularly compelling because the design involved no confounded variation of novelty. This robust difference should be addressed by any model of learning that purports to reflect learning by natural intelligent organisms.

A connectionist model with attentional learning

The advantage of intradimensional shift over extradimensional shift suggests that there is learned attention to dimensions. A model of learning should implement this explanatory principle. Any model of the relevance-shift experiment will also need to be able to learn the XOR category structure in the first phase of training. This structure is nonlinear in the two relevant dimensions, meaning that no simple additive combination of the two relevant dimensions can accurately compute the correct categories. Instead, conjunctive combinations of dimensional values must be encoded in the model. There has been much research that suggests that people can and do encode configurations of values, also called *exemplars*, during learning (e.g. Nosofsky, 1992). The model to be fitted to the shift-learning data formalizes this notion of exemplar representation, along with the notion of learned attention to dimensions.

The model fit to these data was called AMBRY by Kruschke (1996b) because it is a variant of the ALCOVE model (Kruschke, 1992). The architecture of (part of) AMBRY is shown in Figure 4.4. All aspects of the model have specific psychological motivations, and formalize explicit explanatory principles. Because of this correspondence between model parts and explanatory principles, the principles can be tested for their importance by excising the corresponding aspect of the model. In particular, the attentional mechanism can be functionally removed, and the restricted model can be tested for its ability to fit to data.

Activation propagation

In AMBRY, each dimension is encoded by a separate input node. If ψ_i denotes the psychological scale value of the stimulus on dimension i, then the activation of input node i is simply that scale value:

$$a_i^{in} = \psi_i. \tag{1}$$

Because the experiment counter-balanced the assignment of physical dimensions in Figure 4.1 to abstract dimensions in Figure 4.2, the dimensional values were simply assumed to be 1.0 and 2.0; e.g. for the short car, $\psi_{height} = 1.0$, and for the tall car, $\psi_{height} = 2.0$.

There is one exemplar node established for each of the eight cars. The activation of an exemplar node corresponds to the psychological *similarity* of the current stimulus to the exemplar represented by the node. Similarity drops off exponentially with distance in psychological space, as argued by Shepard (1987), and distance is computed using a city-block metric for psychologically separable dimensions (Garner, 1974; Shepard, 1964). An exemplar node is significantly activated only by stimuli that are fairly similar to the exemplar represented by the node. In other words, each exemplar node has a limited "receptive field" in stimulus space. Formally, the activation value is given by:

$$a_j^{ex} = \exp\left(-c \sum_i \alpha_i |\psi_{ji} - a_i^{in}|\right) \tag{2}$$

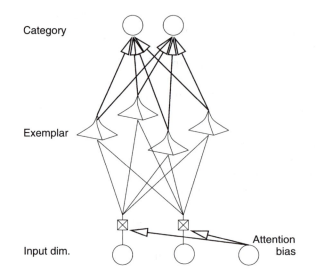

Category

Exemplar

Input dim.

Attention
bias

Figure 4.4.   Architecture of model used for predictions of relevance shift experiments. Thicker arrows denote learned associative weights. The Xs in boxes above the input dimensions represent the multiplicative weighting of the attention on the dimensions.

where c is a constant called the *specificity* that determines the narrowness of the receptive field, where α_i is the *attention strength* on the ith dimension, and where ψ_{ji} is the scale value of the jth exemplar on the ith dimension. Because stimulus values are either 1.0 or 2.0, the values of ψ_{ji} are either 1.0 or 2.0. Figure 4.5 shows the activation profile of an exemplar node in a

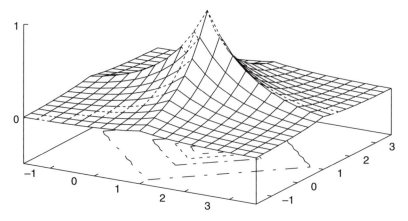

Figure 4.5.   Activation function of an exemplar node. The surface shows a_j^{ex} as a function of a_i^{in} and a_2^{in}, from equation (2) applied to a two-dimensional stimulus space, with $c = 1$, $\alpha_1 = 1$, $\alpha_2 = 1$, $\psi_{j1} = 1$ and $\psi_{j2} = 1$. The diamonds on the plane underneath the surface indicate the level contours of the surface.

two-dimensional stimulus space. It is this pyramid-shaped activation profile that is used to represent the exemplar nodes in Figure 4.4.

Importantly, equation (2) implies that increasing the attention strength on a dimension has the effect of magnifying differences on that dimension, so that differences along the dimension have a larger influence on the similarity. Thus, if a dimension is relevant to a categorization, the attention strength on that dimension can be increased to better distinguish the exemplars from the two categories. On the other hand, an irrelevant dimension can have its attention decreased, so that differences along that dimension do not needlessly impede learning. As will be explained below, AMBRY *learns* how to adjust the dimensional attention strengths to facilitate categorization. The attention strengths are indicated in Figure 4.4 by the arrows from a "bias" node (which is always activated) to the boxes marked with Xs above the input nodes. The boxes are marked with Xs to indicate that each attentional strength is a multiplier on the input.

Activation from the exemplar nodes is propagated to category nodes via weighted connections, illustrated in Figure 4.4 by the arrows from exemplar nodes to category nodes. The activation of each category node is determined by a standard linear combination of weighted exemplar-node activations. Finally, the activations of the category nodes are converted to choice probabilities by a ratio rule, such that the probability of choosing a category corresponds with the activation of the category relative to the total activation of all categories. The mathematical details of these operations are not critical for the present discussion, and can be found in the original article (Kruschke, 1996b).

Learning of attention and associations

The association weights between the exemplar nodes and the category nodes are learned by standard back-propagation of error (Rumelhart et al., 1986). Just as human learners are told the correct answer on each trial, the model is told the desired activation of the category nodes on each trial. Any discrepancy between the desired activation and the model-generated activation constitutes an error. The model then adjusts the dimensional attention values and the associative weights in such a way that the error is reduced as quickly as possible. Not necessarily all the error is eliminated on a single trial. This type of error reduction is called "gradient descent" because it is based on computing the derivative of the error with respect to the attention strengths or associative weights. Formulae for these derivatives are provided by Kruschke (1996b).

Of importance here is to note that the learning of the attention strengths is based on error reduction, and the amount or speed of learning is governed by a single parameter called the attentional learning rate. When this attentional learning rate is fixed at zero, the model has no ability to learn to selectively attend to relevant dimensions (but it can still learn categorizations because of the learnable association weights between exemplars and categories). By testing whether the model can fit the empirical data with its attentional learning rate set to zero, we can discover whether attentional learning is an essential principle in the model.

This model is an algorithmic description of learning. The model makes no claims about physical implementation. Different species might neurally implement the algorithm, or approximations to the algorithm, in different ways. In particular, there is no claim that nodes in the model correspond to neurons in the brain, neither is there any claim that gradient descent on error is implemented as back-propagation of error signals through neural synapses. The model is therefore referred to as a type of *connectionist* model, and is never referred to as a *neural network* model.

Fit of the model

The top graph of Figure 4.6 shows the predictions of AMBRY when fitted to the data shown in Figure 4.3. (In fact, these are the predictions when AMBRY is simultaneously fitted to two other shift conditions, not discussed here. If AMBRY were fitted only to the intra- and extradimensional shifts, the predictions would be even closer to the data.) AMBRY shows the advantage of intradimensional shifts very robustly. It accommodates the data by learning in the first phase to attend to the two relevant dimensions and to ignore the irrelevant dimension. This learned attentional distribution must be unlearned in the extradimensional shift, and therefore the extradimensional shift is more difficult for the model.

Attentional learning is critical to account for the data. When the attentional learning rate is fixed at zero, the best fit of the model exhibits no difference between the types of shift, as can be seen in the bottom graph of Figure 4.6. The best the model can do without attentional learning is settle on the mean of the two types of shift.

BLOCKING OF ASSOCIATIVE LEARNING

Suppose two cues, A and B, are presented to a learner, followed by an outcome. Typically both cues will acquire moderate associative strength with the outcome. On the other hand, if the subject was trained in a previous phase to learn that A by itself predicts the outcome, then the associative strength from B seems to be very weak. It appears that the prior training with A has blocked, i.e. prevented, learning about B, despite the fact that B is now just as predictive of the outcome as A. The phenomenon of blocking, first reported by Kamin (1968), is ubiquitous, occurring in many different procedural paradigms and in many different species.

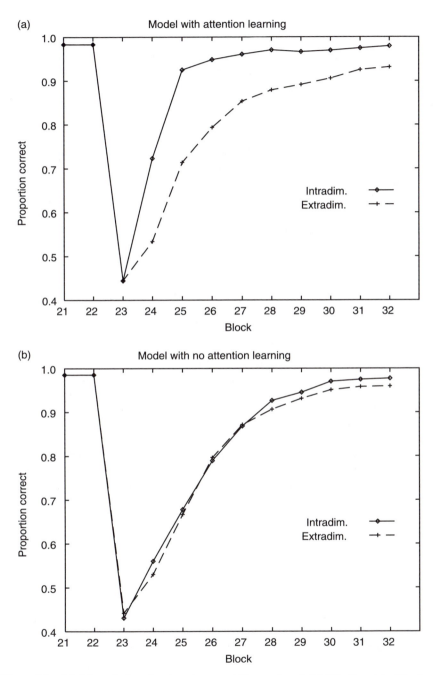

Figure 4.6. Model predictions for the relevance shift experiment. (a) Fit of model with attentional learning. (b) Fit of restricted model with no attentional learning. Adapted from Kruschke, 1996b.

"No empirical finding in the study of animal learning has been of greater theoretical importance than the phenomenon of blocking" (Williams, 1999, p. 618). Blocking is important because it shows clearly that associative learning is not based on merely the co-occurrence of cue and outcome. This fact contradicts a whole raft of learning models that increment associative strength whenever a cue and outcome co-occur.

For more than 30 years there have been two prominent theories of blocking. The dominant theory, formalized in the Rescorla–Wagner model (1972) and equivalent to the delta rule of connectionist models, argues that learning is error-driven. Because the subject has already learned that cue A predicts the outcome, when cue B occurs there is no error in prediction and hence no learning. The Rescorla–Wagner model was motivated to a large degree by the phenomenon of blocking, and the model has been monumentally influential (Miller, Barnet, & Grahame, 1995; Siegel & Allan, 1996).

A competing theory, first suggested by Sutherland & Mackintosh (1971) and extended by Mackintosh (1975), claims that there is in fact something learned about the redundant relevant cue; namely, that it is irrelevant. In other words, subjects learn to suppress attention to the redundant cue. As was emphasized in the previous section regarding intra- and interdimensional shifts, learned attention can be assessed by measuring the difficulty of subsequent learning. Mackintosh & Turner (1971) measured how quickly a previously blocked cue could be learned about by rats, and found evidence in favor of the learned attention theory. Kruschke & Blair (2000) extended and expanded their experimental design in a study with humans, and found robust evidence that people learn to suppress attention to a blocked cue. Learning about a blocked cue was much weaker than learning about a non-blocked control cue.

This ubiquitous learning phenomenon, blocking, involves learned attention. Models of natural learning should incorporate mechanisms of learned attention. The remainder of this section reports previously unpublished results demonstrating the effects of blocking on subsequent learning, and a connectionist model that uses learned attention. As in the previous section, it will be shown that when attentional learning in the model is "turned off", the model cannot exhibit the critical effects.

Experiment design and results

In an experiment conducted in my lab, people had to learn which symptoms indicated certain fictitious diseases. A learning trial might consist of the following sequence of events. First, a list of symptoms is presented on a computer screen, e.g. "back pain" and "blurred vision". The subject would then indicate which disease he/she thought was the correct diagnosis, by pressing a corresponding key. Then the correct response was displayed on the screen. In the initial trials the person would just be guessing, but after several trials she/he could learn the correct diagnoses.

Table 4.1 shows the design of this experiment. Symptoms are indicated by letters, and diseases are indicated by numerals. I will first describe the third phase of training. The central aspect of the third phase is that people must learn to discriminate diseases that share a symptom. Thus, disease 2 is indicated by symptoms B and C (denoted B.C $\rightarrow$ 2), and disease 3 is indicated by symptoms B and D (denoted B.D $\rightarrow$ 3). The two diseases share symptom B, and therefore learning the diseases might be somewhat difficult. The same structure is present for diseases 5 and 6: H.F $\rightarrow$ 5 and H.G $\rightarrow$ 6.

If attention to the shared symptom were suppressed, then discrimination learning should be easier. On the other hand, if attention to the distinctive symptoms were suppressed, then discrimination learning should be harder. The first two phases of training were designed to bring about just such suppression of attention. Notice that in the first phase, symptom A always indicates disease 1, which is denoted A $\rightarrow$ 1. In the second phase, symptom B is paired with symptom A as a redundant relevant cue, i.e. A.B $\rightarrow$ 1. Hence symptom B should by blocked, and should suffer suppressed attention. Hence, subsequent learning of B.C $\rightarrow$ 2 and B.D $\rightarrow$ 3 should be enhanced. By contrast, the first two phases are designed to block the distinctive symptoms F and G, so that learning of H.F $\rightarrow$ 5 and H.G $\rightarrow$ 6 should be worsened.[3]

The final testing phase is an additional assessment of the relative strengths of association established for the diseases that had a blocked shared symptom vs. the diseases that had blocked distinctive symptoms. The test cases C.F, C.G, D.F and D.G present conflicting symptoms, so that their relative strengths can be directly assessed. In these cases, people should select the diseases associated with C and D more than the diseases associated with F and G.

TABLE 4.1
Design of experiment assessing discrimination learning after blocking

Training I	A $\rightarrow$ 1	E $\rightarrow$ 4
Training II (blocking of B, F, and G)	A.B $\rightarrow$ 1	E.F $\rightarrow$ 4
	A.B $\rightarrow$ 1	E.G $\rightarrow$ 4
Training III (discrimination learning)	B.C $\rightarrow$ 2	H.F $\rightarrow$ 5
	B.D $\rightarrow$ 3	H.G $\rightarrow$ 6
	A $\rightarrow$ 1	E $\rightarrow$ 4
Testing	B.C, B.D	H.F, H.G
	A	E
	C.F, C.G, D.F, D.G	

Letters denote symptoms, numerals denote diseases.

There were 40 trials of training phase I, 80 trials of phase II, and 60 trials of Phase III, followed by 20 test trials. There was no test of blocking after phase II because numerous experiments in my lab have shown very robust blocking in this type of procedure (e.g. Kruschke & Blair, 2000). We can safely assume that blocking occurred. The eight symptoms were randomly selected for each subject from the following nine: ear ache, skin rash, back pain, dizziness, nausea, insomnia, bad breath, blurred vision, and nose bleed. Response keys (disease labels) were D, F, G, H, J, and K, randomly assigned to diseases for each subject.

A total of 89 students volunteered to participate for partial credit in an introductory psychology course. The results confirmed the predictions of attentional learning. In the first third of training phase 3, people had higher accuracy on the diseases with a blocked shared symptom (46.3% correct) than on the diseases with the blocked distinctive symptoms (40.2% correct), $t(88) = 2.97$, $p = .004$ (collapsed across all of the third phase, the mean difference in percentage correct was 2.9%).

The final testing phase showed more robust effects of blocking. Table 4.2 shows the choice proportions for the five types of symptom combinations used in the test phase. Of most interest are the conflicting symptom pairs, C.F, C.G, D.F and D.G. In each of these cases a distinctive symptom (C or D) from the diseases with a blocked shared symptom is paired with a distinctive symptom (F or G) from the diseases with blocked distinctive symptoms.

TABLE 4.2

Choice percentages from the test phase of discrimination learning after blocking

Symptoms	Response choice																	
	A			E			C/D			F/G			C/Do			F/Go		
	H	M	R	H	M	R	H	M	R	H	M	R	H	M	R	H	M	R
A	94	95	94	3	1	1	2	1	1	1	1	1	1	1	1	1	1	1
E	3	1	1	95	95	94	1	1	1	1	1	1	0	1	1	1	1	1
BC/BD	1	5	4	1	5	4	74	76	75	5	5	4	10	6	9	9	5	4
HF/HG	1	4	4	1	4	4	7	4	4	71	74	75	7	4	4	13	9	9
CF/CG/DF/DG	2	5	5	2	5	5	49	46	41	33	34	41	7	5	5	6	5	5

Letters in the left column denote symptom combinations. Letters at the tops of the columns denote the symptom corresponding to the disease selected, e.g. response choice "A" means the disease corresponding to symptom A, i.e. disease 1. The response choice "C/D" means the disease corresponding to symptom C if a test case including symptom C was presented, and the disease corresponding to symptom D if a test case including symptom D was presented. Under each choice, the column headed "H" indicates the human choice percentage, the column headed "M" indicates the full model percentage, and the column headed "R" indicates the restricted model percentage with no attention learning.

Attentional theory suggests that learning about symptoms C and D should be faster, hence stronger, than learning about symptoms F and G. Therefore, in these cases of conflict the choices should favor the diseases corresponding with C and D over the diseases corresponding with F and G. The last row of Table 4.2 shows that this result did indeed occur, with 49% of the choices being for the C/D diseases and only 33% of the choices being for the F/G diseases. This difference is highly significant by a binomial test ($z = 4.62$, $p < .001$).

These results, along with those of Kruschke & Blair (2000), show that there is learned attention in blocking (at least in this type of procedure). Because blocking is so pervasive in natural learning, models of learning should address these attentional effects.

A connectionist model with attentional learning

Figure 4.7 depicts the ADIT model introduced by Kruschke (1996a) and extended by Kruschke (2001), referred to here as the EXIT model. EXIT is very similar in spirit to the AMBRY model described in the previous section (Figure 4.4). One difference between the models is that AMBRY used exemplar nodes between the inputs and the categories, whereas EXIT does not. This is merely a pragmatic simplification to reduce the number of free parameters, and is not a theoretical commitment. On the other hand, EXIT does have exemplars between the inputs and the attention nodes. The motivation for this is the idea that learned attentional distributions should be exemplar-specific. For example, when a mushroom is smooth and flat,

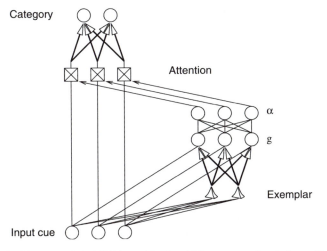

Figure 4.7. Architecture of the EXIT model. The thicker arrows denote learnable associative weights. The Xs in boxes above the input cues represent the multiplicative weighting of the attention on the cues.

attention should be shifted to the flat shape, but attention should not *always* be shifted away from texture to shape.

Another difference between AMBRY and EXIT is that EXIT imposes a capacity constraint on the attention strengths. This capacity constraint in the model is supposed to reflect attentional capacity constraints in humans and other animals: If attention to a feature is increased, it must necessarily be decreased on another feature. This constraint is indicated in Figure 4.7 by the criss-crossing lines between the *gain* nodes and the attention nodes. When a feature is present, the gain node is activated by default, but can also be influenced by learned associations from exemplars. The gains on each feature are then normalized to produce the overall attention to each feature.

One last but important enhancement of EXIT is that attention shifts are executed rapidly within a trial, although they may be learned only gradually across trials. Thus, when corrective feedback is provided on a trial, the error drives a relatively large shift in attention before any associative weight changes are made. This shifted distribution of attention acts as the target values to be learned by the associative weights between the exemplars and the gain nodes. This gives EXIT one more free parameter: An attentional shift rate, distinct from the attentional learning rate.

Complete mathematical details of the model are provided elsewhere (Kruschke, 2001), but it might be useful here to describe the influence of attention in the formulae for categorization and associative weight change. These two formulae show clearly the separate roles of attention for response generation and for learning. Responses are generated proportionally to the activation of the category nodes, and these nodes are activated according to the summed weighted activation of the input cues. Formally, the activation of the kth category node is determined as:

$$a_k^{\text{cat}} = \sum_i w_{ki} \alpha_i a_i^{\text{in}} \tag{3}$$

where w_{ki} is the associative weight from the ith cue to the kth category, α_i is the attention allocated to the ith cue, and a_i^{in} is the activation of the ith cue. Notice that a cue has an influence on the category choice only to the extent that the cue is attended to. Associative weight changes are also affected by attention. The change in the associative weight from the ith cue to the kth output (denoted Δw_{ki}) is given by:

$$\Delta w_{ki} = (t_k - a_k^{\text{cat}}) \, \alpha_i a_i^{\text{in}} \tag{4}$$

where t_k is the *teacher* value (correct response) for the kth category node. Notice that a weight from a cue is changed only to the extent that the cue is being attended to. Thus, the model only learns about what is being attended to, and the model attends to whatever reduces error best.

In summary, processing in the EXIT model occurs as follows. Cues are presented and activate the corresponding input nodes. By default, the corresponding attention gain nodes are then activated, modulated by any learned redistribution of attention for exemplars similar to the stimulus. The normalized (capacity-constrained) attention then multiplicatively gates the cue activations propagated to the category nodes. Category node activations are mapped to response probabilities as in AMBRY. When the correct classification is provided, the error first drives a relatively large attention shift. After this shift is completed, the associative weights to the attentional gain nodes are adjusted to try to learn this new distribution of attention, and the associative weights to the category nodes are adjusted to try to diminish any remaining predictive error.

Fit of the model

The model was fitted to the testing phase data of Table 4.2 (and not to the third phase learning data) with each test type weighted by the number of distinct cases contributing to the type. The best fitting predictions of the model mirror the data quite well. In particular, EXIT shows a strong preference for C/D diseases over F/G diseases in the conflicting symptom cases (see the last row of Table 4.2). Although not fitted to the third learning phase, EXIT, like humans, shows a small (2.2%) advantage for the diseases that had their shared symptom blocked.

Figure 4.8 displays data from the conflicting symptom tests (CF/CG/DF/DG) of Table 4.2 in the form of a bar graph; (a) displays the human choice percentages; (b) displays the predictions of EXIT. In the human data, the two bars for the C/D and F/G choices are at distinctly different heights, as they are in the predictions of EXIT.

Importantly, when the attentional learning rate of EXIT is fixed at zero (but attentional shifting is still allowed), the critical effects cannot be produced by the model. The best fitting predictions of this "no attention" restricted version of the model are also shown in Table 4.2 and in Figure 4.8c. Notice that there is *no* difference between C/D and F/G response proportions for conflict tests (last row of table). Moreover, there is *zero* difference between groups in the third learning phase when attention learning was disallowed. Thus, attention learning is crucial for the model to exhibit the effects observed in people.

THE INVERSE BASE RATE EFFECT

The learning behavior reviewed above can be thought of as irrational and suboptimal. Consider the advantage of intradimensional over extradimensional shift. The two structures in the second phase of learning (see Figure

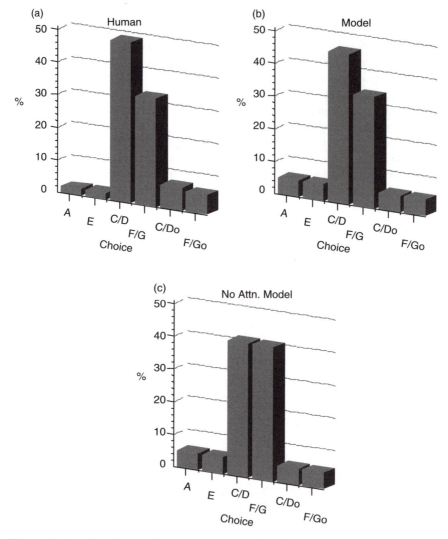

Figure 4.8. Results of the conflicting symptom tests of the blocking experiment. Data from last row of Table 4.2.

4.2) are isomorphic, and so one might think that an optimal learning device should learn them equally efficiently. Consider the phenomenon of blocking. The redundant relevant cue in phase 2 (see Table 4.1) is, after all, perfectly predictive of the outcome, and so a rational and optimal learner should learn about the cue. Moreover, the two pairs of diseases that share a symptom in phase 3 are isomorphic, and so they should be learned equally well.

Another prominent example of apparently irrational learning is the inverse base rate effect. Suppose that very frequently symptoms I and PE occur together and always indicate disease E (I.PE → E), as shown in the left panel of Figure 4.9. On some rare occasions, symptoms I and PL occur, and when they do, they always indicate disease L (I.PL → L). Notice that symptom I is shared by both diseases, and therefore is an imperfect predictor of the diseases. Symptom PE is a perfect predictor of disease E, and symptom PL is a perfect predictor of disease L. The left panel of Figure 4.9 shows this structural symmetry.

After learning these diseases, experiment participants are asked to make diagnoses for novel combinations of symptoms, such as PE.PL and I by itself. For symptom I by itself, people tend to choose disease E, which is appropriate because disease E has a larger base rate, i.e. a higher frequency of occurrence. For symptoms PE.PL, however, people strongly tend to choose the rare disease L. This pattern of results was dubbed the "inverse base rate effect" by Medin & Edelson (1988). This effect is found in disease diagnosis procedures (Kruschke, 1996a; Medin & Edelson, 1988), in a random word association procedure (Dennis & Kruschke, 1998), and in a geometric figure association procedure (Fagot, Kruschke, Depy, & Vauclair, 1998), so it is a very robust phenomenon. It has not yet been reported in other species, however.

Kruschke (1996a) explained the inverse base rate effect as a consequence of rapidly shifting attention. One strong consequence of different base rates is that people tend to learn about the frequent disease before they learn about the rare disease. Thus, people learn early that symptoms I and PE each have a moderate associative strength with disease E. Then people learn later about cases of the rare disease, I.PL → L. As argued in the introductory discussion of learning about mushrooms, people shift attention away from the symptom I already associated with the common disease E, and learn predominantly about the distinctive symptom of the rare disease, thereby building up a strong association from symptom PL to disease L. This asymmetry in the learned associations about the diseases is illustrated in the right panel of Figure 4.9. Consequently, when tested with PE.PL, the strong association from PL to L dominates the moderate association from PE to E. Further empirical and modeling results added supportive evidence to this explanation in terms of rapidly shifting attention.

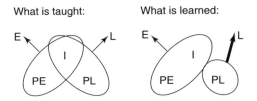

Figure 4.9.   Structure of categories in the inverse base rate effect.

The emphasis of Kruschke (1996a) was rapidly shifting attention during single trials of learning, rather than on learned redistributions of attention. Nevertheless, the notion that attentional redistributions are learned suggests that additional learning *subsequent* to the inverse base rate effect should be impacted by learned attention shifts. In particular, for symptom pair I.PL, attention should be shifted away from I to PL, so that subsequent learning about I in the context of PL should be difficult. On the other hand, for symptom pair I.PE, attention is not strongly shifted away from I, so that subsequent learning about I in the context of PE should be relatively easy. Results of an experiment that tests this prediction are presented here. It will be shown that the results can be fitted by EXIT with attentional shifting, but when attentional shifting is "turned off", the restricted model fails.

Experiment design and results

Table 4.3 shows the design of an experiment that assesses learned attention in a phased-training version of the inverse base rate effect. The first two phases force people to learn I.PE $\to$ E before learning I.PL $\to$ L, instead of relying on base rates to accomplish indirectly this ordering of learning. The design incorporates two copies of the same basic structure, so, for example, the first phase consists of I1.PE1 $\to$ E1 and I2.PE2 $\to$ E2. After the second training phase, there is a test phase to measure the magnitude of the inverse base rate effect. This much of the design is a replication of previous studies (e.g. Kruschke, 1996a, experiment 2).

The third phase of training breaks new ground. Half the subjects went on in this phase to learn that symptoms I1 and I2 were relevant to diagnosing new disease N1 and N2, in the context of PE1 and PE2. This was predicted to be relatively easy because there should be some attention to I1 and I2 in the

TABLE 4.3
Design of experiment assessing learned attention in the
phased inverse base rate effect

Training I	I1.PE1 $\to$ E1	I2.PE2 $\to$ E2
Training II	I1.PE1 $\to$ E1	I2.PE2 $\to$ E2
	I1.PL1 $\to$ L1	I2.PL2 $\to$ L2
Testing	I, PE.PL, etc.	
Training III (easy, I in PE)	I1.PE1 $\to$ N1	I2.PE1 $\to$ N2
	I1.PE2 $\to$ N1	I2.PE2 $\to$ N2
Training III (hard, I in PL)	I1.PL1 $\to$ N1	I2.PL1 $\to$ N2
	I1.PL2 $\to$ N1	I2.PL2 $\to$ N2

E, L, and N denote disease. I, PE, PL denote symptoms.

company of PE1 and PE2. The other half of the subjects learned that I1 and I2 were relevant in the context of PL1 and PL2. This was predicted to be relatively difficult because attention to I1 and I2 should be suppressed in the company of PL1 and PL2.

There were 40 trials of training phase I, 80 trials of phase II, 28 trials of the testing phase, and 80 trials of Phase III. Symptoms and response keys were selected as in the blocking experiment.

A total of 83 students volunteered to participate for partial credit in an introductory psychology course. Six subjects' data were excluded from further analysis because they failed to reach 80% correct in the last half of the second phase of training. This left 38 subjects in the "easy" condition and 39 in the "hard" condition. There were no differences between groups in the first two phases of learning. Table 4.4 shows the choice percentages in the test phase, collapsed across the two groups. For test case I, choices for E were far greater than choice for L (75% vs. 17%), $\chi^2(1,245)/4 = 25.15$, $p < .001$. For test case PE.PL, choices for L were far greater than choices for E (67% vs. 28%), $\chi^2(1,262)/4 = 11.13$, $p < .001$. For test case PE.PLo, choices for Lo were far greater than choices for E (59% vs. 32%), $\chi^2(1,225)/4 = 5.60$, $p < .025$. Thus, the inverse base rate effect is strongly in evidence.

The main novel result regards the relative ease of learning in the third phase. Collapsed across all blocks of the third phase, the mean percentages

TABLE 4.4

Results from test phase of experiment assessing discrimination learning after blocking, with prediction of model in parentheses

Symptoms	Response choice											
	E			L			Eo			Lo		
	H	M	R	H	M	R	H	M	R	H	M	R
I.PE	93	94	93	3	2	3	2	2	2	1	2	2
I.PL	12	9	3	85	85	93	0	3	2	3	3	2
I	75	84	44	17	5	45	5	5	6	3	5	6
PE.PL	28	24	39	67	68	39	1	4	11	4	4	11
PE.PLo	32	24	50	6	4	1	3	4	1	59	68	48
I.PE.PL	52	48	43	43	46	43	1	3	7	4	3	7
I.PE.PLo	63	61	67	5	3	5	3	3	2	29	33	26

Results are collapsed across pairs 1 and 2. For example, symptom I refers to cases of I1 and I2. If I1 was presented, then choices E, L, Eo and Lo refer to diseases E1, L1', E2 and L2, respectively. If I2 was presented, then choices E, L, Eo and Lo refer to diseases E2, L2, E1 and L1, respectively. PE.PLo indicates cases of PE1.PL2 and PE2.PL1 combined. Under each choice, the column headed "H" indicates the human choice percentage, the column headed "M" indicates the full model percentage, and the column headed "R" indicates the restricted model percentage with no attention learning.

correct were 82.7% for the "easy" group and 76.2% for the "hard" group. These are reliably different ($t(75) = 2{:}10$, $SE_{diif} = .031$, $p = .040$ two-tailed for unequal-variance corrected df of 62.10). This difference cannot be attributed to group differences in the initial phases, because there were no hints of differences between groups in the first two phases.

Fit of the model

The model, EXIT, was fitted to the testing data and to the third phase training data. Table 4.4 shows that the model predictions fit the testing data well, with the model exhibiting a robust preference for E when given symptom I alone, a strong preference for L when presented with symptom pair PE.PL, and a strong preference for Lo when presented with PE.PLo. The model also fitted the learning in the third phase well, predicting 80.9% correct in the easy condition and 72.5% correct in the hard condition, compared with 82.6% and 76.2% by humans.

Selected (bold font) data from Table 4.4 are presented graphically in Figure 4.10. It can be seen from Figure 4.10a and b that the model reproduces the pattern of results seen in the human data quite well.

When the attention shifting was turned off, so that the shift rate had a fixed value of zero (and hence there was no attentional learning, either), the restricted model was entirely unable to show the trends of interest. Table 4.4 shows that the model without attention exhibits *no* preference for E when given symptom I alone, *no* preference for L when presented with symptom pair PE.PL, and *no* preference for Lo when presented with symptom pair PE.PLo. The model also shows *no* difference between groups in the third phase of learning, predicting 78.2% correct in the easy condition and 78.3% correct in the hard condition. Yet again we see that attentional mechanisms are critical for the model to fit the data.

Figure 4.10c shows clearly the failure of the restricted model to capture the preferences shown by humans. Without attention shifting and learning, the model can learn the training patterns but generalizes nothing like people do, either in the test phase or in the subsequent training phase.

SUMMARY AND CONCLUSION

The preceding sections provided three illustrations of the importance of attentional shifts and attentional learning in models of natural learning. In all three experiments, attentional learning in one phase was assessed by examining the ease of learning in a subsequent phase. If people have learned to attend to one feature or ignore another feature, then subsequent learning about the attended-to feature should be easier than learning about the ignored feature. In the first illustration, an advantage of intradimensional

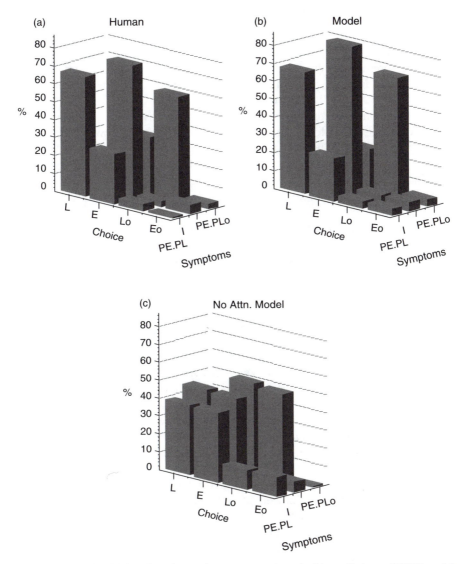

Figure 4.10. Selected data from inverse base rate experiment, with predictions of EXIT model with or without attentional shifting and learning.

shift over extradimensional shift was demonstrated with an experiment (Kruschke, 1996b) that avoided a problem common to all previous designs, i.e. confounded changes in novelty. The second illustration showed that the pervasive phenomenon of blocking involves learned suppression of attention to the blocked cue. The experiment demonstrated that discrimination learning was easier when the shared cue was previously blocked than when the distinctive cues were previously blocked. The third illustration suggested that the rapid attention shifting evident in the inverse base rate effect also involves learned attention shifts, because subsequent learning about the imperfect predictor was more difficult in the context of the later learned (attended to) distinctive cue than in the context of the earlier learned (less strongly attended to) distinctive cue.

All three phenomena—intradimensional shift advantage, blocking, and the inverse base rate effect—have been found in a variety of procedural paradigms and settings. The first two have been found in a variety of animal species (and the third is relatively recent and has not yet been systematically sought in other species). Therefore, attentional learning is a widespread phenomenon and should not be ignored by those who wish to model natural learning.

In all three illustrations, connectionist models that directly implemented attentional shifting and learning fitted the data nicely. When the attentional shifting and learning was "turned off", the models could not exhibit the signature effects observed in the human data. The modeling adds supportive evidence to the veracity of the attentional theory.

Relation to other learning models

There have been a variety of connectionist models of associative learning proposed in recent years, some of which incorporate notions of attention, yet none of which address the type of attentional phenomena described here.

Gluck & Bower (1988) proposed a simple linear associator, that learned by the delta rule, as a model of apparent base rate neglect in human learning. Their seminal article initiated a series of further investigations by several researchers, demonstrating the robustness of the empirical effect and of the model's ability to address it. Yet it turned out that their model cannot account for results from a modest parametric variation of their experimental design, and instead an enhanced model that incorporates rapidly shifting attention is sufficient (Kruschke, 1996a).

Shanks (1992) proposed a variation of a linear associator, called the attentional connectionist model (ACM), in which the attention allocated to a cue is inversely related to the cue's base rate. Thus, the attention allocated to a cue corresponds to the cue's surprisingness or novelty. This notion of attention in the ACM is quite different from the notion expounded in this chapter. The attention in ACM does not shift rapidly in response to categorization errors. Kruschke (1996a) showed that the ACM does not fit data from an experiment examining apparent base rate neglect. Nevertheless, future empirical data might demand the inclusion of ACM-style novelty-based attention in addition to rapidly shifting error-driven attention.

Nosofsky, Gluck, Palmeri, McKinley, & Glauthier (1994) described a model that maintains separate learning rates for each feature and each combination of features. These individual learning rates, or associabilities, are adjusted in response to error. This interesting approach was first proposed by Sutton and colleagues (e.g. Gluck, Glauthier, & Sutton, 1992; Jacobs, 1988). The model was able to capture aspects of a classic learning study that the authors replicated, but the model did not fit the data quantitatively as well as ALCOVE. This approach is intriguing and deserves further investigation. It might be particularly challenged, however, by learning phenomena that are produced by *rapid* attention shifts or by exemplar-specific learned attention.

Some neurally-inspired models of learning, such as those of Schmajuk & DiCarlo (1992) and Gluck & Myers (1997), implement types of attentional modulation in learning. In these models, however, the attentional modulation affects all cues simultaneously, and does not rapidly select component cues within an array. It may well turn out that both types of attentional mechanism are needed in a comprehensive model of learning.

The configural model of Pearce (1994) incorporates exemplar nodes similar to AMBRY, and it incorporates attentional normalization similar to EXIT, but it does not incorporate any kind of shifting selective attention. It therefore is unable to address the effects highlighted in this chapter.

The rational model of categorization (Anderson, 1990) is motivated by normative calculation of conditional probabilities, such that the learner is assumed to be accumulating statistics about feature and category co-occurrences, and then classifying items according to their Bayesian probabilities. The rational model can be implemented in a network framework not unlike a connectionist model (Anderson, 1990, p. 137). The model can account for many findings in learning, but one phenomenon it does not address is the inverse base rate effect. In particular, it fails to show an inverse base rate effect for test symptoms PE.PLo, whereas humans show a strong effect (see Table 4.4 and Figure 4.10). The rational model has no mechanism for shifting or learning attention.

Mackintosh's (1975) classic model for attention learning was invented as a direct formal expression of intuitions about how attention works, based on empirical findings. The formalism was not couched in any larger-scale framework to explain what the model mechanism accomplished computationally, or how the attentional mechanism related to the associative weight learning mechanism. Connectionist modeling adds such a larger-scale perspective. The EXIT model described in this chapter has an architecture motivated by psychological principles similar to Mackintosh's. But the mechanisms for attention shifting, attention learning, and associative weight learning are all derived by a common goal: error reduction. It turns out that a special case of EXIT is very nearly identical to the formulae proposed by Mackintosh (1975) (see Kruschke, 2001).

Attentional shifting and learning are rational

Attention shifts and learned attention are good for the rapid learning of new associations without damaging previously learned associations. While this accelerates learning, it can also lead to apparently irrational behaviors. The irrationality of intradimensional shift advantage, blocking, and the inverse base rate effect has been described above. There are many other examples. Consider a situation wherein a cue is only imperfectly correlated with an outcome. The extent to which people (and other animals) learn to utilize the cue decreases when other, irrelevant, cues are added (e.g. Castellan, 1973; Wagner, Logan, Haberlandt, & Price, 1968). For an optimal learner, the presence of irrelevant information should not affect the ultimate utilization of relevant information, yet for natural learners it does. Kruschke & Johansen (1999) reviewed a number of related phenomena in probabilistic category learning, and addressed a panoply of irrational behavior with a connectionist model called RASHNL (which stands for Rapid Attention SHifting 'N' Learning). The rash shifts of attention facilitate the rational goal of rapid learning, but also lead to over- or under-commitments to various sources of information. Thus, a model that is driven purely by rapid error reduction can generate a number of seemingly irrational behaviors, just like people and many other animals. The pervasiveness of these learning phenomena, across situations and across species, suggests that it would be irrational for connectionist modelers to ignore attentional learning.

Notes

1. An alternative possible solution would be to encode the entire configuration of features in each type of mushroom, and to disallow any generalization on the basis of partially matched configurations. In this way, knowledge about smooth round mushrooms would not interfere with knowledge about smooth flat mushrooms, despite the fact that both pieces of knowledge include the feature smoothness. A problem with this approach is that knowledge does not generalize from learned cases to novel cases, yet generalization is perhaps the most fundamental goal of learning in the first place. For a discussion of configural and elemental learning, see Chapter 2 by Shanks in this volume.
2. The original design used by Kruschke (1996b) also included two other types of shift: A complete reversal of all categories, and a change to another XOR structure with the previously irrelevant dimensions relevant and one previously irrelevant dimension relevant. These additional types of shift were useful for testing other hypotheses about shift learning.
3. Strictly speaking, the design does not constitute blocking of F and G, because these two symptoms are not perfectly correlated with the disease in phase 2 (symptom B, however, does conform strictly to a blocking design). Despite this departure from a strict blocking design, the theoretical implications regarding attentional learning remain the same.

REFERENCES

Ackley, D. H., Hinton, G. E., & Sejnowski, T. J. (1985). A learning algorithm for Boltzmann machines. *Cognitive Science, 9,* 147–169.

Anderson, J. R. (1990). *The adaptive character of thought.* Hillsdale, NJ: Lawrence Erlbaum Associates Inc.

Castellan, N. J. (1973). Multiple-cue probability learning with irrelevant cues. *Organizational Behavior and Human Performance, 9,* 16–29.

Dennis, S., & Kruschke, J. K. (1998). Shifting attention in cued recall. *Australian Journal of Psychology, 50,* 131–138.

Fagot, J., Kruschke, J. K., Depy, D., & Vauclair, J. (1998). Associative learning in baboons (*Papio papio*) and humans (*Homo sapiens*): Species differences in learned attention to visual features. *Animal Cognition, 1,* 123–133.

Garner, W. R. (1974). *The processing of information and structure.* Hillsdale, NJ: Lawrence Erlbaum Associates, Inc.

Gluck, M. A., & Bower, G. H. (1988). From conditioning to category learning: An adaptive network model. *Journal of Experimental Psychology: General, 117,* 227–247.

Gluck, M. A., Glauthier, P. T., & Sutton, R. S. (1992). Adaptation of cue-specific learning rates in network models of human category learning. In *Proceedings of the 14th Annual Conference of the Cognitive Science Society* (pp. 540–545). Hillsdale, NJ: Lawrence Erlbaum Associates, Inc.

Gluck, M. A., & Myers, C. E. (1997). Psychobiological models of hippocampal function in learning and memory. *Annual Review of Psychology, 48,* 481–514.

Hopfield, J. (1982). Neural networks and physical systems with emergent collective computational abilities. *Proceedings of the National Academy of Sciences USA, 79.*

Jacobs, R. A. (1988). Increased rates of convergence through learning rate adaptation. *Neural Networks, 1,* 295–307.

Kamin, L. J. (1968). 'Attention-like' processes in classical conditioning. In M. R. Jones (Ed.), *Miami symposium on the prediction of behavior: Aversive stimulation* (pp. 9–33). Coral Gables, FL: University of Miami Press.

Kruschke, J. K. (1992). ALCOVE: An exemplar-based connectionist model of category learning. *Psychological Review, 99,* 22–44.

Kruschke, J. K. (1996a). Base rates in category learning. *Journal of Experimental Psychology: Learning, Memory, & Cognition, 22,* 3–26.

Kruschke, J. K. (1996b). Dimensional relevance shifts in category learning. *Connection Science, 8,* 201–223.

Kruschke, J. K. (2001). Toward a unified model of attention in associative learning. *Journal of Mathematical Psychology, 45,* 812–863.

Kruschke, J. K., & Blair, N. J. (2000). Blocking and backward blocking involve learned inattention. *Psychonomic Bulletin & Review, 7,* 636–645.

Kruschke, J. K., & Johansen, M. K. (1999). A model of probabilistic category learning. *Journal of Experimental Psychology: Learning, Memory, & Cognition, 25,* 1083–1119.

Mackintosh, N. J. (1965). Selective attention in animal discrimination learning. *Psychological Bulletin, 64,* 124–150.

Mackintosh, N. J. (1975). A theory of attention: Variations in the associability of stimuli with reinforcement. *Psychological Review, 82,* 276–298.

Mackintosh, N. J., & Turner, C. (1971). Blocking as a function of novelty of CS and predictability of UCS. *Quarterly Journal of Experimental Psychology, 23,* 359–366.

Medin, D. L., & Edelson, S. M. (1988). Problem structure and the use of base-rate information from experience. *Journal of Experimental Psychology: General, 117,* 68–85.

Miller, R. R., Barnet, R. C., & Grahame, N. J. (1995). Assessment of the Rescorla–Wagner model. *Psychological Bulletin, 117,* 363–386.

Minsky, M. L., & Papert, S. A. (1969). *Perceptrons.* Cambridge, MA: MIT Press (1988 expanded edition).

Nosofsky, R. M. (1992). Exemplars, prototypes, and similarity rules. In A. F. Healy, S. M. Kosslyn, & R. M. Shiffrin (Eds.), *Essays in honor of William K. Estes: vol. 2. From learning processes to cognitive processes* (pp. 149–167). Hillsdale, NJ: Lawrence Erlbaum Associates Inc.

Nosofsky, R. M., Gluck, M. A., Palmeri, T. J., McKinley, S. C., & Glauthier, P. (1994). Comparing models of rule-based classification learning: A replication of Shepard, Hovland, and Jenkins (1961). *Memory & Cognition, 22,* 352–369.

Pearce, J. M. (1994). Similarity and discrimination: A selective review and a connectionist model. *Psychological Review, 101,* 587–607.

Rescorla, R. A., & Wagner, A. R. (1972). A theory of Pavlovian conditioning: Variations in the effectiveness of reinforcement and non-reinforcement. In A. H. Black, & W. F. Prokasy (Eds.), *Classical conditioning: Ii. Current research and theory* (pp. 64–99). New York: Appleton-Century-Crofts.

Rosenblatt, F. (1958). The perceptron: A probabilistic model for information storage and organization in the brain. *Psychological Review, 65,* 386–408.

Rumelhart, D. E., Hinton, G. E., & Williams, R. J. (1986). Learning internal representations by error propagation. In J. L. McClelland & D. E. Rumelhart (Eds.), *Parallel distributed processing* (Vol. 1, pp. 318–362). Cambridge, MA: MIT Press.

Schmajuk, N. A., & DiCarlo, J. J. (1992). Stimulus configuration, classical conditioning, and hippocampal function. *Psychological Review, 99,* 268–305.

Shanks, D. R. (1992). Connectionist accounts of the inverse base-rate effect in categorization. *Connection Science, 4,* 3–18.

Shepard, R. N. (1964). Attention and the metric structure of the stimulus space. *Journal of Mathematical Psychology, 1,* 54–87.

Shepard, R. N. (1987). Toward a universal law of generalization for psychological science. *Science, 237,* 1317–1323.

Siegel, S., & Allan, L. G. (1996). The widespread influence of the Rescorla–Wagner model. *Psychonomic Bulletin & Review, 3,* 314–321.

Slamecka, N. J. (1968). A methodological analysis of shift paradigms in human discrimination learning. *Psychological Bulletin, 69,* 423–438.

Sutherland, N. S., & Mackintosh, N. J. (1971). *Mechanisms of animal discrimination learning.* New York: Academic Press.

Wagner, A. R., Logan, F. A., Haberlandt, K., & Price, T. (1968). Stimulus selection in animal discrimination learning. *Journal of Experimental Psychology, 76,* 171–180.

Williams, B. A. (1999). Associative competition in operant conditioning: Blocking the response–reinforcer association. *Psychonomic Bulletin & Review, 6,* 618–623.

Wolff, J. L. (1967). Concept-shift and discrimination-reversal learning in humans. *Psychological Bulletin, 68,* 369–408.

SECTION TWO

Memory

CHAPTER FIVE

The division of labor between the neocortex and hippocampus

Randall C. O'Reilly
University of Colorado, Boulder, CO, USA

INTRODUCTION

In addition to addressing specific patterns of behavioral and neural data, neural network models are valuable for their ability to establish general principles of functional neural organization. In particular, computational models can explain how differences in the structuring and parameters of neural networks can lead to qualitatively different, often mutually incompatible, capabilities. To the extent that different computational capacities require fundamentally different kinds of neural networks, the brain could have either a *compromise* or a *trade-off* between the different network properties, or it could *specialize* different brain areas for different functions to avoid such a trade-off. Critically, this kind of computational approach to functional neural organization enables one to understand both *what* is different about the way different neural systems learn, and *why*, from a functional perspective, they should have these differences in the first place. Thus, the computational approach can go beyond mere description towards understanding the deeper principles underlying the organization of the cognitive system.

This chapter explores computational trade-offs to understand the functional organization of brain areas involved in learning and memory, specifically the hippocampus and various areas of the neocortex. These trade-offs are based on a set of computational principles, derived from a convergence of biological, psychological, and computational constraints, for understanding how neural systems subserve learning and memory. These principles were first developed in McClelland, McNaughton, & O'Reilly (1995), and have been refined several times since then (O'Reilly, Norman, & McClelland, 1998; O'Reilly & Rudy, 2000, 2001; O'Reilly & Munakata, 2000). The computational principles have been applied to a wide range of learning and memory phenomena across several species (rats, monkeys, and humans). For example, they can account for impaired and preserved learning capacities with hippocampal lesions in conditioning, habituation, contextual learning, recognition memory, recall, and retrograde amnesia.

The chapter begins with a concise exposition of the principles, adapted from O'Reilly & Rudy (2000), and then discusses in somewhat more detail a set of specific simulations from O'Reilly & Munakata (2000) that illustrate these principles. It concludes with an overview of recent and ongoing applications of the models to a variety of cognitive neuroscience phenomena.

THE PRINCIPLES

Several levels of principles are presented, building from those that are most obvious from a mechanistic perspective. Only basic neural network mechanisms are needed to understand these principles. Specifically, we assume networks having a number of units that communicate via propagation of activation signals along weighted connections to other units. Furthermore, we assume that learning occurs through changes to the connection weights through widely-known mechanisms, as discussed below. See O'Reilly & Munakata (2000) for a recent, in-depth treatment that covers the biological bases of these mechanisms.

Learning rate, overlap, and interference

The most basic set of principles can be motivated by considering how subsequent learning can interfere with prior learning. A classic example of this kind of interference can be found in the AB–AC associative learning task (e.g. Barnes & Underwood, 1959). The A represents one set of words that are associated with two different sets of other words, B and C. For example, the word *window* will be associated with the word *reason* in the AB list, and associated with *locomotive* in the AC list. After studying the AB list of associates, subjects are tested by asking them to give the appropriate B associate for each of the A words. Then, subjects study the AC list (often over multiple iterations), and are subsequently tested on both lists for recall of the associates after each iteration of learning the AC list. Subjects exhibit some level of interference on the initially learned AB associations as a result of learning the AC list, but they still remember a reasonable percentage (see Figure 5.1a for representative data).

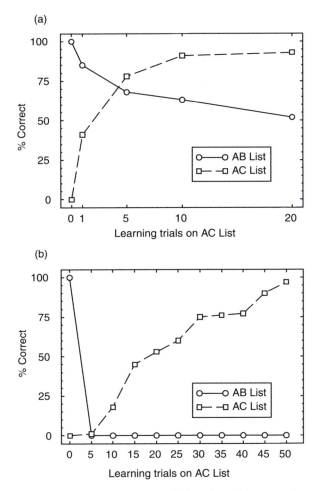

Figure 5.1. Human and model data for AB–AC list learning. (a) Humans show some interference for the AB list items as a function of new learning on the AC list items. (b) Model shows a catastrophic level of interference. Data from McCloskey & Cohen (1989). Reprinted with permission from O'Reilly & Munakata (2000), MIT Press.

The first set of principles concern the ability of a network to rapidly learn new information with a level of interference characteristic of human subjects, as in the AB–AC task. Specifically, we consider the effects of *overlapping representations* and *rate of learning*. Overlapping representations arise in distributed patterns of neural activity over multiple units, where subsets of units are shared across different representations. For example, one would imagine that there are shared units across the AB and AC patterns in the AB–AC task (deriving from the shared A element). Rate of learning refers to the size of weight changes made during learning. Both of these factors affect interference as follows:

- Overlapping representations lead to interference (conversely, separated representations prevent interference).
- A faster learning rate causes more interference (conversely, a slower learning rate causes less interference).

The mechanistic basis for these principles within a neural network perspective is straightforward. Interference is caused when weights used to encode one association are disturbed by the encoding of another (Figure 5.2a). Overlapping patterns share more weights, and therefore lead to greater amounts of interference. Clearly, if entirely separate representations are used to encode two different associations, then there will be no interference whatsoever (Figure 5.2b). The story with learning rate is similarly straightforward. Faster learning rates lead to more weight change, and thus greater interference (Figure 5.3). However, a fast learning rate is necessary for rapid learning.

Integration and extracting statistical structure

Figure 5.3 shows the flip side of the interference story, *integration*. If the learning rate is low, then the weights will integrate over many experiences, reflecting the *underlying statistics* of the environment (McClelland et al.,

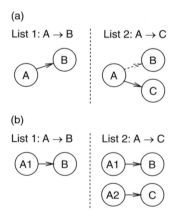

Figure 5.2.   Interference as a function of overlapping (same) representations vs. separated representations. (a) Using the same representation to encode two different associations (A → B and A → C) causes interference—the subsequent learning of A → C interferes with the prior learning of A → B because the A stimulus must have stronger weights to C than to B for the second association, as is reflected in the weights. (b) A separated representation, where A is encoded separated for the first list (A1) vs. the second list (A2) prevents interference.

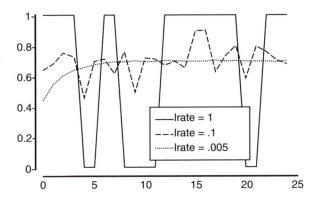

Figure 5.3. Weight value learning about a single input unit that is either active or not. The weight increases when the input is on, and decreases when it is off, in proportion to the size of the learning rate. The input has an overall probability of being active of .7. Larger learning rates (.1 or 1) lead to more interference on prior learning, resulting in a weight value that bounces around substantially with each training example. In the extreme case of a learning rate of 1, the weight only reflects what happened on the previous trial, retaining no memory for prior events at all. As the learning rate gets smaller (.005), the weight smoothly averages over individual events and reflects the overall statistical probability of the input being active.

1995; White, 1989). One can think of this in terms of computing a statistical average—each term in the average contributes by a small factor of $1/n$. As n gets larger, each term contributes less. Similarly, if a neural network is to compute the average or expected characteristics of the environment, each experience must contribute something like n (where n is the total number of experiences) to the overall representation. Furthermore, overlapping representations facilitate this integration process, because the same weights need to be reused across many different experiences to enable the integration produced by a slow learning rate. This leads to the next principle:

- Integration across experiences to extract underlying statistical structure requires a slow learning rate and overlapping representations.

Episodic memory and generalization: Incompatible functions

Thus, focusing only on pattern overlap for the moment, we can see that networks can be optimized for two different, and incompatible, functions: avoiding interference, or integrating across experiences to extract generalities. Avoiding interference requires separated representations, while integration requires overlapping representations. These two functions each have clear functional advantages, leading to a further set of principles:

- Interference avoidance is essential for *episodic* memory, which requires learning about the specifics of individual events and keeping them separate from other events.
- Integration is essential for encoding the general statistical structure of the environment, abstracted away from the specifics of individual events, which enables *generalization* to novel situations.

The incompatibility between these functions is further evident in these descriptions (i.e. encoding specifics vs. abstracting away from them). Also, episodic memory requires relatively rapid learning—an event must be encoded as it happens, and does not typically repeat itself for further learning opportunities. This completes a pattern of opposition between these functions: episodic learning requires rapid learning, while integration and generalization requires slow learning. This is summarized in the following principle:

- Episodic memory and extracting generalities are in opposition. Episodic memory requires rapid learning and separated patterns, while extracting generalities requires slow learning and overlapping patterns.

Applying the principles to the hippocampus and neocortex

Armed with these principles, the finding that neural network models that have highly overlapping representations exhibit *catastrophic* levels of interference (McCloskey & Cohen, 1989; see Figure 5.1b) should not be surprising. A number of researchers showed that this interference can be reduced by introducing various factors that result in less pattern overlap (e.g. French, 1992; Kortge, 1993; McRae & Hetherington, 1993; Sloman & Rumelhart, 1992). Thus, instead of concluding that neural networks may be fundamentally flawed, as McCloskey and Cohen (1989) argued (and a number of others have uncritically accepted), McClelland et al. (1995) argued that this catastrophic failure serves as an important clue into the structure of the human brain.

Specifically, we argued that because of the fundamental incompatibility between episodic memory and extracting generalities, the brain should employ two separate systems that each optimize these two objectives individually, instead of having a single system that tries to strike an inferior compromise:

- The hippocampus rapidly binds together information using pattern-separated representations to minimize interference.
- The neocortex slowly learns about the general statistical structure of the environment using overlapping distributed representations (see also Sherry & Schacter, 1987 for a similar conclusion).

This line of reasoning provides a strikingly good fit to the known properties of the hippocampus and neocortex, respectively (see Norman & O'Reilly, in press; O'Reilly et al., 1998; O'Reilly & Rudy, 2001, for some examples).

Sparse conjunctive representations

The *conjunctive* or *configural* representations theory provides a converging line of thinking about the nature of hippocampal function (O'Reilly & Rudy, 2001; Rudy & Sutherland, 1995; Sutherland & Rudy, 1989; Wickelgren, 1979). A conjunctive/configural representation is one that binds together (conjoins or configures) multiple elements into a novel unitary representation. This is consistent with the description of hippocampal function given above, based on the need to separate patterns to avoid interference. Indeed, it is clear that pattern separation and conjunctive representations are two sides of the same coin, and that both are caused by the use of *sparse* representations (having relatively few active neurons) that are a known property of the hippocampus (O'Reilly & McClelland, 1994; O'Reilly & Rudy, 2001).

To understand why a sparse representation can lead to pattern separation (using different neurons to encode different representations) and conjunctivity, we consider two related explanations. First, consider a situation where the hippocampal representation is generated at random with some fixed probability of a unit becoming active. In this case, if fewer units are active, the odds that the same units will be active in two different patterns will go down (Figure 5.4). For example, if the probability of becoming active for one pattern (i.e. the sparseness) is .25, then the probability of becoming active for both patterns would be $.25^2$ or .0625. If the patterns are made more sparse, so that the probability is now .05 for being active in one pattern, the probability of being active in both patterns falls to .0025. Thus, the pattern overlap is reduced by a factor of 25 by reducing the sparseness by a factor of 5 in this case. However, this analysis does not capture the entire story, because it fails to take into account the fact that hippocampal units are actually driven by weighted connections with the input patterns, and therefore will be affected by similarity (overlap) in the input.

A more complete understanding of pattern separation can be achieved by considering the concept of a unit's *activation threshold*—how much excitation it requires to overcome the inhibitory competition from other units (Marr, 1969; O'Reilly & McClelland, 1994). To produce sparse representations, this threshold must be relatively high (e.g. because the level of inhibition is relatively strong for a given amount of excitatory input). Figure 5.5 shows how a high inhibitory threshold leads simultaneously to both pattern separation and conjunctive representations, where the hippocampal units depend critically on the conjunction of active units in the input. A high threshold leads to conjunctive representations because only those units having the closest

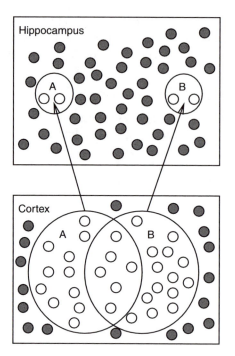

Figure 5.4. Pattern separation in the hippocampus. Small circles represent units, with active ones in white, inactive ones in grey. Circles A and B in the cortex and hippocampus indicate two sets of representations composed of patterns of active units. In the cortex, they are overlapping, and encompass a relatively large proportion of active units. In the hippocampus, the representations are sparser, as indicated by their smaller size, and thus overlap less (more pattern separation). Also, units in the hippocampus are conjunctive and are activated only by specific combinations of activity in the cortex. Reprinted with permission from O'Reilly & Munakata (2000), MIT Press.

alignment of their weight patterns with the current input activity pattern will receive enough excitation to become activated. In other words, the activation a unit receives must be a relatively high proportion of the total number of input units that are active, meaning that it is the specific combination or conjunction of these inputs that are responsible for driving the units. Figure 5.5 illustrates this effect in the extreme case where only the most excited receiving unit gets active. In reality, multiple (roughly 1–5%) units are activated in the hippocampus at any given time, but the same principle applies (see O'Reilly & McClelland, 1994, for a detailed analysis).

To summarize:

• Sparse hippocampal representations lead to pattern separation (to avoid interference) and conjunctive representations (to bind together features into a unitary representation).

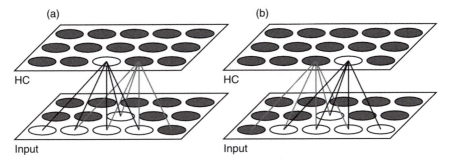

Figure 5.5. Conjunctive, pattern-separated representations result from sparseness (active units are represented in white, inactive ones in gray). The extreme case, where only one receiving unit (in the upper layer, representing the hippocampus) is allowed to be active, is shown here for simplicity. Each receiving unit has roughly the same number of randomly distributed connections from the input units. The two shown here have overlapping input connections, except for one unique unit each. Thus, two very similar input patterns sharing all the overlapping units and differing only in these unique units, shown in (a) and (b), will get completely nonoverlapping (separated) memory representations. In this way, the conjunctive memory representation resulting from sparseness produces pattern separation. Reprinted with permission from O'Reilly & Munakata (2000), MIT Press.

This principle will be explored in greater detail in the context of a specific simulation described below.

Pattern completion: Recalling a conjunction

Pattern completion is required for recalling information from conjunctive hippocampal representations, yet it conflicts with the process of pattern separation that forms these representations in the first place (O'Reilly & McClelland, 1994). Pattern completion occurs when a partial input cue drives the hippocampus to complete to an entire previously encoded set of features that were bound together in a conjunctive representation. For a given input pattern, a decision must be made to recognize it as a retrieval cue for a previous memory and perform pattern completion, or to perform pattern separation and store the input as a new memory. This decision is often difficult, given noisy inputs and degraded memories. The hippocampus implements this decision as the effects of a set of basic mechanisms operating on input patterns (Hasselmo & Wyble, 1997; O'Reilly & McClelland, 1994), and it does not always do what would seem to be the right thing to do from an omniscient perspective, knowing all the relevant task factors.

Learning mechanisms: Hebbian and error-driven

To more fully explain the roles of the hippocampus and neocortex, we need to understand how learning works in these systems (the basic principles just described do not depend on the detailed nature of the learning mechanisms; White, 1989). There are two basic mechanisms that have been discussed in the literature, Hebbian and error-driven learning (e.g. Gluck & Myers, 1993; Marr, 1971; McNaughton & Morris, 1987; Schmajuk & DiCarlo, 1992). Briefly, Hebbian learning (Hebb, 1949) works by increasing weights between co-active neurons (and usually decreasing weights when a receiver is active and the sender is not), which is a well-established property of biological synaptic modification mechanisms (e.g. Collingridge & Bliss, 1987). Hebbian learning is useful for binding together features active at the same time (e.g. within the same episode), and has therefore been widely suggested as a hippocampal learning mechanism (e.g. Marr, 1971; McNaughton & Morris, 1987).

Error-driven learning works by adjusting weights to minimize the errors in a network's performance, with the best example of this being the *error back-propagation* algorithm (Rumelhart, Hinton, & Williams, 1986). Error-driven learning is sensitive to task demands in a way that Hebbian learning is not, and this makes it a much more capable form of learning for actually achieving a desired input/output mapping. Thus, it is natural to associate this form of learning with the kind of procedural or task-driven learning in which the neocortex is often thought to specialize (e.g. because amnesics with hippocampal damage have preserved procedural learning abilities). Although the back-propagation mechanism has been widely challenged as biologically implausible (e.g. Crick, 1989; Zipser & Andersen, 1988), a recent analysis shows that simple biologically-based mechanisms can be used to implement this mechanism (O'Reilly, 1996), so that it is quite reasonable to assume that the cortex depends on this kind of learning.

Although the association of Hebbian learning with the hippocampus and error-driven learning with the cortex is appealing in some ways, it turns out that both kinds of learning play important roles in both systems (O'Reilly, 1998; O'Reilly & Munakata, 2000; O'Reilly & Rudy, 2001). Thus, the specific learning principles adopted here are that both forms of learning operate in both systems:

- Hebbian learning binds together co-occurring features (in the hippocampus) and generally learns about the co-occurrence statistics in the environment across many different patterns (in the neocortex).
- Error-driven learning shapes learning according to specific task demands (shifting the balance of pattern separation and completion in the hippocampus, and developing task-appropriate representations in the neocortex).

It is the existence of this task-driven learning that complicates the picture for nonlinear discrimination learning problems.

A summary of principles

The above principles can be summarized with the following three general statements of neocortical and hippocampal learning properties (O'Reilly & Norman, 2002; O'Reilly & Rudy, 2001):

1. *Learning rate.* The cortical system typically learns slowly, while the hippocampal system typically learns rapidly.
2. *Conjunctive bias.* The cortical system has a bias towards integrating over specific instances to extract generalities. The hippocampal system is biased by its intrinsic sparseness to develop conjunctive representations of specific instances of environmental inputs. However, this conjunctive bias trades off with the countervailing process of pattern completion, so the hippocampus does not always develop new conjunctive representations (sometimes it completes to existing ones).
3. *Learning mechanisms.* Both cortex and hippocampus use error-driven and Hebbian learning. The error-driven aspect responds to task demands, and will cause the network to learn to represent whatever is needed to achieve goals or ends. Thus, the cortex can overcome its bias and develop specific, conjunctive representations if the task demands require this. Also, error-driven learning can shift the hippocampus from performing pattern separation to performing pattern completion, or vice versa, as dictated by the task. Hebbian learning is constantly operating, and reinforcing the representations that are activated in the two systems.

These principles are focused on distinguishing neocortex and hippocampus—we have also articulated a more complete set of principles that are largely common to both systems (O'Reilly, 1998; O'Reilly & Munakata, 2000). Models incorporating these principles have been extensively applied to a wide range of different cortical phenomena, including perception, language, and higher-level cognition. In the next sections, we explore these principles in the context of two implemented models, one representing a basic cortical network, and the other a hippocampal network based on the neurobiology of the hippocampal system. Both networks are tested on the AB–AC interference task as described earlier.

NEOCORTICAL MODEL OF THE AB–AC TASK

As we mentioned previously, the McCloskey and Cohen (1989) catastrophic interference model can be interpreted as a good example of what would happen to a neocortical network with distributed, overlapping representations on the AB–AC task. In this section, we examine a similar such model, developed in O'Reilly & Munakata (2000), that enables us to explore the important parameter of the sparseness, and thereby the level of pattern separation or overlap in the network's representations. Therefore, this network provides a concrete demonstration of some of the central principles outlined above.

Basic properties of the model

The basic framework for implementing the AB–AC task is to have two input patterns, one that represents the A stimulus, and the other that represents the "list context" (Fig. 5.6). Thus, we assume that the subject develops some internal representation that identifies the two different lists, and that this serves as a means of disambiguating which of the two associates should be produced. These input patterns feed into a hidden layer, which then produces an output pattern corresponding to the B or C associate. We use a distributed representation of random bit patterns to represent the word stimuli (Fig. 5.7). The list context patterns for all the items on the AB list are all similar random variations of a common underlying pattern, and likewise for the AC items. Thus, the list context patterns are not identical for each item on the same list, just very similar (this reflects the fact that even if the external environmental context is constant, the internal perception of it fluctuates, and other internal context factors, like a sense of time passing, change as well).

To train the network, O'Reilly & Munakata (2000) initially used default parameters for the Leabra algorithm, which incorporates a comprehensive set of standard neural network mechanisms (O'Reilly, 1998, 2001; O'Reilly & Munakata, 2000). These mechanisms include a combination of both Hebbian and error-driven learning rules, and, most relevant for the present purposes, a k-winner-takes-all (kWTA) inhibition function that can be used to explore different levels of representational sparseness. The default parameters specify a k value that produces an overall activation level of roughly 25%, meaning in the present network that 12 out of the 50 hidden units are active for any given input pattern (i.e. $k = 12$ winners). This activation level typically produces very good results on learning tasks typical of what we think the neocortex excels at—encoding efficient features for representing visual scenes, learning to recognize objects, learning to pronounce written words, etc. (see O'Reilly & Munakata, 2000, for many such models). All of these tasks involve extracting regularities over many instances of experience.

Figure 5.8a shows typical results with these standard parameters. You can see that just as the network starts to learn the AC list (after first acquiring the AB list), performance on the AB list deteriorates dramatically. This replicates the McCloskey & Cohen (1989) finding that a "generic" neural network does not do a good job of capturing the human data (Fig. 5.1). With the generic network as a baseline, we can now test the idea that different parameters can reduce the level of interference. The intention here is to illuminate the

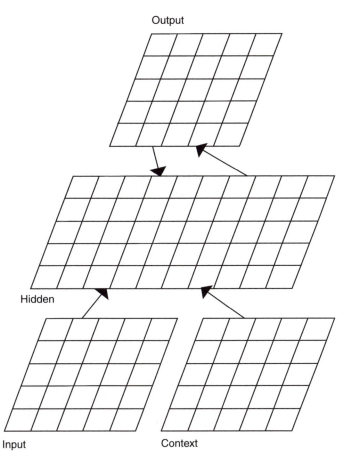

Figure 5.6.   Network for the AB–AC list learning task, with the input layer representing the A stimulus, the context input representing the list context, and the output being the B or C word associate, depending on the list context. Reprinted with permission from O'Reilly & Munakata (2000), MIT Press.

principles underlying these interference effects, and show how they could potentially be reduced—although we will see that they have relatively small effects in this particular context.

The primary source of interference in this network is the pattern overlap, resulting from the 25% activity level. Specifically, items on the AC list will activate and reuse the same units from the AB list, altering their weights to support the C associate instead of the B. Thus, by reducing the extent to which the hidden unit representations overlap (i.e. by making them *sparser*), we might be able to encourage the network to use separate representations for learning these two lists of items. To make the representations sparser, the k

(a)

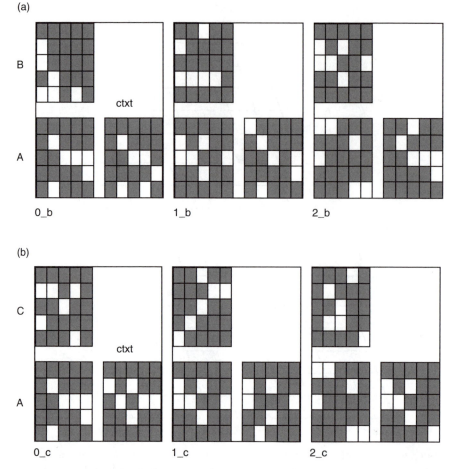

(b)

Figure 5.7. Training patterns for the AB–AC list learning task, showing the first three out of 10 patterns for (a) the AB list and (b) the AC list. Notice that the A input is the same across both lists, but it is paired with a B output on the AB list, and a C output on the AC list. The context input is a random permutation of a different random pattern for each list.

parameter in the kWTA function can be reduced to 4 instead of the default value of 12, resulting in an 8% overall activation level. Note that because the network depends on distributed representations for learning, one cannot reduce the activation much further without impairing learning performance.

O'Reilly & Munakata (2000) found that just reducing the k parameter to 4 did not actually make that much of a difference, because nothing was done to encourage it to use *different* sets of four units to represent the different associates. One way we can encourage this is to increase the variance of the initial random weights, making each unit have a more quirky pattern of

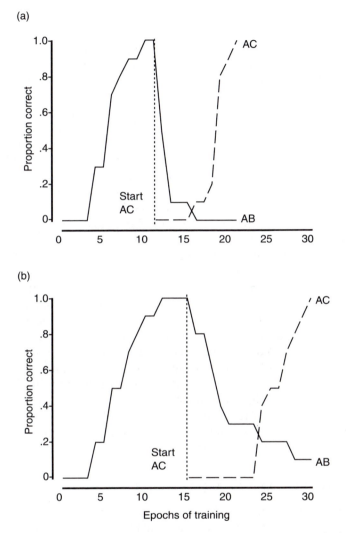

Figure 5.8. Example training results for two different parameter regimes. For both cases, the AB training is automatically terminated at 100% accuracy, switching to AC training. (a) With 24% hidden activity and default parameters, the hidden representations are highly overlapping, and this produces rapid and complete interference on the AB list as the network starts learning AC. (b) With sparser activity (8%) and other optimized parameters, as described in the text, the onset of AB interference is slowed and asymptotic levels are reduced. However, these effects are not particularly dramatic, and do not match human performance.

responses that should encourage different units to encode the different associates. Another thing that can be done to improve performance is to enhance the contribution of the list context inputs relative to the A stimulus, because this list context disambiguates the two different associates. This can be achieved by a weight-scaling parameter in Leabra, and it can be thought of as reflecting strategic focusing of attention by the subject. Finally, increased amounts of Hebbian learning might contribute to better performance because of the strong correlation of all items on a given list with the associated list context representation, which should be emphasized by Hebbian learning. This could lead to different subsets of hidden units representing the items on the two lists, because of the different context representations. The balance of Hebbian and error-driven learning is controlled by a normalized scaling parameter, and the default level is .01 Hebbian and .99 error-driven—we can increase this to .05 Hebbian and .95 error-driven (note that the small weighting factor on Hebbian learning is typically used because Hebbian learning provides much larger and more consistent weight changes relative to error-driven learning).

Figure 5.8b shows typical results from the network with all the parameter changes just described—O'Reilly & Munakata (2000) found that these parameters produced the best results. The main results of these parameters were to delay the onset of interference, and to improve the final level of performance on the AB list after learning about AC. However, it is obvious that this network is still not performing at the level of human subjects, who still remember roughly 60% of the AB list after learning the AC list. In the next section, we show that the remaining limitations of the present network are probably due to the architecture of the network, because a network with an architecture based on the biology of the hippocampus is able to perform at the level of human subjects on this task.

HIPPOCAMPAL MODEL OF THE AB–AC TASK

The hippocampal formation has a distinctive and relatively well-known anatomical structure. Furthermore, considerable neural recording data has been obtained from the hippocampus, providing information about important parameters, such as the relative activation levels in different areas of the hippocampus (Table 5.1). The somewhat remarkable thing about the model described here is that by incorporating these features of the hippocampal biology, we find that the resulting model performs quite well on rapid learning tasks like the AB–AC task, without suffering catastrophic levels of interference (O'Reilly & Munakata, 2000). A complete explication of the computational features of the biological structure of the hippocampus is beyond the scope of this chapter (see O'Reilly & McClelland, 1994, for one such treatment), but a few of the main points are

TABLE 5.1

Rough estimates of the size of various hippocampal areas and their expected activity levels in the rat, and corresponding values in the model. Rat data from Squire et al. (1989), Boss et al. (1985, 1987), and Barnes et al. (1990)

Area	Rat		Model	
	Neurons	Activity (%)	Units	Activity (%)
EC	200,000	7.0	96	25.0
DG	1,000,000	0.5	250	1.6
CA3	160,000	2.5	160	6.25
CA1	250,000	2.5	256	9.4

covered here, followed by a description of how the model performs on the AB–AC task.

Basic properties of the model

The model is based on what McNaughton has termed the "Hebb–Marr" model of hippocampal function (Hebb, 1949; Marr, 1969, 1970, 1971; McNaughton & Morris, 1987; McNaughton & Nadel, 1990). This model provides a framework for associating functional properties of memory with the biological properties of the hippocampus. Under this model, the two basic computational structures in the hippocampus are the feedforward pathway from the entorhinal cortex (EC) to area CA3 (via the dentate gyrus, DG), which is important for establishing the encoding of new memories, and the recurrent connectivity within CA3, which is primarily important for recalling previously stored memories.

Figure 5.9 shows the structure of the model, and an example activation pattern (see O'Reilly & Munakata, 2000, for the original presentation of this specific model, and O'Reilly et al., 1998; O'Reilly & Rudy, 2001, for similar ones). Table 5.1 shows that the model layers are roughly proportionately scaled, based on the anatomy of the rat, but the activation levels are generally higher (less sparse) to obtain sufficient absolute numbers of active units for reasonable distributed representations, given the small total number of units. The model is implemented using the same basic Leabra mechanisms as the earlier cortical model, with the activity levels enforced by setting appropriate k parameters in the kWTA inhibition function. Only Hebbian learning is used because it is sufficient for simple information storage, but it is likely that the hippocampus can also take advantage of error-driven learning in more complex tasks (O'Reilly & Rudy, 2001).

We can summarize the basic operations of the model by explaining how the encoding and retrieval of memories works in terms of the areas and

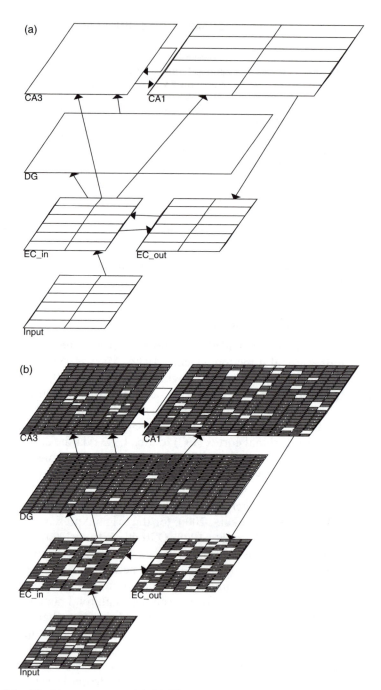

Figure 5.9. The hippocampus model. (a) The areas and connectivity, and the corresponding columns within the input, EC, and CA1. (b) An example activity pattern. Note the sparse activity in the DG and CA3, and intermediate sparseness of the CA1. Reprinted with permission from O'Reilly & Munakata (2000), MIT Press.

projections of the hippocampus. The general scheme for encoding is that activation comes into the EC from the cortex, and then flows to the DG and CA3, forming a pattern-separated representation across a sparse, distributed set of units that are then bound together by rapid Hebbian learning within the recurrent collaterals (also, learning in the feedforward pathway helps to encode the representation). Simultaneously, activation flows from the EC to the CA1, forming a somewhat pattern-separated but also *invertible* representation there—i.e. the CA1 representation can be inverted to reinstate the corresponding pattern of activity over the EC that originally gave rise to the CA1 pattern in the first place (McClelland & Goddard, 1996). An association between the CA3 and CA1 representations is encoded by learning in the connections between them.

Having encoded the information in this way, retrieval from a partial input cue can occur as follows. Again, the EC representation of the partial cue (based on inputs from the cortex) goes up to the DG and CA3. Now, the prior learning in the feedforward pathway and the recurrent CA3 connections leads to the ability to complete this partial input cue and recover the original CA3 representation. This completed CA3 representation then activates the corresponding CA1 representation, which, because it is invertible, is capable of recreating the complete original EC representation.

If, on the other hand, the EC input pattern is novel, then the weights will not have been facilitated for this particular activity pattern, and the CA1 will not be strongly driven by the CA3. Even if the EC activity pattern corresponds to two components that were previously studied, but not together, the conjunctive nature of the CA3 representations will prevent recall (O'Reilly et al., 1998).

In addition to capturing the rough sizes of the different hippocampal areas, the model incorporates rough approximations of the detailed patterns of connectivity within the hippocampal areas (e.g. Squire, Shimamura, & Amaral, 1989). The *perforant path* projections from EC to DG and CA3 are broad and diffuse, but the projection between the DG and CA3, known as the mossy fiber pathway, is sparse, focused, and topographic. Each CA3 neuron receives only around 52–87 synapses from the mossy fiber projection in the rat, but it is widely believed that each synapse is significantly stronger than the perforant path inputs to CA3. In the model, each CA3 unit receives from 25% of the EC, and 10% of the DG. The lateral (recurrent) projections within the CA3 project widely throughout the CA3, and a given CA3 neuron will receive from a large number of inputs sampled from the entire CA3 population. Similarly, the Schaffer collaterals, which go from the CA3 to the CA1, are diffuse and widespread, connecting a wide range of CA3 to CA1. In the model, these pathways have full connectivity. Finally, the interconnectivity between the EC and CA1 is relatively point-to-point, not diffuse like the projections from EC to DG and CA3 (Tamamaki, 1991).

This is captured in the model by a columnar structure and connectivity of CA1.

The functional properties of these various connectivity patterns have been analyzed (for details, see McClelland & Goddard, 1996; O'Reilly & McClelland, 1994; O'Reilly et al., 1998). We focus on just one example here, which is the broad and diffuse nature of the perforant pathway connectivity between EC and DG, CA3. This connectivity produces the same kind of effect as increasing the variance of weights that was explored in the neocortical network—it ensures that individual DG and CA3 neurons receive from a broadly distributed, and essentially random, subset of inputs. Thus, these neurons will encode different random conjunctions, and because of the extreme competition due to sparse activation levels, different such conjunctive units will be activated for even relatively similar input patterns. This produces pattern separation, and thereby avoids the interference problems that plague the neocortical network.

Performance on the AB–AC task

Now we describe how all of this hippocampal circuitry, as captured in the O'Reilly & Munakata (2000) model, performs on the AB–AC paired associates list learning task. If this circuitry enables the hippocampus to learn rapidly using pattern-separated representations that avoid interference, the model should be able to learn the new paired associates (AC) without causing undue levels of interference to the original AB associations, and it should be able to do this much more rapidly than was possible in the cortical model.

The model is trained in much the same way as the cortical model was. During training, the input patterns presented to the *input* layer of the network were composed of three components. The first and second components represented the A and B or C associates, respectively, while the third was a representation of the list context. The item representations were simple random bit patterns as in the cortical network, and the list context was similarly a slightly perturbed version of two different list-prototype patterns. During testing, the second associate (either B or C) was omitted, requiring pattern completion in the hippocampus to fill it in (in the EC_out layer) based on the partial cue of the A stimulus and the context.

Each epoch of training consists of the 10 list items from either the AB or the AC list. There were five initial epochs of training to learn the AB list to 100% accuracy, and then five more epochs to subsequently learn the AC list to 100% accuracy. The network's performance can be measured in terms of how much of the second associate (B or C) is produced in response to an input of the first associate (A) and context during testing. O'Reilly & Munakata (2000) measured this in terms of two variables: stim_err_on and stim_err_off. stim_err_on measures the proportion of units that were erroneously activated in EC_out (i.e. active but not present in the target associate pattern), and stim_err_off measures the proportion of units that were erroneously *not* activated in EC_out (i.e. not active in the network's response, but present in the target pattern). When both of these measures are near zero, then the network has correctly recalled the target associate pattern. A large stim_err_on indicates that the network has *confabulated* or otherwise recalled a different pattern than the cued one. This is relatively rare in the model (O'Reilly et al., 1998). A large stim_err_off indicates that the network has failed to recall much of the probe pattern. This is common, especially for untrained patterns.

Fig. 5.10 shows a plot like those shown previously (Figs 5.1, 5.8), graphing testing performance on the originally-learned AB list items as the network learns the AC list. As this figure makes clear, this hippocampal network model can rapidly learn new information without suffering extensive amounts of interference on previously learned information.

If you were to observe the network as it is tested on the testing items (missing the second associate), you would see the EC_in layer initially activated by the first associate and the list context. Then, this activation flows up to the CA3 layer, where pattern completion via recurrent collaterals and feedforward projections results in the activation of the original, complete CA3 representation for this item as developed during training. This completed CA3 representation then activates the CA1 representation via learned associations, and the CA1 can then fill in the missing parts of the EC_out

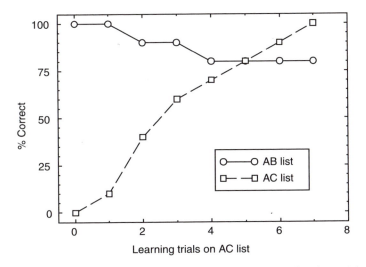

Figure 5.10. Results in the hippocampal model of training on the AC list after training on the AB list. Testing performance on the AB items decreases due to interference as the AC list is learned, but this interference is by no means catastrophic.

pattern. In addition to the "inner loop" of CA3 pattern completion, there is an "outer loop" of pattern completion that occurs through partial EC_out activation feeding back into EC_in and then back up through the hippo-campal system again.

We can obtain additional insight into the hippocampus by observing the model's responses to novel (unstudied) items. To do this, we also tested the network on a set of novel *lure* items in addition to the AB and AC list items. Fig. 5.11 shows testing results on AB items and lure items, with the stim_err_on plotted on the *y* axis against stim_err_off on the *x* axis. Each event shows up as a dot at a particular location. To the extent that these dots are in the lower left-hand corner, the network is recalling accurately. You can see that the trained items produce low amounts of both types of error, and the lures produce high amounts of off-errors (i.e. they simply fail to activate units). This very sharp separation between trained items and lures has important implications for the performance of the hippocampus in memory tests, and is substantiated by analyses of behavioral data (see O'Reilly et al., 1998, for more discussion).

Summary and discussion

The O'Reilly & Munakata (2000) model demonstrates that the unique bio-logical properties of the hippocampus can lead to rapid learning of list items while minimizing interference effects. Because the hippocampal system employs sparse representations, it encodes the list items with highly

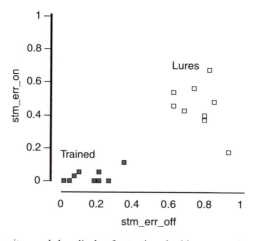

Figure 5.11. Composite graph log display for testing the hippocampal network, showing two kinds of errors—units that should be off but were erroneously on (stm_err_on), and units that should be on but were erroneously off (stm_err_off). The training items have relatively few of both types of errors, and the lure items are mostly inactive (high stm_err_off). Reprinted with permission from O'Reilly & Munakata (2000), MIT Press.

conjunctive, pattern-separated representations. These representations are the key to avoiding interference, as they use different sets of weights to encode items on different lists. In addition to pattern separation, this model demonstrates the crucial, complementary function of pattern completion, which is required to retrieve the previously learned paired associates. We also observed that the network exhibits a very clear separation between trained and novel items, which can be contrasted with a more graded memory signal, as we discuss in a later section. In short, this network behaves much more like the human episodic memory system than the simple cortical network explored previously. This performance supports the idea that the brain needed to develop two complementary learning systems to satisfy the complementary learning objectives of rapid learning of separate events and slow integration across episodes to extract general statistics.

OTHER APPLICATIONS OF THE PRINCIPLES

The principles of complementary cortical and hippocampal learning mechanisms have been applied to a number of different domains, as briefly summarized in the following sections. In most cases, the same neural network model as we have just described was used to simulate the empirical data, providing a compelling demonstration that the principles are sufficient to account for a wide range of findings.

Rapid incidental conjunctive learning tasks

The principles we have outlined clearly suggest that the hippocampus should be most important for tasks that involve the rapid learning of conjunctive information, as is characteristic of human episodic memory. When we encode the events of our daily lives, we do so without expending deliberate effort, and we do so rapidly because these events are by definition fleeting in nature—we need to encode them as they happen. They are also conjunctive in nature, because they bind together all the many elements of an event into a unitary representation that says, "all these things were present at the same time" (e.g. a particular room, furniture, collection of people, actions, etc.).

Fortunately, a number of tasks that capture the *rapid, incidental conjunctive learning* characteristics of the hippocampus have been recently developed in animals. With the use of selective hippocampal lesions in these tasks, experimenters have confirmed that the hippocampus is critical for this function. In these tasks, subjects are exposed to a set of features in a particular configuration, and then the features are rearranged. Subjects are then tested to determine whether they can detect the rearrangement. If the test indicates that the rearrangement was detected, then one can infer that the subject learned a conjunctive representation of the original configuration.

Perhaps the simplest demonstration comes from the study of the role of the hippocampal formation in exploratory behavior. Control rats and rats with damage to the dorsal hippocampus were repeatedly exposed to a set of objects that were arranged on a circular platform in a fixed configuration relative to a large and distinct visual cue (Save, Poucet, Foreman, & Buhot, 1992). After the exploratory behavior of both sets of rats habituated, the same objects were rearranged into a different configuration. This rearrangement reinstated exploratory behavior in the control rats but not in the rats with damage to the hippocampus. In a third phase of the study, a new object was introduced into the mix. This manipulation reinstated exploratory behavior in both sets of rats. This pattern of data suggests that both control rats and rats with damage to the hippocampus encode representations of the individual objects and can discriminate them from novel objects. However, only the control rats encoded the conjunctions necessary to represent the spatial arrangement of the objects, even though this was not in any way a requirement of the task. Several other studies of this general form have found similar results in rats (Good & Bannerman, 1997; Hall & Honey, 1990; Honey & Good, 1993; Honey, Watt, & Good, 1998; Honey, Willis, & Hall, 1990). In humans, the well-established incidental context effects on memory (e.g. Godden & Baddeley, 1975) have been shown to be hippocampus-dependent (Mayes, MacDonald, Donlan, & Pears, 1992). Other hippocampal incidental conjunctive learning effects have also been demonstrated in humans (Chun & Phelps, 1999).

We have shown that the same neural network model constructed according to our principles and tested on the AB–AC task, as described above, exhibits a clear hippocampal sensitivity in these rapid incidental conjunctive learning tasks (O'Reilly & Rudy, 2001). By extension, we therefore believe that the model accounts for the involvement of the hippocampus in episodic memory in humans.

Contextual fear conditioning

Evidence for the involvement of the hippocampal formation in the incidental learning of stimulus conjunctions has also emerged in the contextual fear conditioning literature. This example also provides a simple example of the widely discussed role of the hippocampus in spatial learning (e.g. McNaughton & Nadel, 1990; O'Keefe & Nadel, 1978). Rats with damage to the hippocampal formation do not express fear to a context or place where shock occurred, but will express fear to an explicit cue (e.g. a tone) paired with shock (Kim & Fanselow, 1992; Phillips & LeDoux, 1994; but see Maren, Aharonov, & Fanselow, 1997). Rudy & O'Reilly (1999) recently provided specific evidence that, in intact rats, the context representations are conjunctive in nature, which has been widely assumed (e.g. Fanselow, 1990;

Kiernan & Westbrook, 1993; Rudy & Sutherland, 1994). For example, we compared the effects of preexposure to the conditioning context with the effects of preexposure to the separate features that made up the context. Only preexposure to the intact context facilitated contextual fear conditioning, suggesting that conjunctive representations across the context features were necessary. We also showed that pattern completion of hippocampal conjunctive representations can lead to generalized fear conditioning. Furthermore, a recent study showed that rats can condition to a *memory* of a context, while they are actually located in a novel environment (Rudy & O'Reilly, 2001). The memory is activated via pattern completion from a bucket that was reliably associated with the context during preexposure.

We have simulated the incidental learning of conjunctive context representations in fear conditioning using the same principles as described above (O'Reilly & Rudy, 2001). For example, Fig. 5.12 shows the rat and model data for the separate vs. intact context features experiment from Rudy & O'Reilly (1999), with the model providing a specific prediction regarding the effects of hippocampal lesions, which has yet to be tested empirically.

Conjunctions and nonlinear discrimination learning

One important application of the conjunctive representations idea has been to *nonlinear discrimination problems*. These problems require conjunctive representations to solve because each of the individual stimuli is ambiguous (equally often rewarded and not rewarded). The negative patterning problem is a good example. It involves two stimuli, A and B (e.g. a light and a tone), which are associated with reward (indicated by +) or not (−). Three different trial types are trained: A+, B+, and AB−. Thus, the conjunction of the two stimuli (AB) must be treated differently from the two stimuli separately (A+, B+). A conjunctive representation that forms a novel encoding of the two stimuli together can facilitate this form of learning. Therefore, the fact that hippocampal damage impairs learning the negative patterning problem (Alvarado & Rudy, 1995; McDonald, Murphy, Guarraci, Gortler, White, & Baker, 1997; Rudy & Sutherland, 1995) would appear to support the idea that the hippocampus employs pattern-separated, conjunctive representations. However, it is now clear that a number of other nonlinear discrimination learning problems are unimpaired by hippocampal damage (Rudy & Sutherland, 1995).

The general explanation of these results according to the full set of principles outlined above is that:

- The explicit task demands present in a nonlinear discrimination learning problem cause the cortex alone (with a lesioned hippocampus) to learn the task via error-driven learning.

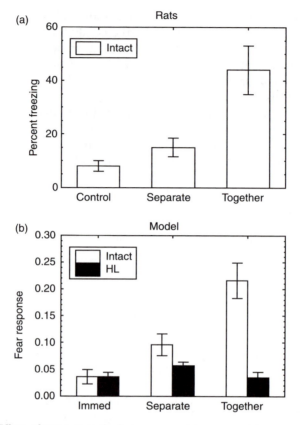

Figure 5.12. Effects of exposure to the features separately compared to exposure to the entire context on level of fear response in (a) rats (data from Rudy & O'Reilly, 1999) and (b) the model (from O'Reilly & Rudy 2001). The immediate shock condition (Immed) is included as a control condition for the model. Intact rats and the intact model show a significant effect of being exposed to the entire context together, compared to the features separately, while the hippocampally lesioned model exhibits slightly more responding in the separate condition, possibly because of the greater overall number of training trials in this case.

- Nonlinear discrimination problems take many trials to learn, even in intact animals, allowing the slow cortical learning to accumulate a solution.
- The absence of hippocampal learning speed advantages in normal rats, despite the more rapid hippocampal learning rate, can be explained by the fact that the hippocampus is engaging in pattern completion in these problems, instead of pattern separation.

We have substantiated this verbal account by running computational neural network simulations that embodied the principles developed above

(O'Reilly & Rudy, 2001). These simulations showed that in many, but not all, cases, removing the hippocampal component did not significantly impair learning performance on nonlinear discrimination learning problems, matching the empirical data. To summarize, this work showed that it is essential to go beyond a simple conjunctive story and include a more complete set of principles in understanding hippocampal and cortical function. Because this more complete set of principles, implemented in an explicit computational model, accounts for the empirical data, this data provides support for these principles.

Dual-process memory models

The dual mechanisms of neocortex and hippocampus provide a natural fit with dual-process models of recognition memory (Aggleton & Brown, 1999; Aggleton & Shaw, 1996; Holdstock, Mayes, Roberts, Cezayirli, Isaac, O'Reilly, & Norman, 2002; Jacoby, Yonelinas, & Jennings, 1997; Norman & O'Reilly, in press; O'Reilly et al., 1998; Vargha-Khadem, Gadian, Watkins, Connelly, Van Paesschen, & Mishkin, 1997). These models hold that recognition can be subserved by two different processes, a *recollection* process and a *familiarity* process. Recollection involves the recall of specific episodic details about the item, and thus fits well with the hippocampal principles developed here. Indeed, we have simulated distinctive aspects of recollection using essentially the same model (Norman & O'Reilly, in press; O'Reilly et al., 1998). Familiarity is a nonspecific sense that the item has been seen recently—we argue that this can be subserved by the small weight changes produced by slow cortical learning. Current simulation work has shown that a simple cortical model can account for a number of distinctive properties of the familiarity signal (Norman & O'Reilly, in press).

One specific and somewhat counter-intuitive prediction of our principles has recently been confirmed empirically in experiments on a patient with selective hippocampal damage (Holdstock et al., 2002). This patient showed intact recognition memory for studied items compared to similar lures when tested in a two-alternative forced-choice procedure (2AFC), but was significantly impaired relative to controls for the same kinds of stimuli using a single-item, yes–no (YN) procedure. We argue that because the cortex uses overlapping distributed representations, the strong similarity of the lures to the studied items produces a strong familiarity signal for these lures (as a function of this overlap). When tested in a YN procedure, this strong familiarity of the lures produces a large number of false alarms, as was observed in the patient. However, because the studied item has a small but reliably stronger familiarity signal than the similar lure, this strength difference can be detected in the 2AFC version, resulting in normal recognition performance in this condition. The normal controls, in contrast, have an intact hippocampus, which performs pattern separation and is able to distinguish the studied items and similar lures regardless of the testing format.

COMPARISON WITH OTHER APPROACHES

A number of other approaches to understanding cortical and hippocampal function share important similarities with our approach, including for example the use of Hebbian learning and pattern separation (e.g. Alvarez & Squire, 1994; Burgess & O'Keefe, 1996; Hasselmo, 1995; McNaughton & Nadel, 1990; Moll & Miikkulainen, 1997; Touretzky & Redish, 1996; Treves & Rolls, 1994; Wu, Baxter, & Levy, 1996). These other approaches all offer other important principles, many of which would be complementary to those discussed here so that it would be possible to add them to a larger, more complete model.

Perhaps the largest area of disagreement is in terms of the relative independence of the cortical learning mechanisms from the hippocampus. There are several computationally explicit models that propose that the neocortex is incapable of powerful learning without the help of the hippocampus (Gluck & Myers, 1993; Rolls, 1990; Schmajuk & DiCarlo, 1992), and other more general theoretical views that express a similar notion of limited cortical learning with hippocampal damage (Cohen & Eichenbaum, 1993; Glisky, Schacter, & Tulving, 1986; Squire, 1992; Sutherland & Rudy, 1989; Wickelgren, 1979). In contrast, our principles hold that the cortex alone is a highly capable learning system that can, for example, learn complex conjunctive representations in the service of nonlinear discrimination learning problems. We think the growing literature on preserved learning with focal hippocampal damage supports the idea that the cortex by itself is a powerful learning system.

SUMMARY

We have shown that a small set of computationally motivated principles can account for a wide range of empirical findings regarding the differential properties of the neocortex and hippocampus in learning and memory. These principles go beyond accounting for data by providing clear reasons why the brain has the specialized areas that it does, and what the mechanistic differences are between these areas.

ACKNOWLEDGEMENTS

Supported by ONR Grants N00014-00-1-0246 and N00014-03-1-0428, and NIH Grants MH061316-01 and MH64445.

REFERENCES

Aggleton, J. P., & Brown, M. W. (1999). Episodic memory, amnesia, and the hippocampal–anterior thalamic axis. *Behavioral and Brain Sciences, 22,* 425–490.

Aggleton, J. P., & Shaw, C. (1996). Amnesia and recognition memory: A re-analysis of psychometric data. *Neuropsychologia, 34,* 51–62.

Alvarado, M. C., & Rudy, J. W. (1995). A comparison of kainic acid plus colchicine and ibotenic acid induced hippocampal formation damage on four configural tasks in rats. *Behavioral Neuroscience, 109,* 1052–1062.

Alvarez, P., & Squire, L. R. (1994). Memory consolidation and the medial temporal lobe: A simple network model. *Proceedings of the National Academy of Sciences, USA, 91,* 7041–7045.

Barnes, C. A., McNaughton, B. L., Mizumori, S. J. Y., Leonard, B. W., & Lin, L.-H. (1990). Comparison of spatial and temporal characteristics of neuronal activity in sequential stages of hippocampal processing. *Progress in Brain Research, 83,* 287–300.

Barnes, J. M., & Underwood, B. J. (1959). Fate of first-list associations in transfer theory. *Journal of Experimental Psychology, 58,* 97–105.

Boss, B. D., Peterson, G. M., & Cowan, W. M. (1985). On the numbers of neurons in the dentate gyrus of the rat. *Brain Research, 338,* 144–150.

Boss, B. D., Turlejski, K., Stanfield, B. B., & Cowan, W. M. (1987). On the numbers of neurons in fields CA1 and CA3 of the hippocampus of Sprague–Dawley and Wistar rats. *Brain Research, 406,* 280–287.

Burgess, N., & O'Keefe, J. (1996). Neuronal computations underlying the firing of place cells and their role in navigation. *Hippocampus, 6,* 749–762.

Chun, M. M., & Phelps, E. A. (1999). Memory deficits for implicit contextual information in amnesic subjects with hippocampal damage. *Nature Neuroscience, 2*(9), 844–847.

Cohen, N. J., & Eichenbaum, H. (1993). *Memory, amnesia, and the hippocampal system.* Cambridge, MA: MIT Press.

Collingridge, G. L., & Bliss, T. V. P. (1987). NMDA receptors—their role in long-term potentiation. *Trends in Neurosciences, 10,* 288–293.

Crick, F. H. C. (1989). The recent excitement about neural networks. *Nature, 337,* 129–132.

Fanselow, M. S. (1990). Factors governing one-trial contextual conditioning. *Animal Learning and Behavior, 18,* 264–270.

French, R. M. (1992). Semi-distributed representations and catastrophic forgetting in connectionist networks. *Connection Science, 4,* 365–377.

Glisky, E. L., Schacter, D. L., & Tulving, E. (1986). Computer learning by memory-impaired patients: Acquisition and retention of complex knowledge. *Neuropsychologia, 24,* 313–328.

Gluck, M. A., & Myers, C. E. (1993). Hippocampal mediation of stimulus representation: A computational theory. *Hippocampus, 3,* 491–516.

Godden, D. R., & Baddeley, A. D. (1975). Context-dependent memory in two natural environments: On land and under water. *British Journal of Psychology, 66,* 325–331.

Good, M., & Bannerman, D. (1997). Differential effects of ibotenic acid lesions of the hippocampus and blockade of n-methyl-D-aspartate receptor-dependent long-term potentiation on contextual processing in rats. *Behavioral Neuroscience, 111,* 1171–1183.

Hall, G., & Honey, R. C. (1990). Context-specific conditioning in the conditioned-emotional-response procedure. *Journal of Experimental Psychology: Animal Behavior Processes, 16,* 271–278.

Hasselmo, M. E. (1995). Neuromodulation and cortical function: Modeling the physiological basis of behavior. *Behavioural Brain Research, 67,* 1–27.

Hasselmo, M. E., & Wyble, B. (1997). Free recall and recognition in a network model of the hippocampus: Simulating effects of scopolamine on human memory function. *Behavioural Brain Research, 89,* 1–34.

Hebb, D. O. (1949). *The organization of behavior*. New York: Wiley.

Holdstock, J. S., Mayes, A. R., Roberts, N., Cezayirli, E., Isaac, C. L., O'Reilly, R. C., & Norman, K. A. (2002). Under what conditions is recognition spared relative to recall after selective hippocampal damage in humans? *Hippocampus, 12,* 341–351.

Honey, R. C., & Good, M. (1993). Selective hippocampal lesions abolish the contextual specificity of latent inhibition and conditioning. *Behavioral Neuroscience, 107,* 23–33.

Honey, R. C., Watt, A., & Good, M. (1998). Hippocampal lesions disrupt an associative mismatch process. *Journal of Neuroscience, 18,* 2226–2230.

Honey, R. C., Willis, A., & Hall, G. (1990). Context specificity in pigeon autoshaping. *Learning and Motivation, 21,* 125–136.

Jacoby, L. L., Yonelinas, A. P., & Jennings, J. M. (1997). The relation between conscious and unconscious (automatic) influences: A declaration of independence. In J. D. Cohen, & J. W. Schooler (Eds.), *Scientific approaches to consciousness* (pp. 13–47). Mahwah, NJ: Lawrence Erlbaum Associates, Inc.

Kiernan, M. J., & Westbrook, R. F. (1993). Effects of exposure to a to-be-shocked environment upon the rat's freezing response: Evidence for facilitation, latent inhibition, and perceptual learning. *Quarterly Journal of Psychology, 46B,* 271–288.

Kim, J. J., & Fanselow, M. S. (1992). Modality-specific retrograde amnesia of fear. *Science, 256,* 675–677.

Kortge, C. A. (1993). Episodic memory in connectionist networks. *Proceedings of the Twelfth Annual Conference of the Cognitive Science Society* (pp. 764–771). Hillsdale, NJ: Lawrence Erlbaum Associates, Inc.

Maren, S., Aharonov, G., & Fanselow, M. S. (1997). Neurotoxic lesions of the dorsal hippocampus and Pavlovian fear conditioning. *Behavioural Brain Research, 88,* 261–274.

Marr, D. (1969). A theory of cerebellar cortex. *Journal of Physiology (London), 202,* 437–470.

Marr, D. (1970). A theory for cerebral neocortex. *Proceedings of the Royal Society (London) B, 176,* 161–234.

Marr, D. (1971). Simple memory: A theory for archicortex. *Philosophical Transactions of the Royal Society (London) B, 262,* 23–81.

Mayes, A. R., MacDonald, C., Donlan, L., & Pears, J. (1992). Amnesics have a disproportionately severe memory deficit for interactive context. *Quarterly Journal of Experimental Psychology, 45A,* 265–297.

McClelland, J. L., & Goddard, N. H. (1996). Considerations arising from a complementary learning systems perspective on hippocampus and neocortex. *Hippocampus, 6,* 654–665.

McClelland, J. L., McNaughton, B. L., & O'Reilly, R. C. (1995). Why there are complementary learning systems in the hippocampus and neocortex: Insights from the successes and failures of connectionist models of learning and memory. *Psychological Review, 102,* 419–457.

McCloskey, M., & Cohen, N. J. (1989). Catastrophic interference in connectionist networks: The sequential learning problem. In G. H. Bower (Ed.), *The psychology of learning and motivation* (Vol. 24, pp. 109–164). San Diego, CA: Academic Press.

McDonald, R. J., Murphy, R. A., Guarraci, F. A., Gortler, J. R., White, N. M., & Baker, A. G. (1997). Systematic comparison of the effects of hippocampal and fornix-fimbria lesions on the acquisition of three configural discriminations. *Hippocampus, 7,* 371–388.

McNaughton, B. L., & Morris, R. G. M. (1987). Hippocampal synaptic enhancement and information storage within a distributed memory system. *Trends in Neurosciences, 10*(10), 408–415.

McNaughton, B. L., & Nadel, L. (1990). Hebb–Marr networks and the neurobiological representation of action in space. In M. A. Gluck, & D. E. Rumelhart (Eds.), *Neuroscience and connectionist theory* (Chap. 1, pp. 1–63). Hillsdale, NJ: Lawrence Erlbaum Associates, Inc.

McRae, K., & Hetherington, P. A. (1993). Catastrophic interference is eliminated in pretrained networks. *Proceedings of the Fifteenth Annual Conference of the Cognitive Science Society* (pp. 723–728). Hillsdale, NJ: Lawrence Erlbaum Associates, Inc.

Moll, M., & Miikkulainen, R. (1997). Convergence-zone episodic memory: Analysis and simulations. *Neural Networks, 10,* 1017–1036.

Norman, K. A., & O'Reilly, R. C. (in press). Modeling hippocampal and neocortical contributions to recognition memory: A complementary learning systems approach. *Psychological Review.*

O'Keefe, J., & Nadel, L. (1978). *The hippocampus as a cognitive map.* Oxford, UK: Oxford University Press.

O'Reilly, R. C. (1996). Biologically plausible error-driven learning using local activation differences: The generalized recirculation algorithm. *Neural Computation, 8*(5), 895–938.

O'Reilly, R. C. (1998). Six principles for biologically-based computational models of cortical cognition. *Trends in Cognitive Sciences, 2*(11), 455–462.

O'Reilly, R. C. (2001). Generalization in interactive networks: The benefits of inhibitory competition and Hebbian learning. *Neural Computation, 13,* 1199–1242.

O'Reilly, R. C., & McClelland, J. L. (1994). Hippocampal conjunctive encoding, storage, and recall: Avoiding a trade-off. *Hippocampus, 4*(6), 661–682.

O'Reilly, R. C., & Munakata, Y. (2000). *Computational explorations in cognitive neuroscience: Understanding the mind by simulating the brain.* Cambridge, MA: MIT Press.

O'Reilly, R. C., & Norman, K. A. (2002). Hippocampal and neocortical contributions to memory: Advances in the complementary learning systems framework. *Trends in Cognitive Sciences, 6,* 505–510.

O'Reilly, R. C., Norman, K. A., & McClelland, J. L. (1998). A hippocampal model of recognition memory. In M. I. Jordan, M. J. Kearns, & S. A. Solla (Eds.), *Advances in neural information processing systems 10* (pp. 73–79). Cambridge, MA: MIT Press.

O'Reilly, R. C., & Rudy, J. W. (2000). Computational principles of learning in the neocortex and hippocampus. *Hippocampus, 10,* 389–397.

O'Reilly, R. C., & Rudy, J. W. (2001). Conjunctive representations in learning and memory: Principles of cortical and hippocampal function. *Psychological Review, 108,* 311–345.

Phillips, R. G., & LeDoux, J. E. (1994). Lesions of the dorsal hippocampal formation interfere with background but not foreground contextual fear conditioning. *Learning and Memory, 1,* 34–44.

Rolls, E. T. (1990). Principles underlying the representation and storage of information in neuronal networks in the primate hippocampus and cerebral cortex. In S. F. Zornetzer, J. L. Davis, & C. Lau (Eds.), *An introduction to neural and electronic networks* (pp. 73–90). San Diego, CA: Academic Press.

Rudy, J. W., & O'Reilly, R. C. (1999). Contextual fear conditioning, conjunctive representations, pattern completion, and the hippocampus. *Behavioral Neuroscience, 113,* 867–880.

Rudy, J. W., & O'Reilly, R. C. (2001). Conjunctive representations, the hippocampus, and contextual fear conditioning. *Cognitive, Affective, and Behavioral Neuroscience, 1,* 66–82.

Rudy, J. W., & Sutherland, R. J. (1994). The memory coherence problem, configural associations, and the hippocampal system. In D. L. Schacter, & E. Tulving (Eds.), *Memory systems 1994* (pp. 119–146). Cambridge, MA: MIT Press.

Rudy, J. W., & Sutherland, R. J. (1995). Configural association theory and the hippocampal formation: An appraisal and reconfiguration. *Hippocampus, 5,* 375–389.

Rumelhart, D. E., Hinton, G. E., & Williams, R. J. (1986). Learning representations by back-propagating errors. *Nature, 323,* 533–536.

Save, E., Poucet, B., Foreman, N., & Buhot, N. (1992). Object exploration and reactions to spatial and nonspatial changes in hooded rats following damage to parietal cortex or hippocampal formation. *Behavioral Neuroscience, 106,* 447–456.

Schmajuk, N. A., & DiCarlo, J. J. (1992). Stimulus configuration, classical conditioning, and hippocampal function. *Psychological Review, 99*(2), 268–305.

Sherry, D. F., & Schacter, D. L. (1987). The evolution of multiple memory systems. *Psychological Review, 94*(4), 439–454.

Sloman, S. A., & Rumelhart, D. E. (1992). Reducing interference in distributed memories through episodic gating. In A. Healy, S. Kosslyn, & R. Shiffrin (Eds.), *Essays in honor of W. K. Estes* (pp. 227–248). Hillsdale, NJ: Lawrence Erlbaum Associates, Inc.

Squire, L. R. (1992). Memory and the hippocampus: A synthesis from findings with rats, monkeys, and humans. *Psychological Review, 99*, 195–231.

Squire, L. R., Shimamura, A. P., & Amaral, D. G. (1989). Memory and the hippocampus. In J. H. Byrne, & W. O. Berry (Eds.), *Neural models of plasticity: Experimental and theoretical approaches* (pp. 208–239). San Diego, CA: Academic Press.

Sutherland, R. J., & Rudy, J. W. (1989). Configural association theory: The role of the hippocampal formation in learning, memory, and amnesia. *Psychobiology, 17*(2), 129–144.

Tamamaki, N. (1991). The organization of reciprocal connections between the subiculum, field CA1 and the entorhinal cortex in the rat. *Society for Neuroscience Abstracts, 17*, 134.

Touretzky, D. S., & Redish, A. D. (1996). A theory of rodent navigation based on interacting representations of space. *Hippocampus, 6*, 247–270.

Treves, A., & Rolls, E. T. (1994). A computational analysis of the role of the hippocampus in memory. *Hippocampus, 4*, 374–392.

Vargha-Khadem, F., Gadian, D. G., Watkins, K. E., Connelly, A., Van Paesschen, W., & Mishkin, M. (1997). Differential effects of early hippocampal pathology on episodic and semantic memory. *Science, 277*, 376–380.

White, H. (1989). Learning in artificial neural networks: A statistical perspective. *Neural Computation, 1*, 425–464.

Wickelgren, W. A. (1979). Chunking and consolidation: A theoretical synthesis of semantic networks, configuring in conditioning, S–R versus cognitive learning, normal forgetting, the amnesic syndrome, and the hippocampal arousal system. *Psychological Review, 86*, 44–60.

Wu, X., Baxter, R. A., & Levy, W. B. (1996). Context codes and the effect of noisy learning on a simplified hippocampal CA3 model. *Biological Cybernetics, 74*, 159–165.

Zipser, D., & Andersen, R. A. (1988). A backpropagation programmed network that simulates response properties of a subset of posterior parietal neurons. *Nature, 331*, 679–684.

CHAPTER SIX

Category-specific semantic memory impairments: What can connectionist simulations reveal about the organization of conceptual knowledge?

E. Charles Leek
University of Wales, Bangor, UK

INTRODUCTION

Connectionist networks have been used to support far-reaching claims about human cognitive function (Bechtel & Abrahamsen, 1991; Ellis & Humphreys, 1999; Rumelhart & McClelland, 1986; Schneider, 1987; Smolensky, 1988). In this chapter we focus on one particular application of the approach: the use of connectionist networks to simulate the patterns of performance shown by brain-damaged patients with acquired cognitive impairments (e.g. Cohen, Farah, Romero, & Servan-Schreiber, 1994; Devlin, Gonnerman, Andersen, & Seidenberg, 1998; Ellis & Humphreys, 1999; Farah, O'Reilly, & Vecera, 1993; Harley, 1998; Hinton & Shallice, 1991; Humphreys, Freeman, & Muller, 1992; Humphreys, Olson, Romani, & Riddoch, 1996; Mayall & Humphreys, 1996; McLeod, Plunkett, & Rolls, 1998; Mozer & Berhmann, 1990; Olson & Caramazza, 1994; Patterson, Seidenburg, & McClelland, 1989; Plaut & Shallice, 1993; Seidenburg, & McClelland, 1989; Tyler, Moss, Durrant-Peatfield, & Levy, 2000).

Studies of patients with neurological disorders have shown that brain damage does not necessarily result in a generalized deterioration of cognitive function, but can lead to highly selective forms of impairment. The patterns of impaired and preserved abilities that are observed provide constraints on hypotheses about the organization and structure of the cognitive system, and about how the system may be impaired by brain damage (Caramazza, 1986; Shallice, 1988). In so-called connectionist neuropsychology, the aim is to examine specific hypotheses about cognitive function through simulated lesions to neural networks, rather than to real brains. This is achieved by examining the effects of damage to a network that instantiates a particular theoretical claim about some aspect of cognitive processing. Theory evaluation is based on a comparison between the output of the "lesioned" network and behavioural data from actual neuropsychological case studies. One appealing aspect of the technique is that, in principle, it is possible to experimentally control the locus and extent of damage to the system—obviously an option that is not available in human lesion studies! But despite its allure, there is continuing debate about the contribution that connectionist neuropsychology can make to theory development in cognitive science (Besner, Twilley, McCann, & Seergobin, 1990; Coltheart, Curtis, Atkins, & Haller, 1993; Fodor & Pylyshyn, 1988; Lamberts & d'Ydewalle, 1990; Massaro, 1988; McCloskey, 1991; Olson & Caramazza, 1994; Olson & Humphreys, 1997; Pinker & Prince, 1988). Much of this debate has taken place in the context of connectionist simulations of language acquisition and disorders of reading and writing (e.g. Patterson et al., 1989; Plaut & Shallice, 1993; Seidenberg & McClelland, 1989). However, the issues that have been raised also have far-reaching implications for the evaluation of connectionist simulations in other domains.

In this chapter we will consider some types of connectionist networks, and their use in simulations of category-specific semantic memory disorders in neurological populations. The chapter is organized as follows. First, we briefly review some of the evidence from neuropsychological studies of patients with category-specific impairments. Second, we critically examine in some detail one attempt to simulate these disorders by lesioning a connectionist network. Third, we discuss some of the ways in which network simulations of category-specific deficits may contribute to the future development of theories of knowledge representation.

NEUROPSYCHOLOGICAL STUDIES OF SEMANTIC MEMORY IMPAIRMENTS

Category-specific deficits for living things

Some of the most remarkable forms of acquired cognitive impairments are those that result in the apparent loss of knowledge about specific categories of objects (for reviews, see Caramazza, Hillis, Leek, & Miozzo, 1994; Forde & Humphreys, 1999; Forde & Humphreys, 2002; Saffran & Schwartz, 1994; Shelton & Caramazza, 1999). Although several early cases are described in the literature (e.g. Dennis, 1976; Neilsen, 1946; Yamadori & Albert, 1973), one of the first detailed study of semantic category-specific impairment was reported by Warrington & Shallice (1984). They described the cases of four patients who had sustained brain damage as a result of a herpes simplex viral infection. The most striking finding was in two patients (JBR and SBY) who were impaired in producing and understanding the names of objects. Remarkably, their difficulties did not extend equally to all classes of objects, but were more pronounced for some categories than others. Both patients performed poorly in naming and defining objects from the biological or living categories of animals, vegetables and fruits, but performed relatively well with nonliving things (or artefacts), such as kitchen items, furniture, tools, and clothing. For example, one of the patients, JBR, accurately named or defined 45/48 (94%) of nonliving things, but only 2/48 (4%) of living things. SBY showed a similar pattern of performance.

Several other apparent cases of disproportionate impairment for biological kinds (or living things) have since been described in patients with varying brain pathologies (stroke, head trauma, viral infection, and degenerative disease), and in studies employing a variety of different behavioural tasks and stimulus materials (e.g. Basso, Capitani, & Laiacona, 1988; Caramazza & Shelton, 1998; Damasio, Grabowski, Tranel, Hichwa, & Damasio, 1996; De Renzi & Lucchelli, 1994; Farah, Hammond, Mehta, & Ratcliff, 1989; Farah, McMullen, & Meyer, 1991; Gainotti & Silveri, 1996; Hart & Gordon, 1992; Hillis & Caramazza, 1991; Kolinsky, Fery, Messina, Peretz, Evinck, Ventura, & Morais, 2002; Laiacona, Barbarotto, & Capitani, 1993; Laiacona, Capitani, & Barbarotto, 1997; McCarthy & Warrington, 1988; Moss, Tyler, Durrant-Peatfield, & Bunn, 1998; Moss, Tyler, & Jennings, 1997; Pietrini, Nertempi, Vaglia, Revello, Pinna, & Ferro-Milone, 1988; Samson, Pillon, & De Wilde, 1998; Sheridan & Humphreys, 1993; Silveri, Daniele, Giustolisi, & Gainotti, 1991; Silveri & Gainotti, 1988; Sirigu, Duhamel, & Poncet, 1991).

Category-specific deficits as artefacts of stimulus variables

Despite the striking nature of these impairments, their theoretical significance has remained the subject of controversy. Several authors have argued that these cases do not, in fact, reflect a genuine category-specific impairment, but rather arise because of confounding factors (Forde, Francis, Riddoch, Rumiati, & Humphreys, 1997; Funnell & Sheridan, 1992; Gaffan & Heywood, 1993; Stewart, Parkin, & Hunkin, 1992). For example, Funnell & Sheridan (1992) presented the case study of a 20 year-old woman, SL, who had suffered right hemisphere brain damage as a result of a car accident and subsequent craniotomy. SL was shown to perform significantly better at naming pictures of living things than nonliving things. However, in a subsequent experiment, when SL had to name a further set of 48 pictures of objects that had been matched across categories in terms of word frequency, familiarity and visual complexity, the category effect went away: SL performed poorly in naming low-familiarity items, regardless of whether they were living or non-living things. Similarly, Stewart et al. (1992) reported the case study of a patient, HO, who, like the patients described by Warrington & Shallice (1984), had suffered brain damage as a result of herpes simplex encephalitis. HO also showed a category effect in picture naming (65% correct for living things, and 86% correct for nonliving). However, in subsequent testing, HO's apparent disproportionate impairment for living things resolved when he was tested on another set of stimulus materials that had been matched for word frequency, familiarity, and visual complexity. On the basis of this evidence, it has been argued that apparent category-specific impairments for living things arise solely because objects from biological categories tend to be more visually complex, and less familiar, than artefacts (Forde et al., 1997; Gaffan & Heywood, 1993).

THE CASE AGAINST THE ARTEFACT HYPOTHESIS

Although these studies suggest that the failure to adequately control relevant stimulus variables may account for some reported cases of apparent selective impairment for living things, there is other evidence that not all category-specific deficits can be accounted for in this way.

Category effects across equated stimulus materials

One source of evidence comes from case reports showing that the disproportionate difficulty for living things that is observed in some patients holds up even when stimulus variables, such as word frequency, visual complexity, and familiarity, are equated across categories (Caramazza & Shelton, 1998; Farah, Meyer, & McMullen, 1996; Funnell & De Mornay Davies, 1997; Gainotti & Silveri, 1996; Hart & Gordon, 1992; Kurbat, 1997; Laiacona, Barbarotto, & Capitani, 1993; Sartori, Miozzo, & Job, 1993, Sheridan & Humphreys, 1993). For example, in one study, Funnell & De Mornay Davis (1997) retested JBR, the patient originally reported by Warrington & Shallice (1984). When JBR was asked to name sets of pictures of living and nonliving things that had been matched for familiarity and word frequency, his impairment for living things remained, at least for low-familiarity items.

The double dissociation: Selective impairments for nonliving things

Perhaps the strongest evidence that category-specific impairments can reflect genuine effects of semantic category comes from case reports of patients who show the contrasting pattern of performance, i.e. a disproportionate impairment with nonliving relative to living things. One of the clearest demonstrations of this double dissociation comes from two patients reported by Hillis & Caramazza (1991). PS was a 45 year-old president of a small business who suffered a closed head injury following a blow to the head. This resulted in damage to the left and right temporal lobes as well as to the right frontal cortex. The other patient, JJ, was a 67 year-old former business executive who had suffered a stroke, resulting in damage to the left temporal cortex and basal ganglia. Both patients showed evidence of category-specific impairment on a variety of experimental tasks. The contrasting nature of their deficits is most clearly shown in picture naming, where both patients were tested using the same stimulus materials (see Fig. 6.1).

PS is most severely impaired in naming animals, birds, vegetables, and fruits, while he performs reasonable well in naming foods, body parts, clothing, transportation, and furniture. In contrast, JJ is very good at naming animals and birds but relatively poor with foods, body parts, clothing, and furniture. The contrasting category-specific deficits shown by these patients were not restricted to language production tasks, but were also evident in comprehension. For example, JJ and PS showed contrasting patterns of performance in word–picture matching, and in providing verbal definitions of objects in response to their spoken names. Although disproportionate impairments for living things have been more frequently reported in the neuropsychological literature than the reverse dissociation, JJ is not the only patient to show the contrasting pattern of performance. Several other cases have also been reported (e.g. Cappa, Frugoni, Pasquali, Perani, & Zorat, 1998; Gonnerman, Andersen, Devlin, Kempler, & Seidenburg, 1997; Lambon-Ralph, Howard, Nightingale, & Ellis, 1998; Moss & Tyler, 2000;

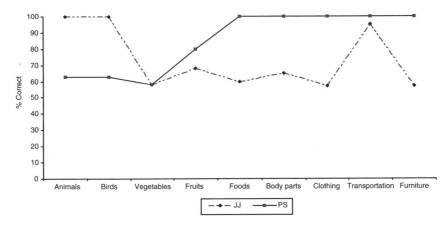

Figure 6.1. The spoken picture-naming performance (percentage correct) of the patients JJ and PS (Hillis & Caramazza, 1991) at 13 months post-onset, as a function of semantic category. After Hillis & Caramazza (1991).

Sacchett & Humphreys, 1992; Warrington & McCarthy, 1983, 1987; Yamadori & Albert, 1973).

These data clearly challenge the hypothesis that category-specific impairments arise solely because of stimulus artifacts: JJ's impairment disproportionately affects objects from categories that have been assumed to be more familiar and less difficult to visually discriminate (Funnell & Sheridan, 1992; Gaffan & Heywood, 1993; Stewart et al., 1992). In contrast, JJ performs relatively well in naming animals and birds, objects that have been assumed to be less familiar and more visually complex.

What is specific about category-specificity?

One further interesting aspect of the empirical data needs to be mentioned. While the apparent disproportionate impairment for living things may be quite striking, there is also evidence, is some patients, that their disorders do not break down neatly in terms of a clear living/nonliving distinction (e.g. Leek & Pothos, 2001; Mahon & Caramazza, 2001; Warrington & McCarthy, 1987). For example, as Fig. 6.1 shows, although JJ was generally worse at naming nonliving than living things, he remained relatively good at naming items from the categories of transportation. In addition, he performed quite poorly in naming fruits and vegetables. In contrast, PS, who was disproportionately impaired at naming living things, had no difficulty naming body parts and foods. Such fractionation among impaired and preserved categories has also been reported in several other cases (e.g. Hillis & Caramazza, 1991; Sacchett & Humphreys, 1992; Warrington & McCarthy, 1987; Warrington & Shallice, 1984). JBR (Warrington & Shallice, 1984), who was disproportionately impaired with living things, was also poor at naming musical instruments, fabrics, and gemstones. There are also some case reports of patients whose deficits are seemingly restricted to particular categories of objects within the living/nonliving distinction (e.g. Dennis, 1976; Farah & Wallace, 1992; Hart, Berndt, & Caramazza, 1985; Shelton, Fouch, & Caramazza, 1998). For example, Hart et al. (1985) described a patient, MD, whose impairment in naming and picture classification tasks was restricted solely to items from the categories of fruits and vegetables. In another case, Shelton et al. (1998) have reported a patient with an apparent selective sparing of knowledge for body parts. These observations undermine a characterization of the data from category-specific impairments in terms of a clean living/nonliving distinction (e.g. Leek & Pothos, 2001; Mahon & Caramazza, 2001; Warrington & McCarthy, 1987).

IMPLICATIONS FOR THEORIES OF SEMANTIC MEMORY

We have briefly reviewed some of the main findings from studies of brain-damaged patients with apparent category-specific impairments. While some cases may be explained in terms of confounding variables, this possibility cannot account for all of the behavioural data. The existence of a double dissociation, and of cases of category-specific impairment across controlled sets of stimulus materials, suggests that these deficits can reflect genuine effects of semantic category. Furthermore, although there is evidence that some patients show a disproportionate impairment with living relative to nonliving things (and vice versa), category-specific impairments do not always break down neatly in terms of a strict living/nonliving distinction. One question that can be asked is how conceptual knowledge is represented in the brain, such that damage leads to the specific patterns of impaired and preserved performance that is found in these patients.

Semantic memory as a structured feature network

One widely held assumption is that mental representations of conceptual knowledge consist of structured networks of semantic features or attributes. This assumption has been used to account for a range of empirical observations about concept acquisition, categorization, prototypicality judgements, and attribute verification in normal subjects (e.g. Collins & Loftus, 1975; Collins & Quillian, 1969, Jackendoff, 1990; McRae, de Sa, & Seidenberg, 1997; Rips, Shoben, & Smith, 1973; Rosch & Mervis, 1975; Tversky, 1977). However, few models concerning the organization of conceptual knowledge make explicit claims about the ways in which semantic memory can be impaired following brain damage. We will consider two general hypotheses that have been discussed in the literature on category-specific impairments.

The taxonomic categories hypothesis

According to the taxonomic categories hypothesis, conceptual knowledge belonging to different semantic categories is encoded in functionally and neuroanatomically distinct structures (e.g. Caramazza & Shelton, 1998; Santos & Caramazza, 2002). The hypothesis is schematically illustrated in Fig. 6.2(a), in the context of a general model of some of the processes involved in picture naming. On this account, taxonomic distinctions among categories are a first-order organizational principle of semantic memory, and of the way that semantic representations are encoded in the brain.

For example, conceptual knowledge about living things may be stored in one functionally distinct system of representations, and knowledge about

(a)   (b)

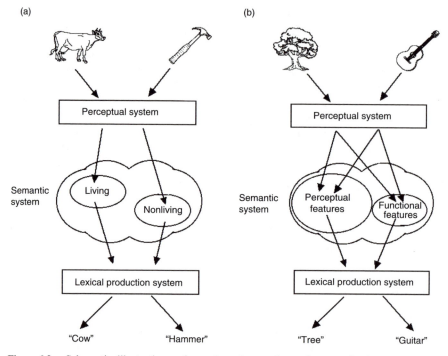

Figure 6.2. Schematic illustrations of two hypotheses about the organization of semantic memory. (a) A variant of the taxonomic categories hypothesis. (b) A variant of the sensory/functional hypothesis.

artefacts stored in another. One might also postulate the existence of other taxonomic distinctions within these broad groupings. The system encoding representations of living things may also contain distinct subsystems for animals, fruits, vegetables, and other biological categories. Similarly, the system that encodes information about artefacts may contain subsystems for transportation, furniture, clothing, and so on. In principle, this hypothesis seems to provide a relatively straightforward account of category-specific deficits. An impairment for particular categories of objects would follow from selective damage to the neural structures that encode semantic representations of those objects. But this version of the taxonomic categories hypothesis is unsatisfactory in a number of respects. For example, the taxonomic distinctions that are assumed to be encoded in the brain are largely motivated by the data that the hypothesis must explain, i.e. by the patterns of performance that have been found in brain-damaged patients with category-specific disorders. Although there is some support, on evolutionary grounds, for the possibility that specialized mechanisms exist for the encoding of information about biological kinds (Caramazza & Shelton, 1998; Santos & Caramazza, 2002), there is no obvious motivation for the assumption that specialized mechanisms also exist for the representation of other categories, such as clothing and musical instruments. In addition, the taxonomic categories hypothesis does not provide a clear explanation for the patterns of associations and dissociations among categories that have been reported, such as the associations between impairments for "living" things and musical instruments (e.g. Basso, Capitani, & Laiacona, 1988; Farah, Meyer, & McMullen, 1996; Stewart et al., 1992; Warrington & Shallice, 1984), and between deficits for "living" things and preserved knowledge of body parts (e.g. Basso et al., 1988; Hillis & Caramazza, 1991; Silveri & Gainotti, 1998; Stewart et al., 1992; Swales & Johnson, 1992; Warrington & Shallice, 1984).

Categories as an emergent property of semantic structure

Another challenge to the taxonomic categories hypothesis is that it is not necessary to postulate taxonomy as a first-order organizational principle of knowledge representation in order for category-specific impairments to arise. These deficits could stem from the way in which semantically related concepts are mapped across an underlying system of conceptual primitives that does not contain an explicit taxonomic organization. For example, we might assume that some of our knowledge of objects relates to their perceptual characteristics, such as their shape, size and colour, while other features represent information about the functional use of objects, e.g. <used for sitting>, and associative properties, e.g. <lives in trees>, <found in Africa>. We might further assume that semantically related concepts from the same category are likely to share more semantic features with each other than with objects from other categories (e.g. Flores d'Arcais & Schreuder, 1987). Given these assumptions, categorical distinctions may reflect overlap in the semantic representations of objects from the same semantic categories, i.e. categorical distinctions might be regarded as an emergent property of the system, rather than as a first-order organizational principle. There are several versions of this basic proposal. On some versions it is assumed that different types of features are mapped across a unitary modality-neutral semantic store that is accessible from all sensory input modalities (e.g. Caramazza, Hillis, Rapp, & Romani 1990; Humphreys & Riddoch, 1988). An alternative account is that different types of features are encoded in distinct modality-specific stores defined either by knowledge type (e.g. visual, functional) and/or by the sensory modality of knowledge acquisition (e.g. Allport, 1985; McCarthy & Warrington, 1988; Shallice, 1988; Warrington & Shallice, 1984). In the next section, we will consider in more detail one variant of the former proposal: The sensory/functional hypothesis.

Sensory/functional hypothesis

On this hypothesis, semantic representations of objects are distributed across modality-specific semantic stores that are defined in terms of the types of features they encode (Farah & McClelland, 1991; Hart & Gordon, 1992; Humphreys & Forde, 2001; Shallice, 1988; Warrington & Shallice, 1984; Warrington & McCarthy, 1983). One variant of the hypothesis is illustrated in Figure 6.2(b), which contains separate semantic stores for sensory or perceptual properties of objects, and for functional information relating to object use. Selective impairments for living and nonliving things are assumed to derive from an asymmetry in the representation of living and nonliving things across the underlying modality-specific stores. Specifically, it is assumed that the semantic representations of living things are more heavily weighted in terms of visual sensory features than functional features (Labov, 1973). In contrast, representations of nonliving things are assumed to be more heavily weighted in terms of functional than visual features. Thus, selective damage to the modality-specific store that encodes visual sensory features is more likely to impair representations of living things than nonliving things. In contrast, damage to the modality-specific store that encodes functional features will result in a disproportionate impairment for nonliving things. The hypothesis also provides a possible explanation for the apparent associations among impaired and preserved categories found in some patients. For example, impairments with musical instruments might be more likely to co-occur with deficits for living than nonliving things, because musical instruments, like objects from animate categories, arguably tend to be distinguished from one another largely on the basis of sensory attributes, such as their visual appearance and the sound that they make. In contrast, body parts, like many inanimate objects, may tend to be more heavily weighted in terms of functional properties than other biological kinds (Farah & McClelland, 1991; Warringon & McCarthy, 1983), and therefore more vulnerable to impairments affecting functional knowledge.

However, the sensory/functional hypothesis also seems to make at least one prediction that is not clearly consistent with some of the behavioural data: Patients with selective damage to one of the modality-specific stores should have preserved access to other types of semantic information about objects in the unaffected modalities. For example, patients who are disproportionately impaired in naming artefacts following a loss of information about the functional properties of objects should still be able to access preserved information about the sensory properties of those objects. In other words, according to the sensory/functional hypothesis, there should be an interaction between category and modality or knowledge type (Shelton & Caramazza, 1999). Although this prediction appears to receive support from some case studies (e.g. Basso et al., 1988; De Renzi & Lucchelli, 1994; Farah et al., 1989; Silveri & Gainotti, 1988), other evidence suggests that the inter-action is not reliable. Several reports have shown that when semantic attrib-utes and objects are equated in terms of familiarity, patients who appear to be disproportionately impaired with living things fail to show the predicted cat-egory by modality interaction (Caramazza & Shelton, 1998; Funnell & De Mornay Davies, 1997; Laiacona et al., 1997; Sheridan & Humphreys, 1993), i.e. they are impaired at retrieving both sensory and functional information about the same objects. Thus, while the sensory/functional hypothesis appears to offer a plausible explanation for some aspects of the empirical data from studies of category-specific disorders, other aspects of the data are rather less well accounted for. Later we will consider how connectionist implementations of cognitive hypotheses about knowledge representation, and the simulation of category-specific impairments, might provide insights about this, and other, intriguing aspects of the behavioural data on category-specific disorders.

CONNECTIONIST SIMULATIONS OF CATEGORY-SPECIFIC IMPAIRMENTS

So far we have considered some of the main aspects of the empirical data from studies of brain-damaged patients with acquired category-specific impairments. We now turn to connectionist simulations of these disorders, and critically examine the contribution that these simulations may make to our understanding of category-specific impairments and to theories of know-ledge representation. Several network simulations of category-specific impairments have been reported (e.g. Devlin, Gonnerman, Andersen, & Seidenberg, 1998; Farah & McClelland, 1991; Harley, 1998; Hinton & Shallice 1991; Moss, Tyler, & Devlin, 2002; Plaut & Shallice, 1993; Small, Hart, Gordon, & Hollard, 1993; Tippett, McAuliffe, & Farah, 1995; Tyler, Durrant-Peatfield, Levy, Voice, & Moss, 1996; Tyler et al., 2000; Zorzi, Perry, Ziegler, & Coltheart, 1999). The allure of the approach to the study of semantic memory derives, in part, from the characteristics of pattern repre-sentation in connectionist networks (e.g. Bechtel & Abrahamsen, 1991; Ellis & Humphreys, 1999; McLeod et al., 1998; Rogers & Plaut, 2002; Rumelhart & McClelland, 1986). In particular, connectionist architectures can represent complex mental representations as distributed networks of interconnected units, comparable with the predominant assumption that conceptual structures consist of overlapping representations of semantic features (e.g. Collins & Loftus, 1975).

In connectionist neuropsychology the aim is to test a specific theoretical claim about the organization and structure of a set of mental processes (e.g. those supporting reading, writing, visual object recognition, or semantic memory) by implementing the proposed system in a neural network. The theoretical hypothesis is then empirically evaluated through a comparison between network performance and behavioural data (e.g. Ellis & Humphreys, 1999; McLeod et al., 1998; Rogers & Plaut, 2002). As we have seen, models of normal cognitive function may be constrained by studies of the patterns of preserved and impaired performance of brain-damaged patients. Similarly, in connectionist neuropsychology, theoretical claims are evaluated in terms of the ability of a lesioned or damaged network to simulate patient data.

There are several apparent advantages of the approach. For example, it is, in principle, possible to lesion networks in very precise and theoretically motivated ways. This allows the researcher more opportunity to generate empirical predictions about the behaviour of the system under investigation following damage. Furthermore, emphasis is placed on specifying theoretical hypotheses at a level of detail that will allow for implementation in a functioning network. Thus, as we will see later in this chapter, a network may be used to generate empirical predictions that may not be immediately obvious from the theory because of the complexity of processes that have been hypothesized. However, as we will also see, the approach is not without its critics (e.g. McCloskey, 1991; Olson & Caramazza, 1994; Olson & Humphreys, 1997). One area of contention concerns the nature of the comparison between network performance and empirical data from lesion studies on which connectionist neuropsychology is based. A central issue is how the interpretation of network performance (or output) is related back to the theoretical claim about cognitive function that the network is being used to evaluate. In order to explore these issues in more detail, we will focus our discussion on one attempt to use a connectionist network to simulate acquired category-specific deficits. In particular, we illustrate our case through a critical examination of the Farah & McClelland (1991) simulation (hereafter, FM91), and their attempt to use the FM91 network to evaluate one variant of the sensory/functional hypothesis. The purpose of this critique is not to raise issues that only apply to the FM91 simulation, but to illustrate a range of issues that also apply to other simulations of cognitive functions, not only in the domain of category-specific deficits, but in other areas as well. We first describe the architecture of the FM91 network, and examine in some detail the correspondence between the network's performance and the neuropsychological data from studies of category-specific deficits. We then consider the theoretical significance of the network, and examine the contribution that the network may make to our understanding of semantic memory and the origins of category-specific disorders. Finally, we discuss some ways in which future simulations, using lesioned networks, may be usefully employed to advance theory development in our understanding of knowledge representation and category-specific impairments.

The Farah & McClelland (1991) network

The aim of the FM91 network was to examine whether category-specific impairments for living and nonliving things can arise from a semantic system that has no inherent category-specific taxonomically defined components, but rather consists of representations that are mapped across modality-specific stores of visual and functional semantic features—consistent with the sensory/functional hypothesis.

Network architecture

The simulation was based on an auto-associative network. The functional architecture of the network is illustrated in Fig. 6.3. It contained two pools of 24 "visible" units[1] that were used both to present input vectors to the network and to record associated output patterns. There was also a layer of 80 semantic units, used to encode two types of putatively modality-specific semantic features. One type of unit was dedicated to encoding visual properties of objects, and the other type was used to encode functional properties. There were bidirectional connections among units both between and within pools, but no direct connections between the two pools of "visible" units.

The number of units dedicated to visual and functional features of objects in the semantic layer was based on ratings obtained from judges, who were asked to underline references to visual and functional attributes of objects in dictionary definitions. On the basis of these ratings, the basic FM91 network had 60 visual semantic and 20 functional semantic units, giving a ratio of visual to functional units of 3:1. The network was trained to encode

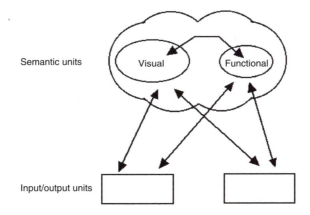

Figure 6.3. The functional architecture of the FM91 network. After Farah & McClelland (1991).

representations of 20 concepts grouped into two categories denoting 10 living and 10 nonliving things.

Network representations

Each concept consisted of a randomly generated pattern of vectors across the "visible" units and a subset of the semantic units. The distribution of visual and functional features for each living and nonliving concept was consistent with the assumptions of the sensory/functional hypothesis: Notably, representations of concepts in the two categories were asymmetrically distributed across the sensory and functional semantic units. Concepts belonging to the category of living things were represented by an average of 2.68 visual features and 0.35 functional features. In contrast, concepts belonging to the category of nonliving things were represented by an average of 1.57 visual features and 1.1 functional features. Thus, representations of living things contained a ratio of 7.7:1 visual to functional features, while representations of nonliving things contained a ratio of 1.4:1. In the network representations, consistent with these ratios, living things were represented by an average of 16.1 visual and 2.1 functional units, and nonliving things were represented by an average of 9.4 visual and 6.7 functional units. The representations of all concepts encoded in the network contained both visual and functional semantic memory units.

Training the network

The network was trained using a supervised learning procedure. On each training cycle, a vector corresponding to one of the 20 concepts was presented to one of the sets of visible units, and the network was allowed to settle for 10 cycles. The weights were then incrementally adjusted using the delta rule (Rumelhart & McClelland, 1986) to minimize the difference between the desired and observed vector patterns across the visible units. The activation levels of all units were updated simultaneously according to a nonlinear activation function.

THE PERFORMANCE OF THE FM91 NETWORK

Effects of selective damage to the visual and functional semantic units

Once the network had been trained to produce the desired semantic patterns for each concept, and their associated output vectors, the semantic units were lesioned in order to simulate the effects of brain damage to the hypothesized semantic system. This involved fixing the activation values of varying proportions of *either* the visual or functional semantic units to zero, so that they could no longer contribute to generating the appropriate semantic or output representations in response to an input pattern. The network's performance was then assessed by presenting the network with the input vectors for each concept across one pool of visible units, and measuring the accuracy of the resulting output patterns. The network's performance for each concept was scored as correct if the output vector it produced matched the desired pattern more closely than the vectors of any of the other concepts on which the network was trained. Figure 6.4 shows the performance of the network for each category of objects as a function of the proportion of damage to *either* the visual or the functional semantic units.

As Figure 6.4 shows, damage to the visual semantic units impairs the network's performance with living things more than nonliving things. In contrast, selective damage to the functional semantic units results in impaired performance with nonliving things, but not living things. Thus, the lesioned network appears to show a double dissociation for living and nonliving things following selective impairment. These contrasting patterns of performance seem qualitatively similar to the double dissociation found in brain-damaged patients with category-specific impairments. Thus, on the basis of the network's performance we might argue that the simulation provides support for the sensory/functional hypothesis. That is, the network seems to show that category-specific deficits can arise following selective impairment to a semantic system that has no category-specific components (Farah, 1994; Farah & McClelland, 1991).

CRITICAL EVALUATION

Impressive as the results of the FM91 simulation seem to be, how closely does the network's performance actually compare with the behavioural data? And to what extent does the simulation provide an explanation of category-specific deficits?

The severity of impairments for living and nonliving things

In fact, a closer inspection of the network's performance suggests that it does not accurately simulate certain aspects of the relevant patient data. In particular, as Figure 6.4 shows, there is a clear asymmetry in the severity of selective impairments for each category. In the first place, it is apparent that damage to roughly 40% or more of the visual semantic units impairs both living and nonliving things, but always results in a disproportionate impairment for living things. In contrast, damage to the same proportions of functional semantic units, while resulting in an impairment for nonliving things, never affects performance with living things, i.e. it does not seem possible to

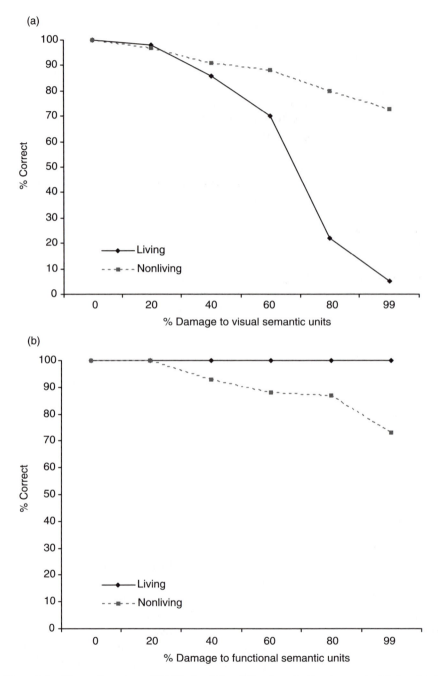

Figure 6.4. The performance of FM91 simulation following selective damage to (a) the visual semantic and (b) functional semantic units.

selectively lesion the network in such a way that will produce a deficit for living things but no impairment for nonliving things.

In addition, as Fig. 6.5 shows, the network's performance suggests that selective impairments for living things should be more severe, relative to unimpaired categories, than impairments for nonliving things.

After maximal damage to the functional semantic units, performance with nonliving things remains at 73% correct, while maximal damage to the visual semantic units results in a performance level at only 5% correct for living things. Most importantly, neither of these aspects of the network's perform-ance seem to be consistent with the behavioural data from some of the reported cases of category-specific impairment. For example, consider again the performance of JJ and PS, the patients described by Hillis & Caramazza (1991). As previously shown in Fig. 6.1, at 13 months post-onset, both patients showed an approximately equal level of severity between impaired and preserved categories. Furthermore, PS, who was disproportionately impaired with living things (animals, birds, vegetables, and fruits), performed at ceiling in naming nonliving things (clothing, transportation, and furni-ture). In addition, some patients who show a disproportionate impairment for nonliving things are more impaired on this category than maximal dam-age to the functional semantic units in the network seems to allow. This is

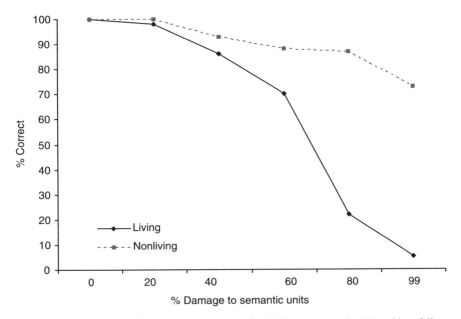

Figure 6.5. The severity of impairments shown by the FM91 simulation for living things follow-ing selective damage to the visual semantic units, and nonliving things following damage to the functional semantic units.

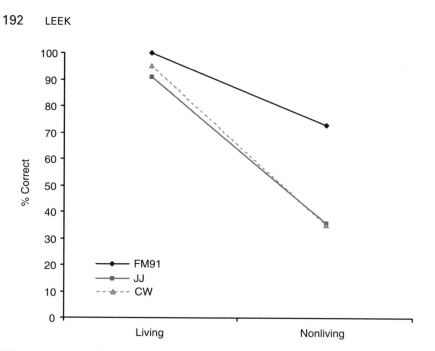

Figure 6.6.   The performance of the patients JJ (Hillis & Caramazza, 1991) and CW (Sacchett & Humphreys, 1992) with living and nonliving things in a spoken picture-naming task (administered at 6 and 2 months post-onset, respectively), and the FM91 simulation following damage to 99% of the functional semantic units.

illustrated in Fig. 6.6, which compares the effects on performance with living and nonliving things following damage to 99% of the functional semantic units in the network, and the picture-naming performance of the patients JJ (Hillis & Caramazza, 1991) and CW (Sacchett & Humphreys, 1992).[2]

How should we interpret these apparent discrepancies between the network's performance and the patient data? To what extent do they undermine the claim that the FM91 network provides support for the sensory/functional hypothesis?

Quantitative comparisons between network performance and patient data

One might argue that it is inappropriate to make such a seemingly direct quantitative comparison between the absolute levels of network performance and the patient data. Indeed, we might, with some justification, raise the same objection to theoretical claims based on a precise quantitative comparison between the levels of impairment shown by two patients on a given behavioural task. For example, differences in performance might be due to other factors that are unrelated to the putative effects of the patients' brain damage, such as their premorbid levels of ability, educational background, sex, age, etc.

So, is our comparison between the FM91 network's performance and those of individual patients with category-specific deficits any more valid? For one thing, there are many factors that could influence the absolute level of performance shown by a lesioned network: the network encodes a relatively small set of concepts in relation to the number of representations that are likely to be stored in the human semantic system. The semantic representations in the network are also based on a limited set of features, and distributions of visual and functional features between living and nonliving things were only roughly approximated using ratings of dictionary definitions. Indeed, we might assume that the network's absolute levels of performance might be more similar to the patients had it been trained on a larger, more elaborate stimulus set, and had more extensive sets of ratings been used to determine the ratios of visual and functional knowledge for each category. The network's performance is also likely to have been influenced by other arbitrary parameters of the simulation, such as the particular learning algorithm that was used, and the number of units in each layer of the architecture. None of these factors were explicitly motivated by the theoretical hypothesis that the network claims to instantiate, i.e. the sensory/functional hypothesis does not specify how many feature units there are, or how associations among different features are learned. In short, we might decide to place little weight on apparent discrepancies between the network's performance and the behavioural data, on the grounds that they arise as a result of theoretically irrelevant aspects of the simulation.

However, as it stands, this argument is not entirely satisfactory. If we are willing to attribute discrepant aspects of the network's performance to arbitrary and irrelevant parameters of the simulation, then we must be able to demonstrate that the same factors cannot also account for those aspects of the network's performance that do seem to be consistent with the behavioural data. For example, could the same arbitrary parameters also account for the category-specific effects shown by the network? This possibility is illustrated by the performance of another simulation, described by Hinton & Shallice (1991). In their study, a recurrent network was trained to output patterns of vectors corresponding to semantic representations of objects belonging to five categories of objects. When lesioned, one version of the network remained accurate with only a single category of objects (foods). However, this apparent category specificity did not arise in a second network that only differed from the first in the values of its initial starting weights. Perry (1999) has also drawn similar conclusions about the role of arbitrary parameters in determining network performance from the analysis of another simulation of category-specific disorders described by Devlin et al. (1998).

Evaluating network performance: A question of transparency under analysis

The main point that emerges from our discussion so far is that in order to fully evaluate the theoretical implications of a connectionist simulation, the network must be transparent under analysis (McCloskey, 1991). That is, we must be able to determine what factors underlie network performance so that we can understand how the network does what it does. There are several possibilities that arise when interpreting the performance of the FM91 simulation, e.g:

- The network's performance might be solely determined by parameters of the simulation that are not specified by the theoretical hypothesis under examination. In the present case these include the learning algorithm, the number of units in the network, the weight update procedure, the nonlinear activation function applied to units in the network, the scoring procedure, and the number of concepts on which the network was trained.[3]
- The network might also fail to accurately simulate certain aspects of the behavioural data, because the theoretical assumptions of the sensory/functional hypothesis have not been correctly instantiated in the network. In this case, while the hypothesis itself may provide an adequate account of the data, the simulation cannot be regarded as a satisfactory test of the hypothesis.
- The network might fail to accurately simulate the relevant behavioural data because of fundamental limitations in the theoretical hypothesis that the network instantiates. In this case, the problematic aspects of network's performance may be of considerable relevance.

Given these possibilities, let us take a closer look at some of the factors that might determine the performance of the FM91 simulation.

NETWORK PARAMETERS AND NETWORK PERFORMANCE

The number of training epochs

The influence of one parameter that is examined in the evaluation of the FM91 simulation is the number of training epochs that the network was given prior to being lesioned. The version of the network that we have been considering so far was damaged after completing 100 training epochs. Fig. 6.7 shows the effects on the performance of the network following selective damage to the functional semantic units after 50 and 200 training epochs.

After 50 epochs, selective damage to the functional semantic units does

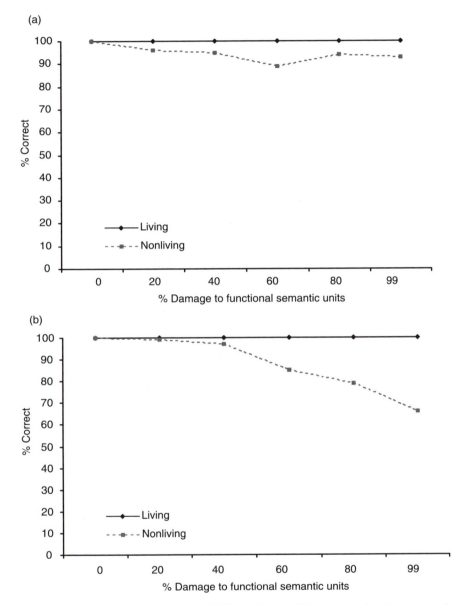

Figure 6.7. The performance of the FM91 simulation following selective damage to the functional semantic units after (a) 50 training epochs, (b) 200 training epochs.

not produce a clearly disproportionate impairment for nonliving relative to living things. In contrast, although after 200 epochs a selective impairment for nonliving things begins to emerge, it is still less severe than the comparative deficit for living things observed following damage to the visual semantic units shown earlier in Fig. 6.4. Thus, although the number of training epochs does affect the pattern of performance shown by the lesioned network, this parameter does not seem to account for the problematic asymmetry in the severity of the double dissociation shown by the network.

The effects of training with and without weight decay

Another aspect of the simulation that was explored by Farah & McClelland (1991) was the influence of the weight decay procedure on network performance. The variant of the simulation examined earlier was trained using a weight decay procedure. This involved reducing the size of the weights on the connections between units by some proportion of their total value at the end of each training epoch. One other variant of the basic FM91 network was trained without using weight decay. Its performance following selective damage to the visual and functional semantic units is shown in Fig. 6.8.

Damage to this variant of the network resulted in more severe deficits, particularly for nonliving things. For example, damage to 99% of the functional semantic units in the basic network resulted in 73% correct performance for nonliving things, but in the variant trained without weight decay, the same amount of damage resulted in only 25% correct performance. As shown in Fig. 6.9(a), this is a much closer match to the patterns shown by the two patients, JJ and CW, described earlier.

But how should the effect of this parameter on network performance be interpreted? And what implications does this have for the conclusions that can be drawn from the FM91 simulation as a test of theory? One question that must be examined is whether a network parameter such as weight decay influences some property of the implementation, like the patterns of weights among units, in a way that remains consistent with the assumptions of the theory under investigation, viz. the sensory/functional hypothesis. Arguably, the absence of weight decay, as Farah & McClelland (1991) suggest, might be expected to produce a network that is less resistant to damage, since individual weights in the connections among units are more likely to take on disproportionate importance in the mappings among the different layers of the network. In this case, weight decay clearly has important consequences for the way in which the network encodes representations. What is less clear is whether the success of the simulation depends on this parameter. If it does, we must determine how it fits with the sensory/functional hypothesis. As it turns out, although the network's performance following damage to the

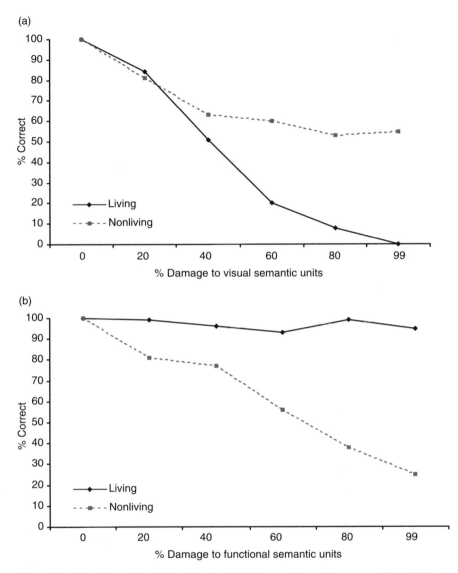

Figure 6.8. The effects of training without weight decay on the performance of the FM91 network following selective damage to (a) the visual semantic and (b) the functional semantic units.

functional semantic units more closely resembles the data from the patients JJ and CW, training the network without weight decay also changes its pattern of performance following selective damage to the visual semantic units. Fig. 6.9(b) shows the performance of the patient JBR (Warrington & Shallice, 1984) and that of the FM91 network (trained without weight decay)

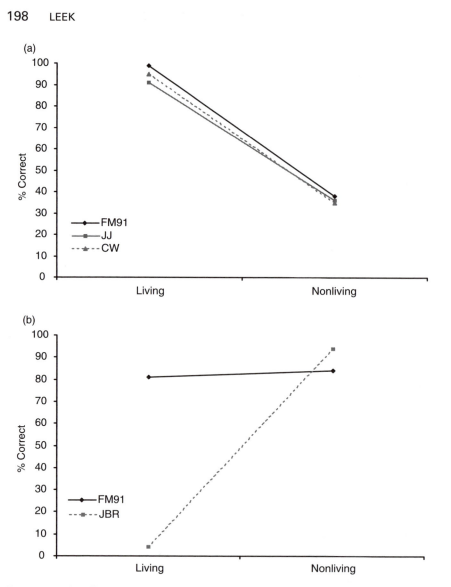

Figure 6.9.   The effects of training without weight decay. The performance of the FM91 network following selective damage to (a) 80% of the functional semantic units compared to the patients JJ (Hillis & Caramazza, 1991) and CW (Sacchett & Humphreys, 1992) in picture naming, (b) 20% of the visual semantic units compared to the patient JBR (Warrington & Shallice, 1984).

following damage to 20% of the visual semantic units. Although the patient and the network show comparable levels of performance with nonliving things, JBR also clearly shows an impairment with living things, while the network does not. Thus, not only is the relation between weight decay and the theoretical implications of the simulation unclear, but also, as we have seen, changing this parameter of the network results in performance that more closely matches some aspects of the data, but weakens the match in other ways.

The simulation as a test of the sensory/functional hypothesis

Another possibility raised earlier was that the seemingly discrepant aspects of the network's performance reflect a fundamental limitation on the explanatory power of the sensory/functional hypothesis (assuming that the hypothesis has been correctly instantiated in the network). In this case, the quantitative comparison that was made between the severity of deficits shown by the network and the performance of individual patients may have important theoretical implications. It would suggest that the sensory/ functional hypothesis (as instantiated in the network) can account for some, but not all, of the relevant behavioural data. Farah & McClelland (1991) do not claim that the sensory/functional hypothesis, or its implementation in the network, should be regarded as the instantiation of a fully fledged theory of semantic memory: among other things, the hypothesis does not make any explicit claims about how conceptual knowledge is acquired. Neither does it specify how semantic representations are internally structured, beyond the assumption that representations of living things and nonliving things differ in their weightings of visual and functional information. Even so, in order to accept the simulation as providing support for the sensory/functional hypothesis, we must be able to show that the category-specific performance of the network, i.e. the double dissociation, follows from the assumptions of the sensory/functional hypothesis and, furthermore, that those assumptions are correctly instantiated in the network. On the one hand, it may seem reasonable to assume that the double dissociation arises from the asymmetry in the *number* of visual and functional features that are contained in the representations of living and nonliving things. This asymmetry follows from a core assumption of the sensory/functional hypothesis. On the other hand (and putting aside the role of arbitrary network parameters—see above) the network's performance might also be determined by other theoretically relevant characteristics of the semantic representations that are instantiated, but which *do not* necessarily follow from assumptions of the sensory/functional hypothesis. For example, although the semantic representations were arbitrarily mapped across particular units, it must be assumed that the representations for concepts from the same category shared—at least to some extent—some proportion of semantic feature units, i.e. that their representations overlapped. This argument is based on a consideration of the number of semantic units that were available (60 visual and 20 functional), the number of concepts on which the network was trained (10 living and 10 nonliving), and on the average number of visual and functional units that were recruited in the representations of objects from the two categories (16.1 visual and 2.1 functional units for living things, and 9.4 visual and 6.7 functional units for nonliving things). Given these details, we must presume that representations of living things tended to share more visual semantic units than they did functional semantic units. The same is also likely to be true for the representations of nonliving things. However, the degree of overlap across visual semantic units must be greater for living than nonliving things, while the reverse must be true across the functional semantic features. Thus, in the network, representations of living and nonliving things are not only asymmetrical in terms of the number of visual and functional units that they employ, but also in terms of the extent to which units of each type overlap with one another. In addition, these two factors (the numbers of units and the overlap of representations) may, in principle, be manipulated independently. One could hold the number of features dedicated to the representations of each category constant, while manipulating the degree of feature overlap among concepts encoded across those features (and vice versa). While only one factor (the number of units/amount of features) follows from the sensory/functional hypothesis, both could account for the category-specific performance of the FM91 network. The asymmetry in the degree of overlap among the semantic representations of living and nonliving things in the network is likely to make living things less resistant to damage following selective impairment of the visual semantic units. Conversely, the higher intercorrelation of functional units for nonliving things, may make this category more susceptible to impairment following selective damage to the functional semantic units. Unfortunately, since feature overlap varies systematically with category in the FM91 simulation, it is difficult to determine which factor contributes to network performance. Consequently, the implications of the FM91 simulation as a test of the sensory/functional hypothesis remain unclear.

Valid implementation of the cognitive hypothesis: The case of the modified network

So far we have discussed the problem of evaluating network performance in relation to a cognitive hypothesis: we have considered the issue of transparency (McCloskey, 1991), i.e. how we can understand what determines network ouput, and we have described some of the difficulties in determining whether network performance is attributable to specific theoretically relevant aspects of the simulation (some of which may not follow directly from the sensory/functional hypothesis) or arbitrary network parameters. Before leaving this discussion, it is also worth considering another related issue— whether the hypothesis under examination has been *appropriately instantiated* in the network. To illustrate the importance of this point, we will briefly consider the performance of another modified version of FM91. The performance of the modified version is shown in Fig. 6.10. Interestingly, it shows a double dissociation in deficits between living and nonliving things, as well as levels of severity of impairment that are comparable to those found in patients JJ and CW described earlier.

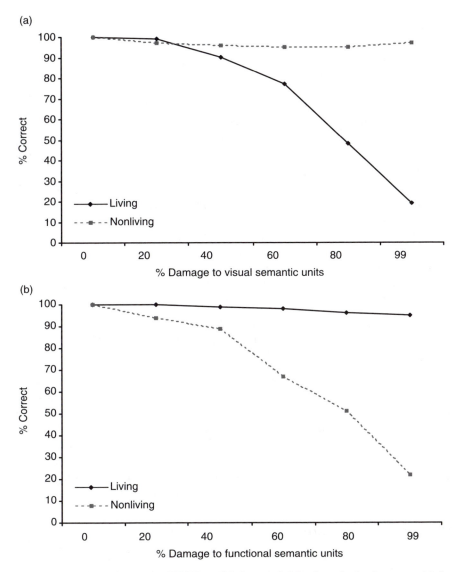

Figure 6.10. The performance of FM91 modified network following selective damage to (a) the visual semantic and (b) the functional semantic units.

However a closer examination of the modified network's architecture reveals that it differs from the basic network in several theoretically relevant ways. Most importantly, in the modified network, the number of semantic units has been arbitrarily set at 40 in each modality. In addition, the ratio of visual and functional features underlying the representations of living and nonliving things was also changed. In the modified network, living things were represented by a ratio of 2.65:1 visual:functional units, and nonliving things by a ratio of 1:2.06. Given these ratios, it should be apparent that the modified network—despite providing a more accurate simulation of the patient data—does not provide a valid test of the sensory/functional hypothesis. The asymmetry in the distribution of semantic units between the two categories of objects results in a system which has, arguably, category-specific components: the visual modality encodes almost exclusively semantic representations of living things, while the functional modality predominantly encodes representations of nonliving things. Thus, it is not surprising that the network produces a reliable double dissociation when selectively lesioned, and its performance cannot be taken as support for a model of semantic memory that does not posit (taxonomic) category-specific components. A relevant theoretical issue that arises from this observation is that, rather than providing support for the sensory/functional hypothesis, we could take the performance of the FM91 simulation as demonstrating the need to posit (at least some form of) taxonomic organization in semantic memory in order to adequately model the relevant behavioural data from category-specific impairments (e.g. Caramazza & Shelton, 1998; Shelton & Caramazza, 1999).

WHAT CONNECTIONIST NETWORKS CAN REVEAL ABOUT THE ORGANIZATION OF SEMANTIC MEMORY

While great caution must be taken in evaluating connectionist simulations of human performance, this does not mean that the approach cannot provide theoretically significant insights about the nature of cognitive processing. In fact, there is at least one further aspect of the FM91 network that merits discussion, not only because it may have important implications for hypotheses about the organization of semantic memory, but also because it provides a good example of the kind of contribution that connectionist neuropsychology may make to theory development in cognitive science.

Representation in connectionist networks

This aspect of the FM91 network relates to Farah & McClelland's (1991) analysis of the effects of partial damage to the semantic representations in the basic network, and the consequences of this damage for the network's ability to access preserved information. Earlier in our discussion, we noted that the sensory/functional hypothesis seems to predict that there should be an interaction between modality of knowledge and category-specificity, i.e. patients with disproportionate impairments with living things, following selective damage to the visual semantic system, should, by hypothesis, remain unimpaired in accessing preserved functional semantic information about both living and nonliving things. In contrast, patients with apparent disproportionate difficulty with nonliving things, following selective impairment to the functional semantic store, should have access to preserved visual information about both nonliving and living things. While this prediction appears to have been confirmed in some case reports (Basso et al., 1988; De Renzi & Lucchelli, 1994; Farah et al., 1989; Silveri & Gainotti, 1988), other evidence suggests that the modality by category interaction is unreliable (e.g. Caramazza & Shelton, 1998; Funnell & De Mornay Davies, 1997; Laiacona et al., 1997; Sheridan & Humphreys, 1993). These later studies have shown that patients with selective impairments for living things may be equally impaired in accessing both visual and functional semantic information.

It is interesting to note, then, that the basic FM91 network, when lesioned, also *fails* to show a category by modality interaction. This is demonstrated by an analysis of the consequences of selective damage to either the visual or functional semantic units on the ability of the network to recover the remaining preserved portion of the encoded semantic representations. The analysis was based on lesioning one set of semantic units, presenting the network with an input vector, and then determining the resulting match between the observed and correct patterns of activation across the impaired and preserved semantic units. Fig. 6.11 shows the effects of selective damage to the visual and functional semantic units on the network's ability to generate the correct representations across both pools of units. Values along the ordinate axis represent the degree of match between the desired and observed patterns of activation (where 100 corresponds to a perfect match).

Selective damage to the visual semantic units impairs the network's ability to produce the correct pattern of activation across both the impaired and preserved semantic units. A similar pattern is found following damage to the functional semantic units. Farah & McClelland (1991) suggest that this result can be understood in terms of the effects of reducing the amount of activation or collateral support from the impaired units that is necessary to fully activate the preserved semantic features. In other words, when one set of semantic units are deprived of a significant proportion of their input, it becomes more difficult for those units to reach criterion levels of activation, even though they have not been damaged. This aspect of the network's performance, as we have seen, does not appear to follow from the theoretical assumptions of the sensory/functional hypothesis. Rather, it seems to derive

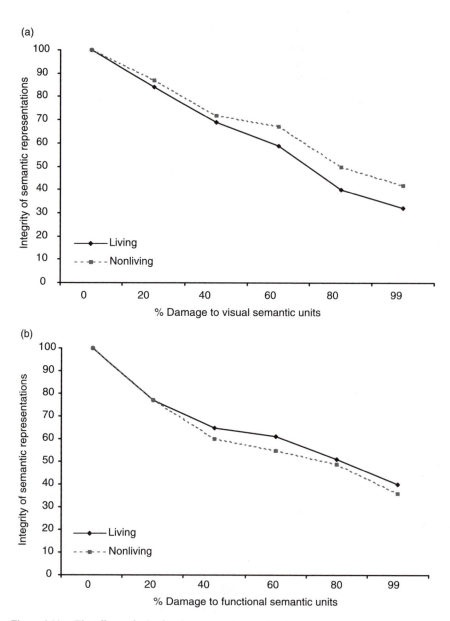

Figure 6.11. The effects of selective damage to the (a) visual semantic, (b) functional semantic units in the FM91 simulation, on the integrity of the semantic representations across both pools of units. After Farah & McClelland (1991).

from inherent properties of the connectionist architecture on which the network is based and, in particular, on the way in which activation is computed across distributed representations (Farah & McClelland, 1991). It also provides one example of how connectionist networks can provide a powerful tool for exploring the relationship between the complex internal properties of mental representations and the effects that damage to those representations has on behavioural performance.

Research from a variety of domains suggests that knowledge representations have a rich and complex internal structure (e.g. Caramazza et al., 1990; Devlin et al., 1998; Jackendoff, 1990; Keil, 1989; Malt & Smith, 1984; McRae et al., 1997; McRae & Cree, 2002; Moss et al., 2002; Rosch & Mervis, 1975). One source of complexity comes from the differential weighting of semantic features in conceptual representations. For example, some features will tend to have more importance than others in distinguishing among exemplars of semantically related concepts (Caramazza et al., 1990; Devlin et al., 1998; McRae et al., 1997; Moss et al., 1997; Rosch & Mervis, 1975; Tyler et al., 1996, 2000; Tyler & Moss, 1997): a semantic feature such as <capable of reproduction> may be an important distinctive property of biological kinds, and therefore facilitate the distinction between living and nonliving things. The importance of particular features also seems to vary depending on the level of discrimination required. The same feature, <capable of reproduction>, will be associated with all exemplars of biological kinds, and so will not facilitate within-category discriminations (e.g. it does not help us distinguish between a butterfly and a plant). In contrast, other types of features, such as, <has seeds>, <has fur> or <has udders> may play an important role in distinguishing among different taxonomic subgroups of biological kinds. Thus, it is likely that the relative importance of individual features will play a role in determining semantic structure, and the ease with which discriminations are made at different levels of categorization. In addition, the consequences of damage to the semantic system may vary depending on the features affected and the nature of the task (Leek & Pothos, 2001).

A further constraint on the nature of semantic structure is the degree of intercorrelation among features of different objects (e.g. Devlin et al., 1998; Gelman, 1988; Keil, 1989; McRae et al., 1997; McRae & Cree, 2002; Moss et al., 1997, in press; Rosch & Mervis, 1975; Tyler et al., 1996, 2000; Tyler & Moss, 1997); i.e. the extent to which the presence of one particular feature predicts the presence of another. There is empirical evidence that categories differ in the extent to which they share features (e.g. McRae et al., 1997; Moss et al., 2002). For example, McRae et al. (1997) have presented a detailed analysis of the intercorrelations among features that subjects list as semantic attributes of different types of objects. They found that features associated with biological kinds, such as animals, were more highly correlated with one another than features associated with artefacts, such as items of furniture.

For example, a biological kind that has fur is also likely to have teeth and claws (e.g. Devlin et al., 1998; McRae et al., 1997; McRae & Cree, 2002). In contrast, an inanimate object that has legs will not necessarily also have a seat (as legs are found on many different kinds of inanimate objects in addition to chairs and stools). The ability of certain classes of connectionist architectures (e.g. Hinton & Shallice, 1991; Hopfield, 1982; Plaut & Shallice, 1993) to capture and encode statistical covariation, and the distributional character- istics of complex feature patterns (e.g. Leek & Pothos, 2001), highlights one area where the approach, accompanied by detailed analyses of network func- tioning, is likely to provide a valuable tool for investigating the structure of knowledge representation in the brain, and the effects of damage to those representations (Devlin et al., 1998; Leek & Pothos, 2001; McCloskey, 1991; McRae et al, 1997; Moss et al., 2002; Plaut & Shallice, 1993).[4]

The conceptual structure account

Some recent work by Tyler, Moss, and colleagues (e.g. Moss et al., 2002; Tyler et al., 2000) demonstrates one particularly promising approach using connectionist architectures to investigate the patterns of breakdown in repre- sentations that encode complex patterns of feature intercorrelation and dis- tinctiveness. Their hypothesis, which they call the conceptual structure account (Moss et al., 2002; Tyler et al., 2000), does not posit the existence of subsystems of features defined either by modality (e.g. McCarthy & Warrington, 1988) or knowledge type, as in the sensory/functional hypothesis examined in the FM91 simulation by Farah & McClelland (1991). Rather, categorical distinctions among concepts are determined by complex patterns of intercorrelations among object properties within a unitary distributed fea- ture space. It is argued that living things tend to have highly intercorrelated properties but weakly correlated distinctive features. In contrast, nonliving things have fewer intercorrelated properties but strong associations among distinctive features. As we discussed above, these attributes of concept struc- ture may have important consequences for understanding the patterns of category-specific impairment that emerge following brain damage. For example, concepts with highly intercorrelated features may be more resistant to damage than those with weakly intercorrelated features. This is because features that are highly intercorrelated receive mutual activation (Devlin et al., 1998; Moss et al., 2002; Tyler et al., 2000).

Tyler et al. (2000) have tested some predictions of this account in a simpli- fied simulation using an auto-associative network (containing input, hidden and output layers) trained using back-propagation (Rumelhart et al., 1986). In brief, the network encoded representations for 16 semantic vectors in which the patterns of intercorrelation among units (representing perceptual and functional attributes of objects), and feature distinctiveness, were varied across concepts. Eight vector patterns each were used to approximate representations of "living" and "nonliving" things. The proportions of shared to distinctive features were higher for living than nonliving concepts. In addition, for nonliving things, distinctive perceptual attributes were strongly correlated with particular functions, whereas for living things, distinctive perceptual properties were uncorrelated with other features. After training, the effects of *random* damage to varying proportions of connections among units were simulated. Interestingly, the network showed worse performance with living than nonliving things, except at the most extreme levels of damage (where more than 60% of connections were "lesioned"), where performance was worse with nonliving than living things. These results are encouraging in that the network simulates an apparent double dissociation following random damage, rather than damage that is targeted to particular classes of units (as in FM91). However, as Tyler et al. (2000; see also Moss et al., 2002) acknowledge, at present interpretation of network performance is limited because the current simulation deals only with a small number of vector patterns. It also largely remains to be seen what contribution arbitrary network parameters—rather than theoretically relevant aspects of representational structure—make to network performance. Finally, as with the FM91 simulation, the network described by Tyler et al. (2000) does not accurately simulate at least one aspect of the relevant patient data. Most notable, like the FM91 simulation, is the apparent asymmetry in the severity of deficits for living and nonliving things, in contrast to the patterns reported for at least two patients described earlier, JJ and PS (Hillis & Caramazza, 1991).

GENERAL CONCLUSIONS

In this chapter, we have focused our evaluation of connectionist neuropsychology on the Farah & McClelland (1991) simulation of category-specific semantic memory impairments. We have seen that, while the network seems to simulate some aspects of the behavioural data, it does not provide an adequate *explanation* for category-specific impairments, even over the limited range of data (such as the living/nonliving dissociation) against which it has been evaluated. Moreover, we have also suggested that the network is not transparent under analysis (McCloskey, 1991), i.e. it is not possible to determine clearly which factors determine network performance, or to assess the relative contribution of theory-relevant properties and arbitrary network parameters. These issues are by no means unique to the FM91 network, but rather apply to the evaluation of any connectionist (or non-connectionist) simulation of behavioural data (Coltheart et al., 1993; Lamberts & d'Ydewalle, 1990; Massaro, 1988; McCloskey, 1991; Olson & Humphreys, 1997; Olson & Caramazza, 1994; Pinker & Prince, 1988). However, other aspects of the FM91 simulation illustrate that connectionist simulations of neurological disorders can provide a valuable tool for theory development in this domain. In particular, semantic representations seem to have a complex internal structure that is likely to constrain the ways that they break down following brain damage. The properties of some classes of connectionist networks, and their ability to capture and encode statistical regularities among features, suggest that detailed analyses of network performance may play an important role in developing hypotheses about the structure of knowledge representations, and about the consequences of damage to those representations on behavioural performance in particular contexts.

ACKNOWLEDGEMENTS

The author would like to thank Michele Miozzo, Alfonso Caramazza, Michael McCloskey, and Brenda Rapp, for numerous discussions at Johns Hopkins about many of the issues raised in this chapter, and Martha Farah for making available details of the network output from the FM91 simulation. The preparation of this chapter was supported by a grant from the Wellcome Trust (GR065697).

Notes

1. The term "visible" units is used here only as a shorthand to distinguish between the input/output pools and the semantic layer. It should not be confused with the more specific use of the term in the context of classes of networks that contain hidden units, such as in Bolzmann machine architectures (Bechtel & Abrahamsen, 1991).
2. This does not preclude the possibility that additional damage to the visual units might be sufficient to produce a selective deficit to nonliving things that is comparable to those observed in these patients. However, given the disproportionate weighting of living to nonliving things in the visual semantic units, such additional damage is also highly likely to impair performance with living things considerably.
3. Although not discussed here, it is also relevant to consider the extent to which the correspondence between network and patient performance varies according to the method used to evaluate network output (i.e. how a determination is made about the accuracy of output vectors in the lesioned network).
4. However, as McCloskey (1991) points out, analyses consisting solely of descriptions of network parameters, such as the input and output vectors, unit activation functions, training procedures and so on, do not constitute explanations of network functioning.

REFERENCES

Allport, D. A. (1985). Distributed memory, modular subsystems and dysphasia. In S. K. Newman and R. Epstein (Eds.), *Current perspectives in dysphasia*. Edinburgh: Churchill Livingstone.

Basso, A., Capitani, E., & Laiacona, M. (1988). Progressive language impairment without dementia: A case with isolated category-specific semantic defect. *Journal of Neurology, Neurosurgery and Psychiatry, 51,* 1201–1207.

Bechtel, W., & Abrahamsen, A. (1991). *Connectionism and the mind: An introduction to parallel processing in networks.* Cambridge, MA: Blackwell.

Besner, D., Twilley, L., McCann, R. S., & Seergobin, K. (1990). On the association between connectionism and data: Are a few words necessary? *Psychological Review, 97,* 432–446.

Cappa, S. F., Frugoni, M., Pasquali, P., Perani, D., & Zorat, F. (1998). Category-specific naming impairment for artefacts: A new case. *Neurcase, 4,* 391–397.

Caramazza, A. (1986). On drawing inferences about the structure of normal cognitive systems from the analysis of impaired performance: The case for single-patient studies. *Brain and Cognition, 5,* 41–66.

Caramazza, A., Hillis, A., Leek, E. C., & Miozzo, M. (1994). The organization of lexical knowledge in the brain: Evidence from category and modality-specific deficits. In L. Hirschfeld, & S. Gelman (Eds.), *Mapping the mind: Domain specificity in cognition and culture* (pp. 68–84). Cambridge: Cambridge University Press.

Caramazza, A., Hillis, A. E., Rapp, B. C., & Romani, C. (1990). The multiple semantics hypothesis: Multiple confusions? *Cognitive Neuropsychology, 7,* 161–189.

Caramazza, A., & Shelton, J. R. (1998). Domain-specific knowledge systems in the brain: The animate–inanimate distinction. *Journal of Cognitive Neuroscience, 10,* 1–34.

Cohen, J. D., Farah, M. J., Romero, R. D., & Servam-Schreiber, D. (1994). Mechanisms of spatial attention: The relation of macrostructure to microstructure in parietal attentional deficits. *Journal of Cognitive Neuroscience, 6,* 377–387.

Collins, A. M., & Loftus, E. F. (1975). A spreading-activation theory of semantic processing. *Psychological Review, 82,* 407–428.

Collins, A. M. & Quillian, M. R. (1969). Retrieval time from semantic memory. *Journal of Verbal Learning and Verbal Behaviour, 8,* 240–247.

Coltheart, M., Curtis, B., Atkins, P., & Haller, M. (1993). Models of reading aloud: Dual-route and parallel distributed-processing approaches. *Psychological Review, 100,* 589–608.

Damasio, H., Grabowski, T. J., Tranel, D., Hichwa, R. D., & Damasio, A. R. (1996). A neural basis for lexical retrieval. *Nature, 380,* 499–505.

Dennis, M. (1976). Dissociated naming and locating of body parts after left anterior temporal lobe resection: An experimental case study. *Brain and Language, 3,* 147–163.

De Renzi, E., & Lucchelli, F. (1994). Are semantic systems separately represented in the brain? The case of living category impairment. *Cortex, 30,* 3–25.

Devlin, J., Gonnerman, L., Andersen, E., & Seidenberg, M. (1998). Category-specific semantic deficits in focal and widespread brain damage: A computational account. *Journal of Cognitive Neuroscience, 10,* 77–94.

Ellis, R., & Humphreys, G. (1999). *Connectionist psychology: A text with readings.* Midsomer Norton: Psychology Press.

Farah, M. J. (1994). Neuropsychological inference with an interactive brain: A critique of the locality assumption. *Behavioural and Brain Sciences, 17,* 43–104.

Farah, M. J., Hammond, K. M., Mehta, Z., & Ratcliff, G. (1989). Category-specificity and modality-specificity in semantic memory. *Neuropsychologia, 27,* 193–200.

Farah, M. J., & McClelland, J. L. (1991). A computational model of semantic memory impairment: Modality specificity and emergent category specificity. *Journal of Experimental Psychology: General, 120,* 339–357.

Farah, M. J., McMullen, P. A., & Meyer, M. M. (1991). Can recognition of living things be selectively impaired? *Neuropsychologia, 29,* 185–193.

Farah, M. J., Meyer, M. M., & McMullen, P. A. (1996). The living/nonliving dissociation is not an artifact: Giving an *a priori* implausible hypothesis a strong test. *Cognitive Neuropsychology, 13,* 137–154.

Farah, M. J., O'Reilly, R. C., & Vecera, S. P. (1993). Dissociated overt and covert recognition as an emergent property of a lesioned neural network. *Psychological Review, 100,* 571–588.

Farah, M. J., & Wallace, M. A. (1992). Semantically-bounded anomia: Implications for the neural implementation of naming. *Neuropsychologia, 30,* 609–621.

Flores d'Arcais, G. B., & Schreuder, R. (1987). Semantic activation during object naming. *Psychological Research, 49,* 153–159.

Fodor, J. A., & Pylyshyn. Z. W. (1988). Connectionism and cognitive architecture: A critical analysis. *Cognition, 28,* 3–71.

Forde, E. M. E., Francis, D., Riddoch, M. J., Rumiati, R. I., & Humphreys, G. W. (1997). On the links between visual knowledge and naming: A single case study of a patient with a category-specific impairment for living things. *Cognitive Neuropsychology, 14,* 403–458.

Forde, E. M. E., & Humphreys, G. W. (1999). Category-specific recognition impairments: a review of important case studies and influential theories. *Aphasiology, 13,* 169–193.

Forde, E. M. E., & Humphreys, G. W. (2002). *Category-specificity in mind and brain.* Hove: Psychology Press.

Funnell, E., & De Mornay Davies, P. (1997). JBR: A reassessment of concept familiarity and a category-specific disorder for living things. *Neurocase, 2,* 461–474.

Funnell, E., & Sheridan, J. S. (1992). Categories of knowledge? Unfamiliar aspects of living and nonliving things. *Cognitive Neuropsychology, 9,* 135–153.

Gaffan, D., & Heywood, C. A. (1993). A spurious category-specific visual agnosia for living things in normal humans and nonhuman primates. *Journal of Cognitive Neuroscience, 5,* 118–128.

Gainotti, G., & Silveri, M. C. (1996). Cognitive and anatomical locus of lesion in a patient with a category-specific semantic impairment for living beings. *Cognitive Neuropsychology, 13,* 357–389.

Gelman, S. A. (1988). The development of induction within natural kind and artifact categories. *Cognitive Psychology, 20,* 65–95.

Gonnerman, L. M., Andersen, E. S., Devlin, J. T., Kempler, D., & Seidenberg, M. S. (1997). Double dissociation of semantic categories in Alzheimer's disease. *Brain and Language, 57,* 254–279.

Harley, T. A. (1998). The semantic deficit in dementia: Connectionist approaches to what goes wrong in picture naming. *Aphasiology, 12,* 299–318.

Hart, J., Berndt, R. S., & Caramazza, A. (1985). Category-specific naming deficit following cerebral infarction. *Nature, 316,* 439–440.

Hart, J., & Gordon, B. (1992). Neural subsystems for object knowledge. *Nature, 359,* 60–64.

Hillis, A. E. & Caramazza, A. (1991). Category-specific naming and comprehension impairment: A double dissociation. *Brain, 114,* 2081–2094.

Hinton, G. E. & Shallice, T. (1991). Lesioning an attractor network. Investigations of acquired dyslexia. *Psychological Review, 98,* 74–96.

Hopfield, J. J. (1982). Neural networks and physical systems with emergent collective computational abilities. *Proceedings of the National Academy of Sciences, USA, 79,* 2554–2558.

Humphreys, G. W., & Forde, E. M. E. (2001). Hierarchies, similarity, and interactivity in object recognition: "Category-specific" neuropsychological deficits. *Behavioral and Brain Sciences, 24,* 453–509.

Humphreys, G. W., Freeman, T. A. C., & Muller, H. J. (1992). Lesioning a connectionist network of visual search: Selective effects on distracter grouping. *Canadian Journal of Psychology, 46,* 417–460.

Humphreys, G. W., Olson, A., Romani, C., & Riddoch, M. J. (1996). Competitive mechanisms of selection by space and object: A neuropsychological approach. In A. F. Kramer, M. G. H. Coles, & G. D. Logan (Eds.), *Converging operations in the study of visual attention*. Washington, DC: American Psychological Association.

Humphreys, G. W., & Riddoch, M. J. (1988). On the case for multiple semantic systems: A reply to Shallice. *Cognitive Neuropsychology, 5,* 143–150.

Jackendoff, R. (1990). *Semantic structures*. Cambridge, MA: MIT Press.

Keil, F. C. (1989). *Concepts, kinds, and cognitive development*. Cambridge, MA: MIT Press.

Kolinsky, R., Fery, P., Messina, D.; Peretz, I., Evinck, S., Ventura, P., & Morais, J. (2002). The fur of the crocodile and the mooing sheep: A study of a patient with a category-specific impairment for biological things. *Cognitive Neuropsychology, 19,* 301–342.

Kurbat, M. A. (1997). Can the recognition of living things being selectively impaired? *Neuropsychologia, 35,* 813–827.

Labov, W. (1973). The boundaries of words and their meanings. In C. J. Bailey & R. Shuy (Eds.), *New ways of analysing variation in English*. Washington, DC: Georgetown University Press.

Laiacona, M., Barbarotto, R., & Capitani, E. (1993). Perceptual and associative knowledge in category-specific impairment of semantic memory: A study of two cases. *Cortex, 29,* 727–740.

Laiacona, M., Capitani, E., & Barbarotto, R. (1997). Semantic category dissociations: A longitudinal study of two cases. *Cortex, 33,* 441–461.

Lamberts, K., & d'Ydewalle, G. (1990). What can psychologists learn from hidden-unit nets? *Behavioural and Brain Sciences, 13,* 499–500.

Lambon-Ralph, M. A., Howard, D., Nightingale, G., & Ellis, A. (1998). Are living and nonliving category-specific deficits causally linked to impaired perceptual or associative knowledge? Evidence from a category-specific double dissociation. *Neurocase, 4,* 311–338.

Leek, E. C., & Pothos, E. (2001). What is specific about category-specificity? Fractionating patterns of impairments and the spurious living/nonliving dichotomy. *Behavioural and Brain Sciences, 24* (3), 487–488.

Mahon, B., & Caramazza, A. (2001). The sensory/functional assumption or the data: Which do we keep? *Behavioural and Brain Sciences, 24,* (3), 488–489.

Malt, B., & Smith, E. (1984). Correlated properties in natural categories. *Journal of Verbal Learning and Verbal Behaviour, 23,* 250–269.

Massaro, D. W. (1988). Some criticisms of connectionist models of human performance. *Journal of Memory and Language, 27,* 213–234.

Mayall, K. A., & Humphreys, G. W. (1996). A connectionist model of alexia: Covert recognition and case mixing effects. *British Journal of Psychology, 87,* 355–402.

McCarthy, R. A., & Warrington, E. K. (1988). Evidence for modality-specific meaning systems in the brain. *Nature, 334,* 428–430.

McCloskey, M. (1991). Networks and theories: The place of connectionism in cognitive science. *Psychological Science, 2,* 387–395.

McLeod, P., Plunkett, K., & Rolls, E. T. (1998). *Introduction to connectionist modelling of cognitive processes*. Oxford: Oxford University Press.

McRae, K., de Sa, V. R., & Seidenberg, M. S. (1997). On the nature and scope of featural representations for word meaning. *Journal of Experimental Psychology: General, 126,* 99–130.

McRae, K., & Cree, G. S. (2002). Factors underlying category-specific semantic deficits. In E. M. E. Forde, & G. W. Humphreys (Eds.), *Category-specificity in mind and brain*. Hove: Psychology Press.

Moss, H. E., & Tyler, L. K. (2000). A progressive category-specific semantic deficit for non-living things. *Neuropsychologia, 38,* 60–82.

Moss, H. E., Tyler, L. K., & Devlin, J. T. (2002). The emergence of category-specific deficits in a distributed semantic system. In E. M. E. Forde, & G. W. Humphreys (Eds.), *Category-specificity in mind and brain*. Hove: Psychology Press.

Moss, H. E., Tyler, L. K., Durrant-Peatfield, M., & Bunn, E. M. (1998). Two eyes of a see-through: Impaired and intact semantic knowledge in a case of selective deficit for living things. *Neurocase, 4,* 291–310.

Moss, H. E., Tyler, L. K., & Jennings, F. (1997). When leopards lose their spots: Knowledge of visual properties in category-specific deficits for living things. *Cognitive Neuropsychology, 14,* 901–950.

Mozer, M. C., & Behrmann, M. (1990). On the interaction of selective attention and lexical knowledge: A connectionist account of neglect dyslexia. *Journal of Cognitive Neuroscience, 2,* 96–123.

Neilsen, J. M. (1946). *Agnosia, apraxia, aphasia: Their value in cerebral localisation.* New York: Harper.

Olson, A., & Caramazza, A. (1994). Representation and connectionist models: The NET spell experience. In G. D. A. Brown, & N. C. Ellis (Eds.), *Handbook of spelling: Theory, process and intervention.* Chichester: Wiley.

Olson, A., & Humphreys, G. W. (1997). Connectionist models of neuropsychological disorders. *Trends in Cognitive Science, 1,* 222–228.

Patterson, K. E., Seidenberg, M. S., & McClelland, J. L. (1989). Connections and disconnections: Acquired dyslexia in a computational model of reading processes. In R. G. M. Morris (Ed.), *Parallel distributed processing: Implications for psychology and neuroscience.* London: Oxford University Press.

Perry, C. (1999). Testing a computational account of category-specific deficits. *Journal of Cognitive Neuroscience, 11,* 312–320.

Pietrini, V., Nertempi, P., Vaglia, A., Revello, M. G., Pinna, V., & Ferro-Milone, F. (1988). Recovery from herpes simplex encephalitis: Selective impairment of specific semantic categories with neuroradiological correlation. *Journal of Neurology, Neurosurgery and Psychiatry, 51,* 1284–1293.

Pinker, S., & Prince, A. (1988). On language and connectionism: Analysis of a parallel distributed processing model of language acquisition. *Cognition, 28,* 59–108.

Plaut, D. C., & Shallice, T. (1993). Perseverative and semantic influences on visual object naming errors in optic aphasia: A connectionist account. *Journal of Cognitive Neuroscience, 5,* 89–117.

Rips, L. J., Shoben, E. J., & Smith, E. E. (1973). Semantic distance and the verification of semantic relations. *Journal of Verbal Learning and Verbal Behaviour, 12,* 1–20.

Rogers, T. T., & Plaut, D. C. (2002). Connectionist perspectives on category-specific deficits. In E. M. E. Forde, & G. W. Humphreys (Eds.). *Category-specificity in mind and brain.* Hove: Psychology Press.

Rosch, E., & Mervis, C. B. (1975). Family resemblances: Studies in the internal structure of categories. *Cognitive Psychology, 7,* 573–605.

Rumelhart, D. E., & McClelland, J. L. (1986). *Parallel distributed processing: Explorations in the microstructure of cognition: Vol. 1, Foundations.* Cambridge, MA: MIT Press.

Sacchett, C., & Humphreys, G. W. (1992). Calling a squirrel a squirrel but a canoe a wigwam: A category-specific deficit for artefactual objects and body parts. *Cognitive Neuropsychology, 9,* 73–86.

Saffran, E., & Schwartz, M. (1994). Of cabbages and things: Semantic memory from a neuropsychological perspective. In C. Umilta, & M. Moscovitch (Eds.), *Attention and Performance XV: Conscious and nonconscious information processing.* Cambridge, MA: MIT Press.

Samson, D., Pillon, A., & De Wilde, V. (1998). Impaired knowledge of visual and nonvisual attributes in a patient with a semantic impairment for living entities: A case of true category-specific deficit. *Neurocase, 4,* 273–290.

Santos, L. R., & Caramazza, A. (2002). The domain-specific hypothesis: A development and comparative perspective. In E. M. E. Forde, & G. W. Humphreys (Eds.), *Category-specificity in mind and brain.* Hove: Psychology Press.

Sartori, G., Miozzo, M., & Job, R. (1993). Category-specific impairments? Yes. *Quarterly Journal of Experimental Psychology, 46A,* 489–504.

Schneider, W. (1987). Connectionism: Is it a paradigm shift for psychology? *Behaviour Research Methods, Instruments and Computers, 19,* 73–83.

Seidenberg, M. S., & McClelland, J. L. (1989). A distributed, developmental model of word recognition and naming. *Psychological Review, 96,* 523–568.

Shallice. T. (1988). *From neuropsychology to mental structure.* Cambridge: Cambridge University Press.

Shelton, J. R., & Caramazza, A. (1999). Deficits in lexical and semantic processing: Implications for models of normal language. *Psychonomic Bulletin and Review, 6,* 5–27.

Shelton, J. R., Fouch, E., & Caramazza, A. (1998). The selective sparing of body part knowledge: A case study. *Neurocase, 4,* 339–351.

Sheridan, J., & Humphreys, G. W. (1993). A verbal-semantic category-specific recognition impairment. *Cognitive Neuropsychology, 10,* 143–184.

Silveri, M. C., Daniele, A., Guistolisi, L., & Gainotti, G. (1991). Dissociation between knowledge of living and nonliving things in dementia of the Alzheimer's type. *Neurology, 41,* 545–546.

Silveri, M. C., & Gainotti, G. (1988). Interaction between vision and language in category-specific impairment. *Cognitive Neuropsychology, 5,* 677–709.

Sirigu, A., Duhamel, J. R., & Poncet, M. (1991). The role of sensorimotor experience in object recognition: A case of multimodal agnosia. *Brain, 114,* 2555–2573.

Small, S., Hart, J., Gordon, B., & Hollard, A. (1993). Performance variability in a diffusely lesioned model of semantic representation for object naming. *Neurology, 43,* 404.

Smolensky, P. (1988). On the proper treatment of connectionism. *Behavioural and Brain Sciences, 11,* 1–74.

Stewart, F., Parkin, A. J., & Hunkin, N. M. (1992). Naming impairment following recovery from herpes simplex encephalitis: Category-specific? *Quarterly Journal of Experimental Psychology, 44A,* 261–284.

Swales, M., & Johnson, R. (1992). Patients with semantic memory loss: Can they relearn lost concepts? *Neuropsychological Rehabilitation, 2,* 295–305.

Tippett, L. J., McAuliffe, S., & Farah, M. J. (1995). Preservation of categorical knowledge in Alzheimer's disease: A computational account. *Memory, 3,* 519–533.

Tulving, E. (1972). Episodic and semantic memory. In E. Tulving, & W. Donaldson (Eds.), *Organisation of memory.* New York: Academic Press.

Tversky, A. (1977). Features of similarity. *Psychological Review, 84,* 327–352.

Tyler, L. K., Durrant-Peatfield, M., Levy, J., Voice, J. K., & Moss, H. E. (1996). Distinctiveness and correlations in the structure of categories: Behavioural data and a connectionist model. *Brain and Language, 55,* 89–92.

Tyler, L. K., & Moss, H. E. (1997). Functional properties of concepts: Studies of normal and brain-damaged patients. *Cognitive Neuropsychology, 14,* 426–486.

Tyler, L. K., Moss, H. E., Durrant-Peatfield, M. R., & Levy, J. P. (2000). Conceptual structure and the structure of concepts: A distributed account of category-specific deficits. *Brain and Language, 75,* 195–231.

Warrington, E. K., & McCarthy, R. A. (1983). Category-specific access dysphasia. *Brain, 106,* 859–878.

Warrington, E. K., & McCarthy, R. A. (1987). Categories of knowledge: Further fractionations and an attempted integration. *Brain, 110,* 1273–1296.

Warrington, E. K., & Shallice, T. (1984). Category specific semantic impairments. *Brain, 107,* 829–853.

Yamadori, A., & Albert, M. L. (1973). Word category aphasia. *Cortex, 9,* 112–125.

Zorzi, M., & Perry, C., Ziegler, J., & Coltheart, M. (1999). Category-specific deficits in a self-organizing model of the lexical semantic system. In D. Heincke, G. W. Humphreys, & A. C. Olson (Eds.), *Connectionist models in cognitive neuroscience*. London: Springer-Verlag.

CHAPTER SEVEN

Connectionist models of short-term memory for serial order

Mike Page
University of Hertfordshire, Hatfield, UK

Immediate serial recall is one of the best-known tasks in cognitive psychology. Participants are typically given a sequence of familiar verbal items that they are then asked to recall in the correct order. Among many theorists, Alan Baddeley and colleagues have perhaps been the most successful in identifying the cognitive components underlying this simple task (Baddeley, 1986; Baddeley & Hitch, 1974). Within their more general working memory (WM) model, they have identified a subsystem that they call the phonological loop. This comprises a phonological store and an articulatory control process that is assumed to refresh the contents of the store via a process usually identified with active rehearsal. The WM model has been extremely useful in identifying those components of short-term memory that subserve immediate serial recall (ISR). Nonetheless, Baddeley's account is a verbal one and thus suffers the problems of a purely verbal model. In particular, it does not describe any detailed mechanism by which serial recall is actually implemented and hence cannot explain some of the detailed patterns present in the ISR data. A number of researchers have sought to provide more quantitative models of immediate serial recall. In some cases, these researchers have tried to keep their models close to Baddeley's verbal characterization, essentially supplying a mechanism by which the verbal model might be implemented. In others, the modellers have tried to use their simulations to call into question some of the assumptions of the verbal model.

In this chapter I will review several recent models of immediate serial recall. For the most part, these have been instantiated as connectionist models and thus fall naturally within the remit of this chapter. I will also describe one mathematical model that has not been characterized as connectionist (Henson, 1998). I do so partly to give a more complete survey of the models that compete in this area of application, and partly because I believe that this mathematical model shares a sufficiently large family resemblance with the connectionist models that its implementation as a connectionist model would be reasonably straightforward.

For each model, I will first describe those aspects of its implementation crucial to its performance. (For a more detailed account, it will be necessary to refer to the original papers.) In the case of the connectionist models, I will try to identify certain implementational choices that the authors have made and to motivate these choices in the context of the modelling task. As will become apparent, due to a certain amount of co-evolution of these models over several years, it is now the case that most of the models can do a reasonably good job of modelling the basic effects seen in the ISR data. I will give brief accounts of the principal results for each model. Nonetheless, there are aspects of the available data that certain of the models find difficult to simulate, either due to some characteristic property of the model itself, or because the models' authors deemed the particular data in question to fall outside the domain of application of the memory component being modelled.

In a companion chapter elsewhere (Page & Henson, 2001), we have discussed in detail how some of the models described here deal with two aspects of the ISR data: first, the rapid drop in recall performance and disappearance of the phonological similarity effect (PSE) over short, filled retention intervals; and second, the positional bias in the pattern of between-list intrusion errors. Most models were able to cope with one or other of the effects but found it difficult to account for both. The only model to have simulated both explicitly is Henson's start–end model (Henson, 1998), which takes advantage of a two-store structure (labile phonological and longer-lasting positional) similar, but not identical, to that that suggested in our own work (e.g. Page & Norris, 1998b). This two-store structure is appropriate because the data suggest a dissociation between the effects of phonological similarity and the presence of positional intrusions, a dissociation that makes modelling difficult for models built around a single store. Rather than revisit this discussion in the current chapter, I will briefly mention the relevant issues when describing each of the models.

There are, however, some other desiderata that might be used in choosing between the models, and these will be discussed more fully in what follows. The first concerns the effect on recall of irrelevant sound (IS) and, more specifically, irrelevant speech. It is well known that immediate serial recall of, for example, a list of items presented visually, is adversely affected by an irrelevant and, typically, meaningless speech stimulus (such as foreign language speech) presented auditorily during list presentation (Baddeley &

Salamé, 1986; Colle & Welsh, 1976; Salamé & Baddeley, 1982, 1986). This is in spite of the fact that participants are advised to ignore the irrelevant stimulus, having been accurately informed that it has nothing to do with the task in hand. The effect is not limited to speech stimuli, and has been shown to result from other sequential stimuli, such as irrelevant tone sequences (e.g. Jones & Macken, 1993). Recent work in our group (Norris, Baddeley, & Page, 2004) has extended this result to show several additional points of note. First, the irrelevant sound effect can be seen even when the IS itself is presented after the end of the stimulus list but before recall (cf. Macken, Mosdell, & Jones, 1999). This is true even if rehearsal is prevented during this retention interval by requiring participants to read aloud digits appearing at a rapid rate (two per second). Second, this retroactive effect of irrelevant sound can be seen even after retention intervals sufficient to cause a marked drop in performance and to result in the disappearance of any phonological similarity effect. Finally, such a long-lasting effect of irrelevant sound is only seen under circumstances in which, *ex hypothese*, the material to be remembered has at some point resided in the phonological store; this is evidenced by the fact the long-lasting effect of IS is eliminated by articulatory suppression during visual input. Models need to be tested against data. As I describe each of the models, therefore, I shall suggest ways in which they might, or might not, be able to simulate this pattern of results.

One further aspect that might be used to choose between models is prompted by the question "What is short-term sequential memory for?" While much has been done to investigate the intricacies of ISR, it would be somewhat self-regarding to assume that evolution has equipped humans with the capacity for ISR solely to keep cognitive psychologists in gainful employ. One of the best motivated accounts of the evolutionary importance of ISR has been proposed by Baddeley, Gathercole, & Papagno (1998), who suggest that the phonological loop is critical for language learning. More specifically, they have identified a number of pieces of evidence that support the view that the phonological loop is crucially involved in the learning of vocabulary. This evidence is drawn from various strands of research. First, research has shown that so-called "short-term memory patients", such as PV (Baddeley, Papagno, & Vallar, 1988; Vallar & Baddeley, 1984a, 1984b), SC (Trojano & Grossi, 1995) and SR (Baddeley, 1993), who are characterized by extremely poor performance on auditory ISR tasks, are also impaired in their ability to learn new vocabulary (typically vocabulary from another language). This link with the phonological loop has been investigated directly by Papagno, Valentine, & Baddeley (1991), who have shown that articulatory suppression, designed to interfere with phonological recoding, can be used to disrupt the learning, by normal participants, of visually presented vocabulary. More indirect evidence has been provided by Baddeley et al. (1998), who have reviewed evidence that nonword repetition ability and span in children (both considered good measures of phonological loop capacity) can be used to predict vocabulary size, with cross-lagged correlations between the measures suggesting a direction of causality consistent with the phonological loop/ vocabulary-learning hypothesis.

Given this proposed link between ISR, at least as mediated by the phonological loop, and the learning of vocabulary, it is worth comparing the computational models of the loop with reference to the degree to which they are structured so as to support the long-term learning of sequences to which they are, perhaps repeatedly, exposed. While such a comparison between models is necessarily more speculative than one that looks directly at the ability of the models to account for particular quantitative data, it is nonetheless instructive to seek to extend the models to the naturalistic demands of long-term learning, even in cases where such an extension has not yet been entertained by the models' authors.

The models that I will describe are: the latest version of the Burgess & Hitch model (BH; Burgess & Hitch, 1999); Brown, Preece, & Hulme's oscillator-based associative recall model (OSCAR; Brown, Preece, & Hulme, 2000); Page & Norris's primacy model (PM; Page & Norris, 1998b); Farrell & Lewandowsky's serial-order-in-a-box model (SOB; Farrell & Lewandowsky, 2002); and Henson's start–end model (SEM; Henson, 1998).

BURGESS & HITCH (1999)

Burgess & Hitch's (1999) model is a reworking and an extension of their influential earlier model (Burgess & Hitch, 1992), that was the first model to attempt a connectionist simulation of ISR within a working memory framework. The later model addresses certain problems with its predecessor, most notably problems regarding the shape of the simulated serial position curves and the detail of the phonological similarity effect. The BH model is a localist connectionist model (see Page, 2000, for a discussion of the distinction between localist and distributed models), having localist representations of list items and of their constituent phonemes. Nonetheless, one of the critical components of the BH model is a distributed representation of context, arranged such that contexts corresponding to neighbouring points in time (e.g. neighbouring list positions) exhibit a higher degree of (vector) similarity than do contexts corresponding to points more separated in time. The structure of the BH model is illustrated in Fig. 7.1. There is a field of item nodes connected together in an inhibitory arrangement such that only one item can have sustained positive activation at any given time. This "winner-takes-all" layer implements what Houghton (1990) has called a competitive queue (cf. Grossberg, 1978; Glasspool, Chapter 8, this volume). Item nodes receive activation from several separate sources. Most importantly, they can be activated via learned, weighted connections from the layer of nodes

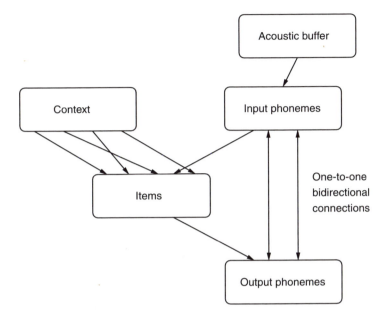

Figure 7.1.   The structure of the Burgess & Hitch (1999) model.

representing a contextual signal. They can also be activated either directly, by visual presentation of the corresponding lexical item, or indirectly (via the nodes labelled "input phonemes"), by item presentation in the auditory modality. The item nodes also have outward-going connections to the nodes corresponding to their constituent phonemes (labelled "output phonemes"), with these nodes in turn being connected bidirectionally and in a one-to-one fashion to the corresponding input-phoneme nodes. All connections other than those linking the input phonemes with the output phonemes are modifiable via a Hebbian-like learning rule and have different components representing short-term (fast-decaying) and long-term (slow-decaying) weights.

The operation of the network can be briefly summarized as follows. On presentation of a list item, the item node that best responds to that item is activated. At the same time, any previously activated item is suppressed by giving it a large inhibitory input that decays at a given rate thereafter. If the item was presented auditorily, then its constituent input phonemes will have been activated, leading to activation in the corresponding output phonemes. If presentation was visual, the output phonemes, and hence the input phonemes, will have been activated via the long-term weights linking the activated item node to its constituent output phonemes. The context units are set to a state appropriate to the current input position and all modifiable weights are adjusted by the Hebbian-like learning rule mentioned above. When the next item in the list arrives, a new item node is selected, the previously active item is suppressed, the input and output phoneme nodes change to reflect the phonemic constituents of the new item, the context units are altered so as to reflect the next list position, and all modifiable weights and inhibitory signals are decayed by the relevant factors. Learning of the appropriate context-to-item and item-to-phoneme weights then proceeds as before. This cycle is carried out for each of the items in the to-be-remembered list.

When list recall is required, any active item is suppressed, the activations of the phoneme nodes are set to zero and the context units are set to a state representing the first list-position. The item nodes thus have two sources of input. First, there is weighted input from the context units, such that items are activated to the extent that the context pattern with which they were associated during list presentation is similar to (i.e. overlaps with) the current context pattern. Second, there is residual inhibitory input from the decaying suppression that was applied during input, such that items from earlier in the list, that have had more time to recover from suppression, will be less suppressed than later list items. This latter input is a new feature of the BH model and leads to the possibly surprising result that the simulated memory span of the BH model is scarcely affected by the absence of the context units. This ordinal (i.e. nonpositional) ordering mechanism is reminiscent of the mechanism underlying the primacy model (Page & Norris, 1998b, described below) and helps the BH model implement the fill-in property required for accurate modelling of serial position curves (Henson, Norris, Page, & Baddeley, 1996; Page & Norris, 1998b).

Recall is a two-phase process: the item that is most activated by the combination of positional context and residual inhibition quashes activation in other items nodes (winner-takes-all dynamics). Activation then flows from the selected item node to its constituent output phonemes, thence to its constituent input phonemes, that in turn boost the input to the selected item and, importantly, other item nodes to the extent that the corresponding items share consituent phonemes with the selected item. Another competition is then held across the input items to select, this time under noisy conditions, the item with the largest net input. It is therefore at this second stage that items phonologically similar to the correct item can be inadvertently selected.

The BH model is better able than its predecessor to model the major pattern of results found across ISR tasks. The model is not, however, without its deficiencies. Even though Burgess and Hitch eschew any attempt to fit their model quantitatively to the experimental data, it is clear, for example, that the serial position curves that the model produces do not show the marked asymmetry of those found experimentally. Elsewhere (Page & Henson, 2001) we have identified what is perhaps a more fundamental problem with the model, namely its inability to model simultaneously both the absence of a phonological similarity effect after reasonably short delays and the presence of positional bias in the pattern of between-list intrusions. The basic problem is that in the BH model the two effects result from the operation of the same system, thus making it difficult to model the observed dissociation. As noted in the introduction, I would like to concentrate here on other matters, namely the modelling of the irrelevant sound effect and on the issue of long-term learning.

In common with the majority of modellers of ISR, Burgess & Hitch (1999) do not choose to model the irrelevant sound effect. This is perhaps because the data have hitherto offered rather fewer constraints than are found in modelling certain other effects. Nonetheless, we believe our recent data on the retroactive effects of IS provide such constraints. First, we must hypothesize a locus for the implementation of the IS effect itself. Data analysis reveals that the effect of IS is found both in an increased number of order errors and an increased number of omission errors (see e.g. Page & Norris, 2003). In addition, the overall effect of IS does not change much with serial position, perhaps increasing slightly, in line with the overall number of errors. These considerations suggest two possible loci for the IS effect in the BH model.

The first possibility is that IS disrupts the weights in the context–item pathways. This assumption might be justified for irrelevant sound simultaneous with the presentation of the context–item pairs, but seems less justified in the case in which IS is presented between presentation and recall (i.e. when IS shows its retroactive effect). Why should IS affect context–item associations when neither context nor item is active at the time of IS presentation? Let us assume, however, that IS can affect context–item associations in this way. The fact that IS has a long lasting effect—extending across retention intervals of 9–12 s (at which time performance is asymptotic and the phonological similarity effect has gone)—implies that IS should have a reliable effect on both the short-term and the long-term weight components of the context–item associations. Such an assumption would explain why the IS is larger at short retention intervals but still reliable at longer intervals. However, it cannot explain why articulatory suppression (AS) should abolish the effect of IS for visual materials at both short and long retention intervals. In the BH model, articulatory suppression at input has a deleterious effect on the learning of the short-term weights between input phonemes and items (I assume that the long-term weights here are sufficiently robust to remain largely unaffected). There is nothing about articulatory suppression as modelled, therefore, that can abolish a disruption by IS, if IS is held to affect the context–item associations. Indeed, it seems possible (without the benefit of simulation) that AS might even exacerbate the IS effect in the BH model, if the IS effect is modelled in this way.

Let us turn, therefore, to the second possible locus of the IS effect, namely the connections between the input phonemes and the items. It transpires that as a result of its rather unusual two-phase recall process, the BH model will show effects on both order and item errors of disruption of these connections. Nonetheless, questions similar to those raised with regard to the first account can be raised again here. The data show that for a visually presented list, with AS during the list as well as during an additional 9 s retention interval, 6 s of IS presented centrally in the retention interval has no effect on recall performance. Since long-term connections would be the only input phoneme–item links operative under these conditions (any changes to the short-term equivalents having been blocked by AS), the lack of an effect of IS in this condition implies a negligible effect of IS on these long-term connections. Now consider the condition in which the list is presented in the absence of AS (such that short-term phoneme–item connections are established), but still with AS and IS accompanying the retention interval. We have surmised that IS has a negligible effect on the long-term weights, so the reliable effect of IS in this condition must be due to its effects on short-term phoneme–item connections, if the interface between input phonemes and items is to be the locus of the IS effect. But there are at least two problems here. The first is similar to that raised above, i.e. why should IS effect phoneme–item weights when IS is presented at a time when neither the items nor, probably, the phonemes are active. Second, why would we expect short-term weights to be having an effect after an effective retention interval of, in this case, 12 s (including list presentation time)? Using the BH model parameters, we can see that any short-term weights established during list presentation will have decayed to only 3% of their original values by the time recall is required (note that this value will effectively be reduced further when the combined effect of decay at both item–output phoneme and input phoneme–item connections is taken into account). This decay is consistent with the fact that performance reaches an asymptotic level after retention has been delayed by 9 s or so. But if these connection weights have so substantially decayed, it seems unlikely that the IS effect, which survives the delay, results from their disruption.

The above considerations suggest that it will be difficult for the BH model to capture the detail of the IS effect, just as it has proved difficult for it to capture that of the phonological similarity effect (it predicts a long-lasting PSE, contrary to the data; Page & Henson, 2001). I now move on to a necessarily brief discussion of long-term learning in the BH model.

As discussed above, one of the purposes of the phonological loop is thought to be the supporting of the learning of long-term memorial representations of frequently encountered sequential stimuli, e.g. vocabulary. It is rather difficult to study the learning of vocabulary experimentally, but some work has been done on the effects of stimulus repetition in the ISR task. This work dates back to Hebb (1961), who showed that if a given stimulus list in an ISR experiment was repeated every third list, then performance on recall of that list improved substantially over repetitions. This has become known as the Hebb effect. The natural way for the BH model to simulate such an effect and, indeed, the way the authors suggest it should be modelled, is for the long-term position–item associations to build up between the repeated items and their corresponding list positions. However, Cumming, Page, & Norris (2003) have recently provided data that suggest that such build-up does not take place. They used transfer lists made up of alternate items in the same places as in the learned Hebb list, with remaining items allocated randomly in the other positions. If the BH model of Hebb effects were correct, then there should have been improved performance on those items that maintained their position. In fact performance on such transfer lists was indistinguishable at all list positions from that on control lists. These considerations call into question whether performance improvement in the Hebb task should best be simulated by the strengthening of context–item associations.

On a more speculative note, we might consider that the strengthening of position–item associations is also unlikely to be of general applicability in the naturalistic vocabulary-learning task. Unlike in the experimental set-up for ISR experiments, the positional contexts of items in to-be-learned word-forms are rarely marked as such in the incoming speech stream. Some cues to the starts/ends of words do occur in patterns of stress and at utterance borders, but they are unreliable in general as guides to the location of yet-to-be-learned sequences. Indeed, some recent data indicate that very young infants are able to learn to recognize repeated subsequences in long sequentially organized stimuli (syllable sequences) from which all such boundary cues have been removed (Saffran, Aslin, & Newport, 1996). To extend the context–item association model in such a way as to allow it plausibly to model such abilities seems, at first glance, to be far from trivial. One possibility might involve large numbers of separate context vectors with at least one made available to "start" at each sequence item, in case that item heralds the beginning of some to-be-learned item sequence. The twin requirements, to remain sensitive to new sequences worthy of learning, and to avoid the continual relearning of already familiar sequences, would complicate considerably the structure of such a system. Even supposing regularly occurring sequences could be learned, of what would such a learned sequence consist? Presumably it would comprise a set of strengthened connections from particular contexts to particular items, but if this were the case, how would the sequence knowledge be protected against re-use of the context nodes to code lists other than the learned list? Furthermore, how would recognition of the learned sequence proceed, particularly given that, as the model stands, there are no connections from items back to contexts? (Note that item–context links are a necessary requirement for a recognition process, but are a long way from comprising a sufficient mechanism.) While I am not claiming that any of these behaviours is impossible in the framework of a position–item association model, it certainly seems that such models do not form a natural foundation on which to build models of long-term learning. This is in spite of the fact that long-term sequence learning in naturalistic environments is the very ability the phonological loop is supposed to expedite.

Having spent some time describing the BH model, I now turn to another position–item associative model, namely the OSCAR model (Brown et al., 2000). Because the two models are related, it will be possible to deal more briefly with the latter.

OSCAR

As noted above, the oscillator-based associative recall model (OSCAR; Brown et al., 2000) also performs recall via a mechanism involving position–item associations. While the positional context employed in the BH model is a simple moving window of activation (modified somewhat for hierarchical coding in grouped lists), Brown et al. have gone to considerable lengths to provide a mechanism that generates a positional context by combining the outputs of a number of simple oscillators. In designing this mechanism, they have sought to provide a positional context signal that meets a number of criteria: it should be reinstatable at recall; it should be nonrepeating and, hence, unambiguous; it should use codes with higher mutual similarity to represent positions more closely spaced in time; and it should permit a hierarchical coding of position in grouped lists (e.g. expressing both position-in-list and position-in-group). Note that all these criteria were met by the more simple positional model used by Burgess & Hitch (1999) and form a fairly general statement of the requirements of any position-based recall mechanism. The precise means by which Brown et al. have implemented their positional context signal need not be of concern here. More germane is the means by which this positional information is used in the ISR task.

In connectionist terminology, OSCAR includes distributed representations of both list positions and list items. This is in contrast to the BH model, which uses localist representation of list items. In OSCAR, list items are represented as length-normalized vectors of randomly generated numbers, with the added feature that list items that are phonologically similar are represented by vectors that share a common portion of their corresponding vectors. Position–item associations are mediated by a matrix of connections fully linking elements of the context vector to elements of the item vector. Learning in this matrix is implemented using a Hebbian learning rule that increments the matrix for each list item by an amount equal to the outer product of the relevant context and item vectors. Recall at a given list position is implemented by reinstating (perhaps only partially) the appropriate context signal, passing this vector through the learned weight matrix to give activation across the item layer. This distributed pattern is then compared with each of the patterns representing members of a possible response vocabulary. The best-matching item is then chosen, before being output (subject to a threshold—see below) and suppressed to discourage its subsequent use. (Note that the use of a best-match process and of item-specific response suppression suggests the use of later, localist item codes, this being implicit in Brown et al.'s reference to Houghton's (1990) competitive queuing.)

The "Hebbian matrix" has only a limited capacity to store position–item associations without interference, particularly in cases where the items involved share some common (e.g. phonological) features. In addition, learning rate is modulated across list positions, with learning rate set high at early positions and decreasing exponentially thereafter. This allows OSCAR to model primacy effects in ISR better. Other mechanisms, some of which also assist in the modelling of primacy effects, include: the degradation, by adding noise, of weights in the context–item matrix, with this degradation being applied for each item uttered in a retention interval (if any) and for each item recalled; weight decay, implemented as a multiplicative decrease in the magnitude of weight changes applied each time a new context–item association is added; and an output threshold applied to the strength required of a recalled item for it to be successfully generated at recall.

As has been described elsewhere (Page & Henson, 2001), the fact that the context signal connects directly to a distributed representation of the list items causes difficulties for OSCAR with regard to the modelling of the phonological similarity effect with lists of mixed confusability. This is because the model is, in Page & Norris' (1998b) terminology, a one-stage model. It also has difficulty in accounting for the rapid disappearance of the PSE over short, filled retention intervals (Page & Henson, 2001). Does OSCAR have similar problems accounting for the pattern of results with irrelevant sound?

The first thing to note is that the OSCAR model does not include any description of the effects of either irrelevant sound or articulatory suppression. It is therefore necessary to postulate the likely locus of the effects of such manipulations. Starting with irrelevant sound, the fact that IS affects order and item errors strongly suggests that irrelevant sound should have its effect on OSCAR's context–item weight matrix. This might either be due to some "leakage" of the irrelevant stimuli into the learning of the weight vector, thus adversely affecting its capacity, or it might be due to a increased level of weight decay during the period over which the IS is presented. Either of these could explain the basic effect of simultaneous IS and the retroactive effect of IS in a retention interval. The former explanation might have difficulty explaining the lack of a prospective effect of IS, although the interpretation of this condition is complicated by the fact that Brown et al. (2000) treat the context–weight matrix as being set to zero before the presentation of a given list. (Naturally this assumption would have to be dropped in general, if only to model the data relating between-list positional intrusions that are a major motivating factor for such models based on position–item associations.)

OSCAR has more trouble, however, modelling the data in more detail. One point of difficulty centres on the fact that the magnitude of the IS effect decreases over short retention intervals. For the data presented in Norris et al. (2004), the effect of IS (on recall of four-letter lists) at long delays (9 s, 12 s) is to increase the mean percentage error from 41% to 44%. Unpublished comparison data, taken from a short-retention version of exactly the same task, showed that IS increased errors from 17% to 22%. Whether one views the increase in percentage error in absolute terms or as a proportion of baseline error (in which case the difference is magnified), it is clear that the effect of IS does not increase with time, even though performance at the long retention intervals is very far from being at floor (floor being at least 75% error). Consideration of the OSCAR model suggests that the effect of any manipulation that reduces the signal in, or adds noise to, the context–item weight matrix should have an increased effect the weaker the baseline signal, provided that a floor in performance has not been reached. This implies that OSCAR should predict a increased effect of IS at longer delays, contrary to the data. There are further problems for OSCAR in explaining a continued effect of IS in the absence of an effect of phonological similarity. In OSCAR the context–item weights impinge on phonological representations. If it is these weights that suffer during the presentation of IS, we should expect an effect of PSE everywhere that we find an IS effect, again contrary to the data.

On a related note, we come to the effect of articulatory suppression. The fact that AS eliminates both the phonological similarity effect and the irrelevant sound effect for visual presentation, at both long and short intervals, strongly suggests that ordered recall under these circumstances could not rely on the context–item weights described in the OSCAR model. This implies that the model should be extended to include some modality-neutral item representations (i.e. item representations not reflecting inter-item phonological similarity) whose association with the current context might permit recall, albeit at reduced levels of performance. Such an additional system might indeed be employed as a back-up store when phonological short-term memory has either decayed or has been impeded by AS, and it might even show the pattern of positional intrusions that survives AS (Page & Henson, 2001). But if positional intrusions and back-up performance are attributed to a long-lasting and nonphonological store, what justification remains for using positional-intrusion data to motivate a context–item model of the phonological loop, of the kind that OSCAR represents? I will return to this topic later.

To turn to the second of the questions on which this chapter is focused, is OSCAR likely to provide a mechanism for long-term learning of frequently occurring, sequentially structured stimuli, such as in the Hebb effect or in the learning of vocabulary? The answer is no, for reasons sufficiently similar to those discussed above in relation to the BH model that I will not dwell too much on them here. In OSCAR, changes in the oscillator-based context signal are supposed to represent the ongoing passage of time. This suggests that the second repetition of a to-be-learned stimulus will occur in a context different from that in which it originally appeared. It is possible to make a portion of the oscillators reset themselves at the beginning of each trial in such a way that they represent some coding of within-list position (see Brown et al., 2000, for details of the implementation) but the mechanism is unlikely to permit the build-up of position–item associations without considerable interference from intervening lists and, in the particular implementation of OSCAR described, without overloading the capacity of the context–item weight matrix. OSCAR thus offers no clues as to why the phonological loop should be critically involved in the learning of, for example, vocabulary.

In summary, OSCAR has difficulties simulating either the pattern of results that characterizes the phonological loop component of short-term memory, namely the effects of phonological similarity, irrelevant sound, and delay, and the interactions between these effects. Moreover, for many of the reasons discussed with reference to the BH model, it does not suggest a coherent account of the formation of long-term memory for sequences. Without considerable modification, therefore, OSCAR's role is thus likely to be limited to the modelling of nonphonological short-term/medium-term memory, as seen in tasks such as recency judgement and free recall. This same type of memory might be employed as a back-up mechanism for performing serial-recall tasks when phonological short-term memory is not available.

THE START–END MODEL (HENSON, 1998)

While not strictly a connectionist model, the start–end model (SEM; Henson, 1998) is sufficiently similar in aims and approach that it merits inclusion here. It has the added attraction that it is one of the most complete and successful models of the ISR task, although it buys this success with a degree of complexity in its formulation. Like the two models described above, SEM is based around position–item associations. For SEM, within-list position is represented as a two-dimensional vector, with one dimension representing something like a position's "degree of startness" and the other dimension representing its "degree of endness" (cf. Houghton, 1990; see Glasspool, Chapter 8, this volume, for further discussion of start–end coding). The degree-of-startness is set to unity for the first position and decreases exponentially (with a parametrically variable exponent) with increasing list position. The degree-of-endness increases with list position (with its own, typically different, exponent) before reaching its maximum value (a further parameter) at the final list position. At list presentation, an episodic token is formed for each list item, containing information relating to the item's identity and the two-dimensional vector corresponding to its within-list position. As in the case of the BH and OSCAR models, the positional information can be elaborated to include additional information, such as within-group position for items in grouped lists. There is also an entry in the SEM token that represents a general context in which the item appears. This entry starts at unity and decreases by a given multiple for each "change in context", where a change in context is usually assumed to occur at the start of a new stimulus list. Finally, and crucially, each item in a stimulus list has what is called a phonological activation. This can be conceived as involving a localist representation that activates when its corresponding item is presented and decays thereafter. In fact, in some of the simulations described in Henson (1998) the phonological activation is set to unity if the item was in the most recent list, zero otherwise. In the multitrial version of Henson's model, memory tokens are established and the relevant phonological activation is boosted for each item encountered, whether during stimulus input or during recall.

Having established a set of tokens corresponding to a given list, recall proceeds by setting up a memory cue. The cue is structured in the same way as a token and contains a start-end vector corresponding to the cued list position, an optional start-end vector cueing within-group position, and a context entry that is always unity. Obviously, the cue token contains no item information. Short-term memory tokens are activated to the extent that they are similar to the memory cue. Similarity is calculated as product of the similarities of the tokens' components, with similarity of components equal to a negative exponential function of the Euclidean distance between the corresponding vectors, multiplied by the square root of their vector product (see Henson, 1998). Following activation of the memory tokens by the cue, noise is added and the item type with the highest resulting activation is selected. (The activation of an item type is deemed to be the maximum activation of tokens of that type; this is to deal with repetitions of a given stimulus item and is discussed in detail in the original paper.) Before the selected item is output, there is a second stage of activation and competition, analogous to that proposed in the primacy model (Henson et al., 1996; Norris, Page, & Baddeley, 1995; Page & Norris, 1998b).

In this second stage, each item competes with a strength equal to the sum of three terms: the relevant type activation from the first stage; a noise term; and a term representing phonological short-term memory. This phonological short-term memory term is itself the product of three terms: the item's phonological activation; the phonological similarity that the item shares with the item selected at the first stage; and a term representing the suppression of previous responses. Once the second-stage competition has been run and a winner selected, the selected item is output, contingent on its activation exceeding an omission threshold.

Henson's (1998) model is quite complex, but gives a very full account of a good deal of ISR data. We shall focus here on the two topics of immediate concern, viz. the irrelevant sound effect and the long-term learning of sequences. Henson raises both these issues in the discussion section of his paper. With regard to irrelevant sound, Henson suggests that the effect might be modelled by postulating that irrelevant sound (and, indeed, other changing-state stimuli) interferes with the coding of position and hence disrupts serial recall. Unfortunately, this account is not sufficient to explain the retroactive effect of IS described above—there is no reason why IS should disrupt positional information when it is presented some time after the time at which that positional information has been encoded in its memory tokens. We therefore must look for another locus of the IS effect in SEM. Perhaps IS could be held to increase the rate of change of list context with time. This would have the effect of generally decreasing the cued activation of memory tokens and would have a corresponding effect on both order and item errors in serial recall. But this solution, too, does not capture the effect and suffers from at least two serious problems. The first is that SEM would then predict that articulatory suppression would not be capable of eliminating the effect of irrelevant sound. This is because in SEM, articulatory suppression is held to eliminate the phonological activations of list items, but not their memory tokens. Indeed, Henson suggests that the memory tokens would be functional in the recall of lists presented visually under AS, from which we can infer that anything that affects the memory tokens should survive as an effect under concurrent AS. We can conclude, therefore, that IS cannot affect SEM's memory tokens. The second problem is that even if IS could be plausibly maintained to affect the memory tokens, this would suggest a larger effect size for longer retention intervals, for reasons similar to those discussed above with regard to OSCAR. This is contrary to the data.

So where does IS have its effect in SEM if not in the memory tokens? The only locus remaining is on the short-term phonological representations. Again, several considerations argue against this alternative account. First, Henson (1998) states that the second stage is effectively transparent to non-confusable items, so no effect would be expected unless IS made drastic changes to the phonological activations. Second, if such drastic changes were made, one would expect IS to modulate the phonological similarity effect—it does not (Salamé & Baddeley, 1986). Third, if IS had its effect only on the fast-decaying phonological activations, then there would be no long-lived effect of IS. For all these reasons, IS cannot be modelled by SEM via an effect on phonological activations. As we have ruled out an effect of IS on the memory codes, we are left with no explanation for the pattern of results found with irrelevant sound.

Is SEM any more successful in suggesting an account of long-term memory for sequences. Henson (1998) discusses the topic briefly (p. 115) and concludes that SEM is not particularly suited to the task. SEM simply accrues tokens in memory, with nothing in particular to link an occurrence of an item in a given list position with the occurrence of the same item in the same position several lists later. Being essentially a position–item association model, SEM would also have problems similar to those discussed with reference to BH and OSCAR. For example, Henson mentions that long-term sequence memory might be built up by having a different start and end marker for each sequence (cf. Houghton, 1990). But this raises all the problems of the lack of such markers in naturalistic situations and of the need for marker proliferation, that I discussed briefly above.

In summary, SEM is a detailed and effective model that seeks to simulate in great detail a broad range of ISR data. Its purview includes not just what has classically been termed the "phonological loop" but also recall that proceeds in the absence of phonological activation. Nonetheless, it fails satisfactorily to account for the extended IS effect and offers no clues to how long-term memory for sequences is related to the short-term equivalent. In Page & Henson (2001), we suggested how the advantages of SEM, that are numerous, can be best exploited in combination with a primacy model of the phonological loop. I shall develop this point later when discussing the primacy model.

THE SERIAL-ORDER-IN-A-BOX MODEL (SOB; FARRELL & LEWANDOWSKY, 2002)

The penultimate model to be addressed is the SOB model of Farrell & Lewandowsky (2002). The model is recent and has not been developed to the point where it deals with the interactions between some of the factors familiar from the working memory literature. Nonetheless, it is a thoroughly connectionist model, different in style from others mentioned here, so I will describe its operation, albeit briefly.

SOB is, as its full name suggests, based on the brain-state-in-a-box model of Anderson, Silverstein, Ritz, & Jones (1977). This is an autoassociative network comprising a pool of nodes, each connected to all of the others via modifiable weights. The activations of the nodes can vary continuously between +1 and −1, so that the state of the whole network can be expressed as a point lying within an n-dimensional hypercube of side-length 2 and centred on the origin. This hypercube is the "box" in which the brain state resides. Items are represented in this network by mutually orthogonal patterns of +1 s and −1 s across the network nodes. Thus, although each item is represented in a distributed fashion, all items are orthogonal to all others, reminiscent of a (binary) localist representation. Autoassociative learning of a given item is implemented by clamping the corresponding pattern onto the nodes and by strengthening each of the weighted connections by an amount proportional to the product of the activations of the nodes that it links. The constant of proportionality here is known as the learning rate. This learning procedure establishes the trained pattern as an attractor towards which nonattractor activity patterns might be said to gravitate. To explain, when an initial, nonattractor pattern of activation is placed across the nodes, units start a series of activation updates, with the updated activation of a given node being some nonlinear function of its previous activation and the weighted input to it. It is this update process that causes the pattern to move towards the attractors defined by the weight matrix. Thus, since all item attractors are vertices of the hypercube, initial activation patterns that are not located at a vertex of the hypercube will move towards attractor vertices. As several patterns are autoassociated, with changes to the weight matrix accumulating accordingly, an attractor is established for each. As increasing numbers of such patterns are learned, however, spurious attractors, i.e. attractors that do not correspond to learned patterns, also form. These spurious attractors interfere with the operation of the network to an increasing extent as the capacity of the network is approached.

Farrell & Lewandowsky (2002) use the network as follows. A network is trained with a number of item-patterns at a low learning rate. This is to simulate pretrial learning. Then a subset of these items is chosen for presentation in a list. Each item undergoes a further autoassociative learning episode, with a much increased learning rate. Crucially, the learning rate for a given item decreases with that item's list position, such that early items are more strongly coded. To implement this decrease, Farrell & Lewandowsky modulate the learning by an amount that varies with the "energy" of the pattern-to-be-learned relative to the current weight matrix. This energy is given as a sum, across all weights, of the product of each weight with the activations of the two nodes that it connects (although no network mechanism is suggested to enable this calculation). The value of this energy tends to decrease with the number of patterns previously stored in the weight matrix. Crucially for the operation of the network, therefore, learning is modulated by a factor proportional to the energy of a given pattern. Of course, there is nothing about the network that would prevent a pattern's being learned with a strength inversely proportional to its energy. The fact that Farrell and Lewandowsky have to stipulate the "direction" of the effect of energy on learning rate (as well, in fact, as its magnitude) rather suggests that their claim that SOB is free of explanatory parameters is somewhat exaggerated.

At recall, the network is cued with a random pattern that then, via the activation-update rule, tends to gravitate towards one of the network's learned attractors. Because the attractors associated with early list items are stronger than those associated with later list items, the random pattern is drawn more often to an attractor representing an early item. If no attractor is reached within a given number of update cycles, an omission is assumed to have occurred; if a spurious (i.e. nonlearned) attractor is reached, then an intrusion is assumed. Given that an attractor state is reached on a particular recall attempt, the outer product of this attractor pattern with itself is then added to an inhibitory weight matrix, once again with a strength determined by the energy of the pattern relative to the positive (i.e. noninhibitory) weight matrix. This inhibitory weight matrix is set to zero before each list is recalled and the net weight matrix used in the activation-update rule is the sum of the positive and inhibitory weight matrices. The action of the inhibitory weight matrix is to weaken considerably those attractors corresponding to previously recalled items. Thus, the inhibitory matrix is an implementation of response suppression similar to that included in all the models described above. Farrell & Lewandowsky (2002) make much of the ability of their model to implement effective response suppression, claiming that this runs counter to my earlier suggestion that suppression in distributed models is "difficult" (Page, 2000, p. 467). They fail to acknowledge, however, that their model relies heavily on the fact that the patterns corresponding to list items are mutually orthogonal, a highly specific case that arguably falls outside of my qualification that the difficulty in suppression occurs when the distributed patterns "overlap". Regardless, the combination of a primacy gradient of attractor strength across serial positions and a suppression of previous responses, makes the SOB model similar to the primacy model (Page & Norris, 1998b) described below. The account of various basic serial order effects is also similar.

As noted above, SOB has not been applied to some of the phenomena seen in standard immediate serial recall, such as the phonological similarity effect and the word-length effect. Indeed, Farrell & Lewandowsky (2002) do not actually directly fit their model to any standard ISR data. It is therefore necessary to speculate how the SOB model might be applied to the irrelevant sound data under consideration here. We might suppose that IS presented simultaneously with the stimulus list affects the list-item attractors. Maybe it would make the attractor patterns more similar, at least to the extent that the IS was homogeneous, thus making recall more difficult. But this would seem to run counter to the finding that changing-state IS has a bigger effect than nonchanging-state IS (Jones, 1993; Jones, Beaman & Macken, 1996). Furthermore, how would this extend to IS presented during a retention interval? Maybe IS in a filled retention interval establishes extra attractor states, making it more likely that at recall a state is reached that corresponds to a nonlist item. But if this were the case, why would AS and IS during the retention interval necessarily cause more additional attractor states than AS on its own? And where would the increase in order errors originate that characterizes at least part of the IS effect? Why, too, would AS during the list abolish the effect? I don't intend to attempt to second-guess any further how the IS effect might be incorporated within SOB. Suffice it to say that the model would need to be elaborated considerably.

With regard to the long-term learning of sequences, including the Hebb effect and vocabulary learning, SOB cannot provide a particularly promising point of departure. The autoassociative network used in SOB has serious capacity constraints, and Farrell & Lewandowsky (2002) avoid these by using a new network for each stimulus list. Any build-up of the weight matrix across trials would lead to catastrophic performance on later lists and could not possibly lead to a Hebb-like improvement for repeated lists, or to the establishment of vocabulary-like sequences in memory. SOB would again seem to need considerable elaboration before a link between phonological short-term memory and vocabulary learning could be modelled.

THE PRIMACY MODEL
(PM; PAGE & NORRIS, 1998B)

Finally, we come to the Primacy Model (PM; Page & Norris, 1998a, 1998b). I have left this until last because it is the model with which I am most familiar. As will become clear, the primacy model has not been previously applied to all of the data under discussion here. Nonetheless, I hope to show that it is at least capable in principle of being so applied, contingent on minor modification. It is, of course, true that as a co-author of the original model I have more liberty in proposing possible extensions to the PM than in suggesting modifications to the models listed above. Having said this, I have tried hard to envisage how those other models might be adapted to the data under consideration here, often going well beyond what is proposed in the source papers themselves.

The PM has been described at both a mathematical and a connectionist level (Page & Norris, 1998b; 1998a, respectively), although the distinction between mathematical and connectionist here is rather specious. PM is a localist model in which each list item is represented by a single node (in fact, in an extended model designed to deal with repeats, there will be a node for each list-token, but nothing in the general model described here depends upon this distinction). On presentation of a stimulus list, each node representing a list item activates, with nodes corresponding to early items activating more than nodes corresponding to later items. In recent versions of the model, this primacy gradient of activation is simply a linear function of list position. Additionally, all activations are assumed to be decaying with a half-life of approximately 2 s (this figure is nothing to do with the apocryphal "two-second capacity" of short-term memory, references to which can be found in the literature). Recall of a stimulus list proceeds by a repeated cycle of choosing, under noisy conditions, the node with the largest activation, forwarding the corresponding item to an output stage, and suppressing it to prevent subsequent selection. The second stage includes an omission thresh-old and a mechanism by which phonological errors are generated. This latter process is discussed in detail elsewhere (Page & Henson, 2001; Page & Norris, 1998a; 1998b) and is not the principal focus of discussion here.

In the PM, the primacy gradient is held to be the instantiation of Baddeley's short-term phonological store. Just as in Baddeley's model, it can be refreshed by a process of subvocal rehearsal, which in the PM is simply regarded as a more recent (i.e. less decayed) presentation of the (possibly incorrectly rendered) list. Again, as in Baddeley's model, the primacy gradi-ent becomes ineffective after unrehearsed delays of 3–4 s or so. Elsewhere, the PM has been defended against criticism that it cannot deal with interlist effects, such as the occurrence of positional intrusions (Page & Henson, 2001). Positional effects dissociate from the phonological similarity effect, in that they survive delays sufficient to obliterate the PSE (Page & Henson, 2001). According to an analysis of the data presented in Norris et al. (2004), they also dissociate from the irrelevant sound effect, surviving manipulations such as articulatory suppression with visual stimuli that abolish the IS effect, the PS effect, and the word-length effect. These facts support the view of Page & Norris (1998b) that positional intrusions should not be used to assert that phonological short-term memory relies on position–item associations. That is not to say that there is no position–item association information encoded in memory. Henson (1999) has shown conclusively that there is, and that it is primarily measured relative to the start and end of stimulus lists. Rather, our view is that this positional information is not the principal means by which participants recall span or near-span length lists.

In Page & Henson (2001) we identify the phonological store component of Henson's SEM as being a potential locus for incorporation of the primacy gradient. At present, this fast-decaying component of Henson's model stores either a flat gradient or a recency gradient across list items. It thus stores no information that could be used effectively in ordered recall. There is nothing in SEM that prevents this component storing order as a primacy gradient, a move that would both reconcile SEM with Baddeley's idea that phonological short-term memory is essentially an order-holding store, and allow Henson's model to deal with the IS data described here, with which it otherwise has difficulties (see above). Such a combination of models would also bring to the PM a means of accounting for positional intrusions, a type of error towards which it has (quite deliberately) not been directed hitherto.

So how can the PM account for the data on which we are focusing here? First, how might the PM simulate an effect of irrelevant sound? This is most easily modelled in the primacy model by decreasing all activations in the gradient by a common multiple. This would bring successive activations closer to each other (more order errors) and all activations closer to an omission threshold (more omissions/item errors). What might be the circumstances whereby such a damping of the gradient would take place? Well, possibly when there is another ordered stimulus around also requiring its own (but separately streamed and weakly held) primacy gradient. This would be consonant with Jones' work on the effect of changing state vs. nonchanging state stimuli (Jones, 1993; Jones et al., 1996); a nonchanging state stimulus would be less likely to be represented as an ordered stimulus (as opposed to a repeated stimulus) and hence would not need representing at the level at which primacy gradients are held. To explain our retroactive effect of IS, the damping should be deemed to occur if an irrelevant stream becomes represented at any time between onset of stimulus presentation and response. This is not a particular problem for the PM, since an activation-based representation of the list persists throughout this time period. A dose effect (Bridges & Jones, 1996) might be explained by an increased probability of setting up an ordered representation of the irrelevant stream the longer it goes on. This proposed mechanism has been simulated quantitatively in Page & Norris (2003) and has been shown to produce accurate fits to relevant data.

The fact that the IS effect is entirely abolished by AS with visual presentation would be consistent with our, and Baddeley's, assumption that such a manipulation prevents activation of the phonological loop, here represented by the primacy gradient. But what of the unexpected finding that the IS, once established by entry into the phonological loop, persists over retention intervals sufficient to result in effectively complete decay of the loop, sufficient, indeed, to abolish the phonological similarity effect? This is where the model requires some extension. The current view of Dennis Norris and myself is that some of the performance after long delays is enabled by a long-term memorial representation of the primacy gradient. The form that this long-term memory takes will be discussed below. With regard to the long-term effect of IS, though, the assumption would be that there exists a process of consolidation into long-term memory (LTM) that operates on the primacy gradient over a short period following completion of the list. If the primacy gradient is damped during this period, either by earlier IS during list presentation or by IS following list presentation and concurrent with the consolidation process, then there will be a lower probability of accurate consolidation. This will result in a small effect of concurrent or retroactive IS on delayed recall, smaller as a proportion of overall errors than is the IS effect on immediate recall.

This account raises a further question. If the consolidated version of the primacy gradient is present after a filled retention interval, then why does it not result in a phonological similarity effect with the relevant materials? The answer must remain rather speculative at this stage but there are several possibilities. First, it is plausible that reading information out of long-term memory behaves differently with respect to phonological similarity to the corresponding short-term memory process. For example, recalling the list BBCTV (for those readers for whom BBC and TV are overlearned acronyms) is not as likely to be subject to phonological confusion errors as is recall of the list BVCTB. Precisely why this is the case is a matter for debate. It may be that having a long-term memorial representation of a list, as opposed to a fast-decaying one, permits output of the list in a manner that can be both slower and more able to be compared with what was intended. As Page & Norris (1998a) have pointed out, the genesis of phonological confusion errors may be associated with speech errors in everyday speech, the occurrence of which can be promoted by requiring fast output in the absence of a veridical version of the intended utterance against which that output can be checked. The second possibility is that the presence of a LTM primacy gradient simply modulates the operation of other mechanisms on which recall relies once the phonological loop has been rendered ineffective. For example, in the combined SEM/PM model suggested above, recall for visual items under AS and, to a large extent, any recall following long, filled retention intervals, will depend on Henson's episodic tokens. Recall by this route is, by definition, not affected by phonological similarity, because otherwise the PSE would survive suppression and delay. If the LTM primacy gradient modulates the operation of this route, by priming early items to be recalled first, then it will contribute to recall and to a small effect of IS, but no PS effect would be expected. This completes a rather speculative account of the long-lasting IS effect, and links it with the issue of LTM for sequences, to which I now turn.

The PM stems from a line of research started by Grossberg (1978) and continued by Cohen & Grossberg (1987), Nigrin (1993), and Page (1993, 1994). The focus of this work was the connectionist implementation of long-term memory for sequences, but within this framework a primacy gradient approach to short-term sequence memory was adopted. The PM was, therefore, a direct development from the earlier LTM work. It is fair to say, therefore, that the PM is demonstrably consistent, in broad terms at least, with all of this previous work. The precise details underlying the marriage of the LTM and STM models are still under development, and an in-depth discussion of the minutiae would be out of place here. Nonetheless, it is worth giving a quick sketch of what is intended.

In the models cited above, a familiar sequence, say the letter-list YMCA, is represented in a localist fashion by a single node. The connection strengths to this node from nodes representing the component letters vary as a primacy gradient. That is, the connection from letter Y is stronger than that from letter M that, in turn, is stronger than that from letter C, and so on. This is exactly the same pattern as is found in the primacy gradient activations representing the list in STM. The learning of a frequently presented list, therefore, can simply be seen as competitive learning (see e.g. Page, 2000) of the pattern of activation that results in short-term memory when that list is presented. As is usual in competitive learning networks, the YMCA-node will activate maximally when the stimulus sequence is consistent with the pattern across its weights, i.e. it will activate strongly to presentation of the list YMCA but not to the list CMYA. Moreover, if there are also outgoing connections from the YMCA-node to some output nodes representing the individual letters, with the weights of these connections also forming a primacy gradient, then activating the YMCA-node will cause strong activation of Y, less of M, and so on. Thus, activation of the higher-level node will permit ordered recall via the usual pick-the-biggest-and-suppress mechanism. Nigrin (1993) and Page (1993, 1994) have gone some way towards implementing such models and they are the subject of current work in our group.

I would therefore suggest that the primacy model is well placed to take advantage of the historical links that it enjoys with models of long-term sequence memory. The operation of these models suggests a framework in which to place long-term memory effects. On the repeated presentation of a Hebb list or a novel vocabulary item, either a node learns to respond to the whole sequence or several nodes learn to respond to "chunk-like" subsequences out of which the sequence is made up. Crucially, the establishment of this node relies on the repeated instantiation of the same primacy gradient across the sequence items themselves. Circumstances that prevent the formation of a primacy gradient, such as articulatory suppression with visual presentation, or brain damage characteristic of short-term memory patients such as PV, should hinder the long-term learning of lists and, in particular, of vocabulary. Note, too, that on logical grounds, if a representation of a list is to be built up over several repetitions, then some representation must be laid down on the first encounter. If this were not the case, then nothing could distinguish the first presentation of a list from its first repetition. It is this comparatively long-lasting representation of the first presentation of a list that results from single-trial learning, that is hypothesized to play a role in the long-term IS effect described above.

CONCLUSION

This chapter has had several purposes. First, to describe a number of current connectionist and connectionist-like models of immediate serial recall, particularly with regard to the styles of connectionism on which they are based. Second, to explore how the models might deal with some rather constraining data on the irrelevant sound effect. And third, to speculate as to how the models might be extended to cope with the long-term memory for sequences, a task for which the phonological loop component of short-term memory appears crucial. To summarize, none of BH, OSCAR, SEM or SOB could either give an adequate account of the IS data or readily be extended to long-term memory. The primacy model has close links with models of long-term sequence memory and can, with minor modification, deal, qualitatively at least, with the detail of the irrelevant sound effects. For a complete model of serial recall, rather than a model of the phonological loop component of recall, the primacy model might best be combined with Henson's SEM to take advantage of the latter model's success in modelling positional effects under conditions in which the phonological loop is either absent or only weakly present.

ACKNOWLEDGEMENT

Mike Page gratefully acknowledges the support of the UK Biotechnology and Biological Sciences Research Council via Grant 310/S15906.

REFERENCES

Anderson, J. A., Silverstein, J. W., Ritz, S. A. & Jones, R. S. (1977). Distinctive features, categorical perception, and probability learning: Some applications of a neural model. *Psychological Review, 84*, 413–451.

Baddeley, A. D. (1986). *Working Memory*. Oxford: Oxford University Press/Clarendon Press.

Baddeley, A. D. (1993). Short-term phonological memory and long-term learning: A single case study. *European Journal of Cognitive Psychology, 5*, 129–148.

Baddeley, A. D., Gathercole, S., & Papagno, C. (1998). The phonological loop as a language learning device. *Psychological Review, 105*, 158–173.

Baddeley, A. D., & Hitch, G. (1974). Working Memory. In G. A. Bower (Ed.) *Recent advances in learning and motivation* (Vol. 8, pp. 47–90). New York: Academic Press.

Baddeley, A. D., Papagno, C., & Vallar, G. (1988). When long-term learning depends on short-term storage. *Journal of Memory and Language, 27*, 586–595.

Baddeley, A. D., & Salamé, P. (1986). The unattended speech effect: Perception or memory? *Journal of Experimental Psychology: Learning, Memory and Cognition, 12*, 525–529.

Bridges, A. M., & Jones, D. M. (1996). Word dose in the disruption of serial recall by irrelevant speech: Phonological confusions or changing state? *Quarterly Journal of Experimental Psychology, 49A*, 919–939.

Brown, G. D. A., Preece, T., & Hulme, C. (2000). Oscillator-based memory for serial order. *Psychological Review, 107*, 127–181.

Burgess, N., & Hitch, G. J. (1992). Toward a network model of the articulatory loop. *Journal of Memory and Language, 31*, 429–460.

Burgess, N., & Hitch, G. J. (1999). Memory for serial order: A network model of the phonological loop and its timing. *Psychological Review, 106*, 551–581.

Cohen, M. A., & Grossberg, S. (1987). Masking fields: A massively parallel neural architecture for learning, recognizing and predicting multiple groupings of patterned data. *Applied Optics, 26*, 1866–1891.

Colle, H. A., & Welsh, A. (1976). Acoustic masking in primary memory. *Journal of Verbal Learning and Verbal Behavior, 15*, 17–32.

Cumming, N., Page, M. P. A., & Norris, D. (2003). Testing a positional model of the Hebb effect. *Memory, 11(1)*, 43–63.

Farrell, S., & Lewandowsky, S. (2002). An endogenous distributed model of ordering in serial recall. *Psychonomic Bulletin and Review, 9*, 59–79.

Grossberg, S. (1978). A theory of human memory: Self-organization and performance of sensory-motor codes, maps and plans. In R. Roden, & F. Snell (Eds.), *Progress in theoretical biology* (pp. 223–374). New York: Academic Press.

Hebb, D. O. (1961). Distinctive features of learning in the higher animal. In J. F. Delafresnaye (Ed.), *Brain mechanisms and learning* (pp. 37–46). Oxford: Blackwell.

Henson, R. N. A. (1998). Short-term memory for serial order: The start-end model. *Cognitive Psychology, 36,* 73–137.

Henson, R. N. A. (1999). Positional information in short-term memory: Relative or absolute? *Memory and Cognition, 27,* 915–927.

Henson, R. N. A., Norris, D., Page, M. P. A., & Baddeley, A. D. (1996). Unchained memory: Error patterns rule out chaining models of immediate serial recall. *Quarterly Journal of Experimental Psychology, 49A,* 80–115.

Houghton, G. (1990). The problem of serial order: A neural network model of sequence learning and recall. In R. Dale, C. Mellish, & M. Zock (Eds.), *Current research in natural language generation* (pp. 287–319). London: Academic Press.

Jones, D. M. (1993). Objects, streams and threads of auditory attention. In A. D. Baddeley & L. Weiskrantz (Eds.), *Attention: Selection, awareness and control* (pp. 87–103). Oxford: Oxford University Press.

Jones, D. M., Beaman, C. P., & Macken, W. J. (1996). The object-oriented episodic record model. In S. Gathercole (Ed.), *Models of short-term memory* (pp. 209–237). Hove, UK: Lawrence Erlbaum Associates Ltd.

Jones, D. M., & Macken, W. J. (1993). Irrelevant tones produce an irrelevant speech effect: Implications for phonological coding in working memory. *Journal of Experimental Psychology: Learning, Memory, and Cognition, 19,* 369–381.

Macken, W. J., Mosdell, N., & Jones, D. M. (1999). Explaining the irrelevant-sound effect: Temporal distinctiveness or changing state? *Journal of Experimental Psychology: Learning, Memory, and Cognition, 25,* 810–814.

Nigrin, A. L. (1993). *Neural networks for pattern recognition.* Cambridge, MA: MIT Press.

Norris, D., Baddeley, A. D., & Page, M. P. A. (2004). Retroactive effects of irrelevant speech on serial recall from short-term memory. *Journal of Experimental Psychology: Learning, Memory and Cognition, 30,* 1093–1105.

Norris, D., Page, M. P. A., & Baddeley, A. D. (1995). Connectionist modelling of short-term memory. *Language and Cognitive Processes, 10,* 407–409.

Page, M. P. A. (1993). *Modelling aspects of music perception using self-organizing neural networks.* Unpublished doctoral dissertation, University of Wales, Cardiff, UK.

Page, M. P. A. (1994). Modelling the perception of musical sequences with self-organizing neural networks. *Connection Science, 6,* 223–246.

Page, M. P. A. (2000). Connectionist modelling in psychology: A localist manifesto. *Behavioral and Brain Sciences, 23,* 443–512.

Page, M. P. A., & Henson, R. N. A. (2001). Computational models of short-term memory: Modelling serial recall of verbal material. In J. Andrade (Ed.), *Working Memory in Perspective* (pp. 177–198). Hove, UK: Psychology Press.

Page, M. P. A., & Norris, D. (1998a). Modelling immediate serial recall with a localist implementation of the primacy model. In J. Grainger, & A. M. Jacobs (Eds.), *Localist Connectionist Approaches to Human Cognition.* Mahwah, NJ: Lawrence Erlbaum Associates, Inc.

Page, M. P. A., & Norris, D. (1998b). The primacy model: A new model of immediate serial recall. *Psychological Review, 105,* 761–781.

Page, M. P. A., & Norris, D. (2003). The irrelevant sound effect: What needs modelling and a tentative model. *Quarterly Journal of Experimental Psychology, 56 (A),* 1289–1300.

Papagno, C., Valentine. T., & Baddeley, A. D. (1991). Phonological short-term memory and foreign language vocabulary learning. *Journal of Memory and Language, 30,* 331–347.

Saffran, J. R., Aslin, R. N., & Newport, E. L. (1996). Statistical learning by 8-month-old infants. *Science, 274,* 1926–1928.

Salamé, P., & Baddeley, A. D. (1982). Disruption of short-term memory by unattended speech. *Journal of Verbal Learning and Verbal Behavior, 21,* 150–164.

Salamé, P., & Baddeley, A. D. (1986). Phonological factors in STM: Similarity and the unattanded speech effect. *Bulletin of the Psychonomic Society, 24,* 263–265.

Trojano, L., & Grossi, D. (1995). Phonological and lexical coding in verbal short-term memory and learning. *Brain and Cognition, 21,* 336–354.

Vallar, G., & Baddeley, A. D. (1984a). Fractionation of working memory: Neuropsychological evidence for a phonological short-term store. *Journal of Verbal Learning and Verbal Behavior, 23,* 151–161.

Vallar, G., & Baddeley, A. D. (1984b). Phonological short-term store, phonological processing and sentence comprehension: A neuropsychological case study. *Cognitive Neuropsychology, 1,* 121–141.

CHAPTER EIGHT

Serial order in behaviour: Evidence from performance slips

David W. Glasspool
Cancer Research UK, London, UK

INTRODUCTION

Many types of behaviour have a temporal aspect—it does not matter just what actions are taken, but in what order they are taken. This is true of everyday motor tasks, such as getting dressed or driving a car, as well as being central to all types of linguistic behaviour. The need to deal with the serial ordering of responses is thus of great importance to much of psychology. Yet historically the issue of serial order has received relatively little attention from the cognitive sciences. In a seminal paper of 1951, Karl Lashley described what he termed "the problem of temporal integration" as "the most import-ant and also the most neglected problem of cerebral physiology" (Lashley, 1951, p. 508). Over more recent decades this neglect has persisted, encour-aged no doubt by the ease with which sequence processing may be achieved with conventional computer programming languages. This has tended to fuel a perception amongst cognitive scientists that "the problem of serial order" has been solved or is trivial, and attention has tended instead towards those areas of cognition which are difficult to address using conventional serial computer techniques.

One of the benefits of the recent resurgence of interest in neural networks is the new perspective that has opened up on assumptions about which prob-lems in cognition are "easy" and which are "difficult". From the connection-ist viewpoint, associative memory and pattern recognition, difficult problems for "classical" AI, become tractable or even straightforward. Other tasks—

sequence generation included—that appear simple from the viewpoint of symbolic systems take on an altogether more complex demeanour when they must be tackled from first principles in a connectionist framework.

This new perspective on the difficulty of generating sequential responses has led to a number of connectionist or related low-level computational approaches to generating serial behaviour. In this chapter I am concerned with the question: How well can these different approaches explain *human* serial behaviour? In assessing this, it is primarily the errors made in sequence generation which are of interest.

Given the simple existence of a psychological competence—say, the ability to write a word from memory—there are very few limits on the types of mechanism that might be proposed to account for it. For example, any number of computer programs can be written which will produce a sequence of letters correctly. The higher informational content provided by the errors which the system is prone to make, either in normal operation or when stressed or damaged, reduces the range of possible mechanisms that might underlie the human competence. It is important, however, to distinguish errors that are due to the mis-operation of a cognitive process, and may thus carry information about the nature of that process, from those that are due to a correctly operating process with incorrect information. Misspelling a word simply because one has learned an incorrect spelling, for example, tells us little about the operation of the spelling process. To distinguish the two types of error, the former are often referred to as performance "slips", and it is these with which this chapter will be concerned.

A number of different serial ordering techniques have been applied in computational models that attempt to explain the types of slip typical of human serial behaviour. However, I shall argue that those which have been most successful share a set of high-level features in their mechanisms for generating serial output. Before examining serial ordering mechanisms, the next section reviews some common features of slips in serial behaviour.

SERIAL BEHAVIOUR AND ACTION SLIPS IN PSYCHOLOGICAL DATA

Serial order in human behaviour has been extensively studied by psychologists. The areas considered in this section are those where significant attention has been given to the occurrence of action slips in the performance of serially ordered behaviour—language production, short-term memory, and the control of routine behaviour. These areas can be expected to cover a number of more or less unrelated cognitive mechanisms. It is particularly interesting, then, that the same major features occur in error profiles across different areas. In all, a total of eight common features may be discerned in data from all or most of the above areas, as follows:

1. *Co-activation of sequence elements.*   To Lashley (1951), one of the most striking implications of performance slips in speech production was that the various responses making up a serial sequence (syllables or phonemes in a word, words in a sentence, etc.) are available and primed for production over a significant time period before and after the point where they should be produced. Dell (1986) and Levelt (1989) both review the findings of a number of studies of speech errors. A general finding is that erroneous items in an utterance may be displaced forwards or backwards from their correct position by some distance, often over several intervening items, implying that there is a level in the speech production process at which an extended series of sounds are concurrently present. Further evidence for this position comes from "co-articulation" effects in speech (Benguerel & Cowan, 1974; Moll & Daniloff, 1971). Subject to physical constraints, the vocal tract anticipates up-coming phonemes during articulation, so that the current phoneme tends to take on some of the features of to-be-articulated phonemes. Co-articulation is not simply the result of interaction within physiological mechanisms, as it is language-dependent (Jordan, 1986).

    Evidence for a "window" of activation extending before and after the current position in a sequence of responses is also shown in spelling. Wing & Baddeley (1980) and Hotoph (1980) both found letter movement errors in the spelling slips of normal subjects. Graphemic buffer disorder (GBD), a well-studied neuropathology of spelling, appears to be primarily a deficit in the serial production of letters and again provides evidence for co-activation of letter representations during spelling (Glasspool, 1998).

    In experiments on verbal short-term memory (Page, Chapter 7, this volume), a high proportion of errors typically involve the order of recalled items, rather than the identity of the items (e.g. Aaronson, 1968), which again has been taken as showing that the identities of items in the to-be-recalled sequence are available both before and after their "target" serial positions (Burgess & Hitch, 1992; Glasspool, 1995). Finally, both movement errors and co-articulation effects are also found in slips made by skilled typists (Rumelhart & Norman, 1982).

2. *Effects of serial position.*   In a number of serial tasks, error rates are lower for the first few items in a sequence (a primacy effect) and the last few items (a recency effect). Primacy and recency effects are best known in recall from verbal short-term memory (STM; e.g. Crowder, 1972; Murdock, 1962; Murray, 1966). These effects in STM are not limited to verbal material, however. Hitch (1974) reports a recency effect in short-term memory for the spatial, rather than temporal,

ordering of a set of stimuli, while Healy (1975) found both primacy and recency effects for spatial STM. Primacy and recency also affect STM for sequences of hand movements (e.g. Magill & Dowell, 1977, in serial recall; Wrisberg, 1975, in reverse serial recall; and Wilberg, 1990, in free recall)

Primacy and recency effects also appear in spelling errors. In normal subjects, Wing & Baddeley (1980) found a clear "inverted U" serial position curve, most errors occurring in word-medial positions. In neurological patients with graphemic buffer disorder, spelling error rates also show primacy and recency.

Finally, Brown (1991) argues that there is evidence from the "tip-of-the-tongue" phenomenon that primacy and recency effects may also be present to some extent in speech production.

3. *Effect of sequence and item length.* In a number of tasks a marked effect is found of the length of the sequence being recalled on the accuracy of recall. In verbal STM studies, the greater the temporal length of the target sequence, the greater the chance of an error; thus, recall is poorer for sequences containing more words (the sequence length effect, e.g. Guildford & Dallenbach, 1925) and for those containing words which take longer to say (the word length effect, e.g. Hulme, Maughan, & Brown, 1991). Length effects are not limited to verbal STM. Magill & Dowell (1977) also found an effect of sequence length on recall for three and six item movement sequences.

Wing & Baddeley (1980) found that words with spelling errors produced by normal subjects were reliably longer on average than those without. A reliable effect of word length is also seen in the spelling errors of GBD patients. Similar effects are also found in speech errors (e.g. Gathercole, Willis, Emslie, & Baddeley, 1991).

4. *Errors more often involve the loss of ordering information than the loss of item identity.* In recall from verbal STM it is well known that a higher proportion of errors involve the order of recalled items than the identity of the items. Aaronson (1968), for example, found that 70–80% of errors involved the order of otherwise correctly recalled items. This is also true of "GBD" spelling errors (Glasspool, 1998) and speech errors (e.g. Treiman & Danis, 1988). Ordering errors also occur as slips in high-level action control (see Cooper, Chapter 10, this volume).

5. *Effects of repeats.* Repeated items within sequences are often found to facilitate errors (at least when the repeats are not immediately adjacent, see below). This is true for speech production (Dell, 1984) and verbal STM (the Von Ranschburg effect; Jahnke, 1969). There is some evidence for a similar effect in spelling (Hotoph, 1980), where the

error rate on the second occurrence of repeated pairs of letters is higher than expected from the letter's position alone.

6. *Behaviour of double items.*   Immediate repeats (doublings), either of phonemes or words, are uncommon in normal speech. In other types of serial behaviour where doubling is possible, however, an interesting set of error types occur which suggest that the act of doubling an item is represented separately from the item to be doubled. Thus, both in typing (Rumelhart & Norman, 1982) and in GBD spelling (Caramazza & Micelli, 1990; Jonsdottir, Shallice, & Wise, 1996), errors often involve the wrong letter in a word being doubled (e.g. school → schhol), or a doubling being omitted (school → schol). It is very rare for a double letter to be inserted in a word which does not already contain one. Rumelhart & Norman (1982) suggest that this implies that close repeats involve a specific doubling schema, which is subject to errors in its positioning.

7. *Effect of similarity.*   Speech error and verbal STM data both show a detrimental effect of similarity between items on order information. Verbal STM studies show an effect of phonological similarity— capacity for lists of words is impaired when the words are phonemically similar (e.g. Conrad & Hull, 1964). The principal effect appears to be an increase in movement errors between similar items while leaving non-similar items unaffected (Baddeley, 1968). In speech production, phonemic similarity again facilitates order errors, as does similarity at other linguistic levels (syntactic class for words, syllabic position for phonemes) (Shattuck-Hufnagel, 1979).

8. *Preservation of domain-specific constraints.*   Errors in sequence production are often constrained to some extent by abstract (e.g. syntactic) features of the items in the sequence. For example, items will commonly preferentially exchange with, or be replaced by, items of the same class. In speech production several different levels of constraints may be identified (e.g. phonotactic constraints on which class of phoneme may appear in certain syllabic positions, or syntactic constraints on classes of word or phrase which may appear in certain sentence positions). These constraints are enforced when errors occur on items at these levels (i.e. words swap with words, noun phrases swap with noun phrases, etc.). The preservation of consonant–vowel status in the spelling errors of GBD patients is similar in that a class of items (letters sharing the same consonant/vowel status as the target letter) may preferentially appear in particular serial positions. There exists an analogous effect in the verbal STM literature: When "chunks" exist in STM experiments, errors occur which could be said to respect the chunked status of data, e.g. when the first item in one chunk swaps with the first item in another.

The data reviewed above are striking in two respects. First, the complexity of error patterns suggest that there is more to generating a sequence of responses than simply "reading out" from an ordered list of responses (in traditional computer program style). Second, similar patterns of data from experiments in different modalities seem strongly suggestive of shared general principles of operation in the mechanisms involved in generating serial order in these different areas.

To begin to investigate what these principles of operation might be, however, we need to look at the psychological data in the context of the different mechanisms which have been proposed as models of human serial behaviour.

COMPUTATIONAL MODELS OF SERIAL ORDER GENERATION

Numerous cognitive models have addressed low-level serial behaviour in various psychological domains. These domains are often rather small, as models tend to address particular limited aspects of behaviour, rather than generalized serial processing. Nonetheless, some common principles for the generation of serial order emerge. This section briefly reviews major approaches to sequence generation in the light of the features of human serial behaviour identified above. The approaches reviewed are not exclusively connectionist, although since connectionist modelling requires an account for serial behaviour from first principles, connectionist modellers have been major consumers of this research and have been a major driving force in the field.

Serial buffer models

One intuitive approach to representing serial order assumes a series of "boxes" or "slots", each of which can hold one response and which are accessed one at a time to produce a response sequence. If anything, this idea has been encouraged by the computer metaphor for mind—it is the most obvious way to generate serial behaviour using a standard computer language.

Conrad (1965), for example, proposed a model of short-term verbal memory as a series of boxes into each of which a subject enters an item in a presented sequence. To recall the sequence, the subject simply "reads out" the contents of each box in order. This type of formulation does not fare well as an explanation of slips in sequence production, however. The only prediction of such a model is that, on breakdown, item identities may become degraded. While this would presumably lead to errors, the serial buffer approach on its own can say nothing about what form such errors would take. The buffer model needs to be augmented with additional mechanisms handling structural and algorithmic information to explain the structure of the errors. Conrad, for example, does this by making the assumption that the same mechanisms that lead to acoustic confusion in speech perception also lead to erroneous recall of items from boxes when those items are degraded by decay.

Such models cannot in themselves account for the types of error produced when sequence production breaks down. With the possible exception of length effects, assuming an equal probability of error on each "slot", nontrivial additional performance assumptions are required to achieve any predictions at all.

Chained models

A particularly popular view, especially amongst connectionist modellers, has been that seriality should be generated by linking the current response in a series to previous responses. Three main distinctions may be drawn amongst such chaining mechanisms:

1. Between *response* chaining, where the stimulus for the current response derives from actual responses made previously, and *indirect* chaining, where the stimulus is some previous internal representation.
2. Between *simple* chaining, where the stimulus for a response is the previous response alone, and *compound* chaining, where some combination of previous responses is used.
3. Between *excitatory* chaining, where the occurrence of previous responses excites the current response, and *inhibitory* chaining, where early responses actively inhibit later ones until they are triggered or selected, when their influence is removed and the later response is released from inhibition.

Standard neural networks are very effective at tasks which involve mapping from an input pattern to an output pattern. One obvious way to achieve sequential behaviour from a network is thus to cause the network to map from its current internal pattern of activation (state) to a new state. Many states may then be chained together to form a temporal sequence. This idea forms the basis of the best-known connectionist approaches to serial order, the recurrent networks of Jordan (1986) and Elman (1990).

Jordan's (1986) architecture consists of a three-layer feedforward network, with input, hidden, and output layers of units, and connections between them trained using the back-propagation algorithm. The input layer nodes are split into two groups. One represents the "plan", a pattern which is held constant throughout the sequence and specifies which particular sequence the network is to learn or produce. The other group specifies the current "state" of the network, and these nodes are activated by recurrent connections from the

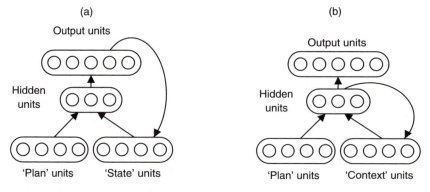

Figure 8.1.   The recurrent network architectures of (a) Jordan (1986) and (b) Elman (1990).

state nodes themselves and from the output nodes (see Fig. 8.1a). This allows the activation pattern of the state nodes to depend on the previous output from the network and on the previous state. Elman's (1990) architecture differs in that, rather than feeding back the activation pattern of the output layer, the Elman net feeds back the previous activation pattern on the hidden units. This is achieved by copying the activation of the hidden units to a set of "context" nodes at each time step (Fig. 8.1b). Since the current state of systems such as these depends to a certain extent on previous states (and thus on previous input) their chaining is not necessarily based just on the current state but may be a function of the entire input and state sequence to date.

Similar recurrent architectures have been developed using other neural network paradigms, e.g. Amit, Sagi, & Usher (1990) have modified a Hopfield net to perform serial chaining. Hopfield nets can settle into stable attractor states, where the pattern of activation across the network becomes self-supporting. This model includes connections that map from one attractor state to another, allowing a chain of attractor states to be assembled, each one providing the stimulus for the next. Amit et al. use this ability to model the rehearsal of sequential input in the Sternberg paradigm (Sternberg, 1966).

The chaining-based model which has perhaps been most used to address slip data is not explicitly connectionist, however. Murdock's "theory of distributed associative memory" (TODAM; Murdock, 1982) is a model of verbal STM which represents items to be stored in memory as vectors with random elements. Items are stored in a memory trace by vector addition, and associated pairs of items are stored by adding the convolution of their vectors to the memory trace. Recall of one of the pair is performed by correlating the trace with the vector representing the other. The basic model is augmented by Murdock (1983) and Lewandowsky & Murdock (1989) to allow serial recall tasks using chaining. A sequence of items is stored by adding to the memory trace both the vector representing each item and the association (represented as the convolution of vectors) between each item and its successor. As each item is retrieved during sequence production, it acts as the cue for its successor.

A two-stage process is used for recall. A similarity metric determines the actual item representation closest to the approximate output, and this is used as the response. If no item is sufficiently determined by the similarity, metric recall is assumed to have failed. When recall is successful, the "deblurred" item representation is used as the cue for the next item's recall, but when recall fails, the approximation yielded by the first stage recall operation is used as the cue. Thus, a cue is always available and it may be possible to continue recall even following an error. Although the model is sometimes able to continue recall following an error, there is no obvious mechanism whereby ordering, and especially exchange, errors might occur. The lack of an explanation for such a ubiquitous phenomenon in human serial behaviour is a serious problem. Murdock (1995) addresses it by introducing remote associations to produce a compound chaining model which is capable of producing exchange errors.

The model produces primacy and recency effects similar in shape and magnitude to those observed in human serial recall (Lewandowsky & Murdock, 1989). The mechanism for recency is the mechanism adopted in the model for general forgetting—as each new item is added to the memory vector, the previous state of the vector is reduced in magnitude by a constant amount. The primacy effect, on the other hand, is due to a mechanism which is entirely ad hoc: The weighting parameters governing the influence of each new item on the memory vector are reduced in each successive serial position.

The question of whether sequencing is carried out by excitatory chains of associations has been vigorously debated since Lashley's (1951) seminal paper.

For example, in the domain of short-term verbal recall, Young (1961, 1962) argued that the stimulus for the production of a response in a sequence is not the preceding response but the ordinal position of the response in the sequence (the "ordinal position hypothesis"). Ebenholtz (1963) supported this position by demonstrating that explicit inter-item associations are not necessary for serial recall. Young (1968) found evidence in long-term memory (LTM) experiments to support the ordinal position hypothesis for LTM too. Learning paired associates (e.g. the pairs EF, CD, AB) does not facilitate the later learning of a list which, if item-to-item chaining were being used, would require the same associations (e.g. ABCDEF). Young concluded that associations are to "place markers", which indicate ordinal position. Slamecka (1964), in a review of the experimental literature, concluded that serial learning proceeds by first learning the identities of the items involved and then fixing their sequential positions. The associations that are learned in serial tasks are most likely to be between each item and "some distinctive symbol designating its relative position in the list", rather than between consecutive items.

In fact, much evidence has now amassed which suggests that little, if any, response chaining occurs in any type of serial behaviour. The data discussed above show evidence that sequencing is not achieved by simple chaining of associations in any modality, the most obvious evidence being the common occurrence of errors in mid-sequence positions. Simple chaining of one response to the next cannot explain how a sequence can continue correctly following an error. Compound response chaining models, however, are not so prone to such problems, since they do not rely only on a single prior response as a cue. However, the probability of further errors will be increased following an initial error, which is at variance with data from serial verbal STM studies (Henson, Norris, Page, & Baddeley, 1996). Henson et al. find that the probability of an error depends only on the position of the item in the sequence, and not on whether or not an error occurred in the previous position. Any theory which holds that any part of the stimulus for a response is the production of the previous response must predict that an error is more likely if the previous response is erroneous, since the stimulus will then be partially degraded. Additionally, evidence from "protrusion" errors in verbal STM (Henson, 1999) suggests that an association exists between each serial position in a sequence and the item to be produced in that position, which is difficult to reconcile with a chaining approach, even when chaining is performed on internal representations rather than outputs.

Another problem for response chaining accounts is the occurrence of exchange errors, common in slips of the tongue, slips of the pen, GBD spelling, typing and verbal STM. Assuming an error of the form ABCD → ACBD, where B and C exchange places, a simple response chaining account would predict that when the erroneous C is produced in the second position, the next response to be activated would be D, via the C to D association.

Indirect chaining, where the stimulus for the next response is not the current response itself but some internal representation related to the current response, does not necessarily suffer from the problems discussed above. However this depends on the locus of errors within the chaining system. For example, in the Elman network of Fig. 8.1b, if an error occurs in the mapping between the hidden units and the output units, an erroneous output may be produced without affecting the cue for the next item (however, if the error occurs earlier in the network, at the level of the hidden, plan or context units, the cue will be affected). However, this does not on its own address the evidence for associations between item identities and serial position, or the common occurrence of exchange errors. Botvinick & Plaut (2003) have recently shown that, given the right representations and training regime, an Elman network may be trained to operate in a manner that can address these factors. However, in this approach, the network is effectively trained not to use chaining to generate serial ordering, and in fact the serial ordering mechanism it acquires appears to be closely related to competitive queuing, which is discussed below.

Lee & Estes' perturbation model

Lee & Estes explicitly introduce the passage of time, rather than associative chaining, as the organizing principle in serial behaviour. Over a number of years they have developed a model of serial recall in verbal STM based on the idea of temporal perturbations in reverberatory cycles. The initial version of the model (Estes, 1972) proposes the idea of a "control element", which represents a sequence in its entirety. Each element in the sequence is activated by association with the control element, rather than with other sequence elements. Sequential activation of the elements is established by a reverberatory loop mechanism: the representation of each item is periodically reactivated at a constant rate. Each item may be perturbed in its timing, to occur either sooner or later than it did on the previous cycle. Over time, the position of an item in the sequence can drift. The start and end points of the sequence are fixed, so that the first and last items may each only be perturbed in one direction.

This active process is sufficient to keep a sequence present in STM. If the sequence is to be stored in LTM and later recalled, a different representation is required. Recall from LTM is held to involve inter-item inhibitory connections which establish inhibitory chaining over the items. This is held to be sufficient to initiate serial recall.

The main problem with this model is the lack of any specified mechanism to implement the reverberatory re-activation of items. The fact that read-out from LTM and immediate recall require different mechanisms is also somewhat unsatisfying. However, the approach does provide an explanation for ordering errors in general and exchanges in particular. The reverberatory mechanism can also explain primacy and recency effects, which are seen as "end effects"—the relative movement of items is limited by the ends of the sequence, allowing greater disruption in the less hindered central section of the sequence. This effect will be discussed further below.

Competitive queuing

I will use the term "competitive queuing" (CQ)[1] to refer to a class of models of serial behaviour which has found application in a number of psychological domains because of their ability to account for many of the common features of slips in serial behaviour identified above. Although there are important differences between implemented CQ models, the following three features are typically present:

1. *A set of refractory response representations.* These constitute a pool of distinct responses or actions from which individual sequences are generated. The nature of the response set depends on the particular problem being modelled. The responses are refractory in that when an item is produced as part of a sequence, it becomes temporarily unavailable for further use.

2. *Parallel response activation and activation gradient.* Responses in a target sequence are activated in parallel at the beginning of recall, but with a gradient of activation over them, such that the sooner a response is to be produced the more active it is. The set of active responses forms the "competitive queue", as the responses compete for output on the basis of their activation level. The relative activation levels may be static throughout production of a sequence or they may change over time.

3. *A competitive output mechanism.* This mechanism has to resolve the response competition in the queue by selecting out the currently most active (dominant) response. This process leads to the subsequent inhibition of the chosen response.

The process of generating a sequence in such a model involves an *activating* or *cueing* mechanism generating a gradient of activations over some subset of item representations, such that the item to be produced first is the most active and the item to be produced last is the least active (see Fig. 8.2). The competitive output mechanism then repeatedly selects for output the most active item. As each item is output it becomes refractory, and hence

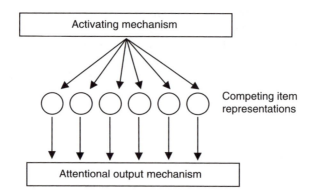

Figure 8.2.   Generic form of CQ models.

temporarily unavailable. In this way the activated items are output in order of their relative activation values, from the most to the least active.

CQ models are amenable to connectionist implementation, although they are not always explicitly connectionist. Models of this form can learn sequences, using simple associative learning rules (Houghton, 1990) as well as back-propagation-type rules (Glasspool, 1998, Glasspool, Shallice, & Cipolotti, 1999).

The CQ paradigm has a number of attractions as a basis for models of serial behaviour in the light of the psychological data discussed earlier: It does not involve associative chaining, it gives rise to the usual effect of sequence length, and it gives a clear and simple account for the high incidence of ordering errors in general, and exchange errors in particular, in serial tasks. Finally, simple versions of the model have given a good account for the higher incidence of errors in medial positions of sequences. The mechanisms behind all these effects will be discussed in detail below.

Not surprisingly, CQ models have been successful in a range of psychological domains, the general principles of the approach often being arrived at independently by different authors. These include:

- *Verbal STM* (Brown, Preece, & Hulme, 2000; Burgess & Hitch, 1992, 1996; Glasspool, 1995; Henson, 1998; Milner, 1961; Page & Norris, 1997, 1998).
- *Typing* (Rumelhart & Norman, 1982).
- *Speech production* (Dell, 1986, 1988; Hartley & Houghton, 1996; Houghton, 1990; Vousden, 1996).
- *Spelling* (Glasspool, Houghton, & Shallice, 1995; Houghton, Glasspool, & Shallice, 1994; Shallice, Glasspool, & Houghton, 1995).
- *Action plans* (Cooper & Shallice, 1997, 2000; Cooper, Shallice, & Farringdon, 1995; Grossberg, 1978; Humphreys & Forde, 1998; Norman & Shallice, 1980, 1986).

CQ models have been successful because they can account for the common features of "slip" errors outlined earlier, which other sequence generation paradigms have problems with. The important question, of course, is precisely what mechanisms CQ models provide for such slips. No two CQ models are exactly alike in their operation or their error mechanisms. However, it is possible to abstract a set of high-level features that can provide a unified account for slips in serial behaviour. To do this it will be necessary first to look in a little more detail at the CQ framework. The most important differences between different CQ models concern the nature of the activating mechanism (see Fig. 8.2). There are two main variants, "static" and "dynamic".

Static mechanisms

Static mechanisms set up a single activation gradient over items, which is then held static during the course of sequence generation. Sequence production is accomplished by virtue of the refractoriness of item representations—as each item is produced, it is removed from the competition for output in the next sequence position, where the next most active item will "win". In such a system it is desirable that items should remain refractory for a long period, as items produced near the beginning of the sequence will have a large input from the activating mechanism, which will still be present towards the end of the sequence. The use of a static activation mechanism places two constraints on a CQ system which may or may not be disadvantageous, depending on the details of the model. First, the final activation level of each successive item in the sequence must be lower than its predecessor. Second, unless there is some means to control the refractory periods of individual item representations (which is generally assumed not to be the case), it is not possible to cater for sequences that contain repeated items.

A clear example of a static mechanism is Page & Norris's (1997, 1998) primacy model of verbal short-term memory, which demonstrates that a considerable amount of data may be explained on a simple model of serial recall (see Page, Chapter 7, this volume). The model associates activation levels with localist representations of words presented to it in sequence. Words near the beginning of the sequence are strongly excited throughout sequence production, while words near the end of the sequence are only weakly active. The difference in activation from each word to the next is given by a fixed ratio. Once a word has been selected for output, it is assumed to be in a refractory state for the duration of the sequence and is subsequently excluded from the output competition. Random noise is added to the activation levels of item representations in order to simulate a degree of uncertainty in the competitive output process, and this introduces errors in sequence production.

The model provides a good account for a number of phenomena associated with verbal STM. Errors involve the movement of items within the sequence, as the wrong item wins the output competition in a particular position, with exchanges particularly common. The span of the model is limited by the uncertain output process—longer sequences provide more opportunity for errors; additionally, assuming the same activation level for the first word in a sequence, the longer a sequence, the smaller the difference between each item and its successor, and hence the greater the likelihood of sequencing errors. A primacy effect is shown, again because the activation difference between items reduces as sequencing progresses. Towards the end of the sequence most items have been output and inhibited, and reduced competition leads to a decrease in errors. The resultant primacy and recency curves closely fit those for visually presented sequences in human subjects. Page & Norris (1998) are also able to account for differences between visual and auditory presentation by making additional assumptions.

A less clear example is given by Rumelhart & Norman (1982), who describe a model of typing that takes a CQ approach to sequence generation. All the letters of a word are activated in parallel, but inhibitory connections are established such that each letter inhibits all later letters. The earlier a letter occurs in the word, the fewer prior letters it has and the less inhibited it is. The gradient of letter activations is fed directly into the motor control response system, where it generates finger movements towards letter keys. The activation gradient in this model is not truly static, since activations change as letters are released from inhibition. However, the activation gradient is monotonic and decreasing, like the gradient in static models.

Dynamic mechanisms

Dynamic mechanisms allow the activation gradient set up over the item representations to vary during the course of sequence generation, in particular removing the constraint on a monotonic activation gradient. The fundamental effect of this is to reduce the reliance on the refractoriness of items for correct sequencing behaviour—some of the work of sequencing is done by the activation mechanism in varying the relative activation levels of items. This can render the sequencing process both more reliable and more flexible. A number of factors may make sequencing more reliable: (a) the number of items competing for output in each sequence position may be reduced by arranging that only a few items are strongly active in each sequence position; (b) the activation level of each successive "winning" item may be brought up to a similar high level, improving noise immunity; and (c) input from the activation mechanism to items early in a sequence may be reduced as sequencing progresses, reducing the need for an excessive refractory period to prevent perseverative errors. Depending on the details of the model, it may be possible to make sequencing more flexible by allowing repeated items to be produced in the same sequence. This requires items that have been produced (and are therefore refractory) to be reactivated by a large activating input.

Young's (1961, 1962) "ordinal position hypothesis" proposes that the stimulus for the production of a response in a sequence is some representation of its ordinal position in the sequence, rather than previous responses, as in chaining models. Henson & Burgess (1997) distinguish two versions of the hypothesis: The position of an item in a sequence may be represented in terms of its position relative to the other items in the sequence (Henson & Burgess term this "*ordinal* representation") or in terms of its absolute position in the sequence regardless of other items (Henson & Burgess's "*positional* representation"). Applied to the activating mechanisms of CQ models, the static form may be classed as encoding an ordinal representation of sequence position, since the position of an item in a sequence depends only on its activation level relative to the activations of the other items (thus, the third most active item will be the third item in the sequence). The dynamic form of activating system introduces a positional element to the representation of ordering in the sequence—since the signal generated by the activating system varies with time, the state of the signal at any moment encodes the current position in the sequence, irrespective of the states of the item representations. However, an ordinal component remains. Although the gradient of item activations varies, it is still the local gradient at any moment which defines which item will be produced in that position. The rate of change of the activation gradient is thus of interest. If the gradient changes very slowly, the system is not very different to a static system and the ordinal component of order representation dominates. If the gradient changes more rapidly, it becomes easier to discriminate successive positions in the sequence from the local state of the gradient, and the positional component comes to dominate. In the extreme case, only the target item would be activated in each sequence position, and a fully positional representation system would result. In models that use a dynamic activating mechanism, a smooth continuum of possibilities exists between the two extremes of a fully positional or fully ordinal representation of item position. This may be thought of in terms of the distinctiveness of consecutive states of the mechanism—the more distinctive, the more rapidly the activation gradient is changing and the further towards the fully positional end of the continuum the model may be placed.

Houghton's (1990) CQ model of speech production uses a simple dynamic form of activating mechanism but encodes position with respect to a small number of positional reference points. This, together with the use of an activation function of limited positional resolution, places the model more towards the "ordinal" than the "positional" end of the continuum. Houghton's model comprises a set of item representations (in this case the items are phonemes), an activating mechanism that establishes a (dynamic) activation gradient over the items, and a competitive output system. Houghton defines an explicit mechanism for this component—a "competitive filter", which consists of a set of nodes interconnected by mutually inhibitory and self-excitatory connections, which establish a winner-takes-all competition over output items. With the addition of random noise to item representations, the model simulates a number of features of speech production errors, notably the effect of word length, a bowed serial error curve, and the phenomenon of co-articulation, with up-coming phonemes primed prior to production. Movement and exchange errors are produced, which can span several intervening phonemes.

The dynamically updated activation gradient is generated by an input signal comprising two nodes, the "initiate" or "I" node and the "end" or "E" node, which vary in activity during sequence production. The I node starts with an activation level of 1.0, and its activation falls exponentially towards 0 as sequence production progresses. The E node takes on a value of 0 at the start of sequence production and approaches 1.0 as the sequence progresses. While the activation levels of I and E nodes unambiguously identify the current position in the sequence, the model used a conventional dot-product activation rule which is able to make only limited use of this positional information. Items near the beginning of the sequence are given strong connections to the I node, and those near the end are strongly connected to the E node. Items in the middle of the sequence, which are more weakly associated with both the I and E nodes, cannot be disambiguated by their relative activation levels alone. Thus, although this approach gives some of the advantages of a positional representation scheme—in particular, repeated items are possible in a sequence, and the tendency for perseverative errors is reduced—the inhibition of the winning item at each time-step during the sequence is still crucial for correct operation.

In the dynamic type of model, the activating mechanism can be viewed as the combination of an input signal embodying information about the position in the sequence, and an activation function which determines how this information affects the activation levels of items. A similar distinction is used in connectionist frameworks, where the activation level of a connectionist node is determined by the net input to the node transformed by an activation function. Houghton (1994) considers the ways in which the distinctiveness of consecutive positions may be increased in CQ models, and points out that two routes are available, corresponding to either increasing the discriminatory power (or positional resolution) of the activation function, so that consecutive states of the same input signal may be more easily discriminated, or increasing the distinctiveness of consecutive states in the signal itself, allowing the same activation function to more easily distinguish consecutive states. Improving positional discrimination can improve both the flexibility and the robustness of the sequencing mechanism, by an extension of the arguments mentioned in the discussion of dynamic forms of activation mechanisms, so this aim has been pursued in a number of CQ models.

OSCAR (Brown, Preece, & Hulme, 2000; Brown & Vousden, 1998; Vousden, 1996) is a model of sequential memory which has been applied to a number of verbal STM paradigms and to speech production (see Page, Chapter 7, this volume, for further discussion). A simple dot-product activation function is used in conjunction with a high-dimensionality input signal, which improves positional resolution. Items are associated with consecutive states of this slowly changing temporal context signal, and the same sequence of context states is reinstated during recall, allowing sequential recall of the learned items. Output is by competitive selection of the most active item, followed by temporary inhibition. The OSCAR model has two major points of novelty compared with prior CQ models: First, the temporal context which provides the overall timing of the model is based upon a set of oscillators, and second, the model uses distributed representations for the internal storage of sequence items (the output of the model uses an essentially localist representation; in CQ models this is effectively forced by the fact that select–inhibit output dynamics are used in the output stages). Brown, Preece, & Hulme (2000) demonstrate a number of verbal STM effects, including the separation of item and order memory, the effects of list length and item similarity, judgements of recency, power-law forgetting, serial position effects, and effects of grouping within lists. Vousden (1996) applies the OSCAR architecture to speech production, and explains the constraints imposed by syllabic structure on speech errors in terms of the periodic nature of the activating mechanism.

A similar approach, using a high-dimensional timing signal to cue sequencing, is employed by Burgess & Hitch (1992, 1996) in a model of verbal STM. Burgess & Hitch use a somewhat simpler changing signal comprising a field of inactive nodes, across which a "window" of high activation is shifted one position per learning or recall time-step. This provides the activating signal in a conventional CQ architecture.

The alternative approach to increasing positional resolution is to improve the positional discrimination of the activating function. Glasspool (1998) and Glasspool & Houghton (submitted) take this approach in a model of spelling. The "I–E" activating signal of Houghton (1990) is used in conjunction with a radial basis function (RBF)-based activating function which is able to sharply discriminate between different combinations of I and E node activation. The benefits of the simple I–E signal (including the simplicity of generating the signal endogenously, and the simple account for primacy and recency effects achieved by assuming that position is encoded relative to the start and end of a sequence) are retained, but the basic performance of the sequencing system is considerably more robust than Houghton (1990). Glasspool (1998) shows that a number of problems with earlier CQ models relate to the undue fragility of sequence generation and are solved by improved positional resolution.

Finally, it is interesting to note that a model taking a similar approach to the generation of sequential behaviour—the production of a dynamic gradient of activations and the selection and inhibition of the most active response—has been successful in a rather different area of psychology. Cooper (Chapter 10, this volume) and Cooper & Shallice (2000) describe an implementation of Norman & Shallice's (1980) contention scheduling system for the control of high-level routine behaviour. Although this model operates at a higher notional level than the others discussed here, the means by which serial ordering of actions is achieved is basically that of CQ. The approach is particularly interesting because it is motivated by ideas concerning the evolution of automatic and of willed behaviour systems, and may offer an independent rationale for the processes underlying CQ.

CQ AS AN EXPLANATORY FRAMEWORK

A range of CQ models, when disrupted, have shown a set of error features consistent with those identified in human serial behaviour at the beginning of this chapter. How, though, does the CQ framework explain these features of serial slips? The details of individual models often obscure the basic principles involved, so here we take a wider view. The foregoing discussion has treated CQ as comprising two key components—activation gradient-based queuing, and competitive output with refractory inhibition. This section explores the contribution of each to the success of CQ mechanisms in modelling psychological data. We will consider in turn each of the common features of human serial behaviour already identified.

Co-activation of sequence elements

It is a basic premise of the CQ approach that items to be sequenced are activated in parallel, and competitive selection and inhibition convert this parallel activation into serial behaviour. CQ systems with static control signals activate all sequence items, whereas those with dynamic control signals activate some subset, the effective size of which depends on the positional resolution of the control signal. Nonetheless, all CQ models involve co-activation of sequence elements to some extent, by definition. Importantly, the set of active elements is not arbitrary. The notion of an activation gradient means that items in the sequence which are close to the target at a particular time will be the most active, and generally the closer the item to the target, the more active it will be (although superimposed on this gradient there may be further patterning reflecting features of the domain of the model, such as the degree of phonemic similarity in the case of verbal STM models; Burgess & Hitch, 1996; Page & Norris, 1997, or syllabic position in speech models, Hartley & Houghton, 1996; Vousden, 1996). This means that positional uncertainty, the basis for movement errors, is centred on the correct position but may be influenced by domain-specific similarity metrics or constraints.

The degree of co-activation of sequence elements is determined essentially by the nature of the activating system, rather than by the competitive output system.

Effects of serial position

CQ models generally exhibit both primacy and recency effects—most errors occur in medial sequence positions. A full analysis of the factors involved has not yet been carried out, but the basic explanations are related to those for primacy and recency in Lee & Estes' reverberatory model and Johnson's distinctiveness model. Depending on the CQ model involved, the major factors are:

- The greater distinctiveness of successive serial positions at the start and end of the sequence compared with those near the middle, due to a greater difference in activation between "winning item" and "best loser" near the start and end of the sequence compared with the middle. This is the case only for certain types of activating mechanism, e.g. in Houghton, Glasspool, & Shallice's (1994) spelling model, I and E nodes create an activating signal which changes more rapidly at the start (I-node falling rapidly) and end (E-node climbing rapidly) than near the middle of the sequence (I and E nodes both changing activation relatively slowly). This leads to greater discriminability and hence wider activation margins in primacy and recency regions. The activating mechanisms used by Burgess & Hitch in their articulatory loop models, by contrast, give rise to a constant difference in activation between winner and closest competitor in all sequence positions.
- The more limited freedom for movement errors near the start and end of the sequence, where there are more options for movement in one direction than the other, compared with positions near the middle where items can move freely in both directions. In terms of the CQ mechanism, this equates to a greater number of items co-activated in parallel with the target item in medial positions, when items both before and after the target are co-activated, than at the start and end, and hence greater competition in medial positions.
- The removal of potential competitors from the pool of active items as each sequence item is selected and inhibited reduces the number of items competing for output. This can lead to a recency effect if recovery from inhibition is relatively slow.

In many (perhaps most) models, two or even all three of these factors are involved in generating primacy and recency effects. For example, in Page & Norris's primacy model, factors (a) and (c) combine: the primacy effect is due to the greater distinctiveness of items near the start of the sequence (i.e. the greater winning margin, as successive activation levels reduce asymptotically towards zero as the sequence progresses). The steeper activation gradient near the start of the sequence leads to less competition than later in the sequence, when the slope is flatter. The recency effect is due to the removal of potential competitors as items are successfully recalled and inhibited, leaving few items to compete for final sequence positions.

Primacy and recency effects thus cannot be easily localized in either the activating system or the competitive output system. In many cases both systems may contribute.

Effect of sequence and item length

All CQ models show a clear effect of sequence length on error rate, errors increasing with longer sequences. Two factors lead to this effect:

- As for any mechanism where errors may occur probabilistically on each sequence item, the greater the number of sequence items, the greater the probability of at least one error. The probability of successfully completing the entire sequence thus declines with increasing length, even if the probability of an error on any particular item is unaffected by sequence length.
- An additional effect more specific to certain formulations of the CQ approach is that longer sequences may be inherently less robust, thus the probability of an error on any particular item in a long list is greater than for the same item in a short list. This effect depends on the type of activation mechanism used. Houghton's I–E activating signal, for example, shows this effect because longer sequences must be coded with the same set of weighted connections as shorter ones, but more distinct activation states must be encoded in this same weight "space". This leads to a shallower activation gradient and increased competition within longer lists. A similar effect occurs in the primacy STM model, but does not occur in Burgess & Hitch's (1992) STM model, for example, where the activation gradient does not vary as a function of sequence length.

Burgess & Hitch (1992) do, however, add a further mechanism for length effects to their rehearsal-based verbal STM model. Weights in the model decay with time during cyclic rehearsal of a sequence, so longer lists experience more decay between rehearsals. This decay is a function of time rather than list length *per se*, so error rates are higher for items that take longer to articulate, as well as for longer lists.

Predominance of ordering errors

It is generally easier for a CQ system to produce an error in the ordering of the items in a sequence than an error involving an item not present in the target sequence. Because sequence items are activated in parallel, the strongest competitor to the target item in any position will generally be another item in the sequence. How strongly items not present in the sequence are able to compete depends on how they are activated. If the only source of activation for nonsequence items is general noise present across all items (as in Houghton's 1990 model) then ordering errors will always be more likely than item errors, because the margin between the target item and its nearest competitor in the absence of noise—another sequence item—must always be smaller than the absolute activation level of the target item, while the magnitude of noise remains the same for both competitor items. In some cases other sources of activation are available, e.g. items (words) in Burgess & Hitch's (1992) STM model receive activation by virtue of their sharing phonemes with the target word. If no within-sequence items receive activation from this source, a nonsequence item that does so will have a greater advantage than usual. Burgess & Hitch still report a greater proportion of order than "item" errors overall, however.

A further factor is the inhibition of items following their output. This tends to cause each item in the sequence to be visited only once, even if in the wrong order. This is not an absolute constraint, of course, as it will depend on how easily items can recover from inhibition. In models where inhibition is relatively transient, erroneous repeats may occur. However, the tendency to visit each item only once, regardless of the actual order, does not appear to be a simple property of any ordering mechanism that does not involve some form of output competition combined with post-output inhibition.

In general, however, the ratio of item identity errors to order errors is a product of the activating mechanism, and may depend on the content of the sequence itself.

Effects of repeats

Some CQ models predict that repeated items should be more prone to errors than other items within a sequence. Two factors contribute to this:

- The inhibition of items following output implies that it will be more difficult to re-activate an item which has already been produced than to activate a "fresh" item. From this we would expect the second item in a repeated pair to be more vulnerable to error than a non-repeated item in the same position. There is some evidence that this is the case in spelling errors (Hotopf, 1980) and verbal STM (Jahnke, 1969; although this is true only for nonimmediate repeats, see below).
- A further factor is the added difficulty of arranging for an item to "win the competition" twice rather than once. A static activation gradient cannot produce this behaviour, so some more complex dynamic

activation system is required, or the sequence must be "chunked" into subsequences that do not contain repeats (this approach is taken by Rumelhart & Norman, 1982). In the former case we might expect that the extra difficulty of re-activating an item would incur a penalty, perhaps in the form of greater vulnerability, although this will depend entirely on the activating mechanism.

Implementational details may or may not allow particular models to exhibit the effect in the final error pattern. In systems with dynamic activating mechanisms, recovery after inhibition can be quite rapid while maintaining robust sequence production. The activation boost given to the repeated item may balance its vulnerability. With rapid recovery from inhibition, the effect of repeating items will also diminish rapidly with the distance between repeats, possibly covering only one or two items. Depending on the dynamics of the activating system it may also be possible for the effect to be counterbalanced to some extent by the reduced number of items competing for output in certain serial positions, since a sequence with a repeated item contains fewer distinct items than a sequence of the same length without repeats. This will tend to reduce the error rate on sequences with repeats. It may be necessary to examine patterns of error incidence in considerable detail in order to disambiguate these possibilities.

Behaviour of double items

While repeated items may be produced by CQ mechanisms if a dynamic activating signal is used, the inhibition of items as they are output makes immediate repeats (doublings) particularly difficult. Syllabic structural constraints in speech production ensure that immediate repeats do not occur at the phonemic level, so the problem does not tend to arise in modelling phonemic speech production. Double letters are common in English spelling, however, and it is interesting that the same gross pattern of errors on double letters is exhibited by typists and in spelling by GBD patients—the property of doubling appears to dissociate from the letter being doubled, so no doubling or more than one doubling may occur, or the wrong letter may be doubled. Rumelhart & Norman's (1982) typing model successfully models such errors, using a doubling schema which is triggered at the appropriate point in word production. However, that model incorporates a powerful external mechanism (segmentation into subword chunks) for handling repeated letters and thus has no intrinsic need for such a mechanism. CQ models with dynamic activating signals can produce nonimmediate repeats but require an additional mechanism for doublings, which provides an independent motivation for the special treatment of double letters. Rumelhart & Norman's doubling schema appears to be the simplest way to treat double items and this general approach has been used in other models (Houghton, Glasspool, & Shallice, 1994; Glasspool & Houghton, submitted) which show the typical error types on double letters in GBD spelling.

Effect of similarity and preservation of domain-specific constraints

In a number of psychological areas, similar items are more prone to confusion in sequence production. The most natural way to express such constraints is typically in terms of a more abstract "schema for order" (Lashley, 1951), in which the category of response that can be produced at any point is restricted to some subset of the responses comprising the behavioural domain. When errors occur in a sequence, the categorical constraints still apply, so that, for instance, if two items are transposed they will tend to be of the same category.

In CQ models, selection of an action for production can only occur when the action wins the activation competition. Any constraint on which actions can be produced when must therefore affect this process. Hence, the obvious way in which categorical constraints can occur in such a model is through the biasing of activation levels for whole classes of response. Glasspool & Houghton (1997) identify two potential sources for such categorical response biasing in CQ, external and internal. In the *external* case, the bias comes from an explicit representation of the stereotyped "template" to which a target sequence must conform. Activation of the template is serially ordered, and it sequentially activates or primes whole classes of response. Many activation-based models of speech and language production have this form, e.g. Dell (1986), Dell, Burger, & Svec (1997), Hartley & Houghton (1996), and MacKay (1987). In the *internal* case, the bias comes from shared features in the internal representations of items, which lead to interference between similar items. Such an explanation for similarity effects is natural in models where items are activated via a feature-based representation (a common approach in connectionist systems).

Any mechanism that tends to bias the activation of a class of responses at certain points during sequence production should lead to serial constraints, so in principle any regularity in the processes that activate item nodes could lead to corresponding regularities in serial errors without affecting the other basic behaviours of CQ systems. Two features of the CQ approach allow serial regularities to be expressed smoothly in this way: Activation-based sequencing, and a lack of associative response chaining. The representation of sequential position by activation level allows activation biases to influence sequence order directly, and the competitive selection of responses under noise means that even small biases can subtly influence error rates. The lack of chaining also allows biases to have a direct and simple effect on performance. Simple response chaining models predict that, following an error, further errors will occur, because the current response contributes to cueing later responses. Thus, an isolated class-preserving exchange error, such as cinema → cimena, with the rest of the word correct (including the intervening vowel), would not be expected to occur.

DISCUSSION

The systems that contribute to the generation of serial behaviour in practice are no doubt both complex and subtle. However, the separation of competitive output from processes that prepare responses for output may allow us to greatly simplify the problem of accounting for slips in serial behaviour. The foregoing discussion shows that both the activating mechanism and the competitive output mechanism contribute to the explanation CQ models can offer for the common features of slips in serial behaviour. In several cases both are involved in a single effect. It is also clear that it is possible to some extent to disentangle the contribution of each system. A number of gross features of slip data can be explained fully or in part by the operation of a competitive output system, letting us concentrate on accounting for more subtle features of the error pattern in a particular domain which may reveal much about the processes contributing to activating responses. Treating CQ as a combination of two assumptions rather than a monolithic theory allows the advantages of the approach, and the shortcomings of other sequencing mechanisms, to be more clearly analysed.

It is interesting to consider possible variations on the CQ theme. There are limited options for varying the basic competitive output mechanism. Localist output item representation appears to be required, because items must be inhibited after output and direct inhibition of a distributed representation will lead to interference with other, noninhibited, item representations. Additionally, movement and exchange errors apparently constrain processes of inhibition to be directly tied to winning a competition over the output items.

There are, however, considerably fewer constraints on the system that establishes the activation gradient. The variety of successful CQ models already demonstrates both static and dynamic activating signals, but other more complex forms are possible. For example, Glasspool (1998) and Glasspool, Shallice, & Cipolotti (1999) outline a more complex system which produces an activation gradient as a result of a "lazy" back-propagation learning rule. Only the minimum of constraints are imposed on the mapping learned by the back-propagation part of the network, allowing an activation gradient to emerge among contenders for each serial output position, which are chosen by a CQ "select-and-inhibit" output mechanism. It would appear that the basic features of CQ sequencing do not place many demands on the precise form of the activation gradient, so long as such a gradient is generated and a competitive select–inhibit output mechanism operates upon it.

The space of possible activating systems is thus far wider than that which has been explored in CQ models to date. A large space of potential models remains unexplored, promising fertile ground for future research. For example, the difficulties of addressing certain data with Elman network models, discussed above, can in part be attributed to their lack of competitive output dynamics. Botvinick & Plaut (2003) have recently shown that an Elman network, coupled with a winner-takes-all output layer, is capable of acquiring positional representations for sequence items. The trained network can be viewed as the activating system in a CQ-like system. Once it has been trained, Botvinick & Plaut's network is capable of immediate serial recall of sequences and operates in a manner that appears to be closely related to CQ models. The relationship of the trained system to the CQ paradigm, and the reasons why this mode of operation is acquired by the network, promise to be rewarding areas for study.

Another area that promises to be an interesting one for future work is the degree to which the type of errors to which a CQ system is prone are affected by aspects of the domain within which it operates. Vousden & Brown (1997) have made an interesting start in this direction with a study of the effect of one parameter in the OSCAR model—the degree of inhibition of items following their production—which seems to be the key to some of the differences between the types of error common in speech as opposed to short-term memory. Increasing the level of inhibition causes the pattern of errors produced by the model to change from one similar to that seen in speech errors to one more typical of short-term memory experiments. Vousden & Brown relate this parameter difference to different task demands in the two areas. Another factor that may be important is the nature and degree of serial "category constraints" in different domains, e.g. the constraint on which category of phoneme may occur in particular syllabic positions.

I have argued that a range of features of slips in serial behaviour can be explained by a small set of assumptions, embodied in the CQ framework. By separating this framework into two components, an activating mechanism and a competitive output mechanism, the explanations for this constellation of features may be more clearly seen. Much of the explanatory contribution comes from the output mechanism, which appears to be well constrained in its form. The investigation of domain-specific activating mechanisms, and their integration and interaction with the CQ output mechanism, is thus a particularly exciting opportunity for future work. Before this can be undertaken, however, there is a more immediate need for a careful investigation into the relationship between the dynamics of the competitive output system and the form of the sequencing errors which result from its disruption. The precise form of slips in serial behaviour, in both normal and damaged systems, should provide a rich source of constraints on the form of the underlying sequencing mechanisms. The challenge is to establish precisely what those constraints are.

Note

1.   The term "competitive queuing" was introduced in a specific model of speech production (Houghton, 1990). Although this was not the first model to use the approach, the label is useful for the broader class of models that generate sequential behaviour using the same basic dynamic process. Here I use the term in this more general sense.

REFERENCES

Aaronson, D. (1968). Temporal course of perception in an immediate recall task. *Journal of Experimental Psychology, 76,* 129–140.

Amit, D. J., Sagi, D., & Usher, M. (1990). Architecture of attractor neural networks performing cognitive fast scanning. *Network, 1,* 189–216.

Baddeley, A. D. (1968). How does acoustic similarity influence short-term memory? *Qurterly Journal of Experimental Psychology, 20,* 249–264.

Benguerel, A. P., & Cowan, H. A. (1974). Co-articulation of upper lip protrusion in French. *Phonetica, 30,* 41–55.

Botvinick, M., & Plaut, D. (2003). Constructive processes in immediate serial recall: A recurrent network model of the bigram frequency effect. In B. Kokinov, & W. Hirst (Eds.), *Constructive memory* (pp. 129–137). Sofia: NBU Press.

Brown, A. S. (1991). A review of the tip-of-the-tongue experience. *Psychological Bulletin, 109,* 204–223.

Brown, G. D. A., Preece, T., & Hulme, C. (2000). Oscillator-based memory for serial order. *Psychological Review, 107(1),* 127–181.

Brown, G. D. A., & Vousden, J. I. (1998). Adaptive analysis of sequential behaviour: Oscillators as rational mechanisms. In M. Oaksford, & N. Chater (Eds.), *Rational models of cognition.* Oxford: Oxford University Press.

Burgess, N., & Hitch, G. J. (1992). Towards a network model of the articulatory loop. *Journal of Memory and Language, 31,* 429–460.

Burgess, N., & Hitch, G. J. (1996). A connectionist model of STM for serial order. In S. E. Gathercole (Ed.), *Models of short-term memory* (pp. 51–72). Hove, UK: Psychology Press.

Caramazza, A., & Miceli, G. (1990). The structure of graphemic representations. *Cognition, 37,* 243–297.

Conrad, R. (1965). Order error in immediate recall of sequences. *Journal of Verbal Learning and Verbal Behaviour, 4,* 161–169.

Conrad, R., & Hull, A. J. (1964), Information, acoustic confusion and memory span. *British Journal of Psychology, 55,* 429–432.

Cooper, R., & Shallice, T. (1997). Modelling the selection of routine action: Exploring the criticality of parameter values. In Langley, P. & Shafto, M. G., (Eds.), *Proceedings of the 19th Annual Conference of the Cognitive Science Society* (pp. 131–136). Stanford, CA.

Cooper, R., & Shallice, T. (2000). Contention scheduling and the control of routine activities. *Cognitive Neuropsychology, 17* (4), 298–338.

Cooper, R., Shallice, T., & Farringdon, J. (1995). Symbolic and continuous processes in the automatic selection of actions. In J. Hallam (Ed.), *Hybrid problems, hybrid solutions, frontiers in artificial intelligence and applications* (pp. 27–37). Amsterdam: IOS Press.

Crowder, R. G. (1972). Visual and auditory memory. In J. Kavanagh, & I. Mattingley (Eds.), *Language by ear and by eye* (pp. 251–275). Cambridge, MA: MIT Press.

Dell, G. S. (1984). Representation of serial order in speech: Evidence from the repeated phoneme effect in speech errors. *Journal of Experimental Psychology: Learning, Memory and Cognition, 10,* 222–233.

Dell, G. S. (1986). A spreading activation theory of retrieval in sentence production. *Psychological Review, 93,* 283–321.

Dell, G. S. (1988). The retrieval of phonological forms in production: Tests of predictions from a connectionist model. *Journal of Memory and Language, 27,* 124–142.

Dell, G. S., Burger, L. K., & Svec, W. R. (1997). Language production and serial order: A functional analysis and a model. *Psychological Review, 104,* 123–147.

Ebenholtz, S. M. (1963). Position mediated transfer between serial learning and a spatial discrimination task. *Journal of Experimental Psychology, 65,* 603–608.

Elman, J. L. (1990). Finding structure in time. *Cognitive Science, 14,* 179–211.

Estes, W. K. (1972). An associative basis for coding and organization in memory. In A. W. Melton, & E. Martin (Eds.), *Coding processes in human memory* (pp. 161–190). Washington, DC: V. H. Winston & Sons.

Gathercole, S. E., Willis, C. S., Emslie, H., & Baddeley, A. D. (1991). The influences of number of syllables and word-likeness on children's repetition of nonwords. *Applied Psycholinguistics, 12,* 349–367.

Glasspool, D. W. (1995). Competitive queueing and the articulatory loop: An extended network model. In J. Levy, D. Bairaktaris, J. Bullinaria, & P. Cairns (Eds.), *Connectionist models of memory and language* (pp. 5–30). London: UCL Press.

Glasspool, D. W. (1998). *Modelling serial order in behaviour: Studies of spelling.* Unpublished doctoral thesis, University of London.

Glasspool, D. W., & Houghton, G. (1997). Dynamic representation of structural constraints in models of serial behaviour. In J. Bullinaria, D. Glasspool, & G. Houghton (Eds.), *Connectionist Representations. Proceedings of the 4th Neural Computation and Psychology Workshop* (pp. 269–282). London: Springer-Verlag.

Glasspool, D. W., and Houghton, G. (submitted). *Serial order and consonant-vowel structure in a model of disordered spelling.*

Glasspool, D. W., Houghton, G., & Shallice, T. (1995). Interactions between knowledge sources in a dual-route connectionist model of spelling. In L. S. Smith, & P. J. B. Hancock (Eds.), *Neural computation and psychology* (pp. 209–226). London: Springer-Verlag.

Glasspool, D. W., Shallice, T., & Cipolotti, L. (1999). Neuropsychologically plausible sequence generation. In D. Heinke, G. W. Humphreys, & A. Olson (Eds.), *Connectionist models in cognitive neuroscience* (pp. 40–51). London: Springer-Verlag.

Grossberg, S. (1978). A theory of human memory: Self-organisation and performance of sensory-motor codes, maps and plans. *Progress in Theoretical Biology, 5,* 233–302.

Guildford, J. P., & Dallenbach, K. M. (1925). The determination of memory span by the method of constant stimuli. *American Journal of Psychology, 36,* 621–628.

Hartley, T., & Houghton, G. (1996). A linguistically constrained model of short-term memory for words and nonwords. *Journal of Memory and Language, 35,* 1–31.

Healy, A. F. (1975). Coding of spatial-temporal patterns in short-term memory. *Journal of Verbal Learning and Verbal Behaviour, 14,* 481–495.

Henson, R. N. A. (1998). Short-term memory for serial order: The start-end model. *Cognitive Psychology, 36,* 73–137.

Henson, R. N. A. (1999). Positional information in short-term memory: Relative or absolute? *Memory and Cognition, 27,* 915–927.

Henson, R. N. A., & Burgess, N. (1997). Representations of serial order. In J. Bullinaria, D. Glasspool, & G. Houghton (Eds.), *Connectionist representations. Proceedings of the 4th Neural Computation and Psychology Workshop* (pp. 283–300). London: Springer-Verlag.

Henson, R. N. A., Norris, D. G., Page, M. P. A., & Baddeley, A. D. (1996). Unchained memory: Error patterns rule out chaining models of immediate serial recall. *Quarterly Journal of Experimental Psychology, 49A,* 80–115.

Hitch, G. J. (1974). Short-term memory for spatial and temporal information. *Quarterly Journal of Experimental Psychology, 26,* 503–513.

Hotopf, W. H. N. (1980). Slips of the pen. In U. Frith (Ed.), *Cognitive processes in spelling* (pp. 287–307). London: Academic Press.

Houghton, G. (1990). The problem of serial order: A neural network model of sequence learning and recall. In R. Dale, C. Mellish, & M. Zock (Eds.), *Current research in natural language generation* (pp. 287–319). London: Academic Press.

Houghton, G. (1994). *Some formal variations on the theme of competitive queueing.* Internal Technical Report, UCL-PSY-CQ1. Department of Psychology, University College London.

Houghton, G., Glasspool, D., & Shallice, T. (1994). Spelling and serial recall: Insights from a competitive queueing model. In G. D. A. Brown, & N. C. Ellis (Eds.), *Handbook of spelling: Theory, process and intervention* (pp. 365–404). Chichester: Wiley.

Hulme, C., Maughan, S., & Brown, C. D. A. (1991). Memory for familiar and unfamiliar words: Evidence for a long-term memory contribution to short-term span. *Journal of Memory and Language, 30,* 685–701.

Humphreys, G. W., & Forde, E. M. E. (1998). Disordered action schema and action disorganisation syndrome. *Cognitive Neuropsychology, 15,* 771–812.

Jahnke, J. C. (1969). The Ranschburg effect. *Psychological Review, 76,* 592–605.

Jonsdottir, M., Shallice, T., & Wise, R. (1996). Language-specific differences in graphemic buffer disorder. *Cognition, 59,* 169–197.

Jordan, M. (1986). Attractor dynamics and parallelism in a connectionist sequential machine. *Proceedings of the 8th Annual Conference of the Cognitive Science Society* (pp. 10–17). Hillsdale, NJ: Lawrence Erlbaum Associates, Inc.

Lashley, K. S. (1951). The problem of serial order in behaviour. In F. Beach, D. Hebb, C. Morgan, & H. Nissen (Eds.), *The Neuropsychology of Lashley* (pp. 506–528: published 1960). New York: McGraw-Hill.

Levelt, W. (1989). *Speaking.* Cambridge, MA: MIT Press.

Lewandowsky, S., & Murdock, B. B. (1989). Memory for serial order. *Psychological Review, 96,* 25–57.

Mackay, D. G. (1987). *The organization of perception and action.* New York: Springer-Verlag.

Magill, R. A., & Dowell, M. N. (1977). Serial position effects in motor short-term memory. *Journal of Motor Behaviour, 9,* 319–323.

Milner, P. M. (1961). A neural mechanism for the immediate recall of sequences. *Kybernetic, 1,* 76–81.

Moll, K. L., & Daniloff, R. G. (1971). Investigation of the timing of velar movements during speech. *Journal of the Acoustical Society of America, 50,* 678–684.

Murdock, B. B. (1962) The serial position effect of free recall. *Journal of Experimental Psychology, 64,* 482–488.

Murdock, B. B. (1982). A theory for the storage and retrieval of item and associative information. *Psychological Review, 89,* 609–626.

Murdock, B. B. (1983). A distributed memory model for serial-order information. *Psychological Review, 90,* 316–338.

Murdock, B. B. (1995). Developing TODAM: Three models for serial-order information. *Memory and Cognition, 23,* 631–645.

Murray, D. J. (1966). Vocalization-at-presentation and immediate recall with varying recall methods. *Quarterly Journal of Experimental Psychology, 18,* 9–18.

Norman, D. A., & Shallice, T. (1980). *Attention to action: Willed and automatic control of behaviour.* Center for Human Information Processing (Technical Report No. 99). University of California at San Diego, CA.

Norman, D. A., & Shallice, T. (1986). Attention to action: Willed and automatic control of behaviour. Reprinted in revised form in R. J. Davidson, G. E. Schwartz, & D. Shapiro (Eds.), *Consciousness and self-regulation* (Vol. 4, pp. 1–18). New York: Plenum.

Page, M. P. A., & Norris, D. G. (1997). A localist implementation of the primacy model of immediate serial recall. In J. Bullinaria, D. Glasspool, & G. Houghton (Eds.), *Connectionist representations. Proceedings of the 4th Neural Computation and Psychology Workshop* (pp. 316–330). London: Springer-Verlag.

Page, M. P. A., & Norris, D. G. (1998). The primacy model: A new model of immediate serial recall. *Psychological Review, 105(4),* 761–781.

Rumelhart, D. E., & Norman, D. A. (1982). Simulating a skilled typist: A study of skilled cognitive-motor performance. *Cognitive Science, 6,* 1–36.

Shallice, T., Glasspool, D. W., & Houghton, G. (1995). Can neuropsychological evidence inform connectionist modelling? Analyses of spelling. *Language and Cognitive Processes, 10,* 195–225.

Shattuck-Hufnagel, S. (1979). Speech errors as evidence for a serial-ordering mechanism in sentence production. In W. E. Cooper, & E. C. T. Walker (Eds.), *Sentence processing: Psycholinguistic studies presented to Merrill Garret* (pp. 295–342). Hillsdale, NJ: Lawrence Erlbaum Associates, Inc.

Slamecka, N. J. (1964). An inquiry into the doctrine of remote associations. *Psychological Review, 71,* 61–76.

Sternberg, S. (1966). High-speed scanning in human memory. *Science, 153,* 652–654.

Treiman, R., & Danis, C. (1988). Short-term memory errors for spoken syllables are affected by the linguistic structure of the syllables. *Journal of Experimental Psychology: Learning, Memeory, and Cognition, 14* (1), 145–152.

Vousden, J., & Brown, G. D. A. (1997). To repeat or not to repeat: The time course of response. In J. Bullinaria, D. Glasspool, & G. Houghton (Eds.), *Connectionist representations. Proceedings of the 4th Neural Computation and Psychology Workshop* (pp. 301–315). London: Springer-Verlag.

Vousden, J. I. (1996). *Serial control of phonology in speech production.* Unpublished doctoral dissertation, University of Warwick, UK.

Wilberg R. B. (1990). The retention and free recall of multiple movements. *Human Movement Science, 9,* 437–479.

Wing, A. M., & Baddeley, A. D. (1980). Spelling errors in handwriting: A corpus and a distributional analysis. In U. Frith, (Ed.), *Cognitive processes in spelling* (pp. 251–285). London: Academic Press.

Wrisberg, J. (1975). The serial position effect in short-term motor retention. *Journal of Motor Behaviour, 7,* 289–295.

Young, R. K. (1961). The stimulus in serial verbal learning. *American Journal of Psychology, 74,* 517–528.

Young, R. K. (1962). Tests of three hypotheses about the effective stimulus in serial learning. *Journal of Experimental Psychology, 63,* 307–313.

Young, R. K. (1968). Serial Learning. In T. Dixon, & D. Horton (Eds.), *Verbal behaviour and general behaviour theory* (pp. 122–148). Englewood Cliffs, NJ: Prentice Hall.

SECTION THREE

Attention and cognitive control

CHAPTER NINE

Computational models of visual selective attention: A review

Dietmar Heinke and Glyn W. Humphreys
Behavioural and Brain Sciences Centre, University of Birmingham, UK

INTRODUCTION

This chapter reviews some of the major computational models of visual attention and highlights how they help to clarify concepts in psychological theories. To do this we focus on some of the major issues and experimental paradigms that have influenced psychologists, including space- vs. object-based attention, stimulus filtering tasks, and visual search. We also discuss how the models can be used to simulate neuropsychological disorders of visual cognition, including agnosia and neglect—disorders that themselves highlight particular theoretical issues, such as the role of parallel grouping processes in vision, the relations between attention and spatial representation, and the interaction between bottom-up and top-down factors in selection. We conclude by evaluating the contribution of the modelling process to understanding cognition.

To provide the framework for our analysis, we first consider the issues and paradigms that have dictated much of the psychological research on visual attention.

Space- vs. object-based attention

Psychological theories traditionally hold that visual selection is spatially based, assuming that selection involves some form of internal spotlight that activates attended regions or leads to the inhibition of unattended regions of visual field (Posner, Snyder, & Davidson, 1980; Treisman, 1988). Strong evidence for spatial selection comes from studies of cueing which show that detection of a target is improved when it is preceded by a spatially valid cue (Posner et al., 1980). On the other hand, experiments have also demonstrated a more object-based style of selection. For instance, the detrimental effects of invalid cues are reduced if cues and targets fall within the same perceptual object (Egly, Driver, & Rafal, 1994), and the costs in detecting two stimuli presented simultaneously relative to when they are presented successively in time are reduced if the stimuli are attributes of a single object (e.g. Duncan, 1984). To capture these results, we need theories that specify not only how both space- and object-based selection operates but, importantly, how these different forms of selection may interact.

Stimulus-filtering tasks

One procedure that has been used extensively to investigate attentional selection in humans has been stimulus filtering, where participants are given a stimulus attribute to use as a cue to select other properties of a target in a display. For instance, subjects may be asked to name the colour of a shape (e.g. a red square). Experimenters may then be interested in the impact on selection of stimuli carrying nontarget attributes (e.g. a blue circle or a red circle), impact on responses to targets, and whether any impact is related to factors such as the response associated with the relevant and irrelevant items. Generally, the effect of the distractors is dependent on their similarity to the relevant target attributes (e.g. Van der Heijden, 1981). On the other hand, the experiments showed that the interference depends on the spatial distance between relevant and irrelevant items (e.g. Eriksen & Eriksen, 1974). Eriksen & Yeh (1985) took these experimental findings as evidence for an imperfect spatial selection process in the shape of a "zoom lens". Stimuli falling in the penumbra of this zoom lens may still be processed to some degree, to generate interference even at the response level. Hence, theories need to explain these aspects of nonspatial (attribute-based) as well as spatial selection.

Visual search

One special kind of filtering task, in which the number of nontarget elements are varied systematically, is visual search. Studies of visual search have been used particularly to assess the question of which visual processes are spatially parallel and which necessitate that selection becomes spatially restricted, so that a target is only detected following some form of serial search (operating across one restricted spatial region at a time) (see Wolfe, 1998, for recent review). Typically, search efficiency is measured using the slope of the function relating reaction time (RT) to the number of distractors present. The slope of the search function, then, depends on the exact nature of the target and the distractors in the display, e.g. if the target is distinguished by a salient feature (feature search), such as a horizontal bar amongst vertical bars, search slopes are shallow or even flat (a result termed 'pop-out' in search). In contrast, if the target is defined by a conjunction of features (e.g. a blue vertical bar amongst green vertical and blue horizontal bars) search is slow and typically linearly related to the number of distractors present. Usually these findings are interpreted as indicating different modes of processing during search. Efficient (flat) search functions are said to reflect spatially parallel processes, whereas linear and steep functions are attributed to spatially serial processes, (e.g. Treisman & Gelade, 1980).

There are numerous theories based on this dichotomy. Here we focus on two theories, each of which has formed the basis for computational models, which we review subsequently. Wolfe & Cave (1990) suggested that the visual system computes for each item in the display its saliency relative to surrounding items. A "saliency map" is then assembled in parallel across a display. The saliency map is also modulated by the observer's "set" for the target, which acts in a top-down manner to raise activation values for relevant attributes. Values in the saliency map are used to direct attention to the most salient item, which is then compared with a memory representation of the target. If the item is not the target, the next most salient item is selected and tested for being a target, and so forth. This serial search process, guided by saliency, is the hallmark of the guided search model.

An alternative account has been proposed by Duncan & Humphreys (1989). They suggested that items are grouped according to their similarity in an early parallel stage of processing. These groups compete for access to a limited capacity visual short-term memory on the basis of the similarity between the stimuli and the memory template of the target. If the group that has won the competition contains the target, the search is terminated; if not, the selection process starts again. In the case of search for a target defined by a salient feature (feature search), the distractor items differ from the memory template for the target, and so tend to create little competition for selection with the target. In addition, if the distractors are homogeneous, they can be grouped and rejected together. As a consequence of both factors, search is efficient and little affected by the number of distractors present (search is spatially parallel). For targets defined only by a conjunction of features, however, search is disrupted by a variety of factors: (a) there can be grouping between the target and the distractors sharing a critical feature, reducing the match between the template of the target and the representation of the display; (b) there is little grouping between distractors that do not share features, disrupting the efficient rejection of distractors; and (c) distractors sharing features with targets will partially activate the target's template, creating competition for selection. The net result is that conjunction search will be relatively inefficient and even spatially serial, selecting each item in the display in turn. Computational versions of these theories will be discussed below.

Neuropsychological disorders

Visual agnosia

In conjunction with studies of visual attention in normal observers, one other important constraint on understanding the mechanisms of visual selection comes from neuropsychology—the study of disorders of cognition. One example of such a disorder is visual agnosia, a term applied to patients with a selective impairment in the visual recognition of common objects (e.g. Farah, 1990; Humphreys, 1999; Humphreys & Riddoch, 1993). Patients with visual agnosia can have difficulties in selecting information from visual displays, due to problems in grouping together relevant visual features and in segmenting apart irrelevant features. This becomes particularly apparent in visual search tasks in which target selection is aided by the efficient grouping and rejection of distractors (e.g. when distractors are homogeneous). Normal subjects show relatively flat search functions under these conditions, and absent responses can even be faster than present (due to fast rejection of distractors) (Duncan & Humphreys, 1989; Humphreys, Quinlan, & Riddoch, 1989; Quinlan & Humphreys, 1987). In contrast, agnosic patients can show inefficient search and they may fail to demonstrate any evidence of fast absent responses (Humphreys, Riddoch, Quinlan, Price, & Donnelly, 1992). This is not due to a breakdown in visual attention *per se*, since such patients can conduct quite efficient serial search, when grouping processes do not act to facilitate search (Humphreys et al., 1992). Thus, the study of such patients can inform us about the contribution of grouping processes to selection. Theories hoping to provide a full account of how visual attention relates to the processes involved in grouping and object recognition need to be able to account for deficits of this sort.

Visual neglect

An example of a more particular disturbance in visual attention *per se* is the neuropsychological disorder of visual neglect. This term is applied to patients who, following damage to the temporoparietal and frontoparietal regions of the brain, may fail to respond to stimuli presented on the side of space opposite to their lesion (see Humphreys & Heinke, 1998; Husain & Kennard, 1996; Robertson & Marshall, 1993; Walker, 1995). Performance can be affected by the position of an object relative to the patient's body (e.g. Karnath, Schenkel, & Fischer, 1991; Riddoch & Humphreys, 1983). This can be interpreted as an impairment of space-based selection, reflecting the coding of objects in a body-centred coordinate schema. In contrast, other patients neglect parts relative to an object, consistent with a spatial deficit in object-based selection, e.g. in neglect dyslexia the impaired identification of letters on the contralesional side of a word can occur even when the word is presented in the ipsilesional visual field (e.g. Young, Newcombe, & Ellis, 1991), suggesting that neglect is then determined by the positions of the letters within the word, rather than in a coordinate system centred on the body. Studies of neglect, then, enable us to explore the relations between different forms of spatial coding in visual selection. There are also other interesting aspects of the syndrome, e.g. studies of word reading demonstrate that knowledge can modulate the severity of neglect, because neglect can be mitigated in reading words compared to reading nonwords (e.g. Sieroff, Pollastek, & Posner, 1988). Hence, neglect provides a means for studying the interaction of bottom-up and top-down processes in selection. Visual extinction is typically a milder problem in visual selection and refers to effects where patients can detect a single stimulus presented on the contralesional side of space, but fail to detect the same item when it is exposed simultaneously with an item on the ipsilesional side (e.g. Karnath, 1988). Recent studies of extinction have demonstrated that effects can vary as a function of grouping between elements in the ispi- and contralesional fields. Extinction is reduced when elements group relative to when they fail to group, and so are treated as separate objects (e.g. Gilchrist, Humphreys, & Riddoch, 1996; Ward, Goodrich, & Driver, 1994). Here again, models need to be able to account for an interaction between grouping and selection, and how selection can be subject to a spatial bias after lesioning.

Attentional vs. representational accounts of neglect.   Psychological theories of neglect have typically characterized the disorder as being due either to damaged visual attention or to an impaired internal representation of space (see Riddoch & Humphreys, 1987, for one discussion). Arguments for an impairment in spatial representation come from studies of so-called object-centred neglect, where patients fail to report features on one side of an object, irrespective of its lateral position in space (Caramazza & Hillis, 1990; Young et al., 1991). In contrast, arguments for a more specific impairment in visual attention comes from studies showing that neglect can be ameliorated by cueing attention to the affected side (Riddoch & Humphreys, 1983). Furthermore, deficits can be exacerbated when attention is paid to the ipsilesional side from where patients seem to have problems in disengaging attention (Posner, Walker, Friedrich, & Rafal, 1984). As we shall show, computational models can demonstrate that the contrast between "attentional" and "representational" aspects of neglect is false; both aspects of neglect can emerge from a spatially specific lesion in models in which attention modulates the elaboration of particular forms of spatial representation.

Organization of this chapter

The computational models we will review here have attempted to account for subsets of the properties and paradigms used to study attention. In this chapter we will introduce the models and elaborate on the explanations they give to the different aspects of attention. In the discussion section we will compare the different models. It should be noted that our focus is on the major models used to simulate behavioural data. Hence, we exclude models which have primarily focused on applying the idea of selective attention to computer vision problems (e.g. Tsotsos et al., 1995) or on modelling the underlying neurobiology of attention (e.g. Braun, Koch, & Davis, 2001; Hamker, in press). We begin by considering models applied to two main paradigms used to study attention in humans—stimulus filtering and visual search tasks. Typically, simulations of such tasks do not contain very elaborate mechanisms for object recognition. Models that incorporate procedures for object recognition as well as attention, then, provide a better account of the way in which object- and space-based selection interact and of how top-down knowledge can modulate bottom-up biases in selection. Consequently, we proceed to discuss these models before proceeding to outline how models can be applied to neuropsychological disorders such as visual agnosia and neglect.

COMPUTATIONAL MODELS OF VISUAL SELECTION

The selective attention model (SLAM)

SLAM was proposed by Phaf, van der Heijden, & Hudson (1990) to model experimental findings from filtering tasks, in which participants are asked to name a specific attribute of one of two objects in the display, with the target item being specified by another attribute (e.g. van der Heijden, 1981). For instance, an experiment may contain three elementary attributes: colour (red, blue), form (disc, square) and position (left, right). A typical display may consist of a red square on the left and a blue disc on the right, and participants are asked to name the colour of the square. The general finding in such filtering tasks is, if items in the display possess the same response attribute (congruent condition, e.g. a red disc and a red square, when the task is to name the colour of the square), then participants perform better than if items have different response attributes (e.g. a blue disc and a red square, the incongruent condition). Phaf et al. (1990) examined whether these congruence effects could emerge in their computational model, incorporating processes that select visual information in parallel over time in a competitive fashion. SLAM's architecture is shown in Fig. 9.1. Input to the model was provided by units that stood for combinations of particular attributes—form and colour, colour and position, and form and position. These input units fed

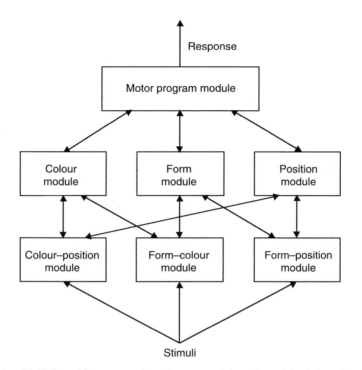

Figure 9.1. SLAM's architecture consists of seven modules. All modules behave in a "winner takes-all" fashion. The units in the input module encode conjunctions of colour–position, form–colour and form–position, for each item. The modules at the next feature stage encode separately colour, form, and position. The output stage was used to simulate motor responses in humans. There were recurrent connections between the modules, forcing SLAM to converge into a consistent state. Adapted from Phaf et al. (1990).

through to feature modules, in which the units responded only to colour, form, or position. Finally, the feature modules fed activation through to motor program modules, used for verbal responses (e.g. red, blue, disc, square, left, and right). Units with each module were inhibitory. Thus, one colour (blue) inhibited other colours (red), one shape other shapes (square to disc), and activation in one location inhibited that in other locations. There were recurrent connections between the modules, forcing SLAM to converge into a consistent state, where all active units fit with the response. For instance, if the answer to the colour of the square is red, then units which stand for red, disc and, left should be active, whereas all other units are suppressed. Excitatory connections generated mutual support between items with shared attributes, whilst inhibitory connections generate competition between items with different attributes. As a result of the mutual support between elements shared by different stimuli, there could be facilitation when separate items processed a common response attribute (concurrent condition). In contrast, in the incongruent condition (blue disc and red square), the time taken for SLAM to converge was lengthened, due to competition between differing attributes in the same domain. Hence, SLAM simulated the basic findings of filtering tasks, where concurrence of attributes speed up reaction times and incongruent attributes delays responses.

In a second set of simulations, Phaf et al. (1990) attempted to model data from the Stroop task (Stroop, 1935). In this task, colour names written in different hues are presented to participants who are asked to name either the word or the hue. If asked to name the hue, RTs are delayed if the word and hue are different, compared when they are the same. In contrast, if asked to name the word, participants show little effect of colour incompatibility. In order to accommodate these findings, Phaf et al. (1990) modified SLAM in two ways. First, they added an input attribute, word, so that the input to SLAM comprised of three additional input modules: word-colour, word-position, word-shape. Second, in order to account for the asymmetry between colour naming and word naming, direct connections between the input stage and the motor stage were added, bypassing the feature module. For the colour-naming task, however, the route via the colour feature module still determined the response of the motor program module. This response is delayed by the strong influence from the direct routes, especially when the word name is incompatible with the colour name. In contrast, for the word-naming task, this direct access process produced responses that were little affected by the colour feature module. Hence, SLAM could mimic the basic Stroop effect. In addition, Phaf et al. (1990) simulated the experimental findings when the ink colour and the word are spatially separated (e.g. Dyer, 1973). In this procedure the Stroop task is turned into a classical filtering task, with subjects being required to attend to the ink colour and to filter out the word. Generally Stroop interference is reduced in these circumstances. The same result emerged in SLAM. When the colour and the word appeared at the same location, it was harder to suppress the irrelevant attribute than when the stimuli fell in separate locations, when the feedback from the position module could selectively suppress the word response. According to Phaf et al. (1990), the position-based feedback implements a type of object-based selection, because the suppression of attributes that are part of the same object is more difficult than the suppression of attributes belonging to different objects. Phaf et al. (1990) suggest that SLAM illustrates how object-based (or attribute-based) and space-based attention can coexist in one model, as both were simulated using the same architecture.

SLAM is a very simple model, but it nevertheless shows how cooperative and competitive interactions can generate apparent "attentional effects" in simulations. Phaf et al. (1990) argue that the model can easily be extended to process more then two items, e.g. by allowing more then two positions to be encoded in input modules. However, it is unclear whether such an extended version of the model could simulate experimental results on selection with multiple items, as in visual search tasks, where intricate patterns of search functions appear. In the following section we will first discuss a serial account of such search functions and then, at the end of this section, show that a parallel, competitive approach to selection can also account for search functions. In addition, objects in SLAM have no explicit spatial coding of their parts. Nevertheless, neuropsychological evidence on neglect indicates that spatial coding within objects is important for human object recognition. As we will show in the rest of the chapter, different architectures have to be used to cope with spatially extended objects.

Guided search (GS) and other models of visual search

The guided search model of Wolfe (1994) is an example of a class of computational models used to account for search in visual scenes, using the idea of a "saliency map", which dictates the order of a subsequent serial search process. Most models within this class focus on physiological aspects of search and/or applications to computer vision (see Koch & Itti, 2001, for a recent review). The guided search model, however, focuses on simulating behavioural data. The model assumes a two-stage model of visual selection, as has long been proposed in psychological theories (James, 1890; Neisser, 1967; Treisman & Gelade, 1980). The first, pre-attentive stage of processing is held to be spatially parallel and to involve the computation of simple visual features. The second stage, in contrast, is held to be attentional in nature, to be spatially serial, and it enables more complex visual representations (involving combinations of features) to be computed. The architecture of guided search is illustrated in Fig. 9.2. In guided search, the pre-attentive stage comprises a series of retinotopic maps that are activated in parallel by the presence of appropriate visual features (colours, lines at particular orientations, and so forth). Each feature map encodes the presence of a particular feature across the display. Additionally, the activation of the maps is enhanced by the differences in features between surrounding items. For instance, if a vertical target line is surrounded by horizontal lines, then activation in the vertical feature map at the target location is higher than if the vertical line was surrounded by vertical distractors. This modulation of activation decreases with the spatial distance between any features. Apart from this bottom-up activation, knowledge of the target in visual search tasks leads to the top-down activation of feature maps for expected target features (e.g. the maps for "red" and "vertical", if the target is a red vertical line). The value that features acquire, then, is a combination of bottom-up and top-down knowledge. Activation values for elements in each feature map are used to signal locations that are worthy of further attention. The greater the activation at a

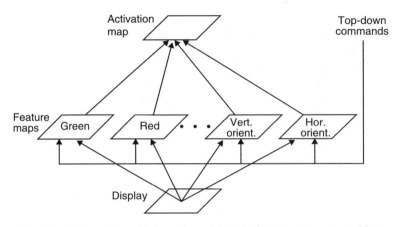

Figure 9.2. Illustration of the guided search model. In the first stage the output of feature maps results from a combination of top-down and bottom-up influences. Bottom-up activation is computed from local feature differences (see text for details). Top-down activation is based on the features of the target in the visual search. The figure gives four examples of possible feature maps: green, red, vertical line, and horizontal line orientations. In the activation map the output of the feature maps is additively overlaid. Search through the display takes place in a serial fashion and follows the activation in the activation map in descending order, either until the activation falls under a threshold or the target is found.

location, the more likely it is that attention will be directed to that location. The activation from all feature maps is topologically summed within an "activation map", which represents the overall saliency of locations in the display. Attention is directed to the location in the field where saliency is highest. If this location contains the target of the search task, the search is terminated. If not, further deployment of attention and subsequent tests for target follow the activation of the saliency map in descending order. This serial search terminates if either the target is found or the activation of the unattended locations in the saliency map falls under a threshold (for details, see Chun & Wolfe, 1996; Wolfe, 1994).

Guided search can be applied to data from visual search in the following manner. Targets that are dissimilar from distractors will produce high activation in their own feature map and within the overall saliency map. Hence, search is then efficient. This allows guided search to account for flat search functions from feature search with dissimilar target–distractor pairs (e.g. a horizontal line target amongst vertical distractors). However, if the targets and distractors are similar to each other, as in so-called conjunction search tasks, when the critical features that specify the target are also borne by distractors (e.g. when the target is a red and vertical line and the distractors are green vertical and red horizontal lines), the corresponding feature maps do not indicate the location of the target, since the features of the target are similar to the distractor features in the same feature maps. Consequently, the summed activation from the feature maps in the saliency map does not highlight the target in the saliency map. Indeed, Wolfe (1994) suggested that neural noise in GS would then lead to distractors being selected before targets, since their saliency value may be higher. As a consequence, serial search functions result. Top-down activation for an expected target can modify this to some degree, since it can activate the features belonging to the target (red and vertical, in our example). The target, having both these features, can still achieve a higher value in the saliency map than distractors that each have only one of the critical features. This can explain why conjunction targets that have features quite different from those of each half set of distractors can be detected efficiently (Wolfe, Cave, & Franzel, 1989). However, if the feature values of the target and each half set of distractors become close, then distractor feature maps may be activated along with the target feature map, losing the target's advantage within the saliency map.

Guided search is able to account for the major contrast between "single feature" and conjunction search and, by means of its top-down activation, is able to accommodate findings of efficient conjunction search when stimuli have quite different values along their feature dimensions. However, there are weaknesses. One is that the mechanism for serial search is not implemented in a manner consistent with the connectionist architecture of the earlier stages of the model. Another is that the model does not have procedures that enable visual features to be grouped, to allow object representations to be constructed. Yet there is considerable psychological evidence that grouping affects early parallel stages of vision, e.g. targets and distractors that are distinguished only by how their features group can still yield parallel search functions (e.g. Enns & Rensink, 1991). Some targets can only be distinguished from distractors when the stimuli group to form discriminably different objects (Donnelly, Humphreys, & Riddoch, 1991; Humphreys & Donnelly, 2000), and targets can be difficult to detect, if they group with distractors (Rensink & Enns, 1995).

Two connectionist models similar in flavour to guided search are the feature gate model of Cave (1999) and the dynamic search model of Deco & Zihl (2001).

As outlined by Cave (1999), the feature gate model uses a pyramidal architecture of feature processing to model visual selection. At each level of the pyramid items are selected and, via an "attentional" gating mechanism, passed on to the next level. This selection mechanism led to a successively reduced number of items and finally to one selected item. Similar to guided search, the selection process at each level was guided in a bottom-up and top-down way. As Cave (1999) pointed out, this architecture is capable of simulating not only the same experiments as guided search, but also several additional experimental findings on divided attention and Eriksen flanker interference. The effects of divided attention are reproduced by gating items through the pyramidal structure from spatially separate locations. The Eriksen flanker interference results from the fact that the attentional gates also pass on information from adjacent locations. Consequently, the flankers will somewhat influence the activation on the top level of the pyramid and delay or speed-up the response of feature gate, depending on the compatibility of the flankers.

The model by Deco & Zihl (2001), like guided search, uses feature maps that can be modulated in a top-down fashion and sums output from feature maps in a "high-level" map. In addition, each feature map implements competitive interactions. This competition leads to a convergence of activation, with one winner in the "high-level" map, marking the location of the target. Reaction times are expressed in terms of the number of iterations taken by the model to produce a winner in the high-level map. Deco & Zihl (2001) reported that the speed of convergence matches the common finding that conjunction searches are slower than single feature search. In a feature search task, the top-down influence suppresses all distractors, making the convergence of the model independent of the number of elements in the input. In a conjunction search, the top-down influence suppresses the elements in each feature map that do not have target features, but convergence within each feature map is still affected by the presence of distractor elements that have the same features as targets and so are not subject to top-down suppression. As a consequence, the convergence of the high-level map was found to depend on the number of items, producing a linear search function. In essence, Deco & Zihl (2001)'s model shows that competitive interactions are capable of simulating search functions even when there is no "spotlight" of attention, so that the serial search mechanism, as assumed in guided search, is not essential. However, Deco & Zihl's (2001) model remains limited to dealing with simple visual features. In the following sections we will discuss models that can cope with more complex objects.

Search via recursive rejection model (SERR)

SERR (Humphreys & Müller, 1993) was set up to simulate effects of grouping on visual search, as suggested by the psychological model of Duncan & Humphreys (1989). The model was mainly based on the architecture of a Boltzmann machine (Hinton & Sejnowski, 1988). In models of this type, units behave in a stochastic fashion with a two-state output activation, either active or inactive. The probability of assuming one of the two states is determined by the size of the input a unit receives from other units. The model used an hierarchical organization to simulate visual search for letter-like stimuli made of horizontal and vertical line elements. Formally, search for a target defined by a particular combination of such features relative to dis-

tractors (e.g. a ⌐ target vs. T distractors) can be described as a conjunction search task, since each letter is composed of the same, more primitive line elements. However, provided that the distractors are homogeneous,
search can be relatively efficient (Humphreys et al., 1989). Search becomes
inefficient primarily when the distractors are heterogeneous (e.g. a ⌐
target vs. T and ⊢ distractors). This suggests that search in this case is
strongly influenced by grouping between distractors. The first set of units in
SERR's hierarchy coded the presence of horizontal and vertical edges on a
retina (see Fig. 9.3). Activation from these units was transmitted through to
units that coded combinations of the first sets of units (L-junctions, line
terminators), and activation from these units was transmitted to further representations of T-junctions formed by combining outputs from particular L-
and line terminator units. In each case, a map of units was constructed to
represent elements across the visual field. Activation from the T-junctions
was then fed into template units, which acted to detect the targets and distractors in the experiments. The target might be a T in one orientation and
the distractor Ts in other orientations. In order to capture grouping effects,
excitatory connections were established between T units within the same map
and inhibitory connections between units standing for the same location but
in different maps. Thus, identical Ts supported one another in the search, and
heterogeneous Ts competed to form separate groups. Additionally, the excitatory connections within the T maps were gated by a "location map", allowing
activation only to spread to locations were there was something in the visual
field. This was done in order to suppress possible "hallucinations" of elements produced by the grouping mechanism. Activation from the letter maps
was transmitted through to template units, set up according to the particular
targets and distractors that might be used in search. At the template level,
there was rapid accumulation of evidence for identical Ts, and slower
accumulation of evidence for each type of T in a heterogeneous set. The
template units themselves were also competitive, so that only one such unit
was incremented on each iteration of the network. A particular target or
distractor was said to be detected when its template unit reached a threshold.
If the first template to reach threshold was the target, search stopped. If it
was a distractor, then the template and associated T units were inhibited and
search continued over the remaining elements until either a target was found
or all the items had been rejected.

SERR was able to simulate patterns of visual search found in human data
with identical (homogeneous) and heterogeneous distractors. With identical
and nonidentical distractors, there was rapid grouping and rejection of the
background items, enabling targets to be detected efficiently, leading to a
efficient search. In contrast, with heterogeneous stimuli several groups of
distractors could be selected before the target might be found. Hence, the
time to detect the target depended on the number of groups that had to be

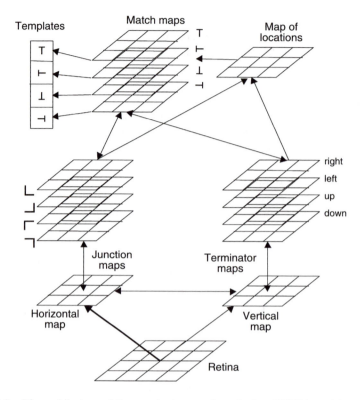

Figure 9.3. The architecture of the search via recursive rejection (SERR) model uses a hierarchical organization to simulate search for letter-like stimuli. The first two maps in SERR's hierarchy code the presence of horizontal and vertical line elements. Activation from these units is transmitted through to maps that encode L-junctions and line terminators, and activations from these maps are combined to activate units corresponding to T junctions in the match maps. Activation from the T-junctions is then fed into template units. The template units accumulate the evidence for each type of T, signalling the presence of a particular item when the relevant template reaches threshold. In order to capture grouping, excitatory connections were established between T units within the same match map and inhibitory connections between same locations across different matched maps. Additionally, the excitatory connections within the match maps were gated by the location map, allowing activation to spread only to locations where there was a stimulus on the retina. Adapted from Humphreys & Müller (1993).

selected serially, before the target was detected. In addition, given the stochastic behaviour of the model, there was some probability that a target present in the field may not be found. This was particularly the case with heterogeneous distractors, which competed strongly for selection. With heterogeneous distractor groups, a target could be temporally inhibited (its corresponding units placed in an inactive state). If the distractors were subsequently selected (and rejected as being nontargets), the model could decide (incorrectly) that no target was present. To prevent errors (false rejections) of this type, the search would have to be repeated. When such repetitions (re-checks) were conducted to match the error rates found in human data, then search with heterogeneous distractors was a linear function of the number of distractors present.

In subsequent work, Müller, Humphreys, & Donnelly (1994) showed that SERR generates a strong reduction in search time when there is more than one target present (e.g. there is a redundancy gain). Müller et al. (1994) found that when two targets were present, search became faster than was ever the case, even on the fastest search trials when a single target was present. This "super-additive" redundancy gain is difficult to explain in models assuming strict serial search of the items present, but it is predicted by SERR (see Miller, 1982; however, see Townsend & Nozawa, 1997 for a different view, which argues that serial models can also produce super-additivity). In SERR, search benefits from the presence of two targets in two ways: (a) multiple targets form mutually supportive groups; and (b) there is a faster accumulation of activation within template units from each grouped target. The "super-additive" results generated by SERR occur because the model has a strong parallel component, accumulating activation simultaneously across the field. In addition, however, SERR incorporates a serial mechanism of successive rejection of selected items, and it can employ recursive re-checking. Hence, SERR can be classified as a hybrid model of visual search. On the one hand, it incorporates parallel, competitive selection and grouping processes, and on the other hand it applies search serially through groups and applies serial re-checking. The ability of the model to simulate linear search functions provides an existence proof that such functions are not necessarily an indication of a strict serial (item-by-item) search process as, for instance, in guided search.

One interesting aspect of the work carried out with SERR is the link between computational modelling and experimentation. For example, SERR's predictions concerning redundancy gains from multiple search targets were verified in empirical studies of human search conducted by Müller et al. (1994). Other predictions derived from the model were examined by Humphreys & Müller (1993). One such prediction concerns search performance when re-checking precesses are prevented by making people respond to a fast deadline. In SERR, this re-checking process takes the form of repeating the search until the error rate declines (see above). When such repetitions are decreased (e.g. because a fast response deadline has to be met), then the error rates rise, particularly when large numbers of distractors are present. Humphreys & Müller (1993) found a similar pattern of errors at larger display sizes in human search under fast deadline conditions. Thus, the model served not only to simulate data, but also as a source of novel empirical predictions.

Despite SERR's success in both capturing prior results and predicting novel findings, the model is limited in several aspects. For example, it employs a fixed processing architecture useful only for searching through T-like targets and distractors. Also, although SERR groups elements to form large perceptual units, these groups are influenced by the local identity of features; they do not serve the process of putting parts together for object recognition. Only identical features are grouped, and there is no grouping between different elements that would together form a shape (e.g. four corner brackets making a square). This constrains the application of the model to a broader set of data on the interrelations between object recognition and attention. The model also encounters problems in "scaling up", since each feature combination is "bound together" by activating a local unit that represents the presence of that combination at a given location in the field. Clearly, this would require a large number of units to represent all possible feature combinations at all possible locations. This issue is essentially concerned with how feature combinations can be "bound" together. SERR accomplishes binding through allocating units in its hardware. We consider next some models that accomplish binding in a different manner and that attempt to address the broader issues concerning the relations between recognition and attention.

Multiple object recognition and attentional selection (MORSEL) (Fig. 9.4)

The MORSEL model, developed by Mozer (1991) and Mozer & Sitton (1998), linked visual attention to object recognition, to provide an explicit account of the interrelations between these two processes. MORSEL essentially contained two modules—one for object recognition, derived from an earlier model termed BLIRNET (Mozer, 1987), and one for visual attention. Object recognition was achieved using a hierarchical coding schema, progressing from position-bound detectors for line orientation and colour, to units at the top end of the hierarchy which respond to combinations of features in a nearly translation-invariant manner (irrespective of the lateral position of items in the field). At each level of the recognition hierarchy, features and locations were pooled so that higher-order units respond to increasing complex features and feature combinations in a manner that gradually became less location-dependent. Many of the simulations performed with the model were concerned with word recognition. For such simulations, units at the top-end of the hierarchy respond to clusters of letters and letter features. These features are "glued" together, using an independent "pull-out" network, trained to classify the distributed representation formed in the recognition system. This "pull-out" network can be thought of as using stored (in this case lexical) knowledge to "clean up" the distributed code, which is formed in a bottom-up manner (although note that this remains a feedforward system; activation from the pull-out network is not used in a

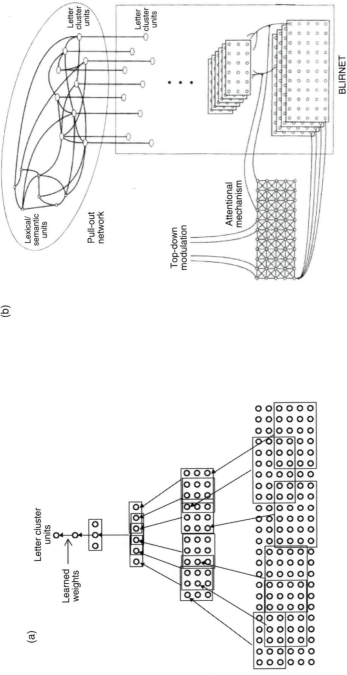

(b)

(a)

Figure 9.4. (a) The object recognition module (otherwise termed BLIRNET) in MORSEL. Object recognition was achieved using a hierarchical coding schema, progressing from position-bound detectors for line orientation and colour, to units at higher levels of the hierarchy which respond to combinations of features, and which are less bound to the locations of features on the retina (adapted from Mozer, 1987). (b) The pull-out network (top) and the attentional mechanism (AM) (bottom) in MORSEL. This "pull-out" network uses stored (lexical) knowledge to "clean up" the distributed code that is formed in a bottom-up manner. The attentional mechanism (AM) modulates activation in the recognition system by raising activation levels for stimuli in attended parts of the visual field over activation levels for stimuli in unattended regions. This space-based, attentional modulation reduces the likelihood of distributed features from multiple stimuli being combined incorrectly to form migration errors. External input into the AM was formed by summing the output from the line-orientation detectors at the first stage of recognition process, for each location in the field. Thus, the external input into the AM network was insensitive to feature properties. Adapted from Behrman, Moscovitch, & Mozer (1991).

top-down manner, to influence feature coding in the model). As Mozer (1991) pointed out, this process of using distributed features to activate stored knowledge can introduce some computational problems in its own right. Consider the problem of word recognition, when there are several words in the field. Each word may be recognized on its own, based on a unique combination of distributed features components. However, when there is activation from multiple words, components in each word may activate some new lexical representation, so that the letters could be miscombined in perception to form a word not actually present. In perceptual report, letters could "migrate" from one letter string to another. There is some evidence from psychological studies indicating that these migration errors can occur when words are presented briefly (see Mozer, 1991). To overcome this problem, a separate "attentional" mechanism (AM) was added. The goal of the AM was to modulate activation in the recognition system by raising activation levels for stimuli in attended parts of the visual field over activation levels for stimuli in unattended parts of the field. The main effect of this space-based, attentional modulation was to reduce the likelihood of distributed features from multiple stimuli being combined incorrectly to form migration errors, since only features of the attended object would be active. This architecture is similar to the structure of the feature gate model, introduced earlier in this chapter, but in feature gate an attentional modulation operates at every level of the recognition network (Cave, 1999). Within the AM network, units had local, excitatory connections, whilst more distant units had inhibitory connections. This connectivity with the network led to activation converging into an "elastic" (as opposed to fixed-size) spotlight, whose size and position depended on external inputs. Input into the AM took the form of summed outputs from the detectors at the first stage of recognition process, for each location in the field. Thus, the AM network was insensitive to feature properties, responding only to the presence of some "thing" at a given region of the field. In addition, Mozer & Sitton (1998) assumed that the input of the feature maps into the AM network could be modulated in a top-down manner from higher cognitive levels (e.g. when a target could be in a particular colour).

Mozer & Sitton (1998) showed that MORSEL could mimic the dichotomy between feature search and conjunction search for orientated colour elements. For the feature search task, the top-down influence suppressed the features of the distractors, so that only the target provided an active input to the AM. This caused the AM to select the target within the same time period, independent of the number of items present in the display. Hence, MORSEL could produce the flat search function typical for feature search. For conjunction search, the top-down signals biased the AM to the target location by (a) activating feature maps containing target features and (b) suppressing feature maps containing distractor features. However, provided that the top-down bias was not overwhelming, distractors still influenced the selection process and the search function showed the usual dependency on the number of items due to competition in the AM. The top-down processing in MORSEL is comparable to the top-down modulation in the guided search model.

One interesting aspect of the simulations of conjunction search in MORSEL is that contrasting effects of the distractors were found as a function of whether many or few distractors were present. With few distractors, search was efficient and little affected by the number of targets. With many distractors, search times increased as a function of each extra distractor. Mozer & Sitton (1998) attributed this rise in search times to increased competition between items in the field, and to increased crosstalk within the recognition network (since when there are more items in the field, inter-item distances will be reduced, so higher-level units are more likely to be activated by neighbouring features). Mozer and Sitton (1998) related these results to data on human visual search by Pashler (1987), who reported a "dog leg" function for conjunction search—reaction times were initially little affected by distractors, but then increased steeply when more distractors were presented. The same result has been interpreted by at least some investigators as indicating the effects of crowding on search for conjunction targets, due to the increased likelihood of features being mis-combined when stimuli are in close spatial proximity (see Cohen & Ivry, 1991). MORSEL provides an explicit account of such feature miscombinations and of how attention is required to reduce them, especially with displays with closely proximal items.

In addition to simulating visual search data, Mozer & Sitton (1998) demonstrated the generality of their approach by showing how MORSEL could be used to simulate other standard paradigms used in attention research, including studies of spatial attention using visual cueing and distractor interference in stimulus-filtering tasks. Visual cueing was simulated by presenting a brief peripheral pre-cue prior to the presentation of a target at either the cued or an uncued location (on valid and invalid trials). Pre-activation of the target's location in the AM facilitated target selection, since less activation was then required when the target appeared. In contrast, invalid cues created some competition for selection of the target's location. The difference between RTs on valid and invalid cue trials mimics human data (Posner et al., 1980). As we have noted earlier, in stimus-filtering tasks distractors can interfere with responses to targets, demonstrated by slowed RTs when targets and distractors require opposite responses (Eriksen & Eriksen, 1974). Mozer & Sitton (1998) showed that such competition effects could emerge in MORSEL, provided that attention did not have a sharp spatial impact on processing in the recognition module, otherwise no interference would occur. As Mozer & Sitton (1998) pointed out, this delivers computational support for the zoom lens model of Eriksen & Yeh (1985), where it was assumed that attention does not focus exclusively on the target and, therefore, allow interference from distractors to occur.

MORSEL is an attempt to link attention to wider aspects of object recognition. However, it conceptualizes attention as a separate mechanism modulating object recognition. The following section will introduce a computational model that combines attention with object recognition in a more interactive way.

Selective attention for identification model (SAIM)

One other model that has attempted to marry object recognition to visual attention is SAIM (Heinke & Humphreys, 1997, 1999, 2003; Humphreys & Heinke, 1998). The architecture of SAIM followed an idea of "dynamic routing circuits" put forward by Olshausen, Anderson, & Van Essen (1993, 1995). They proposed that attention can help to generate translation-invariant pattern recognition by serving as a "window" through which activation from a retinal field must pass before being transmitted through to recognition systems. Provided that the window can be shifted around to different spatial positions, the same units will modulate recognition, irrespective of the lateral positions of objects in the retinal field. Consequently, recognition units do not need to be coded for every location in the field, since the same input will occur across different retinal positions, normalized by the shifting attentional window. To achieve this shifting of an attentional window across space, Olshausen et al. (1993) proposed the existence of two sets of units. One set maps the contents in the visual field into a attentional window or "focus of attention" (FOA); the second set controls the shifting of the FOA. In SAIM these two sets of units were termed the "contents network", representing a partial contents of the visual field, and the "selection network", modulating the units in the contents network (see Fig. 9.5). In SAIM a third network, the "knowledge network", comprised a set of template units corresponding to stored memories for objects. This was added to Olshausen's architecture to integrate a object recognition system into SAIM, and it enabled SAIM to simulate the effects of stored knowledge on selection.

To achieve translation-invariant object recognition, activation in the selection network had to fulfil several constraints: (a) the contents in the visual field should be mapped only once into the FOA; (b) the contents of the FOA should cover only neighbouring areas in the visual field. These constraints led to a network of competitive and cooperative interactions, as depicted in Fig. 9.6. This step followed an idea of using connectionist approaches for soft constraint satisfaction first suggested by Hopfield & Tank (1985). The excitatory interactions ensure the activation of neighbouring units in the selection network, implementing the second constraint. In addition, the first constraint

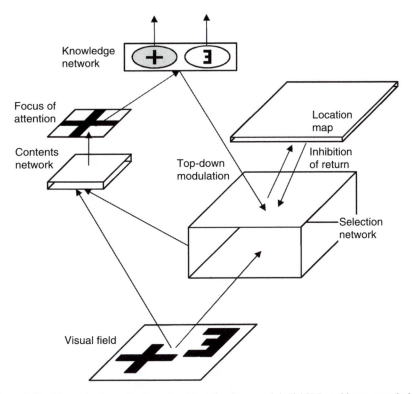

Figure 9.5. The selective attention for identification model (SAIM) achieves translation-invariant object recognition with three modular networks: The contents network maps the contents of the visual field into the focus of attention (FOA). This mapping is translation-invariant. The selection network determines the location in the visual field where elements in content network are mapped into the FOA. The knowledge network possesses stored knowledge in the form of template units and recognizes the contents of the FOA via simple template matching. These three components operate in parallel. The location map stores the locations of objects already attended to and prevents these locations from being selected again. This determines attention-switching behaviour, with old items not being attended for a second time. Adapted from Heinke & Humphreys (2003).

was wired into the selection network through inhibitory interactions limiting the number of units in the selection network allowed to be activated, and consequently restricting the area SAIM can select. This network of inhibitory connections is illustrated in Fig. 9.6. Each row in the network contains units that are responsible for the contents of one location in the FOA. Inhibitory connections between these units ensure that only one location in the visual field is mapped into a given location in the FOA. Similarly, competition between units in the columns of the network ensures that a given position in the visual field is only mapped into one location in the FOA. The remaining

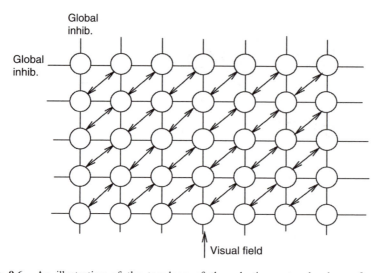

Figure 9.6. An illustration of the topology of the selection network, shown for a one-dimensional visual field. The horizontal and vertical lines between units stand for inhibitory connections within the rows and columns of the network. The arrows stand for excitatory connections between units on diagonals of the network. Every unit receives an input from the visual field in a topological fashion. The connections ensure that the selection network obeys a set of constraints when activating units (see text for details). Adapted from Ellis & Humphreys (1999).

winning units determine the activation transmitted into the FOA through the contents network. Activation in the contents network is multiplied with the activation from the selection network, so that activation from the visual field is only transmitted to the FOA if it is supported by active units in the selection network. When two or more objects are presented, there is competition between the activation they create in the selection network. When top-down support is not taken into consideration (see below), the object that tends to be selected first is the one whose local parts generate most mutual support—either because the object is large or because the parts are arranged quite close to one other. Interactions in the selection network also typically lead to the FOA being aligned with the centre of mass of the selected object.

In addition to operating in a bottom-up manner, SAIM differs from the other models considered here in that it uses top-down object knowledge to influence selection directly, by modulating activation within the selection network. This top-down influence originates from the knowledge network, where stored knowledge was represented by means of a set of template units, connected to units in the FOA. The introduction of the knowledge network adds further constraints to the behaviour of SAIM. Here, the main constraint is that the template unit that best matches the contents of the FOA should be maximally activated and all other units of the knowledge network should be inhibited. This constraint results in two types of connectivity, a simple competitive interaction within the knowledge network, and a top-down modulation of the selection network from the knowledge network. This top-down modulation biases the selection network to favour familiar over nonfamiliar objects.

Having selected one of several objects present, SAIM also incorporates a mechanism for switching attention from a selected object to others in the visual field. This is accomplished by activating units in a "location map" corresponding to the position occupied by the selected object. Once a location unit is activated, it acts to inhibit corresponding positions in the selection network, so that these positions can no longer win the competition to control the mapping of stimuli through to the FOA. At the same time, the template for the selected object is also inhibited. Consequently, another, previously unattended, object then wins the competition for selection, so that attention is switched between objects. This process mimics a form of "inhibition of return", in which attention is biased against returning to locations containing objects that have already been selected (e.g. Klein, 1988; Posner & Cohen, 1984).

The performance of SAIM has been evaluated by measuring the number of iterations that it took a template unit to reach threshold (the reaction time, RT; Heinke & Humphreys, 2003). SAIM showed a bottom-up bias towards large relative to small objects and to objects in which the pixels were densely placed around their centre of mass. These effects are emergent properties of the proximity constraints built into the selection network. Such bottom-up biases generate efficient selection of large, densely-packed stimuli, similar to the evidence of "pop out" for salient targets in human visual search (Treisman & Gelade, 1980). In addition, a variety of other characteristics of human selection were simulated, e.g. Duncan (1980) reported a "multiple object cost", where selection was shown to suffer when multiple relative to single stimuli had to be reported. This cost was most pronounced when the reported elements come from separate objects, and it was not evident when the elements belonged to a single object. SAIM manifests similar effects. There is a cost for the second of two selected objects, when compared with when only that object is presented in the field. However, all the parts of a selected object tended to become available together in the FOA, so there were few costs for reporting multiple attributes of attended objects. In this sense, SAIM manifested a form of object-based selection, even though this was modulated through a spatial attentional window. This was also demonstrated in simulations of the effects of spatial cueing. Basic cueing effects were modelled by a briefly presented cue at a location field followed by a target at either the same or a different location. RTs were facilitated when cues and targets fell at the same location, compared with when they appeared at different locations, capturing data such as those reported by Posner et al. (1980). To examine whether object coding modulated such effects, cues were presented at locations already occupied by an object in the field. On invalid trials, the target could then appear either in the cued object, or at the same distance away but in a previously uncued object. Heinke & Humphreys showed that the spatial effect of the cue could combine with activation from the cued object, to generate an advantage for targets that fell within the cued object relative to those that fell elsewhere. This simulates the data of Egly et al. (1994), typically interpreted in favour of an object-based selection process. Other forms of object-based bias were demonstrated by varying where a cue fell within a subsequently presented shape. Cues were most effective when they fell at the centre of mass of a target, due to SAIM's bottom-up bias to centre its FOA at this position in a shape. Similar effects in human selection were reported by Pavlovskaya, Glass, Soroker, Blum, & Groswasser (1997).

Object-based influences were apparent not only in how attention was allocated within shapes, but also in attentional biases following selection. As we have noted, inhibition of return was implemented by location-based inhibition of selected positions and inhibition of the templates for an attended object. This led not only to attention being biased against selected locations, but also against the objects that formerly occupied those locations, even if they subsequently moved to a new location. Evidence for object- as well as space-based influences in inhibition of return has been documented (Posner et al., 1980; Tipper & Behrmann, 1996; Tipper, Driver, & Weaver, 1991; Tipper, Jordan, & Weaver, 1999). Like MORSEL, SAIM was also able to model forms of filtering by stimulus properties, using space as the medium for selection. For example, the target in an Eriksen flanker task could be selected by pre-activating a location where it would appear, although this activation could not be so high that activation in other (distractors) positions was prevented from creating competition for selection. When a distractor matching the target was presented, this overlaid the target's activation in the FOA, facilitating selection. In contrast, a mismatching distractor could create transient activation in the FOA consistent with its features rather than those of the target. This was sufficient to also create competition at the template level, if the target and distractor had different identification responses. A response competition effect was consequently apparent.

As we have noted, bottom-up biases with the model could be modulated by the top-down influences from the knowledge network. If a target template had a high activation value from the outset of a trial (e.g. due to priming), or if it had high weights from the FOA relative to other templates, then selection would be biased toward this target when compared with other stimuli. This suggests that selection should be biased towards more familiar or recently primed objects. The flip side of this is that familiar objects may be difficult to ignore when the task is to select the less familiar of two stimuli; also, objects similar to the primed stimulus may be misrecognized as the primed item. Again, there are psychological data on (a) biases to select stimuli made familiar by consistent mapping training as targets (Shiffrin & Schneider, 1977), and (b) false positives when targets are similar to primed representations (Schvaneveldt & McDonald, 1981).

In a model such as SAIM, there is a danger that, when there are multiple stimuli in the field, features from different items could be bound together, since they activate higher-order representations in parallel. This binding problem is solved by spatial attention, which limits activation from unattended items. This is similar to the view incorporated into a psychological model such as the "feature integration theory" (Treisman, 1998), in which spatial attention is used to filter out distractors, so that only the features of attended targets are available for binding. However, since SAIM only implements how form information may be coded in vision, it is unable to capture many of the results where feature integration theory has been applied, involving studies in which multiple stimulus dimensions have been varied (e.g. colour as well as form).

NEUROPSYCHOLOGICAL DEFICITS

We have discussed how, in addition to the paradigms used to explore visual attention in normal observers, important evidence on the nature of attention comes from the study of neuropsychological deficits. In the following section we will discuss how the models presented a base account for neuropsychological deficits.

Visual agnosia

Damage to the occipital-temporal areas of the brain is associated with visual agnosia—the impaired recognition of visually presented objects (e.g. Humphreys, 1987; Humphreys & Riddoch, 1993). Humphreys et al. (1992) showed that agnosic patients had impaired visual search, but only under conditions in which grouping normally generates efficient search. This has been modelled by SERR (Humphreys, Freeman, & Müller, 1992) with the effects of the brain lesion simulated by adding noise to the Boltzmann activation functions in the model. The task was to detect a form conjunction target, ⌐, presented amongst homogeneous distractors (T's containing the same features as the target). When the activation functions were noisy, units corresponding to the stimuli had some probability of not being activated, even when the appropriate stimuli were present in the field. Similarly, there was an increased probability that units corresponding to other stimuli were activated. The net result was that grouping between identical distractors was disrupted, making search inefficient. In contrast to this, there was little effect

of increasing the noise in the model on search for targets amongst heterogeneous distractors (e.g. ⊥ vs. T, ⊢, and ⊣). With heterogeneous
distractors, grouping effects could disrupt target detection, especially if the
targets were grouped with distractors. In this case, any loss of the beneficial
effects of grouping were counteracted by the positive effects of breaking up
inappropriate target–distractor groups. Consistent with these simulation
results, Humphreys et al. (1992) reported that search for form conjunction
targets amongst heterogeneous distractors can be relatively little affected in
agnosia (Humphreys et al., 1989). Often one might think that the effects of
neural damage are simply to degrade processing, so that the more difficult of
two tasks becomes even harder. The selective deficit on search with homogeneous, compared with heterogeneous, distractors contradicts this, since the
easier task is then affected. This indicates that, rather than generating a general deterioration, the brain lesion affects a specific process: grouping based
on complex form representations. The effects of lesioning SERR likewise had
a selective effect with homogeneous rather than with heterogeneous distractors, due to the disruption of grouping processes.

Unilateral neglect and extinction

Damage to temporoparietal and frontoparietal regions of the human brain
can be associated with unilateral neglect (a failure to respond to stimuli contralateral to the side of lesion) and extinction (a failure to respond to contralesional stimuli when ipsilesional stimuli are simultaneously present; see our
earlier discussion). These disorders have been simulated in several of the
models we have reviewed.

Extinction

Basic forms of extinction have been modelled, like neglect, by having lesions
alter the spatial competition between stimuli in the visual field. In some
instances, the lesions have simply been less severe to produce extinction,
although in a model such as SAIM neglect and extinction can come about
through lesions to different components of the model. We return to discuss
this point at the close of this section. Humphreys, Olson, Romani, & Riddoch
(1996) introduced spatially specific lesions into the map locations, or into the
maps coding the form conjunctions, in SERR. In this case, the lesions
reduced the probability of units going into an active state. When a single
stimulus was presented to the affected part of space, the lesion was not sufficient to prevent recognition. However, when a different stimulus was placed
in the unimpaired field, it exerted an inhibitory influence on the contralesional item, decreasing the likelihood that it would be detected. Extinction
resulted. Humphreys et al. (1996) also noted that, when the contra- and
ipsilesional stimuli were the same, extinction could be reduced because the

ipsilesional item then supported detection of the contralesional stimulus, due to excitatory connections between items represented in the same form map. As noted in the Introduction, positive effects of grouping on extinction in patients have been reported by (amongst others) Gilchrist et al. (1996), Humphreys & Heinke (1998) and Ward et al. (1994). Such grouping effects arise as a natural consequence of positive interactions in the model between elements that can combine to form larger objects.

MORSEL and SAIM also simulate extinction in quite similar ways. In MORSEL, extinction can be captured by introducing a spatial lesion into the attention module, so that units on one side of space generate less activity than those on the other side (Mozer, 1991). Provided that the lesion is not too large, a single item may still be detected on the affected side whilst being extinguished by competition in the attention map when another item appears on the unaffected side. MORSEL is also able to explain why extinction effects are reduced when elements are part of a familiar object, compared with when they do not. Parts that belong to the same object can be recovered together by the pull-out network, even if one part is degraded (Mozer, 1991). In SAIM, extinction can emerge when lesions affect the processing of inputs coming from one side of the visual field. This leads to a spatial imbalance in the competitive interactions within the network, so that items on the unaffected side tend to win the competition for selection; these items are selected in preference to stimuli that appear on the affected side of space (Heinke & Humphreys, 2003).

Neglect

In MORSEL, neglect arises when a more severe lesion is imposed on the attention network (relative to the lesion that generates extinction). Mozer, Halligan, & Marshall (1997), for example, showed that neglect in bisection tasks could be simulated in terms of where the centre of activation in the attentional network fell with a target line. When a graded lesion was imposed across the network, attention tended to fall on the ipsilesional side of the true centre of the line. The degree of misplacement also increased in larger lines, matching the neuropsychological data (Riddoch & Humphreys, 1983).

In contrast to this, neglect can be induced in SAIM in at least two different ways. One way is to increase the the severity of a "vertical" lesion that can produce extinction in its stronger form. This generates a bias in which stimuli presented in one part of the visual field are favoured for selection over items that fall into the lesioned area. When the lesion is sufficiently severe, there can also be a distortion in the spatial selection process, with a target being mapped into one side of the FOA. This has knock-on effects on the ability to disengage attention, once an object is identified. Normally, as we have noted, attention is disengaged from identified objects by inhibitory feedback. When the input is shifted in the FOA, the inhibitory feedback may no longer inhibit activation from the object first identified, and attention becomes "stuck" on this object. On such occasions, SAIM manifests neglect of an object presented on the contralesional side of two or more stimuli. There is space-based neglect.

A second form of neglect can be generated in SAIM by what we term a "horizontal" lesion, affecting the units in the selection network that modulate the mapping from the visual field into one side of the FOA (Fig. 9.7). In this case, there can be a spatial unbalancing of mapping of information into FOA, leading to a misplaced FOA, so that elements on the contralesional side are not mapped into the FOA. Importantly, this occurs irrespective of the absolute positions of stimuli in the visual field, and it can affect each object present in the field (see Fig. 9.8 for an example). There is a form of "object-based" neglect, that takes place within each selected object.

SAIM is sensitive to grouping between stimuli, with there being facilitatory interactions between parts of a single perceptual group. In SAIM these interactions are based not only on bottom-up relationships (e.g. proximity) but also on top-down activity when two stimuli map onto a common template representation. For instance, in the example shown in Fig. 9.9, SAIM was given templates conforming either to two separate letters (I and T) or to the combined pair of letters (the word IT). Following a lesion there was

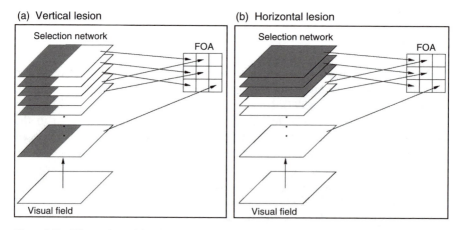

Figure 9.7. Illustration of the "vertical" (a) and "horizontal" (b) lesions used in SAIM. Each layer in the selection network in this illustration is responsible for the contents of one pixel in the FOA. The dark shaded areas illustrate the areas of lesions (reduced weights on connections to those units). The horizontal lesion affects the part of the selection network that is related to the left part of the FOA and this lesion is invariant with respect to the visual field. The vertical lesion affects units responding to one side of the visual field. For a vertical lesion, the mapping into the whole of the FOA can be affected, but only for the left part of the visual field. Adapted from Heinke & Humphreys (2003).

Left field   Right field

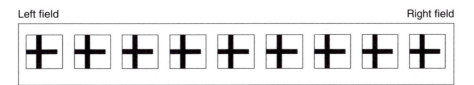

Figure 9.8. Object-based neglect in SAIM. Each window depicts the resulting contents of the FOA for a symmetric cross at different locations in the visual field (from left to right). Irrespective of the cross location in the visual field, the left-most pixel is neglected by SAIM. Adapted from Heinke & Humphreys (2003).

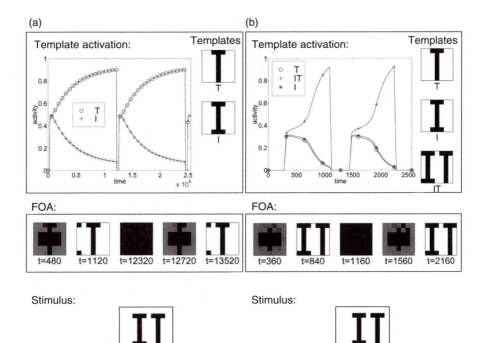

Figure 9.9. This simulation result with SAIM illustrates how a top-down influence in SAIM can modulate left neglect. (a) SAIM was given templates either conforming to two separate letters (I and T); in (b) templates for the letters were used alongside a template for the combined pair of letters (the word IT). After lesioning of the selection network, there was neglect of the letter on the affected side when the stimuli activated separate templates, but not when they activated the same template (the word IT). Here, top-down activation from the template for the word supported units in the selection network for the letter on the affected side, enabling activation to be detected in the FOA of the model. Adapted from Heinke & Humphreys (2003).

neglect of the letter on the affected side when the stimuli activated separate templates but not when they activated the same template (the word IT). Here, top-down activation from the template for the word supported units in the selection network for the letter on the affected side, enabling activation to be detected in the FOA of the model. This top-down activation extends a model such as SERR, where grouping is based only on bottom-up similarity effects. In SAIM, grouping by activating a common template could lead to stimuli being recovered together, even when there is no stronger bottom-up grouping than in other stimuli, that are subject to neglect. The facility for top-down grouping is useful, since equivalent effects have been observed in parietal patients. Sieroff et al. (1988) reported neglect between letters making up nonwords, but not when the letters combined to form words, even though bottom-up grouping should not favour the letters in words. Like SAIM, MORSEL is also able to explain why neglect effects are reduced when elements are part of a familiar object, compared with when they are not (see Mozer, 1991). However, the mechanisms mediating such effects in MORSEL differ from those in SAIM. MORSEL does not employ top-down feedback from the object recognition system to affect selection with the attentional module, but uses the "pull-out" network to recover degraded stimuli even when the attentional module is lesioned. Accordingly, MORSEL, like SAIM, can account for letter recognition being improved in words relative to nonwords in neglect patients. Interestingly, there is now support for SAIM's approach of top-down influence from neurophysiological evidence. Recently McAdams & Maunsell (2000) and Motter (1994) showed that directing attention to stimulus features modulates the responses of neurons in V4 throughout the visual field. This is similar to how SAIM's top-down activation operates, where the top-down modulation influences the behaviour of the selection network throughout the visual field.

There are now also several pieces of neuropsychological evidence indicating that different forms of neglect exist and can be fractionated from one another. One double dissociation was reported by Humphreys & Heinke (1998). In their study, some patients only showed neglect of the contralateral member of a pair of objects, but had no neglect of each object. In contrast, other patients manifested neglect of each object, but did not neglect whole objects. Patients with this last form of "within-object neglect" might be worse at identifying the left side of an object in their right field, even relative to their identification of the right side of an object in their left field (see also Driver, Baylis, & Rafal, 1992). Humphreys & Riddoch (1994, 1995) even reported a dissociation between neglect within and between separate objects in a single patient who had suffered bilateral brain lesions. This patient neglected the left side of selected objects, whilst also omitting whole objects presented on his right side. These double dissociations can be simulated in SAIM, because neglect between and within objects is caused by distinct lesions. The vertical lesion causing neglect between objects will not necessarily cause within-object neglect; similarly the (horizontal) lesion will generate object-based neglect without effects of the visual field. Heinke & Humphreys (2003) even simulated the dissociation with a single patient, by introducing a "vertical" lesion affecting the right side of space and a "horizontal" lesion affecting the left.

Object-based neglect can also be simulated in MORSEL if there is a graded lesion across its attentional field (Mozer et al., 1997). With such a graded lesion, the right side of each object will be relatively more activated than the left side, even when the object is shifted laterally across the visual field. There can be neglect of left-side features even when the object falls in the right visual field. However, it is difficult to see how MORSEL can account for the double dissociation where a whole object on the right side and left parts of objects on the left side can be ignored, as it has been done with SAIM. This is a limitation of using a simple attentional mechanism confined to a two-dimensional representation of the field, where a spatial lesion can be introduced in a single way.

DISCUSSION

Emergent properties and existence proofs

We have presented a number of connectionist models of visual attention, which have been applied to different psychological paradigms with both normal observers and neuropsychological patients. The models incorporate a number of common ideas, in particular that "attentional" behaviour arises out of competitive interactions between units in networks. In such networks, there is typically no single "attentional module" that imposes selectivity on perception and action; rather, attentional behaviour is an emergent property of competitive interaction in networks. An exception to this approach is MORSEL, which has an attentional module separate from its identification components. Another exception is guided search, which does not contain a competitive mechanism between stimuli. According to the "competitive" approach to attention, "attention" may infiltrate multiple levels of information processing, where competition takes place. This contrasts with traditional psychological models, which have tended to posit a single locus of attention acting either "early" or "late" in processing (see Broadbent, 1958; Deutsch & Deutsch, 1963, respectively). For example, in SAIM there is competition between multiple stimuli to fall within a spatial window of attention. Cueing the window to an area of space biases this competition so that unattended stimuli are filtered—a form of "early" attention. Nevertheless, multiple stimuli in the field can activate their stored representations in parallel, with competition between templates to control the response. This implements a form of "late" selection, as evidenced by simulations of response

competition in the Eriksen flanker task. The model thus shows how traditional psychological theories are not necessarily mutually contradictory;
selection can be "early" or "late", depending on a variety of conditions, e.g.
the presence of cueing, the familiarity of the objects, and so forth. Similarly,
models such as MORSEL and SAIM demonstrate that effects of spatial
cueing with networks are not necessarily the result of a module devoted to
"engaging", "moving", or "disengaging" attention (e.g. Posner et al., 1980).
In these models, the dynamics of processing can also be altered by lesioning,
so that, for example, the effects of invalid spatial cueing are much larger for
targets presented in the affected rather than the unaffected field (Heinke &
Humphreys, 2003; see also Cohen, Romero, Servan-Schreiber, & Farah, 1994,
for a similar example in a small-scale connectionist model devoted purely to
simulating spatial cueing effects). This interaction of invalid cueing and target field is found in studies using patients with lesions of the parietal lobe
(Posner et al., 1984), and it has been attributed to a deficit in an "attentional
disengagement" mechanism. In MORSEL and SAIM, however, it arises
because the target on the lesioned side is slow to suppress residual activation
from the cue due to the weakened impact of the target following the lesion.
As a consequence, the selection of the target is delayed. The simulations
indicate that we should be cautious in identifying too readily a particular
experimental finding with a particular (and devoted) processing mechanism
(here for attentional disengagement).

Another dichotomy made in psychological models, that can play little role
once processing is implemented in detailed computational terms, is that
between "attentional" and "representational" disorders in neglect. For
instance, consider both MORSEL and SAIM. In both models, neglect is
produced by a bias in spatial selection, so that one part of the visual world is
favoured for attention. In both cases, however, there is a spatial distortion in
selection, so that only a part of space is represented, i.e. activates stored
knowledge. For such models neglect is a disorder of both attention and spatial representation. Similarly, models such as MORSEL and SAIM incorporate mechanisms for both space- and object-based selection. In SAIM these
processes interact directly, so that object knowledge is used to guide spatial
attention by top-down activation of the selection network. In MORSEL
space-based attention (in the attention module) and object-based selection,
e.g. via the pull-out network, are functionally more independent, although
the information that is finally selected is influenced by both factors. For these
models, visual selection is not either space-based or object-based, it is both.

In these respects the models, once implemented, can act as "existence
proofs" for psychological theory (in the above examples, the proofs demonstrate that object- and space-based theories are not incompatible). Another
example of this concerns the implementation of visual search in models such
as SERR, in which there is parallel processing of visual stimuli, with selection

dictated by which elements form the strongest perceptual group. There is then serial selection of each perceptual group. For such a model, linear search functions do not reflect an item-by-item search process; rather, they reflect serial rejection of groups plus some degree of re-checking to maintain error rates at larger display sizes. The simulations here provide an existence proof that linear search functions are not necessarily caused by spatially serial (item-by-item) search, as suggested in the guided search model. This point is made even more strongly in simulations of search that we have carried out with SAIM. We measured the time for a target of distractor template to reach threshold as a function of a number of distractors in the field. The time for both the target and distractor templates to reach threshold varied linearly with the size of the distractor set, even though there was not even serial selection of grouped items—the target template reached threshold first when it was present and the distractor threshold was attained first when no target was present. The effect of the distractor set size in target and distractor selection in SAIM arises because when multiple items are present, there are systematic increases in the competition for attention within the selection network and between the templates for the stimuli. Again, the simulations demonstrate that linear search functions can be generated by spatially parallel search mechanisms.

Comparisons between models

The models we have discussed have, in some cases, been applied to rather different tasks (filtering by stimulus properties, visual search, multiple word identification, etc.). This makes it difficult to compare them directly. In particular, it is problematic to argue that one model is superior to another, given the multiple differences that exist. For example, consider SAIM and SERR. One criterion on which models may be judged is the rule of Occam's razor (William of Occam, 1285–1347/49), that "entities should not be multiplied beyond necessity". The model that employs the fewest, simplest mechanisms should be the best. A somewhat different criterion is that the model should take into account as much psychological evidence as possible. SAIM and SERR differ in terms of these criteria. SERR is simpler in terms of its processing architecture and its processing dynamics. On the other hand, SAIM covers a broader number of tasks (object recognition, word recognition, visual search) and it is not configured to process just one particular type of stimulus (L- and T-like items). Judgement about which model is better is determined by the question being asked—as a model of a particular search task, then probably SERR, since SERR, unlike SAIM, incorporates form-based grouping; as a more general model applicable to many objects, and as a solution to the binding problem, then probably SAIM.

Another approach to comparing between models is to ask whether one model is able to provide a better account of a particular experimental result that they both attempt to address. One example here concerns the simulations of neglect within and between perceptual objects. As we have noted, these contrasting forms of neglect can be found not only in different patients, but even in the same patient. The observed double dissociation can be simulated relatively easily in SAIM, since its architecture lends itself to lesioning in different ways (vertical vs. horizontal lesions; see Fig. 9.7). These contrasting forms of lesioning essentially affect the selection of stimuli in different reference frames: a retinal frame (vertical lesion) and an object-based frame (horizontal lesion). Lesioning in these different ways generates spatial deficits in the different reference frames, leading to neglect either within a single object or between separate objects. In contrast to this, MORSEL employs only a single (retinal) frame of reference for both object recognition and attention. Object-based deficits in neglect are then brought about by graded lesioning, so that there are relative biases in selection between the different parts of objects. We have argued that, in this framework, it is not clear how patterns of double dissociation could emerge, especially within a single patient. We suggest that, at least as far as modelling these different forms of neglect is concerned, SAIM provides a more natural account.

Another issue relevant to the modelling enterprise concerns how parameters are used in order to capture particular sets of results. Ideally, these parameters should be kept constant throughout all simulations to prove the generality of the model. However, alteration of parameters can be allowed for accounting of altered experimental set-ups. For instance, in order to account for knowledge-based biases on selection, the initial setting for SAIM's knowledge network was modified so that one template unit was favoured over others, making the selection network more likely to select the corresponding item. On the other hand, in these simulations the increased influence of the template unit had to be restricted to limit the likelihood of false alarms, especially if stimuli had features similar to the "primed" target. In a sense, this restriction represents a case of fitting parameters to the data— an example of modifying parameters in a less favourable way. However, since it seems plausible to argue that any intelligent system would have to strike a balance between useful top-down influences and a top-down influence that becomes ineffective because it overwrites bottom-up input. Hence, here the process of fitting the parameters to the data is a necessary way of constraining the model. As a next step, however, one would want to evaluate whether changes, e.g. in object familiarity, can be captured by variations in the critical parameter. That is, modellers need to move beyond fitting the data to a single datum to test whether qualitative changes in parameter values are appropriate. There are other examples of modifying parameters to accommodate experimental data that we have covered in this chapter, particularly the simulations of flanker interference in the "Eriksen" paradigm (Eriksen & Eriksen,

1974). Flanker interference has been observed in both MORSEL and SAIM. In SAIM the spatial location of the target location was primed to reflect the knowledge of participants about the location of the target, and targets would be selected in preference to distractors. This seems a plausible assumption, based on the standard Eriksen flanker procedure, where the location of targets is known in advance by observers. However, the magnitude of spatial priming had to be limited, otherwise any competitive interference from distractors would be eliminated. This can be considered as a somewhat arbitrary fitting of parameters to the data, to generate interference effects of appropriate size. This argument also applies to MORSEL, where the efficiency of selection in the attentional module had to be reduced to generate the interference effect. Although it is of course important for models to demonstrate that they are capable of simulating a broad range of human data, it is clear that the resulting conclusions are more interesting and general when they emerge from intrinsic properties of models, using the same set of parameters.

Finally, an important aspect of computational modelling is that it can enable researchers to draw in constraints that come from outside the parent discipline. For example, our focus in this chapter has been on computational models of cognitive data, and we have not discussed models that attempt to capture neurophysiological data. However, it is certainly possible for models in this area to be linked to such data (e.g. Deco & Zihl, 2001). Models also capture some of the motivating computational principles that presumably guide selection and object recognition (see Marr, 1982), and so can link to work in artificial intelligence as well as in psychology. By incorporating such constraints, models will move beyond being "mere" implementations of a particular psychological theory to become a framework for understanding attention, from the single cell to the system level (see Seidenberg, 1993, for an in-depth discussion of this).

Modelling neuropsychological data

In the field of attention, computational models have been evaluated not only by comparing their results to data from normal observers, but also by simulating neuropsychological data. In these simulations the effects of brain lesions have been modelled in a variety of ways, including adding noise to the activation values (in SERR; Humphreys & Müller, 1993) and reducing the weights on connections (e.g. in SAIM; Heinke & Humphreys, 2003). At present it is not clear how best to simulate the effects of brain lesions in models, and alternative procedures could include eliminating connections or adding varying degrees of noise across each iteration of a network (Olson & Humphreys, 1997). One relevant issue is whether the lesion should selectively affect processing in one part of a model or whether it should exert a more pervasive influence. Humphreys et al. (1992) changed a global parameter affecting all stages of their model, to simulate agnosia. In contrast, reduced weights on connections in one part of the field may be useful for simulations of neglect, since this deficit appears to reflect a spatial imbalance in selection. It remains for future work to establish how different forms of simulated lesion may capture the contrasting effects of brain damage on human performance.

CONCLUSION

In this review we have highlighted contributions of computational models to research on visual selective attention. These contributions include demonstrating that traditional dichotomies such as space-based vs. object-based attention, early vs. late selection, and representational vs. attentional accounts of visual neglect do not necessarily hold. In each case, selective processing in the models arises from competitive mechanisms in which units interact to gain control of behaviour, and attention can be an emergent property of the network and not a distinct module in its own right. The models can provide detailed accounts of both normal and abnormal selection and some models can also do this across a range of different tasks. We conclude that computational models do provide a useful contribution to research in this area.

ACKNOWLEDGEMENTS

This research was supported by the Medical Research Council (MRC), UK, and the European Union.

REFERENCES

Behrman, M., Moscovitch, M., & Mozer, M. C. (1991). Directing attention to words and non-words in normal subjects and in a computational model: Implications for neglect dyslexia. *Cognitive Neuropsychology, 8,* 213–248.

Braun, J., Koch, C., & Davis, J. L. (Eds.). (2001). *Visual attention and cortical circuits.* Cambridge, MA: MIT Press.

Broadbent, D. E. (1958). *Perception and communication.* London: Pergamon.

Caramazza, A., & Hillis, A. E. (1990). Levels of representation, co-ordinate frames, and unilateral neglect. *Cognitive Neuropsychology, 7*(5/6), 391–445.

Cave, K. R. (1999). The FeatureGate model of visual selection. *Psychological Research, 62,* 182–194.

Chun, M. M., & Wolfe, J. M. (1996). Just say no: How are visual searches terminated when there is no target present? *Cognitive Psychology, 30,* 39–78.

Cohen, A., & Ivry, R. B. (1991). Density effects in conjunction search: Evidence for a coarse location mechanism of feature integration. *Journal of Experimental Psychology: Human Perception and Performance, 17*(4), 891–901.

Cohen, J. D., Romero, R. D., Servan-Schreiber, D., & Farah, M. J. (1994). Mechanisms of spatial attention: The relation of macrostructure to microstructure in parietal neglect. *Journal of Cognitive Neuroscience, 6*(4), 377–387.

Deco, G., & Zihl, J. (2001). Top-down selective visual attention: A neurodynamical approach. *Visual Cognition, 8*(1), 119–140.

Deutsch, J. A., & Deutsch, D. (1963). Attention: Some theoretical considerations. *Psychological Review, 70*, 80–90.

Donnelly, N., Humphreys, G. W., & Riddoch, M. J. (1991). Parallel computation of primitve shape descriptions. *Journal of Experimental Psychology: Human Perception & Performance, 17*(2), 561–570.

Driver, J., Baylis, G. C., & Rafal, R. D. (1992). Preserved figure–ground segmentation in visual matching. *Nature, 360*, 73–75.

Duncan, J. (1980). The locus of interence in the perception of simultaneous stimuli. *Psychological Review, 87*, 272–300.

Duncan, J. (1984). Selective attention and the organization of visual information. *Journal of Experimental Psychology: General, 113*(4), 501–517.

Duncan, J., & Humphreys, G. W. (1989). Visual search and stimulus similarity. *Psychological Review, 96*(3), 433–458.

Dyer, F. N. (1973). Interference and facilitation for color naming with separate bilateral presentations of the word and color. *Journal of Experimental Psychology, 46*, 314–317.

Egly, R., Driver, J., & Rafal, R. D. (1994). Shifting visual attention between objects and locations: Evidence from normal and parietal subjects. *Journal of Experimental Psychology: Human Perception and Performance, 123*, 161–177.

Ellis, R., & Humphreys, G. (1999). *Connectionist psychology.* Hove, UK: Psychology Press.

Enns, J., & Rensink, R. (1991). Preattentive recovery of three-dimensional orientation from line drawings. *Psychological Review, 98*(3), 335–351.

Eriksen, B. A., & Eriksen, C. W. (1974). Effects of noise letters upon the identification of a target letter in a nonsearch task. *Perception & Psychophysics, 14*, 155–160.

Eriksen, C. W., & Yeh, Y.-Y. (1985). Allocation of attention in the visual field. *Journal of Experimental Psychology: Human Perception and Performance, 11*(5), 583–597.

Farah, M. J. (1990). *Visual agnosia: Disorders of object recognition and what they tell us about normal vision.* Cambridge, MA: MIT Press.

Gilchrist, I., Humphreys, G. W., & Riddoch, M. J. (1996). Grouping and extinction: Evidence for low-level modulation of selection. *Cognitive Neuropsychology, 13*, 1223–1256.

Hamker, F. H. (in press). The re-entry hypothesis: Linking eye movements to visual perception. *Journal of Vision.*

Heinke, D., & Humphreys, G. W. (1997). SAIM: A model of visual attention and neglect. In *Proceedings of the 7th International Conference on Artificial Neural Networks—ICANN'97* (pp. 913–918). Lausanne, Switzerland: Springer-Verlag.

Heinke, D., & Humphreys, G. W. (1999). Modelling emergent attentional properties. In D. Heinke, G. W. Humphreys, & A. Olson (Eds.), *Connectionist models in cognitive neuroscience—the 5th neural computation and psychology workshop* (pp. 240–251), University of Birmingham, UK. London: Springer-Verlag.

Heinke, D., & Humphreys, G. W. (2003). Attention, spatial representation and visual neglect: Simulating emergent attention and spatial memory in the selective attention for identification model (SAIM). *Psychological Review, 110*(1), 29–87.

Hinton, G. E., & Sejnowski, T. J. (1988). Learning and relearning in Boltzmann machines. In *Parallel distributed processing: Explorations in the microstructure of cognition: Vol. 1, Foundations.* A Bradford Book. Cambridge, MA: MIT Press.

Hopfield, J. J., & Tank, D. (1985). "Neural" computation of decisions in optimization problems. *Biological Cybernetics, 52*, 141–152.

Humphreys, G. W. (1987). Objects, words, brains and computers: Framing the correspondence problem in object and word recognition. *Bulletin of the British Psychological Society, 40*, 207–210.

Humphreys, G. W. (1999). The neuropsychology of vision. In G. W. Humphreys (Ed.), *Case studies in the neuropsychology of vision* (pp. xi–xiii). Hove, UK: Psychology Press.

Humphreys, G. W., & Donnelly, N. (2000). 3-D constraints on spatially parallel shape perception. *Perception & Psychophysics, 62*(5), 1060–1085.

Humphreys, G. W., Freeman, T. A. C., & Müller, H. M. (1992). Lesioning a connectionist model of visual search: Selective effects on distractor grouping. *Canadian Journal of Psychology, 46,* 417–460.

Humphreys, G. W., & Heinke, D. (1998). Spatial representation and selection in the brain: Neuropsychological and computational constraints. *Visual Cognition, 5*(1/2), 9–47.

Humphreys, G. W., & Müller, H. J. (1993). SEarch via Recursive Rejection (SERR): A connectionist model of visual search. *Cognitive Psychology, 25,* 43–110.

Humphreys, G. W., Olson, A., Romani, C., & Riddoch, M. J. (1996). Competitive mechanisms of selection by space and object: A neuropsychological approach. In A. F. Kramer, M. G. H. Coles, & G. D. Logan (Eds.), *Converging operations in the study of visual selective attention.* Washington, DC: American Psychological Association.

Humphreys, G. W., Quinlan, P. T., & Riddoch, M. J. (1989). Grouping processes in visual search: Effect with single and combined-feature targets. *Journal of Experimental Psychology: General, 118,* 258–279.

Humphreys, G. W., & Riddoch, M. J. (1993). Interactive attentional systems and unilateral visual neglect. In I. Robertson, & J. Marshall (Eds.), *Unilateral neglect: Clinical and experimental studies* (pp. 139–167). Hove, UK: Lawrence Erlbaum Associates, Ltd.

Humphreys, G. W., & Riddoch, M. J. (1994). Attention to within-object and between-object spatial representations: Multiple side for visual selection. *Cognitive Neuropsychology, 11*(2), 207–241.

Humphreys, G. W., & Riddoch, M. J. (1995). Separate coding of space within and between perceptual objects: Evidence from unilateral visual neglect. *Cognitive Neuropsychology, 12*(3), 283–311.

Humphreys, G. W., Riddoch, M. J., Quinlan, P. T., Price, C. J., & Donnelly, N. (1992). Parallel pattern processing in visual agnosia. *Canadian Journal of Psychology, 46,* 67–103.

Husain, M., & Kennard, C. (1996). Visual neglect associated with frontal lobe infarction. *Journal of Neurology, 243,* 652–657.

James, W. (1890). *The principles of psychology.* New York: Dover.

Karnath, H.-O. (1988). Deficits of attention in acute and recovered visual hemi-neglect. *Neuropsychologica, 26,* 27–43.

Karnath, H.-O., Schenkel, P., & Fischer, B. (1991). Trunk orientation as the determining factor of the "contralesional" deficit in the neglect syndrome and as the physical anchor of the internal representation of body orientation in space. *Brain, 114,* 1997–2014.

Klein, R. (1988). Inhibitory tagging system facilitates visual search. *Nature, 334,* 430–431.

Koch, C., & Itti, L. (2001). Computational modelling of visual attention. *Nature Reviews: Neuroscience, 2,* 194–203.

Marr, D. (1982). *Vision: A computational investigation into the human representation and processing of visual information.* San Francisco, CA: W. H. Freeman.

McAdams, C. J., & Maunsell, H. R. (2000). Attention to both space and feature modulates neuronal responses. *Journal of Neurophysiology, 46,* 1751–1755.

Miller, J. (1982). Divided attention: Evidence for coactivation with redundant signals. *Cognitive Psychology, 14,* 247–279.

Motter, B. C. (1994). Neural correlates of attentive selection for color or luminance in extrastriate area V4. *Journal of Neuroscience, 46,* 2178–2189.

Mozer, M. (1991). *The perception of multiple objects: A connectionist approach.* Cambridge, MA: The MIT Press.

Mozer, M. C. (1987). Early parallel processing in reading: A connectionist approach. In M. Coltheart (Ed.), *Attention and Performance XII*. Hove, UK: Psychology Press.

Mozer, M. C., Halligan, P. W., & Marshall, J. C. (1997). The end of the line for a brain-damaged model of unilateral neglect. *Journal of Cognitive Neuroscience, 9*(2), 171–190.

Mozer, M. C., & Sitton, M. (1998). Computational modeling of spatial attention. In H. Pashler (Ed.), *Attention* (pp. 341–393). Hove, UK: Psychology Press.

Müller, H. J., Humphreys, G. W., & Donnelly, N. (1994). SEarch via Recursive Rejection (SERR): Visual search for single and dual form-conjunction targets. *Journal of Experimental Psychology: Human Perception and Performance, 20*(2), 235–258.

Neisser, U. (1967). *Cognitive psychology*. New York: Appleton-Century-Crofts.

Olshausen, B., Anderson, C. H., & Van Essen, D. C. (1995). A multiscale dynamic routing circuit for forming size- and position-invariant object representations. *Journal of Computational Neuroscience, 2*, 45–62.

Olshausen, B. A., Anderson, C. H., & Van Essen, D. C. (1993). A neurobiological model of visual attention and invariant pattern recognition based on dynamic routing of information. *Journal of Neuroscience, 13*(11), 4700–4719.

Olson, A., & Humphreys, G. W. (1997). Connectionist models of neuropsychological disorders. *Trends in Cognitive Science, 1*, 222–228.

Pashler, H. (1987). Detecting conjunctions of color and form: Reassessing the serial hypothesis. *Perception & Psychophysics, 41*(3), 191–201.

Pavlovskaya, M., Glass, N., Soroker, I., Blum, B., & Groswasser, Z. (1997). Coordinate frame for pattern recognition in unilateral spatial neglect. *Journal of Cognitive Neuroscience, 9*(6), 824–834.

Phaf, H. R., van der Heijden, A., & Hudson, P. (1990). SLAM: A connectionist model for attention in visual selection tasks. *Cognitive Psychology, 22*, 273–341.

Posner, M. I., & Cohen, Y. (1984). Components of visual orienting. In H. Bouma, & D. G. Bowhuis (Eds.) *Attention and Performance X* (pp. 531–556). Hove, UK: Psychology Press.

Posner, M. I., Snyder, C. R. R., & Davidson, B. J. (1980). Attention and the detection of signals. *Journal of Experimental Psychology: General, 109*(2), 160–174.

Posner, M. I., Walker, J. A., Friedrich, F. J., & Rafal, R. D. (1984). Effects of parietal injury on convert orienting of attention. *Journal of Neuroscience, 4*(7), 1863–1874.

Quinlan, P. T., & Humphreys, G. W. (1987). Visual search for targets defined by combination of color, shape and size: An examination of the tasks constraints on feature and conjunction search. *Perception & Psychophysics, 41*, 455–472.

Rensink, R. A., & Enns, J. (1995). Pre-emption effects in visual search: Evidence for low-level grouping. *Psychological Review, 102*, 101–130.

Riddoch, M. J., & Humphreys, G. W. (1983). The effect of cueing on unilateral neglect. *Neuropsychologia, 21*, 589–599.

Riddoch, M. J., & Humphreys, G. W. (1987). Visual object processing in a case of optic aphasia: A case of semantic access agnosia. *Cognitive Neuropsychology, 4*, 131–185.

Robertson, I., & Marshall, J. C. (1993). *Unilateral neglect: Clinical and experimental studies*. Hove, UK: Psychology Press.

Schvaneveldt, R. W., & McDonald, J. E. (1981). Semantic context and the encoding of words: Evidence for two modes of stimulus analysis. *Journal of Experimental Psychology: Human Perception & Performance, 7*, 673–687.

Seidenberg, M. S. (1993). Connectionist models and cognitive theory. *Psychological Science, 46*, 228–235.

Shiffrin, R. M., & Schneider, W. (1977). Control and automatic human information processing: II. Perceptual learning and automatic attending and a general theory. *Psychological Review, 84*, 127–190.

Sieroff, E., Pollastek, A., & Posner, M. I. (1988). Recognition of visual letter strings following injury to the posterior visual spatial attention system. *Cognitive Neuropsychology, 5,* 427–449.

Stroop, J. R. (1935). Studies of interference in serial verbal reactions. *Journal of Experimental Psychology, 18,* 643–662.

Tipper, S. P., & Behrmann, M. (1996). Object-centered not scene-based visual neglect. *Journal of Experimental Psychology: Human Perception and Performance, 22,* 1261–1278.

Tipper, S. P., Driver, J., & Weaver, B. (1991). Object-centered inhibition or return of visual attention. *Quarterly Journal of Experimental Psychology, 43A,* 289–299.

Tipper, S. P., Jordan, H., & Weaver, B. (1999). Scene-based and object-centred inhibition of return: Evidence for dual orienting mechanisms. *Perception & Psychophysics, 61,* 50–60.

Townsend, J. T., & Nozawa, G. (1997). Serial exhaustive models can violate the race model inequality: Implications for architecture and capacity. *Psychological Review, 104*(104), 595–602.

Treisman, A. (1988). Features and objects: The fourteenth Bartlett memorial lecture. *Quarterly Journal of Experimental Psychology, 40A*(2), 201–237.

Treisman, A. (1998). Feature binding, attention and object perception. In G. W. Humphreys, J. Duncan, & A. Treisman (Eds.), *Brain mechanisms of selective perception and action* (Vol. 353, pp. 1295–1306). London: The Royal Society.

Treisman, A. M., & Gelade, G. (1980). A feature-integration theory of attention. *Cognitive Psychology, 12,* 97–136.

Tsotsos, J. K., Culhane, S. M., Wai, W. Y. K., Lai, Y., Davis, N., & Nuflo, F. (1995). Modeling visual attention via selective tuning. *Artificial Intelligence, 78,* 507–545.

van der Heijden, A. H. C. (1981). *Short term visual information forgetting.* London: Routledge & Kegan Paul.

Walker, R. (1995). Spatial and object-based neglect. *Neurocase, 1,* 371–383.

Ward, R., Goodrich, S., & Driver, J. (1994). Grouping reduces visual extinction: Neuropsychological evidence for weight-linkage in visual selection. *Visual Cognition, 1*(1), 101–129.

Wolfe, J. M. (1994). Guided search 2.0: A revised model of visual search. *Psychonomic Bulletin & Review, 1*(2), 202–238.

Wolfe, J. M. (1998). Visual Search. In H. Pashler (Ed.), *Attention* (pp. 13–74). Hove, UK: Psychology Press.

Wolfe, J. M., & Cave, K. R. (1990). Deploying visual attention: The guided search model. In A. Blake, & T. Troscianko (Eds.), *AI and the eye* (pp. 79–103). Chichester: Wiley.

Wolfe, J. M., Cave, K. R., & Franzel, S. L. (1989). An alternative to the feature integration model for visual search. *Journal of Experimental Psychology: Human Perception & Performance, 15,* 419–433.

Young, A. W., Newcombe, F., & Ellis, A. W. (1991). Different impairments contribute to neglect dyslexia. *Cognitive Neuropsychology, 8,* 177–192.

CHAPTER TEN

The control of routine action: Modelling normal and impaired functioning

Richard P. Cooper
Birkbeck, University of London, London, UK

INTRODUCTION

Behavioural routines, from brushing one's teeth to travelling to work, pervade our daily lives. Such routines comprise well-practised, perhaps even stereotyped, sequences of actions that may be analysed at a number of levels. Consider the routine task of brushing one's teeth. At a gross level, this involves a series of identifiable steps: get brush, apply paste, brush, rinse mouth, rinse brush, put brush down, and dry mouth. Each step, however, may be analysed separately. Applying paste, for example, involves picking up the tube of paste, opening it, applying some paste to the brush head, closing the paste tube, and putting the tube down. Even apparently simple acts, such as picking up the brush, can be decomposed into combinations and sequences of reaching, grasping, retracting, etc.

There appears, however, to be a qualitative distinction between the decomposition of simple acts such as picking an object up, and more complex acts such as brushing one's teeth. This distinction is apparent in several ways:

1. The "local physics" of the environment (e.g. the shape of the brush's handle) affects the lower level (how we reach and grasp), but not the higher level (picking up the brush and using it).
2. The timing of subactions at the lower level is critical to their success (e.g. we must open our grip whilst reaching and close it only once

reaching is complete). At the high level, timing is less critical and interruption or interleaving is even possible.

3. Low-level actions are not subject to lapses or slips in normally functioning individuals. (In picking up an object, one does not occasionally unintentionally fail to perform the reach subaction.) As discussed below, actions at the higher level are subject to characteristic errors, especially when attention is diverted.

4. Everyday use of language (in both describing action and in requesting others to make actions) does not normally refer to actions at the level of reaching, grasping, retracting, etc.

Cooper & Shallice (2000) provide further arguments for distinguishing between these two levels and treating them as separate domains of action. This chapter focuses on control of action at the higher level, with particular emphasis on routine action and the model of Cooper & Shallice (2000). The chapter begins by describing the empirical phenomena that any theory of the control of action at this level must address. Several current approaches to action control at the higher level are then described, with the focus being on the theory of Norman & Shallice (1980, 1986). A detailed presentation of the structure and functioning of the Cooper & Shallice (2000) model, which derives from the Norman & Shallice theory, follows. The model is evaluated in the General Discussion, where inadequacies are identified and related models considered.

THE PHENOMENA TO BE EXPLAINED

Any account of the control of action at the higher level must account for data from at least three areas: error, learning, and impairment. The account must explain the everyday slips and lapses common in the behaviour of neurologically intact individuals; it must account for the effects of practice on performance (and in particular for the automatization of action with practice); and it must account for the varieties of breakdown in action control observed following neurological insult.

Slips and lapses in action at the higher level

Momentary slips and lapses in action are common in everyday tasks. Most people will admit to lapses, such as entering a room and failing to remember why one went into the room in the first place, or finding oneself doing one thing when moments before one had intended to do another. Such slips and lapses are not amenable to standard laboratory investigation—they are relatively infrequent and are difficult to evoke under controlled conditions. They have, however, been investigated through the use of naturalistic diary studies.

For example, Reason (1979, 1984) conducted a number of diary studies in which participants were required to note down action lapses when they occurred, recording details of time, place, current intentions, etc. Reason was able to classify the reported errors into a number of categories, including: perceptual confusions, e.g. putting shaving cream, instead of toothpaste, on a toothbrush; spatial confusions, e.g. turning on an electric fire instead of a transistor radio located nearby; insertion errors, e.g. attempting to remove spectacles that were not being worn; omission errors, e.g. attempting to boil a kettle without plugging it in; perseverative errors, i.e. unnecessary repetition of a previously completed action, such as putting two tea-bags in a single cup; and capture errors, e.g. starting to do one thing but becoming side-tracked and doing another. A number of other error types were also reported.

Data on slips and lapses of action provide valuable insights into the functioning of the action control system. Reason argued, on the basis of participants' states as reported at the time of these slips and lapses, that the conditions that evoke action slips are relatively uniform: "during the execution of some automatized task in a familiar setting in which attention has been claimed by some internal preoccupation or by some external distraction" (Reason, 1984, p. 547). Any theoretical account of action control must explain why the system is prone to the kinds of errors reported by Reason's participants when performing automatized tasks without full attention. Indeed, Reason (1984) interpreted the results of his diary study with reference to his own proto-theory of the control of automatized tasks.

The effects of practice

Reason's (1984) claim that slips and lapses arise in the execution of *automatized tasks* brings into focus the notion of automatization. Consider an everyday activity such as brushing one's teeth. This is a task that many people carry out twice a day. As such, it is, to many people, an extremely well-practised or automatized task. The control processes that apply during the execution of such well-practised tasks may be contrasted with those that apply during the execution of novel or nonroutine tasks. Automatized tasks require minimal explicit attention—one may successfully brush one's teeth while reading one's post—but are subject to the slips and lapses noted by Reason (1979, 1984). Nonroutine tasks, such as planning a route that avoids roadworks or locating an error in a mathematical proof, on the other hand, generally consume full attention—two such tasks cannot be performed in tandem—but are not susceptible to slips and lapses.

Many (if not all) tasks that begin as nonroutine can be automatized through practice. Consider the task of driving a car. A new driver learning to master changing the gears typically has difficulty talking whilst changing gears. Once some experience has been acquired, the two tasks can generally

be combined with little effect upon each other, although errors (such as changing up instead of down or mistiming the use of the clutch) may occasional
occur. This situation illustrates two obvious facts; first, that it is possible to
carry out two unrelated tasks simultaneously, and second, that such dual-task
performance is aided by practice. The situation is obviously somewhat more
complicated than this. For example, although a skilled driver may be able to
talk while driving, smooth simultaneous execution of the two tasks will break
down if an attentionally demanding situation (e.g. a car accident or
unfamiliar roadworks ahead) should arise. Thus, even automatized tasks can
be attentionally demanding when the context differs from the norm.

Norman & Shallice (1980, 1986) refer to automatized tasks as "routine",
and distinguish between routine behaviour and controlled or nonroutine
behaviour. The latter is attentionally demanding, and necessary when negoti-
ating situations that are unfamiliar or require particular care. Automatic or
routine behaviour, by contrast, can be performed with little or no overt attention and can on occasion be performed in parallel with other tasks with little
or no interaction, but is only possible in situations that are highly familiar
and where the required response is well-practised.

The distinction between routine and nonroutine behaviour has parallels in
the domain of attention. Shiffrin, Schneider, and colleagues (e.g. Schneider &
Fisk, 1982; Schneider & Shiffrin, 1977; Shiffrin & Schneider, 1977, 1984)
have performed a number of studies on automatic and controlled processing
of visual information. Automatic processing is held to be fast, occur in parallel, not be limited by working memory capacity, and be beyond voluntary
control. Controlled processing, by contrast, is effortful, capacity-limited, and
under willed control. Controlled processing occurs when dealing with novel
or inconsistent information. Automatic processes only operate when the visual input is very familiar. The parallels between control of visual processing
and control of action are so strong that several authors (e.g. MacKay, 1985;
Shallice, 1994) suggest that the same control processes operate for all routine
activities.

The routine/nonroutine, or automatic/controlled, distinction provides a
second hurdle for theories of the control of action. Any such theory
should account for the qualitative differences in behaviour that arise when
performing in a routine, as opposed to a nonroutine, manner.

Impairments of action control at the higher level

A final source of data to be accounted for by theories of action control
concerns characteristic breakdowns of the action control system. Neurological impairment may lead to a number of distinct forms of breakdown in
action control. For a theory of action control to be viable, it must therefore
account for the varieties of breakdown that have been observed to occur.

These include disorders resulting from neurological insult, such as utilization behaviour (Lhermitte, 1983; Shallice, Burgess, Schon, & Baxter, 1989), ideational apraxia (De Renzi & Lucchelli, 1988), action disorganization syndrome (Humphreys & Forde, 1998; Schwartz et al., 1991, 1995, 1998) and strategy application disorder (Shallice & Burgess, 1991), as well as disorders arising from neurochemical imbalances, such as slowed action initiation in Parkinson's disease (Bloxham, Mindel, & Frith, 1984; Jahanshahi, Brown, & Marsden, 1992; Sheridan, Flowers, & Hurrell, 1987) and stereotypy in amphetamine psychosis (Lyons & Robbins, 1975; Randrup & Munkvad, 1967).

In patients exhibiting utilization behaviour, actions appear to be disproportionately driven by aspects of the environment. Thus, Lhermitte (1983) reported a patient who, when presented with three pairs of spectacles, proceeded to put on all three pairs at once. Shallice et al. (1989) investigated whether this behaviour could be attributed to the patient misunderstanding the doctor's intentions. They placed a number of household objects on a tray at one end of a table. Two neuropsychologists then sat with a patient (who had shown signs of utilization behaviour) at the other end of the table, and carried out a standard neuropsychological assessment. During the assessment the patient spontaneously used many of the objects on the tray. This usage ranged from simple toying behaviours to taking a packet of playing cards from the tray and dealing four cards to each person at the table.

A rather different disorder of action control is discussed by De Renzi & Lucchelli (1988). Ideational apraxia involves a combination of problems. Perhaps the most striking of these is a tendency to produce object-inappropriate actions. Thus, De Renzi & Lucchelli report instances of a bottle-opener being used as a stirrer and a coffee filter being used as a spoon. The mislocation of action, as in attempting to light a candlestick instead of a candle, was also common. Other difficulties exhibited by De Renzi & Lucchelli's patients included general perplexity, clumsiness, and sequence errors (including omission errors).

In a series of papers, Schwartz et al. (1991, 1995, 1998) have reported a number of patients (generally with frontal lobe injuries) who show general disorganization of routine activities. This disorganization manifests itself in large numbers of errors that are similar to the lapses and slips seen in normals. Thus, Schwartz et al. (1991) describe the disorganization of patient HH whilst engaged in two routine tasks, preparing and eating his institutional breakfast, and brushing his teeth. HH produced action sequences that contained numerous independent acts (i.e. actions that were task-relevant but that did not contribute towards a directly subsequent goal, such as picking up and shaking a sugar pack, and then adding cream to the coffee mug, before returning to add sugar), as well as a variety of errors, including substitution errors (e.g. putting cream into his orange juice), anticipation errors (e.g. drinking his "coffee" before he had added coffee granules to the boiling water) and omission errors (e.g. failing to open the cream container before attempting to pour from it). While many of his errors could be interpreted as utilizations, HH's actions were purposive in that they mostly contributed towards his current goal (i.e. breakfasting or tooth-brushing). The coherence of HH's actions improved during the 6 weeks over which he was studied, although significant action disorganization was still evident at the end of the period.

The strategy application disorder concerns action breakdown at a somewhat higher level of control. Shallice & Burgess (1991) reported two patients who could perform many standard neuropsychological assessment tasks at normal or better levels, but who showed severe disruption in apparently simple "multiple-subgoal" tasks. These tasks involved completion of several open-ended subtasks in a limited amount of time and subject to certain scheduling constraints. Although the patients had no difficulty with the individual subtasks, they were unable to schedule them effectively.

Each of the above impairments arises after neurological insult involving physical damage to neural structures and/or tissue. Action control may also be affected by neurochemical disorders, e.g. in Parkinson's disease action initiation is typically greatly slowed (e.g. Bloxham et al., 1984; Jahanshahi et al., 1992; Sheridan et al., 1987). It is widely accepted that this is related to either a deficiency of, or a decreased sensitivity to, the neurotransmitter dopamine, and treatment of Parkinsonism with L-dopa, a precursor of dopamine, alleviates the symptom.

A second disorder of action arising from neurochemical imbalances results from high doses of amphetamines. Such doses have been observed to lead to stereotyped behaviour in all mammals (Randrup & Munkvad, 1967), ranging from sniffing and head movements in rats to manipulative movements in higher primates. In a review of the behavioural effects of amphetamines, Lyon & Robbins (1975) interpret stereotypy in terms of an increased rate of responding coupled with a reduced set of response categories. Curiously, the neurophysiological effects of amphetamines include an increase in the concentration of dopamine and related neurotransmitters in the synaptic cleft (Robbins, 1982). There is therefore neurophysiological evidence to suggest that amphetamine psychosis and the slowed action initiation in Parkinson's patients are in some sense opposite ends of a continuum, with normal behaviour somewhere in between.

THEORIES OF HIGHER-LEVEL ACTION CONTROL

A number of theories of the high-level control of action have been proposed. These include activation-based theories (MacKay, 1985; Norman & Shallice, 1980, 1986), recurrent network theories (Botvinick & Plaut, 2002; Schneider & Detweiler, 1987; Schneider & Oliver, 1991) and production system theories

(Anderson & Lebiere, 1998; Kieras & Meyer, 1997; Meyer & Kieras, 1997; Newell, 1990). This section reviews some of these theories. A more complete survey may be found in Cooper (2002).

Norman and Shallice: Contention scheduling and supervisory attention

The dominant theory of higher-level action control is the activation-based theory of Norman & Shallice (1980, 1986). The theory constitutes an amalgam of Shallice's (1972) early work on control processes and Norman's (1981) work on action slips and lapses. In addition, the theory is consistent with the proto-theory developed by Reason (1984).

Norman & Shallice argue that routine and non-routine action are controlled by separate systems. Contention scheduling (CS), the system held to control routine behaviour, is effectively a conflict resolution mechanism that operates upon a hierarchically organized set of action schemas. Each schema corresponds to an abstracted behavioural routine (such as brushing one's teeth), and consists of a set of component schemas (e.g. picking up the brush, applying paste, etc.). Schemas compete within an interactive activation network (McClelland, 1992), i.e. they have activation values that may be excited or inhibited by various factors, and active schemas tend to inhibit less active competing schemas. When schemas become sufficiently active, they are selected. Selected schemas effectively control the behaviour of CS by selectively exciting their component subschemas. Once selected, a schema will remain in that state until a competing schema's activation exceeds that of the selected schema. At the lowest level the schema hierarchy interfaces with the effector system, with low-level schemas corresponding to action primitives, such as *pick up* or *unscrew*. Selection of such schemas results in performance of the corresponding action.

Several factors may excite or inhibit schemas within the hierarchy. The basic mechanism of competition is due to lateral inhibition (i.e. inhibition of a schema from competing schemas) and self-activation (i.e. excitation generated by each schema in order to sustain its activation in the face of lateral inhibition). Together, these influences lead to at most one schema from each set of competitors being highly active at a time. In addition, schemas are held to receive excitation from two further sources: the internal representation of the environment, and selected schemas at higher levels in the hierarchy (termed "source schemas" by Norman & Shallice, 1986).

Competition within the schema hierarchy is defined in terms of overlapping resource requirements: two schemas compete if they require the same cognitive or effective resources. Cognitive resources include special-purpose cognitive modules (e.g. a language module). Effective resources include hands and/or fingers.

Control of nonroutine action is held to require input from a second system, the supervisory attentional system (SAS). In nonroutine situations the SAS may modulate the behaviour of CS by directly exciting or inihibiting schemas at any level in the CS network. Prototypical controlled action is therefore held to involve the SAS directly, exciting low-level schema nodes in sequence. In fact, routine action is also held to involve direct excitation of schemas by the SAS, but in this case the excitation is targeted at schemas high in the hierarchy, and the excitation need not be maintained for the duration of the schema: once CS has been "configured" by SAS to perform a task, CS can be left to function autonomously.

The SAS performs a number of other high-level functions, including planning and monitoring. It differs from CS in being limited in the number of things it can do in parallel. Within CS, several schemas may be active and controlling behaviour at one time, provided those schemas do not compete. In contrast, SAS can only attend to one task at a time. The internal detail of the functioning of SAS is poorly specified, although in recent work Shallice & Burgess (1996) have attempted to decompose the system into functional subcomponents.

The CS/SAS theory is motivated by the slips, lapses, and errors in action selection described in the preceding sections. It is therefore able to provide an informal account of many of the main phenomena. For example, utilization behaviour and capture errors will arise if top-down influences (from source schemas to their component subschemas) are too weak in comparison with triggering from the environment. Similarly, perseverative errors will arise if schema deselection fails: If a high-level schema is not deselected when its component subschemas have been completed, it will continue to excite those subschemas, triggering repeated actions.

MacKay: Content, sequence and timing systems

MacKay (1985) proposed a theory of action control that has much in common with that of Norman & Shallice (1980, 1986). The theories agree on an activation-based hierarchy of schemas as the basic mechanism for organizing and controlling behaviour. MacKay's theory differs in being more well-specified at the lower level, but less well-specified at the higher level. Three kinds of nodes are posited: content nodes (corresponding to Norman & Shallice's action schemas), sequence nodes (which trigger schema nodes in the appropriate order), and timing nodes (which activate sequence nodes and determine the rate of behaviour). The primary difference between the theories is the use of separate timing and sequence nodes.

Although content nodes within MacKay's theory parallel schema nodes within the theory of Norman & Shallice, content nodes do not compete. Instead, sequencing is controlled by separate nodes that trigger, in sequence, the subnodes of an active content node. Sequence nodes are themselves triggered by timing nodes, which serve to coordinate actions that occur in parallel.

Errors in action are accounted for in a way analogous to that of Norman & Shallice: utilization behaviour and capture errors, for example, are claimed to result from environmental triggering of content nodes that overrides their sequential triggering, and ideational apraxia is claimed to result from damage to connections between sequence nodes.

Schneider et al.: The CAP architecture

A rather different theory of control processes is advanced by Schneider and colleagues (Detweiler & Schneider, 1991; Schneider & Detweiler, 1987; Schneider & Oliver, 1991). The theory, embodied in the CAP architecture, is actually a general theory of cognitive control processes, and has been applied to the control of working memory (Schneider & Detweiler, 1987), attention (Shedden & Schneider, 1990), and multiple-task performance (Detweiler & Schneider, 1991).

Several broad assumptions underlie the CAP architecture:

1. Information is stored and processed in a network of modules that are dedicated to different forms of processing (e.g. visual, auditory, and motor). The modules are interconnected and interact. In addition, each module is internally modular and organized into levels. All modules are assumed to function in parallel.
2. There is local specialization of function within modules. Submodules perform specialized processing on restricted classes or ranges of inputs.
3. Control mechanisms exist which modulate the flow of information between and within modules. The mechanisms act by receiving activity signals from the various modules and sending control signals back to the modules. The control signals may attenuate a module's output or modify the level of feedback within a module. The former alters the activity of a module by gating its output, whereas the latter alters the module's response to new signals. With low feedback new signals can control the module, but with high feedback existing signals will tend to swamp all but the most persistent of new signals.
4. Submodules are implemented as simple three-layered feedforward connectionist networks. The transfer from controlled to automatic processing involves learning, by the appropriate networks, of the input/output mappings that constitute a task. Once the requisite skill and knowledge have been encoded in a submodule, that submodule may directly control behaviour.

5. Weights in the submodules are influenced by several different learning-rate constants. Following Hinton & Plaut (1987), this allows the submodules to learn quickly while reducing interference between new and existing knowledge.
6. The control mechanisms are implemented with recurrent networks. These networks sequence behaviour by attenuating and altering feedback of the various modules and submodules.

Certain aspects of the CAP architecture are broadly consistent with the positions of Norman & Shallice and MacKay. Thus, the notion of hierarchically organized submodules may be mapped onto the concept of a schema hierarchy. Similarly, the distinction between routine and nonroutine behaviour is attributed to the operation of two distinct systems. The primary difference between the theories concerns CAP's assumptions 3 and 6: that subsystems are controlled through attenuation and feedback modification, and that these signals are generated by recurrent networks.

Meyer and Kieras: The EPIC architecture

Each of the above theories of control has a connectionist flavour. Meyer & Kieras (1997: see also Kieras & Meyer, 1997) propose a thoroughly nonconnectionist theory of executive control processes. EPIC consists of a central processor that receives input from peripheral perceptual devices and sends output to peripheral motor devices. The central processor is a production system interpreter that operates on a set of *if–then* style rules. The production system has unlimited processing power and no conflict resolution mechanism: it processes in parallel all matching rules on each processing cycle.

EPIC was developed in part to explore certain aspects of behaviour on psychological refractory period tasks, and to show that the detailed timing properties of that behaviour did not require the assumption of a limited capacity central processor. Although it successfully achieves this, and therefore questions an assumption present in all of the above theories (i.e. that nonroutine behaviour is controlled by a limited-capacity central processor), it is silent on the three aspects of behaviour outlined at the beginning of this chapter (slips and lapses, learning, and impairments). We therefore do not consider it in detail.

MODELLING ROUTINE ACTION: THE COOPER & SHALLICE (2000) MODEL

Only one of the above theories, that of Norman & Shallice, has been developed into a fully-fledged model of routine action.[1] The basic model, as a model of routine action, is task-independent. In order to evaluate the model, however, performance of a specific task must be considered. To this end, Cooper & Shallice (2000) describe the model in detail and consider its behaviour in the routine task of preparing coffee (see also Cooper, Shallice, & Farringdon, 1995). This section presents a slight variant of the Cooper & Shallice model. Subsequent sections describe its behaviour in an extended task: that of preparing and eating a breakfast consisting of cereal and coffee.

The primary components of the model are three competitive networks: the schema network, the object representation network, and the resource network. Nodes in the schema network correspond to action schemas, as described above. Each schema has a corresponding node, and the nodes are organized hierarchically, with source schema nodes dominating their component schema nodes. Nodes in the object representation network correspond to the internal representations of objects that affect the system's behaviour. Cooper & Shallice (2000) make the simplifying assumption that this network includes nodes for all and only the objects present in the current task situation. Nodes in the resource network correspond to the cognitive and effective resources available to the contention scheduling system. In the context of the simulations reported here, this network can be reduced to two nodes, corresponding to the left and right hands.

Schemas and the schema network

It is assumed that people possess a (large) number of action schemas, and that for each action schema there is a node in the schema network. Schemas are purposive, i.e. goal-directed, and the hierarchical structuring of schemas is derived from goal–subgoal relations. Consider a schema for adding sugar from a sugar bowl to a coffee mug. The goal of this schema is to sweeten the coffee. The schema might have four components: *pick up* a teaspoon, *dip* the teaspoon into a sugar bowl, *empty* the teaspoon into the coffee mug, and *discard* the teaspoon. Because each component is itself a schema, each component has a goal. These goals are in fact the subgoals of the original higher-level schema, and successful completion of the higher-level schema requires successful completion of the subgoals, rather than successful completion of the component schemas—the subgoals may be achieved through the operation of other schemas. This is clearer when higher levels are considered. For example, several schemas may be employed to achieve the goal of sweetening a mug of coffee, including one for adding sugar from a sugar bowl, one for adding sugar from a packet, and one for adding artificial sweetener. Thus, schemas are defined as having a goal and a set of subgoals. The components of a schema are defined indirectly as those schemas that achieve a subgoal of the higher-level schema.

Schemas at the interface between cognitive and motor action are referred to as basic-level schemas. Each such schema has a corresponding action, and

the corresponding actions have argument roles (i.e. placeholders for the specific objects that they should be applied to and the specific resources that
should be used) and resource requirements. The schema for *dip* referred to
above, for example, has a corresponding *dip* action. This action has a resource
requirement (a hand to use as an effector) and two argument roles, the
effector to do the dipping (which, hopefully, is a hand that is holding a
suitable spoon) and something to dip into (which, hopefully, is an accessible
source of sugar).

The object representation networks

Objects may serve many functional roles. A mug of black coffee, for example,
can serve as both a source of black coffee and a target when adding milk. The
model distinguishes different functional roles by requiring representations of
an object to have separate activation values for each possible functional role.
Thus, in the breakfast model, which employs three functional roles (source,
target, and implement), the representation of the coffee mug will have three
distinct activation values: one as a source, one as a target, and one as an
implement. Normally the activation of the mug as an implement will be near
rest. The activation as source and target will depend on whether the mug is
empty. The object representation "network" is therefore better described as a
set of networks. There are no dependencies between these networks: the activity of a node in one network is entirely independent of the activity of a
corresponding node in another network.

Activation flow

Basic properties of activation

Nodes in the schema, object representation and resource networks have
associated activation values. These values are subject to a number of excitatory or inhibitory influences, as discussed below. The influences alter the
activation values of nodes subject to three principles. Activation values cannot be excited above a maximum value; activation values cannot be inhibited
below a minimum value; and with no input, activation values tend towards a
resting value. In the simulations reported below, the maximum activation is
1.0, the minimum is 0.0, and the rest activation is 0.1. Activation values may
be inhibited to below the resting value, but once below that value they will
recover to the resting value if inhibition is removed. Similar remarks apply to
activation values above the resting level. The rate at which activation values
recover towards their resting value is a parameter of the model. Full
mathematical details are given in Cooper & Shallice (2000).

Activation flow within networks

All nodes in all networks are subject to two influences: self-influence and lateral influence. Self-influence is generally an excitatory influence that prevents active nodes from reverting to rest. It is proportional to a node's own activation, and so is greatest for the most active nodes. Lateral influence is generally an inhibitory influence. The degree of inhibition on any node is dependent on the activation of its competitors. If two nodes are competing, then the inhibition of the more active node on the less active node will be greater than the inhibition of the less active node on the more active node. The conditions under which nodes compete are defined below.

In addition to self- and lateral influences, nodes within the schema network may receive a top-down influence. Specifically, selected schemas excite their component schemas if and only if the preconditions of the component schemas have been met. The degree of excitation is proportional to the selected schema's activation, and inversely proportional to the number of component schemas.

Activation flow between networks

Nodes may also receive excitation (or inhibition) from other nodes in other networks. Thus, object representation and resource nodes receive excitation (or inhibition) from schema nodes, and schema nodes receive excitation (or inhibition) from object representation and resource nodes. The flow of excitation and inhibition between the networks is determined by schema-specific triggering functions. These functions determine, for each schema, the situations that trigger that schema. Situations may be simple, consisting of the presence of an object with given features (e.g. the presence of a spoon), or complex, consisting of multiple objects and resources in specific configurations (e.g. the presence of a nonempty spoon being held by one hand). If a schema's triggering function is satisfied, then the schema's node receives activation from the object representations or resources that satisfy the function. This flow of activation is two-way, so if an object representation or resource excites/inhibits a schema node then that schema will excite/inhibit the object representation or resource nodes.

The degree of excitation/inhibition that flows between networks is determined by the nodes participating in the interaction. A highly active schema will strongly excite the object representations and resources that trigger it. Similarly, object representations that have been inhibited to below rest activation will inhibit schemas that they trigger.

Triggering functions reflect affordances: a schema is triggered by a situation if and only if the schema can be performed in the situation. At the lowest level of the schema hierarchy (i.e. the level corresponding to actions such as *pick up, pour, tear*, etc.) an object representation/resource combination triggers a schema if and only if the object (in its current state) and resource can be used by the schema. At higher levels, object representations and resources trigger schemas if and only if they trigger a component subschema of the schema.

Although SAS functions have not been implemented, it is assumed that the SAS can also directly excite or inhibit nodes in any network. Automatic functioning requires excitation by the SAS of a node high in the schema hierarchy corresponding to the intended action (e.g. the "prepare cereal" node). Inhibition of a prepotent response requires inhibition by the SAS of the node corresponding to the response.

Competition

Competition between nodes within each network ensures that, in the normally functioning system, at most one node within each set of competing nodes is highly active at any time. As discussed above, competition is effected by a lateral influence that operates between competing nodes. The lateral influence on any node is proportional to the sum of the difference between rest activation and the activation of each competing node. If a node is highly active, it will tend to strongly inhibit its competitors; if it is near rest, it will have little effect on its competitors; and if it is below rest, it will excite its competitors.

Schema nodes compete if they: (a) are alternative means of satisfying a single goal; (b) share resource requirements; or (c) share a subgoal. The purpose of the first clause is to prevent two alternative means of achieving a single goal from becoming active at the same time. The second clause is a direct restatement of the Norman & Shallice (1980, 1986) definition of the conditions under which schemas compete. The third clause is required as resource requirements are marked only on basic-level schemas (i.e. those at the lowest level of the hierarchy, corresponding directly to actions). If two schemas share a subgoal, they will normally also share resource requirements, and hence should compete.[2]

Object representation nodes compete within each functional role. Thus, in the breakfast model all object representations compete within the source functional role, all object representations compete within the target functional role, and all object representations compete within the implement functional role.

The current model assumes that resources are independent. There is therefore no competition in the resource node network.

Schema selection and deselection

Following Norman & Shallice (1980, 1986), a schema node is selected when its activation exceeds a threshold. For the simulations reported below, this threshold is 0.6. Once selected, a schema remains in that state, even if its activation falls below the selection threshold, until its activation is exceeded by a competitor. It is then deselected.

The selection process serves two functions: it alters activation flow within the schema network and, when a basic-level schema is selected, it triggers the execution of basic actions. Thus, once selected, a schema may excite its component schemas. Under normal functioning this excitation will lead to one of the component schemas becoming highly active (and hence selected), and so on, until a basic-level schema is selected. This basic-level schema will then trigger execution of the corresponding action, before being inhibited and deselected. A further basic-level schema may then be selected, leading to execution of a further action, and so on.

Several possibilities exist for mechanisms that might implement appropriate activation flow from selected schemas. Cooper & Shallice (2000) take the influence of selected schemas on their component schemas to be excitatory if the component schema's preconditions have been achieved and zero otherwise. The inhibition of a schema once its goal has been achieved is effected by reversing the self-influence (i.e. making it inhibitory) for any selected schema whose goal has been achieved. Cooper & Shallice (2000) note, however, that the inhibitory mechanisms are a matter of implementation. To illustrate this point, an alternative mechanism for inhibition is employed here. In the simulations reported below, self-influence is always excitatory. The influence of a selected schema on its component schemas, however, is assumed to be inhibitory for any component schema whose goal has been achieved. This inhibition ensures that component schemas are deselected once they have been completed, allowing other schemas to be selected and action to progress.

Serial order and serial order constraints

Competition ensures that the model does not attempt to perform two competing actions at the same time (in fact, because all basic-level schemas in the breakfasting task require use of the same resource—the hands—competition ensures that only one action is ever attempted at a time). Several factors work together to ensure that sequencing of actions is appropriate. First, triggering of schemas from the environment ensures that actions that are physically possible are more likely to become active than actions that are not physically possible. Thus, the schema corresponding to *put down* will not be triggered by the environment unless something is actually being held, and the schema corresponding to *pick up* will only be triggered by the environment if there is a free hand and a small object in view. Second, as noted above, a schema's component schemas may have preconditions that influence the flow of excitation from a selected schema node to its component schema nodes, biasing the system towards selecting those component schemas whose preconditions have been satisfied.

To illustrate the effects of environmental triggering and serial order constraints, consider the schema for adding sugar to coffee, as described above. This has four components: *pick up* (a teaspoon), *dip* (the teaspoon into a sugar bowl), *empty* (the teaspoon into the coffee mug), and *discard* (the teaspoon). This schema will normally be selected when the hands are empty and all objects for adding sugar are available. At this point, environmental triggering is excitatory for *pick up* (as it is physically possible) and inhibitory for all other schemas (as their corresponding actions are not physically possible). The *pick up* schema will therefore be selected and its corresponding action executed. *Pick up* will then cease to receive excitation from *add sugar from bowl to coffee* (as the goal of *pick up* has been achieved). It will continue to receive some excitation from the environment (assuming that one hand is still empty). Both *dip* and *discard* will now receive excitatory triggering from the environment. However, because the precondition of *discard*—that something has been added to the coffee—has not been achieved, it will not receive excitation from *add sugar from bowl to coffee*, and so *dip* is more likely to be selected. Selection of *empty* and then *discard* will follow, at which point the goal of *add sugar from bowl to coffee* (i.e. sweeten coffee) will have been achieved, and *add sugar from bowl to coffee* will be inhibited.

Performing basic actions

The inclusion of object representation and resource networks represents an extension to the original theory of Norman & Shallice. The networks serve two purposes: to provide a means by which the system's representation of the environment may trigger schemas, and to allow selection of the objects over which selected schemas operate. Both of these functions are necessary for a complete implementation of the theory. Although the former was explicitly discussed in the statement of the original theory, a precise mechanism was not specified. The latter was left implicit.

In the current model, selection of a basic-level schema leads to execution of its corresponding action. Before the action can be executed, however, its argument roles must be filled. Each argument role of an action has a selection restriction. Only objects or resources that satisfy an argument role's selection restriction can be assigned to that argument role. The *dip* action, for example, has two argument roles. One must be filled by a resource, which is a hand that is holding a spoon. The other must be filled by a source object, which is a nonempty open container. Argument roles are filled with the most active resource or object that satisfies their selection restriction. When adding sugar from the sugar bowl, for example, and the *dip* schema is selected, the sugar bowl will be the most active nonempty open container (in the functional role of source). Similarly, a hand holding a teaspoon will be the most active appropriate resource. Once objects and resources are assigned to an action, the action is executed. This leads to changes in the world, and the system's representation of the world, and hence changes in the pattern of triggering activity received by the schema network.

Argument selection can fail in two ways. First, it may be that there are no objects satisfying a selection restriction. For example, both hands may be empty when a hand holding a spoon is required. This kind of failure leads to omission of the action. Second, incorrect arguments may be selected because they are more active than the correct arguments. This kind of failure leads to an argument substitution error, as when shaving cream, instead of toothpaste, is applied to a toothbrush.

BEHAVIOUR OF THE COOPER & SHALLICE MODEL

The model as described above is quite complex, and many components must interact appropriately for the model to function as intended. In order to test the model fully, however, it must be applied to a specific task, and the physical world in which that task is to be carried out must also be simulated. This section describes the model's behaviour on a breakfasting task. The task is routine, and similar to that in which Schwartz et al. (1991, 1995) observed action disorganization in neurological patients.

The breakfasting task

The breakfasting task is an extension of the coffee preparation task considered by Cooper & Shallice (2000). The task involves four subtasks: preparing coffee (á la Cooper & Shallice, 2000), taking a sip of coffee, preparing cereal, and consuming a spoonful of cereal. The task is only a slight simplification of breakfasting as it may occur in everyday life. The schema hierarchy consists of 24 schemas, comprising 12 high-level schemas (*eat breakfast, prepare coffee, prepare cereal, drink from mug, consume from bowl, add sugar from packet, add sugar from bowl, add coffee from packet, add coffee from jar, add milk from carton, stir coffee* and *put cereal into mouth*) and 12 basic-level schemas (*pick up, put down, dip, empty, eat from spoon, stir, pour, tear, screw open, screw closed, swap hands* and *drink*). There are 13 objects in the simulated world (a sugar packet, a salt packet, a coffee packet, a sugar bowl, a cereal bowl, a plate of toast, a glass of juice, a coffee mug, a coffee jar with lid, a milk carton, a spoon, and a stirrer), several of which are distractor objects.

Normal functioning

Fig. 10.1 shows the actions and arguments selected in a typical run of the normally functioning model. The numbers on the left indicate the cycle number at which each action was executed. As can be seen from the list of actions, the model first picks up the milk carton. It then tears it and pours some milk into the cereal bowl (which already contained cereal). After putting the milk carton down the model adds sugar to the cereal from a sugar packet (cycles 314–358) and eats some cereal (cycles 416–452). The model then moves on to the coffee-related tasks.

The *eat breakfast* schema (which has four subgoals: to prepare coffee, to drink coffee, to prepare cereal, and to eat cereal) was provided with constant excitation for the duration of this run.[3] This excitation rapidly led to the *eat breakfast* schema becoming highly active and hence selected. This is seen more clearly in Fig. 10.2, which shows the activation profiles of all schemas throughout the duration of the task. The smooth curves correspond to higher-level schemas. The spiked curves correspond to basic-level schemas which, once selected, are immediately performed and inhibited.

The line on Fig. 10.2 that rises from 0.1 (rest activation) to near maximum

217: *pick_up* milk_carton
236: *tear* milk_carton
243: *pour* milk *into* cereal_bowl
257: *put_down* milk_carton
314: *pick_up* sugar_packet
335: *tear* sugar_packet
344: *pour* sugar *into* cereal_bowl
358: *put_down* sugar_packet
416: *pick_up* spoon
430: *dip_spoon_into* cereal_bowl
436: *consume* cereal
452: *put_down* spoon
603: *pick_up* coffee_packet
623: *tear* coffee_packet
631: *pour* coffee *into* coffee_mug
646: *put_down* coffee_packet
717: *pick_up* milk_carton
737: *pour* milk *into* coffee_mug
777: *put_down* milk_carton
828: *pick_up* sugar_packet
848: *pour* sugar *into* coffee_mug
880: *put_down* sugar_packet
951: *pick_up* coffee_mug
960: *drink_from* coffee_mug
975: *put_down* coffee_mug

Figure 10.1.   Normal behaviour of the model in the breakfast task, generated with the following weightings of activation sources: self = 0.30; lateral = 0.30; top-down = 0.36; environmental = 0.04.

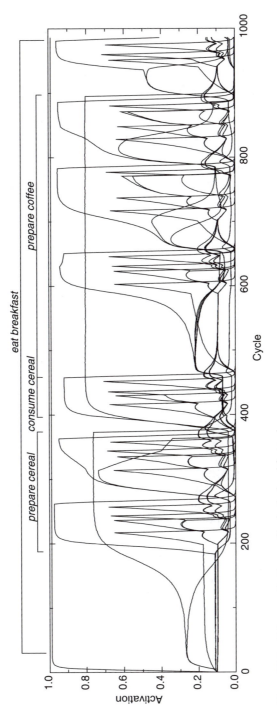

Figure 10.2. Schema activation profiles in the breakfast task.

activity over the first few cycles represents the activity of the *eat breakfast* schema. Once this schema is selected, the schemas corresponding to the two subgoals of *eat breakfast* whose preconditions are satisfied (*prepare coffee* and *prepare cereal*) receive top-down excitation. The activity of these schemas can be seen to rise to about 0.25 over the first 20 cycles, before competitive effects draw the schemas apart. One schema (in this case that of *prepare cereal*) wins the competition and suppresses the other (*prepare coffee*), which remains suppressed until *prepare cereal* is complete and deselected (approximately cycle 375). At this point *prepare coffee* has no active competitors, and so its activation rises and in due course it is selected.

Note that in fact two high-level schemas become active shortly after cycle 375. The second is that of *consume cereal*, which begins to receive top-down activation once its precondition (*prepare cereal*) is complete. Both schemas become active because (on the definition given here) they do not compete. However, *consume cereal* does compete with the components of *prepare coffee*, and so the components of *prepare coffee* remain inactive until *consume cereal* is complete. The three components of *prepare coffee* are then selected and effected in turn, before *drink coffee* is finally selected.

Slips and lapses

It was suggested above that supervisory control is not normally necessary when performing routine actions, but that in the absence of such control action slips and lapses may arise. In fact, the model requires sustained excitation of the top-most schema throughout the task. If such excitation decays or is otherwise not sustained, the activation of the top-most schema will fall until it is deselected, and activity at the lower levels will cease. This situation corresponds to one form of action lapse identified by Reason (1979, 1984): decay of intention. Intuitively it corresponds to the situation when one realizes one is doing something without knowing why one is doing it.

Other modes of failure of the model lead to other types of slips and lapses. The following failures are possible:

- Failure to inhibit a prepotent response: something in the environment triggers execution of an unintended routine, which is not inhibited by supervisory control. This may occur at multiple levels. At high levels it may result in capture errors. At the lowest level it results in toying, utilization behaviour, or even sequence errors (if the environmentally triggered action is one that would naturally occur later in a sequence).
- Failure to sufficiently specify an argument or inhibit an inappropriate argument: if a schema is not sufficiently precise in its argument specification, inappropriate object representations may be activated, leading to object substitution errors.

- Failure to deselect a completed schema: if a schema is not deselected on completion, then a routine may be performed multiple times, leading to perseverative behaviour.

The first two of these modes of failure occur when performing routine tasks in nonroutine situations. Such situations have not been investigated within the model, but the prediction is that input will be required from the SAS to ensure correct performance.

Impaired functioning

Action disorganization syndrome

Schwartz et al. (1991, 1995) suggest that action disorganization syndrome, as observed in their patients HH and JK, can be explained in terms of an impairment of the CS system. Specifically, they suggest that action disorganization is a result of reduced top-down excitation within the system. The Cooper & Shallice model allows this suggestion to be tested, and Cooper & Shallice (2000) provide a detailed analysis of the model's behaviour in the coffee preparation task when the balance between top-down and environmental triggering is disrupted. Consistent with Schwartz et al.'s suggestion, it was found that when this balance favours environmental triggering, the model behaves in a manner similar to that of action disorganization patients. An illustrative replication of these results in the breakfast task is shown in Fig. 10.3, which shows the behaviour of the model when top-down influence is reduced (from 0.36 to 0.32) and environmental triggering is increased (from 0.04 to 0.08).

The model begins by toying with the spoon (picking it up and then putting it down again). It then picks up the teaspoon and dips it into the sugar bowl, but puts it down again before completing the sugaring act. It then goes on to successfully add coffee granules to the mug of boiling water, and drink the "coffee", omitting to add milk and failing to successfully add sugar. The model then moves on to cereal preparation. It succeeds in adding milk and sugar to the cereal, but then proceeds to eat the sugar from the teaspoon, instead of the cereal. The model exhibits qualitatively the same mix between structured behavioural routines (e.g. adding the coffee granules) and unstructured independent actions (toying with the sugar) as observed by Schwartz et al. (1991, 1995) in patients HH and JK.

Amphetamine psychosis

Robbins & Sahakian (1983) interpret the effects of psychomotor stimulants (including amphetamines) in terms of the Norman & Shallice (1980, 1986) theory. They note that amphetamine-like stimulants lead to increased activity

59: *pick_up* spoon
363: *put_down* spoon
432: *pick_up* teaspoon
476: *dip_spoon_into* sugar_bowl
496: *put_down* teaspoon
549: *pick_up* coffee_packet
567: *tear* coffee_packet
579: *pour* coffee *into* coffee_mug
588: *put_down* coffee_packet
633: *pick_up* coffee_mug
643: *drink_from* coffee_mug
656: *put_down* coffee_mug
699: *pick_up* milk_carton
716: *tear* milk_carton
727: *pour* milk *into* cereal_bowl
737: *put_down* milk_carton
786: *pick_up* sugar_packet
805: *tear* sugar_packet
817: *pour* sugar *into* cereal_bowl
826: *put_down* sugar_packet
905: *pick_up* teaspoon
921: *consume* sugar
935: *put_down* teaspoon

Figure 10.3. Impaired behaviour of the model in the breakfast task, illustrating action disorganization, generated with the following weightings of activation sources: self = 0.30; lateral = 0.30; top-down = 0.32; environmental = 0.08.

in the striatal dopamine system, and suggest that this increased activity facilitates the excitation, and hence selection, of schemas within the contention scheduling (CS) system. A different suggestion of the effects of increased dopamine activity on a CS-like system comes from Joseph, Frith, & Waddington (1979), who suggest that dopamine over-activity leads to a breakdown in inhibitory competition. The Robbins & Sahakian proposal may be tested within the model by increasing the self-influence on schemas. The Joseph et al. proposal may be tested by decreasing the lateral influence. In fact, both modifications lead to similar behaviour. Cooper & Shallice (2000) found that the critical factor in determining model performance is not the absolute level of either self-influence or lateral influence, but the ratio between the two. When the proportion of self-influence relative to lateral influence is increased, the model does exhibit behaviours reminiscent of amphetamine psychosis in that the rate of responding increases.

There are relatively few response categories available within either the coffee preparation domain (as investigated by Cooper & Shallice, 2000) or the breakfast task (as presented here). It is therefore not currently possible to determine whether the damaged model also exhibits the second characteristic of amphetamine psychosis, a reduction in the set of response categories.

Slowed action initiation

As noted above, dopamine imbalance is implicated in both amphetamine psychosis and Parkinson's disease, and dopamine depletion or decreased dopamine receptivity is held in part to be responsible for slowed action initiation in Parkinsonism. The relation between dopamine and lateral inhibition or self-activation suggested in the previous section implies that slowed action initiation should result from increasing the proportion of lateral inhibitory influence with respect to self-influence.

The behaviour of the model with increased lateral influence and decreased self-influence is shown in Fig. 10.4. Comparing this with Fig. 10.2, one can see that all actions are performed successfully and in an appropriate order.[4] The key point to recognize is that action initiation (measured in cycle time) in Fig. 10.4 takes more than twice as long as in Fig. 10.2 (481 cycles as opposed to 217 cycles), but the time between task initiation and task completion (681 cycles in Fig. 10.4 and 758 cycles in Fig. 10.2) is not similarly affected.

Although it is too simplistic to suggest that amphetamine psychosis is due simply to an excess of dopamine and impaired action initiation is due simply to a deficiency of dopamine, the model does suggest that both disorders

481: *pick_up* coffee_packet
501: *tear* coffee_packet
509: *pour* coffee *into* coffee_mug
524: *put_down* coffee_packet
613: *pick_up* milk_carton
632: *tear* milk_carton
640: *pour* milk *into* coffee_mug
654: *put_down* milk_carton
712: *pick_up* sugar_packet
732: *tear* sugar_packet
740: *pour* sugar *into* coffee_mug
754: *put_down* sugar_packet
802: *pick_up* coffee_mug
807: *drink_from* coffee_mug
822: *put_down* coffee_mug
872: *pick_up* milk_carton
887: *pour* milk *into* cereal_bowl
922: *put_down* milk_carton
978: *pick_up* sugar_packet
999: *pour* sugar *into* cereal_bowl
1040: *put_down* sugar_packet
1127: *pick_up* teaspoon
1141: *dip_spoon_into* cereal_bowl
1147: *consume* cereal
1162: *put_down* teaspoon

Figure 10.4. Impaired behaviour of the model in the breakfast task, illustrating slowed action initiation, generated with the following weightings of activation sources: self = 0.28; lateral = 0.32; top-down = 0.36; environmental = 0.04.

involve an imbalance of the same general kind. An imbalance in one direction slows action initiation, while an imbalance in the other leads to increased rates of responding.

Other neurological impairments

As noted above, action disorganization syndrome shares some behavioural similarities with utilization behaviour, and the transcript of actions in Fig. 10.3 illustrates simple utilization behaviour (toying with the spoon). Utilization at the basic-level can therefore be accounted for in terms of reduced top-down excitation (or increased environmental triggering). Higher-level utilization behaviour (such as dealing from a deck of cards, as observed by Shallice et al., 1989) requires a more complex explanation. Flow of top-down activation must be intact within the behavioural sequence for the complete task (e.g. of dealing from a pack of cards) if the task is to be completed without error. One possibility consistent with the model is that such high-level utilizations result from the failure to explicitly inhibit inappropriate environmentally triggered schemas.

Inappropriate or insufficient excitation of object representations by schemas can lead to the misuse of objects as in ideational apraxia. Such misuse will essentially occur through errors of object selection. Whilst this may contribute to ideational apraxia, it is likely that the explanation is more complex, as ideational apraxics typically also show deficits in direct tests of object use (De Renzi & Lucchelli, 1988). It would appear that it is not just the excitation of objects by schemas that is at fault in ideational apraxia, but also the triggering of schemas by object representations. Inappropriate or failed triggering of schemas by objects will lead to selection of inappropriate schemas, and hence object misuse.

The obvious interpretation of the strategy application disorder of Shallice & Burgess (1991) within the CS/SAS theory is one of a breakdown of supervisory function with intact CS processing, and this is the interpretation offered by Shallice & Burgess. The disorder is therefore not one that should be explained by the CS model. It does, however, provide support for the CS/SAS distinction.

GENERAL DISCUSSION

Relation of the Cooper & Shallice model to the Norman & Shallice theory

The original verbally-specified theory of Norman & Shallice was, like most verbally-specified theories within cognitive psychology, incompletely specified. It did not, for example, provide mathematical equations for the behaviour of activation, or mechanisms for the selection of arguments. The

Cooper & Shallice model faithfully implements all aspects of Norman & Shallice theory—all theoretical statements of the theory are embodied in the model—but also includes details that go beyond the theory. Some of these details are purely implementational, necessary for computational completeness but not of theoretical relevance. Others represent true extensions to the Norman & Shallice theory.

Extensions of the implementational kind include the equations used for calculating the activation of nodes given the various inputs, the mechanisms for inhibiting a schema's node once the schema has been executed and the mechanisms for recording subgoal completion. The implementation of each of these aspects of the theory is necessary for a complete working model but tentative in that alternative, equally valid, approaches to their implementation exist. Empirical data is not currently available to distinguish between the competing alternatives, and in some cases it is unclear whether discriminating data could in principle be obtained (cf. Cooper, Fox, Farringdon, & Shallice, 1996).

Extensions of the theoretical kind include the goal-orientated nature of schemas (i.e. that schemas have goals and that the components of a schema are those schemas that achieve one of the schema's subgoals), the representation of objects within an interactive activation network paralleling that of schemas, and the subsequent use of activity in the object representation network to trigger schemas and vice versa.

Relation of the Cooper & Shallice model to other models involving serial order

The model described above simultaneously addresses a range of computational constraints. First, the domain of action selection requires sequential behaviour. Second, most theorists agree that sequential behaviour is hierarchically structured and controlled (although see Botvinick & Plaut, 2002, for an alternative view). Third, sequential hierarchically-structured behaviour operates over objects that must be bound to (or otherwise associated with) individual actions as they are performed. None of these concerns would present any difficulties to a purely symbolic approach (such as EPIC). However, such an approach is unlikely to be able to account for the patterns of error and breakdown described above.

This is not to say that a purely connectionist approach would necessarily fare any better. Simple recurrent network models (e.g. Elman, 1990; Jordon, 1986), which have been advocated in other sequential domains and which serve a sequencing function in the CAP architecture (Detweiler & Schneider, 1991; Schneider & Detweiler, 1987), face two difficulties when applied to the domain of routine action. They must coordinate object and action domains in the presence of resource constraints, and they must account for the full range of error types, including omission errors. The former problem is one of how to represent the task of routine action. The latter is a problem because simple recurrent networks are most powerful when sequential behaviour involves generating chains of outputs, where one output primes the next. Houghton & Hartley (1996) have argued, following Lashley (1951), that models that sequence on the basis of chaining cannot account for the range of errors produced by human participants on a variety of tasks. Omission errors, which Schwartz et al. (1998) have argued are particularly common in their frontal patients, would seem particularly difficult to obtain with a chaining model. Nevertheless, Botvinick & Plaut (2002) have developed a simple recurrent network model of the coffee preparation task (as modelled by Cooper & Shallice, 2000) and demonstrated that, following suitable training, the model is capable of generating the full range of error types. Further evaluation of this model remains to be performed, but one difficulty concerns the relation of the model to systems involved in nonroutine action. In particular, it is unclear how control signals might interact with the model to modulate performance of isolated task segments (e.g. of deliberately adding extra sugar when preparing coffee for someone with a sweet tooth, and when that precise task has never previously been performed), or how other cognitive systems might interact to detect and correct action slips and lapses.

Numerous authors have used the mechanisms of interactive activation to provide alternative approaches to sequential behaviour. Although interactive activation networks were first used by McClelland & Rumelhart (1981) to model static responses (in the domain of letter and word perception), Rumelhart & Norman (1982) demonstrated how the same mechanism could be applied to a sequential task (that of typing). Indeed, there are many similarities between the Cooper & Shallice model and that of Rumelhart & Norman: both models employ hierarchically-structured schemas to group action sequences, and both models include feedback from the response system (the resource network in the Cooper & Shallice model) to the schema hierarchy. The models differ in the mechanism for controlling sequencing and the extent of the schema hierarchy. Rumelhart & Norman control sequencing through inhibition of items later in the sequence by items earlier in the sequence. This contrasts with the use of preconditions and environmental triggering in the Cooper & Shallice model. The difference may be attributed to domain differences (environmental triggering cannot disambiguate possible keys to press whilst typing), but the issue is open to debate. The extent of the schema hierarchy is also determined by the domain. Rumelhart & Norman require just two levels (key-press schemas and word schemas). The number of levels in the Cooper & Shallice model is domain-dependent. The breakfast model presented above has four levels, but the lunch box model of Cooper et al. (in press) has five levels, the coffee preparation model of Cooper & Shallice

(2000) has three levels, and Cooper (1998) presents a model of the same form with just two levels.

Another interactive activation model of action selection is that of Maes (1989). Nodes in this model correspond to various competences, and activation flows between the nodes according to standard interactive activation principles. Like both the Cooper & Shallice model and the Rumelhart & Norman model, conflicting nodes inhibit each other. Maes' model also makes use of symbolic preconditions to bias sequential behaviour, in a manner similar to that employed by Cooper & Shallice. However, in contrast to the Cooper & Shallice model, there is no hierarchical structuring or argument selection in Maes' model: all nodes correspond to base-level actions with bound arguments.

The Cooper & Shallice model is also related to the "competitive queuing" models of Houghton and colleagues (Glasspool, 1998; Hartley & Houghton, 1996; Houghton, 1990; Houghton, Glasspool & Shallice, 1994; Shallice, Glasspool & Houghton, 1995). Notions of selection and inhibition after selection are common to all of these models. The principal differences are again due to differences in domains. Within the competitive queuing models, the hierarchical organization is limited to just two levels (words and letters in the spelling models) (Glasspool, 1998; Houghton, 1990; Houghton, Glasspool & Shallice, 1994; Shallice, Glasspool & Houghton, 1995) and phonemes and syllables in the speech production model (Hartley & Houghton, 1996), argument and resource selection are not required, and serial order is effected by a varying context signal (rather than gating of activation flow via symbolic preconditions). The competitive queuing models are further distinguished by the inclusion of a learning mechanism. As discussed below, the lack of a learning mechanism is a significant limitation of the Cooper & Shallice model.

Limitations of the Cooper & Shallice model

Notwithstanding the success of the model described above in producing well-formed action sequences, there are a number of limitations of the model that remain to be addressed. Some of these relate to simplifications made for the purpose of implementation and pose no great difficulties. Others raise conceptual or theoretical issues to which future research must be directed.

The treatment of goals, and in particular the way in which subgoals are effectively ticked off as the schemas that achieve them are deselected, is a gross simplification and clearly insufficiently flexible. The model treats goals as atomic symbols, but they are better understood as conditions that may or may not be true, given the current state of the world. The current treatment fails to allow for situations in which subgoals are optional, in which they must be repeated multiple times, or in which they may already have been achieved.

Thus, the schema for adding sugar from the sugar bowl to the coffee mug has precisely four components: *pick up* spoon, *dip* spoon into bowl, *empty* spoon into mug, and *discard* spoon. The schema will not function correctly if it is selected when a spoon is already being held or when the sugar bowl is covered by its lid. In a similar way, it is not possible to represent the fact that drinking coffee involves taking multiple sips until the coffee mug is empty (this is why the breakfasting task did not require drinking all of the coffee or eating all of the cereal). Recent work (Cooper et al., in press) demonstrates that the treatment of goals can be elaborated without detriment to the rest of the model.

A number of questions are also posed by the model's treatment of object representations. The simplest of these concerns the number of functional roles required. It is unclear whether the three functional roles used in the breakfasting task will prove to be sufficient for all tasks. More seriously, there is at present no empirical or theoretical justification for any specific set of functional roles. A more complex difficulty is raised by the role of visual attention. As a first pass, visual attention may serve to modulate the activation of object representations. The form that such modulation should take, however, is unclear.

There are strong parallels between activation processes in the schema network and in the object representation network, but the concept of selection, which is crucial in the schema network, has no parallel in the object representation or resource networks. Cooper et al. (in press) show that mechanisms to allow for the selection and deselection of objects within the scope of higher-level schemas that make use of those objects are also consistent with the general CS framework. Such mechanisms allow, for example, a specific coffee mug to be selected as a target for the duration of coffee preparation, and then inhibited once coffee preparation is complete. This "binding" of arguments is an intuitively desirable feature of an action selection system.

Perhaps the most serious difficulty with the model as described here is its lack of a learning mechanism. Learning, and in particular the transfer from controlled to automatic processing, was highlighted in the introduction as one of the core phenomena that a theory (and hence model) of action selection should address. The Norman & Shallice (1980, 1986) theory distinguishes between controlled and automatic action, but is virtually silent on the mechanisms underlying transfer from controlled to automatic. Nevertheless, and in the light of the Cooper & Shallice model, some comments on learning may be made. First, one may assume that the lowest level of the schema hierarchy is fixed (or acquired early in development). Learning then involves the creation of new schema nodes (superordinate to existing schema nodes), along with their associated triggering functions and ordering constraints. Schema nodes for nonroutine action sequences (complete with ordering constraints) may be created by the SAS (perhaps as part of the process of executing the action sequence, and not necessarily with the purpose of learning the sequence). Triggering functions map states of the current representation of the world to schemas, and, assuming a feature-based representation of the world, could be encoded in, and learned by, a two-layer feedforward network mapping between the object representation network and the schema network. Cooper & Glasspool (2001) have demonstrated that simple reinforcement learning can be used with such a representation to learn triggering functions of basic-level schemas. Whether these putative mechanisms can be extended to account for learning of complete schema hierarchies remains to be demonstrated.

CONCLUSION

The problem of action control is far from trivial. It requires the integration of endogenous constraints (including an agent's goals or intentions, the availability of an agent's effectors, and agent-specific preferences for particular action orderings), exogenous constraints (most notably from the structure of the environment) and task constraints (e.g. preconditions that must be achieved before an action can be carried out). This chapter has presented an interactive activation model of routine action selection that is capable of integrating these constraints in the generation of routine yet flexible behaviour.

The model also provides a qualitative account of many of the errors observed in everyday routine action, both in normals and in several classes of neurologically impaired individuals. Thus, the model can account for "absent-mindedness", as well as aspects of action disorganization syndrome, utilization behaviour, ideational apraxia, amphetamine psychosis, and Parkinsonism. These strengths justify further development of the model, especially in areas such as the representation of goals and the transfer of behaviour from controlled to automatic modes of functioning.

ACKNOWLEDGEMENTS

I am grateful to Tim Shallice, Myrna Schwartz, Stephanie Warrick, and Peter Yule for extensive discussion of the model presented here. Preparation of the chapter was assisted by grants from the US National Institutes of Health (#R01 NS31824–05) to Myrna Schwartz and from the Royal Society (RSRG 20546) to Richard Cooper.

Notes

1. The theory of Schneider and colleagues is embodied in a number of models, but none of these relate to routine action. The Meyer & Kieras theory is embodied in a model of the psychological refractory period task, but again has not been applied to routine action. The only other current model of routine action, that

of Botvinick & Plaut (2002), is not obviously identifiable with any of the above theories. The Botvinick & Plaut model is discussed further in the General Discussion.

2.   Although this approach to schema competition is adequate, it is not ideal. Cooper et al. (in press) employ a conceptually simpler definition within a revised version of the model.

3.   In a complete implementation (i.e. one that included the SAS) this excitation would come from the SAS.

4.   Note that the subtasks in Fig. 10.4 are performed in a different order to those in Fig. 10.2. However, neither order violates any task constraints.

REFERENCES

Anderson, J. R., & Lebiere, C. (1998). *The atomic components of thought*. Mahwah, NJ: Lawrence Erlbaum Associates, Inc.

Botvinick, M., & Plaut, D. C. (2002). Representing task context: Proposals based on a connectionist model of action. *Psychological Research, 66*, 298–311.

Bloxham, C. A., Mindel, T. A., & Frith, C. D. (1984). Initiation and execution of predictable and unpredictable movements in Parkinson's disease. *Brain, 107*, 371–384.

Cooper, R. P. (1998). Visual dominance and the control of action. In M. A. Gernsbacher, & S. J. Derry (Eds.), *Proceedings of the 20th Annual Conference of the Cognitive Science Society* (pp. 250–255). Madison, WI: Cognitive Science Society Incorporated.

Cooper, R. P. (2002). Order and disorder in everyday action: The roles of contention scheduling and supervisory attention. *Neurocase, 8*, 61–79.

Cooper, R. P., Fox, J., Farringdon, J., & Shallice, T. (1996). A systematic methodology for cognitive modelling. *Artificial Intelligence, 85*, 3–44.

Cooper, R. P. & Glasspool, D. W. (2001). Learning action affordances and action schemas. In R. M. French, & J. Sougné (Eds.), *Connectionist models of learning, development and evolution* (pp. 133–142). London: Springer-Verlag.

Cooper, R. P., Schwartz, M. F., Yule, P., & Shallice, T. (in press). The simulation of action disorganisation in complex activities of daily living. *Cognitive Neuropsychology*.

Cooper, R. P., & Shallice, T. (2000). Contention scheduling and the control of routine activities. *Cognitive Neuropsychology, 17*, 297–338.

Cooper, R. P., Shallice, T., & Farringdon, J. (1995). Symbolic and continuous processes in the automatic selection of actions. In J. Hallam (Ed.), *Hybrid problems, hybrid solutions* (pp. 27–37). Amsterdam: IOS Press.

De Renzi, E., & Lucchelli, F. (1988). Ideational apraxia. *Brain, 111*, 1173–1188.

Detweiler, M., & Schneider, W. (1991). Modelling the acquisition of dual-task skill in a connectionist/control architecture. In D. L. Damos (Ed.), *Multiple-task performance* (pp. 69–99). London: Taylor & Francis.

Elman, J. L. (1990). Finding structure in time. *Cognitive Science, 14*, 179–211.

Glasspool, D. W. (1998). *Modelling serial order in behaviour: Studies of spelling*. Unpublished PhD Thesis, Department of Psychology, University College London.

Hartley, T., & Houghton, G. (1996). A linguistically constrained model of short-term memory for nonwords. *Journal of Memory and Language, 35*, 1–31.

Hinton, G. E., & Plaut, D. C. (1987). Using fast weights to deblur old memories. In *Proceedings of the 9th Annual Conference of the Cognitive Science Society* (pp. 177–186). Seattle, WA: Cognitive Science Society Incorporated.

Houghton, G. (1990). The problem of serial order: A neural network model of sequence learning and recall. In R. Dale, C. Mellish, & M. Zock (Eds.), *Current research in natural language generation* (Ch. 11, pp. 287–319). London: Academic Press.

Houghton, G., Glasspool, D. W., & Shallice, T. (1994). Spelling and serial recall: Insights from a competitive queuing model. In G. D. A. Brown, & N. C. Ellis (Eds.), *Handbook of spelling: Theory, process and intervention* (pp. 365–404). Chichester: Wiley.

Houghton, G., & Hartley, T. (1996). Parallel models of serial behaviour: Lashley revisited. *PSYCHE, 2,* 25.

Humphreys, G. W., & Forde, E. M. E. (1998). Disordered action schema and action disorganisation syndrome. *Cognitive Neuropsychology, 15,* 771–811.

Jahanshahi, M., Brown, R. G., & Marsden, C. D. (1992). Simple and choice reaction time and the use of advance information for motor preparation in Parkinson's disease. *Brain, 115,* 539–564.

Jordon, M. I. (1986). *Serial order: A parallel distributed processing approach.* Technical Report 8604, Institute for Cognitive Science, University of California at San Diego, CA.

Joseph, M. H., Frith, C. D., & Waddington, J. L. (1979). Dopaminergic mechanisms and cognitive deficits in schizophrenia: A neurobiological model. *Psychopharmacology, 63,* 273–280.

Kieras, D. E. & Meyer, D. E. (1997). A computational theory of executive cognitive processes and multiple-task performance: part 2. Accounts of the psychological refractory-period phenomenon. *Psychological Review, 104,* 749–791.

Lashley, K. (1951). The problem of serial order in behavior. In L. A. Jeffress (Ed.), *Cerebral mechanisms in behavior* (pp. 112–136). New York: Wiley.

Lhermitte, F. (1983). Utilisation behaviour and its relation to lesions of the frontal lobes. *Brain, 106,* 237–255.

Lyons, M., & Robbins, T. W. (1975). The action of central nervous system stimulant drugs: A general theory concerning amphetamine effects. In W. B. Essman, & L. Valzelli (Eds.), *Current developments in psychopharmacology* (pp. 80–163). New York: Spectrum Publications.

MacKay, D. G. (1985). A theory of the representation, organization and timing of action with implications for sequencing diosorders. In E. A. Roy (Ed.), *Neuropsychological studies of apraxia and related disorders* (pp. 267–308). Amsterdam: Elsevier Science/North Holland.

Maes, P. (1989). How to do the right thing. *Connection Science, 1,* 291–323.

McClelland, J. L. (1992). Toward a theory of information processing in graded, random, interactive networks. In D. E. Meyer, & S. Kornblum (Eds.), *Attention and performance, XIV* (pp. 655–688). Cambridge, MA: MIT Press.

McClelland, J. L., & Rumelhart, D. E. (1981). An interactive activation model of context effects in letter perception: Part 1. An account of basic findings. *Psychological Review, 88,* 375–407.

Meyer, D. E., & Kieras, D. E. (1997). A computational theory of executive cognitive processes and multiple-task performance: part 1. Basic Mechanisms. *Psychological Review, 104,* 3–65.

Newell, A. (1990). *Unified theories of cognition.* Harvard: Harvard University Press.

Norman, D. A. (1981). Categorization of action slips. *Psychological Review, 88,* 1–15.

Norman, D. A., & Shallice, T. (1980). *Attention to action: Willed and automatic control of behavior.* Chip report 99, University of California, San Diego, CA.

Norman, D. A., & Shallice, T. (1986). Attention to action: Willed and automatic control of behavior. In R. Davidson, G. Schwartz, & D. Shapiro (Eds.), *Consciousness and self regulation: Advances in research and theory* (Vol. 4, pp. 1–18). New York: Plenum.

Randrup, A., & Munkvad, I. (1967). Evidence indicating an association between schizophrenia and dopaminergic hyperactivity in the brain. *Orthomolecular Psychiatry, 1,* 2–7.

Reason, J. T. (1979). Actions not as planned: The price of automatization. In G. Underwood, & R. Stevens (Eds.), *Aspects of consciousness* (Ch. 4, pp. 67–89). London: Academic Press.

Reason, J. T. (1984). Lapses of attention in everyday life. In W. Parasuraman, & R. Davies (Eds.), *Varieties of attention* (Ch. 14, pp. 515–549). Orlando, FL: Academic Press.

Robbins, T. W. (1982). Sterotypies: Addictions or fragmented actions? *Bulletin of the British Psychological Society, 35,* 297–300.

Robbins, T. W., & Sahakian, B. J. (1983). Behavioural effects of psychomotor stimulant drugs: Clinical and neuropsychological implications. In I. Creese (Ed.), *Stimulants: Neurochemical, behavioural, and clinical perspectives,* New York: Raven, 301–338.

Rumelhart, D. E., & Norman, D. A. (1982). Simulating a skilled typist: A study of skilled cognitive-motor performance. *Cognitive Science, 6,* 1–36.

Schneider, W., & Detweiler, M. (1987). A connectionist/control architecture for working memory. In G. H. Bower (Ed.), *The psychology of learning and motivation* (pp. 53–119). Orlando, FL: Academic Press.

Schneider, W., & Fisk, A. D. (1982). Concurrent automatic and controlled visual search: Can processing occur without resource cost? *Journal of Experimental Psychology: Learning, Memory and Cognition, 8,* 261–278.

Schneider, W., & Oliver, W. L. (1991). An instructable connectionist/control architecture: Using rule-based instruction to accomplish connectionist learning in a human time scale. In K. Van Lehn, (Ed.), *Architectures for intelligence* (Ch. 5, pp. 113–145). Hove, UK: Lawrence Erlbaum Associates.

Schneider, W., & Shiffrin, R. M. (1977). Controlled and automatic human information processing. I: Detection, search and attention. *Psychological Review, 84,* 1–66.

Schwartz, M. F., Montgomery, M. W., Buxbaum, L. J., Lee, S. S., Carew, T. G., Coslett, H. B., Ferraro, M., Fitzpatrick-De Salme, E. J., Hart, T., & Mayer, N. H. (1998). Naturalistic action impairment in closed head injury. *Neuropsychology, 12,* 13–28.

Schwartz, M. F., Montgomery, M. W., Fitzpatrick-De Salme, E. J., Ochipa, C., Coslett, H. B., & Mayer, N. H. (1995). Analysis of a disorder of everyday action. *Cognitive Neuropsychology, 12,* 863–892.

Schwartz, M. F., Reed, E. S., Montgomery, M. W., Palmer, C., & Mayer, N. H. (1991). The quantitative description of action disorganisation after brain damage: A case study. *Cognitive Neuropsychology, 8,* 381–414.

Shallice, T. (1972). Dual functions of consciousness. *Psychological Review, 79,* 383–393.

Shallice, T. (1994). Multiple levels of control processes. In C. Umilta, & M. Moscovitch (Eds.), *Attention and performance, XV: Conscious and nonconscious information processing* (pp. 395–420). Cambridge, MA: MIT Press.

Shallice, T., & Burgess, P. W. (1991). Deficits in strategy application following frontal lobe lesions. *Brain, 114,* 727–741.

Shallice, T., & Burgess, P. (1996). The domain of supervisory processes and temporal organization of behaviour. *Philosophical Transactions of the Royal Society of London, B351,* 1405–1412.

Shallice, T., Burgess, P. W., Schon, F., & Baxter, D. M. (1989). The origins of utilisation behaviour. *Brain, 112,* 1587–1598.

Shallice, T., Glasspool, D. W., & Houghton, G. (1995). Can neuropsychological evidence inform connectionist modelling? Analyses of spelling. *Language and Cognitive Processes, 10,* 195–225.

Shedden, J. M., & Schneider, W. (1990). A connectionist model of attentional enhancement and signal buffering. In *Proceedings of the 12th Annual Conference of the Cognitive Science Society* (pp. 566–573). Cambridge, MA: Cognitive Science Society Incorporated.

Sheridan, M. R., Flowers, K. A., & Hurrell, J. (1987). Programming and execution of movements in Parkinson's disease. *Brain, 110,* 1247–1271.

Shiffrin, R. M., & Schneider, W. (1977). Controlled and automatic human information processing. II: Perceptual learning, automatic attending and a general theory. *Psychological Review, 84,* 127–190.

Shiffrin, R. M., & Schneider, W. (1984). Automatic and controlled processing revisited. *Psychological Review, 91,* 269–276.

SECTION FOUR

Language processes

CHAPTER ELEVEN

Integrating multiple cues in language acquisition: A computational study of early infant speech segmentation

Morten H. Christiansen and Suzanne Curtin
Cornell University, Ithaca, NY, and University of Pittsburgh, PA, USA

INTRODUCTION

Considerable research in language acquisition has addressed the extent to which basic aspects of linguistic structure might be identified on the basis of probabilistic cues in caregiver speech to children. In this chapter, we examine systems that have the capacity to extract and store various statistical properties of language. In particular, groups of overlapping, partially predictive cues are increasingly attested in research on language development (e.g. Morgan & Demuth, 1996). Such cues tend to be probabilistic and violable, rather than categorical or rule-governed. Importantly, these systems incorporate mechanisms for integrating different sources of information, including cues that may not be very informative when considered in isolation. We explore the idea that conjunctions of these cues provide evidence about aspects of linguistic structure that is not available from any single source of information, and that this process of integration reduces the potential for making false generalizations. Thus, we argue that there are mechanisms for efficiently combining cues of even very low validity, that such combinations of cues are the source of evidence about aspects of linguistic structure that would be opaque to a system insensitive to such combinations, and that these mechanisms are used by children acquiring languages (for a similar view, see Bates & MacWhinney, 1987). These mechanisms also play a role in skilled language comprehension and are the focus of so-called "constraint-based" theories of sentence processing (Cottrell, 1989; MacDonald, Pearlmutter, &

Seidenberg, 1994; Trueswell & Tanenhaus, 1994) that emphasize the use of probabilistic sources of information in the service of computing linguistic representations. Since the learners of a language grow up to use it, investigating these mechanisms provides a link between language learning and language processing (Seidenberg, 1997).

In the standard learnability approach, language acquisition is viewed in terms of the task of acquiring a grammar (e.g. Gold, 1967; Pinker, 1994). This type of learning mechanism presents classic learnability issues: there are aspects of language for which the input is thought to provide no evidence, and the evidence that does exist tends to be unreliable. Following Christiansen, Allen, & Seidenberg (1998), we propose an alternative view in which language acquisition can be seen as involving several simultaneous tasks. The *primary* task—the language learner's goal—is to comprehend the utterances to which he/she is exposed for the purpose of achieving specific outcomes. In the service of this goal, the child attends to the linguistic input, picking up different kinds of information, subject to perceptual and attentional constraints. There is a growing body of evidence that, as a result of attending to sequential stimuli, both adults and children incidentally encode statistically salient regularities of the signal (e.g. Cleeremans, 1993; Saffran, Aslin, & Newport, 1996; Saffran, Newport, & Aslin, 1996). The child's *immediate task*, then, is to update its representation of these statistical aspects of language. Our claim is that knowledge of other, more covert aspects of language is derived as a result of how these representations are combined through multiple-cue integration. Linguistically relevant units (e.g. words, phrases, and clauses), emerge from statistical computations over the regularities induced via the immediate task. On this view, the acquisition of knowledge about linguistic structures that are not explicitly marked in the speech signal—on the basis of information, that is—can be seen as a third *derived task*. We address these issues in the specific context of learning to identify individual words in speech. In the research reported below, the immediate task is to encode statistical regularities concerning phonology, lexical stress, and utterance boundaries. The derived task is to integrate these regularities in order to identify the boundaries between words in speech.

The remainder of this chapter presents our work on the modelling of early infant speech segmentation in connectionist networks trained to integrate multiple probabilistic cues. We first describe past work exploring the segmentation abilities of our model (Allen & Christiansen, 1996; Christiansen, 1998; Christiansen et al., 1998). Although we concentrate here on the relevance of combinatorial information to this specific aspect of acquisition, our view is that similar mechanisms are likely to be relevant to other aspects of acquisition and skilled performance. Next, we present results from two new sets of simulations.[1]

The first simulation involves a corpus analysis inspired by the Christiansen et al. (1998) model, and which provides support for the advantage of integrating multiple cues in language acquisition. In the second simulation, we demonstrate the model's robustness in terms of dealing with noisy input beyond what other segmentation models have been shown capable of dealing with. Finally, we discuss how multiple-cue integration works and how this approach may be extended beyond speech segmentation.

THE SEGMENTATION PROBLEM

Before an infant can even start to learn how to comprehend a spoken utterance, the speech signal must first be segmented into words. Thus, one of the initial tasks confronting the child when embarking on language acquisition involves breaking the continuous speech stream into individual words. Discovering word boundaries is a nontrivial problem, as there are no acoustic correlates in fluent speech to the white spaces that separate words in written text. There are, however, a number of sublexical cues that could potentially be integrated in order to discover word boundaries. The segmentation problem therefore provides an appropriate domain for assessing our approach, insofar as there are many cues to word boundaries, including prosodic and distributional information, none of which is sufficient for solving the task alone.

Early models of spoken language processing assumed that word segmentation occurs as a by-product of lexical identification (e.g. Cole & Jakimik, 1978; Marslen-Wilson & Welsh, 1978). More recent accounts hold that adults use segmentation procedures in addition to lexical knowledge (Cutler, 1996). These procedures are likely to differ across languages, and presumably include a variety of sublexical skills. For example, adults tend to make consistent judgements about possible legal sound combinations that could occur in their native language (Greenburg & Jenkins, 1964). This type of phonotactic knowledge may aid in adult segmentation procedures (Jusczyk, 1993). Additionally, evidence from perceptual studies suggests that adults know about and utilize language-specific rhythmic segmentation procedures in processing utterances (Cutler, 1994).

The assumption that children are not born with the knowledge sources that appear to subserve segmentation processes in adults seems reasonable, since they have neither a lexicon nor knowledge of the phonological or rhythmic regularities underlying the words of the particular language being learned. Therefore, one important developmental question concerns how the child comes to achieve steady-state adult behaviour. Intuitively, one might posit that children begin to build their lexicon by hearing words in isolation. A single word strategy, whereby children adopt entire utterances as lexical candidates, would appear to be viable very early in acquisition. In the Bernstein-Ratner (1987) and the Korman (1984) corpora, 22–30% of child-directed utterances are made up of single words. However, many words, such as determiners, will never occur in isolation. Moreover, this strategy is hopelessly underpowered in the face of the increasing size of utterances directed toward infants as they develop. Instead, the child must develop viable strategies that will allow him/her to detect utterance–internal word boundaries, regardless of whether or not the words appear in isolation. A more realistic suggestion is that a bottom-up process, exploiting sublexical units, allows the child to bootstrap the segmentation process. This bottom-up mechanism must be flexible enough to function despite cross-linguistic variation in the constellation of cues relevant for the word segmentation task.

Strategies based on prosodic cues (including pauses, segmental lengthening, metrical patterns, and intonation contour) have also been proposed as a way of detecting word boundaries (Cooper & Paccia-Cooper, 1980; Gleitman, Gleitman, Landau, & Wanner, 1988). Other recent proposals have focused on the statistical properties of the target language that might be utilized in early segmentation. Considerable attention has been given to lexical stress and sequential phonological regularities—two cues also utilized in the Christiansen et al. (1998) segmentation model. In particular, Cutler and her colleagues (e.g. Cutler & Mehler, 1993) have emphasized the potential importance of rhythmic strategies to segmentation. They have suggested that skewed stress patterns (e.g. the majority of words in English have strong initial syllables) play a central role in allowing children to identify likely boundaries. Evidence from speech production and perception studies with preverbal infants supports the claim that infants are sensitive to rhythmic structure and its relationship to lexical segmentation by 9 months (Jusczyk, Cutler & Redanz, 1993). A potentially relevant source of information for determining word boundaries is the phonological regularities of the target language. A study by Jusczyk, Friederici, & Svenkerud (1993) suggests that between 6 and 9 months, infants develop knowledge of phonotactic regularities in their language. Furthermore, there is evidence that both children and adults are sensitive to, and can utilize, such information to segment the speech stream. Work by Saffran, Newport, & Aslin (1996) show that adults are able to use phonotactic sequencing to differentiate between possible and impossible words in an artificial language after only 20 minutes of exposure. They suggest that learners may be computing the transitional probabilities between sounds in the input and using the strengths of these probabilities to hypothesize possible word boundaries. Further research provides evidence that infants as young as 8 months show the same type of sensitivity after only 3 minutes of exposure (Saffran, Aslin, & Newport, 1996). Thus, children appear to have sensitivity to the statistical regularities of potentially informative sublexical properties of their languages, such as stress and phonotactics, consistent with the hypothesis that these cues could play a role in bootstrapping segmentation. The issue of when infants are sensitive to particular cues, and how strong a particular cue is to word boundaries, has been addressed by Mattys, Jusczyk, Luce, & Morgan (1999). They examined how infants would respond to conflicting information about word boundaries. Specifically, Mattys et al. (experiment 4) found that when sequences which had good prosodic information but poor phonotactic cues were tested against sequences that had poor prosodic but good phonotactic cues, the 9 month-old infants gave greater weight to the prosodic information. Nonetheless, the integration of these cues could potentially provide reliable segmentation information, since phonotactic and prosodic information typically align with word boundaries, thus strengthening the boundary information.

Segmenting using multiple cues

The input to the process of language acquisition comprises a complex combination of multiple sources of information. Clusters of such information sources appear to inform the learning of various linguistic tasks (see contributions in Morgan & Demuth, 1996). Each individual source of information, or *cue*, is only partially reliable with respect to the particular task in question. In addition to previously mentioned cues—phonotactics and lexical stress—utterance boundary information has also been hypothesized to provide useful information for locating word boundaries (Aslin et al., 1996; Brent & Cartwright, 1996). These three sources of information provide the learner with cues to segmentation. As an example, consider the two unsegmented utterances (represented in orthographic format):

> *Therearenospacesbetweenwordsinfluentspeech#*
> *Yeteachchildseemstograspthebasicsquickly#*

There are sequential regularities found in the phonology (here represented as orthography) which can aid in determining where words may begin or end. The consonant cluster *sp* can be found both at word beginnings (*spaces* and *speech*) and at word endings (*grasp*). However, a language learner cannot rely solely on such information to detect possible word boundaries. This is evident when considering that the *sp* consonant cluster also can straddle a word boundary, as in *cats pyjamas*, and occur word-internally, as in *respect*.

Lexical stress is another useful cue to word boundaries. For example, in English most bisyllabic words have a trochaic stress pattern with a strongly stressed syllable followed by a weakly stressed syllable. The two utterances above include four such words: *spaces*, *fluent*, *basics*, and *quickly*. Word boundaries can thus be postulated following a weak syllable. However, this source of information is only partially reliable, as is illustrated by the iambic stress pattern found in the word *between* from the above example.

The pauses at the end of utterances (indicated above by #) also provide useful information for the segmentation task. If children realize that sound sequences occurring at the end of an utterance always form the end of a word, then they can utilize information about utterance final phonological sequences to postulate word boundaries whenever these sequences occur *inside* an utterance. Thus, knowledge of the rhyme *eech#* from the first example utterance can be used to postulate a word boundary after the similar sounding sequence *each* in the second utterance. As with phonological regularities and lexical stress, utterance boundary information cannot be used as the only source of information about word boundaries, because some words, such as determiners, rarely, if ever, occur at the end of an utterance. This suggests that information extracted from clusters of cues may be used by the language learner to acquire the knowledge necessary to perform the task at hand.

A COMPUTATIONAL MODEL OF MULTIPLE-CUE INTEGRATION IN SPEECH SEGMENTATION

Several computational models of word segmentation have been implemented to address the speech segmentation problem. However, these models tend to exploit solitary sources of information, e.g. Cairns, Shillcock, Chater, & Levy (1997) demonstrated that sequential phonotactic structure was a salient cue to word boundaries, while Aslin, Woodward, LaMendola, & Bever (1996) illustrated that a back-propagation model could identify word boundaries fairly accurately, based on utterance final patterns. Perruchet & Vinter (1998) demonstrated that a memory-based model was able to segment small artificial languages, such as the one used in Saffran, Aslin, & Newport (1996), given phonological input in syllabic format. More recently, Dominey & Ramus (2000) found that recurrent networks also show sensitivity to serial and temporal structure in similar miniature languages. On the other hand, Brent & Cartwright (1996) have shown that segmentation performance can be improved when a statistically-based algorithm is provided with phonotactic rules in addition to utterance boundary information. Along similar lines, Allen & Christiansen (1996) found that the integration of information about phonological sequences and the presence of utterance boundaries improved the segmentation of a small artificial language. Based on this work, we suggest that the integration of multiple probabilistic cues may hold the key to solving the word segmentation problem, and discuss a computational model that implements this solution.

Christiansen et al. (1998) provided a comprehensive computational model of multiple-cue integration in early infant speech segmentation. They employed a simple recurrent network (SRN; Elman, 1990), as illustrated in Fig. 11.1. This network is essentially a standard feedforward network equipped with an extra layer of so-called context units. At a particular time

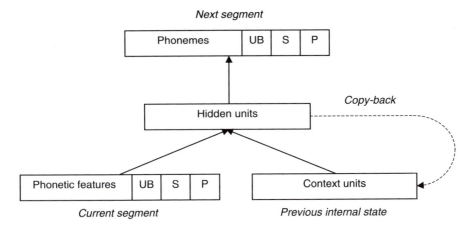

Figure 11.1. Illustration of the SRN used in Christiansen et al. (1998). Arrows with solid lines indicate trainable weights, whereas the arrow with the dashed line denotes the copy-back weights (which are always 1). UB refers to the unit coding for the presence of an utterance boundary. The presence of lexical stress is represented in terms of two units, S and P, coding for secondary and primary stress, respectively. Adapted from Christiansen et al. (1998).

step, *t*, an input pattern is propagated through the hidden unit layer to the output layer (solid arrows). At the next time step, *t* + 1, the activation of the hidden unit layer at the previous time step, *t*, is copied back to the context layer (dashed arrow) and paired with the current input (solid arrow). This means that the current state of the hidden units can influence the processing of subsequent inputs, providing a limited ability to deal with integrated sequences of input presented successively.

The SRN model was trained on a *single* pass through a corpus consisting of 8181 utterances of child-directed speech. These utterances were extracted from the Korman (1984) corpus (a part of the CHILDES database; MacWhinney, 2000) consisting of speech directed at preverbal infants aged 6–16 weeks. The training corpus consisted of 24,648 words distributed over 814 word types and had an average utterance length of 3.0 words (see Christiansen et al., 1998, for further details). A separate corpus, consisting of 927 utterances and with the same statistical properties as the training corpus, was used for testing. Each word in the utterances was transformed from its orthographic format into a phonological form and lexical stress was assigned using a dictionary compiled from the MRC Psycholinguistic Database, available from the Oxford Text Archive.[2]

As input, the network was provided with different combinations of three cues, dependent on the training condition. The cues were: (a) phonology, represented in terms of 11 features on the input and 36 phonemes on the output;[3] (b) utterance boundary information, represented as an extra feature

(UB) marking utterance endings; and (c) lexical stress, coded over two units as either no stress, secondary or primary stress (see Figure 11.1). The network was trained on the *immediate task* of predicting the next phoneme in a sequence, as well as the appropriate values for the utterance boundary and stress units. In learning to perform this task, it was expected that the network would also learn to integrate the cues such that it could carry out the *derived task* of segmenting the input into words.

With respect to the network, the logic behind the derived task is that the end of an utterance is also the end of a word. If the network is able to integrate the provided cues in order to activate the boundary unit at the ends of words occurring at the end of an utterance, it should also be able to generalize this knowledge so as to activate the boundary unit at the ends of words which occur *inside* an utterance (Aslin et al., 1996). Fig. 11.2 shows a snapshot of SRN segmentation performance on the first 37 phoneme tokens in the training corpus. Activation of the boundary unit at a particular position corresponds to the network's hypothesis that a boundary follows this phoneme. Black bars indicate the activation at lexical boundaries, whereas the grey bars correspond to activation at word internal positions. Activations above the mean boundary unit activation for the corpus as a whole (horizontal line) are interpreted as the postulation of a word boundary. As can be seen from the figure, the SRN performed well on this part of the training set, correctly segmenting out all of the 12 words save one (/slipI/ = *sleepy*).

In order to provide a more quantitative measure of performance, accuracy

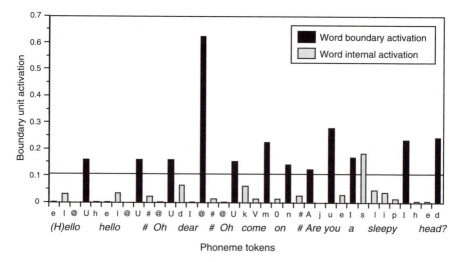

Figure 11.2.   The activation of the boundary unit during the processing of the first 37 phoneme tokens in the Christiansen et al. (1998) training corpus. A gloss of the input utterances is found beneath the input phoneme tokens. Adapted from Christiansen et al. (1998).

and completeness scores (Brent & Cartwright, 1996) were calculated for the separate test corpus, consisting of utterances not seen during training:

$$Accuracy = \frac{Hits}{Hits + FalseAlarms}$$

$$Completeness = \frac{Hits}{Hits + Misses}$$

Accuracy provides a measure of how many of the words the network postulated were actual words, whereas completeness provides a measure of how many of the actual words the net discovered. Consider the following hypothetical example:

$$\# t h e \# d o g \# s \# c h a s e \# t h e c \# a t \#$$

where # corresponds to a predicted word boundary. Here, the hypothetical learner correctly segmented out two words, *the* and *chase*, but also falsely segmented out *dog, s, thec*, and *at*, thus missing the words *dogs, the*, and *cat*. This results in an accuracy of $\frac{2}{2+4} = 33.3\%$ and a completeness of $\frac{2}{2+3} = 40.0\%$.

With these measures in hand, we compared the performance of nets trained using phonology and utterance boundary information—with or without the lexical stress cue—to demonstrate the advantage of getting an extra cue. As illustrated by Fig. 11.3, the phon-ub-stress network was significantly more accurate (42.71% vs. 38.67%) and had a significantly higher completeness score (44.87% vs. 40.97%) than the phon-ub network. These results thus demonstrate that having to integrate the additional stress cue with the phonology and utterance boundary cues during learning provides for better performance.

To test the generalization abilities of the networks, segmentation performance was recorded on the task of correctly segmenting novel words. The three-cue net was able to segment 23 of the 50 novel words, whereas the two-cue network was only able to segment 11 novel words. Thus, the phon-ub-stress network achieved a word completeness of 46%, which was significantly better than the 22% completeness obtained by the phon-ub net. These results therefore support the supposition that the integration of three cues promotes better generalization than the integration of two cues. Furthermore, the three-cue net also developed a trochaic bias, and was nearly twice as good at segmenting out novel bisyllabic words with a trochaic stress pattern in comparison to novel words with an iambic stress pattern.

Overall, the simulation results from Christiansen et al. (1998) show that the integration of probabilistic cues forces the networks to develop representations that allow them to perform quite reliably on the task of detecting

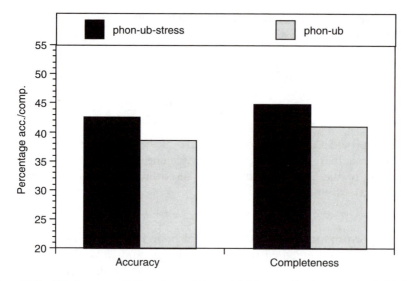

Figure 11.3. Word accuracy (left) and completeness (right) scores for the net trained with three cues (phon-ub-stress; black bars) and the net trained with two cues (phon-ub; grey bars).

word boundaries in the speech stream.[4] This result is encouraging, given that the segmentation task shares many properties with other language acquisition problems that have been taken to require innate linguistic knowledge for their solution, and yet it seems clear that discovering the words of one's native language must be an acquired skill. The simulations also demonstrated how a trochaic stress bias could emerge from the statistics in the input, without having anything like the "periodicity bias" of Cutler & Mehler (1993) built in. Below, in our first simulation, we present a corpus analysis that sheds further light on how the integration of the cues provided by lexical stress and phonology may change the representational landscape to facilitate distributional learning.

SIMULATION 1: STRESS CHANGES THE REPRESENTATIONAL LANDSCAPE

Rhythm is a property of the speech stream to which infants are sensitive at a very young age (Jusczyk, 1997; Morgan & Saffran, 1995; Nazzi, Bertoncini, & Mehler, 1998). Infant research has shown that at age 1–4 months infants are sensitive to changes in stress patterns (Jusczyk & Thompson, 1978). Moreover, English infants have a trochaic bias at age 9 months, yet this preference does not appear to exist at 6 months (Jusczyk, Cutler, & Redanz, 1993), suggesting that at some point during age 6–9 months, infants begin to orientate to the predominant stress pattern of the language. One possible assumption is that the infant has a rule-like representation of stress that assigns a trochaic pattern to syllables, allowing the infant to take advantage of lexical stress information in the segmentation of speech.

Arguments supporting the acquisition of stress rules are based on child production data that show systematic stages of development across languages and children (Demuth & Fee, 1995; Fikkert, 1994). The consistent nature of stress development supports the postulation of rules in order to account for the production data (Hochberg, 1988). However, the question remains as to what extent this data provides insight into early acquisition processes. We believe that, by drawing on the perceptual and distributional learning abilities of infants, an alternative account emerges, establishing a basis for constraints on stress assignment. We present a corpus analysis investigating how lexical stress may contribute to statistical learning and how this information can help infants group syllables into coherent word units. The results suggest that infants need not posit rules to perform these tasks.

Infants' sensitivity to the distributional (Saffran, Aslin, & Newport, 1996) and stress-related (Jusczyk & Thompson, 1978) properties of language suggests that infants' exposure to syllables that differ in their acoustic properties (i.e. for lexical stress: the change in duration, amplitude, and pitch) may result in differing perceptions of these syllable types. We propose that infants' perceptual differentiation of stressed and unstressed syllables results in a *representational* differentiation of the two types of syllables. This means that the same syllable will be represented differently, depending on whether it is stressed or unstressed. Lexical stress thus changes the representational landscape over which the infants carry out their distributional analysis, and we employ a corpus analysis to demonstrate how this can facilitate the task of speech segmentation.

Simulation details

We used the Korman (1984) corpus that Christiansen et al. (1998) had transformed into a phonologically transcribed corpus with indications of lexical stress. Their training corpus forms the basis for our analyses.[5] We used a whole-syllable representation to simplify our analysis, whereas Christiansen et al. used single phoneme representations.

All 258 bisyllabic words were extracted from the corpus. For each bisyllabic word we created two bisyllabic nonwords. One consisted of the last syllable of the previous word (which could be a monosyllabic word) and the first syllable of the bisyllabic word, and one of the second syllables of the bisyllabic word and the first syllable of the following word (which could be a monosyllabic word). For example, for the bisyllabic word /slipI/ in /A ju eI slipI hed/, we would record the bisyllables /eIsli/ and /pIhed/. We did not record bisyllabic nonwords that straddled an utterance boundary, as they are not likely to be perceived as a unit. Three bisyllabic words occurred only as single word utterances, and, as a consequence, had no corresponding non-words. These were therefore omitted from further analysis. For each of the remaining 255 bisyllabic words, we randomly selected a single bisyllabic non-word for a pairwise comparison with the bisyllabic word. Two versions of the 255 word–nonword pairs were created. In one version, the *stress condition*, lexical stress was encoded by adding the level of stress (0–2) to the representation of a syllable (e.g. /sli/ → /sli2/). This allows for differences in the representations of stressed and unstressed syllables consisting of the same phonemes. In the second version, the *no-stress condition*, no indication of stress was included in the syllable representations.

Our hypothesis suggests that lexical stress changes the basic representational landscape over which infants carry out their statistical analyses in early speech segmentation. To operationalize this suggestion, we have chosen to use mutual information (MI) as the dependent measure in our analyses. MI is calculated as:

$$MI = \log\left(\frac{P(X, Y)}{P(X)P(Y)}\right)$$

and provides an information theoretical measure of how significant it is that two elements, X and Y, occur together given their individual probabilities of occurrence. Simplifying somewhat, we can use *MI* to provide a measure of how strongly two syllables form a bisyllabic unit. If *MI* is positive, the two syllables form a strong unit: a good candidate for a bisyllabic word. If, on the other hand, *MI* is negative, the two syllables form an improbable candidate for a bisyllabic word. Such information could be used by a learner to inform the process of deciding which syllables form coherent units in the speech stream.

Results

The first analysis aimed at investigating whether the addition of lexical stress significantly alters the representational landscape. A pairwise comparison between the bisyllabic words in the two conditions showed that the addition of stress resulted in a significantly higher *MI* mean for the stress condition ($t(508) = 2.41, p < .02$)—see Table 11.1. Although the lack of stress in the no-stress condition resulted in a lower MI mean for the nonwords compared to the stress condition, this trend was not significant, $t(508) = 1.29, p > .19$. This analysis thus confirms our hypothesis, that lexical stress benefits the learner by changing the representational landscape in such a way as to provide more information that the learner can use in the task of segmenting speech.

The second analysis investigated whether the trochaic stress pattern provided any advantage over other stress patterns—in particular, the iambic stress pattern. Table 11.2 provides the *MI* means for words and nonwords for

TABLE 11.1
Mutual information means for words and
nonwords in the two stress conditions

Condition	Words	Nonwords
Stress	4.42	−0.11
No stress	3.79	−0.46

TABLE 11.2
Mutual information means for words and nonwords from the stress condition as a
function of stress pattern

Stress pattern	Words	Nonwords	No. of words
Trochaic	4.53	−0.11	209
Iambic	4.28	−0.04	40
Dual	1.30	−1.02	6

the bisyllabic items in the stress condition as a function of stress pattern. The trochaic stress pattern provides for the best separation of words from non-words, as indicated by the fact that this stress pattern has the largest difference between the *MI* means for words and nonwords. Although none of the differences were significant (save for the comparison between trochaic and dual[6] stressed words, $t(213) = 2.85$, $p < .006$), the results suggest that a system without any built-in bias towards trochaic stress nevertheless benefits from the existence of the abundance of such stress patterns in languages such as English. The results indicate that no prior bias is needed toward a trochaic stress pattern because the presence of lexical stress alters the representational landscape over which statistical analyses are done, such that simple distributional learning devices end up finding trochaic words easier to segment.

The segmentation model of Christiansen et al. (1998) was able to integrate the phonological and lexical stress cues so as to take advantage of the change in the representational landscape that their integration affords. No separate, built-in trochaic bias was needed. Instead, the integration of the three probabilistic cues—phonology, utterance boundary, and lexical stress information—within a single network allowed the trochaic bias to emerge through distributional learning. Of course, both the input to the Christiansen et al. model and the corpus analyses involved idealized representations of speech, abstracting away from the noisy input that a child is faced with in real speech. In the next simulation, we therefore explore the model's ability to segment speech when presented with more naturalistic input, and demonstrate that this type of statistical learning device can in fact cope with noisy input.

SIMULATION 2: COPING WITH CO-ARTICULATION

Ultimately, any model of speech segmentation must be able to deal with the high degree of variation that characterizes natural fluent speech. Our earlier work, as reported above (Allen & Christiansen, 1996; Christiansen, 1998; Christiansen et al., 1998) has established that SRNs constitute viable models of early speech segmentation. These models, like most other recent computational models of speech segmentation (e.g. Aslin et al., 1996; Brent, 1999; Brent & Cartwright, 1996; Perruchet & Vinter, 1998), were provided with idealized input. This is in part due to the use of corpora in which every instance of a word always has the same form (i.e. it is a so-called *citation form*). While this is a useful idealization, it abstracts away from the considerable variation in the speech input that a child is faced with in language acquisition. We therefore now present simulations involving a phonetically transcribed speech corpus that encoded the contextual variation of a word, more closely approximating natural speech. More specifically, we gleaned the adult utterances from the Carterette & Jones (1974) corpus—a part of the CHILDES database (MacWhinney, 2000). These utterances consist of informal speech among American college-aged adults.[7]

The goal of the current simulation is to establish whether the success of the word segmentation model discussed here is dependent on the use of the simplified citation form input. Comparisons are made between networks exposed to a corpus incorporating contextual variation (i.e. co-articulation) and networks exposed to a citation form version of the same corpus. If the SRN is to remain a viable model of word segmentation, no significant difference in performance should arise in these comparisons.

Simulation details

The network was provided with the three probabilistic cues, discussed in the previous sections, for possible integration in the segmentation task: (a) *phonology*, represented in terms of an 18 value feature geometry; (b) *lexical stress*, represented as a single separate feature indicating the presence of primary vowel stress; and (c) *utterance boundary information*, represented as a separate feature (UB) which was only activated when pauses occurred in the input.

The simulations involved two training conditions, depending on the nature of the training corpus. In the *co-articulation* condition, the SRN was trained on the phonetically transcribed UNIBET version of the Carterette & Jones (1974) corpus. This transcription did not include lexical stress—a cue that contributed significantly to successful SRN segmentation performance in Christiansen et al. (1998). However, lexical stress was indirectly encoded by the use of the reduced vowel *schwa* (/6/ in UNIBET), so we chose to encode all vowels save the *schwa* as bearing primary stress.[8] Utterance boundaries were encoded whenever a pause was indicated in the transcript. In the *citation form* condition, the SRN was trained on a corpus generated by replacing each word in the orthographic version of the Carterette & Jones corpus with a phonological citation form derived via the Carnegie-Mellon Pronouncing Dictionary (cmudict.0.4)—a machine-readable pronunciation dictionary of North American English which includes lexical stress information. This procedure was similar to the one used to generate training corpora for the models reported in Christiansen et al. (1998). These pronunciations were subsequently translated into UNIBET format. Four vowels which were weakly stressed according to the dictionary were replaced with the UNIBET *schwa* and encoded as stressless, whereas the other vowels were encoded as stressed. Whereas the phonetically transcribed version of the Carterette & Jones corpus included indications where pauses occurred within a single turn, the orthographic version did not include such indications. We therefore counted the number of pauses occurring in each turn in the phonetically transcribed version, and randomly inserted the same number of pauses into the appropriate turn in the citation form version of the corpus.[9]

The overall corpus consisted of 1597 utterances, comprising 11,518 words. Test corpora were constructed by setting aside 10% of the utterances (the same utterances in both training conditions). Thus, the training corpora consisted of 1438 utterances (10,371 words) and the test corpora of 159 utterances (1147 words). In order to provide for more accurate test comparisons between the SRNs trained under the two conditions, utterance boundaries were inserted by hand in the citation form test corpus in the exact same places as found in the co-articulation test corpus. The networks in both training conditions were trained on two passes through their respective training corpus, corresponding to 74,746 sets of weight updates. Identical learning parameters were used in the two training conditions (learning rate: .1; momentum: .95) and the two nets were given the same initial weight randomization within the interval [−.2, .2].

Results

In this simulation, we investigated whether the SRN model of early segmentation could perform as well in the co-articulation condition as in the citation form condition. Fig. 11.4 shows the accuracy and completeness scores for the two networks. The co-articulation SRN obtained an accuracy of 25.27% and a completeness of 37.05%. The citation form SRN reached an accuracy of 24.33% and a completeness of 40.24%. There were no significant differences between the accuracy scores ($\chi^2 = 0.42, p > .9$) or the completeness scores ($\chi^2 = 2.46, p > .19$). Thus, the SRN model of word segmentation was able to cope

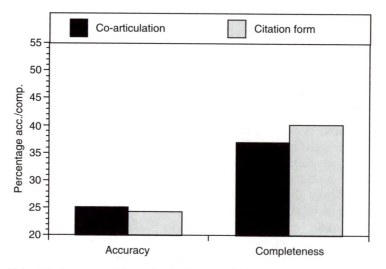

Figure 11.4. Word accuracy (left) and completeness (right) scores for the co-articulation net (black bars) and the citation form net (grey bars).

successfully with variation in the form of co-articulation, suggesting that it provides a good basis for discovering word boundaries in input that is closer to natural speech than the input used in previous computational models.

The results show that our model performs well on the segmentation task—despite being faced with input characterized by considerable variation. This outcome is important, because it demonstrates that the model provides a robust mechanism for the integration of multiple cues, whereas previous models have not been shown to be able to cope satisfactorily with co-articulation. For example, although the connectionist model by Cairns et al. (1997) was trained on a corpus of conversational speech, in which assimilation and vowel reduction had been introduced into the citation forms using a set of rewrite rules, it performed poorly in comparison with the present model (e.g. when pauses were included, their model discovered 32% of the *lexical* boundaries, whereas our model discovered 79% of the lexical boundaries). Our results suggest that connectionist networks provide a useful framework for investigating speech segmentation under less than ideal circumstances. In contrast, it is not clear that other computational frameworks can readily provide the basis for such investigations. For example, statistical optimization models, such as the DR algorithm (Brent & Cartwright, 1996) and the INCDROP model (Brent, 1999), use stored representations of previously encountered lexical units to segment subsequent input. Consequently, these models would end up storing several different phonological versions of the same word in the lexicon if presented with input incorporating co-articulation, as in the above simulation. Likewise, memory-based segmentation models, such as PARSER (Perruchet & Vinter, 1998), which segments out the longest section of the input that matches a stored unit, would also suffer from similar problems (although the frequency weights attached to such units may provide some relief).

Of course, there is much more to the variation in the speech stream than we have addressed here. For example, the input to our co-articulation nets varied in terms of the individual phonemes making up a word in different contexts, but in real speech co-articulation also often results in featural changes across several segments (e.g. the nasalization of the vowel segment in *can*). Future work must seek to bring the input to segmentation models closer to the actual variations found in fluent speech, and we have sought to take the first steps here.

GENERAL DISCUSSION

In this chapter, we have suggested that the integration of multiple probabilistic cues may be one of the key elements involved in children's acquisition of language. To support this suggestion, we have discussed the Christiansen et al. (1998) computational model of multiple-cue integration in early infant speech segmentation and presented results from three simulations that further underscore the viability of the approach. The corpus analysis in the first simulation showed how lexical stress changes the representational landscape to facilitate word segmentation over a distributional learning device incorporating multiple-cue integration. Previous results obtained from the Christiansen et al. model attest that this model is able to take advantage of such changes in the representational landscape. The second simulation demonstrated that the model is capable of dealing with noisy inputs that are more closely related to the kind of input to which children are exposed. Taken together, we find that the Christiansen et al. model, in combination with the simulations reported here, provide strong evidence in support of multiple-cue integration in language acquisition. In the final part of this chapter, we discuss two outstanding issues with respect to multiple-cue integration—how it works and how it can be extended beyond speech segmentation.

What makes multiple-cue integration work?

We have seen that integrating multiple probabilistic cues in a connectionist network results in more than just a sum of unreliable parts. But what is it about multiple-cue integration that facilitates learning? The answer appears to lie in the way in which multiple-cue integration can help constrain the search through weight space for a suitable set of weights for a given task (Christiansen, 1998; Christiansen et al., 1998). We can conceptualize the effect that the cue integration process has on learning by considering the

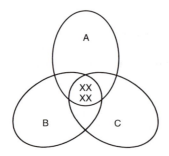

Figure 11.5. An abstract illustration of the reduction in weight configuration space that follows as a consequence of accommodating several partially overlapping cues within the same representational substrate. Adapted from Christiansen et al. (1998).

following illustration. In Fig. 11.5, each ellipse designates for a particular cue the set of weight configurations that will enable a network to learn the function denoted by that cue. For example, the ellipse marked A designates the set of weight configurations that allow for the learning of the function *A* described by the A cue. With respect to the simulations reported above, A, B, and C can be construed as the phonology, utterance boundary, and lexical stress cues, respectively.

If a network using gradient descent learning (e.g. the back-propagation learning algorithm) was only required to learn the regularities underlying, say, the A cue, it could settle on any of the weight configurations in the A set. However, if the net was also required to learn the regularities underlying cue B, it would have to find a weight configuration that would accommodate the regularities of both cues. The net would therefore have to settle on a set of weights from the intersection between A and B in order to minimize its error. This constrains the overall set of weight configurations that the net has to choose between—unless the cues are entirely overlapping (in which case there would not be any added benefit from learning this redundant cue) or are disjunct (in which case the net would not be able to find an appropriate weight configuration). If the net furthermore had to learn the regularities associated with the third cue, C, the available set of weight configurations would be constrained even further.

Turning to the engineering literature on neural networks, it is possible to provide a mathematical basis for the advantages of multiple-cue integration. Here multiple-cue integration is known as *"learning with hints"*, where hints provide additional information that can constrain the learning process (e.g. Abu-Mostafa, 1990; Omlin & Giles, 1992; Suddarth & Holden, 1991). The type of hints most relevant to the current discussion is the so-called *"catalyst hints"* type. This involves adding extra units to a network, such that additional correlated functions can be encoded (in much the same way as the lexical stress units encode a function correlated with the information provided by the phonological input with respect to the derived task of word segmentation). Thus, catalyst hints are introduced to reduce the overall weight configuration space that a network has to negotiate. This reduction is accomplished by forcing the network to acquire one or more additional related functions, encoded over extra output units. These units are often ignored after they have served their purpose during training (hence the name "catalyst" hint). The learning process is facilitated by catalyst hints because fewer weight configurations can accommodate both the original target function and the additional catalyst function(s). As a consequence of reducing the weight space, hints have been shown to constrain the problem of finding a suitable set of weights, promoting faster learning and better generalization.

Mathematical analyses in terms of the Vapnik-Chervonenkis (VC) dimension (Abu-Mostafa, 1993) and vector field analysis (Suddarth & Kergosien, 1991) have shown that learning with hints may reduce the number of hypotheses a learning system has to entertain. The VC dimension establishes an upper bound for the number of examples needed by a learning process that starts with a set of hypotheses about the task solution. A hint may lead to a reduction in the VC dimension by weeding out bad hypotheses, and reduce the number of examples needed to learn the solution. Vector field analysis uses a measure of "functional" entropy to estimate the overall probability for correct rule extraction from a trained network. The introduction of a hint may reduce the functional entropy, improving the probability of rule extraction. The results from this approach demonstrate that hints may constrain the number of possible hypotheses to entertain, and thus lead to faster convergence.

In sum, these mathematical analyses have revealed that the potential advantage of using multiple-cue integration in neural network training is twofold: First, the integration of multiple cues may reduce learning time by reducing the number of steps necessary to find an appropriate implementation of the target function. Second, multiple-cue integration may reduce the number of candidate functions for the target function being learned, thus potentially ensuring better generalization. As mentioned above, in neural networks this amounts to reducing the number of possible weight configurations that the learning algorithm has to choose between.[10] Thus, because the phonology, utterance boundary, and lexical stress cues designate functions that correlate with respect to the derived task of word segmentation in our simulations, the reduction in weight space not only results in a better representational basis for solving this task, but also leads to better learning and generalization. However, the mathematical analyses provide no guarantee that multiple-cue integration will necessarily improve performance. Nevertheless, this is unlikely to be a problem with respect to language acquisition because, as we shall see next, the input to children acquiring their first language is filled with cues that reflect important and informative aspects of linguistic structure.

Multiple-cue integration beyond word segmentation

Recent research in developmental psycholinguistics has shown that there is a variety of probabilistic cues available for language acquisition (for a review, see contributions in Morgan & Demuth, 1996). These cues range from cues relevant to speech segmentation (as discussed above) to the learning of word meanings and the acquisition of syntactic structure. We briefly discuss the two latter types of cues here.

Golinkoff, Hirsh-Pasek, & Hollich (1999) studied word learning in children of 12, 19, and 24 months of age. They found that perceptual salience and social information in the form of eye gaze are important cues for learning the meaning of words. The study also provided some insights into the developmental dynamics of multiple-cue integration. In particular, individual cues are weighted differently at different stages in development, changing the dynamics of the multiple-cue integration process across time. At 12 months, perceptual salience dominates—only names for interesting objects are learned, while other cues need to correlate considerably for successful learning. Seven months later, eye gaze cues come into play, but the children have problems when eye gaze and perceptual salience conflict with each other (e.g. when the experimenter is naming and looking at a perceptually uninteresting object). Only at 24 months has the child's lexical acquisition system developed sufficiently that it can deal with conflicting cues. From the viewpoint of multiple-cue integration, this study thus demonstrates how correlated cues are needed early in acquisition to build a basis for later performance based on individual cues.

There are a variety of cues available for the acquisition of syntactic structure. Phonology not only provides information helpful for word segmentation, but also includes important probabilistic cues to the grammatical classes of words. Lexical stress, for example, can be used to distinguish between nouns and verbs. In a 3000-word sample, Kelly & Bock (1988) found that 90% of the bisyllabic trochaic words were nouns, whereas 85% of the bisyllabic iambic words were verbs (e.g. the homograph *record* has stress on the first syllable when used as a noun, and stress on the second syllable when used as a verb). They furthermore demonstrated that people are sensitive to this cue. More recent evidence shows that people are faster and more accurate at classifying words as nouns or verbs if the words have the prototypical stress patterns for their grammatical class (Davis & Kelly, 1997). The number of syllables that a word contains also provides information about its grammatical class. Cassidy & Kelly (1991) showed that 3 year-olds are sensitive to the probabilistic cue that English nouns tend to have more syllables than verbs (e.g. *gorp* tended to be used as a verb, whereas *gorpinlak* tended to be used as noun). Other important cues to nounhood and verbhood in English include differences in word duration, consonant voicing, and vowel types—and many of these cues have also been found in other languages, such as Hebrew, German, French, and Russian (see Kelly, 1992, for a review).

Sentence prosody can also provide important probabilistic cues to the discovery of grammatical word class. Morgan, Shi, & Allopenna (1996) demonstrated using a multivariate procedure that content and function words can be differentiated with 80% accuracy by integrating distributional, phonetic, and acoustic cues. More recently, Shi, Werker, & Morgan (1999) found that infants are sensitive to such cue differences. Sentence prosody also provides cues to the acquisition of syntactic structure. Fisher & Tokura (1996) used multivariate analyses to integrate information about pauses, segmental variation and pitch and obtained 88% correct identification of clause boundaries. Other studies have shown that infants are sensitive to such cues (see Jusczyk, 1997, for a review). Additional cues to syntactic structure can be derived through distributional analyses of word combin-ations in everyday language (e.g. Redington, Chater, & Finch, 1998), and from semantics (e.g. Pinker, 1989).

As should be clear from this short review, there are many types of prob-abilistic information readily available to the language learner. We suggest that integrating these different types of information, similarly to how the segmen-tation model was able to integrate phonology, utterance boundary, and lex-ical stress information, is also likely to provide a solid basis for learning aspects of language beyond speech segmentation. Indeed, a recent set of simulations inspired by the modelling described here have demonstrated that the learning of syntactic structure by an SRN is facilitated when it is allowed to integrate phonological and prosodic information in addition to distri-butional information in a small artificial language (Christiansen & Dale, 2001). Specifically, an analysis of network performance revealed that learning with multiple-cue integration resulted in faster, better, and more uniform learning. The SRNs were also able to distinguish between relevant cues and distracting cues, and performance did not differ from networks that received only reliable cues. Overall, these simulations offer additional support for the multiple-cue integration hypothesis in language acquisition. They demon-strate that learners can benefit from multiple cues, and are not distracted by irrelevant information. Moreover, this work has recently been scaled up to deal with actual child-directed speech (Reali, Christiansen, & Monaghan, 2003).

CONCLUSION

In this chapter, we have presented a number of simulation results that demonstrate how multiple-cue integration in a connectionist network, such as the SRN, can provide a solid basis for solving the speech segmentation problem. We have also discussed how the process of integrating multiple cues may facilitate learning, and have reviewed evidence for the existence of a plethora of probabilistic cues for the learning of word meanings, grammatical class, and syntactic structure. We conclude by drawing attention to the kind of learning mechanism needed for multiple-cue integration.

It seems clear that connectionist networks are well suited for accommodating multiple-cue integration. First, our model of the integration of multiple cues in speech segmentation was implemented as an SRN. Second, and perhaps more importantly, the mathematical results regarding the advantages of multiple-cue integration were couched in terms of neural networks (although they may also hold for certain other, nonconnectionist, statistical learning devices). Third, in the service of immediate tasks, such as encoding phonological information, connectionist networks can develop representations that can then form the basis for solving derived tasks, such as word segmentation. Symbolic, rule-based models, on the other hand, would appear to be ill-equipped for accommodating the integration of multiple cues. First, the probabilistic nature of the various cues is not readily captured by rules. Second, the tendency for symbolic models to separate statistical and rule-based knowledge in dual-mechanism models is likely to hinder integration of information across the two types of knowledge. Third, the inherent modular nature of the symbolic approach to language acquisition further blocks the integration of multiple cues across different representational levels (e.g. preventing symbolic syntax models from taking advantage of phonological cues to word class).

As attested by the other chapters in this volume, connectionist networks have provided important insights into many aspects of cognitive psychology. In particular, connectionism has shown itself to be a very fruitful, albeit controversial, paradigm for research on language (see e.g. Christiansen & Chater, 2001b, for a review; or contributions in Christiansen & Chater, 2001a; Christiansen, Chater, & Seidenberg, 1999). Based on our work reported here, we further argue that connectionist networks may also hold the key to a better and more complete understanding of language acquisition, because they allow for the integration of multiple probabilistic cues.

Notes

1. Parts of the simulation results have previously been reported in conference proceedings (simulation 2, Christiansen & Curtin, 1999; and simulation 1, Christiansen & Allen, 1997).

2. Note that these phonological *citation forms* were unreduced (i.e. they do not include the reduced vowel *schwa*). The stress cue therefore provides additional information not available in the phonological input.

3. Phonemes were used as output in order to facilitate subsequent analyses of how much knowledge of phonotactics the net had acquired.

4. These results were replicated across different initial weight configurations and with different input/output representations.

5. Christiansen et al. (1998) represented function words as having primary stress, based on early evidence suggesting that there is little stress differentiation of content and function words in child-directed speech (Bernstein-Ratner, 1987). More recently, Shi, Werker, & Morgan (1999) have found evidence in support of such differentiation. However, for simplicity we have retained the original representation of function words as having stress.

6. According to the Oxford Text Archive, the following words were coded as having two equally stressed syllables: *upstairs, inside, outside, downstairs, hello*, and *seaside*.

7. It would, of course, have been desirable to use child-directed speech as in Christiansen et al. (1998), but it was not possible to find a corpus of phonetically transcribed child-directed speech.

8. This idealization is reasonable, because most monosyllabic words are stressed and most of the weak syllables in the multisyllabic words from the corpus involved a *schwa*. Further support for this idealization comes from the fact that the addition of vowel stress implemented in this manner significantly improved performance, compared to a training condition in which no stress information was provided.

9. Note that the random insertion of utterance boundaries may lead to the occurrence of utterance boundaries where they often do not occur normally (not even as pauses), e.g. after determiners. Because the presence of pauses in the input is what leads the network to postulate boundaries between words, this random approach is more likely to improve rather than impair overall performance, and thus will not bias the results in the direction of the co-articulation training condition.

10. It should be noted that the results of the mathematical analyses apply independently of whether the extra catalyst units are discarded after training (as is typical in the engineering literature) or remain a part of the network, as in the simulations presented here.

REFERENCES

Abu-Mostafa, Y. S. (1990). Learning from hints in neural networks. *Journal of Complexity, 6,* 192–198.

Abu-Mostafa, Y. S. (1993). Hints and the VC Dimension. *Neural Computation, 5,* 278–288.

Allen, J., & Christiansen, M. H. (1996). Integrating multiple cues in word segmentation: A connectionist model using hints. In *Proceedings of the Eighteenth Annual Cognitive Science Society Conference* (pp. 370–375). Mahwah, NJ: Lawrence Erlbaum Associates, Inc.

Aslin, R. N., Woodward, J. Z., LaMendola, N. P., & Bever, T. G (1996). Models of word segmentation in fluent maternal speech to infants. In J. L. Morgan, & K. Demuth (Eds.), *Signal to syntax* (pp. 117–134). Mahwah, NJ: Lawrence Erlbaum Associates, Inc.

Bates, E., & MacWhinney, B. (1987). Competition, variation, and language learning. In B. MacWhinney (Ed.), *Mechanisms of language acquisition* (pp. 157–193). Hillsdale, NJ: Lawrence Erlbaum Associates, Inc.

Bernstein-Ratner, N. (1987). The phonology of parent–child speech. In K. Nelson, & A. van Kleeck (Eds.), *Children's language* (Vol. 6). Hillsdale, NJ: Lawrence Erlbaum Associates, Inc.

Brent, M. R. (1999). An efficient, probabilistically sound algorithm for segmentation and word discovery. *Machine Learning, 34,* 71–106.

Brent, M. R., & Cartwright, T. A. (1996). Distributional regularity and phonotactic constraints are useful for segmentation. *Cognition, 61,* 93–125.

Cairns, P., Shillcock, R. C., Chater, N., & Levy, J. (1997). Bootstrapping word boundaries: A bottom-up approach to speech segmentation. *Cognitive Psychology, 33,* 111–153.

Carterette, E., & Jones, M. (1974). *Informal speech: Alphabetic and phonemic texts with statistical analyses and tables.* Berkeley, CA: University of California Press.

Cassidy, K. W., & Kelly, M. H. (1991). Phonological information for grammatical category assignments. *Journal of Memory and Language, 30,* 348–369.

Christiansen, M. H. (1998). Improving learning and generalization in neural networks through the acquisition of multiple related functions. In J. A. Bullinaria, D. G. Glasspool, & G. Houghton (Eds.), *Proceedings of the Fourth Neural Computation and Psychology Workshop: Connectionist representations* (pp. 58–70). London: Springer-Verlag.

Christiansen, M. H., & Allen, J. (1997). Coping with variation in speech segmentation. In A. Sorace, C. Heycock, & R. Shillcock (Eds.), *Proceedings of GALA 1997: Language acquisition: Knowledge representation and processing* (pp. 327–332). Edinburgh: University of Edinburgh Press.

Christiansen, M. H., Allen, J., & Seidenberg, M. S. (1998). Learning to segment speech using multiple cues: A connectionist model. *Language and Cognitive Processes, 13,* 221–268.

Christiansen, M. H., & Chater, N. (Eds.) (2001a). *Connectionist psycholinguistics.* Westport, CT: Ablex.

Christiansen, M. H., & Chater, N. (2001b). Connectionist psycholinguistics: Capturing the empirical data. *Trends in Cognitive Sciences, 5,* 82–88.

Christiansen, M. H., Chater, N., & Seidenberg, M. S. (Eds.) (1999). Connectionist models of human language processing: Progress and prospects. *Cognitive Science, 23* (4, Special Issue), 415–634.

Christiansen, M. H., & Curtin, S. (1999). The power of statistical learning: No need for algebraic rules. In *Proceedings of the 21st Annual Conference of the Cognitive Science Society* (pp. 114–119). Mahwah, NJ: Lawrence Erlbaum Associates, Inc.

Christiansen, M. H., & Dale, R. A. C. (2001). Integrating distributional, prosodic and phonological information in a connectionist model of language acquisition. In *Proceedings of the 23rd Annual Conference of the Cognitive Science Society* (pp. 220–225). Mahwah, NJ: Lawrence Erlbaum Associates, Inc.

Cleeremans, A. (1993). *Mechanisms of implicit learning: Connectionist models of sequence processing.* Cambridge, MA: MIT Press.

Cole, R. A., & Jakimik, J. (1978). How words are heard. In G. Underwood (Ed.), *Strategies of information processing* (pp. 67–117). London: Academic Press.

Cooper, W. E., & Paccia-Cooper, J. M. (1980). *Syntax and speech.* Cambridge, MA: Harvard University Press.

Cottrell, G. W. (1989). *A connectionist approach to word sense disambiguation.* London: Pitman.

Cutler, A. (1994). Segmentation problems, rhythmic solutions. *Lingua, 92,* 81–104.

Cutler, A. (1996). Prosody and the word boundary problem. In J. L. Morgan, & K. Demuth (Eds.), *From signal to syntax* (pp. 87–99). Mahwah, NJ: Lawrence Erlbaum Associates, Inc.

Cutler, A., & Mehler, J. (1993). The periodicity bias. *Journal of Phonetics, 21,* 103–108.

Davis, S. M., & Kelly, M. H. (1997). Knowledge of the English noun–verb stress difference by native and nonnative speakers. *Journal of Memory and Language, 36,* 445–460.

Demuth, K., & Fee, E. J. (1995). *Minimal words in early phonological development.* Unpublished manuscript, Brown University and Dalhousie University.

Dominey, P. F., & Ramus, F. (2000). Neural network processing of natural language: I. Sensitivity to serial, temporal and abstract structure of language in the infant. *Language and Cognitive Processing, 15,* 87–127.

Elman, J. L. (1990). Finding structure in time. *Cognitive Science, 14,* 179–211.

Fikkert, P. (1994). *On the acquisition of prosodic structure.* Dordrecht, The Netherlands: Institute of Generative Linguistics.

Fisher, C., & Tokura, H. (1996). Prosody in speech to infants: Direct and indirect acoustic cues to syntactic structure. In J. L. Morgan, & K. Demuth (Eds.), *Signal to syntax* (pp. 343–363). Mahwah, NJ: Lawrence Erlbaum Associates, Inc.

Gleitman, L. R., Gleitman, H., Landau, B., & Wanner, E. (1988). Where learning begins: Initial representations for language learning. In F. J. Newmeyer (Ed.), *Linguistics: The Cambridge Survey* (Vol. 3, pp. 150–193). Cambridge, UK: Cambridge University Press.

Gold, E. M. (1967). Language identification in the limit. *Information and Control, 10,* 447–474.

Golinkoff, R. M., Hirsh-Pasek, K., & Hollich, G. (1999). Emergent cues for early word learning. In B. MacWhinney (Ed.), *Emergence of language.* Mahwah, NJ: Lawrence Erlbaum Associates, Inc.

Greenburg, J. H., & Jenkins, J. J. (1964). Studies in the psychological correlates of the sound system of American English. *Word, 20,* 157–177.

Hochberg, J. A. (1988). Learning Spanish stress. *Language, 64,* 683–706.

Jusczyk, P. W. (1993). From general to language-specific capacities: The WRAPSA model of how speech perception develops. *Journal of Phonetics, 21,* 3–28.

Jusczyk, P. W. (1997). *The discovery of spoken language.* Cambridge, MA: MIT Press.

Jusczyk, P. W., Cutler, A., & Redanz, N. J. (1993). Infants' preference for the predominant stress patterns of English words. *Child Development, 64,* 675–687.

Jusczyk, P. W., Friederici, A. D., & Svenkerud, V. Y. (1993). Infants' sensitivity to the sound patterns of native language words. *Journal of Memory & Language, 32,* 402–420.

Jusczyk, P. W., & Thompson, E. (1978). Perception of a phonetic contrast in multisyllabic utterances by two-month-old infants. *Perception & Psychophysics, 23,* 105–109.

Kelly, M. H. (1992). Using sound to solve syntactic problems: The role of phonology in grammatical category assignments. *Psychological Review, 99,* 349–364.

Kelly, M. H., & Bock, J. K. (1988). Stress in time. *Journal of Experimental Psychology: Human Perception and Performance, 14,* 389–403.

Korman, M. (1984). Adaptive aspects of maternal vocalizations in differing contexts at ten weeks. *First Language, 5,* 44–45.

MacDonald, M. C., Pearlmutter, N. J., & Seidenberg, M. S. (1994). The lexical nature of syntactic ambiguity resolution. *Psychological Review, 101,* 676–703.

MacWhinney, B. (2000). *The CHILDES Project* (3rd ed.). Mahwah, NJ: Lawrence Erlbaum Associates, Inc.

Marslen-Wilson, W. D., & Welsh, A. (1978). Processing interactions and lexical access during word recognition in continuous speech. *Cognitive Psychology, 10,* 29–63.

Mattys, S. L., Jusczyk, P. W., Luce, P. A., & Morgan, J. L. (1999). Phonotactic and prosodic effects on word segmentation in infants. *Cognitive Psychology, 38,* 465–494.

Morgan, J. L., & Demuth, K. (Eds.) (1996). *From signal to syntax*. Mahwah, NJ: Lawrence Erlbaum Associates, Inc.

Morgan. J. L., & Saffran, J. R. (1995). Emerging integration of sequential and suprasegmental information in preverbal speech segmentation. *Child Development, 66,* 911–936.

Morgan, J. L., Shi, R., & Allopenna, P. (1996). Perceptual bases of rudimentary grammatical categories: Toward a broader conceptualization of bootstrapping. In J. L. Morgan, & K. Demuth (Eds.), *From signal to syntax* (pp. 263—281). Mahwah, NJ: Lawrence Erlbaum Associates, Inc.

Nazzi, T., Bertoncini, J., & Mehler, J. (1998). Language discrimination by newborns: Towards an understanding of the role of rhythm. *Journal of Experimental Psychology: Human Perception and Performance, 24,* 1–11.

Omlin, C., & Giles, C. (1992). Training second-order recurrent neural networks using hints. In D. Sleeman, & P. Edwards (Eds.), *Proceedings of the Ninth International Conference on Machine Learning* (pp. 363–368). San Mateo, CA: Morgan Kaufmann.

Perruchet, P., & Vinter, A. (1998). PARSER: A model for word segmentation. *Journal of Memory and Language, 39,* 246–263.

Pinker, S. (1989). *Learnability and cognition*. Cambridge, MA: MIT Press.

Pinker, S. (1994). The language instinct: How the mind creates language. New York: William Morrow.

Reali, F., Christiansen, M. H., & Monaghan, P. (2003). Phonological and distributional cues in syntax acquisition: Scaling up the connectionist approach to multiple-cue integration. In *Proceedings of the 25th Annual Conference of the Cognitive Science Society*. Mahwah, NJ: Lawrence Erlbaum Associates, Inc.

Redington, M., Chater, N., & Finch, S. (1998). Distributional information: A powerful cue for acquiring syntactic categories. *Cognitive Science, 22,* 425–469.

Saffran, J. R, Aslin, R. N., & Newport, E. L. (1996). Statistical learning by 8-month-old infants. *Science, 274,* 1926–1928.

Saffran, J. R., Newport, E. L., Aslin, R. N. (1996). Word segmentation: The role of distributional cues. *Journal of Memory and Language*, *35*, 606–621.

Seidenberg, M. S. (1997). Language acquisition and use: Learning and applying probabilistic constraints. *Science, 275,* 1599–1603.

Shastri, L., & Chang, S. (1999). *A spatiotemporal connectionist model of algebraic rule-learning* (TR-99–011). Berkeley, CA: International Computer Science Institute.

Shi, R., Werker, J. F., & Morgan, J. L. (1999). Newborn infants' sensitivity to perceptual cues to lexical and grammatical words. *Cognition, 72,* B11–B21.

Suddarth, S. C., & Holden, A. D. C. (1991). Symbolic-neural systems and the use of hints for developing complex systems. *International Journal of Man–Machine Studies, 35,* 291–311.

Suddarth, S. C., & Kergosien, Y. L. (1991). Rule-injection hints as a means of improving network performance and learning time. In L. B. Almeida, & C. J. Wellekens (Eds.), *Proceedings of the Networks/EURIP Workshop 1990* (Lecture Notes in Computer Science, Vol. 412, pp. 120–129). Berlin: Springer-Verlag.

Trueswell, J. C., & Tanenhaus, M. K. (1994). Towards a lexicalist framework of constraint-based syntactic ambiguity resolution. In C. Clifton, L. Frazier, & K. Rayner (Eds), *Perspectives on sentence processing* (pp. 155–179). Hillsdale, NJ: Lawrence Erlbaum Associates, Inc.

CHAPTER TWELVE

Language production, lexical access, and aphasia

Gary S. Dell
University of Illinois, Champaign, IL, USA

Language users, with few exceptions, acquire two skills very early in life—how to comprehend and how to produce spoken utterances. Production, which is the subject matter of this chapter, is less often studied than comprehension, but has long been the object of connectionist modelling. Some production data, such as certain properties of slips of the tongue, are easily explained by connectionist principles. However, as we will see, there are other aspects of production that challenge simple connectionist accounts.

This chapter will first present a general framework for language production, building on the seminal contributions of Bock (1982), Garrett (1975), Levelt (1989) and others. Next, a recent connectionist model of one aspect of the production process, the lexical access of single words, will be described. This model, which is one that I have worked on for some time (e.g. Dell, Schwartz, Martin, Saffran, & Gagnon, 1997; Foygel & Dell, 2000), illustrates the utility of spreading activation in accounting for production error data from both normal speakers and from patients with aphasia. This lexical access model, however, does not adequately address three key issues for connectionist models of language: temporal sequence, linguistic structure, and learning. The final part of the chapter will examine language production data related to these issues, and discuss the prospects for connectionist accounts of the data.

LANGUAGE PRODUCTION

Speaking is undoubtedly the most complex thing that people routinely do. Consider an utterance as simple as, "Illinois is flat". It takes less than 2 s to move one's articulatory organs through the sequence of gestures needed to produce this sentence. Yet, the mental operations leading up to its articulation call on a bewildering variety of knowledge sources and processing mechanisms. Although these operations are only beginning to be understood, the last 25 years has seen much progress, and it is now possible to give a rough outline of the production process (see Bock, 1995, for a review).

The act of speaking involves three main stages, each of which is composed of several subprocesses (see Fig. 12.1). The first stage is *conceptualization*, i.e. deciding what to say. This stage constructs a preverbal message, a conceptual representation of the utterance. For "Illinois is flat" the message would contain the proposition that the land in the US state of Illinois has the property of being flat. It would further indicate that this proposition is to be asserted, as opposed to, for example, questioned. The processes involved in message construction are a part of the general cognitive operations involved in the planning of behavior. We say things to have effects on the world, specifically on the beliefs and, ultimately, the behaviors of other people. For example, we may wish to dissuade a friend from bringing their skis on a visit to Illinois.

The second stage, the *formulation* stage, turns a message into linguistic form. So this stage moves from "what to say" to "how to say it". Formulation involves two substages, *grammatical encoding* and *phonological encoding*. During grammatical encoding, lexical items are selected and arranged so as to express the meaning. These processes might identify the proper noun, ILLINOIS, and the adjective FLAT. Furthermore, the constraints of English grammar would be consulted to place these words into a structure that identifies word order and phrase membership, and specifies additional function morphemes. For example, some relevant grammatical constraints would be that proper nouns do not take determiners, such as, "The Illinois", or that one uses the simple present tense when making timeless statements such as, "Illinois is flat".

During phonological encoding, the sounds of the lexical items are retrieved and organized for articulation, resulting in a phonetic plan for the utterance. The sounds of the word "Illinois", for example, must be organized into syllables and groups of syllables that identify the rhythmic structure of the word, e.g. (I′ lə) (nɔj′). This structure determines timing and stress. Furthermore, the organization of a word's sounds is influenced by surrounding words. In our example, most speakers would say [Ilənɔjz] for "Illinois is".

Key parts of the formulation stage involve the access of information from the mental lexicon, a speaker's store of knowledge of words. Current theory (e.g. Levelt, Roelofs, & Meyer, 1999) assumes that lexical access is a two-step

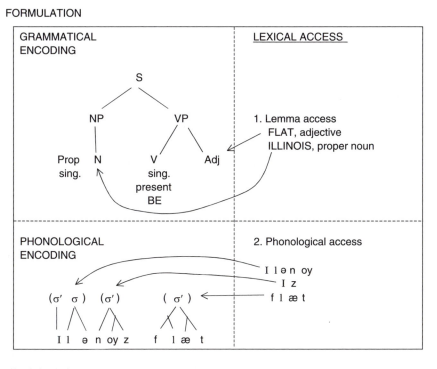

Figure 12.1. Components of language production. Adapted from Levelt (1989).

operation, one step associated with grammatical encoding and one with phonological encoding. The first step, *lemma access*, takes as input a conceptual representation, and selects a *lemma*, a holistic representation of a lexical item that specifies its syntactic category (noun, verb, etc.) and features that play a syntactic role, such as, in English, whether or not a noun is plural, or, in Italian, a noun's gender. The retrieved lemmas, in conjunction with other characteristics of the message, assemble the grammatical structure of the utterance (e.g. Kempen, 1997). The second step, *phonological access*, takes each lemma and retrieves its sequence of speech sounds. These sounds are the building blocks of phonological encoding (e.g. Roelofs, 1997).

The final production stage is *articulation*. The phonetic plan of the utterance must be turned into movements of the articulators to produce speech. A speaker can, as well, translate the phonetic plan into motor imagery without overt articulation. This leads to inner speech. Most people can produce sufficiently detailed speech-motor imagery that they can hear "slips of the tongue" in their inner speech (Dell & Repka, 1992).

The production framework presented in Figure 12.1 has received much support from controlled experiments. Some studies measured how quickly people can produce words or sentences under various circumstances (e.g. Griffin & Bock, 1998; Kempen & Huijbers, 1983; Levelt et al., 1999; Roelofs & Meyer, 1998; van Turennout, Hagoort, & Brown, 1998). Others examined the choices that speakers make when there are different ways of expressing a message (e.g. Bock, 1986; Bock & Griffin, 2000; Ferreira, 1996; Ferreira & Dell, 2000). This experimental work has helped identify the representations that are associated with each production component and the time-course of the entire process.

The earliest support for this production framework, however, did not come from experiments. It came from analyses of errors in natural speech (Dell & Reich, 1981; Fromkin, 1971; Harley, 1984; Garrett, 1975; MacKay, 1970). These studies examined collections of slips of the tongue, such as exchanges of speech sounds ("thollow hud" for "hollow thud") or substitutions of one word for another ("Liszt's second Hungarian restaurant" where "Hungarian rhapsody" was intended). Other studies focused on errors made by aphasic speakers (see Garrett, 1984; Schwartz, 1987, for reviews). Most normal and aphasic speech errors can be placed within the formulation stage, and thus an examination of their properties can tell us about the organization of this production component. Specifically, errors involving misordering, substitution, deletion, or addition of speech sounds can be associated with phonological encoding, while errors in which whole words are replaced by other words, or where words are misordered, are typically assigned to grammatical encoding. As we will see, accounting for the facts associated with these errors has been a major goal of connectionist models of production. For this reason, this chapter will focus more on error data than on other data, such as response time.

Of the three production stages, formulation has most often been the target of connectionist modelling. There are no connectionist models of conceptualization, and articulation has only rarely been treated in connectionist terms (see e.g. Guenther, 1995). For models of formulation, there are a few dealing with the grammatical encoding of multi-word utterances (Chang, 2002; Chang, Dell, Bock, & Griffin, 2000; Gordon & Dell, 2003; Houghton, 1993; Schade, 1992). But most formulation models have ignored grammatical processes and focused, instead, on the access of single words or lists of unrelated words or nonwords (Berg & Schade, 1992; Dell, 1986; Dell, Juliano, & Govindjee, 1993; Gupta & MacWhinney, 1997; Harley, 1993; Hartley & Houghton, 1996; Houghton, 1990; Levelt, Roelofs, & Meyer, 1999; Plaut & Kello, 1999; Rapp & Goldrick, 2000; Roelofs, 1992, 1997; Vousden, Brown, & Harley, 2000). The next section illustrates this work by presenting the lexical access model of Foygel & Dell (2000), a model designed to account for the errors of aphasic patients.

A MODEL OF LEXICAL ACCESS IN APHASIC SPEAKERS

The discreteness debate

There are two competing views of lexical access in production. The first, the discrete view, emphasizes the distinction between lemma and phonological access. It is hypothesized that these processes do not overlap in time and that they retrieve information in a modular fashion (Levelt et al., 1991). The access of a lemma, such as FLAT (adj), is completely finished before phonological access (f l ae t) begins. Furthermore, the lemma access stage is unaffected by the phonological properties of words, whereas the phonological access stage is unaffected by their semantic properties. The alternative nondiscrete view accepts the distinction between the access of a word's syntactic/semantic properties and its phonological properties, but denies that these are discrete and modular stages. Instead, processing is thought to be *cascaded*—phonological access can commence before lemma access is completed (e.g. Caramazza, 1997; Humphreys, Riddoch, & Quinlan, 1988)—and *interactive*—phonological information about partially retrieved lemmas can influence lemma selection via feedback (e.g. Dell & O'Seaghdha, 1991; Harley, 1984; Stemberger, 1985). Proponents of the cascaded and interactive views have tended to frame their theories in connectionist terms. Spreading activation is a natural mechanism for nondiscrete processing, as seen in one of the original connectionist models in psychology, the interactive activation model of visual word recognition (McClelland & Rumelhart, 1981).

Much of the research on the question of discreteness in lexical access has come from experimental paradigms in which subjects name pictured objects. Some of these studies have supported the discrete view by showing that lemma access has an earlier time-course than phonological access. For example, Schriefers, Meyer, & Levelt (1990) found that response times to name a pictured object can be affected by presenting auditory distractor words while a person is in the act of retrieving the picture's name. However, a semantic distractor, such as "dog" for a picture of a CAT, has an influence beyond that of an unrelated word only when it is presented early in the picture-naming event, and phonological distractors, such as "cap", only differentially affect response times if they occur later in the process. These results suggest that lexical access moves from a phase in which semantic information is important (lemma access) to one in which a word's form is important (phonological access) (see also van Turennout, Hagoort, & Brown, 1998).

Other experimental findings are more consistent with the nondiscrete view. Peterson & Savoy (1998) showed that phonological information is accessed for semantic competitors of sought-after words. When speakers correctly named a picture of a FROG, there was activation of the sounds of words such as TOAD, as seen in facilitated response times to phonologically related probes such as TOE. This activation suggests cascaded processing (see also Cutting & Ferreira, 1999; Damian & Martin, 1999; Jescheniak & Schriefers, 1998).

Support for interaction between lemma and phonological access has come from examining errors of lexical access. Martin, Gagnon, Schwartz, Dell, & Saffran (1996) showed that picture-naming errors that bear a semantic relation to the target tend to be phonologically similar as well. For example, a picture of a SNAIL is erroneously called a "snake". This is an experimental demonstration of the mixed-error effect, a statistical tendency for whole-word slips of the tongue to resemble their targets both semantically and phonologically (Dell & Reich, 1981; Harley, 1984). The mixed-error effect is suggestive of interaction during lexical access. Semantic influences on errors would, on all accounts, be located at lemma access or some previous stage. If semantic errors also exhibit phonological influences in excess of chance expectations, it suggests that phonological information is contributing to decisions at the earlier level, i.e. that there is interactive feedback.

The semantic–phonological aphasia model

The semantic–phonological aphasia model (Foygel & Dell, 2000) is an interactive two-step account of the picture-naming errors made by aphasic patients. This model maintains the distinction between the lemma and phonological access steps that is central to discrete views of lexical access, but each of the steps is achieved by interactive spreading activation and hence can account for the data that motivate nondiscrete views.

The semantic–phonological model is a later version of one by Dell et al. (1997). Both models make the same assumptions about normal lexical access, but differ in their account of aphasic deficits. The next subsection describes the account of normal access that both models share. This is followed by subsections describing the specific properties of the semantic–phonological model, and an evaluation of that model's fit to aphasic data.

Normal lexical access assumptions

Lexical access occurs through spreading activation in a network such as that shown in Fig. 12.2. The network contains separate layers of units for semantic features, words, and phonemes. The connections are excitatory and bidirectional. Top-down connections link semantic features to words, and words to their phonemes. Bottom-up connections do the reverse, thus providing interactive feedback.

Lemma and phonological access are separate steps. Lemma access begins with a jolt of 10 units of activation to the semantic features of the target. Activation spreads throughout the network for eight time steps, according to a noisy, linear activation rule, specifically:

$$A(j, t) = A (j, t - 1) (1 - q) + \Sigma\, w (i, j)\, A (i, t - 1) + \text{noise} \qquad (1)$$

where $A(j,t)$ is the activation of unit j at time step t, q is the decay rate, and $w(i,j)$ is the connection weight from the source unit i to the receiving unit j. During each time step, each unit's activation level is perturbed by normally distributed noise with a mean of zero and a standard deviation proportional to the unit's activation.[1] The activation rule [equation (1)] applies to all network units. Hence, the input semantic features, like all other units, are subject to decay, noise, and influence from neighboring activated units.

During lemma access, the target word, here assumed to be CAT, will normally obtain the most activation. However, the natural action of the network activates other words, and other words' phonemes and semantic features. *Semantic* neighbors, such as DOG, obtain some activation from shared

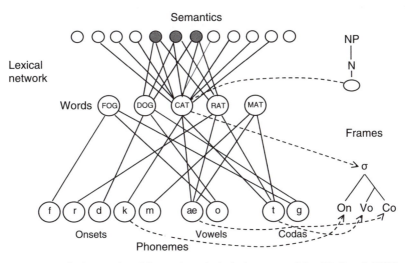

Figure 12.2. Lexical network and frames from the lexical access models of Dell et al. (1997) and Foygel & Dell (2000). CAT is the illustrated target.

semantic units. Furthermore, because activation spreads from words to phonemes during lemma access (cascading) and feeds back from phonemes to words (interactivity), phonologically related or *formal* neighbors of the target, such as MAT, become activated. *Mixed* semantic–phonological neighbors of the target, such as RAT, gain activation from both top-down semantic and bottom-up phonological influences. Consequently, mixed neighbors are especially activated, which gives the model its mechanism for the mixed error effect.

After eight time steps, the most highly activated word unit of the proper syntactic category is selected. This completes lemma access. When naming pictures of objects, nouns are the proper category, and so the most activated noun is selected. Most likely, the selected word is the target (CAT). However, due to noise, a semantic (DOG), formal (MAT), or mixed (RAT) word could be incorrectly selected instead, provided that it is a noun. If the noise is extreme, an unrelated word such as LOG could be selected.

Phonological access begins with a jolt of activation (100 units) to the selected word unit. This jolt introduces a large nonlinearity in the spreading activation process. In essence, it enables the words to act as nonlinear "hidden" units. These kinds of units are required because semantic-to-phonological mappings for words are largely unsystematic. Words with similar semantics tend not to have similar phonological forms.

After the jolt to the selected word, activation spreads for eight more time steps. Following this, the most activated phonemes are selected and linked to slots in a *phonological frame*. The implemented model encoded only single-syllable consonant, vowel, coda (CVC) words, such as CAT. The possible phonemes were organized into sets of onsets, vowels, and codas, and the most active of each set was linked to the appropriate slot in a CVC frame. This selection and linkage concludes the phonological access step.

For the purposes of model evaluation, six categories of responses were considered: (a) correct responses (CAT), indicating correct lemma and phonological access; (b) semantic errors (DOG), which reflect a semantic mis-selection at lemma access and correct phonological access; (c) formally related word errors (MAT), which could either indicate selection of a formally related word at lemma access, followed by correct phonological access, or correct lemma access followed by the mis-selection of a few phonemes during phonological access; (d) mixed errors (RAT), which likely occur during lemma access, but could in principle result instead from correct lemma access followed by an error in phonological access; (e) unrelated words (LOG), which are most likely errors of lemma access that are correctly pronounced; (f), nonwords (LAT), which result from erroneous phonological access.

The model was initially set up to simulate normal speakers' picture-naming errors. This required specification of the lexical network and values for connection weights and decay rate.[2] The data came from 60 normal speakers tested by Dell et al. They had been given 175 pictures from the Philadelphia Naming Test (PNT; Roach et al., 1996) to name, and their errors were placed in the six response categories. Table 12.1 shows the proportions obtained for the categories, the proportions generated by the model, and the model's parameter values. In both the model and the data, errors are infrequent and occur mostly in the semantic and mixed categories.

Aphasic lexical access

Dell et al. tested 21 fluent aphasic patients on the PNT and categorized their errors in the same manner as for the normal speakers. All of the aphasic subjects experienced some difficulty in word retrieval during speaking, making more errors than normals on the task. However, the patients varied greatly in both overall performance and the distribution of error types. Table 12.2 gives three of the patients' response distributions. These patients illustrate both variation in correctness (contrast GL with the other two) and variation in error pattern, independently of correctness (contrast LH's mostly nonword error pattern, with IG's primarily semantic pattern). The goal of the semantic–phonological model was to provide an account of this variation, using the model of normal performance as a starting point.

Dell et al. hypothesized that patient error patterns reflect quantitative variation between the normal error pattern, i.e. the pattern in Table 12.1, and a "random" pattern. They called this claim the *continuity thesis*. The random pattern is the proportion of the response categories that would be observed if

TABLE 12.1
Semantic–phonological model and naming data from control subjects

	Correct	Semantic	Formal	Nonword	Mixed	Unrelated
Data	.969	.012	.001	.000	.009	.003
Model	.972	.013	.001	.000	.014	.000

Model parameters: s = .0698; f = .1000; q = .6.
Data from Dell et al. (1997). Adapted from Foygel & Dell (2000).

TABLE 12.2
Error category proportions for three patients tested on the Philadelphia naming test

Patient	Correct	Semantic	Formal	Nonword	Mixed	Unrelated
LH	.69	.03	.07	.15	.01	.02
IG	.69	.09	.05	.02	.03	.01
GL	.28	.04	.21	.30	.03	.09

Adapted from Dell et al. (1997).

there were no influence of lexical knowledge on word-form retrieval, but the retrieved forms nonetheless respected the general phonological character-istics of words, such as length and phonotactic constraints. The random pattern thus reflects the opportunities afforded by the lexicon, such as the relative number of semantic or formal neighbors that words have, and the proportion of phonologically legal strings that are words. Dell et al. esti-mated that the random pattern for English object naming would be 80% nonwords, and that most of the remaining 20% would be unrelated words, followed by, in order, formally related words, semantically related words, and mixed words. For example, if the target is CAT, a random output would likely be a nonword such as MOG, and would be extremely unlikely to be a string that corresponds to a mixed error, RAT.

For a model, the random pattern is the proportion of the response cat-egories that would occur if noise is overwhelming. Then, the error propor-tions would only reflect the opportunities present in the model's lexicon. Given this perspective, it is important that the model's random pattern be similar to that of the real lexicon, i.e. with random outputs, the large majority of the model's strings should be nonwords, and any strings that happen to be words should tend to be unrelated to the target. The network neighborhoods for the normal version of the model were chosen to make the model's random pattern similar to estimates of the random pattern for English.

The continuity thesis is a claim about the possible error patterns in apha-sia. Assuming six response categories, a particular pattern is a point in six-dimensional space. The normal pattern in one point in the space and the random pattern is another point. For the continuity thesis to hold, the pos-sible patterns should correspond to a simple continuous region connecting these two points.[3] The semantic–phonological model is a method for generat-ing such a region. The model specifies how the normal model can be "lesioned", and this lesioning defines the region between the normal and the random points.

According to the semantic–phonological model, aphasic deficits corres-pond to reduced connection weights in the network. Specifically, there are two lesionable parameters, the lexical–semantic weight (s) and the lexical–phonological weight (f).[4] Thus, each patient's lexical access deficits can be characterized by the extent to which activation flows between semantic and word nodes, and the extent to which activation flows between word and phoneme nodes. The theory of aphasic naming deficits in the semantic–phonological model thus aligns with the two steps of lexical access. Par-ameter s is the weight of connections that are largely responsible for lemma access, and this parameter is distinct from f, which is the weight of connec-tions associated with phonological access. However, the alignment of the parameters with lexical access steps is not perfect. Because of the cascaded and interactive nature of the model, the phonological weights are in play during lemma access, as are the semantic weights during phonological access.

Model properties

Fig. 12.3, from Foygel and Dell (2000), shows how the model's errors vary as a function of the semantic and phonological weights. Each panel shows one of the six response categories (light areas indicate higher probability). The normal point is near the lower right of each panel, where the parameters are near their normal values, and the random pattern is associated with low values toward the upper left.

The upper right of each panel corresponds to a lesion solely in the semantic weights. This lesion creates word errors of all types, as opposed to nonword errors. To see this, consider what happens when semantic weights are vanishingly small, but the phonological weights are intact. The activation level of the word units is entirely determined by noise, and so the selected word is random. This word, though, is given the normal jolt of activation that is due the selected word and so it undergoes nearly normal phonological encoding. The result is word, but no nonword, errors. When the semantic weights are less drastically lesioned, semantic, mixed, and formal errors are more common than unrelated words. Formal and mixed errors, in particular, are promoted by phoneme-to-word feedback from the target word. When phonological rather than semantic weights are lesioned, there is incorrect phonological access of the selected words, resulting in mostly nonwords and some formals (see left side of the panels).

To gain a further understanding of the model's properties, Foygel & Dell analyzed its error space by projecting it onto a best-fit plane computed from the first two principal components of the model distributions, which accounted for over 99% of the variance. The projected distribution and component coefficients are shown in Fig. 12.4. The three corners of the region correspond to the normal point, the random point, and a third point, labeled "word errors" in the figure, at which lemma access is maximally disrupted, but phonological access is normal.

The fact that the region is low-dimensional and runs from the normal to the random points shows that the model instantiates the continuity thesis. Furthermore, one can use the component coefficients to characterize the model's functional dimensions. The first component's coefficients have a high positive value for the correct category, revealing this component to be one of general severity of the deficit. The second component distinguishes word errors (positive coefficients) from nonword errors (high negative coefficients) and thus serves to distinguish the type of lesion, semantic vs. phonological. Thus, the model has mechanisms for variation in both overall severity of damage and type of damage. The next question is whether these mechanisms have any support in the data.

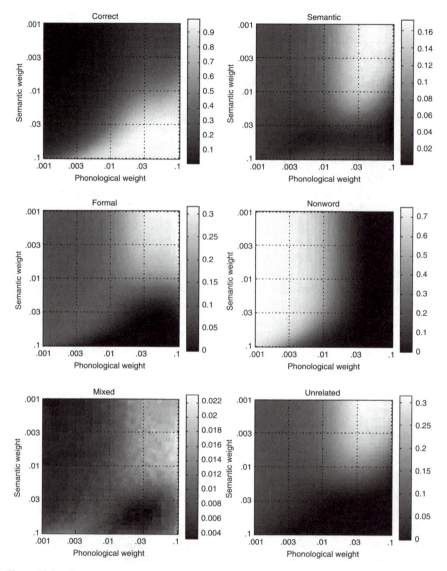

Figure 12.3. Response proportions from the semantic–phonological model as a function of semantic and phonological weights. From Foygel & Dell (2000). Reprinted from the *Journal of Memory and Language, 43*, Foygel, D., & Dell, G. S., Models of impaired lexical access in speech production, 182–216, Copyright © 2000, with permission from Elsevier.

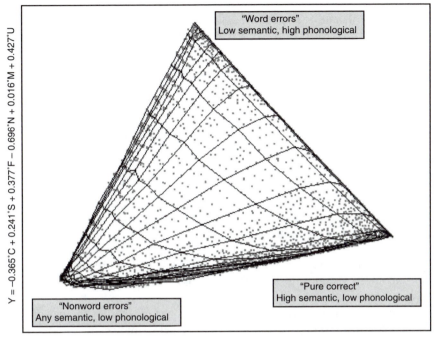

$$X = 0.811^{\circ}C - 0.025^{\circ}S - 0.119^{\circ}F - 0.562^{\circ}N - 0.001^{\circ}M - 0.104^{\circ}U$$

Figure 12.4. Projection of error types onto the best-fit plane, defined by the first two principal components (x and y axes, respectively). The coefficients defining each component are given on the axes (C = correct, S = semantic, F = formal, N = nonword, M = mixed, U = unrelated). From Foygel & Dell (2000). Reprinted from the *Journal of Memory and Language*, *43*, Foygel, D., & Dell, G. S., Models of impaired lexical access in speech production, 182–216, Copyright © 2000, with permission from Elsevier.

Model tests

Fogyel & Dell tested the semantic–phonological model in several ways. First, they asked whether the naming data from Dell et al.'s 21 patients could be fitted by the model, i.e. for each patient, they sought values of s and f that make the model's six category proportions close to the patient's proportions. To the extent that this is possible, it suggests that the patient variation can be explained by the model. When best-fitting parameters (minimizing χ^2) were determined, the patients were fairly well fitted by the model. The root mean squared deviation (RMSD) between patient and model proportions ranged from .005 to .093, with a mean of .030. Table 12.3 shows the model proportions and chosen parameters for the three patients discussed earlier. These three patients have, on average, a degree of fit similar to that of the entire group of 21 patients. Notice that the patient with the predominance of nonwords, LH, is assigned more of a lesion in the phonological weights

TABLE 12.3
Fit of the semantic–phonological model to the three patients from Table 12.2

Patient/model parameters	Correct	Semantic	Formal	Nonword	Mixed	Unrelated	RMSD
LH	.690	.030	.070	.150	.010	.020	
s = .0237							
f = .0178	.671	.057	.066	.177	.009	.020	.0175
IG	.690	.090	.050	.020	.030	.010	
s = .0198							
f = .0340	.795	.086	.054	.013	.014	.038	.0449
GL	.280	.040	.210	.300	.030	.090	
s = .0093							
f = .0154	.272	.102	.157	.323	.014	.133	.0397

Adapted from Foygel & Dell (2000).

($f = .0178$) than in the semantic weights, ($s = .0237$). In contrast, the patient who had more semantic errors, IG, gets the reverse lesion ($f = .0340$, $s = .0198$).

The second test that Foygel & Dell did was to see whether the parameters assigned for the naming task could predict performance in another task, word repetition. In a repetition task, the examiner says a word, and the patient simply repeats it. Eleven of Dell et al.'s patients were given the 175 words of the PNT to repeat. Their responses were categorized exactly the same way as their picture-naming responses were.

The basis for predicting repetition from naming is the two-step nature of the lexical access theory. Naming involves both lemma and phonological access. Repetition, by assumption, involves only phonological access. Thus, for each patient, one can take the model as parameterized for naming, and run it through only the phonological access step to get predicted proportions for repetition. This analysis assumes that the patients successfully recognize the word that they are told and that all errors result from their attempt to say it. Although this assumption is not true for all aphasic patients, it seemed to be warranted for the patients in Dell et al.'s repetition study.

The repetition predictions were successful, particularly given that no new parameters were estimated from the data to derive the predicted proportions. The RMSD ranged from .005 to .132, with a mean of .035. Table 12.4 shows the predicted and obtained repetition for the one patient from the set in Table 12.3 who was also tested on repetition, IG, and another whose degree of fit was close to the median, JL. Notice that IG, the patient to whom the model assigned a semantic lesion based on naming performance, does much better in repetition (95% correct) than in naming (69%). This is exactly right from the perspective of the semantic–phonological model's account of the

TABLE 12.4
Repetition data for two patients and fits of the semantic–phonological model

Patient/model parameters	Correct	Semantic	Formal	Nonword	Mixed	Unrelated	RMSD
JL	.890	.000	.020	.030	.000	.000	
s = .0255							
f = .0221	.878	.000	.028	.090	.002	.000	.0254
IG	.950	.000	.020	.020	.000	.000	
s = .0198							
f = .0340	.970	.000	.013	.016	.001	.000	.0088

Adapted from Foygel & Dell (2000).

relationship between naming and repetition. If most naming errors are associated with lemma access, then one expects repetition, which relies on phonological access, to be much better.

Although the semantic–phonological model provided a good account of the naming and repetition patterns in Dell et al.'s patients, none of the patients were assigned pure phonological or semantic lesions. Thus, these cases do not provide a strong test of the model's claims that f and s can be independently lesioned. Fogyel & Dell did, however, identify two patients in the literature that represented clearer examples, and whose naming data had been scored appropriately. The patients and the model fits are shown in Table 12.5. JBN (Hillis, Boatman, Hart, & Gordon, 1999) seems to have a pure phonological deficit; the phonological weight is only 3.5% of normal, while the semantic weight is normal. As expected, this patient's errors are overwhelmingly phonological (nonwords and some formally related words).

TABLE 12.5
Naming error proportions for JBN (Hillis et al., 1999) and MB (Schwartz & Brecher, 2000) and fits of the semantic–phonological model

Patient/model parameters	Correct	Semantic	Formal	Nonword	Mixed	Unrelated	RMSD
JBN	.380	.000	.060	.530	.030	.000	
s = .0698							
f = .0035	.372	.018	.069	.524	.010	.007	.0126
MB	.731	.074	.046	.000	.034	.040	
s = .0184							
f = .0437	.799	.085	.062	.002	.014	.038	.0303

Note: The data from JBN are from Hillis et al.'s picture-naming test, and those from MB are from the second administration of the picture-naming test.
Adapted from Foygel & Dell (2000).

Although not as clear an example, MB (Schwartz & Brecher, 2000) represents the opposite lesion. She makes no nonword errors, along with word errors in every category. The assigned model parameters show a marked semantic deficit. Thus, the dissociations allowed by the model seem to occur in patients.

A final test examined the interactive nature of the model. Phoneme-to-word feedback in the model is responsible for the mixed-error effect, the tendency for semantic and phonological factors to combine to promote word level errors during lemma access. Dell et al. had shown that this effect was present in some patients, but not in others (see also Rapp & Goldrick, 2000). Foygel & Dell demonstrated that this distinction is preserved in the semantic–phonological model. Specifically, the patients in the group that Dell et al. found to have a mixed-error effect were assigned by the semantic–phonological model to a region of the model's parameter space in which the phonological weights were relatively stronger than the semantic weights. The other patients had relatively weaker phonological weights. This is just what would be expected. Strong phonological weights are needed to deliver phonological feedback to the word level during lemma access, and promote mixed errors.

In summary, the semantic–phonological model illustrates the potential of an interactive two-step approach to lexical access. Much of this potential comes from the model's connectionist character. Spreading activation offers a natural way for the retrieval of a target word to activate related words. The interactive spread of activation, in particular, provides an account of formal influences on errors of lemma access, such as the mixed-error effect. However, the model has several limitations, particularly in its account of phonological processes, and these illustrate some of the challenges that connectionist models of production face. The remaining sections of the chapter focus on three of these: *temporal sequence, linguistic structure,* and *learning.*

TEMPORAL SEQUENCE

Spoken language is inherently sequential. Sentences are sequences of words, and words are sequences of sounds. The semantic–phonological model is only a model of lexical access and hence does not sequence words. It does, however, make claims about the representation and access of the serial order of sounds within words. Specifically, the model activates the sounds of its words in parallel, rather than sequentially. Information about the order of these sounds is coded by means of positional categories associated with the phonemes and the frame slots to which the selected units are linked (for background on frame-and-slot models see Dell, 1986; MacKay, 1982; Shattuck-Hufnagel, 1979). The frame identifies the hierarchical and sequential structure of the word, e.g. that it is a single-syllable word with an onset consonant (C), a vowel (V), and a coda (C) consonant (CVC), in that order. The phoneme units belong to the categories of onsets, vowels, and codas, and it is assumed that only units with the appropriate category can link to a corresponding slot in the frame. In connectionist models such as the semantic–phonological model, this necessitates having a different unit for the onset and coda version of each consonant.

The frame-and-slot approach in Foygel & Dell's model, however, fails to take note of several important issues concerning serial order. How is the order of slots in the frame represented? What about words whose syllables are not CVCs? How is the order of syllables in a multi-syllabic word determined? If different units are required for the same phoneme, depending on its position, in what sense is the onset and coda version the same phoneme? In addition, there are several empirical phenomena showing that a fully parallel approach to phonological encoding in production is incorrect. Instead, there seems to be some form of sequential phonological activation (for reviews, see Meyer, 1990, 1991; Sevald & Dell, 1994; Wheeldon & Levelt, 1995).

An example of a sequential influence on phonological encoding is the *initialness effect* on speech errors (MacKay, 1970; Shattuck-Hufnagel, 1983; Vousden et al., 2000). The initial sounds of words and syllables are more vulnerable to phonological movement errors than noninitial sounds (e.g. the error "sue sholes" for "shoe soles", which is an exchange of word- and syllable-initial sounds). Another example is the *sequential interference effect* (O'Seaghdha & Marin, 2000; Sevald & Dell, 1994). Speakers find it harder to repeat a pair of words that share beginning sounds (e.g. "pick pit pick pit . . .") than a pair sharing final sounds ("pick tick pick tick . . ."). One can explain the greater difficulty of initial sharing only by assuming that there is some difference between the beginnings and the ends of word forms. More generally, these and other empirical findings suggest that some aspect of phonological encoding is sequential, contrary to the semantic–phonological model, which assumes parallel activation of sounds and relies on a frame-and-slot mechanism to sort out serial order.

Control–signal models provide an alternative to parallel activation. These models replace the static word units in the semantic–phonological model with units that generate a time-varying control signal. This signal allows for sequential retrieval of a word's sounds. The first control–signal model of phonological access in production was that of Houghton (1990), illustrated in Fig. 12.5. There are three layers of units in this model, word–control–signal units, phoneme units, and a competitive filter. Each word is represented by two control–signal units, a *start* and an *end* unit. At the beginning of a phoneme sequence, the start unit will be on and the end unit will be off, and this state will gradually evolve into the reverse by the word's end. Words are learned by associating the sequence of phoneme units with the control–signal

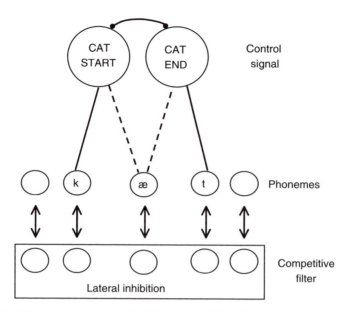

Figure 12.5.   The control–signal model of Houghton (1990), illustrated for the word CAT.

units by a Hebbian learning process. The word–initial phoneme will thus get strong weights to the start unit, medial phonemes will have weights to both units, and final ones will connect primarily to the end unit. At the beginning of access, the control–signal's state will ensure that the first phoneme is the most activated one. The activations of all of the phoneme units are then passed on to the competitive filter, which uses lateral inhibitory connections to select the most activated phoneme, presumably the initial one at the beginning of a word. Then, the selected phoneme is suppressed. This is necessary to prevent erroneous reselection of a phoneme. Finally, the control–signal state is updated and the entire process continues, with the result that the second phoneme gains the most activation, is selected and then suppressed, and so on until the end of the word.

Houghton's control–signal model is truly sequential and hence is consistent with the findings suggesting sequential access during phonological encoding. More importantly, though, it addresses the serial ordering issues that were ignored by approaches such as the semantic–phonological model. The control–signal model is, in principle, capable of representing phoneme order for all lexical items. Furthermore, there is no need for different units for phonemes occurring in different positions. The model allows, for example, the access of the same unit for [d] in the word DID.

However, the frame-and-slot mechanism used by Foygel & Dell does have some advantages over the control–signal approach. These have to do with the production phenomena related to linguistic structure, which is the topic of the next section.

LINGUISTIC STRUCTURE

The frame-and-slot approaches to the order of sounds in words give an account of three aspects of phonological speech errors, the *vowel–consonant effect*, the *syllable-position effect*, and the *phonotactic regularity effect*. The vowel–consonant effect is a constraint that vowels replace vowels, e.g. CAT is spoken as [kUt], and consonants replace consonants, e.g. CAT is spoken as [gaet]. The syllable-position effect is a tendency for phonemes in particular syllable positions (onset, vowel, coda) to move to corresponding positions, e.g. the coda [s] in "house" moves to a coda position in the error "lighthouse" spoken as "licehouse". Phonotactic regularity refers to the fact that phonological speech errors only rarely create sound combinations that violate the phonotactic patterns of the language. Thus, the error "dlorm" for "dorm" (Stemberger, 1983) is exceptional.

What these three phenomena have in common is that they illustrate how speech errors are governed by linguistic structure. To explain them, a model must be sensitive to the phonology of the language being spoken. This is what the frame provides. It enforces constraints on the ultimate shape of syllables that are encoded, e.g. it only allows vowels in vowel locations and consonants in consonant locations. Furthermore, the use of positional categories such as onset and coda in the frame offers a mechanism for the syllable-position effect. And finally, the frame can be associated with other constraints, such that phonotactically impossible sequences such as word initial [dl] are prevented.

Given the useful features that frames provide, it would be desirable to combine these with control–signal accounts of serial order within words. A model by Hartley & Houghton (1996) has done just this. The model, shown in Fig. 12.6, retains the idea from Houghton (1990) that the input to the model is a time-varying signal across a pair of units. This signal is now explicitly associated with the distinction between the onset of a syllable (one unit) and vowel–coda combination or rhyme (the other unit). The control–signal units are connected to phoneme units and to slots in a generic *syllable template*. This template implements the frame. It consists of units for five positions in a maximal English syllable CCVCC, with each unit associated with the kind of phoneme that can go in that position. The template units are activated one at a time, and each, when activated, sends a signal to all phonemes that are consistent with that slot. This signal then combines with activation sent directly to the target phonemes (first to those of the onset, and then those of the rhyme), effectively ordering the target phonemes in a way that is sensitive to linguistic structure.

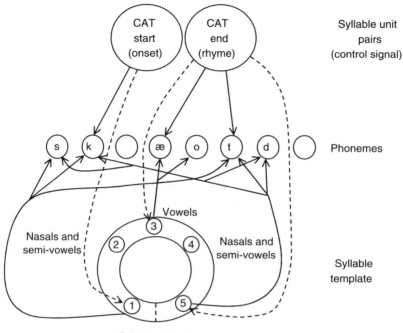

Figure 12.6.   The model of Hartley & Houghton (1996), showing the structures and connections relevant for the syllable CAT.

The Hartley & Houghton model, and other connectionist-like models that implement frame-like structures (e.g. Gupta & MacWhinney, 1997; Levelt et al., 1999; Roelofs, 1997; Schade, 1992, 1999), go a long way towards provid-ing an account of sequential and structural effects on phonological encoding. However, from a connectionist perspective, there is something unsatisfying about explicit implementations of frames. Many connectionist models seek to have linguistic structure emerge from general principles of learning and cognition, rather than directly building it in (Elman et al., 1996; MacWhinney, 1999; Seidenberg & MacDonald, 1999). Can the same be done for phonological frames?

Initial attempts to develop connectionist models of phonological encoding in production without explicit frames met with limited success. Dell et al. (1993) trained simple recurrent networks (e.g. Elman, 1990; Gupta & Cohen, 2002; Jordan, 1986) by back-propagation to map between distributed repre-sentations of words and sequences of phonological features. After training with short words from limited vocabularies (50–412 English words), the model was able to learn the mapping fairly well. Importantly, the errors that occurred when noise was added to the connection weights exhibited some of the structural properties that suggest frames. For example, the errors tended to be phonotactically regular. CAT might be encoded as [gaet] or [ket], but never as [tkae]. This effect arises because of the model's featural representations of phonemes and its learning mechanisms. Consider the phonotactic regularity effect. The units and connections that code each word's form are used to code the forms of related words. Hence, the retrieval of a word's form is influenced by the properties of many other similar words. This induces a bias for the model's errors to follow the general characteristics of the language's word forms, and hence the errors obey phonotactics constraints.

There is, however, a major problem with the recurrent network models of phonological encoding. They cannot produce phoneme movement errors, particularly exchanges. Consider the error, "heft lemisphere" for "left hemisphere". In frame-based models of phonological encoding that can encode more than one word or syllable (e.g. Dell, 1986), exchanges result from interactions between frame-insertion operations and post-selection suppression. If [h] replaces [l] in "left", the [h] rather than the [l] is suppressed after being inserted in the frame slot for onset. Consequently, when the next syllable's onset slot is being filled, the [h] may be less active than it should be. Specifically, the [l], which was passed over when "left" was encoded, may be more active than [h] resulting in the complete exchange, "heft lemisphere". The recurrent network models have nothing analogous to the suppression of a phoneme that has been associated with a particular slot and hence do not produce exchanges.

A recent model may offer an "emergentist" account of frames, an account that is consistent with the existence of exchanges and the effects of linguistic structure on errors. Vousden et al. (2000) have proposed that the time-varying components of phonological encoding, such the control–signal syllable pairs and the syllable template in the Hartley & Houghton (1996) model, can emerge from sets of oscillators that control timing in motor systems (e.g. Brown, Preece, & Hulme, 2000). Specifically, Vousden et al.'s model, OSCAR (for oscillator-based associative recall), assumes that during phonological encoding, phonemes (as sets of features) acquire weighted connections to two sets of oscillators, one that constitutes a nonrepeating control signal, and a set that repeats with the period of a syllable. The links between elements of the nonrepeating signal and the phonological features activate the phonological content of each syllable in sequence, much like the start and end units in Houghton (1990). The links between the repeating signal and the features are analogous to those between the syllable template slots and the phonemes in Hartley & Houghton's model.

Consider how OSCAR would phonologically encode the phrase "tin cup". First, the sequence of features in these syllables would be associated with oscillator states, and then the sequence would be produced. For the association process, the oscillators would be set to some initial state, and the features of the [t] would be linked to that state by Hebbian learning. Then the signal emanating from the oscillators would change due to their own internal dynamics, and the features of [I] would be linked to that new state, and so on until the end of the phrase. Crucially, because some of the oscillators repeat with the period of a syllable, the signal state at the time of [t] will be similar to (share elements with) the state at the time for [k] in "cup". Also, the states at [I] and [n] would be similar to those at [ʌ] and [p], respectively.

After this association process, actual production begins. The initial state of the oscillators is reinstated, and this state changes over time, as determined by the oscillators' dynamics, recalling the sequence of features associated with each state. At the beginning, the activation flows to features that were linked to this initial state, those of [t]. Because of the repeating syllable component of the oscillators, however, some activation will flow to [k], in addition to [t]. If there is some noise in the system, the [k] may replace the [t], thus creating a substitution from a corresponding syllable position, here onset to onset. OSCAR, like all of the other phonological encoding models, assumes that there is suppression of the selected output. Hence, an initial error such as "tin cup" being produced as "kin . . ." may lead to a completed exchange ". . . tup" when the oscillators reach the state corresponding to the onset of the second syllable.

Thus, we see that error phenomena related to linguistic structure may be accommodated in models of phonological encoding. Dynamic control signals that correspond to the cyclical aspects of production, such as the syllable, can function as phonological frames. In particular, the OSCAR model seems to have a great deal of promise in this respect.

LEARNING

The third challenge facing connectionist models of production is that of learning. How does a model build its vocabulary and acquire the skills of producing words and sentences?

The semantic–phonological aphasia model did not address learning. However, some of the other models of phonological encoding in production have learning mechanisms. In the models of Houghton (1990) and Hartley & Houghton (1996), the sequence of phonemes for a word or syllable is learned through a single presentation of the sequence. The model "hears" the sequence, stores it via Hebbian learning, and then can produce it later. This ability to acquire a sequence in one presentation distinguishes these models from the recurrent network production models (e.g. Dell et al., 1993), which use back-propagation and require many trials to acquire a sequence. Single-trial learning accords with the fact that people can repeat a sequence simply from hearing it once. Not only that, we can learn a word and its meaning from hearing it just once or twice in context (Carey, 1978).

The control–signal models' ability to learn a sequence from a single presentation is made possible by the assumption that the units that represent heard phonemes are the same units that represent spoken phonemes. So, the connections between phonemes and lexical control signals acquired during input are the same as those that direct output. Although this proposal provides a good account of the acquisition of word forms, there are contrary data. Some neuropsychological evidence suggests that the connections between lexical and phonological units are separate for input and output (e.g. Nickels & Howard, 1995). Patients with phonological output deficits can sometimes be largely unimpaired in phonological input tasks. In fact, the semantic–phonological model makes exactly this assumption in its account of repetition deficits: The presented word is assumed to be correctly recognized (strong input phoneme-word weights), while production performance is very errorful (weak phonological weights on the output side). Clearly, there is need for a better understanding of the relations among the acquisition, production, and recognition of word forms (see Gupta & MacWhinney, 1997; Plaut & Kello, 1999).

Another aspect of learning in production that is typically not addressed by connectionist models is post-acquisition learning. Language learning really never stops. The production system, in particular, continually adapts to its current demands. Some of these adaptations can be understood as lexical priming or frequency effects, effects that alter the availability of a particular word form. Words that are common or have been recently produced are associated with lower error rates or faster retrieval times (Jescheniak & Levelt, 1994).

Other learning effects, however, cannot be due to the priming of a single word form. For example, consider the difficulty a speaker has in saying a tongue-twister such as "Chef's sooty shoe soles". This difficulty is greatly alleviated by practicing the phrase four or five times. In fact, not only are errors reduced as a function of practice, but their character changes. Difficult tongue-twisters tend to be associated with perseveratory substitutions of phonemes or words (e.g. ". . . shoe sholes"). After practice, anticipatory substitutions (e.g. "sef's sooty . . .") are more common than perseveratory ones. This *anticipatory practice effect* can be accounted for by a learning mechanism that enables phrasal units to gain more activation with practice, along with a post-selection suppression mechanism that is effective, regardless of amount of practice (Dell, Burger, & Svec, 1997). Hence, upcoming units end up being relatively more activated that previously spoken ones. However, alternative accounts, such as one in which practice increases the efficiency of suppression, cannot be ruled out.

Another example of adaptive learning was demonstrated by Dell, Reed, Adams, and Meyer (2000). They had speakers recite strings of syllables, such as "hes feg meng ken" in time with a metronome in a 4-day experiment. On each day the speakers recited 96 such strings three times each. Each string was composed of four CVC syllables, and always contained the same eight consonants. Two of these, [h] and [ŋ], are required by the phonotactics of English to occur in only one syllable position; [h] must be an onset, and [ŋ] must be a coda. Two other sounds, [f] and [s], were also given restricted distributions throughout the experiment. Half of the speakers always experienced [f] as an onset and [s] as a coda, and half experienced the reverse assignment. Thus, the study created artificial experiment-wide phonotactic constraints on these two sounds. The remaining sounds, [m], [n], [k], and [g], could occur both as onsets and as codas.

The data of interest in Dell et al.'s experiment were errors in which consonants moved from one syllable to another. As expected, the misplacements of [ŋ] and [h] kept to their syllable position 100% of the time. This is the phonotactic regularity effect on errors; an error string such as [ŋ eg] violates English phonotactics and hence does not occur. Movements of [m], [n], [k], and [g] exhibited a weaker tendency to retain their original syllable position— 68% of the time. This is the syllable position effect referred to earlier. The novel result in the study concerned movements of [f] and [s], the phonemes whose positions were restricted within the experiment. These kept to their syllable position 98% of the time, far in excess of the 68% of the time that the other consonants retained their position.

This error sensitivity to the experiment-wide distribution of sounds seems to be a form of learning, one that adapts the production system to what it has recently produced. Moreover, the learning occurs quite rapidly. On the first day of testing, there were 184 misplacements of [f] and [s]. Only four of these were movements to the incorrect syllable position. Dell et al. suggested that each utterance of a syllable tunes the production system to favor the production of that and similar syllables. The effect of the tuning lasts for longer than a single trial sequence (three repetitions of the four-syllable string), and it accumulates with the tuning associated with other utterances. The overall effect is to adapt the system to recent experience. In fact, one can speculate that the constraint that errors be phonotactically well formed is the result of recent speaking experience, instead of abstract phonological knowledge acquired early in childhood.

Thus, learning in production is associated with several empirical phenomena. These will continue to challenge models of production. A key question concerns the relation between acquisition and later learning. Can models of the acquisition of production skills also account for the learning and adaptation that occur later in life? Or vice versa? Connectionist models, by virtue of their explicit learning and processing mechanisms, should be extremely important tools for answering this question.

CONCLUSIONS

This chapter began by presenting a recent connectionist model of lexical access in production, the semantic–phonological model. This model emphasized the two-step nature of access, but allowed each access step to be carried out by interactive activation. Although that model provided a good account of the basic error categories associated with the access of single words by normal and aphasic speakers, it suffered from a number of limitations, particularly with respect to its mechanisms for phonological processes. Models that make use of time-varying control signals have promise in addressing these limitations, by providing for effects of linguistic structure and temporal sequence on phonological encoding. Ultimately, though, production models need to take greater advantage of connectionist learning mechanisms and address data that are informative about how the language production system changes with experience.

ACKNOWLEDGEMENTS

Preparation of this chapter was supported by grants NSF SBR 98–73450 and NIH DC-00191. The author thanks Linda May and Judy Allen for work on the manuscript.

Notes

1. Specifically, the noise was the sum of two components, intrinsic noise (sd = .01, mean = 0) and activation noise (sd =. 16A(j,t), mean = 0). In essence this makes noise increase linearly with activation, but there is still some noise when activation is zero.
2. The weight and decay parameters in Table 12.1 are from the version of the model by Foygel & Dell, and are slightly different from those used by Dell et al. Other parameters were given previously in the text and are the same as those used by Dell et al.
3. "Simple" is difficult to define precisely here. But the extent to which the region has few dimensions and is monotonic would contribute to simplicity.
4. The earlier model of Dell et al. had also assumed two lesionable parameters, a single global connection weight, and the decay rate.

REFERENCES

Berg, T., & Schade, U. (1992). The role of inhibition in a spreading activation model of language production, Part 1: The psycholinguistic perspective. *Journal of Psycholinguistic Research, 22,* 405–434.

Bock, J. K. (1982). Towards a cognitive psychology of syntax: Information processing contributions to sentence formulation. *Psychological Review, 89,* 1–47.

Bock, J. K. (1986). Syntactic persistence in language production. *Cognitive Psychology, 18,* 355–387.

Bock, J. K. (1995). Sentence production: From mind to mouth. In J. L. Miller, and P. D. Eimas

(Eds.), *Handbook of perception and cognition, Vol. 11: Speech, language and communication* (pp. 181–216). Orlando, FL: Academic Press.

Bock, J. K., & Griffin, Z. M. (2000). The persistence of structural priming. *Journal of Experimental Psychology: General, 129,* 177–192.

Brown, G. D. A., Preece, T., & Hulme, C. (2000). An oscillator-based model of memory for serial order. *Psychological Review, 107,* 127–181.

Caramazza, A. (1997). How many levels of processing are there in lexical access? *Cognitive Neuropsychology, 14,* 177–208.

Carey, S. (1978). The child as word learner. In M. Halle, J. Bresnan, & G. Miller (Eds.), *Linguistic theory and psychological reality.* Cambridge, MA: MIT Press.

Chang, F. (2002). Symbolically speaking: A connectionist model of sentence production. *Cognitive Science, 26,* 609–651.

Chang, F., Dell, G. S., Bock, J. K., & Griffin, Z. M. (2000). Structural priming as implicit learning: A comparison of models of sentence production. *Journal of Psycholinguistics, 29,* 217–229.

Cutting, J. C., & Ferreira, V. S. (1999). Semantic and phonological information flow in the production lexicon. *Journal of Experimental Psychology: Learning, Memory, and Cognition, 25*(2), 318–344.

Damian, M. F., & Martin, R. C. (1999). Semantic and phonological codes interact in single word production. *Journal of Experimental Psychology: Learning, Memory, & Cognition, 25*(2), 1345–1361.

Dell, G. S. (1986). A spreading activation theory of retrieval in language production. *Psychological Review, 93,* 283–321.

Dell, G. S., Burger, L. K., & Svec, W. R. (1997). Language production and serial order: A functional analysis and a model. *Psychological Review, 104*(1), 123–147.

Dell, G. S., Juliano, C., & Govindjee, A. (1993). Structure and content in language production: A theory of frame constraints in phonological speech errors. *Cognitive Science, 17,* 149–195.

Dell, G. S., & O'Seaghdha, P. G. (1991). Mediated and convergent lexical priming in language production: A comment on Levelt et al. *Psychological Review, 98,* 604–614.

Dell, G. S., Reed, K. D., Adams, D. R., & Meyer, A. S. (2000). Speech errors, phonotactic constraints, and implicit learning: A study of the role of experience in language production. *Journal of Experimental Psychology: Learning, Memory, and Cognition, 26,* 1355–1367.

Dell, G. S., & Reich, P. A. (1981). Stages in sentence production: An analysis of speech error data. *Journal of Verbal Learning and Verbal Behavior, 20,* 611–629.

Dell, G. S., & Repka, R. (1992). Errors in inner speech. In B. Baars (Ed.), Experimental slips and human error: Exploring the architecture of volition (pp. 237–262). New York: Plenum.

Dell, G. S., Schwartz, M. F., Martin, N., Saffran, E. M., & Gagnon, D. A. (1997). Lexical access in aphasic and nonaphasic speakers. *Psychological Review, 104,* 801–838.

Elman, J. L. (1990). Finding structure in time. *Cognitive Science, 14,* 179–211.

Elman, J. L., Bates, E. A., Johnson, M. H., Karmiloff-Smith, A., Parisi, D., & Plunkett, K. (1996). *Rethinking innateness: A connectionist perspective on development.* Cambridge, MA: MIT Press.

Ferreira, V. S. (1996). Is it better to give than to donate? Syntactic flexibility in language production. *Journal of Memory and Language, 35,* 724–755.

Ferreira, V. S., & Dell, G. S. (2000). The effect of ambiguity and lexical availability on syntactic and lexical production. *Cognitive Psychology, 40,* 296–340.

Foygel, D., & Dell, G. S. (2000). Models of impaired lexical access in speech production. *Journal of Memory and Language, 43,* 182–216.

Fromkin, V. A. (1971). The non-anomalous nature of anomalous utterances. *Language, 47,* 27–52.

Garrett, M. F. (1975). The analysis of sentence production. In G. H. Bower (Ed.), *The psychology of learning and motivation* (Vol. 9, pp. 133–177). New York: Academic Press.

Garrett, M. (1984). The organization of processing structure of language production: Application to aphasic speech. In D. Caplan, A. Lecours, & A. Smith (Eds.), *Biological perspectives on language*. Cambridge, MA: MIT Press.

Gordon, J. K., & Dell, G. S. (2003). Learning to divide the labor: An account of deficits in light and heavy verbs production. *Cognitive Science, 27,* 1–40.

Griffin, Z. M., & Bock, J. K. (1998). Constraint, word frequency, and the relationship between lexical processing levels in spoken word production. *Journal of Memory and Language, 38,* 313–338.

Guenther, F. H. (1995). Speech sound acquisition, co-articulation, and rate effects in a neural network model of speech production. *Psychological Review, 102,* 594–621.

Gupta, P., & Cohen, N. J. (2002). Skill learning, repetition priming, and procedural memory: Theoretical and computational analysis. *Psychological Review, 109,* 401–448.

Gupta, P., & MacWhinney, B. (1997). Vocabulary acquisition and verbal short-term memory: Computational and neural bases. *Brain & Language, 59*(2), 1267–1333.

Harley, T. A. (1984). A critique of top-down independent levels models of speech production: Evidence from non-plan-internal speech errors. *Cognitive Science, 8,* 191–219.

Harley, T. A. (1993). Phonological activation of semantic competitors during lexical access in speech production. *Language & Cognitive Processes, 8*(3), 1291–1309.

Hartley, T., & Houghton, G. (1996). A linguistically-constrained model of short-term memory for nonwords. *Journal of Memory and Language, 35,* 1–31.

Hillis, A. E., Boatman, D., Hart, J., & Gordon, B. (1999). Making sense out of jargon: A neurolinguistic and computational account of jargon aphasia. *Neurology, 53,* 1813–1824.

Houghton, G. (1990). The problem of serial order: A neural network model of sequence learning and recall. In R. Dale, C. Mellish & M. Zock (Eds.), *Current research in natural language generation* (pp. 287–319). London: Academic Press.

Houghton, G. (1993). *A constraint-satisfaction model of grammatical role assignment in language production.* Unpublished manuscript.

Humphreys, G. W., Riddoch, M. J., & Quinlan, P. T. (1988). Cascade processes in picture identification. Special Issue: The cognitive neuropsychology of visual and semantic processing of concepts. *Cognitive Neuropsychology, 5*(1), 67–104.

Jescheniak, J. D., & Levelt, W. J. M. (1994). Word frequency effects in speech production: Retrieval of syntactic information and of phonological form. *Journal of Experimental Psychology: Learning, Memory and Cognition, 20,* 824–843.

Jescheniak, J. D., & Schriefers, H. (1998). Discrete serial versus cascaded processing in lexical access in speech production: Further evidence from the coactivation of near-synonyms. *Journal of Experimental Psychology: Learning, Memory, and Cognition, 24*(5), 1256–1274.

Jordan, M. I. (1986). Attractor dynamics and parallelism in a connectionist sequential machine. In *Proceedings of the Eighth Annual Conference of the Cognitive Science Society* (pp. 531–546). Hillsdale, NJ: Lawrence Erlbaum Associates, Inc.

Kempen, G. (1997). *Grammatical performance in human sentence production and comprehension.* Unpublished manuscript.

Kempen, G., & Huijbers, P. (1983). The lexicalization process in sentence production and naming: Indirect election of words. *Cognition, 14,* 185–209.

Levelt, W. J. M. (1989). *Speaking: From intention to articulation.* Cambridge, MA: MIT Press.

Levelt, W. J. M., Roelofs, A., & Meyer, A. S. (1999). A theory of lexical access in speech production. *Behavioral and Brain Science, 21,* 1–38.

Levelt, W. J. M., Schriefers, H., Vorberg, D., Meyer, A. S., Pechmann, T., & Havinga, J. (1991). Normal and deviant lexical processing: Reply to Dell & O'Seaghdha (1991). *Psychological Review, 98,* 615–618.

MacKay, D. G. (1970). Spoonerisms: The structure of errors in the serial order of speech. *Neuropsychologia, 8,* 323–350.

MacKay, D. G. (1982). The problems of flexibility, fluency, and speed–accuracy trade-off in skilled behaviors. *Psychological Review, 89,* 483–506.

MacWhinney, B. (Ed.) (1999). *The emergence of language.* Mahwah, NJ: Lawrence Erlbaum Associates, Inc.

Martin, N., Gagnon, D. A., Schwartz, M. F., Dell, G. S., & Saffran, E. M. (1996). Phonological facilitation of semantic errors in normal and aphasic speakers. *Language and Cognitive Processes, 11,* 257–282.

McClelland, J. L., & Rumelhart, D. E. (1981). An interactive activation model of context effects in letter perception: Part 1. An account of basic findings. *Psychological Review, 88,* 375–407.

Meyer, A. S. (1990). The time course of phonological encoding in language production: The encoding of successive syllables of a word. *Journal of Memory and Language, 29,* 524–545.

Meyer, A. S. (1991). The time course of phonological encoding in language production: Phonological encoding inside a syllable. *Journal of Memory and Language, 30,* 69–89.

Nickels, L. A., & Howard, D. (1995). Phonological errors in aphasic naming: Comprehension, monitoring and lexicality. *Cortex, 31*(2), 1209–1237.

O'Seaghdha, P. G., & Marin, J. W. (2000). Phonological competition and cooperation in form-related priming: Sequential and nonsequential processes in word production. *Journal of Experimental Psychology: Human Perception and Performance, 26,* 57–73.

Peterson, R. R., & Savoy, P. (1998). Lexical selection and phonological encoding during language production: Evidence for cascaded processing. *Journal of Experimental Psychology: Learning, Memory, & Cognition, 24,* 539–557.

Plaut, D. C., & Kello, C. T. (1999). The emergence of phonology from the interplay of speech comprehension and production: A distributed connectionist approach. In B. MacWhinney (Ed.), *The emergence of language.* Mahwah, NJ: Lawrence Erlbaum Associates, Inc.

Rapp, B., & Goldrick, M. (2000). Discreteness and interactivity in spoken word production. *Psychological Review, 107,* 460–499.

Roach, A., Schwartz, M. F., Martin, N., Grewal, R. A., & Brecher, A. (1996). The Philadelphia Naming Test: Scoring and rationale. *Clinical Aphasiology, 24,* 121–133.

Roelofs, A. (1992). A spreading-activation theory of lemma retrieval in speaking. *Cognition, 42,* 107–142.

Roelofs, A. (1997). The WEAVER model of word-form encoding in speech production. *Cognition, 64,* 249–284.

Roelofs, A., & Meyer, A. S. (1998). Metrical structure in planning the production of spoken words. *Journal of Experimental Psychology: Learning, Memory, and Cognition, 24,* 922–939.

Schade, U. (1992). *Konnektionismus—Zur Modellierung der Sprachproduktion.* Opladen: Westdeutscher-Verlag.

Schade, U. (1999). *Konnektionistische Sprachproduktion.* Wiesbaden: Deutscher Universitäts Verlag.

Schriefers, H., Meyer, A. S., & Levelt, W. J. M. (1990). Exploring the time-course of lexical access in production: Picture–word interference studies. *Journal of Memory and Language, 29,* 86–102.

Schwartz, M. F. (1987). Patterns of speech production deficit within and across aphasia syndromes: Applications of a psycholinguistic model. In M. Coltheart, R. Job, & G. Sartori (Eds.), *The cognitive neuropsychology of language.* Hillsdale, NJ: Lawrence Erlbaum Associates, Inc.

Schwartz, M. F., & Brecher, A. (2000). A model-driven analysis of severity, response characteristics and partial recovery in aphasics' picture naming. *Brain and Language, 73,* 62–91.

Seidenberg, M. S., & MacDonald, M. C. (1999). A probabilistic constraints approach to language acquisition and processing. *Cognitive Science, 23,* 569–588.

Sevald, C., & Dell, G. S. (1994). The sequential cuing effect in speech production. *Cognition, 53,* 91–127.

Shattuck-Hufnagel, S. (1979). Speech errors as evidence for a serial-order mechanism in sentence production. In W. E. Cooper, & E. C. T. Walker (Eds.), *Sentence processing: Psycholinguistic studies presented to Merrill Garrett* (pp. 295–342). Hillsdale, NJ: Lawrence Erlbaum Associates, Inc.

Shattuck-Hufnagel, S. (1983). Sublexical units and suprasegmental structure in speech production planning. In P. F. MacNeilage (Ed.), *The production of speech* (pp. 109–136). New York: Springer-Verlag.

Stemberger, J. P. (1983). *Speech errors and theoretical phonology: A review.* Bloomington, IN: Indiana University Linguistics Club.

Stemberger, J. P. (1985). An interactive activation model of language production. In A. W. Ellis (Ed.), *Progress in the psychology of language* (Vol. 1, pp. 143–186). Hillsdale, NJ: Lawrence Erlbaum Associates Inc.

van Turennout, M., Hagoort, P., & Brown, C. M. (1998). Brain activity during speaking: From syntax to phonology in 40 milliseconds. *Science, 280,* 572–574.

Vousden, J. I., Brown, G. D. A., & Harley, T. A. (2000). Serial control of phonology in speech production: A hierarchical model. *Cognitive Psychology, 2,* 101–175.

Wheeldon, L. R., & Levelt, W. J. M. (1995). Monitoring the time course of phonological encoding. *Journal of Memory and Language, 34,* 311–334.

CHAPTER THIRTEEN

Computational models of reading

Marco Zorzi
University of Padova, Italy

INTRODUCTION

Experimental psychologists have been interested in reading research for more than 30 years. It was readily recognized that reading is a complex cognitive skill based on a number of different functions and components. For instance, upon presentation of a printed word, we can immediately understand its meaning, e.g. in silent reading, and we can sound it out if asked to do so, e.g. in reading aloud. However, we can read aloud words that we have not seen before, including novel (although pronounceable) combinations of letters. We can also decide whether or not a given letter string is a real word. Because reading is the result of a complex cognitive activity, one main thrust of reading research has been directed towards fractionating the reading process into several subcomponents.

In this chapter, I review recent progress in developing computational models of (oral) reading of isolated words. The chapter is organized as follows: The first part is an overview of the empirical background and of the traditional (verbal) theories of reading; in the second part three recent computational models are reviewed and evaluated with respect to a number of benchmarks, based on experimental studies on normal subjects as well as brain-damaged patients; in the third part the models are compared to highlight similarities and differences; in the fourth, final part I briefly discuss the issue of adjudication between models and some future directions of the modelling enterprise.

Psychology of reading

There is an incontrovertible fact about languages that use the alphabetic writing system: letters and letter patterns (e.g. graphemes) largely correspond to speech units (e.g. phonemes). However, in some languages the correspondence between orthography and phonology is not always straightforward. A theoretically relevant distinction among the many alphabetic languages is the degree of *consistency* of the spelling–sound mappings, i.e. how much the spelling–sound (grapheme–phoneme) correspondences are constant across the whole vocabulary. When an appropriate set of spelling–sound conversion rules is used with languages like Italian, Spanish, or Serbo-Croatian, the derived (or *assembled*) pronunciation is in most cases correct; that is to say, readers of these languages can reliably assemble the correct pronunciation of a given word even when it is unfamiliar to them (i.e. it has not been encountered before).[1] The orthographic systems of these languages are referred to as "*shallow*" (Frost, Katz, & Bentin, 1987). By contrast, in languages like English or French ("*deep*" orthographies), the correspondences between graphemes and phonemes can be multiple and less systematic, e.g. the graphemes *au, aux, eau, eaux, o*, correspond to a single phoneme /o/ in French. In English these correspondences are in some cases irregular (e.g. the vowels in PINT, HAVE) or arbitrary (e.g. the vowel in COLONEL). In fact, the major locus of inconsistency in English is the vowel (see Treiman, Mullenix, Bijeljac-Babic, & Richmond-Welty, 1995; Venetzky, 1970): a single vowel grapheme often maps onto several phonemes, e.g. EA in MEAN, HEAD, STEAK is pronounced as /i/, /e/, /eI/,[2] respectively. For instance, the /e/ pronunciation of EA in HEAD is atypical, and is therefore an exception to the most typical EA → /i/ rule. Therefore, it is possible to distinguish between *regular* words, where using spelling–sound correspondences would yield the correct pronunciation, and *exception* words, where using the same correspondences would yield a wrong pronunciation (a so-called *regularization* error; e.g. reading PINT to rhyme with MINT).

Dual-route models

Readers could not be confident about the pronunciation of written words if only correspondence rules were used in reading. In fact, skilled readers can usually read exception words such as PINT, HAVE, COLONEL perfectly well. However, it is also clear that they know and use correspondence rules, because they will read similar looking nonwords (e.g. KINT, MAVE, SOLONEL) in a way which reflects, not the individual exception words, but the phonological values the letters standardly represent. Such observations have led to "dual-route" models of reading, which postulate two routes from spelling to sound (see e.g. Baron & Strawson, 1976; Besner & Smith, 1992; Coltheart, 1978, 1985; Forster, 1976; Morton & Patterson, 1980; Paap &

Noel, 1991; Patterson & Morton, 1985). One, usually referred to as the lexical route, is thought to operate by retrieving word pronunciations from an internal lexicon. It is therefore based on a word-specific association mechanism, and contains any learned word. The phonological form is thus "addressed" from the visual word form as a whole; therefore, it has been considered a look-up procedure, and its product has been called *addressed* (or *retrieved*) *phonology*.

It is widely agreed (but see Van Orden, Pennington, & Stone, 1990) that the lexical route can also operate through the mediation of word meanings. In this lexical–semantic route the printed form accesses the semantic representation of that word, which in turn activates the corresponding phonology; therefore, this procedure has been usually referred to as *reading via meaning*. The distinction between a lexical–semantic route and a direct lexical (i.e. nonsemantic) route was first suggested by a case study of acquired dyslexia described in 1980 by Schwartz, Saffran, & Marin (note that this distinction means that the dual-route model is in fact a three-route model). Most theorists assume that the semantic route contributes little to word naming in skilled readers, since, being indirect, it is slow in delivering a word pronunciation (but see Patterson, Graham, & Hodges, 1994; Plaut, McClelland, Seidenberg, & Patterson, 1996). However, Strain, Patterson, & Seidenberg (1995) demonstrated some impact of a semantic variable (imageability) in reading low-frequency exception words (i.e. the words that usually yield the longest naming latencies); this finding has been recently replicated across different orthographic systems (Shibahara, Zorzi, Hill, Wydell, & Butterworth, 2003). In the lexical route, orthographic, semantic, and phonological representations of words are functionally independent and are stored in the orthographic input lexicon, semantic system, and phonological output lexicon, respectively. The orthographic input lexicon contains units that represent the orthographic form (i.e. the spelt form) of any written word known by the reader; this allows the identification and recognition of familiar letter strings.

The second route (the sublexical or nonlexical route) is described as a letter-to-sound mapping, resulting in the *assembled phonology*, which is based upon explicit rules specifying the dominant (e.g. most frequent) relationships between letters and sounds (for reviews, see Carr & Pollatsek, 1985; Patterson & V. Coltheart, 1987). This knowledge about the common spelling–sound relationships in the language can be applied on any string of letters in order to derive a set of sounds that are assembled into a phonological code. The assembly route can be used on both known words (and will yield the correct pronunciation if they follow the standard pronunciation rules—so-called "regular" words) and novel items (new words, nonwords). Thus, the lexical route can handle all known words including exceptional spelling–sound relationships and provides the unusual /&/ in HAVE, whereas the assembled route produces the /eI/ in MAVE on the basis of words such as GAVE, WAVE, SAVE, SLAVE, etc.

Among dual-route theorists there is a large consensus on the modules involved in word recognition and naming, but not on the internal operations of those modules (Carr & Pollatsek, 1985), particularly in regard to the assembly mechanism. One main issue is the nature of the spelling–sound rules involved in phonological assembly. According to Coltheart (1978; Coltheart, Curtis, Atkins, & Haller, 1993) the spelling–sound correspondence system operates on a set of rules that translates individual graphemes into the corresponding phonemes. The term "grapheme" refers to letters and letter groups (or *functional spelling unit*; see Venetzky, 1970) that represent a single phoneme. Therefore, print-to-sound transcoding involves segmentation and conversion rules that operate on grapheme–phoneme correspondences (GPC): each individual grapheme is associated to its most frequent phonemic realization. However, recent evidence suggests that the spelling–sound mapping in English cannot be solely described in terms of grapheme–phoneme correspondences. Treiman et al. (1995) have demonstrated that a larger orthographic unit, referred to as word body or rhyme (i.e. the homologue of the rhyme in spoken syllables, i.e. the vowel and any following consonants), is a better guide to pronunciation than the isolated graphemes, and that this unit plays a role in skilled reading. Although a consideration of the rhyme units makes English spelling–sound mapping somewhat more systematic, there is no doubt that the many exception words can be only dealt with by the readers on a whole-word basis.

If both lexical and sublexical processes act in parallel on any input string, then exception words will (by definition) lead to disagreements between the two readings. That is, the output produced by the lexical procedure conflicts with the incorrect pronunciation ("regularization") generated by the assembled procedure; such interference would lead in turn to longer reaction times. The idea of conflicting outputs represents the classic explanation for the so-called regularity effect: subjects are slower to read irregularly spelled words than regular words (Glushko, 1979; Paap & Noel, 1991; Seidenberg, Waters, Barnes, & Tanenhaus, 1984; Taraban & McClelland, 1987). However, the regularity effect tends to be weak or altogether absent for high frequency words (Seidenberg et al., 1984). The standard account of this frequency by regularity interaction is that the lexical route is much faster than the assembly route: therefore, for high-frequency words, the addressed (lexical) phonology can be output before any interference from the assembly route may arise. Thus, some models assume a "horse race" between the two outputs (e.g. Paap & Noel, 1991), where the response is determined by the first process to finish. Other models propose that the output of the two processes is pooled continuously until a phonological representation sufficient to drive articulation is generated (e.g. Monsell, Patterson, Graham, Hughes, & Milroy, 1992).

Lexical analogy models

A second class of models assumes a single process in spelling-to-sound translation, denying the existence of functionally separated lexical and sublexical processes. In an important paper, Glushko (1979) found that the pronunciation of words and nonwords is influenced by knowledge of other words with similar spelling patterns. Letter strings which share the word body (vowel and final consonants) with exception words yielded longer naming latencies. This effect was termed the "consistency effect", because performance is determined by the consistency of spelling–sound relationships of the neighbourhood of similarly spelled words. Since most of the exception words are also inconsistent, it was argued that the regular exception distinction is psychologically useless: what is important is whether a word is consistent or inconsistent with the orthographic and phonological structure that it activates. Furthermore, subjects gave an irregular pronunciation to a significant number of the inconsistent nonwords, i.e. nonwords containing substrings with more than one common pronunciation (e.g. "OVE" may be pronounced as in STOVE, WOVE, GROVE, etc., or LOVE, GLOVE, SHOVE). These results have been taken as strong evidence against the dual-route model: if GPC rules are used by the subjects, all nonwords should have been given regular pronunciations.

The notion of abstract rules that are independent from lexical knowledge (a basic assumption of classic dual-route models) was challenged by the results of other studies (e.g. Campbell & Besner, 1981; Kay & Marcel, 1981; Rosson, 1983). For instance, Kay & Marcel (1981) demonstrated that reading nonwords with inconsistent word bodies can be influenced by the presentation of their word neighbours, i.e. real words that share the same bodies (e.g. HEAF preceded by DEAF was more likely to be pronounced as /hef/, rather than as the more standard /hif/). These observations led to *lexical analogy* models (Glushko, 1979, 1980; Henderson, 1982; Kay & Marcel, 1981; Marcel, 1980). These models propose that the pronunciation of novel items (nonwords) can be assembled on the basis of lexical knowledge, i.e. the pronunciation would be synthesized from a "cohort" of similar looking words activated by the input.

A variety of attempts have been made to accommodate these challenging results. Later versions of dual-route theories have assumed that pronunciation rules can involve orthographic units of different sizes. For instance, Patterson & Morton (1985) proposed two distinct levels of orthographic structure, i.e. graphemes and word bodies. With regard to single-route models, Shallice and colleagues (Shallice & McCarthy, 1985; Shallice, Warrington, & McCarthy, 1983) proposed that spelling–sound conversion can proceed in parallel through a number of levels involving different kinds of orthographic units, from graphemes to whole words. This hypothesis was named the *multiple level position* (Shallice et al., 1983).

However, as noted by Patterson & Coltheart (1987), the latest lexical analogy models (e.g. Humphreys & Evett, 1985) incorporated the assumption that the translation procedure for a nonword is different from that for a known word. At that point, the theories became difficult to distinguish, partly due to their lack of detail or computational implementation. It is for this reason that the computational modelling of reading performance initiated by Seidenberg & McClelland (1989) has become so important. Computational models are much more explicit and can be tested on any number of words and nonwords, of varying degrees of regularity, consistency, etc., to produce highly detailed simulations of human performance. It is in the context of such explicit models that the theoretical debate concerning the number of routes and the nature of the computations in the reading has been re-opened. Recent experimental studies have been deeply influenced by computational theories, because important theoretical issues can be more easily formalized and a priori predictions can be readily derived from implemented models.

Neuropsychology of reading

Reading research has been greatly influenced by cognitive neuropsychology. Acquired dyslexia is a reading disorder following focal (usually in the left hemisphere) or widespread brain damage in patients who premorbidly had normal reading abilities. A dyslexic syndrome can manifest either as a deficit in attributing the correct sound (phonology) or the correct meaning to a written word. These two forms may present either in isolation or simultaneously, and may have different degrees of severity (for review see Denes, Cipolotti, & Zorzi, 1999).

Acquired disorders of reading have been generally discussed in the framework of dual-route models (e.g. papers in Coltheart, Patterson, & Marshall, 1980, and in Patterson, Marshall, & Coltheart, 1985). The central tenet of these models, that is the existence of two different processes for the computation from print to sound, has been particularly useful in explaining two different forms of acquired dyslexia: phonological dyslexia and surface dyslexia. These two forms are particularly relevant for computational modelling because they represent the two sides of a neuropsychological double dissociation that is taken as evidence for independent processes in the functional architecture. However, as discussed later in the chapter, computational models have also been used by some authors to offer alternative explanations of the two syndromes (for review, see Patterson & Lambon Ralph, 1999).

Phonological dyslexia

In this syndrome, the reading disorder is specific for nonwords, while word reading is significantly retained. This dissociation is interpreted as the result of selective damage to the letter–sound conversion mechanism, i.e. the phonological assembly route. The first case of phonological dyslexia was described by Beauvois & Derouesné (1979), but the purest example is patient WB, described by Funnell (1983). WB showed an almost perfect performance in word reading, while he was completely unable to read any nonword aloud, neither could he give the sounds of single letters.

Typical errors produced by phonological dyslexics in reading nonwords include lexicalization errors (e.g. *mook–book*), i.e. the production of a real word that is visually and/or phonologically similar to the target. Phonological dyslexics also show an effect of visual similarity on the processing of pseudo-homophones (i.e. nonwords that sound like real words, e.g. *brane*). The advantage of a pseudohomophone over a control nonword is modulated by its visual similarity to the source word (e.g. patient LB; Derouesné & Beauvois, 1985).

Surface dyslexia

The main characteristic of this syndrome, described for the first time by Marshall & Newcombe (1973) is that regular word and nonword reading is significantly better than exception word reading. Irregular words tend to be pronounced in a way that reflects the phonological values assigned to the individual graphemes through spelling–sound conversion rules (e.g. PINT is read as /pInt/ instead of /paInt/). The classic interpretation of these regularization errors is that the lexical route is impaired, so that reading can be accomplished only through the phonological assembly route. The purest examples of the syndrome are patients MP (Behrmann & Bub, 1992; Bub, Cancelliere, & Kertesz, 1985) and KT (McCarthy & Warrington, 1986).

Surface dyslexia is often associated with a semantic deficit and/or anomic aphasia. The reading performance of surface dyslexics is sensitive to word frequency: typically, it shows a frequency–regularity interaction, whereby performance in reading exception words worsens as word frequency decreases (Behrmann & Bub, 1992; Bub et al., 1985; Kay & Patterson, 1985; Marshall & Newcombe, 1973; McCarthy & Warrington, 1986). Such findings have been considered to be evidence that the lexical route can still deliver the correct pronunciation for some exception items.

COMPUTATIONAL MODELS

A new promising approach for understanding reading and its disorders comes from the development of computational models. Computational models are much more explicit than traditional verbal theories (e.g. box and arrows models). In contrast to the loose formulation of these latter models, computational models need to be explicit in any implementational detail; in addition, they can produce highly detailed simulations of human performance (e.g. they can be explicitly tested on any number of stimuli), and the performance after a "lesion" to the model can be readily compared to the behaviour of neuropsychological patients.

The theoretical side of reading research has been given substantial impetus by the development of different (and alternative) computational models of visual word recognition and reading aloud (e.g. Coltheart, Curtis, Atkins, & Haller, 1993; Coltheart, Rastle, Perry, Langdon, & Ziegler, 2001; Grainger & Jacobs, 1996; Norris, 1994; Plaut, McClelland, Seidenberg, & Patterson, 1996; Seidenberg & McClelland, 1989; Van Orden, Pennington, & Stone, 1990; Zorzi, Houghton, & Butterworth, 1998a, 1998b). As a consequence, recent empirical research has been deeply influenced by computational theories, partly because they provide a unique opportunity to generate novel (and falsifiable) detailed predictions. The seminal work in this respect is Seidenberg & McClelland's (1989) parallel distributed processing (PDP) model, which exploited a connectionst (or PDP) approach to modelling reading.[3]

More recently, three models have been shown to account for a variety of empirical data from both adult skilled oral reading and neuropsychological disorders of reading following brain damage: Seidenberg & McClelland's (1989) PDP model and its successor, described by Plaut et al. (1996), the dual-route cascaded (DRC) model of Coltheart et al. (1993, 2001), and the connectionist dual-process model of Zorzi et al. (1998a). The main characteristics of these models are reviewed below.

Benchmarks for computational models of reading

Typically, a model is tested by presenting one or several lists of stimuli (words or nonwords) taken from a published study. Dependent measures of the model's performance are error rates and reaction times (RT). The latter are simply the number of cycles taken by the model to produce a stable phonological output for each presented stimulus. Thus, the model's naming latencies are collected for each item and subsequently analysed with appropriate statistics to assess the significance of the effect(s). In some cases, models can be evaluated at the item level, by regressing model's latencies onto human latencies (e.g. Coltheart et al., 2001; Spieler & Balota, 1997; Zorzi, 2000). Finally, the performance after a "lesion" to the model can be readily compared to the behaviour of neuropsychological patients.

As noted before, reading research has produced a vast amount of empirical data during the past 30 years. A successful computational model of reading should be able to account for at least a number of "standard" phenomena, i.e. the empirical findings (from both experimental psychology and neuropsychology) that are relatively uncontroversial and replicated. The list presented below is intended as a benchmark against which computational models can be tested and compared. The list is not exhaustive and is restricted to naming studies.

1. *Frequency effect.* Reading is faster for high-frequency words than for low-frequency words (Forster & Chambers, 1973).
2. *Lexicality effect.* Reading is faster for regular words than for non-words (Forster & Chambers, 1973; McCann & Besner, 1987).
3. *Frequency by regularity interaction.* Reading is faster for regular words than for irregular words when these are low in frequency, whereas the regularity effect is smaller or absent for high-frequency words (Paap and Noel, 1991; Seidenberg et al., 1984; Taraban & McClelland, 1987).
4. *Consistency effects.* Reading is faster for words which have a word body that is pronounced the same way in all English words (consistent) than for words in which the body is pronounced differently in other words (Glushko, 1979; Jared, McRae, & Seidenberg, 1990); the same effect is found for nonwords (Andrews & Scarratt, 1998; Glushko, 1979; Treiman, Kessler, & Bick, 2003). The body consistency effect is modulated by the ratio between "friends" (neighbours having the same pronunciation of the word body) and "enemies" (neighbours having a different pronunciation of the word body) (Jared et al., 1990). It can be observed for both high- and low-frequency words and is independent of the effect of consistency defined at the level of individual letter–sound correspondences (i.e. regularity) (Jared, 1997, 2002).
5. *Position of irregularity effect.* The size of the regularity effect declines as a function of the position in irregular words of their exceptional grapheme–phoneme correspondence (Coltheart & Rastle, 1994; Cortese, 1998; Rastle & Coltheart, 1999).
6. *Nonword length effect.* It has long been known that word length affects naming latencies (e.g. Frederiksen & Kroll, 1976). More recently, Weekes (1997) used monosyllabic stimuli and found that word length interacts with lexicality: the length effect is significant only for the nonword stimuli.
7. *Surface dyslexia.* The ability to read exception words is selectively impaired, and it shows a typical frequency–regularity interaction; regular word and nonword reading can be perfectly retained (e.g. McCarthy & Warrington, 1986).
8. *Phonological dyslexia.* The ability to read nonwords is selectively impaired; word reading (both regular and exception) can be perfectly retained (e.g. Funnell, 1983).

The "triangle" model

The computational framework described by Seidenberg & McClelland (1989) has been referred to as the "triangle model" (see Fig. 13.1). The model assumes the existence of two pathways from spelling to sound: One pathway is a direct mapping from orthographic to phonological representations, whereas the second pathway maps from print to sound via the representation of word meanings.

The model is implemented in a neural network format: large ellipses in the figure represent layers of "visible" units, whereas small ellipses represent "hidden" units (e.g. Rumelhart, Hinton, & Williams, 1986). Unfortunately, the semantic pathway was not implemented by Seidenberg & McClelland. Their attempt to simulate many aspects of skilled oral reading using a single network mapping spelling onto sound (the bold part of Figure 13.1) led many authors to refer to it as the "single-route PDP model". Indeed, the model was intended to represent a strong challenge to dual-route theories (e.g. Patterson, Seidenberg, & McClelland, 1990; Seidenberg & McClelland, 1989, 1990). More recently, the development of the successor of the model (Plaut et al., 1996) has made clear that only the interaction between two pathways can provide an account for some empirical data (see below). Nonetheless, it is still strongly reaffirmed that the triangle framework does not resemble a dual-route model.

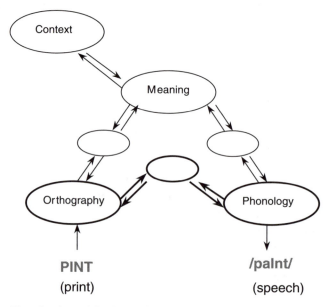

Figure 13.1. The triangle model, adapted from Seidenberg & McClelland (1989). The part of the model implemented by Seidenberg & McClelland (also Plaut et al., 1996) is shown in bold.

Seidenberg & McClelland (1989)

The Seidenberg & McClelland (1989; hereafter SM) PDP model of reading aloud represents a nontraditional theory of the mapping from spelling to sound. The strongest claim of SM is that the phonology of any given word (regular or exception) or nonword can be computed from its orthographic representation by a single process. This process is spread of activation through a three-layer neural network, where the activation patterns over input and output units represent the written form and the phonological form of the word, respectively. The knowledge about spelling–sound mappings is distributed in the network, and resides in the connections that link the processing units. According to Plaut et al. (1996), the model can be thought of as an integration of lexical analogy and multiple levels theories, as it denies the existence of separate lexical and sublexical (or nonlexical) procedures.

SM trained the network on a set of nearly 3000 monosyllabic English words using the back-propagation learning algorithm (Rumelhart et al., 1986). Training items were presented to the network with a probability reflecting a logarithmic function of the Kucera & Francis (1967) word frequency norms. Orthographic and phonological representations for words (and nonwords) consisted of activation patterns distributed over a number of primitive representational units, following the triplet scheme of Wickelgren (1969).

The SM model was shown to account for various facts about the reading performance of normal subjects. In particular, it showed the classic interaction between frequency and regularity, an effect that was previously taken as evidence supporting the dual-route model. The explanation offered by the SM model did not call upon the competition between two processing routes; indeed, it did not involve two routes at all. The explanation of SM was that the computation of the phonological representation of a high-frequency exception word such as HAVE is not affected by knowledge of similarly-spelled regular words such as GAVE, because the large number of exposures to the word itself during training has sufficient impact on the connection weights to wash out the effects of the exposure to the regular word neighbours. In contrast, the number of exposures to a low-frequency exception word such as PINT is not sufficient to overcome the impact on the weights of the regular word neighbours such as HINT and MINT.

However, the model has been criticized by several authors (see e.g. Besner, Twilley, McCann, & Seergobin, 1990; Coltheart et al., 1993). For instance, the phonological representation in the model was based upon Wickelfeatures, a scheme that Pinker & Prince (1988) argued strongly against. In effect, the model failed to give an output that could plausibly be used as the basis of an articulatory process. The phonological output had to be compared with the desired output to compute a phonological error score; this error score was then used to determine the best match amongst a set of candidates, including the correct pronunciation or several possible pronunciation errors. As pointed out by Coltheart et al. (1993), this procedure would miss errors which are not included in the list of possible errors (e.g. output containing a wrong number of phonemes).

The criticisms to the SM model, however, have largely focused on its non-word reading performance and on its ability to account for neuro-psychological data. Besner et al. (1990) tested the model on several lists of nonwords and found that it performed very poorly. About 40% of the non-words presented were not read correctly, and in some cases the errors pro-duced by the model consisted of phonemes which were completely arbitrary with respect to the orthographic input (e.g. POTE $\Rightarrow$ /paIt/, KEDE $\Rightarrow$ /yid/, TROAD $\Rightarrow$ /traIt/). Consequently, they rejected the SM claim to have pro-vided a plausible single-route model. Moreover, they pointed out that the model's performance was more similar to that of a phonological dyslexic patient than that of a normal reader, arguing that this was due to the absence of a nonlexical route (i.e. the model was reading many words on an idio-syncratic "whole word" basis, and had failed to abstract a generally effective spelling–sound mapping procedure from its training).

Several authors (e.g. Coltheart et al., 1993) criticized the intrinsic difficulty of the SM model to account for the neuropsychological double dissociation between nonword reading and exception word reading (i.e. phonological vs. surface dyslexia). Patterson, Seidenberg, & McClelland (1989) showed that a lesion to the model (performed by removing a variable proportion of hidden units) had a larger disruptive impact on exception word reading than on regular word reading. However, regular word reading was not spared and the errors produced by the model in reading exception words were far from a close match to those produced by surface dyslexic subjects such as KT (Behrman & Bub, 1992). Furthermore, surface dyslexics show very good nonword reading. As pointed out by Coltheart et al. (1993), the attempt to lesion the model to simulate surface dyslexia is *a priori* unsuccessful, given that the intact model showed "impaired" nonword reading (a key feature of the phonological dyslexic syndrome).

Plaut, McClelland, Seidenberg, & Patterson (1996)

As previously discussed, the debate on computational models has focused on nonwords, and the ability of the models to generate appropriate readings of novel items has become a major theoretical benchmark (e.g. Seidenberg, Plaut, Petersen, McClelland, & McRae, 1994). The Plaut, McClelland, Seidenberg, & Patterson model (1996)—hereafter PMSP—has been pre-sented as an improved version of the SM model. The new model overcomes some of the limitations of the SM model, e.g. it can read nonwords at a level of performance similar to human subjects (see also Seidenberg et al., 1994). This point is of particular importance because it counters the arguments of Besner et al. (1990) and Coltheart et al. (1993), that the poor performance of the SM model was to be ascribed to the lack of a separate nonlexical procedure.

The PMSP model is different from the SM model in numerous important ways. The most important is the representational redesign: Plaut and colleagues abandon the highly distributed Wickelfeature representation in favour of a more localist coding of orthographic and phonological units. The representation of phonology is based on phonemes and segmented according to the syllabic structure, i.e. output nodes are organized to represent onset (i.e. beginning consonants), vowel, and coda (i.e. consonants following the vowel) positions. A similar organization is adopted for the orthographic representation, with the input nodes coding for individual graphemes (rather than letters), i.e. single nodes stand for whole groups of letters, e.g. WH, CH, AY, EA, CK, TCH, etc. PMSP motivate the new representational scheme with the need to condense spelling–sound regularities in order to improve generalization. Indeed, the task of learning grapheme–phoneme correspondences is made easier by hand-coding graphemes that correspond to single phonemes.

The PMSP model is based on the same three-layer architecture of SM. However, one version of the model allows for recurrent connections and the network is trained using a continuous version of the back-propagation through time learning algorithm (Pearlmutter, 1989). One important feature of this kind of network is that activation spreads gradually from input through output nodes and the network takes a certain number of cycles to settle to a final (stable) output state. PMSP take the settling time (number of cycles) for any given orthographic input as a measure of naming latency (RT). This represents a significant improvement over the SM model. Of some interest also is the analysis of the recurrent network performed by Plaut et al. A recurrent network usually develops attractors in the output space that correspond to the trained patterns. However, PMSP found that the attractors developed by the network were "componential", i.e. they corresponded to word segments rather than to whole words. This would explain the network's ability to generalize to novel patterns.

Evaluation of the model

All simulation studies reported by PMSP (except for the simulation of surface dyslexia) are based on the phonological pathway (i.e. the orthography–phonology network) in isolation.

1. *Frequency effect*: YES. The effect is the result of the training regime (how often a word is presented during training is a function of its frequency[4]), which in turn affects the associative strength of the mapping between orthographic and phonological representations.

2. *Lexicality effect*: YES. The model shows shorter settling times for words compared to nonwords. However, the effect has not been investigated by PMSP.

3. *Frequency–regularity interaction*: YES. See section on the SM model above for an explanation of the effect. In general, factors that increase the summed input to the network's units (e.g. high frequency) improve performance, but the asymptotic nature of the activation function produces a relative insensitivity to variation in other factors (e.g. regularity) (for a formal analysis, see Plaut et al., 1996). Note also that PMSP treat regularity as one of the extremes on the consistency continuum (see section "Consistency vs. regularity" below).

4. *Consistency effects*: YES. The model shows a body consistency effect, both for high- and low-frequency words (Coltheart et al., 2001; Jared, 2002). The effect depends on neighbourhood characteristics and is present for both regular words and nonwords. It appears, however, that the model is not sensitive to the effect of consistency defined at the level of individual letter–sound correspondences (Jared, 1997; Zorzi, 2000).

5. *Position of irregularity effect*: NO. The model does not show the interaction between regularity and position of the irregular grapheme (Coltheart et al., 2001; Zorzi, 2000).

6. *Nonword length effect*: NO. Plaut et al. (1996) showed that the PMSP model is sensitive to word length: the attractor network version of the model takes more time to settle on the final pronunciation as the number of letters increases. Plaut et al. demonstrated the length effect by regressing the number of letters onto the model's naming latencies. Number of letters was positively correlated with naming latency and accounted for a unique proportion (0.8%) of its variance. However, the model does not show the correct form of interaction between lexicality and word length found by Weekes (1997; see Coltheart et al., 2001).[5]

7. *Surface dyslexia*: YES. A lesion to the phonological pathway produces a mild version of surface dyslexia. However, when the model is lesioned to the extent required to match the performance of a severe surface dyslexic patient such as KT, the model's performance drops substantially on regular words and nonwords (Plaut et al., 1996). The repeated failures to simulate surface dyslexia with a single network led PMSP to develop a "dual-route" (yet nontraditional) explanation of surface dyslexia, which is based on the Patterson & Hodges (1992) hypothesis, that the integrity of phonological representations is dependent on an interaction between meaning and phonology. PMSP trained the orthography-to-phonology (O–P) network with an additional external input to the phoneme units that represented the

contribution of a (putative) semantic pathway (Plaut et al., 1996, simulation 4). Furthermore, the magnitude of this external input increased in the course of training, to simulate an increased competence of the putative semantic pathway. PMSP showed that in this version of the model the O–P network is relieved from mastering low-frequency exception words, because the correct output for these words is provided by the semantic pathway. They argued that, as the semantic pathway's competence improves, the phonological pathway becomes specialized for regular words; this results in a redistribution of labour between semantic and phonological pathways. Therefore, when a lesion completely eliminates the contribution of the semantic pathway, the severity of the dyslexic pattern exhibited by the O–P network is a function of the redistribution of labour between the semantic and the phonological pathways that has occurred prior to the lesion. The PMSP account of surface dyslexia is further discussed in the third part of this chapter.

8. *Phonological dyslexia*: YES. Harm & Seidenberg (2001) have recently simulated the performance of phonological dyslexic patients in a full implementation of the triangle model. The lesion (addition of noise) was produced at the phonological level, to implement the hypothesis that phonological dyslexia is caused by an impairment in the representation of phonological information (e.g. Farah, Stowe, & Levinson, 1996; Patterson & Marcel, 1992). The reading performance of the lesioned model is a direct consequence of the fact that nonwords have a less stable phonological representation than words. Note, however, that the syndrome might also be simulated with a lesion to the O–P network, in line with the standard dual-route account of phonological dyslexia.

The dual-route cascaded (DRC) model

In response to the "single-route" models of Seidenberg, McClelland, and colleagues (Plaut et al., 1996; Seidenberg & McClelland, 1989), Coltheart and colleagues (Coltheart et al., 1993; Coltheart & Rastle, 1994; Coltheart et al., 2001; Rastle & Coltheart, 1999) have developed a computational implementation of the dual-route theory. In this model, known as the DRC (dual-route cascaded) model, lexical and nonlexical routes are implemented as different and functionally independent components (see Fig. 13.2). Moreover, the two routes operate on different computational principles: serial, symbolic processing in the nonlexical route, and spreading activation in the lexical route. The nonlexical route (named GPC route) performs serial parsing and grapheme–phoneme conversion, can be used on any string of letters and is necessary for reading nonwords; the lexical route operates through cascaded

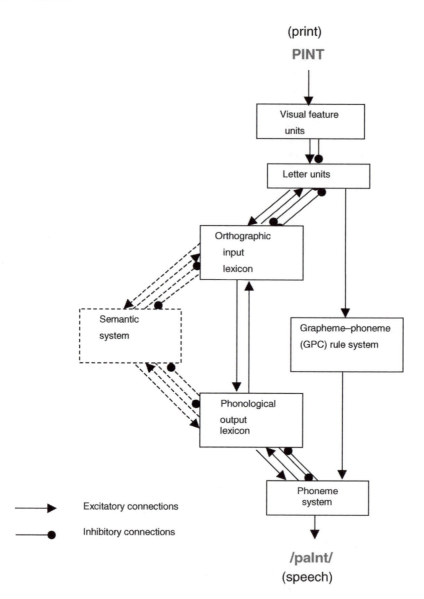

Figure 13.2.   The dual-route cascaded (DRC) model, adapted from Coltheart, Curtis, Atkins, & Haller (1993). The lexical–semantic route of the model is not implemented (dashed lines).

activation on orthographic word nodes (i.e. orthographic lexicon) and phono-logical word nodes (i.e. phonological lexicon), can be used on known words, and is necessary for reading exception words.

The lexical route is implemented as an interactive activation model, based on the McClelland & Rumelhart (1981; also Rumelhart & McClelland, 1982) word recognition model joined to Dell's (1986) spoken word production model (Coltheart & Rastle, 1994). However, one important limitation of the lexical pathway in DRC is that it presents a static picture of a mature cognitive system, and the problem of how the lexical knowledge is acquired is not addressed (this is a rather general problem for the class of interactive activation models). For instance, frequency effects are simulated by assuming that the resting activation level of any lexical node is a scaled value of its frequency count. In addition, the model incorporates a large number (24) of parameters that have to be tuned by hand.

The GPC route is held to be slow and serial (i.e. it delivers one phoneme at a time) and is therefore regarded as a controlled process, which is resource-demanding and subject to strategic control (e.g. Monsell et al., 1992; Paap & Noel, 1991). Because of this, the interaction between lexical route and GPC route is usually limited to low-frequency words, i.e. for visually familiar words, recognition (and naming) is completed before the assembled phonological code becomes available. Thus, conflicts between lexical and nonlexical routes occur only when words are somewhat unfamiliar and irregular (i.e. low-frequency exception words); this is reminiscent of classic dual-route horserace models (e.g. Paap & Noel, 1991).

The GPC route developed by Coltheart et al. (1993) is based upon explicit grapheme–phoneme rules that are discovered and stored by a specially constructed "learning algorithm" in a single pass through the training database. From a connectionist point of view, an obvious problem with this is how the rules are acquired, which is a complex and *ad hoc* procedure. For example, consider how graphemic parsing is achieved: the first step is to try the match between single letters and phonemes; when a letter–phoneme correspondence is not possible, i.e. one or more letters of the string are left unmatched, the algorithm recursively tries in the next steps to group more letters until it is able to find a proper match to the phoneme, i.e. the cluster of letters (grapheme) that maps to the phoneme. This learning algorithm is able to discover inconsistent print–sound mappings, i.e. cases where a spelling pattern maps onto more than one pronunciation. However, in this case, the less frequent alternatives are simply eliminated at the end of the learning phase, leaving only the most common mapping in the rule set. In the latest version of the model, the set of learned GPC rules are abandoned and replaced by a simpler, hand-coded set of rules (Coltheart et al., 2001; Rastle & Coltheart, 1999).

The DRC model belongs to the family of "classic" dual-route models, which assume the existence of a memory-based system to retrieve stored items and of a "productive" system of linguistic rules that can deal with novel items, indeed following a traditional view in linguistics and in cognitive psychology (e.g. Chomsky, 1957; Pinker, 1991). However, these principles are partly contradicted by the implementation of the lexical route in DRC. The lexical route is a connectionist network based on activation principles, where the activation of nodes at all levels is cascaded, parallel, and bidirectional. This produces a number of "side-effects", e.g. the presentation of a word or nonword produces the activation of a "neighbourhood" of nodes that code similar-looking words. Consistency effects in DRC would be produced by the activation of word neighbours in the lexical route. Interestingly, this is exactly the assumption made by lexical analogy models; however, Coltheart et al. (2001) argue that body consistency can be reinterpreted as an effect of spurious competitive phoneme activations generated by the GPC route (see section "Consistency vs. regularity" below). The coordination of serial (the GPC route) and parallel (the lexical route) processes in DRC indeed causes some additional difficulties for the model. Some form of temporal coordination is needed, and it is assumed that the serial production of the phonemes by the GPC route is tied to the processing in the lexical route (e.g. one phoneme is produced every 17 processing cycles of the lexical route). Furthermore, an additional "interface" process is needed to connect the serial (symbolic) output of the GPC route to the parallel activation of phonemes by the lexical route (note that the phonemes produced by the GPC route cannot have any intrinsic activation value). This process must specify which of the lexically-activated phoneme slots corresponds to each phoneme symbol as it is generated by the GPC mechanism. Some consonants can occur more than once in a given syllable in different positions or "slots" (e.g. *pip*). Therefore the syllabic position (serial order) of symbols coming from the GPC route must be marked in some way so that the appropriate slot is accessed (for the injection of additional activation). All in all, the interface process in such a model is clearly rather complex (perhaps deserving a box of its own in an architectural description of the model) and adds numerous new assumptions to dual-route models. This is an inevitable consequence of having the two routes operate according to such different computational and representational principles: the lexical route parallel, connectionist, and activation-based; the GPC route serial, rule-based, and symbolic.

Evaluation of the model

1. *Frequency effect*: YES. The frequency effect is produced by the standard implementation of interactive activation models, whereby the resting levels of the lexical nodes are set to be a function of word frequency.
2. *Lexicality effect*: YES. Nonwords are processed only by the nonlexical route, which is generally much slower than the lexical route.
3. *Frequency–regularity interaction*: YES. For low-frequency words, the cost of irregularity is much higher than for high-frequency words

because conflicting information delivered by the (slower) nonlexical route has more chance to arrive before lexical processing is completed.

4. *Consistency effects*: NO. The model shows a body consistency effect both for high- and low-frequency words, which has been reinterpreted by Coltheart et al. (2001) as an effect of spurious competitive phoneme activations generated by the GPC route—see section "Consistency vs. regularity" below. However, consistency effects do not depend on neighbourhood characteristics and the model fails to show a consistency effect for regular words (Jared, 2002). Finally, the model fails to show a nonword consistency effect (Treiman et al., 2003).

5. *Position of irregularity effect*: YES. The effect arises in the model because the probability for a phoneme delivered by the nonlexical route to arrive before the word is named decreases as a function of position. That is, because the nonlexical route operates serially from left to right, the incorrect phonemic realization (regularization) of the irregular grapheme in an exception word will have little chance to interfere if it is delivered shortly before naming initiates. In contrast, an irregular grapheme in the initial positions of the word results in greater interference, because its regularized pronunciation is produced much earlier in time, thus having the chance to compete strongly with the correct phoneme activated by the lexical route.

6. *Nonword length effect*: YES. The effect is entirely produced by the serial operation of the nonlexical route. For words, the effect is washed out by the lexical route, thus producing the interaction between lexicality and length.

7. *Surface dyslexia*: YES. When processing in the lexical route is slowed, performance drops significantly for low-frequency exception words. The model provides a good match to the performance of patients MP and KT (Coltheart et al., 2001).

8. *Phonological dyslexia*: YES. When processing in the nonlexical route is slowed (or even abolished), performance drops significantly for nonwords, whereas word reading is retained. Lexicalization errors are produced because the presentation of a nonword stimulus produces activation of the lexical nodes corresponding to its word neighbours. Given sufficient processing time, the subthreshold activation of the lexical node, which is most strongly activated by the nonword stimulus, spreads to the phoneme nodes. The model can also account for data from patient LB (Derouesné & Beauvois, 1985) regarding the effect of pseudohomophony and its interaction with visual similarity (Coltheart, Langdon, & Haller, 1996).

It must also be noted that Coltheart and colleagues, following Grainger & Jacobs's (1996) work with the MROM model, a development of McClelland

& Rumelhart's (1981) interactive activation model, show that the DRC model can produce accurate simulations of a number of studies that used the lexical decision task (Coltheart et al., 2001).

The connectionist dual process model

Zorzi, Houghton, & Butterworth (1998a) developed a connectionist model of reading where a dual-route processing system emerges from the interaction of task demands and initial network architecture in the course of reading acquisition. In this model, the distinction between phonological assembly and lexical knowledge is realized in the form of connectivity (either direct or mediated) between orthographic input and phonological output patterns (for similar treatment of the problem of learning the sound–spelling mapping in writing, see Houghton & Zorzi, 1998, 2003). The model thus maintains the uniform computational style of the PDP models, but makes a clear distinction between lexical and sublexical processes in reading.

Zorzi et al. (1998a) and Houghton & Zorzi (2003) discuss this kind of architecture in relation to the standard multi-layer network that has become quite common in connectionist modelling (e.g. in the reading domain, the network models of Bullinaria, 1997; Plaut et al., 1996; Seidenberg & McClelland, 1989). Multi-layer networks are a generalization of the basic feedforward perceptron of Rosenblatt (1962; for discussion, see Rumelhart et al., 1986). Multi-layer networks have greater representational power than two-layer networks in which the input and output domains are directly connected. The use of an intermediate layer of hidden units laying between input and output permits the learning (in principle) of arbitrary nonlinear mappings. However, a typical multi-layer network is built from a two-layer network, not only by the addition of hidden units and the necessary connections, but also by the removal of the existing direct connections between the input and output layers. However, if the hidden units are added but the direct connections are not removed, the network will still be multi-layer, but with two distinct pathways from input to output, one direct and the other mediated by hidden units.

This architecture has a number of interesting properties that distinguish it from the more common version of multi-layer networks. For instance, learning can take place in both pathways at the same time, but the network tends to partition the learning such that the direct pathway will learn simple (linear) regularities, while the mediated route will respond to idiosyncratic (exception) input–output pairs by recognizing the exceptional inputs and correcting the regular response produced by the direct pathway (Zorzi et al., 1998a). In this case, the network's ability to generalize to novel stimuli tends to be concentrated in the direct pathway. Zorzi et al. (1998a) also showed that damage to the two pathways has different effects, so that double dissociations between regular items and exceptional items (i.e. regular words and nonwords vs. exception words) can be observed. The production of such dissociations has proved extremely challenging for connectionist models based on the standard multi-layer architecture (Bullinaria & Chater, 1995; Plaut et al., 1996).

Zorzi et al. (1998a, 1998b) also studied in great detail the performance of a simple two-layer network (i.e. without hidden units) trained to learn the mapping between orthography and phonology. Zorzi et al. found that this network acquires properties that are considered the hallmark of a phonological assembly process, and named it the two-layer model of phonological assembly (TLA).

The TLA model was trained on a set of nearly 3000 monosyllabic words. Training in the TLA model does not require the back-propagation algorithm; learning is achieved through the simpler delta rule learning procedure (Widrow & Hoff, 1960), which is formally equivalent to a classical conditioning law (the Rescorla–Wagner rule; Sutton & Barto, 1981), and has been directly applied to human learning by a number of authors (for review, see e.g. Gluck & Bower, 1988a, 1988b; Shanks, 1991; Siegel & Allan, 1996). The input to the model is a representation of the spelling of a monosyllabic word. Letters in words are represented using a positional code, where each node represents both a letter and the position in the word occupied by that letter. There are no nodes representing combinations of letters, such as graphemes (e.g. TH, EE, etc.). Thus, the orthographic representation is strictly position-specific, slot-based, and equivalent to that used in the McClelland & Rumelhart (1981) model for the letter detector level. For each possible letter position there is an entire set of letter units, which are supposed to be activated from a preceding feature detector level. However, the positions are defined with respect to orthographic onset (i.e. letters preceding the vowel letter) and orthographic rhyme (or word body, i.e. all letters from the vowel onwards). The first three positions are for the (orthographic) onset representation, and the onset slots are filled from the first slot onwards. The orthographic rhyme, which has a maximum length of five letters (e.g. OUGHT in THOUGHT), is represented on the following five slots. The phonological representation has a similar format, with phonemes in a syllable aligned to phonological onset and rhyme positions. In this case there are three onset positions, and four rhyme positions.

Zorzi et al. (1998a) showed that the TLA network is able to extract the statistically more reliable spelling–sound relationships in English (for a developmental study of this capacity, see also Zorzi et al., 1998b), without forming representations of the individual training items (such as the exception words). Therefore, the assembly route in the dual-process model produces regularized pronunciations (if the input word is an exception word) and is not sensitive to the base frequency of the trained words. The model provides a good match to the nonword reading performance of human sub-jects, and can also read single letters and graphemes. Furthermore, the output of the network reflects the relative consistency of a given mapping. As dis-cussed above, the major locus of inconsistency in pronouncing English words is the vowel (e.g. EA in HEAD, MEAL, GREAT; e.g. Treiman et al., 1995). The model, along with the most common mapping of the vowel, delivers other, alternative, less common mappings, which are activated to a lesser extent.

Because the TLA network is inherently incapable of learning idiosyncratic (exceptional) mappings, the correct pronunciation of exception words must be achieved through a mediated mapping. This can be based on a distributed lexicon (as discussed above, this can be provided by a layer of hidden units laying between input and output) or on lexical nodes (as in traditional dual-route models). This latter solution was adopted by Zorzi et al. (1998a) for modelling a frequency-sensitive lexical pathway and its interaction with the phonological assembly network. Thus, the lexical pathway in the model can be conceptualized as an interactive activation network (for implementation of a lexical pathway for spelling, see Houghton & Zorzi, 2003), or alter-natively, as any network that develops mediated, internal representations for the known words. However, the additional advantage of a (localist) inter-active activation model of the lexical route is that visual word recognition (e.g. perceptual identification and lexical decision task) can be readily simu-lated (Grainger & Jacobs, 1996). Clearly, with regard to word recognition and retrieval of lexical phonology, any advantage of distributed over localist rep-resentations has yet to be demonstrated (for further discussion, see Page, 2000, and accompanying commentaries).

The model's final pronunciation is produced by the phonological decision system (PDS) on the basis of activation competition; this process is sensitive to response competition from alternative mappings, which is postulated to be a causal factor in naming latencies. The structure of this system is identical to the output layer of the TLA, but incorporates features, lateral inhibition and gradual activation decay, which provide a temporal dynamic. The output produced by the TLA model propagates gradually to the PDS, where the activations change over time until one of the units in each activated phoneme group reaches a response threshold. The time that the network takes to settle is taken as a measure of naming latency. The entire model is depicted in Fig. 13.3.

The two processing pathways of the dual-process model are activated in parallel and their phonological output builds up over time in a cascaded fashion. However, in contrast to a classic dual-route horserace model, the processing rates of the two routes are very similar (the assembly route is actually faster than the lexical route). The point of interaction between the two procedures is realized in the PDS, where the on-line competitive

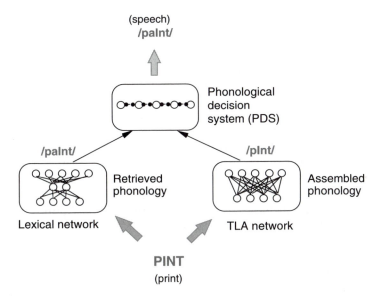

Figure 13.3. The connectionist dual-process model. Adapted from Zorzi, Houghton, & Butterworth (1998a).

interaction between the output of the two processes results in the final phonological code that should drive articulation.

Evaluation of the model

1. *Frequency effect*: YES. The frequency effect is produced by the lexical pathway, whereby the phonology of a given word becomes active (in a gradual fashion) with a speed that is proportional to its frequency. This is similar to interactive activation models.
2. *Lexicality effect*: YES. Nonwords are processed only by the phonological assembly network, whereas words enjoy the combination of two sources of phonological information, i.e. lexical phonology and assembled phonology reinforce each other.
3. *Frequency–regularity interaction*: YES. Competing phonemes produced by the TLA network for exception words interfere with the (correct) phonemes activated by the lexical pathway when they are combined in the PDS. This competition takes time, but the suppression (i.e. inhibition) of incorrect phonemes is accomplished more quickly for high-frequency words.
4. *Consistency effects*: YES. The model shows a body consistency effect for both high- and low-frequency words (Coltheart et al., 2001; Zorzi, 1999a). The effect depends on neighbourhood characteristics and is present for both regular words and nonwords. The consistency effect is

produced by the TLA network, which produces multiple candidates for a given phoneme position as the result of the inconsistency of the spelling–sound mapping. The effect arises from exposure during learning to orthographically similar words that have different pronunciations. For instance, along with the most common mapping of the vowel, the model delivers other, alternative, less common mappings, which are activated to a lesser extent. This produces competition in the PDS, which turns into longer latencies.

5. *Position of irregularity effect*: YES. the effect in the model is generated by the presence of competing phonemes at the position of irregularity, which is modulated by the degree of consistency of the grapheme–phoneme mapping. Thus, it can be interpreted as a position-specific grapheme–phoneme consistency effect. In Rastle & Coltheart's (1999) stimuli, first position irregular words tend to be more inconsistent than second or third position irregular words at the grapheme level (for further discussion, see Zorzi, 2000).

6. *Nonword length effect*: YES. Zorzi (1999a) tested the model with a list of 116 nonwords (assembled with the nonwords used by Rastle & Coltheart, 1998; Weekes, 1997). The number of letters was a significant predictor of the model's latencies (accounting for 4.5% of the variance). Furthermore, the model showed a significant interaction between lexicality and word length on the Weekes (1997) stimuli. Zorzi (1999a) suggested that this effect is produced in the model by the fact that long nonwords contain less frequent letter combinations compared to short nonwords.

7. *Surface dyslexia*: YES. When processing in the lexical route is slowed, performance drops significantly for low-frequency exception words. The model provides a good match to the performance of patients MP and KT (Zorzi et al., 1998a; Zorzi, 1999a).

8. *Phonological dyslexia*: Not simulated. In the simulations with the three-layer network trained with back-propagation, Zorzi et al. (1998a) showed that a lesion to the direct pathway (i.e. the connections linking letter units to phoneme units) results in a severe deficit in nonword reading. However, detailed modelling of phonological dyslexia will require the full implementation of a lexical route similar to that of Houghton & Zorzi's (2003) dual-route model of spelling.

Other models

A number of other studies have presented computational implementations of various aspects of the reading process (e.g. Ans, Carbonnel, & Valdois, 1998; Bullinaria, 1996; Grainger & Jacobs, 1996; Jacobs, Rey, Ziegler, & Grainger, 1998; Norris, 1994). Most notable is the multiple read-out model (MROM) of word recognition developed by Grainger & Jacobs (1996). This model is a development of the original McClelland & Rumelhart (1981) interactive activation model, and incorporates the important features of stochastic processing and multiple response criteria. For instance, response in a lexical decision task can be based on different decision criteria, such as unique identification (i.e. when a single word node reaches response threshold) or summed lexical activation. The reliance on a particular criterion for responding is a stochastic process, which is partly dependent on the nature of the word and nonword stimuli. The MROM model has been shown to account for a wide range of data concerning the lexical decision and the perceptual identification task. More recently, Jacobs et al. (1998) have developed a new version of the model that includes lexical phonological representations (MROM-P).

Norris (1994) developed an implementation of the multiple levels model of reading (e.g. Shallice et al., 1983). The Norris model is implemented as an interactive activation model, where the orthographic input representations include all possible levels, e.g. single letters, graphemes, word bodies, whole words. All these different components are represented explicitly, e.g. the rhyme unit in milk is represented by a single node, ILK, as well by its letter components. Similarly, the phonological representation incorporates all possible levels of representation (e.g. phonemes, onsets, rhymes). The values of the connections in the model are set by hand (this is typical of interactive activation models), using values reflecting the statistical co-occurrences between orthographic and phonological components. Interestingly, in one simulation Norris found that an adequate set of connections could also be learnt though the delta rule learning algorithm. The model's nonword reading performance, however, was still poor compared to that of human readers. Furthermore, the very restricted range of naming latencies produced by the model does not allow a proper (i.e. quantitative) evaluation of the model (Coltheart et al., 2001).

Bullinaria (1996) presented a fuller implementation of the triangle framework, adding to the basic orthography–phonology network a second pathway from spelling to meaning to sound (i.e. the semantic route). The model is a multi-layer recurrent network trained with a variant of the back-propagation learning algorithm. Hidden layers link the three levels of representation (orthographic, phonological, and semantic; see Figure 13.1). One main aim of Bullinaria's study was to explore the division of labour between semantic and phonological pathways. He found that word pronunciation relied entirely on the orthography–phonology pathway, and that access to semantics relied entirely on the orthography–phonology–semantics pathway. These results are interesting from a computational perspective, but are inconsistent with a number of experimental and neuropsychological findings.

COMPARISON OF THE THREE MODELS

Modelling reading aloud is a special case in the growing field of computational cognitive modelling. The SM model is indeed one of the most successful computational models of cognitive functions: this is testified by the huge number of citations, and by the major debate in the reading literature generated by the model. While in the past years the success of a computational model could be judged by simple "proof of simulation", this has now quite changed. A good model should account for data from experimental studies on normal subjects (in terms of both reaction times and error rates), from studies on patients with neuropsychological disorders, and ultimately from developmental studies. However, the strengths of a model must be judged not only in terms of number of facts that it can account for, but also in terms of economy and relative "transparency" of the model: if the model's internal operations are difficult to interpret, little insight can be gained from it (for discussion, see McCloskey, 1991). A further important point regards the novel or differential predictions that models may provide.

Converging principles

Although the architectures and processing assumptions of the three models are remarkably different, a fair degree of convergence towards general processing principles can be individuated. One of such principles is that the interaction between two different sources of phonological information is a necessary assumption for explaining both behavioural and neuropsychological data. That is, upon presentation of a printed word, phonological codes are retrieved through a lexical–semantic pathway (or network) as well as being assembled through a spelling–sound mapping process.

In the DRC model this interaction is still best characterized as a horserace, similarly to the original dual-route "horserace" model (Coltheart, 1978; Paap & Noel, 1991). In the triangle and the dual-process models, on the other hand, the interaction is a sort of pooling process, as proposed in alternative versions of the dual-route model (the "pooling" model, Monsell et al., 1992; the "summation" model, Hillis & Caramazza, 1991). Besides this point, there are major theoretical differences between the models with regard to the characterization of the assembly procedure.

Phonological assembly: Rules or connections?

One theoretically important distinction between the three models concerns the characterization of phonological assembly as a process based on a rule system or an associative network. In both the dual-process model and the triangle model, the assembly route is implemented in a neural network form, where the mapping between orthographic and phonological representations is learnt through exposure to a large corpus of words (in spite of these similarities, the two models differ for a number of important features; see section "Consistency vs. regularity" below). The phonological assembly route in DRC (i.e. the GPC route), however, is a production system, based on a set of explicit rules specifying the dominant (e.g. most frequent) relationships between letters and sounds.

Note that in the TLA component of the dual-process model, the direct connections between letters and phonemes can sometimes be "read out" as pronunciation rules (e.g. initial letter M is always pronounced as /m/). However, most of the sublexical spelling–sound mappings discovered by the network are sensitive to the local context and their size is variable (see Zorzi et al., 1998a). As suggested by Patterson and V. Coltheart (1987), the notion of an abstract rule proposed by nonlexical route theorists may be intended either in the sense of an (implicit?) mapping rule or of an (explicit?) production rule. The network's connections can be regarded as mapping rules, in contrast to the explicit rule system adopted in DRC. The conceptualization of assembly as a system of "flexible (mapping) rules" is not new, e.g. Brown & Besner (1987) suggested that orthographic inputs may be associated with a small number of phonological outputs. The possibility of rules with multiple outputs has also been proposed by Patterson & Morton (1985) in relation to the "body subsystem" contained in their model. Most notably, the idea of multiple outputs is incorporated in the notion of "islands of reliability" in spelling–sound correspondence put forth by Carr & Pollatsek (1985): correspondences are more reliable for some graphemes than for others. Thus, the system would typically specify single outputs for consonants and multiple outputs for vowels. Brown & Besner (1987) explicitly suggested ". . . a system of rules which generates small sets of values for consonants and larger sets of values for vowels" (p. 481). This conceptualization of the assembly procedure is quite compatible with the TLA model. However, it contrasts sharply with the characterization of the GPC route in DRC, which is not sensitive to consistency and delivers a single phoneme for each position.

Phonological assembly: Serial or parallel?

A second and perhaps more important distinction between the three models regards the characterization of phonological assembly as a serial or parallel process. In both the dual-process and the triangle models, the network implementing the spelling–sound mapping route operates in parallel on the orthographic input, at least for monosyllabic words (note that all three models are currently limited to monosyllables). In contrast, the GPC algorithm in DRC operates serially by submitting one letter at a time to the rule system. It is important to note that this feature is a specific theoretical assumption in the DRC model, and that serial processing is not strictly necessary for the rule system to operate. Coltheart & Rastle (1994) and Rastle & Coltheart (1999) have strongly argued for a serial operation of the phonological assembly route. They took the position of irregularity effect as direct evidence for the operation of a serial mechanism. However, Zorzi (2000) has shown that the parallel dual-process model can account for the position of irregularity effect without the assumption of a serial component. Furthermore, the dual-process model provides an alternative explanation of the effect in terms of grapheme–phoneme consistency. The PMSP model cannot account for the position of irregularity effect, but this is likely to be caused by its reduced sensitivity to grapheme consistency (as opposed to body consistency; for discussion, see Zorzi, 2000).

Phonological assembly: Fast or slow?

A third difference between the models regards the characterization of phonological assembly as a slow or as a fast process. This has also important implications for the characterization of the on-line interactions between the two reading routes. As noted, the GPC route is held to be slow and serial, and therefore interaction (e.g. conflict) between the two routes is relegated "to the status of a minor nuisance that mainly plagues laboratory tasks . . ." (Carr & Pollatsek, 1985, p. 9). More generally, the DRC model conforms to classic dual-route models (Baron, 1977; Coltheart, 1978; Meyer, Schvaneveldt, & Ruddy, 1974) in giving a predominant role to the visual route, because the assembly of phonology is believed to be too slow to affect lexical access. A sublexical (or prelexical) activation of phonology (coming from the assembly route) can make some contribution to word recognition only for very low-frequency words, i.e. those that are too slowly dealt with by the lexical route (e.g. Seidenberg et al., 1984). Furthermore, because the GPC route delivers the regular pronunciation of a letter string, the assembled phonology is beneficial only in the case of regular words, while it is detrimental in the case of words with irregular spelling–sound correspondences (Coltheart et al., 1993; Coltheart & Rastle, 1994). On this account, written word recognition in real circumstances is largely a matter of direct visual access from print.

The dual-process model, on the other hand, suggests that processing in the assembly route can be fast and parallel. This is highly consistent with recent proposals depicting phonological assembly as a fast and automatic process (e.g. Perfetti & Bell, 1991; Perfetti, Bell, & Delaney, 1988). Phonological properties of printed words can affect performance in a variety of reading tasks (for review, see Frost, 1998) and the results of several studies suggest a fast and automatic assembly process, preceding word identification (for reviews, see Berent & Perfetti, 1995; Van Orden et al., 1990).

Lexical phonology

In both the triangle and the dual-process models, the output of the phonological assembly network interacts with the phonological code produced by a lexical (or lexical–semantic) pathway. However, it is worth pointing out that the way in which Zorzi et al. (1998a) simulated the contribution of retrieved phonology (i.e. the lexical route) is very similar to the way in which PMSP simulated the contribution of a "semantic" pathway. In both cases, what it really amounts to is a further (frequency-weighted) input to phonology. As argued by Bernstein & Carr (1996), there is nothing compellingly "semantic" in the simulation described by PMSP: rather, these properties can be ascribed to a lexical nonsemantic route. One limitation of the PMSP simulation is the lack of assumptions about the time course of the semantically-driven activation of phonology; that is to say, the input from the two routes to the phonological output begins simultaneously, and this seems rather implausible. Given that the phonological and the semantic pathways are thought to operate in parallel, the phonological pathway should be substantially faster than the semantic pathway, since the latter contains two additional layers of nodes that must be traversed (i.e. the semantic layer and a further layer of hidden units; see Figure 13.1). Full implementations of the triangle model (e.g. Harm & Seidenberg, 2001) are necessary to shed more light on the issue of the "distribution of labour" between the phonological and semantic routes.

Consistency vs. regularity

Within the triangle model, the role of the spelling–sound network implemented by PMSP is indeed that of an assembly procedure, which can be used on any string of letters, including nonwords. However, the PMSP model departs substantially from standard characterizations of phonological assembly, because it can produce the correct pronunciation of exception words and it is sensitive to word frequency. The PMSP model is sensitive to consistency, although the effect is tightly linked with the frequency effect (i.e. a frequency by consistency interaction; see Plaut et al., 1996). Finally, regularity and consistency are conflated in the model; in fact, PMSP treat regularity as one of the extremes on the consistency continuum.

Word frequency has of course no role in the assembly procedure of the DRC model. The regularity effect is produced by the competition of phonemes produced by the GPC route with phonemes produced by the lexical route. Consistency effects would arise in DRC as a result of subthreshold activations in the lexical route generated by the word or nonword stimulus (Coltheart et al., 1993), i.e. a sort of lexical analogy effect. More recently, Coltheart et al. (2001) argued that body consistency can be reinterpreted (at least in DRC) as an effect of spurious competitive phoneme activations generated by the GPC route as a consequence of its serial processing (i.e. a "whammy" effect; Rastle & Coltheart, 1998). For instance, on inconsistent words like DROVE, the GPC route initially translates the vowel without considering the final E; later on, the system produces the correct vowel phoneme, which will compete with the other vowel candidate. However, recent studies have shown that DRC fails to account for consistency effects. Jared (2002) found that the model does not produce an effect for regular inconsistent words and that consistency in DRC is not modulated by neighbourhood type (i.e. the ratio between "friends" and "enemies"). Treiman et al. (2003) reported that readers' pronunciations of vowels in nonwords are influenced by both preceding and following consonants. In a comparison of people's pronunciations with those produced by the computational models, Treiman et al. found that, although none of the models could fully account for the experimental data, all models except DRC captured the overall pattern of performance. Finally, DRC fails to show a nonword consistency effect in the RT data when tested on Glushko's (1979) stimuli (Zorzi, unpublished data).

In the dual-process model, word frequency has no role in the assembly procedure. This is because the connection weights in the two-layer network are influenced by the frequency of the sublexical correspondences but not by the frequency of the whole word. Consistency effects arise within the assembly component for both words and nonwords; this is the result of the existence of multiple mappings (in particular for vowels) that compete at the output level. The regularity effect is produced by the interaction between lexical and assembly processes, when phonemes produced by the TLA network compete with an alternative phoneme produced by the lexical pathway.

The three models can therefore make different predictions with regard to a possible dissociation between consistency and regularity. It would seem that the dual-process model is the only model that predicts a clear dissociation between consistency and regularity. Preliminary evidence for such dissociation comes from Jared's (1997) Experiment 4. The dual-process model can easily account for the independent effects of consistency and regularity in determining the naming latencies and provides a perfect simulation of Jared's results (Zorzi, 1999a). According to Jared, the DRC model "produced robust exception effects with Experiment 4 words, but no regular-consistent effect with words having lower frequency friends than enemies" (p. 524). The PMSP model, on the other hand, showed both consistency and regularity effect, but "tended to exaggerate the effect for exception words with low frequency friends than enemies" (p. 525). In a follow-up study, Jared (2002) found that regularity effects cannot be entirely attributed to consistency. Atypical grapheme–phoneme correspondences influence pronunciation, primarily in the case of low-frequency words for which the correspondence is also unusual in the word body context.

Accounts of surface dyslexia

In both the DRC and dual-process models surface dyslexia is simulated by slowing the activation of lexical phonology. This conforms to the traditional explanation of the syndrome, which is based on the assumption of selective damage to the lexical route. In the triangle model, however, surface dyslexia is simulated by lesioning the semantic route.

The hypothesis that correct exception word reading is dependent upon semantic representations was proposed by Patterson & Hodges (1992) to explain the neuropsychological association between semantic dementia and surface dyslexia. Many patients presenting with semantic impairments are also surface dyslexic (e.g. Funnell, 1996; Graham, Hodges, & Patterson, 1994; Patterson & Hodges, 1992). In PMSP's account of surface dyslexia, differences among patients not only reflect a different severity of the lesion, but also, in particular, their different premorbid reading competence, i.e. the degree of "redistribution of labour" between semantic and phonological pathways.

However, this hypothesis is challenged by the cases of patients showing the corresponding dissociation (i.e. intact reading in the presence of semantic deficits). The patient reported by Schwartz et al. (1980) was able to read exception words that she could not understand. The strongest evidence in support of the independence of semantic and phonological processing comes from a recent study of Cipolotti & Warrington (1995). Their patient DRN, though presenting with a semantic dementia, had a strikingly well-preserved ability to read both regular and exception words that he failed to comprehend. Three other patients with exactly the same characteristics have been later described (Cipolotti & Warrington, 1996; Lambon-Ralph, Ellis, & Franklin, 1995). This pattern, known as lexical nonsemantic reading, is accounted for in the dual-route model by the existence of the lexical nonsemantic route, which can be still intact in the case of damage to the semantic system.

However, Plaut (1997) argues that the different effects of a semantic deficit can be accommodated within an individual differences account, where, for a given individual (i.e. network), the reliance on the semantic pathway for reading exception words depends on a combination of two free parameters of the model: semantic strength and weight decay. Unfortunately, these two parameters are not linked to any measurable characteristics of the individual reader. As a consequence, Plaut's account does not provide any grounds to predict *a priori* the behaviour of a given reader.

One possible explanation for the association between semantic dementia and surface dyslexia is that it reflects pathological involvement of functionally and anatomically closely related brain regions (see also Cipolotti & Warrington, 1995). In other words, this specific form of cortical degeneration would lead to semantic impairments but also (and perhaps invariably) to the disruption of lexical processing (both orthographic and phonological). This hypothesis would seem to gain support from a recent study that compared the reading performance of patients with different types of dementia (Noble, Glosser, & Grossman, 2000). Despite the presence of a semantic impairment, patients with Alzheimer's disease, frontotemporal dementia, and progressive nonfluent aphasia did not show a pattern of reading difficulty consistent with surface dyslexia; only the patients with semantic dementia showed the predicted pattern of reading impairment. However, it is worth noting that the disruption of lexical orthographic and phonological processing in semantic dementia appears to be tightly linked to the loss of word meaning, as demonstrated by the correlation across items between comprehension and exception words reading (Funnell, 1996; Graham et al., 1994) that has been observed in some patients. Funnell (1996) proposed that in surface dyslexics a lexical response is preferred over a sublexical, regularized response only when vestiges of word meaning remain. Patient EP, who presented with semantic dementia (and surface dyslexia), showed knowledge of both lexically derived and sublexically derived pronunciation in reading exception words (e.g. presented with GLOVE, she responded "/gl@Uv/ or /glVv/?"; see Funnell, 1996). When all meaning of a given word was lost, the patient selected a sublexical response, even when she had also produced the correct lexical response. Clearly, further work is necessary to simulate more details of the surface dyslexic syndrome.

CONCLUDING REMARKS

Adjudication between models

The existence of several successful models calls for a research strategy aiming at adjudicating between them. Jacobs & Grainger (1994; also Grainger & Jacobs, 1996) discuss a number of different approaches that can be pursued to adjudicate between competing models. For instance, *descriptive adequacy* refers to the degree of accuracy with which a model predicts a data set. Indeed, recent experimental studies have exploited the availability of computational models to compare human performance (in terms of both pronunciations and RTs) with that of the various models (e.g. Jared, 2002; Treiman et al., 2003). A different criterion for model evaluation is *falsifiability* (Popper, 1935), i.e. a model's ability to generate predictions that can be falsified.

One example of research strategy based on falsificationism and strong inference is the recent study of Rastle & Coltheart (1999), which was designed to investigate a specific assumption, i.e. the serial vs. parallel operation of the phonological assembly process. Clearly, the advantage of such an approach is that, in principle, the falsification of the parallel models would reduce the number of remaining theories to one (i.e. the DRC model).

The "position of irregularity" effect discovered by Rastle & Coltheart (1999; also Coltheart & Rastle, 1994) was predicted by the DRC model because of the specific assumption of serial processing in the phonological assembly route. Following a logic of strong inference, Rastle & Coltheart concluded that their results refute parallel models of reading, such as the PMSP model and the dual-process model.

Indeed, this method can be very effective and should be used whenever possible. In the specific case, however, Rastle & Coltheart's (1999) conclusion was premature, because it was not based on a formal test of the two parallel models. Zorzi (2000) demonstrated that the dual-process model can account for the position of irregularity effect without assuming a serial component, and found an alternative explanation based on positional grapheme–phoneme consistency. Thus, Zorzi's study provides a further demonstration of the importance of the computational approach in experimental cognitive psychology. More generally, two main conclusions can be drawn from this debated issue:

1. The use of a given effect, e.g. a supposedly serial effect, as a proof of a model's specific architectural assumption can be fallacious.
2. Empirical studies aiming at adjudicating between competing models should actually test the competitors (i.e. run the stimuli through the models).

Future directions

The three computational models reviewed in this chapter have been quite successful in simulating a wide range of data from both normal and impaired word reading. However, all models have the potential for extensions and improvements. For instance, one important issue is whether the architectures proposed are general enough to be successfully used on languages different from English (e.g. Ijuin, Fushimi, Patterson, & Tatsumi, 1999; Perry & Ziegler, 2002; Ziegler, Perry, & Coltheart, 2000; Ziegler, Perry & Coltheart, 2003). Other issues that can be explored with these models include: (a) the extension of the approach to modelling spelling (e.g. Houghton & Zorzi, 2003); (b) the simulation of a semantic system (e.g. Harm & Seidenberg, 2001); (c) the simulation of reading performance at the item level (e.g. Coltheart et al., 2001; Spieler & Balota, 1997) to improve the fit to the behavioural data; (d) the account of strategic effects/attentional control of the reading process (e.g. Kello & Plaut, 2003; Lupker, Brown, & Colombo, 1997; Zevin & Balota, 2000; Zorzi, 1999b).

However, although these models represent a great advance over previous verbal–diagrammatic models, an important limitation is that none of these is plausible when looking at issues such as learning procedures and learning environment. For instance, the DRC model is implemented as a static model of the mature reading system; learning was not investigated at all in the model. More interesting in a developmental context are the dual-process and triangle models. The learning properties of these models can be exploited to look at developmental issues (see e.g. Harm & Seidenberg, 1999; Hutzler, Ziegler, Perry, Wimmer, & Zorzi, 2004; Zorzi et al., 1998b). However, data from children's reading has not so far played a large part in the development of the models. In addition, all modelling work carried out by Seidenberg, Plaut, and colleagues is based on feedforward or recurrent multi-layer networks, trained with the back-propagation learning algorithm (Rumelhart et al., 1986). It is well known that this learning algorithm is biologically implausible; this should raise a number of concerns when dealing with any serious attempt to model human learning. A much more serious problem, however, is that connectionist models of reading learn the task of reading aloud through the exposure to a very large corpus of spelling–sound pairs. That is, the input (spelling) and the "desired" output (target pronunciation) for many thousands of words are typically presented several hundreds of times, until the error-correction procedure (e.g. back-propagation) employed as learning algorithm reaches a level of performance that is considered adequate by some external criterion. According to Share (1995), this training regimen is highly implausible. Share (1995) notes that, "Although connectionist models claim to simulate human printed word learning, direct input of target pronunciations for the several thousand words used in the training corpus implies subscription to the dubious direct teaching option ..." (p. 199). That is to say, the kind of "supervised" learning used in all currently implemented models implies that a teacher externally supplies the pronunciation of all words that should be learnt. The idea that several thousands of words can be taught by externally supplying the correct pronunciation is flawed for a great number of reasons (for discussion, see Share, 1995).

Therefore, an important issue for modellers will be the development of models that are constrained to learn in realistic stimulus environments, using only learning rules likely to have some sound psychological or neurobiological basis. Success in this endeavour would open the possibility of assessing the impact of different teaching methods, both for normal children and in remedial treatment of reading disorders.

Notes

1. Note, however, that in "shallow" languages such as Italian and Croatian the assembled pronunciation may be correct at the segmental level (i.e. the phonemes that make up the word) but incorrect at the supra-segmental level (i.e. the

assignment of stress). There is a significant number of words where stress must be lexically assigned, because its placement does not adhere to the statistical regularities of the language (see Colombo, 1992; Colombo & Tabossi, 1992, for Italian; Sbisa, Zorzi, & Tabossi, 1998, for Croatian).

2. Pronunciation keys: /i/ in BEAN, /A/ in BEAR, /O/ in BORN, /u/ in BOON, /3/ in BURN, /I/ in PIT, /e/ in PET, /&/ in PAT, /V/ in BUD, /0/ in POT, /U/ in GOOD, /eI/ in BAY, /aI/ in BUY, /oI/ in BOY, /@U/ in NO, /aU/ in NOW, /tS/ in CHAIN, /dZ/ in JANE, /9/ in THINK, /T/ in THIN, /S/ in SHIP.

3. In fact, the first implemented model of the spelling–sound mapping was NETtalk (Sejnowski & Rosenberg, 1987), but it was not considered as a psychological model of the reading process.

4. An equivalent procedure is to use the frequency value of a given pattern to scale the derivative of the error term calculated by the back-propagation algorithm (Plaut et al., 1996).

5. Plaut (1999) offered an account of the length effect based on a simple recurrent network (Elman, 1990) that is trained to generate a sequence of phonemes as output in response to letter strings. The network is also trained to maintain a representation of its current position within the string, and to use this signal to refixate a peripheral portion of input when it encounters difficulty in generating a pronunciation. One critical issue in this approach is the use of the number of fixations made by the network in pronouncing a word as a measure of naming latency. Furthermore, there is no empirical evidence that readers use more than one fixation in reading monosyllabic words.

REFERENCES

Andrews, S., & Scarratt, D. R. (1998). Rule and analogy mechanisms in reading nonwords: Hough dou peapel rede gnew wirds? *Journal of Experimental Psychology: Human Perception and Performance, 24,* 1052–1086.

Ans, B., Carbonnel, S., & Valdois, S. (1998). A connectionist multiple-trace memory model for polysyllabic word reading. *Psychological Review, 105,* 678–723.

Baron, J. (1977). Mechanisms for pronouncing printed words: Use and acquisition. In D. LaBerge, & S. J. Samuels (Eds.), *Basic processes in reading: Perception and comprehension* (pp. 175–216). Hillsdale, NJ: Lawrence Erlbaum Associates, Inc.

Baron, J., & Strawson, C. (1976). Use of orthographic and word-specific knowledge in reading words aloud. *Journal of Experimental Psychology: Human Perception and Performance, 2,* 386–392.

Beauvois, M. F., & Derouesné, J. (1979). Phonological alexia: Three dissociations. *Journal of Neurology, Neurosurgery and Psychiatry, 42,* 1115–1124.

Behrmann, M., & Bub, D. (1992). Surface dyslexia and dysgraphia: Dual routes, single lexicon. *Cognitive Neuropsychology, 9,* 209–251.

Berent, I., & Perfetti. C. A. (1995). A rose is a reez: The two-cycles model of phonology assembly in reading English. *Psychological Review, 102,* 146–184.

Bernstein, S. E., & Carr, T. H (1996). Dual-route theories of pronouncing printed words: What can be learned from concurrent task performance? *Journal of Experimental Psychology: Learning, Memory, and Cognition, 22,* 86–116.

Besner, D., & Smith, M. C. (1992). Basic processes in reading: Is the orthographic depth hypothesis sinking? In R. Frost, & L. Katz (Eds.), *Orthography, phonology, morphology, and meaning* (pp. 45–66). Amsterdam: Elsevier.

Besner, D., Twilley, L., McCann, R. S., & Seergobin, K. (1990). On the connection between connectionism and data: Are a few words necessary? *Psychological Review, 97,* 432–446.

Brown, P., & Besner, D. (1987). The assembly of phonology in oral reading: A new model. In M. Coltheart (Ed.), *Attention and Performance XII* (pp. 471–489). Hillsdale, NJ: Lawrence Erlbaum Associates, Inc.

Bub, D., Cancelliere, A., & Kertesz, A. (1985). Whole-word and analytic translation of spelling to sound in a non-semantic reader. In K. E. Patterson, J. C. Marshall, & M. Coltheart (eds.), *Surface dyslexia: Neuropsychological and cognitive studies of phonological reading* (pp. 15–34). Hove, UK: Lawrence Erlbaum Associates Ltd.

Bullinaria, J (1997). Modelling reading, spelling and past tense learning with artificial neural networks. *Brain and Language, 59,* 236–266.

Bullinaria, J. (1996). Connectionist models of reading: Incorporating semantics. In *Proceedings of the First European Workshop on Cognitive Modeling* (pp. 224–229). Berlin: Technische Universitat Berlin.

Bullinaria, J. A., & Chater, N. (1995). Connectionist modelling: Implications for cognitive neuropsychology. *Language and Cognitive Processes, 10,* 227–264.

Campbell, R., & Besner, D. (1981). This and that: Constraints on the production of new written words. *Quarterly Journal of Experimental Psychology, 33A,* 375–396.

Carr, T. H., & Pollatsek, A. (1985). Recognizing printed words: A look at current models. In D. Besner, T. G. Waller, & G. E. MacKinnon (Eds.), *Reading research: Advances in theory and practice* (Vol. 5, pp. 1–82). San Diego, CA: Academic Press.

Chomsky, N. (1957). *Syntactic structures.* The Hague: Mouton.

Cipolotti, L., & Warrington, E. K. (1995). Semantic memory and reading abilities: A case report. *Journal of the International Neuropsychological Society, 1,* 104–110.

Cipolotti, L., & Warrington, E. K. (1996, January). *Deterioration of semantic knowledge in surface dyslexia.* Paper presented at the 14th European Meeting for Cognitive Neuropsychology, Bressanone, Italy.

Colombo, L. (1992). Lexical stress effect and its interaction with frequency in word pronunciation. *Journal of Experimental Psychology: Human Perception and Performance, 18,* 987–1003.

Colombo, L., & Tabossi, P. (1992). Strategies and stress assignments: Evidence from a shallow orthography. In R. Frost, & L. Katz (Eds.), *Orthography, phonology, morphology, and meaning* (pp. 319–340). Amsterdam: North Holland.

Coltheart, M. (1978). Lexical access in simple reading tasks. In G. Underwood (Ed.), *Strategies of information processing* (pp. 151–216). London: Academic Press.

Coltheart, M. (1985). Cognitive neuropsychology and the study of reading. In M. I. Posner, & O. S. M. Marin (Eds.), *Attention and Performance XI* (pp. 3–37). Hillsdale, NJ: Lawrence Erlbaum Associates, Inc.

Coltheart, M., Curtis, B., Atkins, P., & Haller, M. (1993). Models of reading aloud: Dual-route and parallel-distributed-processing approaches. *Psychological Review, 100,* 589–608.

Coltheart, M., Langdon, R., & Haller, M. (1996). Computational cognitive neuropsychology and acquired dyslexia. In B. Dodd, L. Worrall, & R. Campbell (Eds.), *Models of language: Illuminations from impairment* (pp. 9–36). London: Whurr.

Coltheart, M., Patterson, K. E., & Marshall, J. C. (1980). *Deep dyslexia.* London: Routledge & Kegan Paul.

Coltheart, M., & Rastle, K. (1994). Serial processing in reading aloud: Evidence for dual-route models of reading. *Journal of Experimental Psychology: Human Perception and Performance, 20,* 1197–1211.

Coltheart, M., Rastle, K., Perry, C., Langdon, R., & Ziegler, J. C. (2001). DRC: A dual route cascaded model of visual word recognition and reading aloud. *Psychological Review, 108,* 204–256.

Cortese, M. J. (1998). Revisiting serial position effects in reading. *Journal of Memory and Language, 39,* 652–665.

Dell, G. S. (1986). A spreading activation theory of retrieval in sentence production. *Psychological Review, 93,* 283–321.

Denes, F., Cipolotti, L., & Zorzi, M. (1999). Acquired dyslexias and dysgraphias. In G. Denes, & L. Pizzamiglio (Eds.), *Handbook of clinical and experimental neuropsychology.* Hove, UK: Psychology Press.

Derouesné, J., & Beauvois, M. F. (1985). The "phonemic" stage in the non-lexical reading process: Evidence from a case of phonlogical alexia. In K. E. Patterson, J. C. Marshall, & M. Coltheart (Eds.), *Surface dyslexia: Neuropsychological and cognitive studies of phonological reading* (pp. 399–458). Hove, UK: Lawrence Erlbaum Associates Ltd.

Elman, J. L. (1990). Finding structure in time. *Cognitive Science, 14,* 179–211.

Farah, M. J., Stowe, R. M., & Levinson, K. L. (1996). Phonological dyslexia: Loss of a reading-specific component of the cognitive architecture? *Cognitive Neuropsychology, 13,* 849–868.

Forster, K. I. (1976). Accessing the mental lexicon. In R. J. Wales, & E. C. T. Walker (Eds.), *New approaches to the language mechanisms.* Amsterdam: North Holland.

Forster, K. I., & Chambers, S. (1973). Lexical access and naming time. *Journal of Verbal Learning and Verbal Behaviour, 12,* 627–635.

Frederiksen, J. R., & Kroll, J. F. (1976). Spelling and sound: Approaches to the internal lexicon. *Journal of Experimental Psychology: Human Perception and Performance, 2,* 361–379.

Frost, R. (1998). Toward a strong phonological theory of visual word recognition: True issues and false trails. *Psychological Bulletin, 123,* 71–99.

Frost, R., Katz, L., & Bentin, S. (1987). Strategies for visual word recognition and orthographic depth: A multilingual comparison. *Journal of Experimental Psychology: Human Perception and Performance, 13,* 104–115.

Funnell, E. (1983). Phonological processing in reading: New evidence from acquired dyslexia. *British Journal of Psychology, 74,* 159–180.

Funnell, E. (1996). Response biases in oral reading: An account of the co-occurrence of surface dyslexia and semantic dementia. *Quarterly Journal of Experimental Psychology, 49A,* 417–446.

Gluck, M. A., & Bower, G. H. (1988a). Evaluating an adaptive network model of human learning. *Journal of Memory and Language, 27,* 166–195.

Gluck, M. A., & Bower, G. H. (1988b). From conditioning to category learning: An adaptive network model. *Journal of Experimental Psychology: General, 117,* 227–247.

Glushko, R. J. (1979). The organization and activation of orthographic knowledge in reading aloud. *Journal of Experimental Psychology: Human Perception and Performance, 5,* 674–691.

Glushko, R. J. (1980). Principles for pronouncing print: The psychology of phonology. In A. M. Mesgold, & C. A. Perfetti (Eds.), *Interactive processes in reading.* Hillsdale, NJ: Lawrence Erlbaum Associates, Inc.

Graham, K. S., Hodges, J. R., & Patterson, K. (1994). The relationship between comprehension and oral reading in progressive fluent aphasia. *Neuropsychologia, 32,* 299–316.

Grainger, J., & Jacobs, A. M. (1996). Orthographic processing in visual word recognition: A multiple read-out model. *Psychological Review, 103,* 518–565.

Harm, M., & Seidenberg, M. S. (1999). Phonology, reading acquisition, and dyslexia: Insights from connectionist models. *Psychological Review, 106,* 491–528.

Harm, M., & Seidenberg, M. S. (2001). Are there orthographic impairments in phonological dyslexia? *Cognitive Neuropsychology, 18,* 71–92.

Henderson, L. (1982). *Orthography and word recognition in reading.* London: Academic Press.

Hillis, A. E., & Caramazza, A. C. (1991). Mechanisms for accessing lexical representations for output: Evidence from a category-specific semantic deficit. *Brain and Language, 40,* 106–144.

Houghton, G., & Zorzi, M. (1998). A model of the sound-spelling mapping in English and its role in word and nonword spelling. In M. A. Gernsbacher, & S. J. Derry (Eds.), *Proceedings of the Twentieth Annual Conference of the Cognitive Science Society* (pp. 490–495). Mahwah, NJ: Lawrence Erlbaum Associates, Inc.

Houghton, G., & Zorzi, M. (2003). Normal and impaired spelling in a connectionist dual-route architecture. *Cognitive Neuropsychology, 20,* 115–162.

Humphreys, G. W., & Evett, L. J. (1985). Are there independent lexical and nonlexical routes in word processing? An evaluation of the dual-route theory of reading. *Behavioral and Brain Sciences, 8,* 689–740.

Hutzler, F., Ziegler, J., Perry, C., Wimmer, H., & Zorzi, M. (2004). Do current connectionist learning models account for reading development in different languages? *Cognition, 91,* 273–296.

Ijuin, M., Fushimi, T., Patterson, K., & Tatsumi, I. (1999). A connectionist approach to Japanese Kanji word naming. *Psychologia, 42,* 267–280.

Jacobs, A. M., & Grainger, J. (1994). Models of visual word recognition—Sampling the state of the art. *Journal of Experimental Psychology: Human Perception and Performance, 20,* 1311–1334.

Jacobs, A. M., Rey, A., Ziegler, J. C., & Grainger, J. (1998). MROM-P: An interactive activation, multiple read-out model of orthographic and phonological processes in visual word recognition. In J. Grainger, & A. M. Jacobs (Eds.), *Localist connectionist approaches to human cognition.* Hillsdale, NJ: Lawrence Erlbaum Associates, Inc.

Jared, D. (1997). Spelling-sound consistency affects the naming of high frequency words. *Journal of Memory and Language, 36,* 505–529.

Jared, D. (2002). Spelling-sound consistency and regularity effects in word naming. *Journal of Memory and Language, 46,* 723–750.

Jared, D., McRae, K., & Seidenberg, M. S. (1990). The basis of consistency effects in word naming. *Journal of Memory and Language, 29,* 687–715.

Kay, J., & Marcel, A. J. (1981). One process not two in reading aloud: Lexical analogies do the work of non-lexical rules. *Quarterly Journal of Experimental Psychology, 33A,* 397–413.

Kay, J., & Patterson, K. E. (1985). Routes to meaning in surface dyslexia. In K. E. Patterson, J. C. Marshall, & M. Coltheart (Eds.), *Surface dyslexia: Neuropsychological and cognitive studies of phonological reading* (pp. 459–508). Hove, UK: Lawrence Erlbaum Associates Ltd.

Kello, C. T., & Plaut, D. C. (2003). Strategic control over rate of processing in word reading: A computational investigation. *Journal of Memory and Language, 48,* 207–232.

Kucera, H., & Francis, W. N. (1967). *Computational analysis of present-day American English.* Providence, RI: Brown University Press.

Lambon-Ralph, M., Ellis, A. W., & Franklin, S. (1995). Semantic loss without surface dyslexia. *Neurocase, 1,* 363–369.

Lupker, S. J., Brown, P., & Colombo, L. (1997). Strategic control in a naming task: Changing routes or changing deadlines? *Journal of Experimental Psychology: Learning, Memory, and Cognition, 23,* 570–590.

Marcel, A. J. (1980). Surface dyslexia and beginning reading: A revised hypothesis of the pronunciation of print and its impairments. In M. Coltheart, K. E. Patterson, & J. C. Marshall (Eds.), *Deep dyslexia.* London: Routledge & Kegan Paul.

Marshall, J. C., & Newcombe, F. (1973). Patterns of paralexia: A psycholinguistic approach. *Journal of Psycholinguistic Research, 2,* 175–199.

McCann, R. S., & Besner, D. (1987). Reading pseudohomophones: Implications for models of pronunciation and the locus of the word-frequency effect in word naming. *Journal of Experimental Psychology: Human Perception and Performance, 13,* 14–24.

McCarthy, R., & Warrington, E. K. (1986). Phonological reading: Phenomena and paradoxes. *Cortex, 22,* 359–380.

McClelland, J. L., & Rumelhart, D. E. (1981). An interactive activation model of context effects in letter perception: Part 1. An account of basic findings. *Psychological Review, 88,* 375–407.

McCloskey, M. (1991). Networks and theories: The place of connectionism in cognitive science. *Psychological Science, 2*(6), 387–395.

Meyer, D. E., Schvaneveldt, R. W., & Ruddy, M. G. (1974). Functions of graphemic and phonemic codes in visual-word recognition. *Memory & Cognition, 2,* 309–321.

Monsell, S., Patterson, K. E., Graham, A., Hughes, C. H., & Milroy, R. (1992). Lexical and sublexical translation of spelling to sound: Strategic anticipation of lexical status. *Journal of Experimental Psychology: Learning, Memory and Cognition, 18,* 452–467.

Morton, J., & Patterson, K. E. (1980). A new attempt at an interpretation, or, an attempt at a new interpretation. In M. Coltheart, K. E. Patterson, & J. C. Marshall (Eds.), *Deep dyslexia* (pp. 91–118). London: Routledge & Kegan Paul.

Noble, K., Glosser, G., & Grossman, M. (2000). Oral reading in dementia. *Brain & Language, 74,* 48–69.

Norris, D. (1994). A quantitative, multiple levels model of reading aloud. *Journal of Experimental Psychology: Human Perception and Performance, 20,* 1212–1232.

Paap, K. R., & Noel, R. W. (1991). Dual route models of print to sound: Still a good horse race. *Psychological Research, 53,* 13–24.

Page, M. (2000). Connectionist modelling in psychology: A localist manifesto. *Behavioural and Brain Sciences, 23,* 443–512.

Patterson, K. E., & Coltheart, V. (1987). Phonological processes in reading: A tutorial review. In M. Coltheart (Ed.), *Attention and performance XII: The psychology of reading* (pp. 421–447). Hillsdale, NJ: Lawrence Erlbaum Associates, Inc.

Patterson, K. E., Graham, H., & Hodges J. R. (1994). Reading in Alzheimer's type dementia: A preserved ability? *Neuropsychologia, 8,* 395–412.

Patterson, K. E., & Hodges, J. R (1992). Deterioration of word meaning: Implications for reading. *Neuropsychologia, 12,* 1025–1040.

Patterson, K. E., & Lambon Ralph, M. A. (1999). Selective disorders of reading? *Current Opinion in Neurobiology, 9,* 235–239.

Patterson, K. E., & Marcel, A. J. (1992). Phonological ALEXIA or PHONOLOGICAL alexia? In J. Alegria, D. Holender, J. Junca de Morais, & M. Radeau (Eds.), *Analytic approaches to human cognition* (pp. 259–274). New York: Elsevier.

Patterson, K. E., Marshall, J. C., & Coltheart, M. (1985). *Surface dyslexia: Neuropsychological and cognitive studies of phonological reading.* Hove, UK: Lawrence Erlbaum Associates Ltd.

Patterson, K. E., & Morton, J. (1985). From orthography to phonology: An attempt at an old interpretation. In K. E. Patterson, J. C. Marshall, & M. Coltheart (eds.), *Surface dyslexia: Neuropsychological and cognitive studies of phonological reading* (pp. 335–359). Hove, UK: Lawrence Erlbaum Associates Ltd.

Patterson, K. E., Seidenberg, M. S., & McClelland, J. L. (1989). Connections and disconnections: Acquired dyslexia in a computational model of reading processes. In R. G. M. Morris (Ed.), *Parallel distributed processing: Implication for psychology and neurobiology* (pp. 131–181). London: Oxford University Press.

Pearlmutter, B. A. (1989). Learning state space trajectories in recurrent neural networks. *Neural Computation, 1*(2), 263–269.

Perfetti, C. A., & Bell, L. C. (1991). Phonemic activation during the first 40 ms of word identification: Evidence from backward masking and masked priming. *Journal of Memory and Language, 30,* 473–485.

Perfetti, C. A., Bell, L. C., & Delaney, S. M. (1988). Automatic (prelexical) phonemic activation in silent word reading: Evidence from backward masking. *Journal of Memory and Language, 27,* 59–70.

Perry, C., & Ziegler, J. C. (2002). Cross-language computational investigation of the length effect in reading aloud. *Journal of Experimental Psychology: Human Perception and Performance, 28,* 990–1001.

Pinker, S. (1991). Rules of language. *Science, 253,* 530–535.

Pinker, S., & Prince, A. (1988). On language and connectionism: Analysis of a parallel distributed processing model of language acquisition. *Cognition, 28,* 73–193.

Plaut, D. C. (1997). Structure and function in the lexical system: Insights from distributed models of word reading and lexical decision. *Language and Cognitive Processes, 12,* 767–808.

Plaut, D. C. (1999). A connectionist approach to word reading and acquired dyslexia: Extension to sequential processing. *Cognitive Science, 23,* 543–568.

Plaut, D. C., McClelland, J. L., Seidenberg, M. S., & Patterson, K. E. (1996). Understanding normal and impaired word reading: Computational principles in quasi-regular domain. *Psychological Review, 103,* 56–115.

Popper, K. R. (1935). *Logik der Forschung.* Berlin: Springer.

Rastle, K., & Coltheart, M. (1998). Whammies and double whammies: The effect of length on nonword reading. *Psychonomic Bulletin and Review, 5*(2), 277–282.

Rastle, K., & Coltheart, M. (1999). Serial and strategic effects in reading aloud. *Journal of Experimental Psychology: Human Perception and Performance, 25,* 482–503.

Rosenblatt, F. (1962), *Principles of neurodynamics.* New York: Spartan.

Rosson, M. B. (1983). From SOFA to LOUCH: Lexical contributions to pseudoword pronunciation. *Memory and Cognition, 11,* 152–160.

Rumelhart, D. E., Hinton, G. E., & Williams, R. J. (1986). Learning internal representations by error propagation. In D. E. Rumelhart, & J. L. McClelland (Eds.), *Parallel distributed processing: Explorations in the microstructure of cognition. Vol. 1: Foundations* (pp. 318–362). Cambridge, MA: MIT Press.

Rumelhart, D. E., & McClelland, J. L. (1982). An interactive activation model of context effects in letter perception: Part 2. The contextual enhancement effects and some tests and extensions of the model. *Psychological Review, 89,* 60–94.

Sbisa, S., Zorzi, M., & Tabossi, P. (1998). *Lexical stress effects in reading Croatian words.* Paper presented at the 10th Congress of the European Society for Cognitive Psychology, Jerusalem, Israel, September.

Schwartz, M. F., Saffran, E. M., & Marin, O. S. M. (1980). Fractionating the reading process in dementia: Evidence for word-specific print-to-sound associations. In M. Coltheart, K. E. Patterson, & J. C. Marshall (Eds.), *Deep dyslexia* (pp. 259–269). London: Routledge & Kegan Paul.

Seidenberg, M. S., & McClelland, J. L. (1989). A distributed, developmental model of word recognition and naming. *Psychological Review, 96,* 523–568.

Seidenberg, M. S., & McClelland, J. L. (1990). More words but still no lexicon: Reply to Besner et al. (1990). *Psychological Review, 97,* 447–452.

Seidenberg, M. S., Plaut, D. C., Petersen, A. S., McClelland, J. L., & McRae K. (1994). Nonword pronunciation and models of word recognition. *Journal of Experimental Psychology: Human Perception and Performance, 20,* 1177–1196.

Seidenberg, M. S., Waters, G. S., Barnes, M. A., & Tanenhaus, M. K. (1984). When does irregular spelling or pronunciation influence word recognition? *Journal of Verbal Learning and Verbal Behaviour, 23,* 383–404.

Sejnowski, T. J., & Rosenberg, C. R. (1987). Parallel networks that learn to pronounce English text. *Complex Systems, 1,* 145–168.

Shallice, T., & McCarthy, R. (1985). Phonological reading: From patterns of impairment to possible procedures. In K. E. Patterson, J. C. Marshall, & M. Coltheart (Eds.), *Surface dyslexia: Neuropsychological and cognitive studies of phonological reading* (pp. 361–397). Hove, UK: Lawrence Erlbaum Associates Ltd.

Shallice, T., Warrington, E. K., & McCarthy, R. (1983). Reading without semantics. *Quarterly Journal of Experimental Psychology, 35A,* 111–138.

Shanks, D. R. (1991). Categorization by a connectionist network. *Journal of Experimental Psychology: Learning, Memory, and Cognition, 17,* 433–443.

Share, D. L. (1995). Phonological recoding and self-teaching: *sine qua non* of reading acquisition. *Cognition, 55,* 151–218.

Shibahara, N., Zorzi, M., Hill, M. P., Wydell, T., & Butterworth, B. (2003). Semantic effects in word naming: Evidence from English and Japanese Kanji. *Quarterly Journal of Experimental Psychology, 56A,* 263–286.

Siegel, S., & Allan, L. G. (1996). The widespread influence of the Rescorla–Wagner model. *Psychonomic Bulletin & Review, 3,* 314–321.

Spieler, D. H., & Balota, D. A. (1997). Bringing computational models of word naming down to the item level. *Psychological Science, 8,* 411–416.

Strain, E., Patterson, K., & Seidenberg, M. S. (1995). Semantic effects in single-word naming. *Journal of Experimental Psychology: Learning, Memory, and Cognition, 21,* 1140–1154.

Sutton, R. S., & Barto, A. G. (1981). Toward a modern theory of adaptive networks: Expectation and prediction. *Psychological Review, 88,* 135–170.

Taraban, R., & McClelland, J. L. (1987). Conspiracy effects in word pronunciation. *Journal of Memory and Language, 26,* 608–631.

Treiman, R., Kessler, B., & Bick, S. (2003). Influence of consonantal context on the pronunciation of vowels: A comparison of human readers and computational models. *Cognition, 88,* 49–78.

Treiman, R., Mullenix, J., Bijeljac-Babic, R., & Richmond-Welty, E. D. (1995). The special role of rhymes in the description, use, and acquisition of English orthography. *Journal of Experimental Psychology: General, 124,* 107–136.

Van Orden, G. C., Pennington, B. F., & Stone, G. O. (1990). Word identification in reading and the promise of subsymbolic psycholinguistics. *Psychological Review, 97,* 488–522.

Venetzky, R. L. (1970). *The structure of English orthography.* The Hague: Mouton.

Weekes, B. S. (1997). Differential effects of number of letters on word and nonword naming latency. *Quarterly Journal of Experimental Psychology, 50A,* 439–456.

Wickelgren, W. A. (1969). Context-sensitive coding, associative memory, and serial order in (speech) behavior. *Psychological Review, 76,* 1–15.

Widrow, G., & Hoff, M. E. (1960). Adaptive switching circuits. *Institute of Radio Engineers, Western Electronic Show and Convention Record, Part 4* (pp. 96–104) New York: IRE.

Zevin, J. D., & Balota, D. A. (2000). Priming and attentional control of lexical and sublexical pathways during naming. *Journal of Experimental Psychology: Learning, Memory, and Cognition, 26,* 121–135.

Ziegler, J. C., Perry, C., & Coltheart, M. (2000). The DRC model of visual word recognition and reading aloud: An extension to German. *European Journal of Cognitive Psychology, 12,* 413–430.

Ziegler, J. C., Perry, C., & Coltheart, M. (2003). Speed of lexical and nonlexical processing in French: The case of the regularity effect. *Psychonomic Bulletin & Review, 10,* 947–953.

Zorzi, M. (1999a). *The connectionist dual-process model: Development, skilled performance, and breakdowns of processing in oral reading.* Unpublished Doctoral Thesis, University of Trieste.

Zorzi, M. (1999b). Routes, races, and attentional demands in reading: Insights from computational models. In M. Hahn, & S. C. Stoness (Eds.), *Proceedings of the Twenty-first Annual Conference of the Cognitive Science Society* (pp. 772–777). Mahwah, NJ: Lawrence Erlbaum Associates, Inc.

Zorzi, M. (2000). Serial processing in reading aloud: No challenge for a parallel model. *Journal of Experimental Psychology: Human Perception and Performance, 26,* 847–856.

Zorzi, M., Houghton, G., & Butterworth, B. (1998a). Two routes or one in reading aloud? A connectionist dual-process model. *Journal of Experimental Psychology: Human Perception and Performance, 24,* 1131–1161.

Zorzi, M., Houghton, G., & Butterworth, B. (1998b). The development of spelling–sound relationships in a model of phonological reading. *Language and Cognitive Processes, 13,* 337–371.

Author index

Subject index